MARKETING
Principles and Practice

DENNIS ADCOCK

AL HALBORG

CAROLINE ROSS

17. 10. 0L

FINANCIAL TIMES

Prentice Hall

An imprint of **Pearson Education**

Harlow, England · London · New York · Reading, Massachusetts · San Francisco · Toronto · Don Mills, Ontario · Sydney
Tokyo · Singapore · Hong Kong · Seoul · Taipei · Cape Town · Madrid · Mexico City · Amsterdam · Munich · Paris · Milan

Pearson Education Limited

Edinburgh Gate
Harlow
Essex CM20 2JE
United Kingdom

and Associated Companies throughout the world

Visit us on the World Wide Web at
www.pearsoneduc.com

First published in 1993
Second edition published 1995
Third edition published 1998
Fourth edition published 2001

© Dennis Adcock, Ray Bradfield, Al Halborg, Caroline Ross, 2001

ISBN 0 273 64677 X

British Library Cataloguing in Publication Data
A CIP catalogue record for this book can be obtained from the British Library.

10 9 8 7 6 5 4 3 2 1
05   04   03   02   01   00

Typeset by 3
Printed by Ashford Colour Press Ltd., Gosport

Contents

Preface

Marketing is a very exciting subject that provides a constant challenge not only to students of the subject but also to practitioners. The authors of the book were delighted therefore to be asked to write a fourth edition of the book, giving them the opportunity to update examples and capture the changes that have affected the subject in the last three years.

This new edition of Marketing Principles and Practice has endeavoured to include many up to date examples, and extensive use has been made of articles from the *Financial Times* newspaper. The articles have been used to highlight the importance of current affairs and how the changes in the environment impact on the actions and direction of marketing practice.

The structure of this edition of the book has not changed dramatically, and although designed for students coming to marketing for the first time, it is complete enough to appeal to a very wide spectrum of readers at all levels.

The case studies and exercises provide an enjoyable way of viewing how marketing can be approached and the wide application that it has.

As authors we hope you enjoy the book, but most of all for those of you who are using the text to study for examinations – we wish you success, and hope the book helps make the subject interesting and easy to understand.

Acknowledgements

The authors are indebted to students at Coventry University and the University of Warwick as well as the other universities who use the text and who have offered helpful and constructive criticism. In presenting the cases to enable discussion on the subject matter, many of the successful older cases have been updated and focused on current issues. Many of the cases are new, some of which are designed to reflect the increasing importance of e-business. All cases have been tested and are offered to stimulate class discussion as well as helping to make the principles of marketing more relevant in practice.

There are a number of colour illustrations in the book, which are examples of marketing in practice. We are indebted to the agencies that have helped in this respect and we would urge all students to continue to study current media as well as articles in the marketing and national press. By considering these against the general principles as presented in this book it is possible to learn more of the subject which is so dynamic and so much fun.

In revising the text we have all relied on others to assist in typing, researching revising and just putting up with us as we worked against publishing deadlines. A special thankyou goes to Ray Bradfield for his contributions to the book. The most important help and support however has been that offered by our respective partners, Marion, Eileen and Kenneth. We thank them for their encouragement and their tolerance.

1

What is marketing?

Marketing: the action or business of bringing or sending to market.
Oxford English Dictionary

This marketing of supplies was the beginning ... of its prosperity.
Harper's Magazine (1984)

INTRODUCTION

Marketing is now entering a new era, the dawning of the 21st century has brought with it a dynamic and exciting new dimension for both consumers and companies alike, a radical change in how companies and their customers interact is possible with the new technology now available. This technological revolution for sourcing information will alter the way in which many companies conduct their business. Marketing will change and develop, as e-commerce becomes increasingly more important.

This textbook will help you to understand how marketing theory can be applied and made to work in practice, with regard to both traditional and new approaches to marketing. The first step is to understand exactly what marketing is. Almost everyone that has been asked the question, 'What is marketing?' is usually willing to hazard a guess, even if they do give the incorrect answer of selling and advertising, or companies trying to force consumers to buy products that they do not want. Marketing encompasses so many things, from the design and delivery of products, how they are priced, packaged and promoted, to the business side of segmenting and targeting customers, and then positioning the product using the strategic tools available. Traditionally these tools, which are the factors that a supplier can control, have been known as the 'marketing mix'. The mix is sometimes seen as comprising categories based on the product, price, place and promotion (the '4Ps'), however most successful organisations would say that 'marketing' means keeping the customers happy, so much so that they keep coming back to you, and in doing so keep your business profitable. For this it is necessary to see the 'product' offered to customers in a wider context of everything the customer receives, both goods and every type of service. To accommodate this thinking it is necessary to widen the marketing mix to include the people who serve customers, and the processes involved in any exchange that takes place.

All the aspects outlined above will be discussed in greater depth in the book, but it is important to realise that marketing affects virtually everyone, it is literally all around, seen in the variety of products for sale, the advertisements on television, newspapers and the Internet, etc. Today the success of an organisation may depend on how well it markets itself and its products, making sure its customers are satisfied, not only with the product or service purchased, but also with the service received and the ancillary packages of delivery and finance that are offered.

It is evident therefore that marketing covers a wide range of activities, in fact everything related to what was once described as providing:

The right product, in the right place, at the right price, and at the right time.

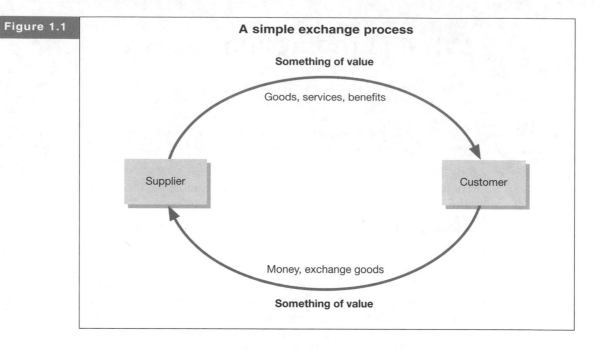

Figure 1.1

A simple exchange process

What is 'right'? From the marketing viewpoint it is right if it gets the *desired response* from the required number of potential customers, efficiently and ethically. As customers we expect to have a choice when we spend our money. We can also choose not to spend any money at all by deciding not to buy a product. When we do decide to buy, an exchange takes place. Money is exchanged for the chosen product and hopefully both parties will feel happy with their side of the bargain (Figure 1.1).

Money is not the only form of exchange – for example, companies as well as individuals can exchange products without money actually changing hands. However, in the majority of marketing exchanges, money is used. Usually, in addition to the actual money spent, it is necessary for the purchaser to invest *time* when making the decision to buy. This might involve visiting a shop or other selling outlet, using the Internet, studying catalogues and sometimes discussing the purchase with family or friends.

Inevitably a specific purchase also means the sacrifice of not being able to buy something else with the money spent (the *opportunity cost* of the purchase).

MARKETING DEFINITIONS

It can therefore be seen that Marketing involves an *exchange process*, and this is central to one of the simplest accepted definitions of Marketing which is:

Marketing is the study of exchange processes especially those associated with the provision of goods and services.

While clearly focused and concise, this definition provides no indication of the potential relevance and scope of the subject. It assumes knowledge that money is usually used as the medium for exchange and makes no mention of the objective of the exchange. This aspect is better addressed in the definition proposed by the celebrated American author of marketing textbooks, Philip Kotler:

Marketing is the human activity directed at satisfying needs and wants through an exchange process. (Kotler, 1980)

Since 1980 Kotler's definition has developed:

Marketing is a social and managerial process by which individuals and groups obtain what they need and want through creating and exchanging products and value with others. (Kotler et al., 1999)

An important addition in these definitions is that *needs* and *wants* are to be satisfied. The major addition is the phrase 'of value', and as this is an important aspect of marketing, it will be explored fully in later chapters.

There are many other useful and equally acceptable definitions. The one preferred by the British Chartered Institute of Marketing (CIM) is:

Marketing is the management process responsible for identifying, anticipating and satisfying customers' requirements profitably.

Both Kotler and CIM focus on the profitable exchange being for the supplier. The term 'profitable' is not being used in the strict accounting sense, but rather as an indication of the importance of both parties having to *benefit* from the exchange.

THE EXCHANGE PROCESS

Economic prosperity and progress depends upon the development of ways by which products can be exchanged between individuals and societies. At the simplest level, this would be restricted to direct exchanges with near neighbours. To increase the opportunity to do this, and the variety of goods available, times and meeting places are established so people can gather to make exchanges. Typically these gatherings became known as fairs or markets. These allowed trade to expand over considerable distances as merchants took products from one market to another. Trade involving the direct exchange of goods is known as barter, and depends upon individuals with complementary products finding one another. For an exchange to take place a person who has a pig and wants some wheat needs to find someone with wheat who wants a pig.

This difficulty is significantly reduced once a means of exchange has some general acceptance. This could be a valued product such as salt (paid to Roman soldiers and from which the word 'salary' is derived), tea, precious stones, something made out of precious metal, or the tokens of value that we accept as money. The use of money allows the person to sell the pig on a day when there is someone wanting to buy a pig and buy the wheat on another day when there is someone wanting to sell wheat. It also allows very precise relative values to be placed on different products, depending upon size, availability and demand. Thus, if there are fewer pigs available the person with the pig may find that what he receives in exchange for it will buy several bags of wheat. Alternatively, on another day, the person could find that to buy one bag of wheat it will be necessary to sell two pigs.

The demand and availability for some products such as wheat, or seasonal products such as vegetables, may well depend upon the weather, with the result that the price may vary significantly from month to month. Other products will not be affected in this way, which means that both sellers and buyers can know an accepted price for these products. This makes it unnecessary for a buyer to visit the market, as goods can be purchased at the accepted price through intermediaries or merchants.

As trade increases so does the number of markets and merchants. This provides individuals with opportunities to choose between many more potential suppliers. It also provides suppliers with opportunities to sell to many more potential customers. Inevitably this means that suppliers and customers become increasingly separated: not only by physical distance and time, but also by culture and attitude. This separation is likely to reduce the benefits derived from the exchange. For the supplier this is because eventually income is reduced by the additional costs involved, and for the purchaser as a result of reduced value being received. Marketing, by focusing on the exchange process, provides ways of analysing this process to maximise the benefit both parties gain from an exchange.

WHAT IS MARKETING?

While it could be argued that the definitions and explanations given earlier in this chapter fully answer this question, it is necessary to adopt a different approach to explain the different ways the term 'marketing' is used. This involves recognising that, in practice, the term is used in four different ways. These are as an organisational function, as a management function, as a business concept and as an accepted business philosophy.

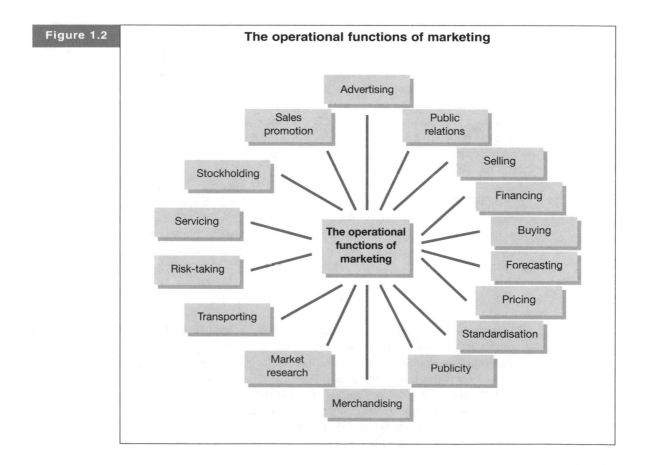

Figure 1.2

The operational functions of marketing

Marketing as an organisational function

Within all types of organisation it is generally considered good management practice to identify activities and responsibilities and allocate these within specific organisational functional areas such as production or accounting. For most organisations, advertising, sales promotion and marketing research would be considered *core marketing function activities*. Other activities would be dependent upon the type of organisation. For example, within a retail organisation the buying function is likely to be classified as a marketing function whereas, in a manufacturing organisation it would normally be considered a production function. Figure 1.2 shows the wide range of tasks, which can be included within the marketing function. Some of these, like the core activities already mentioned, are sufficiently crucial to the function of marketing to warrant at least an individual chapter in this textbook. Others, such as buying may need more explanation. Within all trading organisations the range of products offered to customers is likely to be of crucial importance to the success of the organisation. As it is the buyers who are responsible for making this selection it is logical to consider this as a marketing function within organisations of this type – for instance, wholesalers, retailers and importers.

It is unusual for organisations to have the responsibility for two of the activities shown specifically assigned to an individual department, and yet both can be of critical importance to an organisation in the marketing context. One of the most important is *risk taking*, as most businesses involve the acceptance of risk. A simple example is the local greengrocer who goes to the market on Friday morning to purchase his stock for the weekend. During the summer it is likely that lettuces, tomatoes and the other salad produce will be purchased. How much of each should be bought? It is important that sufficient is purchased to meet the needs of customers since, if the product is sold out there is always the possibility that a disappointed customer will be a lost customer. Equally the greengrocer does not want to have so much left that some of it will have to be discarded. Since the amount sold in Britain is likely to depend upon the weather, the decision will always involve risk. To reduce this risk it is likely that the weather forecast will be consulted before going to the market.

The second activity for which it is unusual for the responsibility to be allocated specifically is standardisation. At first sight this might be seen as having only a limited relevance to marketing. Yet the introduction of well-promoted standards have significantly contributed to the prosperity of many suppliers. Two very different examples would be the introduction of standardised sizes of eggs by the British Egg Marketing Board and the introduction of quality standards by the Japanese optical industry.

Marketing as a management function

Another aspect of marketing is its crucial role in ensuring that the activities of an organisation are clearly directed towards the principal objective of meeting the needs of customers effectively. This is the *planning* and *co-ordinating* role of marketing. This aspect of marketing was specifically identified in 1974 by the pioneering marketing author T. Levitt, in *Marketing for Business Growth*, in which he stated that marketing is not just a business function, it is a consolidating view of the whole business purpose.

It is useful to separate this management aspect of marketing from the philosophy of marketing and the other functions of marketing, since it involves the allocation of resources as well as the co-ordination of effort and therefore has to be carried out at a higher level within an organisation. It can indeed be argued, that marketing as a management function should always be the central task of the most senior management team, whatever this might be called within any specific organisation.

Marketing as a business concept

This third aspect of the term 'marketing' relates to its use with respect to the insights that have resulted from the exchange process having been studied in detail and from many different points of view. From this study theories have been developed which are used to analyse the process of meeting customers' needs and determining how these may be improved. This has involved developing specific terminology to classify individual components of different types of need and ways that these can be met.

It is now accepted that all types of organisation can effectively use these concepts. These include those that manufacture products and those that provide a service, as well as organisations such as charities like Save the Children Fund. Their product is the feeling you have after making a donation, so that even in this situation a real exchange is taking place between the giver and the charity. Such examples illustrate the relevance of marketing to many activities and products. It is now accepted as being equally relevant to industrial and service industries as well as to the public sector and voluntary organisations.

Marketing as an accepted business philosophy

Marketing as a business philosophy recognises the importance of the customer and that business exists to serve customers rather than manufacture products. To be effective this philosophy must be accepted as being crucial in every part of an organisation. Peter Drucker once wrote, 'There is only one valid definition of business purpose: to create a customer.' If you do not have any customers for the product or service your organisation offers, then there is no reason for its continuing existence.

This was recognised in 1776 by Adam Smith, the father of modern economics, who wrote:

> Consumption is the sole end and purpose of all production and the interests of the product ought to be attended to only so far as it may be necessary for promoting those of the customer.

This is still true today and not dependent on the organisation being a manufacturing firm. An example of how this still applies in today's world is the book selling company Amazon.com.

Example   The philosophy of Amazon.com is that the customer is king. Jeff Bezos, the founder of the company, had several areas of the business which were seen as vital to success. One of these was how to attract and keep customers, customer care was seen as being a vital element and a key growth driver of the company. It will be interesting to chart the future performance of the company and observe whether speedy deliveries, a discount on prices, good selection of books and customised service will continue to attract customers in the years to come.

UNDERSTANDING MARKETING AS A STUDENT

In recognising these four aspects of marketing it can be appreciated that any one of them can be the core theme of a basic text on marketing. A review of these will show that many use 'Marketing as a management function' as the core theme. This approach assumes that marketing is primarily a planning activity and as a result there are a number of disadvantages. This text seeks to avoid these by considering all four aspects of the subject in turn. Initially the philosophy of marketing will be explored in the terms of customers, their context and behaviour. Then the concepts of marketing will be introduced, together with the related functions of marketing and finally the co-ordinating and planning aspects of marketing will be considered.

Before it is possible to fully understand the roles of marketing it is necessary to consider what is a *market*. At its simplest a market is a place where goods and services are offered for sale, and buyers consider those offerings. However the idea of a physical trading place is no longer sufficient to encompass every location where an exchange is possible. There are many points of contact between suppliers and potential buyers and all of these are part of the market. It is, therefore, useful to widen the idea of a market to include the complete *market space* occupied by a group of suppliers and their customers. This could include the so-called *virtual market* that exists when customers are purchasing goods over the Internet. George Day, writing in 1994, suggested that:

> Most markets do not have neat boundaries.

And:

> Different customers will have different perceptions of the products offered, and suitable substitutes, thus making it difficult to describe a market in an absolute sense.

What should be avoided is the temptation to define a market solely in terms of a specific product that is being offered for sale. Descriptions such as 'the car market' or 'the soft drink market' tend to lead to thinking that revolves around a particular product class rather than around the *benefits* customers desire, and which that product could satisfy. It will be seen that there are often many different ways to achieve the ultimate marketing goal of customer satisfaction and supplier profit.

MARKETS AND MARKET REGULATION

Customers achieve satisfaction through a beneficial exchange with a supplier. The customer receives something they desire and the cost (sacrifice) is considered worth paying. On the other hand the supplier makes a sale and also receives a satisfactory consideration (price) for the goods or services. Historically local customers knew their local suppliers and were able to judge the quality of goods offered. Both buyer and seller obviously want a good deal, but because they know one another they are likely to see the benefit of being fair to the other party. If there was a problem, that could be sorted out locally and it is apparent that dealing with someone who is known involves less risk than dealing with a stranger.

However trade has now grown to a global scale, and beyond. In particular the trade between strangers, customers and suppliers who have no close intimacy has increased with the growth and development of markets. There is an understandable fear that maybe one party is gaining at the expense of the other, and this has required that rules be introduced to protect customers from problems. In particular, those involved in supervising markets have introduced regulations governing how trade should be conducted. These are designed to ensure that those coming to purchase at their market can trust in that market as a whole and thus encourage '*fair*' trading. There are now universally accepted measures of length, weight and volume, and regulations as to the accuracy of the measures used by traders. The penalties for giving short measure became extremely harsh since to do so could significantly undermine the integrity of an established market. To further encourage good practice many of these regulations have become part of nationally administered laws. Whilst such rules and regulations are now a feature of most traditional market places there is still a long way to go to regulate the Internet.

There are three kinds of markets that require discussion:

- Open markets
- Regulated markets
- Unregulated markets.

Open markets

Both of the parties making an exchange are more likely to consider that the exchange has been beneficial when the exchange has been made within the context of what is known as an 'open market'. This is a market that has all of the following characteristics:

1 Single standardised product
2 Many buyers
3 Many sellers
4 Buyers and sellers have equal access to all available information relevant to the market.

An open market can be established and continue only when both buyers and sellers agree to abide by the rules necessary to maintain the four conditions set out above. This means that the product has to be clearly defined, that membership of the market as a buyer or seller has to be regulated and the rules relating to the availability of information are clearly established and regulated. Because the market is formed to trade in a standardised product, there is an overwhelming emphasis on *prices*. In fact, when there is no way to differentiate a product it becomes a commodity and the price becomes the sole determinant of value. Those markets which set the world price for commodities such as gold, oil, orange juice, wheat, coffee or soya beans, as well as the major stock markets, all have rules which are intended to maintain the 'openness' of the markets. The penalties for infringing these rules are inevitably severe.

However, even in these markets there are opportunities for speculation and for product differentiation. Indeed this is often necessary in order for them to continue as effective markets during times of difficulty. Is a product offered for immediate delivery the same as an identical product being sold now, but for delivery in (say) six months time? These are obviously different in that one might benefit a customer with an immediate need, the other offers the benefit of secure supply in order to meet future requirements. Alternatively a supplier who needs to sell immediately might be seen in a different light to one who is able to store stocks and sell when prices are higher due to changes in the balance of supply and demand.

Example The demand for beer in the UK increases during a hot summer and is significantly depressed if the summer is cold and wet. This would reduce the demand for barley since this is an important ingredient of beer. Furthermore, after a cold wet summer brewers are likely to have unused stocks of the barley purchased in expectation of higher demand. As a result they are likely to postpone purchasing new supplies of barley. The farmer having taken in his crop is likely to need to sell some of it to at least pay for the harvest. If his normal brewer customers are unwilling to buy barley he becomes dependent upon the speculators within the market who will purchase barley believing that because of the poor summer there will be a poor harvest and as a result the price will rise as time passes. Thus, the market is able to function in spite of there being low demand by the actual users of the product.

While there are many examples of open markets, these must be considered exceptions in the context of exchanges normally made by individuals. There are a number of reasons for this:

- First, products purchased are rarely homogeneous. Even potatoes vary by variety and packaging making comparison by the purchaser difficult, which frustrates the first condition of an open market.
- Secondly, the numbers of potential buyers and the demand for products is constantly changing, which frustrates the second condition of an open market.
- Thirdly, the individual purchaser usually has a limited choice of supplier, which frustrates the third condition of the open market.
- Lastly, purchasers rarely have as much information about the market as does the supplier, which contravenes the fourth condition of an open market.

Because of the special conditions within an *open market* there is less scope for marketing and for the many techniques utilised by marketers to create unique offerings in order to satisfy customers.

Regulated markets

The regulations governing an open market are designed to ensure that it is able to operate with none of the participants having an unfair advantage over the others. Regulated markets recognise that there is a lack of balance between the parties and therefore this type of market has rules that are intended to ensure a degree of fair trading. Such regulations are laid out in the Sale of Goods Act that requires products offered to the general public to be fit for the purpose for which they were intended. Thus, the purchaser of a pair of gloves intended for washing up can expect them to be waterproof and have them replaced should those purchased leak.

All developed societies have similar regulations to regulate legal trade. It is therefore usual for manufacturing and trading organisations to have to comply with such regulations which effectively constitute one aspect of the marketing environment in which an exchange, or trade in general, takes place. Legislation and market regulations are not the only environmental variables affecting marketing. Others involve the economic, social and technological variables in a market place, which are discussed in detail in chapters 3 and 4. Since organisations have little influence over these environmental factors they are generally referred to as 'uncontrollable variables'. They contrast the variables such as product quality, service, additional features and price which can be determined by the organisation supplying a given product and, because

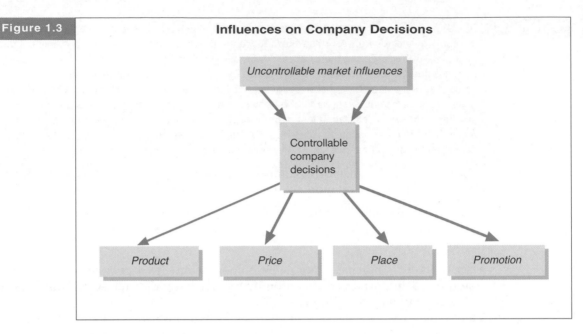

Figure 1.3

Influences on Company Decisions

of this, these marketing activities or variables are known as 'controllable variables'. Figure 1.3 shows the relationship between these two types of variable.

Marketing is involved in developing the controllable variables within the context of the uncontrollable, but regulated market place in order to attract sufficient customers to trade with a specific supply organisation.

Unregulated markets

If there were no regulations then customers would be unprotected and the maxim of 'let the buyer beware' (*caveat emptor*) would apply. There is a distinct difference between an unregulated market and a de-regulated market. In the former the buyer is 'on their own' reacting to offers made such as in a street market or a car boot sale where there is little comeback if products don't perform as expected. De-regulation is the removal of artificial monopoly restrictions in order to encourage free competition and increase customer choice. This has been a feature of a number of markets over recent years, and the results have been dramatic as in the airline sector and now in telecommunications. However the new competitive environment is still regulated, the difference being that those regulations are not restrictive but are based on fair competition.

the Internet is not yet controlled in quite the same way. Because it is international, and the country of origin is not always clear there is still a lack of confidence amongst some customers. Problems persist regarding the reliability of delivery, product quality and the handling of complaints, and the privacy of personal details linked to the possibility of payment fraud. These will be issues that will be the focus of much attention as the Internet grows in importance, and if they are not tackled effectively the growth of e-commerce could be seriously reduced.

Selling and early marketing has traditionally been based on a 'stimulus → response' sequence. In this process the supplier makes an attractive offer (stimulus) in the hope of receiving a positive response (purchase decision) from the customer. This was the basis of much early thinking about marketing, especially in the *fast-moving consumer goods* (fmcg) markets in the middle of the 20th century. It is still relevant in certain markets, and for certain products or services. However the response will depend to a large extent on the confidence a customer has regarding both the product offered and the supplier making the offering. In an unregulated market there is no obvious protection. In such a situation, the marketing role is to promote confidence regarding a supplier so customers are prepared to trade. Many techniques are available, but they all work best in a regulated yet competitive market place. In this type of market the role of marketing is to do more than instill confidence, it is to ensure that an offering is really the best available for a chosen group of customers.

MARKETING TODAY

The four aspects of marketing were earlier described as:

- Marketing as an organisational function
- Marketing as a management function
- Marketing as a business concept
- Marketing as a business philosophy.

Marketing in all these roles has one overriding task – to develop and retain customers for the business and to ensure that satisfactory exchanges take place between the supplier and the chosen customers. There is still a role for marketing in developing offers that customers find irresistible, the use of promotional techniques will always feature strongly in every marketing campaign. However there has been much development regarding the role of marketing over the last few decades. Good marketers understand their customers and base all activities on what can be made acceptable to them. Good marketers work inside their organisations to ensure that the best possible overall offering is developed and that it is supported by all employees of the company. But more importantly, today, good marketers regard customers as *partners* in the exchange process. Customers are not just there to be sold to, but are to be encouraged and developed so that every satisfied customer is an advocate for the supplier, prepared to recommend a favoured company to friends and acquaintances, and willing to purchase again from that organisation. This has led to the development of *relationship marketing*, a concept that focuses on retaining customers not just achieving a sale. Whilst market conditions are not always appropriate for relationship marketing, there are many occasions when such an approach leads to the best marketing option. This aspect of marketing will be discussed further in later chapters.

CONCLUSION

From reading this chapter, you should have grasped a basic understanding of what marketing is. It should also be clear that this involves understanding a number of different aspects of the subject, all of which centre upon the simple basic philosophy that customers are crucial to an organisation's success and this involves interacting with those customers and developing profitable exchanges with them over time. Tom Peters put profit into perspective:

> **Long-term profit *equals* revenue from continuously happy customer relationships *minus* cost.**

Marketing is therefore as we have seen, much more than selling, although some aspects of persuasion and influence are inevitably present. Satisfying customer needs over time, but not at any cost, is an ideal, but this requires that they are customers of your organisation, not your competitors. The obvious problem is that profit is required in any exchange, or at least a cost-effective use of resources. In addition there are wider ethical and moral issues, which will be discussed later. Suffice it to say that business today is not sales at any cost. A prominent US businessman once suggested:

> **There is a new bottom line for business – social approval. Without it, economic victory would be pyrrhic indeed.**

QUESTIONS

1 *How can marketing benefit organisations?*

2 *Describe how the exchange process functions.*

3 *In what ways do you see marketing developing in the future?*

FURTHER READING

Brabbs, C. (2000) 'Coke in One 2 One link to target teens market', *Marketing*, 3 February.

Brown, R. (1987) 'Marketing – a function and a philosophy', *Quarterly Review of Marketing*.

Davidson, H. (1997) *Even More Offensive Marketing*. Penguin.

Day, G. (1994) 'The capabilities of market driven organisations', *Journal of Marketing*, October.

Drucker, P. (1968) *The Practice of Management*, Pan.

Kotler, P., Armstrong, G., Saunders, J. and Wong, V. (1999) *Principles of Marketing*, 2nd European edn., Prentice-Hall.

Levitt, T. (1960) 'Marketing myopia', *Harvard Business Review*, March–April.

Levitt, T. (1974) *Marketing for Business Growth*.

Murphy, C. (2000) 'Why Coca-Cola is no longer it', *Marketing*, 20 January.

Nakamoto, M. and Kehoe, L. (2000) 'Japan to step up production of semiconductors', *Financial Times*, 14 April.

Saunders, R. (1999) *Business the amazon.com way*. Capstone Publishing.

Smith, A. (1976) *The Wealth of Nations*, Macmillan.

Wilson, T. (2000) 'New media choice/Number 10', *Marketing*, 18 May.

Marketing the virtual way

There are many ways in which organisations can try to get the customer to feel more in tune with them, and so more likely to be loyal customers, and it is not only organisations who try to make this happen but also political parties. To this end the government in Britain has a website www.pm.gov.uk and it is becoming increasingly popular. The prime minister at the time of writing is Tony Blair and he has a new message each Friday for the general public who view the site. Also on the site is a page telling how the government feel they have succeeded in many areas.

Other features of the site include photographs of each of the individual cabinet ministers along with a short biography on each, a virtual tour of 10 Downing St – especially the cabinet room. This part of the tour is very novel and to some most interesting, as it offers the view from Mr. Blair's seat as well as close-ups of the furniture, carpets and curtains.

It will be interesting to see future developments on the site, but there is no doubt a government site is here to stay.

Questions

1 *Do you think that the website will help the government to be seen in a favourable light?*

2 *In what ways do you think the government can market itself?*

3 *In what way could the www. pm.gov.uk site be improved for marketing purposes?*

4 *Which other organisations could benefit from having a website such as this?*

CASE STUDY

The Cola wars

There is aggressive worldwide competition between the major suppliers of cola drinks. The 'weapons' used are all aspects of marketing aimed to make individual brands more desirable than competitors.

Coca-Cola has been winning in the volume sales growth, whilst Pepsi Cola takes second place. In the UK although only 60 per cent of the population actually drink colas there are more men than women consumers, and the percentage of drinkers is much higher for the younger age groups when compared to the older age range. Thus the young are the main target market.

For many years Coca-Cola has been the leading brand, outselling Pepsi-Cola by more than two to one in the UK and by four to one worldwide (although in Scotland, the soft drink Irn-Bru is more popular than Coca-Cola). Diet Coke showed a similar dominance over Diet Pepsi. However, more than a decade ago in the US, Pepsi gained significant market share as a result of the effective marketing campaign featuring the 'Pepsi challenge' which concentrated on the product taste. This led to the well-documented launch of the ill-fated New Coke.

However Coca-Cola has now recovered and one of the secrets of its success is its widespread distribution coverage. Former Coke President Bob Woodward pledged 'to put Coke within an arm's reach of desire'. The emphasis on availability complements other aspects of the way Coke is offered.

More recently it has been Pepsi that has changed the presentation of its product with Pepsi Max and project blue – the re-packaging of the product. However the re-launch was reported as not successful. Pepsi worldwide (excluding the USA) made a loss in the year following the

▶

relaunch. Although Max is now performing well, the losses on the other two products (regular and Diet) have been a problem.

Things however have not been running smoothly for Coca-Cola. They suffered bad publicity and a drop in share price after being accused of mishandling a contamination scare in Belgium. The company was forced to destroy millions of cases of both Coca-Cola and Fanta when hundreds of people in Belgium became ill after drinking the products. The bad publicity was more from the fact that it took the company longer than a week to act on the rumours.

In Europe, PepsiCo and Virgin complained that Coca-Cola was using unfair practices. They alleged that Coke used discounts and rebates to entice wholesalers and retailers to grant them exclusive distribution. Similar problems are facing the company in other parts of the world, and in Russia Coke's plants are operating at levels far below capacity.

Coke is using several measures to fight back. The future will see much more use of the traditional glass bottle with its easy-to-recognise shape. 'Enjoy Coca-Cola' will replace the slogan 'Always Coca-Cola' and prices are likely to increase slightly to improve profit margins. Recent major advertising campaigns in the U.K. have encouraged consumers to collect on pack tokens from Coca-Cola and exchange them for a prepaid mobile phone. The mobile phone has a Coca-Cola fascia, and a ring tone that plays the jingle from the Coke television advert.

Pepsi also offered goods to help promote products, they included Sony Mini-Discs and Technics turntables at discounted prices, in return for a specified number of ring-pulls.

It is interesting to watch how the brands develop and how they compete with each other, but in the UK, the war has not been won completely. Companies such as Virgin who produce a variety of soft drinks and Barr's the makers of Irn-Bru are innovative and hungry for success. The future may yet be orange – the colour of Irn-Bru, it has been a runaway success in Scotland, is catching up in England, is especially popular when mixed with vodka in Russia, and is about to be launched in America. The soft drinks war is not static, it is indeed a tough market to be in.

Questions

1 *Given the facts above, what differences do you identify in the UK market between Coke and its competitors?*

2 *Do you think these are the cause of the 'runner up' position of Pepsi?*

3 *What changes do you think Pepsi could make to strengthen its position? – the answer is not to spend more on advertising, which has been tried, although you could discuss the benefits from association, such as those when Pepsi sponsored various international superstars.*

4 *Compare the competition between the following companies from the marketing viewpoint:*
    – Coca-Cola and Pepsi
    – McDonald's and Burger King
    – British Airways and Virgin Atlantic
    – Unilever and Proctor and Gamble.

Marketing orientations

INTRODUCTION

Having examined the different ways in which the term marketing is used, it is now possible to examine in more detail how marketing has evolved and the different descriptions given to each of these stages. The stages are as follows:

- Production
- Product
- Selling
- Marketing.

It is possible that students may be a little confused when comparing these particular areas in different books and articles; this is only because the words used to describe them vary from textbook to textbook, but invariably mean the same thing. These stages can be referred to as the marketing orientations, marketing concepts or marketing management philosophies. The following table identifies and describes the marketing orientations in turn (Table 2.1).

Further approaches include relationship marketing and societal marketing; they are often regarded as successors to the approaches outlined in Table 2.2. All of the

Table 2.1 Marketing orientations

Orientation	Profit driver	Western European timeframe	Characteristics
Production	Production methods	Until the 1950s	The improvement of production and distribution, in order to achieve a reduction in costs and improved efficiency
Product	Quality of product	Until the 1960s	The quality of the product is paramount Focus on product not customers' needs
Selling	Selling methods	1950s and 1960s	Effective selling and promotion are the major drivers to success
Marketing	Needs and wants of customers	1970 to present day	Focus on providing the goods and services that will satisfy the needs and wants of consumers

Table 2.2   Further approaches to marketing

Relationship marketing	Building and keeping good customer relations	1980s to present day	Emphasis is placed on the whole relationship between suppliers and customers The aim is to give the best possible attention, customer services and therefore build customer loyalty
Societal marketing	Benefit to society	1990s to present day	Similar characteristics as marketing orientation but with the added proviso that there will be a curtailment on any harmful activities to society, in either product, production, or selling methods

approaches are briefly outlined in this chapter but both relationship marketing and societal marketing will be covered in more depth later in the book.

PRODUCTION ORIENTATION

Production orientation is often a characteristic of organisations which have developed specific skills or technologies. It often involves manufacturing products in large quantities in order to minimise the costs of production. Providing acceptable quality at the lowest price is seen by many organisations as the main objective. Very often the problems with regard to production orientation, such as dissatisfied customers, are easy to recognise but difficult to correct. This is particularly true with regard to service organisations involving dedicated staff. Generally where a product has mass appeal, production orientation within manufacturing organisations has the effect of providing initial success followed by a significant decline.

There have been some classic examples of this, e.g. the Ford Motor Company of Detroit became the largest manufacturer of automobiles by developing the mass production process. This minimised the cost of production to the extent that no other manufacturer could offer a cheaper or better-value car. In 1927 the company was producing 1.5 million cars per year, twice as many as its nearest rival General Motors. Yet during that year Ford was unable to sell the cars that were being made. Former loyal customers in the USA were choosing one of the more modern vehicles being offered by Ford's competitors. The situation became so serious that Ford was forced to stop their production for 18 months until a new product could be launched. By this time, General Motors had successfully replaced Ford as market leader, which shows that customer loyalty is hard to keep, and also difficult to recover once lost.

These examples explain the production concept extremely well, however a more up-to-date one would be the production orientation currently being followed by the semiconductor industry. Massive investment is currently being undertaken in constructing large new plants and increasing manufacturing facilities in semiconductor manufacturers, the aim being to increase production capacity to keep up with the rapid growth in the industry; this has to a certain extent been fuelled by the strong demand for mobile phones, personal computers and digital cameras. Most of the new semiconductor production is taking place in the USA, Japan and Taiwan where there has also been a transition to copper as the metal that links transistors on a chip; the overriding aspect, however, is that production capability is being massively increased. A quote from Dan Hutcheson, the president of a market research group VSLI Research, sums up the situation very well.

> The market for semiconductor production equipment is so hot that equipment makers don't need to have any sales skills any more. Everything is dependent on how fast equipment producers can take orders and turn them around.

It remains to be seen if overproduction is achieved, whether there will be customer loyalty for any one semiconductor firm or whether the lowest price will win the orders.

PRODUCT ORIENTATION

> We produce excellent, well-designed, quality products which are great value for money. Customers are sure to want our products.

Product orientation occurs where the focus is given to the product rather than to the needs and wants of customers. This has often been the case in high-technology companies where scientists are excited by the superiority or originality of a product but little forethought is given to the appeal to the market. Insufficient consideration is also paid to whether there will be a genuine demand for the product and this has resulted in many products failing when they are launched. In some cases, however, success has been well deserved. James Dyson, whose focus on design and technology resulted in the bagless vacuum cleaner, provides a good example of product orientation and his ballbarrow, although not such a huge financial success, is also a good example.

There are many other older examples of successful product-orientated companies. One regularly cited is Sony of Japan. The founder, Masaru Ibuka was a brilliant inventor and he has said that, 'Merchandising and marketing people cannot envisage a market that does not exist'. Both he and his commercially aware partner, the late Akio Morita, purposely went out to meet potential consumers. They both deliberately visited places where people gathered and talked about product benefits. It might be unusual for a chairperson of a major international company to do market research, but it is claimed that is exactly how Akio Morita found there was a need for a personal and portable tape player. He recognised a need, and in spite of scepticism from his marketing people proceeded to design the 'Walkman'. This success is well known, and has been paralleled in the now common personal CD-players and miniature televisions. Further research will, however, show that this approach has resulted in market failure of a number of Sony developments, in spite of being technically superior to those offered by their competitors. One such product was the Betamax video recorder. This product failed in the market against the VHS system invented by JVC, mainly because it seems that JVC had a better understanding of the importance of the standardisation aspect of marketing. Unlike Sony, JVC actively encouraged other companies to adopt their system. Their agreement with companies in Taiwan and Korea prevented these companies from exporting their products for a number of years, while allowing them to manufacture and sell products in their domestic markets. Immediately the export ban expired these companies began exporting their products and, thus, the price of domestic video recorders dropped. Sony was unable to respond with their existing product, and also failed to secure production of sufficient major movie rights in Betamax format. Within months they were offering VHS recorders as these had become the accepted market standard. This was a crucial lesson for Sony, who when they were launching the Playstation made sure that an entire package of console and games were in place. In order that this would be the case Sony chose a forward-thinking software partner Psygnosis. Sega, on the other hand, then rushed to launch its CD-based console, Saturn, in June 1995 but supported it with only five titles. There ensued a race for superiority and sales but it appears that to date, Sony still has more games than either Sega or Nintendo. It would seem that Sony took the Betamix experience to heart, and has learnt from their mistake. Please see the case study at the end of the chapter for further developments in this market.

Product-orientated companies with potential mass markets very often become production-orientated. This makes them increasingly less able to respond when customers stop buying their products. Most react to this situation by implementing vigorous sales and advertising campaigns thus adopting a sales orientation.

Example   ## Levi-Strauss

Can Levi-Strauss regain its market position?

Philip Martineau, the new Chief Executive at Levi-Strauss, has a problem 'Levi's is a *mythical* brand, but its performance has been poor.' In fact as reported in *Business Week* (13 March 2000) the company has suffered three years of 'tumbling sales, lay-offs, plant closures and a failed attempt to attract the teenage and twenty market with its on-line selling initiative [discontinued in January 2000]'.

The report suggests that 'when fashion shifted to big-pocketed cargo and carpenter pants the [Levi] company hung back – and lost the youth market ... It's fortunes faded faster than a pair of jeans!!!!'

A young customer was reported as saying 'Levi's doesn't make the styles teenagers want. They now prefer baggy pants from JNCO and Kikwear. Levi's styles are too tight and for the older generation like middle aged people'.

So what went wrong? Basically it was the *product orientation* of the company. Since the mid 1990s the traditional five-pocketed jean has steadily lost out to the new fashions. Traditional jeans once represented over 50 per cent of the market, that is now down to below less than 20 per cent. Some stores that sell to the youth market have stopped retailing Levi's.

Martineau admits that Levi's have always been a season behind market trends but they now have completely missed developments. They believed in the 501 and continued with it as sales declined – a real product focus! But things are not easy because there is still a market for traditional jeans. Martineau's difficulty is that traditional jeans no longer appeal to all age groups like they used to. Levi's still need to retain their older customers and yet also wish to attract the younger generation. Is this really possible in the 21st century?

The dilemma for Martineau is that he believes: 'Levi's is too huge a brand to be focused on a narrow segment of the audience [market].'

SALES ORIENTATION

Sales orientation dictates that a business must aggressively promote its products. As the product already exists, sales staff are made responsible for identifying every potential customer. This does not mean that sales representatives are customer-orientated, as that would involve starting with customer needs and not the product.

The approach becomes: 'We have a good product and in this competitive market we must push it hard to achieve our sales goals.'

The authors of this book have extensive experience of selling and do not want to be unfair to the thousands of good salespeople throughout industry. Good sales staff understand the benefits their products offer and use these 'selling points' to convince customers. They also understand competition, as they are at the 'sharp end' of business and often their pay includes an element of commission on actual sales.

Sales orientation can emphasise one of two approaches, a *competitor focus* or a *customer focus*. It may be enough to beat the competition. There are no prizes for being second in a sales negotiation. But if you win the contract, make the sale and see the sales graph rise, there is satisfaction, as described in the case study.

Kenichi Ohmae introduced the concept of a *competitive triangle*. This considers that a customer can choose between a number of different, maybe even dissimilar, products or services. Each customer will choose the one that best meets his/her needs and reject the others. If this is accepted, it is enough that we offer a better match than our competitors (see Chapter 5 for more on the competitive triangle).

Unfortunately, companies, which adopt a sales orientation, inevitably find that this is only effective for a short time but involves significantly increased costs and so is successful only at the expense of the profitability of the organisation.

You might like to consider whether this is the true goal of a marketing-led organisation.

Example	## Job satisfaction

Gary, a Plant Science graduate working for a major pharmaceutical company as a medical representative, got his job through a specialist agency. He describes his work thus:

'Within my own territory I have sole responsibility. I get a quarterly allowance for entertainment/meetings – how I spend this is up to me, but I am expected to get value for money.

I have large quantities of prescription-only samples and free promotional material, which are also my responsibility. I also have a company car, film equipment, company stationery, etc. I work alone for most of the time. At other times I am being field trained, attending sales meetings and large promotional meetings.

My working hours are not defined, but on average I leave the house at 7.30–8.00 am (later if working near home) and get back about 5.00–6.00 pm. I have an hour for lunch, flexible, but usually 1.00 till 2.00 pm. I work a five-day week, but may do meetings or attend exhibitions in the evenings or Saturdays, for which I get extra pay.

I do not have to keep records of hours worked, it doesn't affect salary anyway. I spend Thursday evenings doing administration to be posted on Friday to my manager.

We do the job for money not love. It is not easy, so there is a high drop-out rate. We are expected to be very smart at all times. Promotion is limitless – our managing director started as a rep – but it must be earned by success, and not time served.

You need to get on with people, especially self-important ones, and to work on your own initiative. The ability to read minds is helpful and the ability to speak in public is essential, but it comes with practice anyway. You must be able to drive, and have a clean licence.

Major satisfaction is rare, and only occurred once for me so far, when a doctor came up and thanked me for telling him about a drug because he saved someone's life with it. Most satisfaction comes from nice sales graphs with steep climbing lines on them, and therefore a healthier bank balance.'

MARKETING ORIENTATION

Customers' needs change over time, whether for industrial or consumer products. Maybe we have persuaded a customer to buy our product because it offered the best price or because of some high-pressure selling. Then, as soon as a product that is a better match for the customer's requirement comes on the market, they might drop us in favour of the new product. We have not earned much customer loyalty. If we have worked hard to develop our product to reflect customers' needs then they may not switch so readily. It is up to our company to be both competitor- and customer-orientated. This is called a *marketing orientation* (see Figure 2.1).

To return to the words of Kenichi Ohmae:

Competitive realities are only what you test possible strategies against. You define what you want to do in terms of customers.

Question

Which of these statements best describes a marketing orientation?

- *I make what I can sell.*
- *I sell what I can make.*

We now should begin to understand the importance of marketing orientation and the crucial need to start with the customer in defining the business we are in, and therefore make what we can sell. However, it is much more difficult to implant a marketing orientation in a company than it might seem. Marketing orientation does not occur because a company has a marketing department, or because the managing director says so. It occurs when the customer notices the difference. It happens only when all people in an organisation measure themselves in terms of the benefits offered to customers. It does not matter whether you are directly interfacing with a customer or not. In most organisations a whole range of people have contact with customers. This

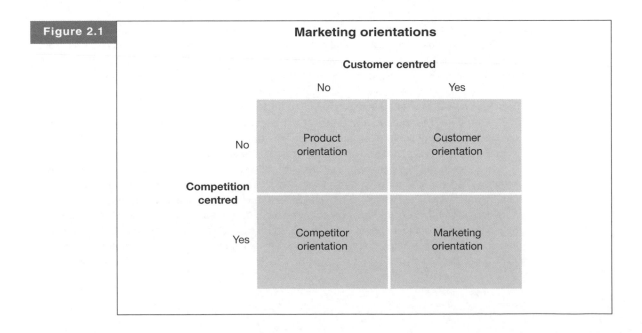

Figure 2.1

Marketing orientations

would include the telephone operator, delivery driver, repair mechanic, or invoice clerk, as well as the usual sales and marketing contacts.

Many organisations are now running customer care programmes, which include all members of staff. Those who are not directly involved in the marketing function can be called part-time marketers because they have a key customer support role. Some organisations do not have any specific marketing staff, yet the company is successful. This happens occasionally in companies where the main focus is on ensuring products supplied and services offered are right for the customers.

Customer relationships are particularly important if you are in a service organisation. One of the differences between a service and a product is the ownership of the core product – that is, the benefit that is received from the product. Another is that the production of the services takes place at the time of delivery. An example of this could be that of a taxi driver. The drivers do not often consider themselves as marketers, but as taxi drivers. In Coventry, a city in England, there are several major taxi firms, but if one particular firm gave prompt, efficient and cheerful service to all its customers, when a taxi is next needed this will be remembered, and then that firm will get repeat business. This is a good example of a part-time marketer at work. A marketing-orientated company will be full of part-time marketers.

Example   ## Wal-Mart stores

Wal-Mart is a classic example of a company that has embraced a *marketing orientation*.
Listed below are some quotes from a report on Wal-Mart.

'Every morning at 5.30 am the previous days results for each region, store, department and merchandise line are provided to managers, who in turn pass on pertinent information to their associates [employees].'

'Stories about Sam Walton and those associates who have made exceptional efforts to please customers are told regularly. These have become the informal way to communicate expectations and behaviours to other associates.'

'Wal-Mart makes the customer the focus of everything they do. The company empowers all associates closest to the customer to do whatever it takes to satisfy them. This can go beyond the normal helpful, friendly service and can include a cashier giving a customer a price reduction based on the customer's word that the product was cheaper elsewhere, or replacing at no charge an item left in the parking lot.'

'Wal-Mart consider themselves to be "students" of customer buying habits, demographics, wants, likes and preferences through data gathering and personal contact. They see their role as the "customer's agent" – seeking out the best products, negotiating the best price, and passing on savings to customers. The policy of EDLP (everyday low prices) drives the company, but price is not the sole determinant of their success'

'The company is willing to try out many new ideas and to adjust them depending upon their success.'

Wal-Mart is a pro-active company that makes exceptional effort to please its customers. They want to make shopping a pleasurable experience and they are willing to change or adapt anything in order to remain relevant to the needs of customers.

FURTHER APPROACHES TO MARKETING

Relationship marketing

As the name suggests this type of approach to marketing is all about building up lasting relationships between suppliers and customers. The subject will be covered in more detail later in the book but is outlined here to help explain how marketing has developed.

One of the main objectives of organisations is to try to keep the customers as happy as possible so that they will keep coming back. A good example to demonstrate this is that of car sales, and in particular the role of the salesperson in the showroom. In many instances a relationship is built up over the years between customers and the same salesperson, so when it is time to buy a new car or upgrade the car, many people automatically return to the same salesperson year after year. One of the authors has bought three cars from the same salesman, even though on one occasion this meant going to a different showroom as the salesman had changed jobs.

With the increase in electronic commerce there will be more customers wishing to buy cars and other products over the Internet. The concept of relationship marketing will still be very important for e-commerce as it has been for the more traditional product outlets. The marketer must ensure that customer interaction is a good experience. This can be encouraged by organisations having an informative, innovative and perhaps interactive web presence, as it is likely to attract attention. Then when people are used to dealing with the company over the Internet, the relationship is strengthened, the good service and efficiency can lead to repeat buying from the customer.

Another way in which retailers especially have been trying to build a relationship with their customers is by introducing loyalty cards and other special reward cards. In Britain, one of the best known examples is Tesco the supermarket chain who offer customers incentives to be loyal by giving rewards when they purchase goods. In the USA fashion retailers such as Beall's and Claire's Accessories offer customers discounts if they can produce a completed loyalty card. These are cards or vouchers that are stamped on each occasion when the customers purchase goods to a certain value. Thus customers have a financial incentive to be loyal and build a lasting relationship with the organisation. There are of course companies who feel that such schemes are not the best route to take, and Safeway, a supermarket chain in Britain, is withdrawing its loyalty card as it is felt that the card no longer has customer appeal.

Societal marketing

The societal marketing orientation is a logical progression from marketing orientation. Marketing orientation focuses on the benefits to particular customers – that is, keeping the customer happy and offering them what they need and want. Societal marketing does all this, but in addition considers the needs of society as a whole. The focus therefore is on a curtailment of any activities that could possibly harm society, and an increase in policies that promote the wellbeing of society as a whole. This type of outlook has been one of the factors that helped the growth of the Body Shop. A range of business activities undertaken by the company included the following:

- The sourcing of raw materials from underdeveloped countries
- An aversion to exploitation of the indigenous population in the underdeveloped countries
- The non-testing of products on animals
- The use of recycled materials for packaging.

It can be seen from these examples that the ethos of societal marketing pervades the company. There is however, some difficulty in saying one organisation has a societal marketing orientation and another has not. It has been argued that cigarette companies, because they put a government health warning on cigarettes, are satisfying their customers needs and wants and being considerate to society as a whole. Heinz, who are currently planning to launch its Linda McCartney vegetarian foods range abroad could also argue that vegetarian foods are good for society. McDonald's is a global brand and is renowned for producing a consistent product, having high standards of cleanliness and service and being societally aware with regard to packaging. There are however pressure groups which target multinational firms that pursue profits for shareholders. McDonald's have been accused of paying low wages to workers, cruelty in the rearing of some of its animals and deliberately targeting children in its advertisements. All of these accusations would deem the company not to be societally marketing-orientated, but pressure groups have admitted that the only reason they target McDonald's is that as it is an industry giant, it can afford to make improvements which could influence other food chains. It would therefore appear that awarding the label of being 'societally aware' to a company is not clear cut and although there is much to recommend the policies of some large companies, there would always appear to be some room for improvement.

The government also has a large influence on the speed and degree to which companies adopt improvements which can benefit society. Government policy with regard to reducing emissions from cars and manufacturing firms can have a huge influence in helping to minimise the pollution in the atmosphere.

The societal marketing concept is therefore one which is very important for the well-being of society in some ways, but has to be carefully considered so that a minority pressure group does not have undue influence stopping something which many others feel may benefit the majority of the population. This is a very topical area and therefore can give rise to further discussion; it is covered in greater depth in a later chapter.

THE ORGANISATIONAL IMPLICATIONS OF MARKETING

If customers are those that purchase, use, or consume a product or service, then clearly to be successful, organisations need to develop and maintain relationships with a variety of different customers. Table 2.3 demonstrates that customers come in many different guises and may be described differently by organisations in different fields. The

Table 2.3 Who is the customer?

Buyer	Sponsor	Patient
Customer	Patron	Pupil
Consumer	Subscriber	Parent
User	Supporter	Motorist
Recipient	Member	Passenger
Adviser	Colleague	Guest
Client	Delegate	Accountant
Viewer	Tourist	Contractor
Reader	Shopper	Distributor
Listener	Householder	Agent
Lender	Taxpayer	Retailer
Banker	Resident	Stockist
Applicant	Ratepayer	Factor
Prospect	Voter	

broad common factor is that they require special treatment from the provider. A customer-orientated approach can therefore apply equally to a food manufacturer or a public sector organisation.

Customer orientation has already been touched on, everyone in the organisation must aim to serve the customer, whether directly or indirectly. This is customer sovereignty: it places the customer effectively at the top of the organisation chart. The substance and credibility of this customer-centredness will be put to the test daily in all sorts of ways (e.g. how long to answer the telephone, promptness of delivery, product quality). The performance and integration of all these activities requires management and training. They cannot be left to chance. Many different types of organisations are putting this into practice – for example, many police stations in Britain have officers in charge of customer service.

Organisations which have adopted the marketing philosophy and are marketing-orientated, will be consistently, over time, developing and improving their relationships with their customers. This requires a commitment to providing customer satisfaction, and the flexibility to respond to customer requirements and changes in the environment in which the organisation operates.

THE MANAGEMENT IMPLICATIONS OF MARKETING

For managers, the application of marketing principles involves both how they operate as individuals, and how they ensure the integration and co-ordination of activities within the organisation. At the individual level, managers within organisations that are marketing-orientated regularly ask questions fundamental to the success of their company such as the following:

- Where are we now?
- Where do we want to get to?
- How do we get there?

These questions can be seen as the starting point for the development of future strategies for the company. When the questions, and answers to them, are analysed they often set the scene for the way forward for the company. It is a good starting point for top management to develop strategies which will lead to competitive advantage in the future. The time frame and cost of any actions to be undertaken can be considered in depth and the most cost-effective and advantageous actions undertaken. Strategy implications with regard to all of these factors are considered in later chapters in more depth.

Obviously the analysis of the organisation's current position is vital, but it is important to consider issues for the future, rather than being focused on the past. This approach is shown in the following questions:

- Who are our existing/potential customers?
- What are their current and future needs?
- How can we satisfy these needs?
- Can we offer a product/service the customer would value?
- Can we communicate with customers?
- Can we deliver a competitive product or service?
- Why should customers buy from us?

It is the responsibility of an organisation's management generally, and its marketing management specifically, to find answers to these questions, and thereby develop solutions to market needs, within the constraints of the organisation's resources and policies. Especially important is the final question, which recognises that customers in most markets have many products from which to choose.

To answer this question we need to first understand the environments in which all organisations operate (see Chapters 3 and 4). We also need to develop a basic knowledge of how people behave when making buying decisions (see Chapters 6 and 7).

At the organisational level, being marketing-orientated commits managers and their customers to:

- a customer orientation
- co-ordinated efforts by all parts of the organisation, and, usually
- a return on investment, rather than sales volume.

An alternative set of key principles is offered by Hugh Davidson, a British writer, who argues that successful marketing requires the application of POISE. That is, marketing should be:

P Profitable
O Offensive (rather than defensive)
I Integrated
S Strategic (= future-orientated)
E Effective (it gets results)

The common thread in these observations, and those of other writers, is the recognition that marketing has to be consciously planned and integrated.

Marketing management is essentially about the co-ordination of customer-directed activities. In particular, good practice and competitive pressure should ensure that a customer focus prevails throughout the organisation. It must be present during each and every activity, rather than fall casualty to the sectional interests and biases of individuals or functional groups. For resource reasons, too, marketing activities should be tightly and smoothly scheduled, without undue delays, cost overruns or other problems that would affect profitability and competitiveness.

Organisationally, marketing involves a set of activities that has to be managed. The management process involved might be generalised as in the following sequence:

1 Research and information
2 Analysis
3 Plans and forecasts } Informed decisions
4 Organisation and co-ordination } Integration
5 Implementation
6 Control } Responsiveness
7 Review } Results – Orientation

The process might be viewed as a continuous cycle of managed activities, guided by key principles. The management task involves planning and co-ordinating the functions of marketing. These, as already discussed, range from more familiar activities such as sales and advertising to specialist fields such as merchandising, research, product development, distribution and customer service.

In practice, these specialist activities will be planned and integrated within an organisation's marketing programme. The exact mix of activities will vary according to the demands of the target market, and will be the subject of major strategic decisions by marketing management.

There is a continuing debate about the relative merits of product management and market management. In the former, a product champion works to maximise objectives through the controllable variables available to the organisation. These controllable variables are another term for the marketing mix, namely product, price, place and promotion. Marketing management focuses on a specific market or market segment and aims to offer the best mix of products to meet the requirement of this group. The merits of these different approaches will be discussed in more detail later, with respect to marketing organisation. There are also organisations with no formal marketing department, but in order to succeed in a dynamic market the key functions are performed either by specialists or by managers who intuitively understand market requirements.

CONCLUSION

Everyone in an organisation needs to be aware of the importance to the organisation of the customers. If this does not happen the firm will fail to grasp the opportunity to reach its full potential. One thing which is very important to remember, is that *marketing is not optional* – for a company to succeed marketing has continued and will continue to play a vital role. It remains to be seen what the full impact of the new technology will bring to the world of marketing, but the marketing orientations are lessons well learned. All sizes of businesses need to put the customer first, not the product nor the production: the customer is the key to success.

QUESTIONS

1   *Describe in your own words the marketing management philosophies outlined in the chapter.*

2   *How does marketing contribute to a company's prosperity?*

3   *From your own experience, name a company that you consider being marketing-oriented. Justify your choice.*

4   *With the growth in business carried out via the Internet, will the traditional view of the marketing concept still be viable?*

FURTHER READING

Beenstock, S. (1998) 'Market raider: how Sony won the console game', *Marketing*, 10 September.

Brown, R. (1987) 'Marketing – a function and a philosophy', *Quarterly Review of Marketing*.

Crawford, A. (1999) 'Times launches £35m schools software offer', *Marketing*, 23 September.

Davidson, H. (1997) *Even More Offensive Marketing*. Penguin.

Drucker, P. (1968) *The Practice of Management*. Pan.

Jardine, A. (1999) 'McDonald's still facing a McLibel backlash', *Marketing*, 16 September.

Kehoe, L. (2000) 'Chip makers gear up for record year', *Financial Times*, 14 April.

Levitt, T. (1960) 'Marketing myopia', *Harvard Business Review*, March–April.

Levitt, T. (1974) *Marketing for Business Growth*.

Morita, A. (1986) *Made in Japan*. Dutton.

Nakamoto, M. and Kehoe, L. (2000) 'Japan to step up production of semiconductors', *Financial Times*, 14 April.

Ohmae, K. (1983) *The Mind of the Strategist*. Pan.

Peters, T. (1988) *Thriving on Chaos*. Macmillan.

Rosier, B. (1999) 'Coke offers website for teachers', *Marketing*, 16 September.

Slater, A. and Kolizeras, K. (1988) *Graduate Careers Information Book*. Sales Careers Services Trust.

Whitfield, P. (1999) 'UB links up with Mirror for £15m schools push', *Marketing*, 16 September.

Williamson, D. (2000) 'The games console: the missing link?', *Revolution*, 27 April.

CASE STUDY

Console game wars

There have been many developments in recent years in the games console market. Microsoft is now a new player in the market and wants a share in the global profits to be made. To achieve a market in this competitive field it is launching the X-box which is a games console with an 8 giga-byte hard drive, and equipped to utilise on-line music and video services as well as having a web capability. Microsoft's group product and marketing manager, Richard Teversham, feels that there will be no real threat to the home personal computer market as home personal computer users are more interested in specification upgrades in computers rather than a plug in and play console. The X-box will plug into the television, be able to run Windows-compatible games as well as play DVDs . Presently major games developers are involved in setting up marketing strategy and it is expected that the X-Box will be the biggest launch in Microsoft history.

Sony, who currently control almost 70 per cent of the games console market, has the Sony PlayStation 2 (PS2), which is also web-enabled and DVD-compatible. The PS2 is designed in order that users can decide the level of technology they desire. The machine was envisaged not to have a modem as standard, but at the same time plays a role in Sony's strategy in that it could sell goods and services from a Sony web department store. This store is likely to sell goods and services, which include on-line financial services.

Sega's web-enabled Dreamcast is positioned as a full entertainment console and appeals to a mass audience. Sega also is investing heavily in intellectual property and is to set up an interactive entertainment company called Sega.com. They see this as an exciting development to give customers something that is not available elsewhere.

Nintendo's next console is code named Dolphin, and at time of writing there is little yet released regarding developments.

All in all it is a very exciting field with strong competition and new developments occurring at a fast pace.

Questions

1   *Given the facts above, what differences do you identify in the UK market (or any market of your choice) between Microsoft's X-box and its competitors?*

2   *What changes do you think Sega could make to increase its sales?*

3   *If you were marketing manager of any of the companies mentioned, how would you make your company the winner?*

4   *Given the current developments in the industry, what do you feel are the main drivers for marketing success?*

CASE STUDY

Marketing and education – societal marketing or merely promotion?

One of the promises the Labour party made to be elected to office in Britain was that there would be a focus on education. It is not only political parties who see education as being a by-word for popularity, but also companies have entered the popularity stakes by publicising their interest in helping schools. In 1999 there was a Books for Schools campaign which resulted in two million books being distributed to 28,000 schools. This initiative was backed by *The Times* and *The Sunday Times* and helped boost the circulation of both newspapers over a 16 week period.

Another initiative was the Software for Schools campaign, which encouraged school children to collect tokens from *The Times, The Sunday Times* and *Times Education Supplement*. The tokens could be exchanged for free software from leading software suppliers, including Microsoft and Lotus. W.H. Smith also supported the campaign with point of sale promotions.

Early in the year 2000 Walkers crisps had a tie-up with *News International* in a Books for Schools scheme which had children and parents saving tokens printed on crisp packets. For several years Tesco has run a successful Computers For Schools promotion.

In March 2000 the Labour government launched a promotion 'Maths Year 2000.' The aim was to help improve the overall maths standards of children. The education and employment secretary David Blunkett supported another promotion, the campaign spearheaded by United Biscuits, owner of the McVitie's and KP Foods brands. Linking with the Mirror Group they invested £15m in providing maths equipment to schools. The United Biscuits promotion was called 'Maths Stuff for Schools' and was supported by a large advertising campaign, with coupons appearing on many of United Biscuits snacks, cakes and biscuit labels, as well as in the Mirror Groups newspapers. Schools could exchange the coupons for mathematical equipment such as protractors, compasses and calculators. One reason why the companies wanted to do this was given by Alison Head, the head of communication at McVities, she stated that 'People believe in cause-related charity. We know that education in schools is a really strong motivator.' Another factor may be the fact that United Biscuits expected the promotion to generate £42m in extra sales across its McVities and KP Foods brands. However, in a recent survey by Mintel Research it was found that 60 per cent of consumers are cynical about companies' motives for cause-related marketing.

This research however has not stopped the flow in promoting products via education. Coca-Cola Schweppes Beverages (CCSB) is taking it a step further and providing teachers with an educational resource website. The aim of the website is to build brand awareness and will be free to teachers at schools, which have Coca-Cola brands in drink machines and canteens. Teachers will be able to download lesson plans and also sheets to handout to pupils on a variety of curriculum subjects – each handout will be linked to a different CCSB brand. A spokesperson from CCSB has stated that 'Each lesson plan has a brand affiliation, but only where it's appropriate. There's not a prerequisite that the teacher has to mention that brand.'

Questions

1 *Are the companies taking action that will benefit society?*

2 *Are the above advertising campaigns ethical?*

3 *What type of marketing management philosophy do you feel the above companies are following? Give reasons for your answers.*

4 *Do you think that this type of promotion would be effective for Further and Higher Education establishments?*

3 The marketing environment

It is the everlasting and unchanging rule of this world that everything is created by a series of causes and conditions and everything disappears by the same rule; everything changes, nothing remains constant.

The teachings of Buddha

INTRODUCTION

The environment plays a major role in the decision making of firms, indeed if companies fail to note what is happening around them they run the risk of having to give profit warnings and perhaps going out of business. If however the company is aware of the environment, and the opportunities that arise because of changes, then there is potential for new sources of revenue. The following is an article from the *Financial Times* which clearly shows how awareness of the environment can help business to adapt and stay in business.

Example | ### Carmakers eye route to twin track revenues | **FT**

Motor industry chiefs are beginning to realise that there are higher profit margins in downstream activities such as loans, insurance and in-car infotainment, writes Tim Burt

Signs of a slowdown in the global automotive industry have encouraged manufacturers to seek new sources of revenue from downstream activities. Falling sales in both North America and Europe have already forced leading carmakers to cut production and squeeze suppliers.

Ford, General Motors (GM) and DaimlerChrysler – the big three in the US – are all restructuring in one way or another. Ford has pledged to cut costs by Dollars 1bn this year, while pushing through an aggressive overhaul in Europe. GM is cutting 15,000 jobs, jettisoning its Oldsmobile brand and reducing European capacity by 400,000 units a year. Neither, however, is facing the sort of challenge confronting DaimlerChrysler. The German-US group is cutting 26,000 jobs at its troubled Chrysler division and warning of further pressures in 2001.

Although the decline in US light vehicle sales has not been as rapid as initially feared, demand remains volatile and there is no help on the horizon in the shape of significant volume or price increases. The same is true in Europe and Asia, where Autopolis, the industry consultants, predicts sales will fall this year and next.

In this difficult trading environment, manufacturers are looking to downstream activities to sustain them through a downturn. Industry leaders such as Jac Nasser, chief executive of Ford Motor Company, and Rick Wagoner, his opposite number at GM, recognise that margins made from selling finance, insurance, parts and even mobile "infotainment" are much higher than from making and selling cars. There are also considerable savings to be achieved in sales, distribution and marketing.

Salomon Schroder Smith Barney, the US investment bank, calculates that distribution in Europe – including advertising, marketing support and transport – represents up to 30 per cent

▶

of a vehicle's pre-tax retail price and almost 27 per cent in the US. If carmakers can cut those costs, then it will greatly reduce unit costs per car, and feed through to the bottom line. A twin-track approach is emerging, therefore, in the auto industry's downstream activities. On the one hand, the manufacturers are exploring new business opportunities in areas such as vehicle financing and in-car internet services.

Income from such business could supplement their existing sources of profit. On the other hand, they are seeking big savings in distribution and marketing activities beyond the factory gate. "Several carmakers are already pursuing plans to rationalise their dealer network in favour of larger, better-funded groups," says John Lawson, head of automotive research at Schroder Salomon Smith Barney. "Most have plans to develop build-to-order manufacturing and all have developed B2C internet sites." So far, however, they have yet to see the benefit of such projects. Internet sales are being used mainly as an information service to connect potential customers to dealers with stock. Build-to-order has proved difficult to implement for mass-market manufacturers which are geared to batch production.

The initiatives may also owe more to the changing regulatory environment than to changing sentiment among the original equipment manufacturers (OEMs). In Europe, for example, the expiry next year of the European block exemption on new car sales will lead to wholesale change in vehicle retailing. If the reforms lead to a free-for-all among dealers and new retail entrants, then manufacturers will have to find alternative ways to protect their revenues. It will also increase the pressure on manufacturers to look for new earnings streams. This is the reason for pilot projects on direct internet sales and the consolidation of dealer activities by some carmakers. That has alarmed some traditional dealers. But they are still likely to play an important role, if only to deliver the vehicles and offer service functions. Other dealers have realised that they must capture more of the product lifecycle.

Put simply, this means retaining the car-buyer as a long-term customer throughout his ownership of the vehicle. At the same time, the manufacturers want to build relationships with the vehicle's second or third owners. They believe they can earn money from recycling vehicles once they reach the end of their lives.

Mr Nasser at Ford calls this bundling of activities and services, including areas such as rapid repair shops and financing, as "adopting the consumer headset". It means that rather than selling a car, manufacturers will, in future, talk about acquiring customers. The key is good customer relationship management (CRM). By improving their CRM activities, the carmakers believe they can derive benefits not only in after-sales but also in production schedules – by building to order – and, eventually, in product development.

For this to work, however, the manufacturers will need to stay in touch with customers for much of their vehicle-buying life. As cars become increasingly sophisticated, so, too, do the technologies that accompany them. And these are seen as another potential revenue source. Examples include General Motor's OnStar multimedia business, which offers voice-activated concierge services, emergency assistance and on-line information on a number of different vehicles. The service, also acquired by other manufacturers, is one of a growing range of premium technologies which, it is hoped, will deliver additional profits and attract new customers. Among the features designed to capture such long-term customers, telematics – embracing everything from navigation systems to in-car e-mail – is just one of the new range of incentives. According to some analysts, global revenues from such services could grow from about Dollars 4bn at present to Dollars 47bn by the end of the decade. Meanwhile, existing downstream operations, particularly in finance and leasing, are likely to become more refined. Having been stung by the impact of falling residual values on leasing contracts, inhouse finance companies, such as Ford Credit and GMAC, may introduce new products that reduce their risk exposure from buy-back guarantees. Not only that, but they can leverage their financial customer base to sell other loans, including mortgages and credit.

Ford Credit, for example, hopes that drive will help to lift earnings by at least 10 per cent this year. All this reflects a structural change in the industry, where a multi-channel approach is emerging in distribution and retailing. Manufacturers are transforming themselves into service providers, where marketing costs will be much more tightly controlled in future.

In part, this is being forced upon them by changes in the regulatory environment. But it also reflects increasing sophistication on the part of carbuyers, who are much more aware of the choices open to them. To woo new customers, a broader service is required. Manufacturers are ready to embrace that challenge because these services – dubbed "product-life management" – could be the key to future profits.

Source: Financial Times, 28 February, 2001 (Copyright: The Financial Times Limited)

The marketing environment factors are often referred to as Social, Technological, Economic and Political variables (STEP). Some authors arrange the variables in a different order, namely Political, Economic, Social and Technological and they are then known as PEST, but it is does not matter which word is used to refer to them. It is difficult or indeed almost impossible for organisations to influence the environment, unless of course the organisations are extremely large and may then be able to exert an influence on government policy. Generally however, organisations have little influence over any of these environmental variables, and they are therefore referred to as uncontrollable variables. This is in contrast to the variables that companies have direct control over, such as product, price, place and promotion, and because of this, these marketing activities or variables are known as the controllable variables. Figure 3.1 shows the relationship between these two types of variable.

THE MARKETING FUNCTION AND THE ENVIRONMENT

Marketing as a function is basically all about matching the offerings of the organisation to the outside world, in particular, the market place. Not surprisingly, many

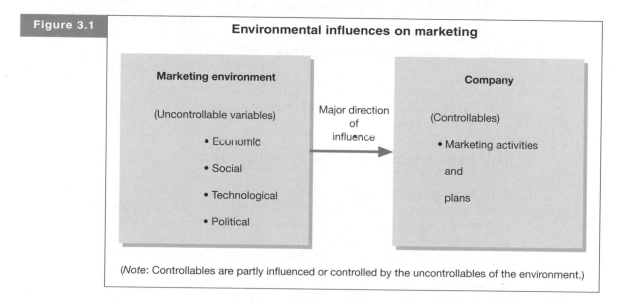

Figure 3.1

Environmental influences on marketing

Marketing environment

(Uncontrollable variables)

- Economic
- Social
- Technological
- Political

Major direction of influence →

Company

(Controllables)

- Marketing activities

and

plans

(*Note*: Controllables are partly influenced or controlled by the uncontrollables of the environment.)

functions within marketing, such as selling, product development and market research, concern themselves with issues, problems and opportunities outside the organisation, and focus on responding to outside events and circumstances. Indeed, Kotler identifies in this external role the need for marketers to develop an 'outside-in' perspective, an ability to work on *external cues and stimuli* to the profit of the whole organisation. Another notable marketing writer, John Howard, emphasises the strategic role of marketing as 'the function by which the firm responds to changes in its environment'.

Response and sensitivity to the environment remains one of the acid-test indicators of success or failure in business in general, and in marketing in particular. The annals of business history and new product development are littered with instances of companies that have lost touch with their markets, misinterpreted or ignored tell-tale signs of change, or become blinded by previous successes and driven by some corporate inertia. Readers might find it instructive to examine a company report, or columnist commentaries on company results, and consider the significant influence on company performance that environmental issues may wield.

At first sight it may seem difficult to see how companies cannot spot the environmental issues that affect their performance. After all, the environment is all about us, literally staring us in the face! Unfortunately, companies all too often become preoccupied with their day-to-day problems, and hard-pressed managers become engrossed in priorities and deadlines more squarely within their responsibility than perhaps marginal changes outside. This is possibly one of the key difficulties with the external environment: it is outside the hubbub of today's business problems, and, excepting the rare instances of sudden change, it tends to present an all too comforting picture of at best gradual change. Sudden changes in the environment are more exceptional and, in any case, cannot be missed! The norm is generally a picture of incremental change over an extended period of time. It is this 'norm' that can prove deceptively dangerous, as the following commentary by Charlotte Villiers demonstrates:

> To look at British industry today is to be reminded of one simple, if rather brutal, analogy that top managers should take to heart: if you put a frog into a pan of cold water and turn on the heat, the frog will happily sit there without noticing the water is getting hot. The result, inevitably, is one boiled, dead frog. But if you drop a frog into some warm water, the frog realises immediately that it is too hot and jumps straight back out again.

The moral of this tale is simply that people do not notice incremental change going on around them until it is too late. Like the doomed frog, many businesses fail to notice what is happening in their environment until their fate is sealed.

THE DIMENSIONS OF THE ENVIRONMENT

In examining the environment in more detail, a basic model will be presented of different dimensions or levels of the environment, each more complex, distant and all-embracing than the previous one. A useful analogy would be to view the marketing environment as a series of subsets within sets, within an ultimate or universal set – the inner subsets are more accessible and familiar to the marketer, the outer sets more indistinct and vague, like a distant landscape. Figure 3.2 illustrates this multidimensional view.

Figure 3.2

Four levels of the marketing environment

Level 1	Level 2	Level 3	Level 4
The company	Company markets	Company stakeholder system	Economic Social Technological Political — The wider environment

Predictably, it is the more distant and complex dimensions of the wider environment (Level 4 in Figure 3.2) that occasion most concern and problems among marketers, and therefore warrant more detailed coverage.

THE COMPANY SETTING (LEVEL 1)

However, the nearer reaches of the marketing environment, Levels 1–3 in Figure 3.2, are important elements of the everyday setting of marketing – Kotler refers to these collectively as the company's *microenvironment*. They are subject to many of the same external factors and Chapter 4 says some more about this aspect of marketing.

Whether organised as a separate department or not, the marketing function operates within an organisational context, and is most effective when well managed, planned and resourced. Within marketing itself, subfunctions such as sales, advertising, research and promotion need to be co-ordinated to produce effective results. The marketing function must integrate with other functions such as production, engineering, purchasing, accounting and personnel. Close working relationships between marketing and functions such as R&D and production will be critical to key ventures, e.g. new product innovation, and will generally affect everyday performance indicators such as customer service. Within this 'inner environment', therefore, a wider role for marketing will be to communicate company-wide the market's requirements and their implications – an aspect of internal marketing. Marketers should be able to assess the organisation's strengths and limitations in major functional specialisms, since important policy issues such as product development and competitive strategy will depend heavily on the commercial exploitation of comparative advantage. Such internal 'audits' of relative strengths and weaknesses will often be routinely made in problem solving and planning, and will commonly be combined with information on the external situation, trends and events.

COMPANY MARKETS (LEVEL 2)

Many companies begin operations within one clearly defined market and develop, through market penetration, by servicing the market more efficiently and knowledgeably. Later growth, however, may depend on finding or developing new markets, and learning to service new types of customer with differing requirements. For other companies, multimarket operations may be entered into from the outset, as a

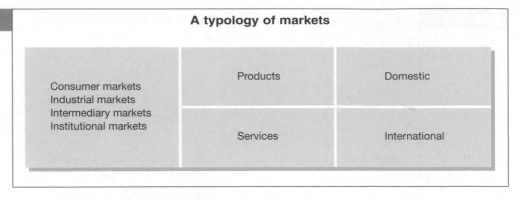

Figure 3.3

A typology of markets

Consumer markets Industrial markets Intermediary markets Institutional markets	Products	Domestic
	Services	International

conscious policy decision. Figure 3.3 presents a simplified view of the types of market that a company might choose to service.

Although most of the terms used are self-explanatory, it is important to note that requirements may differ greatly between the market types – e.g. consumer markets usually involve many more customers, buying for various personal requirements, while industrial markets will involve a smaller number of professional buyers, sourcing for commercial reasons. Intermediary markets involve reseller organisations such as retailers, wholesalers and brokers, selling on to other buyers at a profit. The term 'institutional markets' denotes buyers within institutions such as schools, hospitals, dedicated associations and organisations (e.g. the Church), local authorities and central government. Buyers in such markets may operate through strict rules and procedures and by well-documented plans.

Clearly, the market environment within which a company chooses to operate will vary greatly according to market type. Even if specialising in one market, the company would need to conduct regular research and feedback exercises in order to monitor market changes and turning points.

Last but not least, the competitors a company faces will vary according to the choice of market, or even the corner or sector of the market that it services – competitors are as much part of the market environment as customers.

THE STAKEHOLDER SYSTEM (LEVEL 3)

As the term implies, a company operates within the context of a network of interest groups, each of which has a particular relationship with the organisation, and often conflicting interests and motivations. Figure 3.4 illustrates the stakeholder system for a hypothetical company operating within the prescription medicine field.

Certainly part of this stakeholder system will be the participants in the company's value chain. The concept of the *value chain*, originated by Harvard Professor Michael Porter, models the vertical supply-market system within which a company seeks to fine-tune its performance in the interest of adding customer value and furthering corporate objectives. More detailed comment will be made on value chain analysis below.

It should be stressed that the stakeholder system is a negotiated environment in which company relationships with different parties have to be carefully cultivated and managed. The company effectively has a series of publics – customers, shareholders, suppliers, employers, community bodies, etc. – with which it must maintain contact and ensure mutually productive relations. The marketing significance of this is that the state

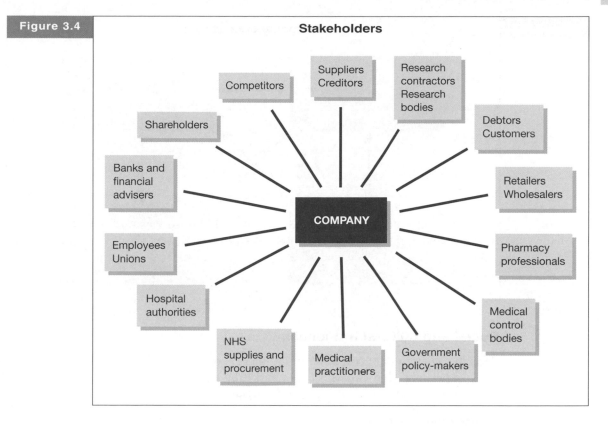

Figure 3.4   **Stakeholders**

of these relationships can exert a powerful influence on success criteria such as brand image, product, acceptability, customer service, trade relations and company reputation.

A WIDER ENVIRONMENT (LEVEL 4)

In the wider environment, sometimes termed the 'macroenvironment', the company is faced by a complex set of uncontrollable variables that collectively shape its markets, its resources and the competitive climate, and that pose challenges and opportunities that may determine the success or failure of the company as a whole.

Figure 3.5 presents a simplified matrix of the four major sets of influences normally identified within the macroenvironment: social, technological, economic and political influences. These four broad categories are conventionally used as generalised headings, each of which encompasses a wide variety of variables – e.g. the social category includes factors at work in society in general, such as demographic and cultural influences. Further, the variables involved may work at different levels of aggregation – sectoral, regional, national and international – and they are likely to be interrelated across the four quadrants – e.g. changes in economic factors like investment may affect technological issues such as innovation (hence the arrows linking the quadrants). The letters denoting the four quadrants form the simple mnemonic STEP, often employed as a basic structure for STEP-analysis in outlining environmental forces relevant to business problems. A more detailed examination will now be made of these four sets of environmental influences.

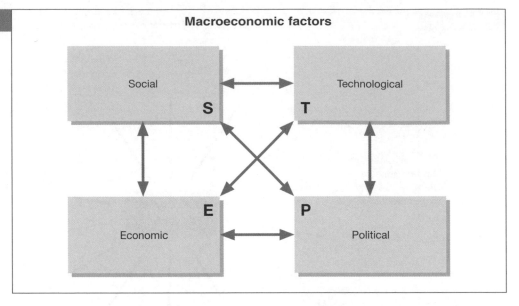

Figure 3.5

Social and cultural influences

Though sometimes difficult to pinpoint, these constitute, literally, the *societywide influences and changes* that can affect the marketing environment. For convenience, they will be divided into two broad areas: demographic factors and cultural factors.

Demographic factors

These concern the *population aggregates and patterns within a society* – population size and make-up. While these factors change only slowly, and are statistically predictable, they nevertheless exert powerful effects on the volume and nature of demand for most products and services. Furthermore, they are the building-blocks of the patterns of lifestyle within a society, and constitute the circumstances in which consumers enact their commercial and social roles. Figure 3.6 presents a summary of the demographic variables of interest to marketers.

Some of these factors will have obvious influences on companies and services in particular markets: for example, the demand for baby-clothes, cots, nursery products, maternity and antenatal services will be directly correlated with birth-rate statistics. Not surprisingly, birth-rate will influence, with a time-lag, the demand for nursery facilities, primary education, toys and playthings, preschool clothes, and paediatric medicine. In like manner, an ageing population – a common phenomenon in industrialised countries – results in increased demand for age-related products and services such as sheltered accommodation, mobility aids, large-print books, pre-retirement counselling and geriatric nursing.

Other factors will exert influences that are less obvious and may vary geographically, or across social groups: especially over time, demographic factors will exhibit multiple influences that may present marketers with either opportunities or threats. An example of such temporal changes is given in Figure 3.7, which shows the changes in UK beer and cider consumption over a recent 13-year period.

Another example again based on alcohol consumption is the trend of increased drinking by females as outlined on page 38.

Figure 3.6

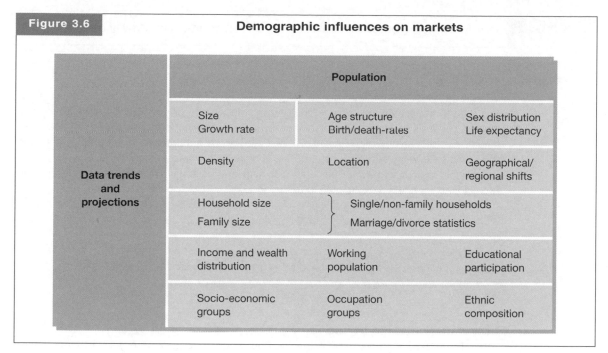

Demographic influences on markets

Figure 3.7

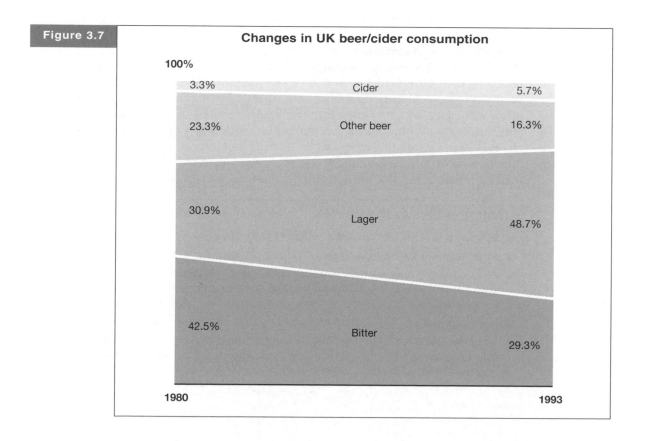

Changes in UK beer/cider consumption

Exercise   Identify the major changes shown in Figure 3.7 and comment on their likely or possible causes.

Example   ### Female alcohol consumption

The growth of alcohol consumption amongst British women is far exceeding that of females in any other European country. The younger women in the age group 18 to 24 are showing the highest increase, mainly it would seem owing to the fact that there are now more females in higher education and in employment. Women are spending more time in the pub: reasons for this could include the social aspect such as, bonding with colleagues and as a way of winding down after a hard day at work. The delay in starting families and the increase in spending power are also factors that have attributed to this trend.

This change in social status of women is also reflected in the purchase of alcohol in supermarkets: women increasingly buy a bottle of wine, and may buy several if there is a special promotion.

This trend is welcomed by pub operators who are making efforts to make pubs more female-friendly, offering a selection of food and with light, airy bars which are less intimidating than the more traditional pubs.

General demographic trends

Certainly in the UK and other industrial countries, recent years have witnessed major movements within the demographic landscape. It is worth noting that, though such changes appear general, and even international, they may not yet be described as irreversible. There seem to be three common factors in these demographic movements.

1 Population age distribution

Many countries have experienced in recent times a slowing in the birth-rate, after a period of high birth statistics in the 1950s and 1960s (the 'baby-boom' post-Second World War period). This combined with an extension of life expectancy related to medical, dietary and economic improvements, resulted in a rightward shift in the population profile, the classic symptoms of an ageing population. Some of these changes have far-reaching economic implications of interest to policy-makers, e.g. the increasing burden of the retired sector (even the 'super-old': 80 years and above) on social services. In Britain, the age of retirement for women is being extended from 60

Demographics in the future

■ **By 2004 30% of the UK population will be 45 to 64 years old.**

■ **By 2020 50% of the UK population will be over 45 years old.**

■ **By early 2000 Europe will have more pensioners than children. They will be healthier and wealthier than previous generations and, Age Concern claims, people in this generation are as old as they act, which is 10 years younger than their chronological age.**

■ **Nowadays, the over-55s account for some 40% of all consumer expenditure.**

■ **No longer is it taken for granted that life ends at retirement. This generation leads a more active and adventurous lifestyle than any previous one, and maturity is bringing an increased range of interests, together with more leisure time to indulge them. Eating out, travel, sports and cultural activities are all feeling the benefits of an ageing population.**

Source: McLuhan (2000)

years old to 65 and this should have the effect of slightly reducing this burden. Another of the problems is the projected decline in the workforce pool, and to help diminish the impact this will have, some companies are actively recruiting older people, one example of this being B&Q, the large do-it-yourself (DIY) supplier. In fact this is a problem encountered not only in Britain, but also in other countries. Florida in the USA has many older workers and retired people holding down both full- and part-time jobs, and many of the shops and smaller businesses have hiring signs outside – ageism does not seem to be a major problem, certainly not in Florida.

The information in the box (p. 38) compiled by Interfocus is a good indication of the demographic changes which will influence the spending pattern of consumers in the future.

2 Household/family composition

In many countries there have been major changes in household and family size and make-up. Social and economic changes have led to later marriages, with fewer

---

Example

M&S hits back over claim of sector turmoil

FT

Retail change in habits highlighted after attack on 'old order'

Marks and Spencer, the struggling high street retailer, has hit back at claims that the sector is in turmoil because companies have failed to respond to demographic shifts.

Verdict, the retail consultancy, said yesterday that retailers had been slow to respond to an ageing population and were continuing to address the market place as though it were static. The comments came in a statement accompanying Verdict's report, *Retail Demographics 2000*. 'It is no coincidence that the retail companies facing the most pressure are those built on the idea of selling the same products, in the same environments in the same way, to the mass market. The penalty for trying to adhere to the old order could well be terminal,' Verdict said. M&S said additional factors had had an impact on the sector.

'While there is no doubt we have to respond to demographic changes, the retail sector has changed,' it said. 'There are now many more players than before and the big supermarkets are now getting into new sectors and selling product they never used to sell.'

'You also have to remember that people's shopping habits have changed and they are spending more on leisure than previously.'

The report warns that retailers stand to lose out if they fail to respond to changes that will see the Friends and Bridget Jones generation of 25 to 39-year-olds diminish by 2m over the next 10 years. The 55 to 69-year-old population is due to increase by 19 per cent, or 1.6m.

Verdict says the falling number of 25 to 39-year-olds will have an effect on mainstream brands – particularly for household or DIY products – because fewer people in this age group will be buying their first home. 'These shifts are all helping to change the nature of the retail economy,' the report says

Source: *Financial Times*, 26 April 2000. (Copyright © The Financial Times Limited)

Questions

1 *Given the performance of M&S recently, do you think that they are responding to demographic changes?*

2 *With regard to the additional factors that are mentioned by M&S, do you think that they are of greater importance than the demographic changes?*

3 *If you were to advise M&S on future strategy, what would you see as the most important areas for change? Give reasons for your answers.*

children. Workforce participation among married women has increased significantly, and many married women nowadays succeed in managing a return to work and career development after maternity breaks. Career couples, with no children, are now quite commonplace – indeed, they have been labelled by advertisers as 'Dinkies' (dual income, no kids), an advertising target group of some apparent interest!

Alongside these changes, the number of non-family households has increased substantially. Some of these households are made up of young careerist adults, or adults choosing singleness, while others represent adults who are divorced or widowed. If note is also taken of the growing number of single-parent families, it is hardly surprising that a researcher definition of 'head of household' is far from the straightforward matter it might have been 30 years ago. Significantly, these household changes have had a major effect on the pattern of demand for a wide range of everyday goods and services.

The article from the *Financial Times* (p. 39) demonstrates the major effect demographic changes are attributed to have had on companies.

3 Geographical shifts

Many 'post-industrial' societies, such as the UK and the USA, have witnessed in recent years a major decline in traditional industrial regions and a parallel growth in 'new-territory' regions based on service industries, e.g. the US Sunbelt and Silicon Valley phenomena. Other countries are experiencing similar movements of people and investment associated with rural depopulation and accelerated urbanisation and industrialisation. Though these phenomena are different, and may even coexist across regions within any one country, their economic and commercial impact may present common symptoms and problems. The marketer must reflect on the medium-term effects of such changes and consider how they affect company development and investment plans.

A major development which may have a significant effect on where people work is the tremendous growth of e-business and the use of the Internet generally. It is now much more common and accepted for people to work from home and perhaps only travel to work very infrequently. This type of working may increase quite dramatically when technological advances such as video conferencing become more widespread and affordable, and as a consequence installed in the home environment as a matter of course.

Cultural factors

Culture within any society is the complex of elements that reflect the society's beliefs and values, perceptions, preferences and behavioral norms. These elements of culture express themselves in people's attitudes and behaviour, in their general lifestyle and in their working lives. Culture is therefore all-embracing and multidimensional, such that neat and exact definitions are difficult and elusive, and better left to specialists such as sociologists and anthropologists.

For the marketer, however, it is necessary to understand that culture will vary within and between societies, so that cultural norms may vary between countries, regions and culture groups or subcultures.

Within a society, culture may be most distinguishable by the prevalent core beliefs and values that people hold, which express themselves in family and friendship relations, in social conventions and rites, in social institutions and the social order itself. Such long-standing facets of culture change very slowly, as they are the product of family upbringing, the education system, national history and political development, religion, and a multiple of other influences such as aesthetic developments, communications and the media.

Below these prevailing core values may be identified a variety of secondary beliefs and values, which tend to be less durable, less universal and more situational. These may be tied in some way to core beliefs, but reflect the development of individual or group choices and feelings – e.g. a belief in education may be rooted in core values, whereas attitudes for or against private education will be an expression of secondary values and beliefs.

These secondary-level beliefs and values are therefore more likely to vary within society, to change over time and be open to change and persuasion. Furthermore, they may be recognisable within the development of subcultures within a society. Subcultures develop in many ways and for different reasons, though they usually entail a grouping of people with common interests, experiences or motivations. Subcultures may therefore be associated with age groupings (the 'youth culture'), regional affiliations (Lancashire versus Yorkshire), religious or ethnic associations, or even situational facets of lifestyle (working mothers, single parents, and students).

Secondary beliefs and values may sometimes exhibit societywide changes over time, effecting a gradual change in a society's general orientation, e.g. in attitudes to work and leisure, an increased interest in self-development and choice, a growth in voluntary sector participation, ecological concern, consumerism, etc.

Environmental awareness is an interesting reflection of how societywide concerns have delivered a powerful message to governments and business leaders in Britain. The 'greening' of consumers has achieved comparable progress across a spread of international markets. A growing number of investors are now stipulating that the companies they invest in are societally aware. Areas therefore which have become much more important in recent years include the vast increase in organic food produced owing to the demand from the market, and also the demand for food which has not been genetically modified. Social responsibility and ethics in marketing is discussed in more detail later in the book.

Exercise

1 As an individual consumer, note the most recent purchase you have made of an environment-friendly product, answer the following questions and be prepared to discuss your purchase:
   – Where did you buy the product?
   – What competing products were on display, and how did they compare on ecology-friendly terms?
     – Did 'going green' involve a price premium?
     – To what extent do you choose green products as a matter of principle?

2 As a student group, devise a simple checklist (twelve headings) by which to assess the 'green policy' of supermarkets. Between the group, visit a few leading supermarket stores and apply the checklist you have developed. Analyse and present your group results in class.

Technological influences

Technology is the touchstone of economic progress, a leading source of competitive advantage commercially, and an indispensable part of everyday lifestyle for the modern consumer. The overriding breakthrough in today's technological terms is the technological revolution for sourcing information. In fact the world's forward thinking organisations are aware that this new technology can have a far-reaching impact on business, and it would seem that fundamental business strategies and operations are now under review. The pace of change has been such that it is likely that most books will be out of date with regard to the new technology before they are even published.

E-business will be examined in more depth in Chapter 4 and examples are used throughout the book to help the reader identify how technology is impacting on traditional marketing methods. Rapid change because of technology has become more readily available to many people, this includes an organisation's customers, suppliers, distributors and in fact anyone who needs to interact with the company.

'Technology' as a term is perhaps misleadingly general, as the technologies encompassed are highly disparate and may vary from the most apparently obscure improvement or technique to the substantive breakthroughs associated with quantum leaps in science and engineering. What cannot be denied is that technology is a major driving force for change, everywhere. Furthermore, technological change appears to be multiplicative, so that the rate of change increases. A simple illustration of this would be to consider the major changes that have taken place in the last twenty or more years – within the lifetime of the average student – through innovations in the fields of information technology (IT), biotechnology, fibre optics, aerospace and materials science. Though developments in these fields have followed different, sometimes faltering, paths, they have in some way combined to produce major changes and challenges, and to raise the commercial stakes of success and failure.

Schumpeter, an American economist, provided an earlier commentary on the commercial realities of technology. He styled technology as a force for 'creative destruction', sweeping aside old products and their providers and replacing them with new competitors and technologies – a dynamic process that has been more recently expounded in the 'five forces' model of Michael Porter, another economist.

To illustrate the competitive force wielded by technology, it is worth observing that many manufacturers have been affected by technology development remote from their own field. Major sectors of the metalworking industry were made obsolete by the development of digital electronics. Weighing machines of all types, typewriters and cash registers are further examples of this.

For many companies, these technological changes have been difficult to detect, especially during periods of erratic economic growth that can conceal the real causes of falls in business activity. Developments in digital electronics have not only changed the form of products, but have also changed the way they are designed and manufactured. Computer-aided design (CAD) not only permits more intricate designs, but also allows these to be manufactured without greatly increased costs. As a result, companies able to invest in these technologies have introduced new products more quickly and competitively. These technologies have also enabled an increase in the variety of products available to the customer. For example, even low-cost items such as plastic patio chairs are now available in dozens of styles.

Technology and research

An everyday marketing perspective on the effects of technology would be the growing consensus that product life cycles are becoming ever shorter. Agreement on exact figures varies, though most marketers would reckon that as many as 80 per cent of products on today's market will have disappeared altogether within ten years. The corollary of this is that company sales and profits are becoming increasingly dependent on a *managed succession of new product introductions*. This, in turn, will hinge on success in the costly and speculative process of R&D and innovation (see example below).

While developments in leading-edge technologies and 'super science' may be associated with high-expenditure efforts in pure research, these high-visibility cases are by no means the standard route by which technology advances. Technology may often move incrementally and diagonally, through a chain process of linking developments, often 'authored' by competitor organisations that jostle for possession of the baton. (Sometimes final leadership position will be the result of a long and costly rivalry between competing systems – witness the confusing contention between Sony, Sega and Nintendo in the games console market.) Furthermore, while commitment and investment is required in programmed research, even high-spending research companies (some pharmaceutical multinationals devote over 25 per cent of turnover to R&D) have found that high budgets alone are not the key to success. In managerial terms, research efforts need to be programmed, monitored for cost-effectiveness and directed towards market needs. The following example although rather lengthy gives an excellent example of the above.

Example | **Where science and mammon collide** | **FT**

As Merck faces the biggest challenge of its history, its chief scientist tells David Pilling about balancing the needs of research and investors

Merck stands apart in the drugs industry. Ask any pharmaceuticals executive which competitor he most admires and nine times out of 10 he will fire back the name of the US company.

At the core of Merck's reputation lies its science. Over the years, it has invented medicines that have become bywords for dependability and safety. (None of its drugs has ever been recalled.) And while it has been as commercially aggressive as the next company, it has maintained a reputation for integrity.

For two decades, the formula has served Merck – and its shareholders – well, but now there is major competition. The history of the drugs business is littered with companies that have suffered hard times or been driven to merger, after the loss of just a single big patent. As if this were not enough, Merck's trial by fire comes at a period of unprecedented change. Rapid advances in the understanding of the links between genes and diseases are opening up new areas for drug research.

Some companies have responded by merging, doubling their research budgets at a stroke. Merck, which has doggedly espoused a go-it-alone credo, suddenly finds itself with an R&D budget only half the size of the new industry leaders.

Glaxo is combining with SmithKline Beecham to form a company with a 7.5 per cent share of the global prescription market, half as much again as Merck. Pfizer, which is gobbling up Warner-Lambert, will boast annual research expenditure of $4.7bn, double Merck's. Moreover, Pfizer is promising earnings growth of at least 25 per cent, a full 10 percentage points above what Merck can hope to offer. For the first time in years, Merck no longer looks like the industry leader.

Not that Dr Scolnick the head of science at Merck is convinced by the arguments that scale will translate into research efficiency. Quite the reverse. But like many of his pressured peers, he has been going over the numbers just to make sure. 'I decided to pull together some data on the products that have come from the sites we have around the world,' he says. 'The thing that's really most striking was that the size of the site has nothing to do with its productivity, absolutely nothing. There's no correlation. None.'

▶

That's a comforting thought for an R&D director with only half as much to spend as his most fearsome competitor. But does that really mean he would not know what to do with Dollars 5bn?

'It is true that if they [Pfizer and Glaxo SmithKline] really organise that $5bn effort well, they have a potential advantage,' he concedes. 'But the caveat is the prefix to the sentence – if they can really do that. I think organising something that big on a global scale is not a trivial exercise.'

Neither does he buy the theory that drug discovery, after years of serendipity, will suddenly become more akin, as some have said, to a production line. Sir Richard Sykes, chairman of Glaxo, has argued that the future of drug discovery will see a direct relationship between what a company puts into R&D and what it gets out at the other end.

'Where would they have been without the mergers?' he asks. 'They would have been worse off. They wouldn't have been in the game.'

Clearly, Merck is not in that position yet. The excellence of its science may still see it through, particularly if some high-profile projects – such as a depression drug in late-stage development – come to fruition.

Yet equally clearly, for the first time in many years, Merck is feeling the pressure. 'We have to enhance our research productivity, there's no question of that,' says Dr Scolnick. 'In spite of the fact that we have been successful and have put out all these terrific drugs, both medically and economically.' He adds: 'I've said to our scientists on several occasions: if they want to preserve our culture, we really need to be [even] more successful than we've been in the past.'

Source: Adapted from *Financial Times*, 21 March 2000. (Copyright © The Financial Times Limited)

Market needs represent the link between invention and innovation. While successful R&D outcomes might prove themselves in a new formulation, a product or process development, real success will not be achieved until users in the market place have adopted the new development. Technological progress therefore ultimately depends on a process of *technology transfer* and *innovation*, both of which involve commercialisation through an understanding of market needs. Here, then, is a critical role for marketing, to direct development efforts and facilitate their commercialisation.

Logically, the needs of the market will be identified by research among customers in that market. Interestingly, this research does not have to be wholly esoteric or technical, as what is sought is an insight into the customer's problems and interests, rather than those of the technologist.

A good illustration of this principle was provided by the Sony Corporation in developing the Walkman. In terms of technology sophistication, the Walkman formula was apparently basic and unexciting – the key element of its success was that it met a latent market need for a cheap, portable cassette-player, at the right moment in time. While Sony sales records doubtless catalogue the real success of the product, the hundreds of copycat versions that have been marketed worldwide are proof enough. Equally, follow-up Sony successes through the Watchman and the Discman are testimony to the market lead developed by the original product. A similar situation exists today with regards to Sony in the games console market.

Market needs in other fields may be signalled by resource shortages, environmental problems and hazards, or the drive to reduce waste. Certainly, in the past, technology itself has presented environmental problems such as pollution and blighted landscapes that now require technological solutions. Given the recent awakening of international concern about the natural environment, it would be no exaggeration to assert that all organisations should consciously review their stance and performance in this regard.

Technology, then, is a major force for change for all organisations. Far removed from the regulated atmosphere of the research laboratory, even the everyday High Street service firm must consider technology in the following terms:

■ How will technological change affect our physical plant, equipment, work routines?
■ How will it affect these issues for our customers, and what will this imply for our operations and offerings?
■ How can we harness technology, or even take a lead role, in developing technology-based competitive advantage?

Exercise

Select one of the following service organisations and consider how technology (a) has affected the way the organisation operates, and (b) offers scope for future competitive advantage:

– solicitors' partnership
– doctors' practice
– travel agency
– high street bank.

The economic environment

The economy is a total system within which material and energy inputs are processed and converted to finished goods and services for distribution and final use. As all business organisations are part of the system, they have a direct interest in monitoring economic developments and guiding their policy decisions accordingly. Most performance-centred organisations incorporate economic data analysis into their business plans and marketing programmes. Often such information is collated as part of a formal *Marketing Information System* (MKIS).

The logic of this is that the current and projected events and trends in the economy – so-called macroeconomic variables – will probably affect the overall level of demand for goods and services, and related aggregates such as stock levels, prices, capacity utilisation and the like. In other markets, often tied to primary resource supplies and distribution (e.g. petroleum) companies make a practice of studying the microeconomic variables within their immediate market or sector.

While microeconomic factors will obviously vary for companies in different sectors, macroeconomic aggregates will present a common backdrop for all companies. Furthermore, as international communications and trade links develop, it is becoming more necessary to talk of the 'world economy' – many Head Offices of large multinationals now operate around the clock, controlling operations across a spread of markets. While economic globalisation is being advanced through international and investment trade links, at the intermediate level regional trade blocs and practices are having marked effects. In the UK, the aftermath of 1992 and the Single European Act (SEA) provides an illustration of the realities of the economic environment for companies within both the UK and the wider European Community (EC). The free movement of goods, services and people is posing challenges within national markets formerly assured as 'home territory', and with it creating greater competition for the producers of goods and services as well as in the labour market.

The economic environment is therefore a complex network of international, domestic and regional influences and dependencies that shape the market potential facing companies. Company performance itself will depend critically on the quality of preparation and decision making that is brought to bear on this potential. The government

| Example | Budget 2000 Red Book: Buoyant activity with rapid growth in demand   FT |

This article sets out the economic background to Budget 2000, providing updated forecasts for the UK and world economies over the next three years. It discusses recent developments in the UK economy and gives a summary of the outlook for growth and inflation . . .

GDP rose by 2 per cent in 1999, exceeding the upper end of the Budget 99 forecast range. Rapid growth in domestic demand, up 3.4 per cent in aggregate and spread fairly evenly among the components of final demand, more than accounted for buoyant activity overall. This was partly offset by somewhat weaker than expected net trade, which reduced growth by 1.7 percentage points. Moreover, claimant unemployment also confounded outside expectations, falling by 140,000 during the course of the year . . .

Household consumption rose by 4 per cent in 1999, in line with the pre-Budget Report forecast, and readily explicable in terms of the fundamental drivers of consumer demand. Growth in real household disposable incomes was somewhat weaker than forecast, despite a sharp rise to 3¼ per cent, which reflected a continued robust expansion in employment incomes and a significant decline in growth in taxes on income as the impact of self-assessment worked through.

Stronger underlying growth in spending therefore led to an unexpected fall in the saving ratio, with rapid gains in household wealth perhaps boosting spending by more than 1 percentage point relative to incomes last year. In particular, house prices accelerated unexpectedly sharply from mid-1999. Falling interest rates in the year to June 1999 also supported above trend consumption growth during the first half of the year.

Source: Extract from *Financial Times*, 22 March 2000. (Copyright © The Financial Times Limited)

Question

In what ways can the above information be used by companies to plan future strategy?

compiles information that can help with these decisions. The extract above from a newspaper article identifies some of the information that is available.

While such data may give a clue to recent economic events, a firmer appraisal to underpin major decisions such as plant investment or international expansion would require methodical analysis of relevant indices, showing turning points, trends and projections, with accompanying commentary and qualifications. Larger companies will retain in-house economists and planners for such purposes, or enlist the services of outsiders such as economic consultants, merchant bankers or venture capitalist organisations.

The significance of the information in the example is that over time they will indicate major economic developments of direct interest to marketers and business people generally. Such 'economy-watching' may enable the vigilant company to respond in time to scenarios such as the following:

■ **Recession**. A downturn in economic activity of variable intensity. The diagnosis may range from a Chancellor's dismissive 'blip' or setback to a world recession. Usual indicators will be a fall or levelling in GNP (and GDP), industrial output, household income, consumer spending and investment expenditure, order-books and notified vacancies. Rises will be recorded in measures such as stocks, unemployment and company bankruptcies.

As spending will be affected, market conditions become thin and more competitive. Though sales for some products and within certain income groups may be little affected, the general picture will be more difficult, while companies in some sectors (e.g. industrial components, machine tools, construction) may suffer heavier reversals through order cancellations, project postponements and stock depletion.

- **Recovery**. The opposite of the above, again varying in intensity and time. Economists will use terms like 'boom', 'upturn' and 'reflation'. Marketers in some sectors will benefit from an early upturn in sales (their sales patterns may provide 'early indicators' of economic activity useful to forecasters, while other sectors, by contrast, may recover late ('lagging indicators'). Major upturns in economic activity may result in 'overheating', with higher costs and prices, import surges, bottlenecks and shortages, and failures through overtrading. Indicators such as investment and stock-levels may vary by sector and according to the 'investment climate'.

- **Inflation**. Rising prices may be associated with buoyant conditions, demand growth and shortages. Although perverse combinations such as 'stagflation' (inflation and recession) are not unknown, severe inflation (hyperinflation, strato-inflation) may rock economic foundations and demand drastic policy remedies such as devaluation, tariffs and IMF assistance.

Example

Equity markets: Rate rises dent consumer confidence   **FT**

Robust income growth will help to underpin the housing market, says Chris Flood

Consumer confidence has been dented by the increases in interest rates since the autumn, but whether this will lead to the much-needed slowdown in consumer spending is open to question. GfK will release its latest survey of consumer confidence on Tuesday. Consumers now appear slightly less optimistic about the state of their own finances over the next 12 months and about the general economic situation. However, the latest official figures showed the growth in household incomes has remained strong during the first quarter of this year, some 6.7 per cent higher than the same period a year ago. This robust income growth will help underpin demand as well as inflation in the housing market. Nationwide building society says annual house-price inflation was running at 17.5 per cent in April, although this should fall to 14 per cent by the end of the year. Nationwide will release May's figures on Tuesday and on Wednesday the Bank of England will provide details of mortgage lending in April. House buyers took out a record £4.1bn in net lending in March.

The number of mortgage approvals (loans approved but not yet made) was 8 per cent higher in March than a year ago, so there is plenty of demand in the pipeline. With expectations of further interest rate increases having lessened recently, the Nationwide argues that higher borrowing costs would only have a 'marginal dampening effect' on the housing market in the short term. The vicious circle, with higher house prices fuelling greater consumer spending, has not yet been broken. The Chartered Institute of Purchasing and Supply report on manufacturing for May, due on Thursday, will reflect deepening gloom among manufacturers.

The April report showed only modest output growth compared with March, with new orders at their lowest level for a year. The strong pound was almost exclusively blamed for a decline in export orders.

Source: Financial Times, 27 May 2000. (Copyright © The Financial Times Limited)

Question

Outline ways in which the increase in interest rates can affect both companies and their customers. Give examples where possible.

The scenarios above are rather simplistic and generalised, and by no means illustrate the real complexities to be met with in practice. More authoritative detail will be found in most economics textbooks. What these pictures do illustrate, though, is the way the economic 'isobars' may change and steepen, domestically and internationally. An added complication for the marketer will be the effect of government policy and also that of the Bank of England in the UK, measures designed to stimulate or manage the economy. While these measures will vary by political preference and according to economic circumstance, they will usually entail manipulation of key instruments such as taxation and expenditure (fiscal policy), interest rates and credit (monetary policy) that will have obvious effects on markets. A good example of an increase in interest rates is given in the article on page 47.

Furthermore, some industries may be subject to microeconomic measures, e.g. in respect of merger control or competition policy, investment or locational incentives. Companies engaged in international marketing will also need to respond to similar economic controls within their overseas markets. Finally, economic policies are likely in future to be more directly influenced by multilateral agencies and agreements and the expansion of common market blocs such as the EC.

The political and legal environment

Some aspects of political and legal environment were covered at the beginning of this chapter. However as an external marketing variable there are other equally important issues. The economic policies cited in the previous section are but one aspect of the political environment, which comprises the controls and checks instituted by central and local government, government agencies and quasi-official bodies. Also of relevance will be the growing influence of international laws and agreements, and at a more local level the activities of various professional and trade bodies, pressure groups and voluntary associations.

Such a regulatory environment may only appear to change slowly, and clear frameworks of rights and representations will usually exist. Nonetheless it is still necessary for marketers to be aware of the policy interpretations of the status quo, and to be attuned to the likely direction and nature of changes to the system. As company stakeholders may sometimes pursue particular interests and grievances through the 'political' system, it is in the interests of companies to frame policies that minimise stakeholder grievances and generally support a record of commercial good practice and social responsibility. In short, companies should seek to demonstrate good corporate citizenship by upholding the letter and the spirit of the law, and generally behaving in a responsible and responsive manner.

The marketing interpretation of such a stance would squarely equate with marketing excellence. This in practical terms might relate directly to a corporate mission statement that guides company activity from higher strategic issues, such as market choice, to everyday performance standards in respect of quality, service levels, customer protocol and the like.

While such autonomous standards of performance are to be commended, some markets and trades have developed general voluntary codes of conduct and control, supported and monitored by a central membership body. Practice within established professions such as medicine and accountancy has long been controlled by strict codes of professional behaviour. Likewise professionals within the Chartered Institute of Marketing have to abide by the Code of Practice.

Self-regulation aside, most governments have developed a body of legislation and enforcement frameworks in respect of industry and trade. In particular, the following areas of control are of direct concern to business:

1 **Legislation in respect of monopoly and competition standards.** In the UK, enforcement powers have in recent years been channelled particularly through the Office of Fair Trading (OFT) and the Monopolies and Mergers Commission (MMC), both vested with wide competition reference powers. As a full EC member, the UK is also subject to Community provisions in respect of these issues: in particular, Article 85 of the Treaty of Rome concerns practices hindering competition, and Article 86 of the Treaty addresses abuses of a dominant market position.

2 **Measures to protect consumers**, whether as groups (e.g. children, patients), individuals, as users of certain products and services (e.g. cigarettes, alcohol, gambling, food, drugs and medicines), or particularly as a target for business activities (mailshots, sales, promotion, etc.). In the UK the original provisions in consumer protection, founded in the law of contract and equity amendments to common law, have been supplemented significantly through legislation that is at least in part attributable to the growth of consumerism.

Additional to these provisions, government bodies exist with statutory and discretionary powers to control the business community in respect of a variety of other issues, from environmental protection and planning restrictions to commercial disclosure and public standards of decency.

Exercise

Try to find articles in the business press which give examples that illustrate the scope of such controls and from these prepare a brief presentation for discussion in class. You may carry out the exercise as a group or individually – if as a group, more extensive reporting will be required, and evidence of teamwork.

Aside from direct action by government and regulatory bodies, companies have in the last twenty or more years had to recognise the increasingly strident concerns of consumerists and related environmental pressure groups and lobbyists. Consumer groups in particular have posed new challenges to marketers, especially through the publication of independent product quality and test information – in the UK, the Consumers' Association, publishers of *Which?*, is very popular and gives information on many products.

CONCLUSION

The marketing environment comprises the playing field upon which competitive marketing takes place. While some of the 'rules' of the playing field may be common knowledge to all players, most 'game-plans' cannot be inspired wholly by mechanistic guidelines. The game is dynamic, and most moves are finally umpired by buyer preferences. Companies need to monitor and decide rational responses to changes in the environment in order to win their colours. The environment will almost invariably wield greater strength than a company can muster, so that pragmatic responses are generally more sensible than Canute-like gestures of defiance. Competitive management can benefit, within the rules, by good intelligence and planning and flexible execution – analysis and monitoring alone are not enough. This is perhaps best summarised by the old adage:

There are three types of companies: those who make things happen; those who watch things happen; and those who wonder what happened.

QUESTIONS

1 *Taking any established product market, consider the various environmental changes that have influenced it over the last 5–10 years.*

2 *Develop a stakeholder map for a typical airline company, and comment on the conflicting interests that the various stakeholders might have in respect of the airline.*

3 *Consider the extent to which demographic changes are likely to influence the commercial success of (a) a supermarket chain, (b) a car manufacturer, (c) a pharmaceutical company.*

4 *Many writers have proposed that the world is rapidly becoming a 'smaller place', as globalisation gathers pace. Consider how such a globalisation process will affect a company's market environment.*

FURTHER READING

Flood, C. (2000) 'Equity markets: rate rises dent consumer confidence: robust income growth will help to underpin the housing market', *Financial Times*, 27 May.

Kotler, P. (1999) *Marketing Management: Analysis, Planning Implementation and Control*. Prentice-Hall.

McLuhan, R. (2000) 'Silver surfers join the Internet party', *Marketing*, 11 May.

Pilling, D. (2000) 'Management pharmaceuticals industry. As Merck faces the biggest challenge of its history – balancing the needs of research and investors', *Financial Times*, 27 May.

Villiers, C. (1989) 'Boiled frog syndrome', *Management Today*, March.

Wright, R. (2000) 'A tradition of mathematical excellence is luring investment', *Financial Times*, 26 April.

CASE STUDY

Hungary's bankable boffins

FT

A tradition of mathematical excellence is luring investment, says Robert Wright

It is the kind of anecdote that makes Hungarians swell with pride. When Enrico Fermi and one of his colleagues left a meeting during the project to design the nuclear bomb, the rest turned to each other. 'Now we can speak Hungarian,' one of them said. It is easy to see the link between Miklos Boda, who tells the story, and the many Hungarian pioneers of early 20th-century science. A highly qualified physicist, Dr Boda looks the part of the central European theoretical researcher. His hair is slightly tousled, his manner faintly distracted. He has inherited a long tradition of excellence in mathematics and physics that has become part of the Hungarian national myth.

Yet, unlike his predecessors, Dr Boda does not have his office in a university research laboratory. He is general manager for the research and development division of Ericsson Hungary, part of the Swedish mobile telephone manufacturer. Among his 250 staff are 70 highly trained mathematicians.

To an outsider it might seem remarkable that even one market-leading high-technology company would choose to base vital research and development in a country that, little more than 10 years ago, was not even a market economy. Yet, according to Gabor Elo, R&D manager in Hungary for Finland's Nokia, nearly every significant mobile phone maker now has some

Hungary-based R&D. The development is particularly remarkable because, Dr Elo says, no other country in Eastern Europe's former Communist bloc has a single such facility. Nokia has three R&D centres in Hungary, all working on software. It employs 350 in R&D, a figure that will rise to 550. Mobile phones are not the only area affected by this development. Among several automotive investments, Audi, Volkswagen's executive car division, is building an engine development centre at Gyor, western Hungary. ZF, a German transmission maker, has a development unit in Eger. In pharmaceuticals, Richter Gedeon, Hungary's leading independent pharmaceuticals company, carries out research on a contract basis for western partners. Yet, while most investors in Hungary claim to be interested in more than the cheap labour – typically one-seventh of the cost in Germany – these investors seem to mean it. Nearly all cite the education system as the main attraction. Students are grounded in scientific basics no longer as fashionable elsewhere.

'One (reason for investing) was the very good education level, mainly the mathematical background,' says Dr Elo of Nokia. 'If you don't have a theoretical background it's very hard to do research in this area. 'The second was the availability. There are very good researchers in southern Europe and other parts of the world, but the availability is not enough for a big R&D market.' The cost of labour comes only third. 'It is not cheap,' Dr Elo says. 'We usually say one person here costs about 70 per cent of the western level.' There are cultural reasons for Hungary's strong tradition of technical and scientific education, Dr Boda of Ericsson believes. While mathematicians are sometimes regarded as 'nerds' in other western nations, in Hungary they are afforded respect, says Dr Boda.

A good research temperament may also have been encouraged by a keenness to innovate born of relative poverty. Ulrich Diller, vice-president of ZF, believes the keenness of Hungarian development staff to improvise works well alongside the different strengths at his company's other development centre, in Detroit. Staff at the US centre show greater commercial awareness, Mr Diller says. 'They can make something out of nothing,' he says of the Hungarians. In highly developed countries, technicians 'can't start with a primitive thing. They only think at the highest level. But [the Hungarians] only think at the lowest level. These you have to bring together and you get a good average.'

More mundane factors also come into play. Many companies see R&D centres as natural follow-ons from investments established in Hungary's mid-1990s investment surge. Audi has bolstered its investment in Gyor, where it makes 90 per cent of its engines, with an engine development centre. Norbert Paulli, area manager for engine development, says, however, that it will do little more than resolve problems thrown up during manufacturing. Core research will remain in Germany. 'If you have any problem during the production of engines, it takes a lot of time to find the designer in Germany who's responsible for solving the problem,' he says. 'Most of the problems during the production process can be solved very quickly if we have well-educated people developing engines here in Hungary.'

Gabor Elo explains how the process has unfolded. 'Every country likes to see more than [simple] commercial things [like] a sales office,' he says. 'But at first, any multinational company comes to sell its products. After that, if it's a reasonable business environment, they come for production. After that, if it's satisfied with the sales and production, comes the strategic, very sensitive business of R&D.'

Yet if Hungary's achievement is impressive after only 10 years as a market economy, it needs to work to keep the investment coming. Managers such as Dr Elo worry whether the hard-pressed Hungarian budget will be able to maintain the existing standard of education. 'We expect the state to keep universities at least at this level,' he says. 'Of course we help a lot. We pay a lot of money to the universities. We need only one thing from the state – that they support universities in launching good students.' The prize could be significant. Hungarians, who played a key role in

▶

planning the atom bomb, a defining technology of the 20th century, may design one just as important to the 21st.

Source: Financial Times; 26 April 2000. (Copyright © The Financial Times Limited)

Questions

1 *From the above article identify the various elements of the marketing environment, which play an important role.*

2 *What will be the marketing environment implications of the new technology developed, if it is accepted and implemented globally?*

3 *How have cultural factors shaped the development of the innovations?*

4 E-business – the technology

When the telephone was invented, people had to think 'out of the box' to see the incredible opportunities it offered. It's easy with hindsight, but the Internet also offers the same opportunities.

Chris Ritchie, Sun's business development manager for e-commerce

INTRODUCTION

The use of the Internet, which is the name given to a global collection of interconnected computer networks, has been growing phenomenally in the last few years and has become an integral part of the lives of many people. Information is distributed over the Internet by means of the world wide web, usually referred to as 'the web'. The capability of this is tremendous and pages containing text, graphics, photographs, sound and video clips can be sent over the Internet. Everyone that is connected to the Internet can share information with each other and can also share communications, databases and take part in transactions etc. In other words the Internet could be described as a worldwide communication technology, a technology which is virtual in that it has no physical home or dimension and users of the Internet can communicate by sending electronic mail or transferring files, and can access information from files. All of which would have seemed very unlikely only a few years ago.

Over the next few years it is expected that the traditional communication devices of personal computers, telephones – both mobile and fixed-line, and televisions as well as interactive games consoles – all of which can be connected to the Internet, will enjoy a surge in popularity. Technology is also set to bring internet connection to cars, houses and refrigerators; it is yet to be seen how all of this will affect households.

REVOLUTIONISING BUSINESS?

The dawning of this new era of e-business, with the giant leaps in capability that it has afforded, to both individuals and organisations alike, has become a major driver in encouraging economic progress. It is set to revolutionise the way in which business is conducted, and also the speed at which business decisions can be made. The following article shows that although this is expected to occur some companies are having difficulties.

Example **Traditional US companies 'struggling with e-commerce'** **FT**

Many traditional US companies are finding it difficult to achieve e-business success because they are having trouble attracting talent and motivating and managing their employees. This is the main finding from a new survey of more than 100 companies by Hewitt Associates, the US management consulting firm.

▶

It found nearly two-thirds of companies believed they were behind non-traditional competitors, such as dotcom enterprises and start-ups, in the use of e-business.

As many as 58 per cent found it hard to align the old and new workplace cultures.

Fifty six per cent of companies believed they faced a challenge in gaining support and guidance from their leaders on new e-business activities.

Forty one per cent added they were struggling to attract the talent they needed for their e-business, and almost as many companies said they found it difficult to get enough talent for that work from their current employees.

More than a third said finding ways to manage their new e-business leadership was a large challenge.

Source: Financial Times, 8 June 2000. (Copyright © The Financial Times Limited)

However, according to British Telecom (BT) the global value of e-business is predicted to increase a thousand times in the next couple of years. E-business means that small companies can become international traders and large companies can deal with each customer personally.

Even though there are difficulties recruiting staff, the new technology is enabling changes to be made in the working lives of many. The following is a brief scenario of how a self-employed person could utilise the new technology:

Example | Self-employed person

David is a heating, ventilation and air conditioning engineer. As with most engineers, he appreciates the opportunities which new technology offers. British Telecom has introduced Asymmetric Digital Subscriber Lines (ASDL) to which David has started to subscribe. This service using broadband access, offers a permanent connection to the Internet, therefore the Internet is instantly available to him and allows voice telephone calls at the same time.

In the morning before he sets out from home David checks his diary, which can be accessed from any net-compatible device, his diary is saved on a scheduling application and entries are secure and permanent. Once driving to his first customer David may use his WAP mobile phone to dial his web service and check his appointments, enter new ones, send and receive e-mails and voice messages. This is a quick and easy way for him to make sure that he does not miss appointments and also ensures that spare parts he needs to order are procured and delivered for him in an efficient manner.

One of the main advantages of using this technology, and the main reason influencing David's decision to subscribe, was that his supplier of parts could send into his inbox a video showing any of the spare parts which David required and the way in which they have to be installed. This saves a lot of hassle for David: he has no need to consult books or spend an inordinate length of time reading complicated instruction leaflets. In addition to this the supplier is located hundreds of miles away, offers the best prices and has a good reputation for technical support. The supplier used target marketing techniques to approach David via the Internet.

In his spare time David enjoys using his interactive television from which he can send e-mails, shop, bank and play games. He considers the subscription fee he pays for ASDL as money well spent.

Example	The web address of mortgage broking company John Charcol is www.charcolon-line.co.uk; traditionally the company did its business through 15 retail branches, but by changing the way it worked and going on-line, the company has almost doubled in size in just over a year. The company selects the best mortgage for people by selecting from a broad range of suppliers – on-line they do not charge a fee.

Another good example of how e-business has changed the way a company approaches business is shown below.

On a wider scale, electronic business (e-business) helps organisations and their partners to merge together with regard to strategy, process, organisation and technology. In a recent survey 90 per cent of top management believed that the Internet would have a huge impact on the global market place. In fact e-business has developed so quickly that it is expected to accelerate into a period of hypergrowth, with the USA leading the way. Britain and Germany are close behind, with Japan, France and Italy a further two years behind them.

the Internet is shifting the balance of power from the firm to the customer. The more information that consumers have the more discerning they are likely to become. Customers will have the ability to carry out a comparison of products and services very quickly. This includes such things as specification, delivery dates and prices.

There is often confusion as to the terms e-business and e-commerce, and they are used interchangeably by many; however, there is a difference. E-business includes e-commerce, but also encompasses business being done throughout the entire value chain, from suppliers of raw materials to manufacturer to customer. In effect, it transforms the day-to-day operations of an organisation. The information that is normally kept safe in each individual department of a company (i.e. from the production, distribution and marketing departments) needs to be visible by all. One of the benefits of this is that when a customer phones the sales department to find out what has happened to the order, it does not take an inordinate length of time to find the answer.

E-commerce can be defined as follows:

E-commerce means conducting business electronically to provide goods, information and services using internet technologies.

OPPORTUNITIES FOR E-BUSINESS

The opportunities that the improvement in technology provides can help organisations in the following ways:

1 Improved communication and collaboration between employees
2 More efficient supply chain management
3 Increased information exchange with suppliers
4 Superior access to new markets and customers.

Improved communication and collaboration

Another major form of communication is the e-mail. This is widely used in both home and office and has replaced the use of the telephone and sending letters in many instances. This can save on both time and money. A letter at best usually is not delivered until the next day, and even if a reply is written and posted back on the same day, the total time taken is three days. An e-mail arrives seconds after it has been sent, if the person responds immediately or later the same day then the information exchange can take place quickly, even on occasion within a few minutes. With regards to saving money the old adage 'time is money' would be appropriate, the longer the time taken to communicate, the more cost is incurred. The costs are for the time of employees, not to mention the paper, envelope and stamps required. For companies this has meant that they have to be prepared to establish customer e-mail management as an application. This involves the company in not only having the ability to receive incoming e-mail messages, but also a system in place which can route the e-mails to the appropriate department – this is usually referred to as the Automated Call Director.

This technology allows communication 24 hours a day should it be desired. Customers and suppliers do not have to be restricted to the traditional 'office hours only' mentality; indeed the modern consumer now expects that business can be done at any hour of the day. The e-mail can also be invaluable as a source of customer feedback, customers will often give ideas about the development of new products as well as tips about fixing web site bugs.

The e-mail is not restricted to business use and has become a favourite means of communication for families – children at school tend to e-mail each other when they get home instead of using the telephone to speak to one another.

More efficient supply chain management

E-business will eventually be used throughout an entire industry's supply chain to link raw material suppliers, manufacturers, assemblers, distributors, marketers and customers.

The objective is to use internet-based technology to optimise the process of logistics, production, and distribution within an organisation. One of the main uses that e-commerce is used for in businesses today is effective *information sharing*. Large organisations have for many years been allowing suppliers and certain customers some knowledge of their systems and private networks for Electronic Data Interchange (EDI). However, by using the Internet, individuals and small firms alike will have access to e-commerce. This is usually achieved in a company by the use of an intranet. An intranet can span many different business locations via use of the Internet.

Firms can share information if they allow specified suppliers or even key customers, to access the company's intranet.

Example	**Hewlett Packard**

Hewlett Packard has an intranet which has more than a hundred private news groups for employees. It can be accessed by more than 125,000 users and the aim is to encourage employees to discuss opportunities for new products and product improvements.

It is not necessary that all of the intranet be visible, as barriers known as firewalls can be built into the system; this then creates what is known as an extranet.

Example	**Uniphar Plc**

Uniphar Plc is a wholesaler of pharmaceutical products to many pharmacies throughout Ireland. Uniphar uses an extranet to give access to recent product, pharmaceutical and medical information to pharmacies. It also has current issues forums with regard to pharmaceuticals and provides the facility to identify the availability of pharmacy locums.

Increased information exchange with suppliers

If a company has an extranet it provides the means by which staff from the organisation and staff from its suppliers can perhaps work on a joint project with a greater degree of openness. The project may be to develop a new product and the extranet helps the collaborative process with regard to product specifications and production methods; it is even possible for the employees of collaborating companies to be working on the same spreadsheet together even though they are working in different locations. There will also be a reduction in time-wasting activities, such as, writing to or visiting each other's sites; this has the advantage of saving both time and money and encourages the sharing of ideas and techniques.

Other technology which can be used is video conferencing. Video conferencing enables people who are many miles apart in distance, to converse with each other as if face to face. This is being increasingly used especially in large firms as an everyday means of communicating; executives no longer have to travel the globe to have business meetings.

Superior access to new markets and customers

Many companies have been trying to develop an e-commerce strategy. There is the opportunity to reach new markets and potentially develop a new distribution channel. To do this one of the first steps that has to be undertaken is the development of a *web site*. This is the shop window, so to speak, that customers using the Internet will access in order to do business with the company. A good web site can make a small business as powerful and competitive as some of the largest organisations. The web site must not be the only form of marketing that the company undertakes, it is as important that the name of the company and what it offers becomes generally well known, and to do this marketing outside the Web should take place. This could take the form of press or radio advertising, and even television advertising now commonly features the web site address of the company in question. It is important that the web site is identified by name, registered with the appropriate body and with relevant search engines. Of course, one of the most important features is that the site must look good, be updated when appropriate, and be fast and easy for customers to use, along with the relevant security features so that customers can order and pay for goods that they may wish to order. There should be easy-to-fill in interactive forms which can help turn a sales prospect into a buyer. Even if the web site is attractive to look at, it must be supported by a secure and integrated *e-business system*. The work behind the scenes will include such things as packing and posting goods, stock control, maintaining databases and financial systems. Some of the features that a web site should incorporate are shown in the box on page 58.

Features of a good web site

1 Registered with search engines and therefore easy to access

2 Looks good and is easy to use

3 Good integration with all company systems

4 Easy to update by company staff

5 Produces company records which can be audited

6 Can interact with visitors to the site

7 Can be controlled and maintained by owner not developer

8 Incorporates security features for financial transactions

9 Has an interactive form for transactions to encourage visitors to purchase

10 Does not take too long to load pictures, etc. when in use.

It is also possible to attract customers to a web site by using banner advertisements or link buttons and these are becoming an important source of revenue for internet providers.

A very useful facility that these web sites offer is the ability to capture *customer information*. It is possible to review the number of 'hits' and the pages which proved most popular to the customers. This information can be invaluable for a company, it can be used to build an excellent overview of the customer base and customer likes and dislikes.

THE IMPACT OF E-BUSINESS ON COST

The use of a fully integrated e-business system within an organisation can result in sizeable cost benefits; the areas where the majority of these cost benefits arise are as follows:

- The costs associated with purchasing production raw materials
- The costs associated with manufacturing and delivering a product or service
- The costs of executing a sale.

According to BT's general manager for electronic government, the UK government could save £13.5 billion over the next three years if it embraced e-business and e-commerce. Many industries are changing to incorporate e-business and will in time harvest these cost changes. Perhaps one of the best known examples is the banking industry: many banks are now providing on-line facilities for many customers.

MOBILE COMMUNICATIONS

As we have seen, mobile communications are being transformed dramatically. Within two years BT predicts that all new mobile phones will be internet-enabled, and by 2003 it is expected that more people will be accessing the web from mobile devices than from desktop computers.

The WAP (wireless application protocol) – is a means of transmitting internet information over mobile devices, and when faster GPRS (general packet radio services) is used then more innovative applications are likely. GPRS is the technology that will make browsing the Internet on a mobile phone much faster and easier to use than it presently is. It will enable the user to be permanently connected to the Internet, and deliver content at speeds five to ten times faster than WAP phones. BT expects summer 2000 to be the launch date of GPRS onto the general market and mobile broadband access to interactive services via universal mobile telecommunications system (UMTS) by 2002. There are many applications for this technology – here are three different and interesting examples.

Example 1 **BskyB**

BskyB has teamed up with Vodafone and BT Cellnet to develop WAP content strategy and is set to deliver sport, news and entertainment content. This will enable a wide audience to have access to the following:

- Live sports results
- Audio commentaries
- Team news and selections
- Betting odds
- Statistics
- Quotes and interviews.

BskyB's director of new media John Swingewood said that 'We want to make Sky's sport, news and entertainment content available on a non-exclusive basis to Vodafone's eight million UK customers. Our relationships are ideal for the development of mobile e-commerce when this becomes available . . .'.

Other digital platforms are also in the pipeline for BskyB, one of which may be plans to launch a sports shop on the Internet to sell a variety of sporting goods; this would include products for golf, football, rugby and cricket etc.

Example 2 **Excite**

Internet portal Excite – dubbed Excite Mobile – is designed to enable users to access personalised information either from their WAP mobile phone or from a computer. The type of content available includes stock prices, weather (both regional and international), TV listings, horoscopes and even film listings for the nearest cinemas.

Example 3 **24/7 Europe**

24/7 Europe has developed an ad server, the developed system incorporates ad serving, management and reporting capabilities, and this will help with regard to delivery, monitoring and control of campaigns. At present the advertising can take the form of a flash screen containing a logo – with the possibility of grapical, colour and location-based ads. An example of this would be a welcome message being sent to users on arrival at an airport by companies like Hertz or Avis asking the traveller whether they would like any other service such as weather reports in addition to car rental.

In theory this could be used as a sophisticated surveillance device. However 24/7 Europe sees mobile advertising as even more measurable than internet advertising, a feature of mobile phones which is set to grow. Indeed it may be that if users want to switch advertising off they may have to pay premium prices for the mobile phone service.

CONCLUSION

This chapter has introduced some of the technology now available to help organisations, and this includes marketing staff. The opportunities available from e-business are definitely available in abundance, but as with every new development and innovation, the practicalities can sometimes seem a little daunting. Bill Gates, the chairman of Microsoft, summed up the situation in his book *Business @ the Speed of Thought*, where it is put forward that only managers who master the digital universe will gain competitive advantage. In fact it is advocated that to make this digital flow happen in a company there are some very important steps to follow. In the book there are twelve steps, but three of the ones which are most important for firms who are on the front line when dealing with customers (this should in fact apply to most organisations) are summarised below:

- Insist that communication flows through e-mail
- Use digital systems to route customer complaints immediately
- Use digital tools to help customers solve problems for themselves.

The use of e-business is a major step forward and it only remains to be seen which companies will thrive and which will die if they do not meet the challenge. In people's daily lives, change with regard to technology uptake may be a little slower, but it is likely that it will happen and probably sooner rather than later.

QUESTIONS

1 *Describe in your own words how the Internet has impacted on the way in which companies interact with (a) suppliers and (b) customers.*

2 *Outline the major ways in which e-business has provided opportunities for organisations to improve the way in which they operate.*

3 *From your own experience, give three examples of web sites which you think are good. Justify your choice.*

4 *What are the latest developments in internet-enabled devices?*

FURTHER READING

BT (2000) *Annual Review for Shareholders*.

Ballam, A. (2000) 'E-commerce dangers, promises and profits', *Management Accounting*, February.

Barrett, S. (2000) 'State of the WAP', *Revolution*, 15 March.

Corboy, M. (1999) 'E-commerce, dispelling the myths and exploiting the opportunities,' *Management Accounting*, November.

Gates, W. H. (1999) *Business @ the Speed of Thought*. Warner Bros.

Lord, R. (2000) 'How to make your service more popular, stop charging for it', *Revolution*, 15 March.

Meadows-Klue, D. (1999) 'Who clicked on what, where, how and why?', the *Daily Telegraph*, 11 September.

Reedy, J., Schullo, S. and Zimmerman, K. (2000) *Electronic Marketing*. The Dryden Press, Harcourt College Publishers.

Roberts, P. (2000) 'E-business: what is it and does it matter to accountants?' *Management Accounting*, February.

Equipment and software trends

Survey – UK call centres: Multimedia set to make their mark

It is almost 30 years since US manufacturer Rockwell launched a new way of doing business with the release of the world's first mass-market automatic call distributor (ACD).

By deftly marrying the call handling power of the private telephone switchboard (PABX) with the processing power of a computer, the company created a method by which enterprises could centralise their customer services enquiries. The call centre was born.

While the price of those first systems has dropped dramatically to bring call centre facilities within reach of a much wider range of businesses, the ACD remains the beating heart of today's call processing industry.

But that is soon set to change as voice-oriented call centres are rapidly replaced by multimedia facilities which manage customer contact using a wide range of media, from today's standard 'live operator' telephone calls to fax, e-mail, automated voice response, real-time web chat, voice-over-IP links and even person-to-person video conferencing. With Datamonitor, the market research company, forecasting exponential growth in European web-enabled call centres from today's figure of around 500 to some 4300 facilities within three years, leading vendors such as Lucent Technologies, Oracle, Nortel Networks and others are moving quickly to integrate tomorrow's technologies into existing offerings.

Among front-runners are interactive voice recognition (IVR), Wap- and Java-enabled applications, intelligent network architectures, advanced customer database systems, integrated messaging and voice-enabled web surfing via voice-over-IP icons that can connect browsing customers to a call centre operator at the touch of a button:

'In an e-commerce environment your competitors are only a click away. That makes an effective response customer contact centre an essential element of a company's success in the electronic market place,' says David Quantrell, vice-president Europe, the Middle East and Africa Nortel Networks' e-business applications division.

Nortel, one of the longest-established vendors of call-centre solutions, was also among the first to release an integrated multimedia system combining voice recognition, text-to-speech processing, call control and reporting, automated e-mail response, and automated fax-back and call-back capabilities.

The product suite also features skills-based call routing – a feature destined to become increasingly important as call-centre teams process customer enquiries through a range of media and, in many cases, a variety of languages.

With globalisation continuing to drive growth in centres with an international reach, software developers are working rapidly to build advanced multi-lingual capabilities into their systems. 'A developer who sticks with one language can't hope to survive in today's market place,' says Alan Pound, director of UK-based Aculab, one of the leading suppliers of speech-processing and network access cards.

Mr Pound says text-to-speech technology is now moving ahead fast, with pleasant, human-sounding voices replacing the Dalek-style delivery that characterised early efforts. 'We now have a very usable, useful technology that's ideal for e-mail readers and systems handling large amounts of rapidly-changing information,' he says.

Automatic Speech Recognition has proved a much harder nut to crack, but Mr Pound says work in the area of neural networks and artificial intelligence is finally yielding fruit. 'Having some context helps a lot because today's systems are relatively good at identifying a human response if they have an idea of what they're going to hear,' he says. Natural free-format language is much more agreeable for the consumer, he adds, but much harder to program.

▶

While technically a hardware vendor, Aculab now employ 10 times as many software developers as nuts-and-bolts engineers, along with a team of linguists who work on training new systems to distinguish homonyms and other complex linguistic constructions. Advances are being made, but Mr Pound says phrases such as 'He moped over his moped' continue to induce considerable confusion in silicon-based systems. But if machines that can understand and talk back are not enough, researchers are already working on software that has the power to detect and adapt to the mood of each incoming caller.

Valery Perushin, a software developer with Arthur Andersen's Centre for Strategic Technology Research in Chicago, has been using neural net systems to analyse voice-prints corresponding to five different emotions – anger, happiness, sadness, fear and 'neutral'. An early prototype system can now register the emotional state of its human interlocutor with 70 per cent accuracy – about the same as a human being. Mr Perushin says he is now working on improving gender-specific and operator-specific recognition, with a view to creating call centre systems that can automatically route customers calling with a complaint or an urgent problem to specially-trained operators. Meanwhile, in the midst of all this high-tech wizardry, the humble ACD is itself undergoing a dramatic transformation. Once a stand-alone box located on the customer's premises, automatic call distribution is evolving into a network service that will be accessed through a new breed of application service provider.

'As ACDs become increasingly complex, not owning the equipment yourself has a number of advantages,' notes Trevor Richer, director of convergent applications with Cable & Wireless. 'For a start, there's no need for a large up-front investment and no ongoing maintenance charges. At the same time, companies get a future-proofed solution that's easier to manage and more flexible in terms of their changing operational requirements.'

If access to ACD services will be increasingly effected on-line, the equipment itself is also rapidly evolving to meet the needs of the multimedia age. As an example, Aspect Communications Corporation, once one of the world's top suppliers of ACDs, now fashions itself as a leading designer of 'multimedia customer relationship portals' – an indication of how pervasive the web has already become in the call-processing industry.

Gary Colville, Aspect's director of marketing for Europe, the Middle East and Africa, says one of today's biggest challenges lies in developing e-business sales systems to minimise the 'abandoned shopping cart' syndrome which currently kills around 60 per cent of all potential on-line transactions.

'New technologies need to be implemented intelligently. Topping-and-tailing of calls using IVR can take 20 per cent off the length of each call, which translates into big savings for large companies,' he says. 'But the same technology used at the wrong time in the customer transaction can cut out your ability to cross-sell and up-sell.'

Mr Colville says web-based information is also driving a lot of voice traffic through traditional call centres as customers 'surf' for information but make a telephone call to place their order.

'Tomorrow's best call centre solutions will be those which can neatly combine the best of all media,' he says. 'Just as the call centre didn't replace the high street, the web will never replace voice interaction with the customer.'

Sarah Parkes

Source: Financial Times, 9 June 2000. (Copyright © The Financial Times Limited)

Question

In what ways can new technology such as that outlined in this case affect both companies and customers? List any advantages and disadvantages of the technology, giving reasons for your answers.

The competitive environment

Not to resemble one's neighbour; that is everything.
Flaubert

INTRODUCTION

In 1985, there appeared in *Business Week* an article entitled 'Forget satisfying the consumer – just outfox the other guy'. This neatly summarises some people's view of marketing. There are no rewards in telling your sales manager, 'I came second in the bid for the contract'; if you did not get the business it does not matter if you come second or twenty-second. The 1970s saw an emphasis on a strong customer focus within marketing organisations. In 1980 Michael Porter of the Harvard Business School published his key book, entitled *Competitive Strategy*, which was quickly followed by Kenichi Ohmae's *The Mind of the Strategist*. Both books have a brief that is wider than marketing *per se*, but both look at the importance of a competitor orientation for any organisation. They make the point that if you forget the competitive environment in which you operate, you could lose your business. This applies not just to private companies, but also the public services in the UK, where government legislation has introduced compulsory competitive tendering (CCT) for many local authority contracts.

Philip Kotler, a most prolific marketing author, also addressed competitive strategy when he jointly authored an article with Ravi Singh entitled 'Marketing warfare in the 1980s'. The parallels between military strategy and business have fascinated writers for a long time. Kotler and Singh suggested various attack and defence strategies that could help win a marketing conflict. These include several alternatives to the direct attack, since a direct assault rarely achieves victory – a view supported by a study of military history.

There are differences between war and business, however, and the Chairman of Electrolux was once reported to have said, 'Unlike the Military, Industry is always at war. If there is peace, they call it a cartel, and, as everyone knows, those are not allowed.'

The early 1980s also saw the publication of Peters and Waterman's book, *In Search of Excellence*. This focused on a survey of a number of then highly successful companies. Although this book says little on beating the competition, it does re-emphasise 'closeness to customers', and building stronger relationships, as some of the key principles of success. However, within this section they do suggest the art of 'nichemanship': 'finding a particular niche where you are better at something than anybody else.' This encapsulates getting ahead of the competition. In their research, Peters and Waterman found that 'a very large proportion of the surveyed companies were superb at dividing their customer base into numerous segments, so that they could provide tailored products and services'. Many successful companies are able to do this with a great deal of precision now owing to the increased use of databases. This is especially true in the retail industry, where the use of customer loyalty cards and credit cards, such as those issued by the supermarket chain Tesco, afford the organisation a great deal of information. The information is gleaned from the customer's application form and the subsequent spending patterns of the consumer. The issues of how customers' make buying decisions will be discussed in Chapters 6 and 7, and segmentation in Chapter 8. What this survey shows is that it may not be possible to win the competitive battle with all your potential customers, but it is possible to be the *preferred product/service for a particular segment of the customer population.*

In Search of Excellence dismisses the move to a more competitive focus, stating: 'The competitor issue is easily put to rest. The excellent companies clearly do more and better competitor analysis than the rest.' It is this ability to understand competitors and predict their actions which is vitally important to all marketing-orientated organisations.

Tom Peters redressed the lack of competitive emphasis in his later book, *Thriving on Chaos*, albeit in a chapter on 'Creative Swiping'. Here he advocates becoming obsessed with competitors – not just the major obvious competitors but all potential competitors. He suggests three tasks:

1 Collect data on competitors
2 Update it regularly
3 Share it widely within the firm.

INDUSTRY STRUCTURE

The performance of an organisation will be influenced by the structure of the industry in which it operates because this will affect the level of competition in that market. Porter (1980) suggested that in addition to analysing what he calls 'jockeying for position' by obvious competitors, there are four other forces which affect the level of competition. These are:

1 The bargaining power of suppliers
2 The bargaining power of customers
3 The threat of new entrants
4 The threat of substitute products or services.

If there is only a small number of key suppliers, perhaps controlling a key ingredient, or a small number of customers, then they can use this to squeeze profitability in an industry. There are other sources of power, but the factors which give rise to this power will change over time, so it is important to continually reassess the situation. As an example, some years ago Tesco supermarkets took over a small regional group called Hillards. The concentration of food retailers who are customers of food manufacturers thus increased. Companies who supplied Hillards but not Tesco were considered as potential suppliers to the wider group. However, since the Hillards' stores were changed to Tesco layout, the predominant change was not in their favour. Certainly this was one example of a change in bargaining power for the food manufacturing industry in relation to its direct customers, the food retailers.

We could also look in detail at the food retailing industry itself. The customers here are families, students, housewives and anyone who purchases food. While there are millions of customers they each spend only a small amount in relation to the turnover of a single large supermarket, let alone a company like Safeway or Tesco with total turnovers in excess of billions of pounds. An individual customer of Hillards might not like the Tesco store that replaced it. However, while all customers have a choice to purchase food wherever they like, the bargaining power of an individual is small and unlikely to affect Tesco's policy. In many cases the choice of supermarket is determined by location and not by the range of items on sale in a particular outlet. Therefore many customers who used the former Hillards store now use it in its 'Tesco' style. In defence of Tesco, it has to be said that during the 1980s it managed very successfully to change its stores, which now attract increasing numbers of customers.

The threat of new entrants can also be studied in the context of food retailing. The 1990s have seen the large German retailer, Aldi, move into the UK, with a long-term plan to open 80 stores in the Midlands and North West. These new stores, with a distinct format, are already attracting customers, and since total food consumption is relatively static they must be winning customers from existing food retailers. Perhaps no obvious substitutes exist in food retailing, but in many industries new ways of applying benefits can be a significant threat, and this could alter the competitive environment in a dramatic way.

THE COMPETITIVE ENVIRONMENT

The competitive environment is likely to be of more immediate importance to marketers than the wider business environment discussed in Chapter 3. The different types of competitive environment can affect the way an organisation markets its products. At one extreme there are markets akin to what economists call 'perfect competition'. Here there are many small firms, which are all too small to have an individual impact on price or performance norms. Usually it is easy to enter or leave such an industry, but the rewards are small owing to the intense competition. In this market, all firms have similar technologies and costs, and the product or service offered is almost impossible to distinguish from others. This is a very difficult market place, since there is no obvious reason why any buyer should choose any particular supplier other than on value and price.

At the other extreme is the monopoly market, where only one supplier exists. The only decision faced by customers is to buy (or not to buy) the product. The recent legal action involving Microsoft is an example of how government can become wary and want to intervene when the strength of a supplier becomes such that it is felt competition is stifled. However, in practice, most markets lie somewhere in between perfect and monopolistic markets.

Exercise

1 Discuss the effect on competition of any industries that have a monopoly or near monopolistic power: is this good for the consumer? Do you feel that the power should be diluted in some way, and if so, how could this be done?

2 Discuss the recent developments in the Microsoft case – how has this affected competition within the industry?

In creating reasons for customers to prefer one product to another, some form of competitive advantage is necessary. Many successful and fast-growing small and medium-sized firms (SMEs), as well as the larger multinationals, feel that they can gain advantages over competitors by being significantly better with regards to customer service, understanding customer needs better and providing a higher quality of product.

The study of competitors and the comparison of the strengths and weaknesses of competitor operations are very important in developing successful marketing plans. Marketing plans are also influenced by the stages of industrial development. In newly emergent industries such as video games, or new forms of entertainment as well as dotcom companies, the emphasis is on developing *customer awareness*. The reason for this is that many potential customers will be first-time buyers or surfers on the web. Growth markets still offer rewards for all competitors, but here the 'jockeying' for a favourable position really begins. As markets mature we find that:

- competition focuses on 'market share' and not market growth, and that;
- customers are usually experienced repeat-buyers who understand the product benefits and know something about the different offerings.

In mature markets there is also an emphasis on competition through modified or improved products, added value or operational efficiency. This becomes more intense as decline sets in, when excess production capacity is apparent and profits are falling. The concept of industry or demand life cycles can be linked to product life cycles, and these will be discussed in greater depth later in the book.

IDENTIFYING COMPETITORS

In order to develop a competitive marketing strategy it is vital that we decide *who our competitors are*. The most obvious competitors are other organisations which offer similar or identical products or services to the same customers as ours. An example of this could be grocery stores who offer on-line shopping at the following web addresses, <www.tescodirect.com> and <www.sainsburys.com>. However, the subject of substitute products and services highlights the *indirect competitors*, who also must be analysed.

It is helpful to define five levels of competitors.

1 Direct competition
2 Close competition
3 Products of a similar nature
4 Substitute products
5 Indirect competition.

Direct competition

Most people would consider that Pepsi Cola is a direct competitor to Coca-Cola. Both companies offer some similar products to the same general market. In this case the production methods employed are also very similar, although the actual formula for the basic cola essence is somewhat different in both companies since these products are in direct competition. Great store is therefore placed by both companies on advertising and gaining an advantage over each other. One way in which Coca-Cola is trying to do this is outlined in the following example.

Example	Coca-Cola has launched a new slogan, 'Coca-Cola: enjoy' to replace its well known 'Always Coca-Cola'. This will be a change for the company, who after seven years are now concentrating on a major new marketing campaign. To support this campaign Coca-Cola is updating its website <www.coca-cola.com> to include many downloadable images, etc. which can be adapted to local markets.

Close competition

Is Pepsi also a competitor to Tango orange drink? Both products offer similar benefits to similar consumers. The difference between orange and cola flavour is easier to recognise than the difference between Coca-Cola and Pepsi, but basically the products are substitutes for each other. In any analysis of drinks, all fizzy drinks need to be considered. Of course, it could be argued that other fizzy drinks include Perrier sparkling mineral water and champagne. Here we would be moving away from a strict interpretation of 'close competition'. Another example which could be considered is that of the websites of <Amazon.com> and <Barnes and Noble.com>, as both companies are sites to visit if one wishes to purchase books, although certainly with Amazon.com there is also a wide variety of other goods to choose from.

Products of a similar nature

Perrier is a naturally sparkling mineral water from Southern France. The water comes up through a field of natural gas, hence the claim to be naturally sparkling as opposed to having added carbon dioxide, which is the case with Pepsi and many other sparkling drinks. However, it is the marketing decision to target Perrier at an adult market, rather than the younger age targeted by Pepsi, which makes Perrier less of a close competitor. Champagne also has an alternative way of producing the fizz. 'Methode Champenoise' is a secondary fermentation of the wine after it has been bottled. But again, it is not the different way of producing the bubbles, rather than the positioning of the product, which makes it less relevant when considering competitors.

Positioning of products is a very powerful tool for companies, and will be discussed in more detail in Chapter 8. At a basic level, positioning is to do with how companies use the marketing mix of product, price, place and promotion in comparison to other companies that offer products of a similar nature. Although the products may be very similar, perhaps it is the pricing or packaging or even the way it is advertised that can alter so dramatically whether customers believe one product to be much better than the other. This shows how the marketing mix is a very powerful tool in the positioning of products, and one that successful companies try to use to their advantage.

Substitute products

Is an ice cream a substitute for a fizzy drink? On a warm summer's day this is a reasonable choice. Marketers need to consider those products, which can substitute in this way. The study of *buyer behaviour* is critical in deciding how wide such a study should go, and will be explained in more depth in Chapters 6 and 7.

Indirect competition

Sometimes it is impossible to guess where competition is coming from. Any product that competes for the same buying power could be considered a competitor. If we consider a student surviving on a limited grant, there may sometimes be a choice between Pepsi Cola and a newspaper, or between going to watch a film or spending the evening in a pub. Perhaps here both examples are relatively low-value items and the distinction is easily made. At a slightly higher level are the types of decisions to be taken about products which cost a great deal more money and the opportunity cost of each decision has be decided. Families may have to decide, for example, whether to change the car or pay for a holiday – the cost of one is in a way the enjoyment forgone from the product that they did not choose.

Another example was a decision by Boots The Chemist to reorganise its stores. The managing director of a company supplying dog biscuits to Boots was told his product would be discontinued even though it was selling well in the stores. The reason was an increase in the space allocated to audio and photographic products, and other 'high-ticket' items. Pet foods were not contributing enough profit per square foot of store and were being completely phased out. This type of competition is almost impossible to assess although it could be said that the dog biscuit company really knew very little about the objectives and needs of the customer. Boots required profit from its shops and obviously the dog biscuits did not contribute sufficiently to this.

> **Exercise**
>
> The following products could be seen as competitors. Which level of competition is involved, and what attention do you think a marketing manager should give to analysing the competitive threat?
>
> (a) A UK rail franchise company considering the threat posed by coach travel.
> (b) A flower shop considering the shop next door which sells fancy chocolate products.
> (c) A Chinese restaurant looking at the range of pre-prepared Chinese meals available in a local supermarket.
> (d) A large brewery company considering home-brew kits.

You could also list other direct or indirect competitors for each of the examples above.

COMPETITOR ANALYSIS

The previous section should demonstrate that it is not always easy to identify who is your competitor for the purpose of understanding their strategies. There is of course one thing which should be considered by all companies, and that is to give customers a *reason to buy from you and not your competitors*. Companies dealing on-line are also in a very competitive environment and one of the major things they must do is to be aware of what their competitors are doing: not only what they are doing but, also, are they providing a good or service faster, or more cheaply, than the competition and is their website easy to navigate? Business guru Tom Peters is right when suggesting that 'excellent companies do better competitor analysis'. The task is to understand the constraints restricting competitors and to predict competitor moves. The objective of this analysis is to find 'points of leverage' which can be used at minimum cost against competitors. It is not appropriate to collect data for its own sake; rather the analysis should focus on those essentials which can help take decisions on how to win in the market place.

It is not necessary at this stage to list the type of data collected in a competitor analysis. The need is specific to any particular set of competitors. It is, however, wider than the obvious marketing issues, and will include issues such as financial strength, operational efficiency and production capability, which could affect a competitor's market performance.

A typical evaluation process could follow the sequence below:

1 Evaluation of competitor's objectives
2 Evaluation of competitor's strategy
3 Evaluation of competitor's success to date
4 Evaluation of competitor's strengths and weaknesses
5 Prediction of future competitor behaviour.

It is the *future responses* that are important for a marketer. However, many firms will behave in a consistent manner, so that studying past actions can help to predict how your competitors might react in the future, and this is of course vital when formulating your organisational plans.

Information on competitors will come from both formal research and informal information channels. The latter includes dialogue with customers, often conveyed in reports from sales staff, but also obtainable from suppliers or other third parties. Although unnecessary data is to be discouraged, an efficient marketing information system is appropriate. The assessment of information needs to be made by a marketing-orientated employer who understands the dynamics of the particular market.

THE COMPETITIVE TRIANGLE

Figure 5.1 is inspired by the work of Kenichi Ohmae. It is an excellent way of remembering that *customers have choices*. From the apex of the triangle customers can assess the different offerings of all companies and their competitors.

Obviously, customers will choose to do business with the company which best matches its requirements. Of course, the workings of customers' decision processes are not simple, and these are discussed in the following chapters. Nevertheless, the match between the various offerings and particular customers, or groups of customers, should not be left to happen by chance. The role of marketers is to try to influence factors in such a way that their organisation's products or marketing offerings are chosen.

The object of this is to try to gain a *sustainable advantage* over competitors. Writing in the *Harvard Business Review* on this subject, Pankaj Ghemawat stated, 'For outstanding performance, a company has to beat the competition. The trouble is that the competition has heard the same message.' He summarises three areas of potential advantage from cross-industry findings:

1 **Product innovation**. Competitors secure detailed information on 70 per cent of all new products within a year of their development. Patenting usually fails to deter imitation. On average, imitation costs a third less than innovation and is a third quicker.
2 **Production**. New processes are even harder to protect than new products. Incremental improvements to old processes are vulnerable too. If consultants are to be believed, 60 per cent to 90 per cent of all 'learning' ultimately diffuses to competitors. Production often blurs competitive advantage: recent studies show that unionised workers pocket two-thirds of the potential profits in US manufacturing.
3 **Marketing non-price instruments**. These are usually ascribed more potency than

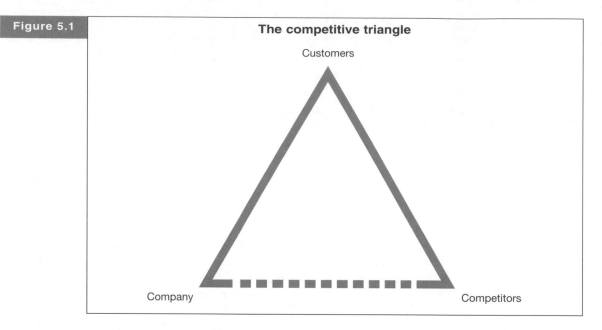

Figure 5.1

The competitive triangle

price changes, partly because they are harder to match. Rivals often react to a particular move, however, by adjusting their entire marketing mix. Such reactions tend to be intense; limited data on advertising suggest that the moves and countermoves frequently cancel out. Another non-price instrument can also be the speed of delivery. This is becoming a major element of competitive advantage especially with regard to some companies which operate on-line.

Example

ZipRound.com is a company that promises delivery of a range of goods in a short space of time, normally within an hour. This is a vast improvement on the timeframe offered by similar on-line companies, the time given by other companies at the time of writing, such as Lastorders.com and the grocery firm TheFoodFerry.com was same-day delivery, whilst it is even longer than this for other major grocery companies.

Nevertheless, Peters still suggests that the goal should be uniqueness. He advises: 'Uniqueness most often comes not from a breakthrough idea, but from the accumulation of thousands of tiny enhancements.'

In the early days of marketing, many organisations looked for the one Unique Selling Point (USP). In fact, as Peters points out, it is much more complex. Therefore, to achieve competitive advantage a marketer needs to be involved with the whole marketing offering, inside and outside the organisation.

MEGA-MARKETING

Kotler suggested that competitive advantage could be gained by altering the external environment. This is undoubtedly possible, as exemplified by Pepsi bringing about the exclusion of Coca-Cola from India for more than a decade. The voluntary agreement limiting car imports from Japan to the UK is another example of reducing competition.

However, the role of the EC Commissioner for Competition is specifically aimed at ensuring that no unfair competitive situations develop. Therefore, most organisations are open to the full power of competition and they have only the internal variables, controlled within their organisation, with which to achieve competitive advantage, as seen by customers outside the organisation.

CONCLUSION

The competitive environment is the most dynamic environment in which an organisation will operate. Other organisations, both nearby and remote, are also planning to offer their products or services, and are aware that success comes from improving on the existing offers. It is in this ever-changing arena that organisations have to strive for ongoing survival.

Companies can decide to try to lead developments and move faster than their rivals into new areas. This requires investment in Research and Development (R&D) and a clear vision of the future. Other organisations will follow fast when new products or services are launched, hoping to improve on an idea with the benefit of seeing customers' reactions. However, laggard companies which react too late find that the market has already moved on.

The study of competitors' activities is vital. But it must be linked to a study of *potential buyers*, how those buyers behave now and how they are likely to behave in the future. This is the subject of Chapter 6. It completes the study of the competitive triangle discussed here. It is necessary for marketers to study both customers and competitors. A focus on one alone is not enough, as it leaves the triangle incomplete. If there is a failure to appreciate the ever-changing competition, then the words of warning at the end of Chapter 3 will be even more relevant: '[There are] those [companies] who wonder what happened.'

QUESTIONS

1 *In a market of your choice, select two leading companies or brands and identify the means by which they compete with each other.*

2 *Do you think a marketer should take the advice: 'Never mind the customer, just outfox the competition'?*

3 *Why do customers still buy branded food products in supermarkets when the retailer's own label is often of similar quality and cheaper?*

4 *To what extent might competition come from unrelated markets in the form of a substitute product?*

FURTHER READING

Brown, P. B., Buell, B., Davis, J. E. and Dreytack, K. (1985) 'Forget satisfying the customer – just outfox the other guy', *Business Week*, 7 November.

Deloitte & Touche (1997) *The Ten Percenters*.

Ghemawhat, P. (1986) 'Sustainable advantage,' *Harvard Business Review*, September–October.

Goddard, C. (2000) 'Speedy delivery shifts up a gear,' *Revolution*, 5 April.

Kotler, P. (1986) 'Mega-marketing', *Harvard Business Review*. –

Kotler, P. (1999) *Marketing Management, Analysis, Planning, Implementation and Control.* Prentice-Hall.

Kotler, P. and Singh, R. (1981) 'Marketing warfare in the 1980s', *Journal of Business Strategy,* Winter.

Ohmae, K. (1983) *The Mind of the Strategist.* Penguin.

Peters, T. (1988) *Thriving on Chaos.* Macmillan.

Pilling, D. and Wolffe, R. (2000) 'Drug abuses: as pharmaceutical companies go to extraordinary lengths to protect expiring patents, regulators are starting to pay close attention', *Financial Times,* 20 April.

Porter, M. E. (1980) *Competitive Strategy.* The Free Press.

CASE STUDY

Drug abuses

FT

As pharmaceutical companies go to extraordinary lengths to protect expiring patents, regulators are starting to pay close attention, say David Pilling and Richard Wolffe

SmithKline Beecham, the company that is merging with Glaxo Wellcome to form one of the world's most powerful drugs groups, will today report strong first-quarter results. But of greater interest to investors will be the little detail appended to the accounts – one relating to a patent.

This month, SmithKline was granted a new US patent on Augmentin, a powerful antibiotic. As a result, its monopoly to produce it could run until 2017, fully 15 years more than expected. The extension is a coup for SmithKline, worth potentially billions of dollars. It is not, however, such good news for patients. In the US, branded Augmentin, which racked up sales of 1.8bn ($1.1bn) last year, costs about $70 for a 10-day course. A generic version might sell for $15.

SmithKline won its extension on Augmentin, first launched in 1981, by filing what is known as a 'submarine' patent. Before its original protection on amoxycillin, the active ingredient of Augmentin, expired, it filed an additional patent covering other elements of the drug, including an acid that stops amoxycillin degrading.

According to one pharmaceuticals' analyst, the 2017 patent is not based on any new discovery but on work conducted in the early 1970s. 'It appears to have got two patent lives for the price of one,' he said. The development is of enormous interest to governments, battling to keep health-care costs down, and to other pharmaceutical companies, which face an unprecedented number of patent expirations.

Warburg Dillon Read estimates that two-fifths of patent-protected drugs will be under direct or indirect generic competition within five years. Because generic manufacturers do not need to recoup the $500m or so it takes to invent a medicine, they can sell them at a fraction of the cost, slashing the originator's sales overnight.

The list of affected medicines includes such well-known products as Prozac, an anti-depressant made by Eli-Lilly (estimated 2000 sales, $2.5bn); Claritin, Schering-Plough's hay fever pill ($2.2bn); and Losec, AstraZeneca's phenomenally successful ulcer medicine ($6bn).

Generic manufacturers are becoming increasingly frustrated. 'The generics industry has a significant opportunity to provide the American public with more affordable medicine,' says Henry Menn of the Generic Pharmaceutical Industry Association in Washington. 'But pharmaceutical companies have instigated a well-funded and well-organised campaign to block generics from entering the market place.' The tactics employed are numerous and complex. One that has attracted increasing attention is the development of 'cleaned-up' versions of old drugs, called single-isomers.

Most drug molecules can exist in two mirror-image forms, only one of which is active. New techniques have been developed to discard the non-active (and possibly harmful) component, enabling drug companies to demonstrate greater potency or fewer side-effects. Branded companies have the benefit of thousands of sales representatives and huge advertising budgets to trumpet even the most marginal advantages. Crucially, the 'new molecule' is treated as a separate drug, with an entirely new patent life.

The strategy has spawned a large number of single-isomer versions of medicines that might otherwise have been on their last legs. These include Prozac Jr; a single-isomer version of Losec called Nexium; and desloratadine, the single-isomer offspring of Claritin. Last Thursday, the US Federal Trade Commission appeared to clear single-isomers of any anticompetitive suspicions by closing a review of Eli-Lilly's exclusive licence to market Prozac Jr.

But the FTC has declared its strong opposition to other practices. Last month, it filed civil charges against Aventis, a Franco-German company, and Abbott Laboratories of the US, as well as against two generic makers, Andrx and Geneva Pharmaceuticals. The pharmaceutical companies were charged with paying the generic manufacturers not to launch cheaper rivals to branded drugs.

The FTC's actions are designed to send a clear signal both to the industry and antitrust lawyers. 'It's fair to say that we are generally concerned about patent-extension strategies that would be anticompetitive,' said one official. 'On the other hand, we think innovation is very important and would not want to take action to deter new products.'

It is a fiendishly complex dilemma for antitrust officials, who are working closely with both the Food and Drug Administration and the Patent Office. Senior antitrust officials in Washington have identified this area as one of the main challenges of a knowledge-based economy. Speaking at a congressional hearing last week, Robert Pitofsky, the FTC's chairman, said: 'The general issue [of technology patents] is the most important and toughest that we are going to face in the next few years. This intersection between antitrust and intellectual property, particularly as the economy moves in the direction of intellectual property, is a tough call.'

In Europe, too, regulators are watchful. Last week, it emerged that the European Commission was looking at one particular strategy being employed by brand companies. When a generic is sent for regulatory approval, it does not normally need an entire dossier of data on safety and efficacy. Instead, it has to prove 'bio-equivalence' with the original branded medicine whose properties are already well established.

The branded medicine is known as the 'reference' product. But pharmaceutical companies have taken to withdrawing this reference product from the market shortly before its patent expires and replacing it with a 'new and improved version' – a capsule, say, instead of a tablet.

When the generic manufacturer seeks regulatory clearance, it runs the risk of rejection on the grounds that there is no longer a marketed reference product with which to compare its medicine. 'This is an extremely anti-competitive action by certain pharmaceutical companies, who are abusing both regulatory and patent laws,' says Greg Perry, director-general of the European Generic Medicines Association. 'It could add billions of euros to healthcare budgets throughout the EU.'

Tom McKillop, chief executive of AstraZeneca, which is accused by the association of employing the tactic to protect Losec, says: 'There's undoubtedly a tension between generics trying to get in as early as possible and the R&D industry trying to defend its intellectual property as long as it can. There's a grey area at the transition point – I don't think that should surprise anyone.' Neither is the generics industry always the innocent victim of predatory practices, he argues. 'The generic boys are all lily white,' he says with heavy irony. 'They're all in it for Joe Public.'

Mr Menn, however, believes generic makers are more sinned against than sinning. He points to tactics such as the filing of 'frivolous' patents as evidence that pharmaceutical companies will resort to anything to keep generics off the shelf. These patents, he says, often cover spurious innovations such as the shape or colour of a pill. They are designed, he alleges, purely to stall generic entry by prolonging litigation.

Pharmaceutical companies, says Mr Menn, would do better to devote the money they spend on

▶

lobbying and litigation to true innovation. Rather than trying to protect old drugs, they should seek to invent the next generation of medicines, he says. He cites Merck, a US drugs group, as a rare example of a company that has adopted this approach. 'Our message is that generic competition is the motivation for innovation,' says Mr Menn. 'The primary focus of the generic blockade is to deny generic drug makers entry into the market place. And that's not good for competition.'

Source : Financial Times, 20 April 2000. (Copyright © The Financial Times Limited)

Questions

1 *Identify the different types of competitive environment displayed in the article.*

2 *How does the competitive enviroment affect the way an organisation markets its products?*

6 Buyer behaviour

I do my thing, and you do your thing. I am not in this world to live up to your expectations.

Fritz Perls

INTRODUCTION

As outlined in previous chapters effective marketing involves focusing organisational activity on the *needs of the potential customer*. This requires an understanding of what determines these needs and how customers respond to them. Indeed, an appreciation of the factors which are most relevant in a decision to buy a particular product is likely to be crucial to the effectiveness of many, if not all, marketing decisions. This aspect of marketing comes within the scope of what is termed 'buyer behaviour'. The subject of buyer behaviour itself has developed to the extent where it is now conventional to study separately consumer buying behaviour, or consumer behaviour, and buying within an organisation, or organisational buyer behaviour. Following this convention, the present chapter will examine consumer buyer behaviour, and Chapter 7 will introduce organisational buyer behaviour.

SOME ISSUES IN BUYER–BEHAVIOUR THEORY

The interested reader will find that there is a voluminous and growing body of literature and ongoing research on buyer behaviour, such that many universities offer whole modules and even degree specialisms based on the subject.

Though the initiation of much of the research has come from the development of marketing itself, valuable and varied combinations have been made by researchers from a number of other academic specialisms, ranging from economics and management theory to psychology, sociology and social anthropology. This multidisciplinary approach is perhaps unsurprising, given the complexity of the field and the multiplicity of research questions that suggest themselves. By way of illustration, within the study of consumer behaviour marketers are interested in questions such as:

■ How can models of buyer behaviour be of use to marketing practitioners?
■ What are the major influences on purchase decisions?
■ Do consumers pass through a sequence of decision stages?
■ If so, do such stages apply equally to all purchase types, or all consumers?
■ What is the relationship between needs, motivation and buying behaviour?
■ How do attitudes affect buying behaviour, and is it necessary to achieve favourable attitude changes before buying takes place?

- How are attitudes formed, and to what extent are they modified, say, by marketing communications or buying experience?
- How and when do consumers seek and use information? How informed are consumers prior to purchasing?
- Is the purchase of a new product or brand approached as a different buying proposition?
- How do buyers evaluate the various alternatives facing them in their buying decisions?
- What is the nature and extent of loyalty among buyers, and how differently do loyal buyers approach their purchase decisions?
- What is the extent of individual versus group-influenced decision making among consumers?

This chapter will seek to provide at least an insight into the answers to such questions. Another factor to consider is the behaviour of consumers as they embark on buying, using electronic means such as the Internet. This will be examined in a little more depth towards the end of this chapter, with specific examples. It is however important to understand the basic theory of consumer buying behaviour before examining some of the more specialist issues, such as the role of marketing communications and e-commerce.

THE SIMPLE BUYING-DECISION PROCESS MODEL

The decision to buy a product, whether it be a soft drink or an item of clothing, involves *responding to a stimulus*. The decision to buy a soft drink may be as a result of being thirsty on a hot day or to be sociable having volunteered to be 'driver' for a night when out with friends at a country pub.

One approach to studying the buying decision process is to *develop a model of it*. The simplest way of doing this is to consider only the stimuli received by the person making the decision and the result – the person does or does not buy. This is a simple version of the classic stimulus–response model of behaviour which assumes that people will generally respond in some predictable way to a stimulus. The person making the decision is thus treated as a 'black box', which is a type of model generally accepted as useful for investigating complex systems which cannot be observed directly, such as the decision-making process of a buyer (see Figure 6.1). It provides a framework which focuses on the inputs, the stimuli and the outcomes of the decision, but offers no insight as to why a decision was made. From elementary economics it might be expected that buying decisions would be made by logically comparing the available choices in terms of cost and value using criteria such as:

- economy of purchase or use
- convenience
- efficiency in operation or use
- dependability in use
- improvement in earnings (e.g. factory equipment).

A review of our own personal buying habits will show that in practice these factors are seldom considered and rarely of paramount importance when we make buying decisions.

Figure 6.1

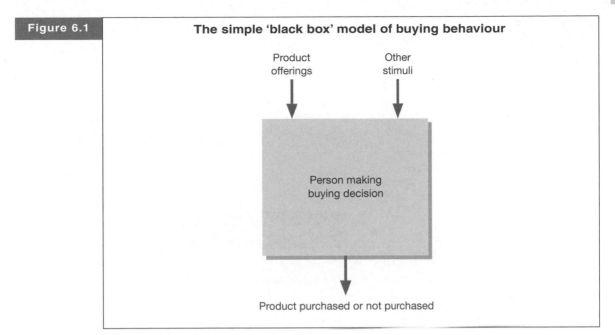

The simple 'black box' model of buying behaviour

Product offerings   Other stimuli

Person making buying decision

Product purchased or not purchased

Exercise

Think of a product you have purchased within the last week or so. Consider carefully why you chose that product. Write down as many reasons as you can to justify your purchase decision. When you have done this, list as many possible alternatives to the product purchased as you can. Remember that not to purchase anything is often an option.

Are you able to justify your choice against each of the alternatives you have listed solely in terms of the economic factors listed? Are there any other explanations? Refer back to your list of reasons as you read the rest of this chapter to see whether there might be a better explanation for your decision. Repeat the exercise for someone very different from yourself who might also have purchased the same product, and consider whether they might have different reasons for their purchase decision.

There are many reasons why economic criteria are ignored when making purchase decisions. Often the person making the decision does not have the necessary information or it is difficult to compare the different products on this basis alone. In some situations, the opinion or behaviour of a third party also has an influence on the purchase decision.

THE PRINCIPAL BUYING-DECISION VARIABLES

While it is not difficult to establish that buying decisions are not generally made on the basis of logical economic criteria, it is considerably more difficult to identify the factors or variables which do affect buying decisions. One reason is that many of these are dependent upon the person making the decision, and hence they are referred to as 'personal buying decision variables'. These personal buying decision variables can be grouped under the following three categories:

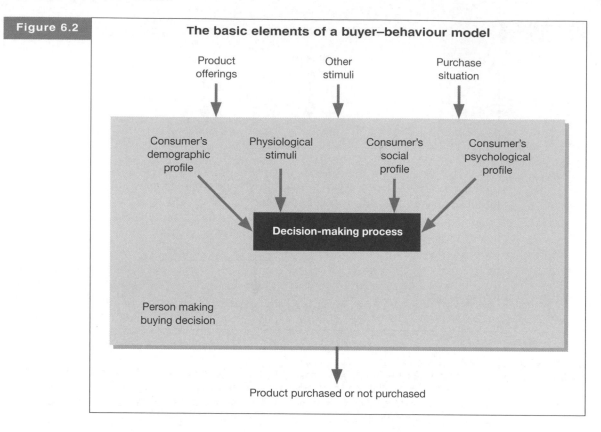

Figure 6.2

The basic elements of a buyer–behaviour model

1 Psychological variables
2 Social influences variables
3 Demographic variables.

In addition, the influence of the purchase situation needs to be recognised; internal stimuli such as thirst or fatigue – the physiological variables – need to be separated from external stimuli such as the aroma of freshly brewed coffee, and the decision process separated from the variables. The basic relationships between these elements are summarised in Figure 6.2.

THE BUYING-DECISION PROCESS

The person who *recognises a need* effectively becomes a *potential customer*. It is the recognition of a need that creates a want. A person may be thirsty so will be in need of a drink, but this may be expressed as wanting a glass of champagne. The creation of a want involves a decision process which can involve some or all of the following seven stages:

1 Recognition of the need – this is a prerequisite of further action.
2 Choice of involvement level – how much time and effort does the need/want justify?
3 Identification of alternatives
4 Evaluation of alternatives
5 Decision – choice made

6 Action

7 Post-purchase behaviour – need to resolve anxieties about choice made.

Most day-to-day purchases involve little or no risk in terms of being dissatisfied with the decision, so justify little time or effort. The choice is made on the basis of the immediately available information.

COMPLEX BUYING BEHAVIOUR

For very high-risk purchases, buyers are likely to go through each stage of the decision-making process. This is termed 'complex buying behaviour' and is seldom adopted because of the time and trouble involved.

An example where this approach might be justified could be the purchase of a wedding present for someone overseas – in the USA, perhaps. Stage 1 comes with the engagement announcement. As the wedding is so far away the need to take extra time and trouble could well be accepted with little thought. Stage 3 might involve finding out how long parcel post takes by sea and air and the relative costs, whether the electrical supply is compatible, and whether a gift list is being circulated around other friends and family members. Stage 4 may involve assessing alternatives which might then be chosen on the basis of the amount of money available for the present. Stage 5, the selection, could be made on the basis of ease of shipment and availability. Stage 6 is the purchase and then, after the present has been purchased, stage 7 might occur when it is being packed since if this is difficult the choice made may well seem less suitable than an alternative which could have been packed and shipped by the supplier.

Another and increasingly used alternative which is less complex would be to purchase the present using e-commerce, where it is relatively easy to order a product and pay for it, and at the same time arrange for it to be delivered to a different address almost anywhere in the world. Depending on the buyers ability and inclination to use computers, this may or may not prove to be an attractive proposition.

INFORMATION SEARCH

Stage 3 of the process – information search – may involve starting from scratch, such as when the product is entirely new or is totally unfamiliar to the buyer. Obvious examples might be skis being purchased by the first-time skier or a hang glider by someone who has only tried the sport once or twice. This is, however, relatively uncommon. Most products are by their nature in some way associated with other products. Thus someone considering buying a new television is likely to consider the brand of their existing television favourably if it has been reliable, unfavourably otherwise. Perhaps the brand of their radio, music centre, CD-player or other similar product would then be at least initially considered. Often car buyers, if they have had good experience of their present car, return to the same manufacturer first to choose the next.

THE EVOKED SET

Those brands, which initially come to mind when considering a purchase, are referred to as the 'evoked set'. Clearly any brands, which most people bring to mind in relation to certain types of product, have a distinct advantage compared with other brands. This is one of the reasons why vast amounts of money are spent by organisations on advertising, to make sure the brand is in the mind of the customer. It is the brands which are regularly within the evoked set of potential purchasers which set the standard that alternative products have to better if they are to be selected.

Howard and Sheth developed the concept of the *evoked set* as a result of their work on the development of a comprehensive buyer-behaviour model.

Exercise | Most people in the UK considering buying a new vacuum cleaner would include Dyson as one of the possible brands. They might not actually evaluate this option, believing the Dyson products would be too expensive, but the brand would be known. What other brands would you initially think of relative to vacuum cleaners? Repeat the exercise for another fairly specific product, for example a small inexpensive new car, personal computer, breakfast cereal, or a soft drink. Compare your list with others considering the same products.

EVALUATION OF ALTERNATIVES

Stage 4 (evaluation of alternatives) is another important part of the process since it will inevitably depend upon making a comparison of only a few specific potential differences between the products. These are known as the 'salient attributes'. Other differences are known as the 'non-salient attributes'. Examples relevant to the choice of a motor vehicle might be the availability of fuel injection, a sunroof or electric windows. Other factors, such as more secure door-locking systems or low-level access to the boot, have until recently been considered non-salient attributes by most buyers, in spite of these features having significantly greater potential for saving inconvenience or injury than the other attributes usually considered salient.

Studies have shown that there are many different evaluation procedures, which are used when making buying decisions. This work has also shown that these tend to be complex, since they involve comparing attributes within the context of brand beliefs and attitudes.

BELIEFS AND ATTITUDES

Other factors significant in the context of evaluating alternatives are the beliefs or attitudes held about the brands. *Beliefs* are perceptions of a brand, which are based on explicit information. *Attitudes* are firmly held ideas, which are often neither confirmed nor explicitly disproved by everyday information sources.

Attitudes are usually seen as multiplex, consisting of at least three elements:

1 a knowledge (= cognitive) component
2 a preference/liking (= affective) component and
3 a conative element that drives the individual towards some behaviour or response.

The relationship between these components is the subject of ongoing research. From a marketing point of view, interest focuses on the influence of salient attitudes – i.e. those of particular relevance to a purchase occasion, brand or marketing proposition. An interesting question concerns the extent to which salient attitudes, say to a brand offering, have to be favourable before a purchase decision can be made. Alternatively, it might be that favourable attitudes could be formed, and certainly reinforced, after the purchase decision, through use experience. In communications theory, these alternatives have been the focus of differing models of how communications may work – i.e. the conversion model versus the reinforcement model. Both views of the communications process have validity, since research evidence indicates that the relationship between attitudes and behaviour is two-way, rather than unidirectional.

THE PURCHASE DECISION

Even when a decision to buy a particular product has been made, the purchase decision can be affected by unanticipated situational factors. These factors can be very diverse such as the cancellation of overtime working or because of the numerous other decisions often directly associated with the purchase: the vendor, the quantity, when and how to pay.

The quantity decision can often involve associated items such as batteries, film for cameras, tape for recording machines, etc. rather than the main item being purchased. Very often the supplier or the vendor removes the need to make these decisions by either including the essentials in the form of a pre-packaged kit or by providing these as a discount on the price. The provision of the associated items as a kit can be considered a marketing strategy, whereas if they are provided as forms of discount this would be a selling strategy.

The timing decision is often linked to the payment decision, and the acceptance of credit cards has to a large extent reduced the importance of these decisions for many purchasers. It is however the emergence of new technology which will have more of an effect on consumers.

Example | **Some applications of e-business**

Increasingly consumers will be able to use their personal computers to purchase tickets, gift certificates and coupons via the web. The delivery for these could be anywhere as long as a machine is connected to the Internet. When they are printed out the consumer can take them for example, to the cinema where bar code readers will read the printed ticket and permit entry to the holder. This type of technology will perhaps have quite an effect on the number of employees required in many places, and may also change the buying behaviour of consumers.

In the USA users of E-Stamp and Stamps.com can buy distinctive marks that serve as proof that they have paid for a package to be sent to a particular location. It is becoming possible to print almost anything that can go on paper and has intrinsic value. The potential for change, not only in the medium used for purchasing goods, but also in customer buying behaviour is ripe for a radical shift in focus.

Question
In what ways do you see the application of the above technology being used, and will it change buyer behaviour?

POST-PURCHASE BEHAVIOUR

The final stage of the complex buying process is post-purchase behaviour. Since it is seldom possible to make a fully rational purchase decision, it is hardly surprising that purchasers often doubt the wisdom of their choice when, finally, the purchase has been made. This leads to minor faults being found with the product itself or its features.

Recognising this, manufacturers have found it beneficial to aim some of their advertising directly at new owners to reassure them that they have made a wise decision. Often motor vehicle manufacturers use this approach: they have appreciated how important an influence existing users can be on potential customers. Other tactics such as the provision of free telephone help-lines, call-out services and 'no-quibble' return policies, such as those adopted by the retailer Marks & Spencer, are aimed specifically at overcoming this problem. It was also within this context that an increasing number of suppliers came to recognise the importance of having good instruction manuals.

THE UTILISATION OF COMPLEX BUYING BEHAVIOUR

It would be logical to assume that complex buying behaviour is generally used for important purchases. Suppliers who believe this applies to their products tend to promote them on the basis of the features and benefits that are the result of the efforts and capabilities of their designers. This approach used to be seen in automobile catalogues, which always included pictures of the engine and details of the technical features of the vehicle.

However, research showed that very few buyers have the knowledge necessary to appreciate the relative importance of this type of information and instead simply assume that competitive products are equivalent with regard to these features. This improved understanding of buyer behaviour can be seen in contemporary catalogues, which seldom refer to these features. Instead, choice is focused specifically on acceptability for purpose (e.g. how many seats) and often to an even greater extent on the perceived prestige of the product. Promotion has also been increasingly focused on this aspect of the product.

DISSONANCE-REDUCING BUYING BEHAVIOUR

When buyers perceive commonplace products as being complex, they are likely to compensate for this by adopting a less involved style of buying behaviour. Usually this reduces the scope of any information search, which means the buying decision is often made from only a small range of the available products. The decision is made with the objective of limiting the possibility of being disappointed with the product. This is called 'dissonance-reducing buying behaviour'. It usually involves selecting a product on the basis of a few obvious, often new, features rather than on the basis of the features actually required. Domestic cookers are a very good example of a product for which this style of buying behaviour is typical. As a result, easily identified features such as automatic timers and light units are emphasised rather than basic performance or ease of use. Because of this, even comparatively low-cost, though useful, features such as thermostatically controlled hobs failed to gain general acceptance. Even more remarkable has been ready acceptance in the UK of 'built-in' ovens, which lack the separate grill that was an essential feature of the traditional British cooker. This is clear evidence that when purchased little or no consideration was given to the way the existing cooker was used, the emphasis was clearly on aesthetics.

Since the purchase choice is likely to be made from a limited range of products it is essential for sellers to promote their brands to ensure they are considered by as many people as possible. This is achieved by emphasising and promoting recognisable brand names. It also means that products that are subject to dissonance-reducing buying behaviour are likely to become increasingly standardised. This is because manufacturers will tend to focus their competitive effort on the features of the products which have the largest market share, rather than on those having the highest performance or most innovative features.

HABITUAL BUYING BEHAVIOUR

For most day-to-day purchases the process is even less involved since there is a whole range of products which are bought mainly as a result of habit. Newspapers, magazines, beverages, petrol and most food products are examples of products that are very often purchased on the basis of habitual buying behaviour. This is something that is encouraged by manufacturers who have a strong brand for their products, and to this end they are willing to spend a great deal of money on advertising budgets to keep the brand firmly in the customers mind. There are an increasing number of firms who are also dedicating more resources to new media, an example being the confectionery brand Nestlé/Rowntree, who are developing websites for several of their brands. It is expected that children who influence the purchase of many sweets such as fruit pastilles and chocolate bars will begin to favour and prefer the brands that have an exciting and innovative website to visit.

VARIETY-SEEKING BUYING BEHAVIOUR

As an alternative to habitual buying behaviour most people adopt a less predictable approach to buying, at least for some of these low-value products. Usually these are products for which there is no clear preference either by the individual making the purchase or, more particularly, by the users of the product (e.g. the family). A typical example of a product in this category is breakfast cereal. Very often this is selected on the basis of buying an alternative to what was purchased on the previous occasion. Another example is the choice of magazine prior to an occasional train journey. Both of these are examples of variety-seeking buying behaviour.

This type of buying behaviour does not apply to high-value items except where the wealth of the individual is such that this would be a trivial purchase. Thus the ordinary car user who changes brand with every purchase is more likely to show dissonance-reducing buying behaviour, in which brand is of little importance, than variety-seeking buying behaviour.

EXPERIENCE BUYING BEHAVIOUR

There has been a move towards organisations recognising that consumers sometimes want more than just the products on offer, they want an 'experience'. The rise in popularity of theme restaurants has shown that the customers want not only the food but also a certain degree of entertainment. The popularity of expensive sports clothing to enable the patrons of sports and fitness clubs to have an enhanced experience at the gym, where the right clothing helps the wearer to feel and look the part, even though their sports and fitness ability may be poor. Airlines are increasingly competing not just on service but on the whole experience of flying with them, from the chauffeur service, the special lounges and the sleeping arrangements.

It is interesting to note how some car manufacturers are now promoting the experience of the drive, how the seat feels, how the engine purrs and the quality and richness of the sound system, and not the particulars such as price and guarantee. Many theme parks with white-knuckle rides are very popular because they can offer customers experiences that are difficult to find anywhere else. All of this type of experience buying behaviour is a step forward from Theordore Levitt's view where customers want solutions and not products. The present view would be that people want to live life to the full, and have a higher self-image than before: they want to realise more potential and see experience buying as a way to do this.

THE PSYCHOLOGICAL FACTORS AFFECTING BUYING DECISIONS

The personality and experience of the individual will inevitably, to some degree, determine buying decisions, which are made by individuals. Within the context of buying behaviour, the areas of specific interest are those concerned with motivation, perception, learning, personality and attitudes.

Individual human behaviour has been studied since ancient times, and for at least the last 100 years by psychologists, sociologists and other behavioural scientists. Within the context of this work, theories have been developed to explain the behaviour of individuals and groups in specific situations such as the workplace. All of those listed as relevant to buyer behaviour are also likely to be studied within the context of human resource management (HRM) and are therefore likely to be familiar to many readers.

MOTIVATION

In contrast to much of the early work on motivation that was concerned with deviant behaviour, Maslow's approach was to consider the factors concerned with the ultimate goal of 'self-actualisation' in terms of a hierarchy. He initially proposed that the individual would endeavour to meet the needs within each level sequentially. However, he recognised that in reality individuals would often be trying to meet the needs within different levels simultaneously. From the viewpoint of buyer behaviour the essential point of the theory is the realisation that there are different classes of need, and the main focus of individuals will depend upon their individual circumstances.

The theory recognises that individuals have limited needs for existence. Thus, at the most basic level, human needs are physiological and concerned with sustenance (food

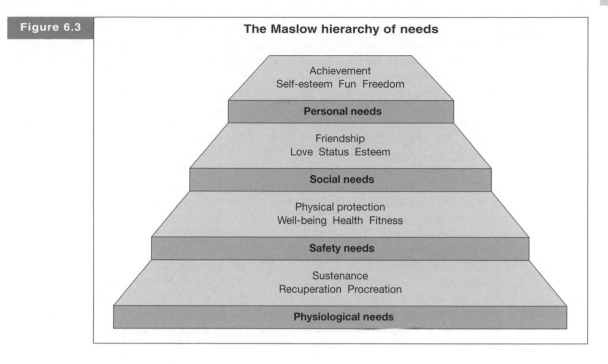

Figure 6.3 The Maslow hierarchy of needs

and drink), recuperation (sleep) and procreation (sex). The theory then proposes that individuals who are able to satisfy these physiological needs will seek to make their situation more secure by trying to satisfy their 'safety' needs, which involve physical protection, ensuring continuity of supply of the basic physiological need, and the physical wellbeing of health and fitness.

Individuals who have satisfied this second-level 'safety' needs, will then tend to focus upon satisfying what are defined as the 'social' needs – love, friendship, status and esteem. Again, once these seem to be satisfied the focus moves to what have been defined as 'personal' needs – achievement, self-esteem, fun, freedom.

The fifth level represents self-actualisation. Maslow saw this as a goal which, for most people, was easily abandoned due to social pressures and other priorities. It provides a link with other self-actualisation theories but is considered of little relevance to buyer behaviour so is usually omitted in this context. The variety of needs defined by Maslow is usually summarised in what is known as the Maslow hierarchy of needs (see Figure 6.3).

The different values attributed to the levels can be used when selecting product benefits. In particular, it has been found that effective advertising messages are often those which appeal to the most appropriate need level. For example, Procter & Gamble found the appeal 'Keeps your baby dry and happy' was more effective than 'Saves you time and trouble' during the initial promotion of their Pampers disposable nappies. In terms of the Maslow theory this can be explained on the basis that the first message appeals at a higher level (the social needs of the mother) than the second, which appeals at the physiological level (the need for rest).

Exercise Take any newspaper colour supplement and see how many of the advertisements can be rated in terms of the Maslow need level to which they are designed to appeal. Clearly some cannot be graded on this basis since they are designed to provide information rather than draw attention to a need or want.

Since one of the main functions of marketing is to ensure that product offerings meet the needs of potential customers, it is clearly essential that great care is taken to understand as fully as possible what these needs are likely to be. Maslow's theory of motivation not only provides a framework which sometimes can be useful for doing this, but also shows that whereas needs can be defined relatively simply they are likely to be expressed as very much more complex and diverse wants.

Consider someone who is thirsty. If that person is climbing in the Pyrenees the need for a drink might be completely met by spring water drunk from cupped hands. To meet the same need while at the Ascot races the same person is likely to want to drink champagne from a crystal glass. The basic need is the same, but in the second case the want recognises the additional needs of meeting the expectations resulting from being part of a social group and perhaps the self-esteem that comes from doing the 'right' thing. The late Rajiv Gandhi earned great respect from the people of India by recognising that his need was the same as every villager and always drank the local water when travelling in rural areas.

The Maslow and other theories of motivation (such as Alderfer's ERG theory (Existence Relatedness and Growth Needs), which is an alternative to Maslow but one which accepts that a hierarchy might not exist, or Herzberg's two-factor theory) are well known, and considered relevant in the context of both HRM and marketing. They are useful for identifying categories and patterns of human needs yet can easily be used to justify the conclusion that 'everyone is different'. Indeed, this is the view taken in Schein's model of 'Complex man' which asserts that:

Human needs fall into many categories and vary according to the stage of development and total life situation. These needs and motives will assume varying degrees of importance to each person creating some sort of hierarchy but this hierarchy is itself variable from person to person, from situation to situation and from one time to another.

While in itself it is of little help to someone trying to solve a specific marketing problem, this does provide a framework for analysing individual buyer behaviour.

PERCEPTION

Individuals literally receive, or sense, information through the five senses: sight, hearing, smell, touch and taste. Perception is the process by which this information is selected, organised and interpreted to produce messages and meanings. As a psychological process, perception is a key prerequisite for information-processing and learning. As such, it is of interest to marketers for the influence it can have on consumer decision making generally, and on the way it can affect antecedent factors such as the reception and understanding of marketing communications.

The senses play a very important role in impulse buying, that is why the smell emanating from fresh bread coming out of an oven is important in supermarkets and can help boost bakery sales. Similarly the sound of French music playing in the background boosts sales of French wine and croissants. A small sample of cheese or other titbit to taste in a supermarket demonstration also helps increase sales of a product.

Not surprisingly, as a person-specific psychological process, perceptions vary somewhat from person to person, even in relation to common stimuli (e.g. in marketing terms, a TV commercial). Psychologists attribute such individual differences in perception to the combined effect of three perpetual subprocesses: selective attention, selective distortion and selective retention:

■ *Selective attention* refers to the means by which people make sense of a mass of stimuli by screening out less meaningful or relevant messages. This is followed by editing in stimuli that are somehow personally appropriate, attractive or noticeable (note that visual cues such as shape, colour and movement may have a role here, hence their interest to marketing communications specialists).
■ *Selective distortion* describes the process by which, consistent with a particular and personal mind-set, individuals will distort information received in order to make it fit their preconceptions, existing beliefs and values.
■ *Selective retention* refers to the tendency for people to retain or memorise only a selection of messages they receive. Usually this selection will be those that are personally meaningful, or deemed to be more supportive of their existing attitudes and beliefs, rather than information at variance with these (which may in any case be distorted by selective distortion).

These three subprocesses help to explain why perception can be highly selective: people see (or hear) what they want to see (or hear). Given such distortions, it is perhaps more understandable why marketing communications need to be well supported by research, and sometimes presented in bold, concentrated bursts in order to break through such perception barriers.

Exercise   Consult any magazine, journal or newspaper and identify a selection of advertisements that appear to be designed to counter, or exploit, perceptual distortions that may occur within the target group. Identify possible distortions, and the way the advertisements relate to these.

LEARNING

Learning refers to consistent changes in an individual's responses as a result of experience, or related changes in the context or pattern of personal memory. Most human behaviour is said to be the product of learning, and so it is highly probable that learning shapes much of the purchase and decision making behaviour that consumers demonstrate. Like perception, learning involves information-processing, and is in turn a major influence on people's beliefs and attitudes.

Research into learning indicates the process of learning as dependent on factors such as stimuli, responses and reinforcement. Stimuli can be internal (e.g. a strong inner drive or need) or external (e.g. a cue such as an advertisement or display, or some associative reminder). Responses may be any action (e.g. purchase) or decision (e.g. a resolution or intention), whether positive or negative (e.g. non-purchase, postponement). Where responses are rewarded by positive feelings and experiences, reinforcement occurs.

This reward–reinforcement process learning theorists term 'operant conditioning', involving reward through a new stimulus or object (e.g. a free sample of a new product). Learning through reinforcement also occurs through 'classical conditioning' (e.g. Pavlov's dogs), where positive associations are developed with an existing experience (the bell at feeding-time) – think of the association effect of exciting music, visual effects, personality testimonies. So-called 'cognitive learning' takes place without reinforcement, while 'vicarious learning' involves learning through the experience, or example, of others. Clearly, learning is a highly complex process, still very much the subject of ongoing research. However, it is almost equally clear that learning, in various forms, may play a significant part in consumer behaviour. This is seen for example in the association–reinforcement effects of marketing communications (everything from packaging design to corporate learning communications efforts) on the 'supplier' side, or the effects of learning through product usage and conditioning, on the buyer side.

PERSONALITY

Personality is the unique psychological make-up of individuals that conditions their behaviour generally, and their responses to particular stimuli and situations. Over the years, researchers have developed a variety of measurement batteries, usually termed 'personality profile inventories', that measure an individual's personality characteristics (or traits), often calibrated along a two-pole scale, e.g. extrovert–introvert, sociable–non-sociable, dominant–subservient, etc.

A major complication with personality research derives from the often complex and confounding differences, and resultant disagreements, among the various schools of theory within the field. *Psychoanalytic theory*, still strongly associated with Freud, emphasises deep-seated impulses and influences through the unconscious mind. *Trait theory* most notably associated with Jung's revisions of Freudian theory, lays emphasis on measuring personality factor (trait) combinations. Other schools of thought focus on social and environmental influences on the individual's personality – hence the continuing 'nature versus nurture' debate in psychology. Some of the theoretical contributions to research have been piecemeal aspects of personality explanation, though useful in their own right, e.g. Maslow's concept of 'self-actualisation'.

An interesting and related concept, that of the 'self-concept', refers to the image people have of themselves, and in turn that which they would wish others to have of them; clearly, advertising themes appear to make various appeals to generalised portrayals of self-concept 'ideal' stereotypes. A comparable notion, that of 'brand personality', has for some time attracted the attentions of marketers and advertising specialists alike. Basically, the interest has lain in investing in a brand a set of associations, similar to the traits (characteristics) that make up a personality. Obviously, the brand associations selected for portrayal would need to be validated by prior research as salient and attractive among sampled target-group respondents. In summary, the detailed research studies into personality as a determinant of buyer behaviour have produced mixed results. While intuitively personality appears to have great potential influence on consumer behaviour, it does, almost by definition, pose major methodological problems in research. Indeed, it has been argued that instrument error or measure unreliability may account for many of the non-significant research findings in the field, rather than absence of a real link with personality variables. As if by consolation, the more recent developments in *psychographics*, which borrow freely from personality constructs, do appear to promise results, especially through their linkage with product use and demographic variables.

DEMOGRAPHIC FACTORS

Buying decisions often depend upon a person's demographic profile. Within this, any of the following variables can be relevant to an individual buying decision.

1 **Age**. There are many needs which are age-dependent, for instance baby food for the very young, mobility aids for the very elderly.
2 **Stage in life cycle**. Furniture purchases are likely to be more dependent upon stage in the life cycle than upon age.
3 **Occupation**. More formal clothing is probably purchased by white-collar workers.
4 **Economic circumstances**. Many products are very much dependent upon perceived discretionary income, e.g. records, theatre tickets, books.
5 **Lifestyle**. This may increase the need for minor luxuries such as champagne as an alternative to, for instance, car ownership.

The retail sector is especially interested in the factors outlined above as the study of demographics plays an important role in the prediction of consumer behaviour and their spending patterns. In the UK there has been a focus of attention for the last 20 years on the group aged late twenties to thirties. The spending potential has now shifted to older, more mature customers. However it is expected that there will be an increasing emphasis placed on middle-aged consumers who are likely to demand more DIY products as well as electrical appliances and home products. It would appear that organisations have to be especially mindful of how they target customers to encourage them to buy, as demographics can have a large influence on customers spending capability.

Generally the lifestyle of many people will be becoming much busier over the next decade and it is expected that this will also have an effect upon the type of products that are bought. The products most likely to see an increase in demand are those which can offer time-saving technology such as personal computers and mobile phones; there may also be an increase in home services such as household cleaning and gardening. The area expected to see a huge increase in popularity is on-line shopping, and it is this that will have an impact on consumer buying behaviour. Different types of typical consumer behaviour are likely to emerge, but as yet there is insufficient research into this area.

| Exercise | Is there any way in which you could identify the different types of consumer behaviour likely to emerge with regard to on-line shopping. One thing to consider is whether everyone who fills a shopping cart on screen abandons his or her orders before actual purchase, or do most continue to complete the transaction? |

THE SOCIAL INFLUENCE VARIABLES

The following social factors will also affect buying decisions made by individuals:

1 **Family background.** Political views, how education is valued, etc.
2 **Reference groups.** Explained below, in terms of aspirational and dissociative reference groups.
3 **Roles and status.** Relative to the product being considered.

The significance and the relevance of reference groups to buying behaviour varies widely according to the type of product being purchased, in particular, whether the product is a necessity or a luxury and whether the product is consumed in private or in public.

Primary reference groups are those groups to which the person is considered to be a full member. Of these the most important is likely to be the immediate family, groups of close friends and co-workers. Primary reference groups are of particular importance with respect to purchases that directly affect the other members of the group – for example, holidays.

Secondary reference groups are those within which contact is more formal and less continuous, such as those resulting from membership of professional associations, trades unions, religious organisations or as a result of where you live or work. Status within such groups is not necessarily automatic so purchases that may imply status within

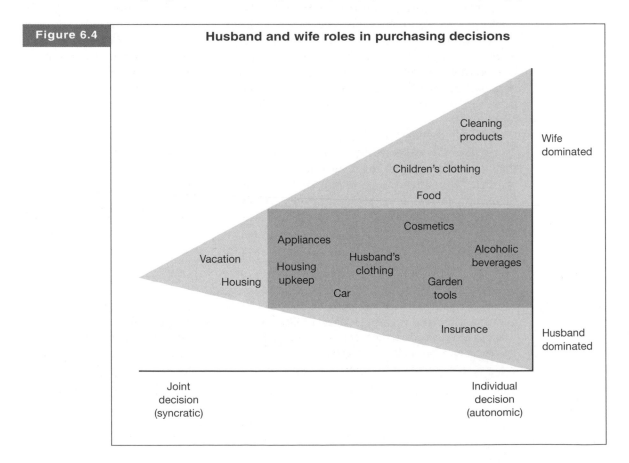

Figure 6.4   Husband and wife roles in purchasing decisions

this type of group are likely to be affected by the expected attitude to the product selected. Menswear could, in general, be considered in this category.

Aspirational groups are those of which the purchaser would like to be considered a member. There is an implied association, however unrealistic, in owning the same brand of tennis racket as a favourite tennis star. The importance of this can be judged, at least in part, by the keenness with which manufacturers wish to sponsor these public heroes. In contrast, dissociative groups are those with which one would prefer not to be associated.

Exercise	Think of different products that could be considered to be in an aspirational group for students, and other products that could be in the dissociative group.

In addition to the factors already mentioned the impact of reference groups on an individual buying decision will depend to some extent on the *degree of risk* perceived. This factor is also likely to affect the way by which the buying decision is reached.

Within the context of the family, as might be expected, the degree to which a buying decision is made by either a husband or wife as individuals or shared between the partners has been shown to depend upon the type of product involved. Research undertaken by Davis and Rigaux in Belgium suggested that the decision making roles of husbands and wives could be classified as in Figure 6.4. Although it would not hold true in some cultures as there would be different weighting between males and females in the decision making process.

E-commerce, e-business and consumer buying

As new technology gains a larger foothold in the way in which business is carried out, the fact that customers should be the prime focus of any successful business has been reinforced. Organisations should be able to provide services through whichever channel the customer wants to use, and if this is by means of the Internet then that should be catered for in an efficient manner. One of the great advantages that may encourage companies to do this is the fact that it can enable much information to be gleaned concerning customers and their behaviour. The type of information that will be available will be:

■ When the customer visited the website
■ Which products and services the potential customer looked at
■ What was actually purchased
■ Any special requirements the customer requested.

An important feature that may encourage more customers to switch to doing business on-line is that it can feel like a one-to-one relationship. An example of this is the Amazon.com site where once you have made a purchase from them the next time you log onto the site you are greeted by name. If companies can build on this type of technology advance and concentrate on customer focus then perhaps better relationships can be built up together with increased customer loyalty and sales. Sandra Vandermerwe, a professor of international marketing and services at Imperial College Management School, has identified four levels at which internet technology can be used:

1 Use the web site like a brochure
2 As an alternative, possibly cheaper sales channel
3 To help customers make a decision – the example given is the way in which ICI lets customers try out paint colours on-line to help them plan their decorations
4 Using the Internet interactively to manage a relationship.

As yet, it remains to be seen whether the above will have a dramatic effect on customer behaviour in the coming years. However, as companies find it increasingly harder to differentiate from competitors with regard to products and services they may find that the use of the Internet, coupled with customer service and making relationships that last, is a key decider in the success of the business. They choose to ignore it at their peril.

Most of the city centre stores now have operational e-commerce sites, they include names such as Marks & Spencer, Boots and Mothercare as well as major banks. The Marks & Spencer site encourages each store to manage the content on the website, so that only products that are currently available will be shown. Customers are also encouraged to email the branch manager of the local M&S store. In general it is expected that as consumers become more used to dealing on-line the volume of business carried out this way will greatly increase.

On-line buyer behaviour

There has already been quite a lot of research carried out into the buying behaviour of consumers shopping on-line. Market analysts Datamonitor carried out a survey into the shopping habits of consumers who prefer to go on-line rather than venture into the city centre. As prices of computers fall many more people are becoming information technology (IT) literate. There is less resistance to learning to use computers, and also increasing in popularity are WAP phones, interactive television, and internet compatible games consoles. This according to the research means that by the year 2004 it is likely that most houses that have personal computers will be connected to the Internet, increasing the number of internet users – and that means potential on-line shoppers of around 100 million in the UK alone.

Further research by Datamonitor concluded that people are shopping animals and categorised them into the following five groups:

■ **The rhino**. Mostly elderly people, usually low income, preferring to pay cash and examine products thoroughly before purchasing them. Have an aversion to going on-line – only a third of them have been on-line, and then only briefly.
■ **The puma.** Usually young and single, having a high income and no fear of shopping on-line – gregarious users of on-line shopping.
■ **The gazelle**. Usually over thirty with a young family. Computer literate but more reserved attitude to shopping on-line, prefers low risk and usually investigates all avenues before making a purchase.
■ **The gorilla.** Spends most of income in traditional bricks and mortar stores, however not averse to trying on-line shopping but likely to spend very conservatively on low-risk, familiar items, perhaps from Amazon.com or Marks & Spencers web pages. Will spend more as confidence builds.
■ **The jackal.** An innovator where new technology is concerned. Very willing to try out the latest web pages and uses on-line shopping in preference to traditional shop-

ping methods. Likely to spend a reasonable amount of money each year on internet shopping.

It remains to be seen if further research in this field will be along the same lines as that outlined above, but it seems certain that on-line buyer behaviour is certainly a different animal from traditional consumer buyer behaviour; it is an interesting field and likely to be the focus of much more attention in the near future.

CONCLUSION

Buyer behaviour provides some valuable insights that can be applied usefully in many marketing situations. It also provides a framework, concepts and a vocabulary which can be used to analyse many marketing issues.

The complexity of the subject, however, is such that it cannot realistically be used prescriptively since it is likely to raise more questions than it answers. There is at least some circumstantial evidence to suggest that attempts have been made to apply these concepts in political campaigns in both the USA and the UK, with little apparent success. This should not be seen to devalue the usefulness of the approach, but rather to emphasise the complexity of the market place and the need to make marketing decisions on the basis, at best, of an incomplete understanding of this evolving research field. Buyer behaviour theory is an exciting field and evolving fast. It remains to be seen if one of the main drivers of change in the field of buyer behaviour is the fact that many consumers are embracing the benefits that new technology is bringing, namely e-commerce. Will the ability to use a new medium alter the buying behaviour of only a few, or will it be the majority?

QUESTIONS

1 *Identify a product that is more appropriate to the 'self-esteem' needs as suggested by Maslow, rather than the more basic needs of a customer.*

2 *Consider a purchase you have made recently and identify the factors that influenced your decision to buy.*

3 *What do you consider is the role of consumer magazines such as* Which? *or* What Computer? *in influencing buyer behaviour?*

4 *How might a knowledge of buyer behaviour theory be of use within (a) selling and (b) product design?*

5 *Identify products which could be said to satisfy 'experience buying behaviour'; is this, in your opinion, a new phenomenon?*

6 *Discuss the ways in which new technology, such as the Internet, will affect consumer buying behaviour.*

FURTHER READING

Andrews, W. (2000) 'Stamp of approval', *Internet World*, March.

Assael, H. (1998) *Consumer Behaviour and Marketing Action*. South-Western Publishing.

Chisnall, Peter M. (1994) *Consumer Behaviour*, 3rd edn. McGraw-Hill.

Eames, L.(2000) 'Consumer shopping animals: what kind of shopping animal are you?', *The Guardian*, 25 May.

Engel, J. F., Blackwell, R. D. and Miniard, P. W. (1995) *Consumer Behaviour*, 8th edn. Dryden Press.

Foxall, G. R., Goldsmith, R. E. and Brown, S. (1998) *Consumer Psychology for Marketing*. International Thompson Business Press.

Jobber, D. and Lancaster, G. (1997) *Selling and Sales Management*. Pitman Publishing.

Lastovika, J. L. and Joachimsthaler, E. A. (1988), 'Improving the detection of personality-behaviour relationships in consumer research', *Journal of Consumer Research*, March.

Mitchell, A. (1998) 'On experience marketing', *Marketing Business*, October.

Peter, J. P. and Olson J. C. (1999) *Consumer Behaviour and Marketing Strategy*, 5th edn. McGraw-Hill.

Rosier, B. (2000) 'Nestlé targets families with sweet brands site', *Marketing*, 20 January.

Solomon, M. R. (1998) *Consumer Behaviour: Buying, Having and Being*, 4th edn. Prentice-Hall.

Williamson, D. (2000) 'M&S rebrands stores with web address', *Revolution,* 1 June.

Safeway to focus on price cuts as it drops loyalty card

FT

Safeway, the UK's fourth biggest supermarket group, yesterday became the first major retailer to abandon its loyalty card scheme. It said the move would help to deliver savings for customers of up to the £110million this year.

Tesco and J Sainsbury, two of its main rivals, said they had no intention of abandoning their loyalty schemes. However, independent consultants suggested Safeway's move could force a closer examination of such schemes by some UK retailers. Carlos Criado-Perez, Safeway chief executive, said the decision to stop giving discount points for every pound spent was 'great news for our clients. People have lost interest in points and don't think they give value. They'll never get tired of great deals.'

Safeway will focus on bigger price cuts on a selected range of products, he said. The price-cutting initiative, launched in the autumn, had helped to drive up same-store sales by 5.7 per cent in the final three months, to March 31, with volume growth of 10 per cent. The sales increase, and news that pre-tax profits would come in at the higher end of expectations at about £245m, helped drive Safeway's shares up by 22p to 230p.

Last year the group reported profits of £350 million. Gill Davies, customer marketing manager at AC Nielsen, consultants, said: 'There has been a lot of money poured into these schemes for questionable gain.'

J Sainsbury said it had accumulated 17 million Reward Cardholders since it launched its scheme in 1996. Tesco said it would be posting extra Tesco cards to 'disappointed Safeway customers'.

Source: Financial Times, 5 May 2000. (Copyright © The Financial Times Limited)

Questions

1 *Given your understanding of the buyer behaviour process, consider the particular variables and influences that might affect buying behaviour related to the shopping experience of going to Safeways.*

2 *In your opinion, would the buyer behaviour exhibited by Safeway shoppers be very similar to the customers of other supermarkets such as Tesco, Sainsbury or Morrisons etc.?*

3 *To what extent, for example, might perception, attitude-formation and learning processes affect purchase behaviour among Safeway users?*

4 *As a related question, could you identify different buyer groups or segments, and if so how might the above decision affect them.*

CASE STUDY

Sainsbury tests the loyalties of Safeway clients

FT

The rivalry between Britain's supermarkets took a new turn yesterday as J Sainsbury made a brazen attempt to poach the 6 million customers belonging to Safeway's soon-to-be-extinct loyalty card scheme.

In an offer that he said was worth a total of £15m, Sainsbury's chief executive told shoppers holding the Safeway ABC card they would immediately receive 500 free Sainsbury reward points if they handed in their cards at the rival supermarket.

'We know from experience that once customers start using the reward card scheme, and its many third-party offers, it becomes an indispensable part of their shopping trip,' said Sir Peter Davis, hailing the reward scheme as an 'integral' part of company policy.

The Sainsbury offer will run from May 13 to June 10, 10 days after the deadline for earning points on the Safeway card expires. The 500 points are worth £2.50 off a shopping bill or can be used in third-party stores in the form of a reward voucher.

Safeway announced the end of its reward card scheme last Thursday. The supermarket justified the move on the grounds that its customers had 'grown bored' of loyalty cards, which it said were increasingly regarded as an irritating gimmick. The company said it preferred to reward shoppers with lower prices.

Safeway yesterday took the Sainsbury move in its stride, saying it was a sign of how effective its six-month campaign to win new customers with price reductions was proving.

'We have obviously rattled them big-style,' it said. 'Our price cuts campaign has won us an extra 750 000 customers a week and at least some of those must be coming from Sainsbury's. It's very flattering.' It said the offer risked backfiring, as the 17 million shoppers who already belonged to Sainsbury's reward scheme were likely to be annoyed by the supermarket's 500-point offer to outside customers.

'We are quite amazed that they are not offering this to their own customers. They are only offering it to our customers, so I imagine they will have a few peeved Sainsbury's customers on their hands.'

Source: Financial Times, 11 May 2000. Copyright © The Financial Times Limited

Questions

1 *Do you think that the Sainsbury customers are likely to be 'peeved', and if so would the strength of feeling be enough to make them change supermarket or alter their buying habits?*

2 *Apart from buyer behaviour what other marketing issues do you think this competitve rivarly between the supermarkets unveils? Do you think that ultimately the competition between the firms will be of benefit to the customer? Give reasons for your answers.*

Organisational buyer behaviour

*No man is an 'land, intire of itself'; every man is a peece of the Continent,
a part of the maine.*

John Donne

INTRODUCTION

As the term implies, organisational buyer behaviour is literally concerned with the processes involved in buying within the context of formal organisations. These organisations have a legal identity in their own right, and will usually have specific resources and procedures with which to conduct all activities within their remit. Specifically, buying and sourcing products and services will usually be managed as a separate activity in support of organisational objectives. A practical definition of organisational buying is:

> **The decision-making process by which business buyers establish the need for purchased products and services, and identify, evaluate and choose among alternative brands and suppliers.** (Kotler, Armstrong, Saunders and Wong, 1999)

As the earlier history of marketing is more closely associated with consumer markets, it is perhaps not surprising that only in more recent times has an interest developed in analysing organisational buyer behaviour. Very early contributions to the field were made by specialist writers on industrial buying, such as Fisher (1976) and Wilson (1968). It is only more recently that the study has been redefined within the context of its essential 'organisational' focus, through an emphasis on analysing the decision-making dynamics of buying, as but one aspect of organisational activities. Indeed, there is still some confusion and ambiguity among marketing theorists in respect of the boundaries and elements of organisational buying behaviour, since some writers appear to 'fudge' the issue by wrongly using 'industrial buyer behaviour' and 'organisational buyer behaviour' interchangeably.

However, the changing technological environment, namely the increasing use of the Internet, is likely to alter the way in which many organisations approach buying, and therefore the buying behaviour will alter and adapt to take account of the new opportunities that this will afford. There is, as yet, a lack of research with regard to the effect of any changes in buying behaviour. However this chapter aims to outline organisational buying behaviour seen from the traditional viewpoint and the newly developing behaviour that buying via the Internet will bring.

For semantic clarity, it will be proposed that 'industrial buyer behaviour' be seen as a subset of 'organisational buyer behaviour'. Further, terms such as 'industrial marketing', 'business marketing' and the most favoured 'business-to-business' (B2B) marketing are best treated as particular marketing subfields. The whole point of such a buyer focus is that it provides a means of improving our understanding of how the buying process works within organisations.

USE OF NEW TECHNOLOGY FOR BUSINESS BUYING

The use of the Internet for business-to-business commerce is growing at a phenomenal rate and is set to reach $1.3 trillion by 2003. There will be many changes to how businesses conduct themselves using this technology – note the increasing use made in offices of email and the decreasing use of fax machines. It is envisaged however that buying behaviour will change radically, as a direct result of using the Internet.

The use of e-commerce by an organisation is often made a lot more beneficial if the technology is used in the correct way – for example, a single company can use an *intranet*. An intranet means that the company uses internet technology within the company, and can link this via firewalls to the public internet. A firewall allows internet access for employees, but allows outsiders access to only limited non-confidential information on the intranet.

Where a company wants to use e-commerce but with only a few trusted suppliers or large customers, an *extranet* can be set up. An extranet is an extended intranet, but it does not allow the general public access to the company system. To help improve the effectiveness and efficiency of transactions within the supply chain, firms will most often use a dedicated extranet.

| Example | One of the first large companies to streamline its supply chain using this type of technology was General Electric (GE) who have to date made massive savings from dealing with suppliers and by saving in printing costs. In 1997 alone the extranet enabled GE Lighting, which is a subsidiary of GE, to source approximately around £1 billion of products and services. This figure is set to soar as more use is made of the extranet for business to business buying. |

Not only can the use of internet technologies be used as above, but they have an extra built-in benefit: the Internet offers businesses the opportunity to add extra benefits to business customers . The benefits include such things as the opportunity to enhance the servicing and support that is necessary in today's environment, to ensure that good customer relations are upheld.

The following is an example of the kind of uses that the technology is being used for within the buying arena.

| Example | In industrial settings when a machine was designed it was understood that the process of sourcing all of the required parts to build the machine would take quite a while. Some parts would have to be purchased and others manufactured. This whole process was difficult to organise and usually took a long while. |
| | With the advent and widespread use of the web, engineers in companies have an enormous amount of information available to them. It is possible now to request quotes electronically, place orders and receive the necessary parts in a fraction of the time that was previously required. This alone will have the potential to help companies slash costs dramatically. |

The above example emphasises the reduction in time taken as a major component in cutting costs. Equally important, however, is the ability of the web to help in sourcing suppliers of particular products. An example of this is outlined below.

Example A site is currently being developed by Ybag.com to target small and medium-sized enterprises (SMEs).

The site will enable SME buyers to type in a request for the products or services that they require and then wait for a reply from prospective suppliers. The providers of the Internet site will make money by charging suppliers every time they offer a quote. A variation on this is the Internet site Mondus.com which offers a similar service to companies, but charges only when a transaction has been completed.

Another site, Biz2Biz.com, is set to become important to manufacturing companies in that it will provide networking trading links, and companies will be able to buy or sell products and services worldwide.

It can therefore be seen that there are many changes in the pipeline which will affect how companies throughout the world approach buying. It cannot be said that the old traditional methods will not have a part to play in the future, indeed there are many companies in the world which have yet to grasp the possibilities that the new technology can bring. There are firms where employees have very little, if any, degree of computer literacy, and yet the business is thriving, albeit usually on a smaller scale than if they embraced the new technology.

As time passes, and the Internet and all that it can offer becomes an integral part of everyone's life, it will be increasingly used in organisations to help run the business, and is likely to bring many changes to the buying procedures used. One of the most likely changes will be a reduction in the number of people required to carry out the buying of products and services for an organisation. Thus the use of the Internet will reduce the time required to source suppliers, this will help reduce complexity, and so save money.

In organisational settings, buying has often been subject to different and more complex influences than is the case with consumer markets. The following section will examine some of these key differences.

SOME DISTINCTIVE CHARACTERISTICS OF ORGANISATIONAL BUYING

Organisational purpose

Organisational buying is usually directly related to the ultimate purpose and objectives of the organisation itself. Buyers have to justify purchases in these terms, even in cases where organisational objectives appear to conflict – e.g. where profit motives are inconsistent with market service or innovation, say, at the level of a particular product or new initiative. Indeed, it is the resolution of such factors that often makes for the complexity of organisational buying situations, making for extended problem solving routines, protracted negotiation and consultation procedures. Goods and services bought by organisations are therefore not selected for themselves or for personal gratification, as in consumer markets, but for their contribution to the *wider delivery/production activity* served by the organisation. In this sense, all purchases by the organisation are intermediate objects, inputs to an ultimate organisational purpose.

Derived demand

Leading on from the above characteristic, it follows that goods and services bought by organisations are subject to a *derived demand*, literally derived from the demand for the final products or services that they deliver. The implication of this relationship is more than academic, since in practice it makes for lagged and sometimes sudden changes in demand, in response to even moderate changes in the demand for final (= consumer) goods and services. This is the accelerator principle of macroeconomics, where, for example, a 5 per cent change in consumer shoe sales may be 'accelerated' back along the supply chain, leading perhaps to a 25 per cent fall-off in the raw materials orders placed by footwear manufacturers.

Concentrated purchasing

Organisational purchases tend to be more concentrated, for a number of reasons. Formal requirements' planning by organisations, combined with the management of stockholdings and careful administration of budgets, tends to make for discrete bundling of purchases and bulk-ordering against volume concessions. Larger industrial customers, though statistically in a minority, may dominate consumption in many markets for intermediate goods; while larger organisations generally have tended to display preferences for centralised purchasing and purchase approval policies. More recently, however, there have been many *internet market places* set up. Buyers and sellers can use these sites to trade anything from horses to motor vehicle parts. This has caused some consternation, and some of the sites that are used as (B2B) market places for the world's largest companies are being investigated, to ensure that no collusion is taking place that would drive prices down to non-competitive levels, or indeed force suppliers to do business on the terms of the big companies alone. This action by the authorities however seems unlikely to deter large companies from linking up to take advantage of the technology now available. The following example shows one of the avenues that companies are exploring.

Example	In the UK large commercial property developers are linking together in order to build an on-line exchange that will aggregate their spending power. The aim is to procure multi-million-pound construction materials and utilities. This initiative should help the developers to save money, as they can be more aggressive with regard to driving deals with suppliers.

Direct dealings

As a generalisation, organisational buyers will more commonly deal direct with suppliers, rather than through intermediaries or third parties. There were, of course, exceptions, as in the case of multilayer wholesaler–retailer markets, industrial supply houses and procurement agencies serving government bodies, such as the Crown Agents in the UK. In recent years this practice has continued to grow, enhanced by the use of e-commerce. It is becoming more common practice for firms to input details of their requirements onto the Internet where they will then receive *offers and prices from suppliers worldwide*.

Specialist activity

Increasingly, organisational buying has become more specialist, in parallel with the growth of purchasing itself as a professional management activity. Unlike consumer markets, therefore, organisational buying will usually be conducted, or at least assisted and directed, by full-time professionals, who are usually up-to-date and well-informed on market, product and trading conditions, and not uncommonly are specialists in a particular product-market field. Moreover, where executives responsible for purchases are not themselves professionals, they will often be able to call on a range of expertise through professionals both within and outside the organisation.

In line with the specialist nature of organisational buying, there will usually be a degree of *formalisation* that ensures that professional and legal standards (e.g. Health and Safety legislation provisions) are adhered to, and organisational policies and managerial controls are heeded.

Multiple purchase influences

In common with many other managerial functions, buying within organisations tends to be an activity subject to *group decision-making influences*, across a number of interested parties, departments and functions within the organisation.

While the principles of co-ordination and good communications would provide for some sharing of decisions, or at least consultation, other factors will also reinforce this. Of some significance will be the need to formally gain authority for purchases, while heavier expenditures or new ventures may represent major risks, which may be better shared, or assessed, through group consensus.

DIFFERENT ORGANISATION TYPES

Though 'organisational buyer behaviour' is used as an umbrella term to cover buying within all organisations, it is both conventional and helpful to identify a general classification of organisational types that display broadly similar buying characteristics. Figure 7.1 presents such a typology.

It should be noted that the four broad types of organisation identified in Figure 7.1 are general categories which could be further broken down into subcategories. For example, the first category could be subdivided into industrial manufacturers and primary producers, such as mining companies and agricultural producers. For simplicity, this subdivision has not been attempted. Notwithstanding this, some commentary on each of the categories will serve to show the diversity of buying behaviour to be met with in practice.

Industrial producers, typified by manufacturing companies, will usually display the most professional treatment of the buying task. Buyers, or purchasing executives, will usually be professionally trained and qualified, commonly working within a separate department, itself organised into specialist sections and tasks (e.g. dealing with specifications, contracts, quotations, forecasting, costing and progress-checking). Price and cost issues are likely to be less significant buying criteria on their own, since quality, performance and delivery issues are more likely to be seen as yardsticks of value. While for some manufacturers a concern for competitiveness and continuity of supplies will lead to the use of a number of suppliers, even for the same component (= multiple sourcing), other companies will seek competitive improvements through concentrating buying through fewer suppliers, or ultimately through one supplier (= single sourcing). Increasingly nowadays, the combination of cost competition, continuous

Figure 7.1

A typology of organisation buyers

Organisational type	Examples	Common buying features
Industrial and producer organisations	Industrial manufacturers, agricultural producers	Quality delivery critical Specialist buyers Reciprocity Vertical linkages common
Commercial and reseller organisations	Retailers Wholesalers Banks and commercial services	Resale margins critical Discounts and volume deals Credit/financing terms Preferred suppliers Specialist buyers
Government and public sector organisations	Central government, municipal authorities	Strict budgetary controls Planned purchasing Competitive tendering Formalised procedures
Institutions	Colleges, hospitals, independent bodies	Budget constraints General management professionalising

quality improvement, quality standards accreditation and collaborative arrangements has made for a dependence by manufacturers on fewer and closer supplier links. These circumstances have made for the conscious development of closer vertical links and partnership relationships between manufacturers and their chosen suppliers, under the banner of supply chain management. Such strategies, inspired originally by the much-vaunted successes of Japanese companies, have centred on the application of systems thinking to achieve 'supply-chain integration' in order to eliminate waste and duplication, and reduce costs and delays within the supply chain.

To illustrate, the approach involves the application of a combination of methods such as electronic data interchange (EDI) for ordering, transport and invoice documentation, preplanned stock replenishment techniques, just-in-time (JIT) parts deliveries and establishing joint user–supplier quality improvement teams. Properly managed, such partnership strategies promise key competitive advantages for each party. However, management of these relationships is by no means simple and uncomplicated, and demands a great deal of trust and information exchange.

Example   British Telecom is keen to encourage close relationships in the B2B sector; to this end they have recently formed joint ventures with two US companies to help them build internet trading communities across Europe. This venture cost in the region of £140 million and involves firms Vertical Net and Internet Capital Group.

Among primary producers, agricultural producers will often have buying requirements that are subject to a range of outside influences, from government-supported subsidy schemes and financing–taxation concessions, to the various services offered by farming co-operatives and associations, agricultural merchants and advisory bodies. The cohesiveness that is often identified among farmers as a group may also act as a powerful word-of-mouth influence on equipment purchase and use, and more generally on farming practice.

A MODEL OF ORGANISATIONAL BUYING BEHAVIOUR

Reseller organisations such as retailers and wholesalers will generally undertake purchases only for selling on to an identified market. While they do not generally physically alter the products they handle, they will seek to *add value through service*. Aside from their stock-in-trade purchases of a range of products for resale, they will also make use of bought-in or contracted services (e.g. distribution, repair services), and will periodically undertake major capital investments for service enhancement, refurbishment, branch growth and resiting. Their purchase decisions in respect of traded goods will be dominated by commercial criteria such as bought-in costs and resale price, profitability (= margins), sales potential and related measures of commercial viability (e.g. stock turnover, sales per square metre, seasonality). Terms of trade (price, delivery, discounts) will be subject to hard negotiation and trade-off between competing suppliers, seeking to establish for the reseller an optimum market position that offers both profit potential and resale customer appeal. The larger retail organisations, with an increasingly dominant position in consumer markets, wield a formidable bargaining power that is matched only by the largest manufacturing suppliers. In recent years companies such as J Sainsburys have taken the lead in developing stronger partnership links with preferred suppliers. Such a strategy bears comparison with the growth of partnering linkages among industrial manufacturers, noted earlier.

Government and public sector organisations probably exhibit the most formality in their buying behaviour. Certainly traditionally, their approaches to purchasing, as in all external dealings, have been highly conservative and slow-moving, often subject to labyrinthine red tape and committee stages, rules and procedures that call for the utmost perseverance on the part of would-be suppliers. However, there are signs that public sector purchasing is now becoming more professional and commercially driven, in response perhaps to the general level of public sector expenditure almost everywhere, moves towards privatisation, and the gradual professionalisation of public sector management itself.

Example   The executive body responsible for co-ordinating central government purchasing, the Buying Agency, is trading with suppliers on an internet portal run by ICL, an IT company. ICL receives a fee on each sale, so that this is a cost-effective approach and massive savings by the government can be made.

Institutions such as colleges, hospitals, voluntary organisations and the like, show through their buying behaviour many parallels with the public sector. Though difficult to generalise, it is probably true to say that purchasing has traditionally been a semi-formalised activity that is seen, as with many a managerial function, as subsidiary to the main purpose of the organisation. Again, as with government organisations, recent external influences and policy changes, such as funding constraints, reorganisations and changes in corporate status, have made purchasing both more professional and competitive, certainly within many western economies.

A SIMPLE MODEL OF ORGANISATIONAL BUYING BEHAVIOUR

A logical and useful approach to studying organisational buying behaviour is to employ a simplified model of the *influences and processes involved*. Though no model can realistically encompass all the complexities to be met across different organisational types and situations, modelling is certainly effective in 'mapping out' the more significant and typical factors at work within a field of study. As testimony to this, marketers have developed in recent years a number of both specialist and general models of organisational buying, some of which will be referred to later in the chapter. For present purposes Figure 7.2 represents a simplified model of organisational buying.

The model illustrated in Figure 7.2 presents a flow-diagram representation of organisational buying behaviour, outlining the more readily recognised influences, decision sequences and outcomes involved. These will now be examined in further detail.

External influences

These consist of both the general environmental factors that affect buying behaviour, and those particular marketing contacts and information inputs that come from suppliers and prospective suppliers.

General environmental influences consist broadly of the STEP (Social, Technological, Economic, Political) factors that were identified as macroinfluences in Chapter 3. It is worth noting, though, that the effect of these influences on the buying function may be somewhat different from the pull they exert on the market-

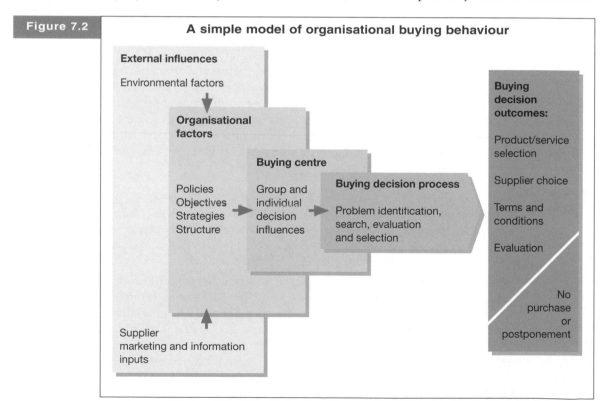

Figure 7.2 — A simple model of organisational buying behaviour

ing side. The challenge for would-be suppliers is therefore to take account of such contrary effects within the marketing programmes that they design for organisational buyers.

Social and cultural environmental influences

These are likely to affect organisational buying in more subtle and indirect ways, over time. For example, the nature of interpersonal dealings and relations, even in business settings, will gradually change as social norms change. However, some organisations – particularly government bodies and community-based organisations (such as schools and hospitals) are likely to work to a mission and purpose that is more explicitly concerned with social issues, values and norms, e.g. in respect of buying for a wider, more diverse customer base.

Technological factors

These factors are no less potent influences on purchasing behaviour within organisations than in other organisational functions. The classical example of technology changes affecting buying requirements would be the challenge facing manufacturers in keeping abreast of technology developments within their industry, and in seeking competitive improvements through technology-led solutions.

Manufacturing organisations with a serious policy commitment to innovation and to technology leadership, and related advances in quality and cost competitiveness, will usually be highly discriminating in their choice of suppliers, insisting that they keep pace in terms of these key issues. Once proved, such buying relationships may graduate further into more permanent partnerships and strategic alliances, offering the provision of mutual advantages through greater competitiveness and accelerated technology transfer, in both directions. Such strategies have now become integral to the search for global competitiveness in industries such as automobile manufacturing, aerospace and electronics. It has been observed, however, that in some cases the long-term benefits of such relationships may not be equally shared by the partners, given that major organisational buyers will often have a bargaining power advantage over individual suppliers.

On a perhaps more modest scale, it is interesting to note comparable buyer–supplier strategies being adopted by leading retailers, with the effect of 'locking in' suppliers through common technology, service and quality improvement standards.

Economic factors

Economic factors will have a powerful effect on purchasing behaviour within all organisations. Where major investment in facilities and plant are concerned, a number of economic criteria will be considered, including interest rates and financing charges, capacity lead-times and staff availability, cost inflation projections and other general indicators of the economic outlook. These factors will also influence everyday purchasing behaviour, certainly in terms of affecting general volumes of demand, budgetary limits and the need for economy and added value.

Political and legal factors

These issues will also come into the picture, both directly and indirectly. *Direct influences* will be seen through the workings of legal restrictions, standards and codes of practice, e.g. in respect of competition law, professional and industrial standards and guidelines. These influences will affect organisations in the private and public sectors alike. Less directly, issues such as social responsibility, ecological awareness and public accountability will affect purchase behaviour, particularly within those organisations that are sufficiently far-sighted and politically aware to incorporate policy guidelines on such matters.

Marketing and information inputs

The purchasing and sourcing process depends heavily on collecting and assimilating various types of information, of direct and indirect relevance to the task in hand. Knowledge and updating on the environmental factors influencing buying will usually filter through to buyers through the organisation's policy and planning functions, through research and information specialists, professional and trade press sources, head office bulletins, consultancy reports and the like.

More specific information on particular procedures and services and the capabilities of prospective suppliers will come through the deliberate search efforts of buyers themselves, or through contact with supplier companies. For simplicity, these information inputs might be divided into supplier sources and third party sources, as illustrated in Figure 7.3.

It should be noted that a number of the 'third-party' information sources used by buyers will be *in-house sources*, involving key users and decision makers, budget-holders, technical advisers and the like. This underlines the significance of group buying decisions, and introduces the role of a buying centre or group, which will be examined in more detail shortly.

It should also be noted that information sources involve both personal and impersonal contacts. Unlike many consumer markets, organisational buying offers suppliers the opportunity to make effective use of personal contact with buyers, subject to staff and resource constraints. Given that word-of-mouth information sources will often be seen by buyers as more credible, suppliers will usually seek to ensure some regular personal contact with buyers and other key influencers within the organisation.

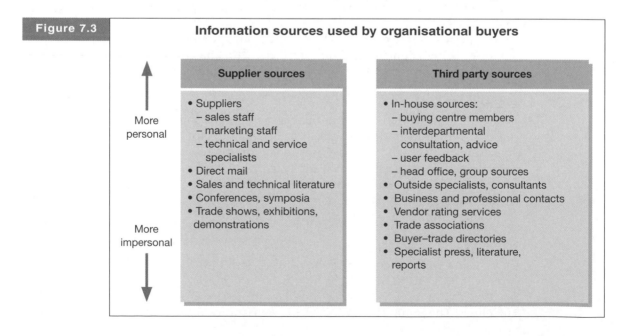

Figure 7.3 — **Information sources used by organisational buyers**

More personal → More impersonal

Supplier sources
- Suppliers
  - sales staff
  - marketing staff
  - technical and service specialists
- Direct mail
- Sales and technical literature
- Conferences, symposia
- Trade shows, exhibitions, demonstrations

Third party sources
- In-house sources:
  - buying centre members
  - interdepartmental consultation, advice
  - user feedback
  - head office, group sources
- Outside specialists, consultants
- Business and professional contacts
- Vendor rating services
- Trade associations
- Buyer–trade directories
- Specialist press, literature, reports

Organisational influences

Like any other managerial specialism or function, purchasing is subject to the organisation's general policies, objectives and strategies. As noted earlier, it is this tie that makes organisational buying more deliberate and specific than buying within consumer markets. While many of the major policies and objectives of an organisation may be very general and broad, they will nevertheless affect the buying task, for instance in respect of the need for cost-effectiveness, justification for returns on expenditure and the standards of managerial performance to be expected. Further, particular policies may be followed that directly affect purchasing – e.g. 'Buy Local' preferences, multiple sourcing, buying policies to support small or local companies and so forth.

Again, most of the apparently 'general' policies and objectives pursued by an organisation will inevitably have some impact on buying patterns, once incorporated into an annual business plan, with accompanying budgets, forecasts and deadlines. A prime example of such an effect would be the implications for buying from the planned development and launch of a new product or service offering. Effectively, such a venture would call for a specific launch plan, with budgets and target dates, for a number of functions, including buying.

Again, selected business growth or improvement strategies are likely to have direct influences on the buying task. For example, a total quality management (TQM) strategy would probably have far-reaching implications for buying, from renewed supplier vetting and selection procedures to perhaps a total overhaul of all existing contracts, buying relationships and control procedures.

Indeed, the increasing adoption of *quality certification systems* continues to exert a major influence on the whole supply chain, from purchasing to after-sales provision, across a spread of both manufacturing and service sectors. In terms of marketing, it has been demonstrated how suppliers can seek competitive advantage through quality registration, and additionally derive worthwhile efficiency gains through better business systems and organisational improvements.

Buying will also be affected by more everyday aspects of organisation such as the rules, systems and procedures employed within the task, staffing levels, departmental organisation and task division. In structural terms, the degree of centralisation imposed by top management may significantly affect the buying function. Centralised management policies will make for more formalised buying procedures that allow less buying autonomy below certain levels in the hierarchy. Obviously, supplier marketing and sales staff would need to be aware of such policies, and to plan their customer contacts accordingly.

The buying centre

Whether or not an organisation has a separate purchasing department, buying will to a greater or lesser extent represent a group-based task, the focus of multiple decision influences from a number of individuals and key executives within different functions across the organisation. Therefore, though purchasing officers may be involved in most purchases, and usually formally progress and implement final buying decisions, they will by no means control or dominate the key buying outcomes in respect of supplier selection, product specifications, terms and conditions. These will be the subject of shared decision making among a buying centre, the make-up of which will likely vary according to the type of purchase and the buying task itself. It is this variability, in group make-up and roles, that adds the essential dynamic to organisational buying, and that poses for suppliers a continuous challenge in their marketing efforts.

Webster and Wind (1992), from their research work on organisational buying, identify five broad roles, and associated buying influences, within the buying centre:

1 **Users** – Those using the product or service, i.e. administrative or operational staff, or their supervisors.
2 **Influencers** – Those influencing key product attributes and criteria, or specifications, through perhaps technical expertise.
3 **Deciders** – Those with the authority to select the product or supplier. For high-ticket purchases these are less likely to be purchasing executives alone.
4 **Gatekeepers** – Those controlling and directing relevant information flows internally, and contact with outsiders such as suppliers. This role could be taken, or shared, by buyers, administrative, secretarial or technical staff.
5 **Buyers** – Typically, purchasing executives charged with administering and progressing the buying task.

It should be stressed that these roles are not necessarily formal or assigned; rather they constitute the effective contribution of different individuals, which is often unplanned. It is another example of the reality of the informal organisation, and is perhaps a fitting reminder that organisations are social entities in which *people interactions* prevail.

It is worth noting that the decision authority within the buying centre may change according to the type of buying decision and task under consideration. Generally this will depend on the complexity of the product to be bought – it is usual for certain members of a buying team to build up expertise in different areas. However, if the complexity of the item to be bought is great, then other technical employees will be asked to assist.

A more widely accepted framework is that originally proposed by Robinson, Faris and Wind (1967), identifying three different types of buying decisions, or 'buyclasses':

1 **New task**. New purchase propositions where the organisation has no previous experience and therefore requires careful search procedures, extended problem solving and shared decision making.
2 **Straight rebuy**. Routine, low-risk, low-involvement repeat purchase decisions with standard information requirements and little shopping comparisons beyond working from a listing of predetermined 'vetted' suppliers. Here, the 'plurality' of the purchase decision may be minimal.
3 **Modified rebuy.** A hybrid of the two previous situations where, for example, there is a record of supplier experience and dealings, though product-design advances make for some re-examination of buying criteria, technical standards and the like. Here, new dimensions of the purchase decision – for instance, design changes – may call for the involvement of relevant specialists such as engineers, technologists and accountants.

Membership of any buying centre may be a moving population, with individuals coming and going even during the life of one purchasing episode, while at any time there may be a number of overlapping centres or groups, dealing with different purchase requirements and tasks. Such a situation can make the supplier's marketing and selling task highly complex, since the target group for promotion and sales contact resembles a moving target. Staying on target demands of the supplier perseverance, up-to-date information and intelligence, and good communications abilities at different levels.

A further imponderable can be the dynamics of interaction within and across the buying group. While organisational goals and policies will be followed by all members of the group, individual influences will be evident, making for conflicts and delays, swings of direction and occasionally even wholesale revisions of the buying agenda.

As an illustration of these individual influences, certainly each 'active' member of the buying centre will behave differently according to their training and experience, their formal position and departmental agenda, as well as more subjective factors such as age, social background and personality. Psychological factors such as perception, motivation and attitudes (e.g. to risk) may therefore become as active in this context as they are within consumer buying situations. We could add yet a further layer of complexity by considering the interplay of these individual influences, through group deliberations involving occasional obstacles of personal chemistry, professional rivalry and even power politics.

As observed, some purchasing episodes will involve a number of functional specialists from across the organisation, which in turn introduces the dynamics of inter-departmental relations, and the territorial tensions and 'tribal' alignments that may exist, even within medium-sized single-sector companies. An interesting issue here is the extent to which purchasing tasks and decisions are devolved, as formal policy, to user functions or departments, formally centralised, or more informally shared through inter-disciplinary group working. Stuart (1991) comments on the need for effective teamwork within and across functional groups, in the interests of decision making outcomes optimal to the whole organisation.

The buying-decision process

Though a simplification, it is useful to envisage the buying decision making process as a six-stage sequence, similar to the problem solving framework sometimes applied to complex consumer purchases. The six stages comprise:

1 **Need identification**. This can come through a number of channels, perhaps through an annual review/plan exercise, a sudden requirement for replacement, a new product, or as a by-product of another programme, such as a quality initiative. It can also come through outside influences, perhaps 'triggered' through successful supplier communication and presentation efforts, or through trade or professional sources, or some combination of these.

2 **Establishing specification**. This is a logical refinement of the first stage, where relevant buying centre members such as users, or influencers in technical or development functions, jointly or separately provide information and guidance on the framing of a set of specifications that meet the needs identified. For more technical problems, a number of alternative designs and technologies may be considered before an agreed specification is produced.

3 **Search activity**. This involves identifying possible products and suppliers that can meet the needs identified in the specification. As we have seen earlier in the chapter there are now more streamlined and efficient ways to do this via the Internet, but in many instances, in more traditional industries, the tried and tested methods are still in use. Buyers are likely to undertake this search process, perhaps aided by

other buying centre members such as gatekeepers. Search activities may range across contacting existing supplier 'accounts', new suppliers, perhaps on recommendation, working through information sources in trade directories, buyer guides, exhibitions, etc. Sometimes the process will be iterative, involving returning to and reworking the specification stage, perhaps in the light of new information or new perspectives on a solution. Such iterations may bring previous group participants back 'on-stage', or introduce new ones.

4 **Evaluation of alternatives**. Identified suppliers and products will be evaluated, both in technical/operational terms, and in respect of price, delivery and capacity issues and service capabilities. A number of buying centre members will be involved in such evaluations, including purchase executives, technical and accounting staff.

5 **Selection and ordering**. A natural follow-on from stage 4, involving choice of some supplier(s) and product(s) to meet the specification. Certainly for major purchases involving significant expenditure with high-risk and long-term commitments, this stage will likely be subject to formal approval, at director or committee level, supported by a comprehensive proposal outlining costs, investment 'payback' details, delivery, service and warranty arrangements and so forth. New task purchases, and some modified rebuy decisions, will also be subject to such formal authorisation. In these situations, the buying specialist's role will be more one of co-ordinating and administering, subject to the selections made by deciders. Obviously, straight rebuy situations will rarely involve such formal approval, nor all of the stages identified.

6 **Post-purchase monitoring**. Here, product and supplier performance will be monitored and periodically reviewed, the need for future changes noted where necessary and remedial action taken on particular problems (e.g. in delivery, quality, warranties). These activities will formally be the responsibility of buyers, assisted as necessary by user feedback and technical advice.

The above sequence of decision making is highly generalised, and would be much simpler for routinised repeat purchases, which probably account for many of the purchases made by the average purchase executive. In these situations, orders would be placed and confirmed by the buyer against standard sampling and inspection procedures, with much less involvement of other parties. However, for modified rebuys and new task situations, the above sequence may be understated, and the total activity may involve quite protracted meetings and face-to-face negotiations, involving many other buying group members.

Buying-decision outcomes

Purchase decision outcomes will translate into orders and contracts specifying selected products and services, and their suppliers, with detailed terms and conditions in respect of price, discounts, delivery and service expectations.

Though straight purchases are most common, some transactions will involve non-ownership options such as lease or rental arrangements, which may be more appropriate in terms of capital outlay, tax advantages or budget planning. Where contracts are entered into, further decision variables will concern the contract period, trial or introductory periods, legal provisions for discontinuation, cost escalation and penalty factors and precise details of service performance.

Finally, for a variety of reasons, the decision outcome may lead to non-purchase, total abandonment of a proposal, or at best postponement or a resolution to start afresh on a somewhat different proposition.

BUYER–SELLER RELATIONSHIPS

Much has been said with regard to the buying behaviour of firms, but it is vital that all firms when selling to others become *customer focused*. Organisations who concentrate solely on internal functions within the company, such as manufacturing or even sales and marketing, do so at their peril. Customer relationship marketing (or management) (CRM) is a concept that is becoming increasingly important. It has been defined by Anderson Consulting as:

Customer relationship management is a discipline that encompasses identifying, attracting and retaining the most valuable customers to sustain profitable growth.

With the growth in the use of the Internet as a medium for sourcing and buying products and services, care must be taken to ensure that customers are treated individually and with attention – for example, emails and calls should be dealt with in a speedy and appropriate manner. As the needs of customers change with time, so should the offering change to reflect those needs.

CONCLUSION

Clearly, organisational buying behaviour is a highly complex subject that defies total explanation through the kind of simple model that has been developed here. Nevertheless, modelling the process is a useful insight into the interactions involved. For a more detailed examination on the subject, the reader is referred to the general model of industrial buyer behaviour developed by Webster and Wind (1992). However the impact of new technology on B2B buying behaviour is not yet fully apparent, things are changing extremely quickly and the full implications are not yet clear.

QUESTIONS

1   *In what ways has the use of the Internet changed business buying behaviour?*

2   *Consider the possible differences in the way that buying decisions might be undertaken within (a) a small manufacturer; (b) a large multinational; (c) a local authority secondary school and; (d) a private hospital.*

3   *Compare and contrast consumer buying behaviour with organisational buying behaviour.*

4   *For any company or organisation with which you are familiar, identify by occupation the people who might perform the following roles for a specific purchase: (i) gatekeeper; (ii) decider; (iii) influencer.*

5   *In what ways might risk affect organisational buying at the level of (a) the organisation, and (b) the individual buyer?*

6   *Identify one major trend within organisational purchasing and consider its implications for marketing practitioners.*

FURTHER READING

Chandiramani, R. (2000) 'BT to create European b2b sites', *Revolution*, 16 February.

Corboy, M. (1999), 'E-commerce dispelling the myths and exploiting the opportunities', *Management Accounting*, December.

Ferguson, W. (1996) 'The impact of the ISO 9000 series standards on industrial marketing', *Industrial Marketing Management*, 25 (4), July.

Fisher, L. (1976) *Industrial Marketing*, 2nd edn. Business Books.

Gallello, D. (2000) 'Engineering on the web', *CADdesk*, 10(1), January.

Kotler, P., Armstrong, G., Saunders, J. and Wong, V. (1999) *Principles of Marketing*, 2nd European edn. Prentice-Hall.

Robinson, P. J., Faris, C. W. and Wind, Y. (1967) *Industrial Buying and Creative Marketing*. Allyn & Bacon.

Simmons, L. (2000) 'Ybag to launch SME site as rival to mondus.com', *Revolution*, 10 May.

Smith, P. (2000) 'Property giants to form procurement exchange', *Revolution*, May.

Webster, F. E. and Wind, Y. (1992) *Organisational Buyer Behaviour*. Prentice-Hall.

Wilson, A. (1968) *The Assessment of Industrial Markets*. Cassell.

CASE STUDY

Competing forces fighting to stop collusion on the net

FT

There is no competition like e-commerce competition, as shown by the choice of 97 differently-priced 'Buns of Steel' aerobics videos listed on the comparison shopping site, www.biddersedge.com. . . .

In theory, perfect information ought to mean perfect competition, with all buyers everywhere able to compare all offers. But as Robert Pitofsky, chairman of the Federal Trade Commission, told an American Bar Association conference of antitrust lawyers, information can be used as easily to collude as to compete.

Shopping bots, for example, could use their chokehold on the market for auction information to display the results from one auction website more prominently than others, perhaps in exchange for payment.

Business-to-business commerce raises a major risk of information abuse, say antitrust lawyers. the Internet provides unprecedented real-time access to information about price, quality and availability of products, reducing the time and money spent on locating deals and negotiating prices.

The risk is that electronic information exchanges may encourage cosy anti-competitive behaviour. It would not be the first time: in 1994, the Justice Department settled a case alleging that the major airlines used their joint electronic fare system to discourage discounting, and travel agents have asked the Justice Department to investigate the anti-competitive aspects of a mega-travel site being formed by airlines.

Joint buying, of the B2B variety, can raise the risk of a 'buyers' conspiracy', says Richard Donovan, antitrust specialist with the law firm Kelley Drye & Warren. In a concentrated industry 'that can be every bit as anti-competitive as agreeing what price they charge consumers for a car,' he says.

Equally challenging for antitrust law is commerce that involves both internet and traditional channels: how will courts decide competition cases where a manufacturer tries to circumvent the middleman, and sell directly to customers on-line? In antitrust lawsuits, where the legal crux of the matter is the definition of the market, courts must decide whether to define the market to include just internet commerce, or just offline commerce, or both.

If two malls that dominate commerce in a Minneapolis suburb merge, for example, will courts consider just the real-world effect of the merger – and decide it is anti-competitive – or factor in competition from the Internet, and decide mergers that create geographical concentrations of power are no longer so worrisome?

Only a few courts have yet considered these questions, and they have tended to define the market to include both on-line and offline commerce. But with manufacturers increasingly competing with retailers, and selling directly on-line, those who lose out are likely to sue in ever larger numbers.

Consider all those retailers who are barred from selling Clinique cosmetic products on-line, for example. Stores such as Bloomingdale's will not forever accept a situation where it cannot sell Clinique's 'age-defying serum' on-line, but only in its stores.

Most legal experts believe a body of antitrust law that has dealt with railroads and mail-order commerce is capable of tackling cyberspace. Cyber-commerce is just so much new wine in old bottles, they say. It's not as though the Internet invented competition, or collusion for that matter. Until the web rewrites rules of human behaviour, existing law should just about manage to cope.

Waldmeir@aol.com

Source: Financial Times, 13 April 2000. (Copyright © The Financial Times Limited)

Questions

1 It has been said that, 'Joint buying, of the B2B variety, can raise the risk of a 'buyers' conspiracy'". Do you think that this is a fair view of the situation?

2 How has the use of new technology enhanced business buying behaviour?

3 Compile a list of advantages and disadvantages of using the Internet for the purpose of industrial buying.

4 How does the above case relate to the principles of organisational buyer behaviour, as outlined in this chapter?

CASE STUDY

Logistics and the supply chain: a transformation in retail trade links   FT

In the networked world of e-commerce, collaboration is the name of the game for retail buyers and their suppliers

Whether they're termed 'B2B portals', 'trading networks', 'procurement hubs' or whatever, the new generation of web-based product sourcing and buying associations that have mushroomed in recent weeks is set to transform retail supply chains.

The traditional adversarial relationship between retail buyers and their suppliers – with each trying to squeeze the other on price or delivery times – has been transformed in the recent years by 'collaborative planning, forecasting and replenishment' schemes where suppliers have access, via the Internet, to the retailer's database to check on promotional progress, branch sales, or forecasts in demand.

Now, this degree of co-operation is extending to inter-retail relationships, with the new web-based trading networks actually set up to automatically aggregate orders from a number of retailers and negotiate the best price and terms from suppliers for the larger volumes involved.

'It's a sort of reverse auction,' says David Stephenson, UK-based, regional director for retail and services with Oracle. 'Retailers input details of their needs and the system automatically

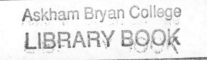

aggregates the orders and invites tenders from suppliers. It also forecasts demand and, eventually, could also be involved in planning distribution.'

Oracle has set up two retail-focused exchanges:

GlobalNetXchange which is a separate legal entity rapidly attracting equity investment from leading retailers worldwide, and RetailMarketXchange which is targeted at the convenience store sector. Sears Roebuck, Carrefour (France), Metro (Germany) and J Sainsbury are already committed to GlobalNetXchange with Royal Ahold (Netherlands) expected to sign shortly. Suppliers are, in theory, welcome to become equity partners as well – although retailers have been the first to participate.

'This is a revolution in retail,' says Arthur C. Martinez, chief executive of Sears Roebuck. 'It will forever redefine supply-chain processes, increase collaboration with suppliers and reduce supply-chain costs.'

Mr Stephenson believes that the network will initially be used for 'goods not for resale' – such as stationery and shopfitting – where procurement tends to be disorganised and costly in many retail businesses, although eventually non-competing retailers may well join together to use the network for sourcing consumer goods. 'The system allows the retail members to issue "private" needs which suppliers can tender for, rather than joining with others to create a large aggregated order,' he explains.

The exchanges were launched in March, so the schemes are still in their infancy, but in the long-term the RetailMarketXchange could certainly present a competitive challenge to the traditional voluntary buying groups in this sector, such as Spar.

This sort of multi-retail trading network is still a little unusual, with earlier ones tending to be developed by a single retailer before being expanded to others in the same sector. Petsmart in the USA has developed a web-based sourcing system with SourcingLink.Net. The technology is based on an established Lotus Notes desktop product, although Steven Pulver, vice-president for sales and services at SourcingLink.Net maintains that the company has 'reinvented itself as an internet company in the past 14 months'.

The Petsmart B2B scheme was introduced last year with the aim of cutting lead times in product development as well as trimming inventory levels. 'Our emphasis is on own label to give a unique product offer,' says Marcia Meyer, the company president, 'so we work closely with suppliers. Our Phoenix buying office has to work with Asian companies with a 15-hour time difference – and European ones with an eight-hour time difference – and we cannot be efficient with just phone or fax.'

Mrs Meyer maintains that while there are many net-based B2B products emerging, few of them are based on real retail needs, accurately mirroring the traditional retail sourcing and supply model electronically. 'SourcingLink.Net is one of the few that does,' she says. 'With a web-based procurement system we are now finding new vendors and we're heavily committed to digital imagery to share product development ideas.'

As with GlobalNetXchange, Petsmart buyers can now 'broadcast' their product requirements over the network and receive offers and suggestions from suppliers worldwide. Over the past year Mrs Meyer's team has sourced more than 900 new product lines electronically and decreased time to market by 50 per cent.

Inventory is down by 20 per cent while the total number of lines on offer has increased by 40 per cent. SourcingLink.Net hosts the Petsmart network and will be opening it to other pet products' retailers worldwide in coming months. It has also been working on a similar scheme with Promodes in France – although since this is now merged with Carrefour (committed to GlobalNetXchange), long-term development may be in doubt.

Many of the new trading networks are hosted, as with Petsmart, by the IT companies providing the software and are similarly highly product specific. Retek, for example, has retail.com, launched last year with early users – including companies such as Selfridges and Storehouse –

tending to come from the clothing sector; i2 Technologies similarly owns SoftgoodsMatrix for the clothing and furnishings sector. This has already attracted companies such as VF Corporation – the world's largest clothing producer – Lee, Wrangler and Bestform.

While some of these networks are predominantly retail driven, others clearly have the initiative coming from suppliers. 'Closed trading communities are limiting, because they benefit the buyer or the seller – but never both,' argues Yanir Aharonson, general manager, of the Israel-based supply chain specialist, Paragon.

'The buyer-orientated trading community restricts access to business processes and restricts suppliers' access outside the buyers' own communities.'

For buyers accessing supplier-based portals there are the same limitations on integrating valuable marketing data and sales information into existing IT systems.

Early data-sharing ventures certainly suffered from this lack of integration and there are also problems about 'ownership' of the data which is being shared. Paragon has set up RetailTrade.net as a semi-independent trading community, arguing that it is more comprehensive by linking a greater diversity of companies into one trading portal. The site is set up by a community co-host or market maker, which creates and maintains the web trading communities by region and by industry-specific markets or groups of markets. Suppliers and buyers register at the site, and then gain access to services and modules worldwide 24 hours a day. The hosts earn income through monthly fees or on a commission basis per transaction.

Rapidly expanding these new trading hubs may be, but they do not solve all supply chain problems. 'These portals can only arrange dates and deals,' says Gilles Serpry, global head of supply chain at Cap Gemini. 'They cannot get the goods from A to B. To do this, retailers will need to take advantage of the newest business models enabled by the Internet.'

Penelope Ody

Source: Financial Times, 3 May 2000. (Copyright © The Financial Times Limited)

Question

In what ways has buying behaviour in the B2B sector changed given the facts outlined above?

Customers, market segmentation and targeting

Divide et impera [Divide and rule].
Ancient political maxim cited by Machiavelli

INTRODUCTION

While marketing as a business philosophy makes the customer central to the objectives of an organisation, it is the concepts of marketing that have been developed from this philosophy which have made marketing so relevant to business and other organisations.

The marketing concepts provide the basic principles and framework within which appropriate decisions can be made by any supplier who wishes to ensure that exchanges made with consumers or customers are mutually beneficial. It is a basic precept of marketing that this must be the principal objective of any supplier who wishes to thrive in a dynamic competitive environment such as is usual today.

It is said that a product is not sold until it has reached the ultimate consumer; in fact, we could go further and say it is not sold until it is *paid for and used by the final consumer*. It is only then that there is any possibility of selling further products to that customer.

In the 1950s the pioneers of mass-marketing, multinational firms such as Procter & Gamble and Coca-Cola, had the power to sell large quantities of standardised goods to a 'homogeneous' mass market, using the promotional attraction of mass media (national press, and especially television). Even earlier, Henry Ford made his fortune by mass-marketing, offering his Model 'T' car in 'any colour as long as it is black'. Now things have changed in the market place. Companies offer products to better suit customers – for example, Coca-Cola now offers caffeine-free, diet, cherry and other variants which combine some or all of these attributes. Ford makes cars, from the Ka, retailing at just under £7000, to the Explorer, a four-wheel drive vehicle retailing at around £28 000 (year 2000 prices), and all of their cars are available in a host of finishes, colours and specifications. At a basic level this could be seen just as an increase in the variety of products offered, but of course the cause of this proliferation is to attempt to meet customer needs more precisely.

If marketing is the satisfying of the needs and wants of customers, then those wants must at least be established, even if they are found to be different for every single consumer. This fact recognises that customers do not always form a homogeneous group, nor are the demands of two, outwardly similar, people necessarily the same. However, as marketing really involves 'profitable or beneficial exchanges' so, as part of the marketing decision process, there must be a view on which customer groups are to be supplied. If different customers have different needs then why not offer them different products to meet those needs? And why not market those products in a way that appeals best to each particular group?

In Chapter 6 it was suggested that the buying decisions of consumers should be linked to relevant characteristics associated with individual buyers, e.g. new mothers buy baby foods, or business suits are purchased by white-collar workers. These examples already illustrate how one specific group could be more likely to buy a particular product than another. It is, of course, sometimes difficult to identify those people who prefer a red car rather than a black car, but these preferences certainly do exist.

WHO ARE OUR CUSTOMERS?

Before an organisation can make any decision associated with marketing a fundamental question must be answered: 'Who are our customers?'

One way to answer this question would be on the basis of Table 1.1 in Chapter 1. This could well be a good initial approach, but it is unlikely to provide an answer that would be useful as the basis for making marketing decisions.

Another approach would be to use the behaviourial criteria that are identified in Chapters 6 and 7 as being relevant to buyer decisions. Identifying the different groups, and so subdividing the market into those groups that can be addressed by a specific marketing strategy, is termed 'segmentation'. Its objective is to select from all possible potential customers those groups that are most likely to need and want to buy a prod-

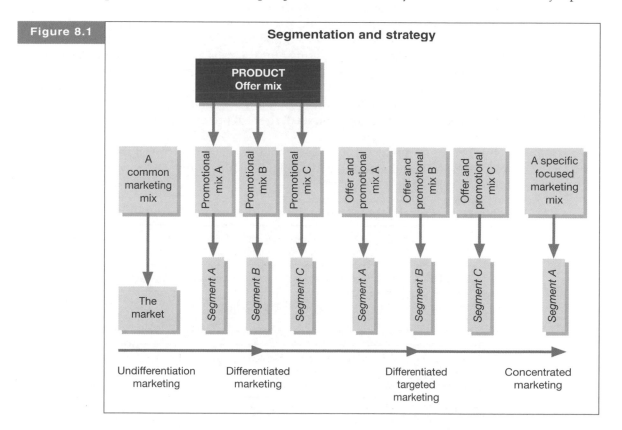

Figure 8.1   **Segmentation and strategy**

uct. The use of different marketing strategies for each distinct segment is known as target marketing, or differentiated marketing (see Figure 8.1).

Each of these different strategies is likely to appeal to very different groups of customers. Consider the type of people who buy food in a delicatessen shop compared with those who regularly shop at a discount food store such as Kwiksave or Aldi. Even if some people use both outlets, the motivations for the visiting of such very different stores will enable those shoppers to be distinguished from those who visit only one of the outlet types mentioned.

This chapter looks at the identification of segments and the benefits of focusing on these segments. It also covers the criteria necessary for a segment to be useful to a marketer.

USEFUL SEGMENTATION

The basic principle of segmentation is very simple. It involves selecting the classification most appropriate to the groups of customers identified. The work involved in doing this is justified only if it can be used to improve marketing effectiveness. To meet this objective the resulting segments must be relevant to the purchase decision, and also capable of being reached by both distribution and communications with some measure of precision.

The traditional approach uses variables, which can be described as geographic and/or demographic. Much of the data collected by the various UK media owners is even today quoted in terms of the socio-economic groupings shown in Table 8.1.

There are many potential problems when using a scale derived from the occupation of the 'head of the household' to determine how people behave. Anyway, the descriptions below are already outdated, using terms such as 'working class'. The classification is also made less easy to use by the changing social order, for instance the move away from the traditional 'husband, wife and 2.4 children' household that prevailed when this classification was started. Now most homes contain either one or two people, and the traditional family group described above represents anything but a majority of homes.

It is becoming more usual to classify consumers on the basis of self-orientation and resources. It is a commercial classification, which has proved very popular with major US advertising agencies (see Figure 8.2).

Table 8.1   Market segmentation, by socio-economic groupings

A	Upper Middle Class	High managerial/administrative/professional, e.g. company director, or established doctor or solicitor
B	Middle Class	Intermediate managerial/administrative/or professional
C1	Lower Middle Class	Supervisory/clerical/junior managerial
C2	Skilled Working Class	Skilled manual workers
D	Working Class	Semi-skilled or unskilled workers
E	Pensioners, casual workers and others	

Source: JICTAR.

Figure 8.2

Value and lifestyle categories (SRI International)

Principle orientated	Status orientated	Action orientated		Resources
	Actualisers			Abundant
Fullfilleds	Achievers	Experiencers		
Believers	Strivers	Makers		
	Strugglers			Minimal

The problems in finding a usable way of describing a segment do not mean that the concept of marketing segmentation is not useful. There are many examples of successful target marketing which can be found. In fact, the industrial product sector is a good example where organisational characteristics (demographic and geographic, such as type of company, size, industry, etc.) can be successfully linked with personal characteristics of personnel who might be: users, influencers, buyers, deciders, or gatekeepers. By identifying how to reach a group of 'deciders' a positive marketing result can be achieved, as in the example below.

Example   A campaign to communicate with the financial controllers of companies with large transport fleets was undertaken by a major tyre company. The company realised financial controllers were a key 'advisor' group and in some cases held the 'decider' role. They were primarily interested in the lowest total cost of operation, not just the cheapest tyre. They could be reached directly, and a campaign was directed at them, emphasising areas they considered important rather than issues important to the transport manager. It proved successful in boosting sales levels.

Returning to the consumer market, another useful set of segments is the ACORN grouping (A Classification Of Residential Neighbourhoods). This is a variation on traditional demographic descriptors, developed in a way that makes communication with this segment easy. It is sometimes termed 'geo-demographics', as it links postcodes (in Britain or other host countries) to the prime characteristics of the occupants of the households. In the UK a total of 38 groupings has been produced, so that a marketing organisation or other user can buy a list of all addresses in a particular category – say, all postcodes which have a majority of 'private flats with single pensioners' (category K38). A mail shot to this segment offering them a relevant product will have a greater success rate than a more random method of contacting this group. Alternatively, a company could collect all the addresses and postcodes of its customers. By analysing these against the ACORN database the predominant categories can be established and plans laid to communicate with other potential customers in the same categories.

Such an exercise can prove very rewarding, but it does not assume that all people in the same postcode groupings behave in the same way. Compare your family with your own neighbours. The use of ACORN does assume, and can demonstrate, that the probability of similarities exist. This is enough to make the database valuable to marketing managers. There are other rival databases such as MOSAIC, PINPOINT and PROFILES, offering similar services.

REQUIREMENTS FOR A USABLE SEGMENT

There is no limit to the number of ways a market may be segmented in particular circumstances, but to be useful a segment must be:

- definable
- sizeable
- reachable
- relevant.

Definable

This means we must be able to describe the market segment, and for this the key characteristics of the segment should show a degree of homogeneity. The segment is of course a subset of a heterogeneous total market, because if the total market were homogeneous there would be no need for segmentation. It is also useful to be able to measure the market size and define the boundaries of the segment.

Sizeable

Is the segment large enough and can it produce the required turnover and profit for your organisation? This criterion depends on the particular organisation, as a minimum revenue of £10m for a brand sold by a large multinational might be required, while another company might find £0.5m an acceptable contribution to turnover. So size is relative, but organisations also need to make profits. It would appear that markets are demanding a continually expanding range of options, models, types, sizes, colours and customisations. That is the challenge of marketing, but useful segments must be assessed in terms of organisational resources and objectives.

Reachable

There must be a way of reaching the segment both effectively and efficiently. This includes the obvious physical distribution of a product, as well as communicating with customers via media or in a direct way. ACORN meets the communication test in some aspects but is not accurate enough in all areas.

Relevant

This is considered the most important test for any described segment. It cannot be considered in isolation from the other criteria as there is no point in describing a relevant segment that cannot be reached. Wilson (1994) introduces a number of criteria by which marketers may make the sometimes difficult choice between identified market segments. The criteria he outlines range from segment durability (or life cycle) and segment price level to customisation costs (including entry investment) and the extent of overlap or interdependency with other segments. On a somewhat different issue of segment selection, Reed (1996) observes that a number of companies are attempting to practice ever-more accurate target marketing, even at the cost of customer deselection through screening criteria. While such approaches depend critically on data accuracy and marketing logic, they hold out the promise, if successful, of reducing costs, concentrating purchases and increasing the impact of promotions such as loyalty schemes.

The message of this section is that although segmentation can be an effective marketing technique, it should be treated carefully. In the era of de-massification, organisations can easily appeal to segments that are too small to be viable, or perhaps too costly to reach. While segmentation can help in the process of understanding customer similarities and differences, careless use could lead to the development of too many product variants, confusion of customers and the failure to capitalise on the real opportunities that such a study of markets and their subsets offer.

SEGMENTATION VARIABLES

In order to describe segments, there are two different approaches that can be used. The first concentrates on the *characteristics of the buyer*. Generally these are classified under one or a combination of the three categories:

- demographic
- geographic
- psychographic and lifestyle.

However, an alternative, but equally powerful, set of variables can be derived, offering a focus on *how customers behave*, and the *benefits sought* by those customers from a product or service. While benefits link closely with lifestyles and psychographics, they do warrant attention as a separate category for classification. So the other two categories are:

- benefit; and
- behaviourial segmentation.

Demographic segmentation

Demographics is the most widely used method of classification of marketing segments. It is the basis for the collection of many government statistics and the standard system used by the media industry. Pym Cornish of RSL, who is an acknowledged authority on demographics, wrote:

> Demographics are often thought of as consisting of no more than the dimensions of sex, age, social grade, region, and a few others that have traditionally been used as a standard market research variable in Britain. But society does not stand still. It has evolved; old generalisations about the family, such as that women look after the house and children while men earn the money, have become less and less true. Yet this does not mean that demographics have become less useful, only that the traditional classifications should be superseded by others that reflect the current structure of society more accurately.

So, in general, the traditional demographic bases are considered to be: gender, age, marital status, socio-economic classification and occupation. To these we must add descriptors such as family type and size, income levels, ethnic origin, education levels and stage in the life cycle. The stage in the life cycle has a heavy weighting with regard to purchases such as home furnishings and DIY items.

For industrial products there are equivalent demographic categories which can be used, such as industry type (SIC – Standard Industrial Codes), turnover and/or profit, numbers of employees and numbers and types of customers.

Such demographic data are relatively easy to obtain. Every 10 years in the UK there is a full census of the population, so that government statistics can be updated. This does not cover issues like lifestyle in great depth, but it does provide a good basis from which to start. Many organisations use *census data* as a basis for decisions on market potential. The type of information provided is called 'secondary data', in that it is collected for one purpose but it is then used for a secondary one. It cannot be stressed too often that the information collected must be relevant to the purchase decision.

The categories that are actually relevant can change, as in the example of Red Stripe lager. This Jamaican lager was originally imported into Britain from the Caribbean. Its price reflected the cost of importing, and it was primarily sold to areas with a high population of Jamaican origin. The brewers, Desnoes and Geddes, then arranged for the product to be brewed under licence in the UK. While they were very careful to maintain the distinctive quality of the lager, it was decided that the price could be modified, and there were opportunities for appealing to a wider number of drinkers. Hence ethnic origin is no longer such a relevant demographic variable for this product.

However, stage in the life cycle does affect consumption of beers and lagers. As people move through the stages of pre-family, family and post-family they change

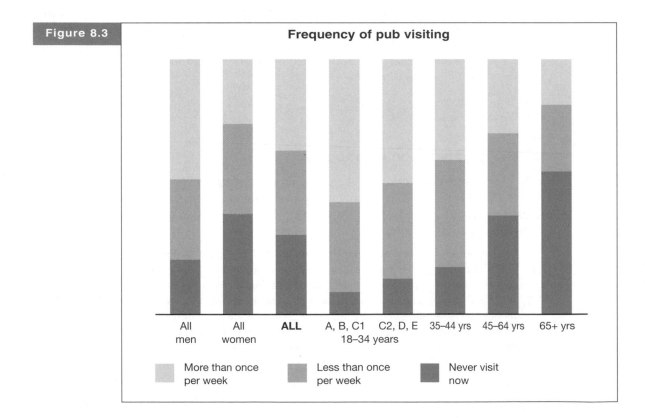

Figure 8.3 Frequency of pub visiting

their drinking habits. Also, some people remain single, or form a relationship but do not marry or have any children. They, too, show changes in drinking according to life cycle. Life cycle is more powerful than age alone in this analysis, as it is able to include relative levels of disposable income and, equally important, leisure time, which a family with children finds is in short supply. Of course the traditional variables do help in describing segments (as, for instance, men drink more beer than women), and there are differences identified by socio-economic groups (see Figure 8.3). In order to describe their customers the major brewers use a combination of demographic data with other bases such as lifestyle (as distinct from life cycle, which is not the same).

Geographic segmentation

This type of classification is often considered as another type of demographic variable. In some ways it is, and the development of geo-demographic bases such as ACORN prove this. Nevertheless it is an obvious grouping, and geographic variables can be considered separately. Issues, such as rural versus urban, warm versus cold, north versus south, can all be considered where appropriate. The consumption of sweet (sugar-based) products is greater in Scotland than in the rest of the UK. Is this perhaps useful information when planning a new confectionery product?

There are also opportunities for the commercial market, such as planning new retail outlets. One company might look for a location in the key area bounded by outlets such as Marks & Spencer, Boots and W. H. Smith, which provides the greatest density of shoppers in many town centres. Another trader might base decisions on the number of suitable customers living within a specific radius or travelling a distance from the centre of a city. Both are dependent on geographic segmentation studies.

It might be appropriate to add a warning regarding large, apparently attractive segments. These naturally attract competitors and may not provide the anticipated level of business. There are many small shops serving a limited geographic area without direct competition and making a reasonable profit. If the business were located in the High Street of a major town, the competition would change the situation, such that although the numbers of potential customers is far greater, the actual custom may not be, and the increased costs involved would decrease profitability.

Psychographic and lifestyle segmentation

Psychographics seeks to classify people according to their personality traits. They are used more in relation to consumer products, but there is no reason why corporate interests, such as a measure of levels of social responsibility, could not be used when considering issues relevant to the segmenting of organisations. There is some debate over whether psychographics should be restricted to issues of sociability, self-reliance, assertiveness and other personality traits, or whether it should be widened to include lifestyles, which cover attitudes, interests and opinions. In general it has over time enveloped lifestyle, and so it is from this perspective that it is discussed. The bringing together of these factors from the two areas provides a more useful and robust segmentation base.

The use of lifestyle characteristics is attractive to the marketer, for two reasons. First, it provides a simple link to the variables used in behavioural theory, e.g. attitudes, perception and social influences. Second, although lifestyles can change over time and over the life cycle of a person, there tends to be a consistency of action in selecting products and services which matches the 'persona' of a consumer at a particular period.

To establish psychographic characteristics, a series of questions are developed and respondents are asked to agree or disagree with statements such as: 'I like to do all my car maintenance', 'Traditional home cooking is best', or 'I worry about environmental issues'. Thus scales are developed from a battery of questions, enabling a detailed picture of attitudes and lifestyle to be constructed. A fuller exposition of the market research procedures required to construct these segments can be found in most standard marketing research texts.

The results of a demographic analysis of whisky drinkers might show they are primarily: class – AB; sex – male; age – 45 plus. A lifestyle study of this category shows it is not homogeneous, and there are many other spirits consumed by the segment, but it could identify key attitudes of those who drink whisky rather than gin.

Benefit segmentation

The idea of segmentation on the basis of the benefit received is wholly consistent with the marketing concept. A motor car purchased as the main or only one for a family will provide a very different benefit from a company car supplied to a single employee, or a car purchased as a second car for a spouse. The benefits received are different and thus the actual car bought will be assessed by very different criteria. Using benefit segmentation these factors can be isolated and this information used to design appropriate products for each group.

In the USA there is a good example of a successful cost/focus strategy based on benefit segmentation, the US hotel chain, La Quinta, which offers a specific product for business travellers. La Quinta have above-average size rooms and good quality construction to ensure minimum external noise in any room. They provide a fast, efficient check-in/out system and certain business facilities required by travelling business people. They are conveniently located on major roads but do not offer restaurants or food service. There is always a 24-hour restaurant nearby if required, but not run by the hotel. La Quinta concentrate on providing a value package for a particular segment, mainly commercial travellers, who require facilities to do an evening's work after a day of meetings, but do not require on-site eating. A restaurant is expensive to run, and so why provide it if the benefit it provides is not required? A similarly focused development in the UK is exemplified by the no-frills, inexpensive tariff, overnight hotels being built by the Trust House group on sites close to their Little Chef restaurants.

Benefit segmentation depends on causal relationships rather than descriptive criteria of segment members. It is as applicable to industrial products or services as to consumer goods and services. In fact, some products span these categories. For instance, a portable calculator could be a consumer item for use by a student, or an industrial product if used in an accounts office. An electrical maintenance service can be offered to a commercial organisation or a private home. A service situation such as this provides the maximum flexibility in target marketing, since each contact between supplier (electrician in this case) and customer is distinct, and the delivery of the service is inseparable from the production. Hence the supplier can provide a precise service to match the benefit required.

In other situations the product is not offered to a discrete segment. An aeroplane could contain passengers who have:

(a) bought tickets at full price

(b) bought discount tickets in advance (APEX) or

(c) bought even cheaper standby tickets or 'bucket-shop' offers.

All groups receive the same prime benefit – air travel to their destination. But the problem regarding full-fare business travellers has been tackled by providing 'Club' or 'Business' class as distinct from 'economy' class. Nevertheless, some passengers buy full economy fares and others are bought at discounted prices. The difference in benefits, such as ability to change times of travel if you hold a full-fare ticket, compared to the possibility of not travelling at all with a standby, illustrate the wider range of benefits which must be explored for the same marketing offering.

Benefit segmentation was popularised many years ago by Russell Haley, who studied the toothpaste market in the USA. He identified four groups (see Table 8.2). From such an analysis, it can be seen how different brands can be designed to meet each of the benefit segments identified above.

Table 8.2 An example of benefit segmentation in the toothpaste market

Segment	Benefit required	Other characteristics
Sensory	Flavour + product appearance	Usually children
Social	Sound bright teeth	Outgoing and active, young (sometimes also smokers)
Worrier	Decay prevention	Heavy users, families
Independent	Low prices	Predominantly male, little loyalty, bought brand on offer

Behaviourial segmentation

A development of psychographic segmentation which concentrates on lifestyle and attitude is to study how people behave with respect to purchasing a particular product. The most obvious approach is to study usage rates and brand loyalty. Questions that can be answered include ones such as, 'How do heavy users differ from light users?' 'Can we isolate brand-loyal consumers?' If we can identify usage levels and link this to other segment criteria, then differentiated marketing strategies can be adopted for each group. Such groups could be:

- heavy users (say every day)
- medium users (maybe once a week)
- light users (say once a month)
- occasional users
- non-users:
  - never used brand
  - lapsed users of brand.

Inevitably a version of the Pareto effect will apply. Perhaps 80 per cent of a company's sales will go to 20 per cent of its customers (heavy users). The temptation is to concentrate on these people, as they provide the bulk of the profitable sales. In fact, they need a marketing mix that retains and reinforces their custom. This will probably be very different from the message to occasional or light users, who may either purchase competitors' products or perhaps not use the product category very often.

Other behaviouristic criteria include:

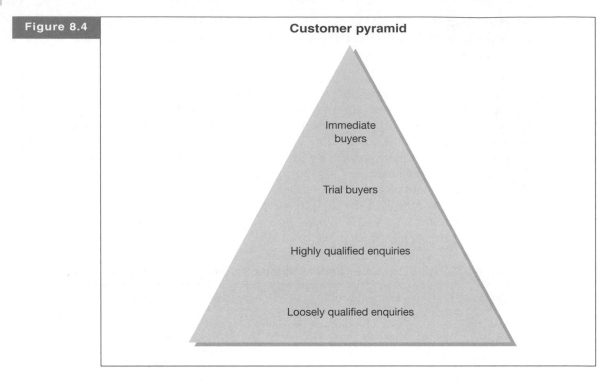

Figure 8.4

Customer pyramid

Immediate
buyers

Trial buyers

Highly qualified enquiries

Loosely qualified enquiries

- loyalty levels
- purchase occasion
- user status
- readiness status.

Purchase occasion is an obvious discriminator with buying behaviour, and therefore should be considered when carrying out a segmentation study.

The behaviour of purchasers buying, say, beer or lager will vary between orders in a public house, occasional purchasing from an off-licence, or regular purchasing as part of a shopping trip. The same is true for an ice cream purchased during the interval in a theatre. In this case the price charged is usually higher than the average retail price, whereas bulk purchase in a freezer centre with the same amount of money could perhaps buy a box of four individual ice creams.

A direct marketing organisation subdivides its mailing list by what they term the 'customer pyramid' (see Figure 8.4). The customer pyramid is one form of measure of readiness to buy, where each requires a different approach from the supplier. Another way of looking at readiness is the AIDA sequence, where customers need to progress from Awareness through Interest to Desire and Action. This progression could take time, and behaviour will be different for potential customers at different stages of this continuum.

TARGET MARKETING

Target marketing is the process of selecting one or more market segments and then developing a product and offer which is aimed specifically at those segments.

Once the target market segments have been identified, the key attitudes of those customers towards the product category should be determined. It is thus clearly essential to define market segments using appropriate criteria, as the very basis of target marketing is dependent on a link between the customers and the segment defined.

Many organisations are aware of how important this targeting can be, and are anxious to build a bond with potential future customers as early as possible. Marketing to children has become more important and increasingly children are having a greater say in purchasing decisions. Research has shown that the influence of children on their parents with regard to purchase decisions has grown by approximately 20 per cent per year for the last ten years, and in the USA this equates to about $200 billion per year. Companies, especially the larger multinationals, therefore see the targeting of children as being a lucrative business and to this end are happy to supply educational material liberally covered with company logos to schools. Shell International are particularly interested in responding to pupils appeals for project work, and some banks see the benefits as being more about community relations and the general social benefit.

Example	**Targeting via children**

Nivea distributed over 1.5 million leaflets to children that offered advice about skin care and protection from the sun during hot weather. The leaflets, although given to children, were actually intended to reach parents, the children being used as an effective communication channel. The company was regarded in this instance as being very philanthropic as they were seen as contributing a health message.

Target marketing provides the bridge between segment selection and product positioning (see Figure 8.5) which is discussed in Chapter 10. Target marketing is the opposite of undifferentiated marketing. This is where the same product is offered to the entire market. Undifferentiated offerings can succeed, but it is usually more effective to offer a variation of the product to suit each relevant market segment. This is especially true in global markets, where major differences of culture and history can also divide potential customers.

As an example, Mars, the chocolate company, feature only men in their promotional material in Saudi Arabia because of the Arab views on showing women. This is an example of differentiated marketing where the basic product is the same but the marketing mix is varied. Target marketing develops this further, including the total marketing mix with variations to the total product offered. Japanese car makers now claim they can personalise a car with regard to so many features that it is possible for every customer to buy a unique product. This could be the ultimate in personalisation, an extreme example of target marketing, and a long way from Henry Ford's bold claim of 'Any colour so long as it is black'. Using modern flexible manufacturing systems, an increasing number of suppliers will be able to define specific target market segments and interact with these ever more precisely.

Companies providing services have always been able to offer personalised products, since the provision of the service is inseparable from the production. Because of this, service products are inherently liable to variations depending upon the individual who actually provides the service. This is why service organisations such as banks, or the McDonald's fast-food restaurant chain, pay so much attention to supplying a standardised range of products. This approach helps to maintain consistency in the quality of service given, and to reduce the risk of the organisation's reputation being

Figure 8.5

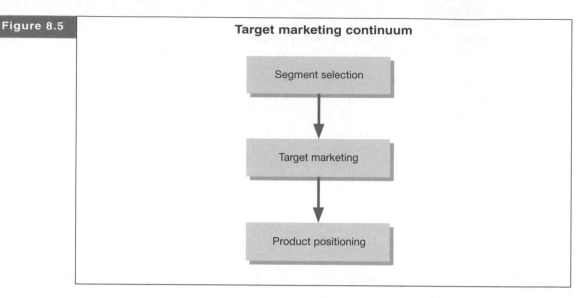

Target marketing continuum

destroyed by a single incidence of poor service, as may happen if this attracts the attention of the media.

On the Internet, target marketing is not quite so clear cut; one way of overcoming the problem is seen by some as undertaking 'viral marketing'. Viral marketing is a way of reaching the target market by allowing a small number of that audience to spread the word about a certain product or brand. This on the Internet is termed 'word of mouse'. The success of this method depends on having something which customers think is cool enough that they really want to tell friends about it: an example of this is given below.

Example   **Viral marketing**

In as little as three years, 40 million people now use hotmail, the free e-mailing system. The way it grew was by people receiving a hotmail from a friend, being impressed by how it worked and deciding to sign up as well.

There are many other cases where the Internet is becoming the communication media used to reach the target market, of course the benefits of the product are emphasied, and in the case of the website of <*www.doctors*.net.uk, doctors are offered high-value content on a closed portal site. The aim of the site is to improve the quality of medical provision in the UK. At the beginning of 2000 there were 23 000 users signed up but the aim is to have recruited 80 per cent of UK doctors (of which there are approximately 100 000) within two years. The <StudentDoctors.Net.UK> is the sister site to this and is targeting the medical students in the UK, who number in excess of 25 000. The site has the benefits of a free ISP, targeted content, email and e-commerce. The benefit to medical schools is that they would be able to make a cost saving of approximately £4 million per year by using the ISP and email facilities. The major advantage of the sites is that they can be personalised, and with regard to the qualified doctors site, this can be according to the users' speciality and seniority. A psychiatrist, for example will be presented with news, job adverts and databases relevant to the psychiatric field

Questions

1 *With the above web sites offering job adverts how will this affect medical journals that tradition-ally had pages dedicated to advertising job vacancies?*

2 *Will this web site reduce the cost to the NHS of advertising – it is estimated that advertising job vacancies cost around £30 million per annum.* Note: *the Overseas Labour Service demands that an advert be placed in more than one journal to prove that no British doctor can fill the post before it goes to someone from overseas.*

3 *Do you think that the pharmaceutical companies would like to be given access to advertise on the site?*

COMPETITIVE ADVANTAGE

The earlier chapters describe how customer needs and wants can change, making exist-ing products obsolete. For example, a competitor may launch a new product that a par-ticular group of customers find more attractive. Because of this, organisations must continually revise their products or services to keep them relevant to the changing needs of customers.

This involves returning to the fundamental marketing questions:

- Who are our existing and potential customers?
- What are their current and future needs?
- How do they judge value?
- When and where can these customers be reached?

Those responsible for products already on the market need to continually ask these basic questions. For example, after being successfully developed on the 'pile it high, sell it cheap' philosophy of its founder, Sir Jack Cohen, the operation of the Tesco supermarket chain was reviewed when Sir Ian McLaurin became chairman. He changed the 'product' by radically revising the groceries and provisions stocked. He discontinued 'Green Shield' stamps and changed the pricing policy. He closed down many older stores and developed new, larger sites with much improved layout. The advertising featured food quality, especially fresh fruit, vegetables and meats. The new Tesco was aimed specifically at the 25–35 age group, seen as a relatively affluent sector of food shoppers. This strategy has succeeded. Tesco is now generally con-sidered as a leader in its field with respect both to the quality of their products and the high market share achieved. This has resulted in a dramatic improvement in both sales and profits for the company. Developments such as these are going on all the time, and they show the importance of marketing that is sensitive to the external environment.

INTERNATIONAL SEGMENTATION

As global influences continue to exert themselves in marketing and in business gener-ally, it is not entirely surprising that recent times have seen a growing interest in the international practice and potential of segmentation. Early interest in applying seg-mentation internationally tended to take the form of crude classification of overseas markets, *en masse*, as target markets to enter: rated as more or less prosperous, more or less accessible, expansionist and so forth. Alternatively, writers on international marketing dispensed with the segmentation issue by inviting international marketers to segment their overseas markets through generally the same approach and variables as within their home markets (e.g. usage, demographics, geography). Such a form of differentiated international marketing became associated with a multimarket strategy within international marketing.

From the mid-1980s onwards, interest was to develop in the whole issue of global marketing and, as a strategy concern within this, global segmentation. One approach to global segmentation has been based on identifying similar segments across markets, Hassan and Blackwell (1994) review a number of other global approaches based on a variety of both conventional criteria (e.g. industrial structure, demographics) and less conventional, cluster-based analyses. An interesting intermediate form of international segmentation has developed in the guise of European segmentation. Of particular note, there has emerged a continuing stream of research studies on so-called 'Euro-consumers', usually based on geo-demographic variables.

CONCLUSION

The various alternative approaches to marketing segmentation have been described under separate headings above. There should be no doubt that these bases are dependent on each other. Effective segmentation could make use of all of the categories, and will usually require a combination of more than one type. By combining the way market segments are analysed it is possible to understand them in great detail, and also to follow changes in the dynamics of those segments. This provides the framework which can be used to answer the question, 'Who is our customer?' and also the basis for identifying potential customers and effectively targeting marketing effort with the objective of developing new loyal customers.

QUESTIONS

1 *How might you segment the market for (a) motor cars, (b) holidays and (c) mobile phones.*

2 *Segmentation leads on to differentiated marketing. How might a company avoid producing too many varieties of a product?*

3 *Do you think demographics alone are a useful way of segmenting the market for educational courses?*

4 *What variables should organisations include in a marketing database to aid segmentation studies?*

FURTHER READING

Ansted, M. (2000) 'Physician know thyself', *Revolution*, 16 February.

Cornish, P. (1990) 'Demographics: not standing still', *Admap*, December.

Dwek, R. (1988) 'Child's play', *Marketing Business*, September.

Haley, R. (1968) 'Benefit segmentation: a decision-orientated research tool', *Journal of Marketing*, 32, July.

Hassan, Salan S. and Blackwell, Roger D. (1994) *Global Marketing Perspectives and Cases*. Dryden Press, Chapters 4 and 5.

Lury, A. (1990) 'Demographics tell me nothing I want to know', *Admap*, December.

Mitchell, A. (1983) *The Nine American Lifestyles*. Macmillan.

Reed, D. (1996) 'Select few', *Marketing Week*, 19(1), March, pp. 53–6.

Wansell, G. (2000) 'The new adlads', *Weekend FT*, The business, 20 May.

Wilson, I. (1994) *Marketing Interfaces: Exploring the Marketing and Business Relationship*. Pitman.

CASE STUDY

Motor industry segmentation   FT

Survey – Germany: Drive towards consolidation continues apace

When Daimler-Benz's Jurgen Schrempp and Chrysler's Robert Eaton agreed merger plans in an Alpine cottage two years ago, the deal took the world by surprise. Observers questioned how the German luxury car-maker would integrate with the American mass car-producer Chrysler, pointing to vast differences in corporate cultures.

Two years later at a press conference in Frankfurt's historic opera house, Mr Schrempp, now chief of the US–German group, announced yet another big deal with Katsuhiko Kawasoe, chief executive of Mitsubishi, Japan's fourth-largest carmaker. This time few people were surprised and no one pointed to the difference in corporate cultures. DaimlerChrysler took just a 34 per cent stake in Mitsubishi and claims to have no plans for a fully-fledged merger.

The merger between Daimler-Benz and Chrysler and the deal between DaimlerChrysler and Mitsubishi are signs of the massive consolidation going on in the global car industry.

But instead of fully-fledged mergers that can be painful and abrasive, many international carmakers have started taking reciprocal stakes to underline close co-operation. This enables them to access each other's client bases and to offer customers a wider range of cars. German carmakers are keen participants in this trend. Shortly after DaimlerChrysler took the stake in Mitsubishi, Volkswagen bought 18.7 per cent of Swedish truck-maker Scania, giving it 34 per cent voting rights.

Analysts were pleased with the deal, although shortly after Robert Buchelhofer, a management board member, pointed out that Volkswagen still lacks presence in the North American truck market.

But while Germany's two largest car makers, DaimlerChrysler and Volkswagen, are joining the global frenzy to size up, offer bigger fleets and create close ties in all crucial regions, two other German companies are doing their own thing.

In a dramatic bid to retain its independence, BMW announced in mid-March 2000 that it would sell its troubled Rover car unit, based in the UK, that it bought for £800m in 1994. It said it had been forced to invest £3bn more since the initial purchase price and absorb endless losses at Rover – £750m last year. BMW will also sell Land Rover, its off-road vehicle subsidiary, to Ford, and produce the next generation Mini in Oxford. The decision to sell Rover signals that BMW is abandoning its dream of becoming a volume carmaker. Instead, it hopes to emerge as a premium car producer in every segment of the market in the next five years. The success of the BMW brand – largely dependent on its best-selling 3-series model – will be applied to a new smaller mid-sized car at the lower end of the market, referred to as the 2-series. It will aim to produce 200,000 of these a year. But compared with production numbers of more than 700,000 for comparable models produced by Volkswagen and Opel, the German General Motors unit, this is still a small figure. In a rapidly consolidating industry, with rising development costs, there is open scepticism whether a manufacturer of BMW's size, excluding Rover, can survive without a partner in the long term.

And yet Porsche, the luxury carmaker, has always felt comfortable in its niche. After flirting with bankruptcy in the early 1990s, it appointed a new chairman, Wendelin Wiedeking, who succeeded in turning the car manufacturer's fortunes around.

▶

Mr Wiedeking implemented radical changes, including a complete overhaul of the manufacturing process and flexible production to respond to cyclical fluctuations. He also sold Porsche's engineering expertise to other companies.

Porsche's ownership structure provides additional stability to the company. Two families hold all of Porsche's voting shares – the Porsches and the Piechs, led by Ferdinand Piech, chairman of Volkswagen. 'We are selling an emotion. Size has nothing to do with profitability,' Mr Wiedeking said recently. But neither the independent nor the merger strategy is failsafe. DaimlerChrysler's first-quarter results, for example, showed how vulnerable the US–German manuufacturer has become to fluctuations in the business cycle of its new partner.

Although the German part of the business won new customers in Europe, its US partner was forced to introduce big discounts to defend market share in the fiercely competitive North American business environment. This pushed the group's first-quarter profits 3 per cent lower.

On the other hand, DaimlerChrysler managed to make serious inroads into the smaller and mid-sized market segment, long considered Volkswagen's turf. After slow initial progress, hampered by safety concerns, both DaimlerChrysler's A-class – designed to rival the Golf – and its Smart compact car are becoming marketing successes, though commercial rewards may take longer to come through.

In the small-car market, DaimlerChrysler is also hoping to profit from its alliance with Mitsubishi. After buying out Volvo, Mitsubishi's former joint venture partner in Europe, Mitsubishi and DaimlerChrysler will each own half of Ned-Car, a passenger car plant in the Netherlands.

Daimler Chrysler's success in expanding downmarket has been remarkable in the fiercely competitive market for small and mid-sized cars in Europe. Determined to make their comebacks in the European car market, US companies such as General Motors and Ford have targeted Germany for a strong push.

Opel said last year it would sacrifice profit to boost market share. As a result it is posing a serious challenge to the prime position of the Volkswagen Golf. That would have been unthinkable a few years ago. But both Ford's German unit and Opel posted losses in 1999. In addition to general price pressures as a result of overcapacity in the car market, the introduction of the euro has forced European carmakers to become more transparent in their pricing structures.

Price differences of up to 30 per cent between European countries are being eroded and several carmakers are being investigated by the European Union's competition authorities. Motor manufacturers have also agreed to reduce carbon dioxide emissions from passenger cars and improve fuel economy by 2008. With pressures such as these, the drive towards consolidation is likely to continue.

Uta Harnischfeger.

Questions

1 *Given the segmentation detailed in the article, examine the various ways in which the car companies can segment the market.*

2 *Take a car manufacturer of your choice, and identify the target market for each car in its range.*

On-line shopping: how to get shoppers to click

FT

On-line grocers must focus on profitable customers and keep costs down, says Alan Mitchell

What is the best business model for on-line grocery shopping within Europe? Retailers contemplating this vast market face an acute dilemma.

On the one hand, there is enormous pent-up demand for home-delivered groceries. Results of a pan-European study of 6,000 shoppers in France, Germany, the Netherlands, Sweden, Switzerland and the UK suggest the service will be a bigger business in Europe than in the US, accounting for more than 10 per cent of all grocery sales within 10 years. On the other hand, the same research, by the Consumer Direct Europe group (whose members include retailers and consumer produce companies such as Interbrew, Kellogg, Le-Shop.ch, Markant Sudwest, Mars, Origin, Procter & Gamble, J Sainsbury and Wincor–Nixdorf), suggests that many customers signing up for the service are inherently unprofitable. As a result, few if any of Europe's 50-plus existing home shopping ventures will ever be commercially viable in their current form, it concludes.

In spite of the proliferation of on-line grocery shopping services such as Webvan, Home Grocer, Streamline and Peapod in the US, Europeans will turn in greater numbers to the new channel.

There are several reasons for this, says Gerhard Hausruckinger, a partner at Roland Berger strategy consultants, who is co-ordinating the Consumer Direct study: greater pressure on time (especially among working women); higher population densities; and the fact that European shoppers are generally more dissatisfied with grocery retailers than their US counterparts.

The British will lead the way with on-line shopping, he predicts, as they and the Germans are more disgruntled with traditional shopping methods than other Europeans. Also the French, who do a lot of top-up shopping at specialist stores, and the Dutch, who like to shop frequently by bicycle, are less attracted to on-line shopping than the British, who tend to shop once a week by car at a superstore, and the Germans, 16 per cent of whom bulk-buy groceries just once a month. The UK also has a relatively high proportion of 'time-starved' consumers – two working parents with children.

But while take-up rates differ, European service providers are similar in one key respect, warns Mr Hausruckinger: they have not come to terms with the economics of on-line grocery shopping, which are 'fundamentally different [from] traditional bricks-and-mortar retailing'. On-line experiments so far deploy a wide range of business models. Some, such as the US start-up Webvan and the UK's J Sainsbury, are investing large sums in sophisticated picking centres and distribution fleets. Others, such as Switzerland's Le-Shop.ch, rely on a third party for fulfilment, thereby reducing the need for large-scale infrastructure investment. Yet others, such as the UK's Tesco, use 'personal shoppers' in existing stores with a fleet of vans operating from each store.

Most charge customers for delivery of orders below a given value. Competitive pressures are driving these charges downwards. Yet, warns Consumer Direct member Kevin Otero, a Procter & Gamble associate director leading the company's response to the channel within Europe, 'there are some groups of consumers that the service does appeal to but [which] you cannot serve in an economically viable fashion. This is why we have seen so many failures in the on-line grocery shopping area.' The 'ideal' on-line shopper from the retailer's point of view is someone who shops regularly and places large orders. Regular orders help the retailer keep customer acquisition costs low. And the larger the order, the easier it is to absorb the cost of taking, assembling and delivering it.

However, across Europe only two consumer segments – parents who both work, and younger, ▶

upmarket IT-literate families – fit this ideal, and together they account for only one in six shoppers. According to the study group, only on-line shopping operators who specifically target these segments will flourish.

'Traditional "please come to us" broadcast advertising is a mistake,' argues Nancy Jain, a Roland Berger consultant working on the project. 'It has to be very specific, targeted marketing. And based on what we know about today's shopper, if you don't recruit at least 50 per cent women you've got a problem.'

Other success factors include internet-only ordering (other order-taking methods are too expensive); a broad range of products; and fulfilment systems operating from dedicated picking warehouses.

Competing operators' assessments of such factors differ, however. According to Mr Otero, on-line retailers can meet most customers' needs with between 30 and 50 percent of a typical superstore's product range. Also, dedicated warehouses can pick much more efficiently from such a reduced range and minimise the out-of-stocks that can plague in-store pick models and lead to unacceptably high levels of customer complaints.

Yet some operators are sticking with the store-based picking model. Tesco admits that dedicated picking warehouses assemble shopping baskets more efficiently, but says they are more expensive overall. Warehouses serve broader geographical areas than individual stores and delivery vans have to travel further. And offering a reduced range of products will in the long term reduce customer choice, it says. Until a critical mass of demand is reached, 'our model comes out the best,' it insists.

Once the operational, marketing and cultural hurdles of the on-line grocery business are cleared the financial rewards of success could be high. Typically, grocery shoppers give only 35–40 per cent of their household's total grocery spend to 'the main shop'. But once they go on-line, that proportion can double.

The downside for traditional bricks-and-mortar retailers is that as soon as home shopping reaches critical mass it could siphon the most profitable big-spending customers out of their stores – to such a degree that auditors may start questioning traditional property-based retailers' depreciation policies, warns Mr Hausruckinger. 'In the interests of their shareholders, traditional operators will have to view their target shoppers as their core assets, rather than their store locations.'

Source: Financial Times, 15 March 2000. (Copyright © The Financial Times Limited.)

Questions

1 *Given the segmentation and targeting policies of the companies that offer on-line shopping, how do you envisage the future unfolding for them?*

2 *How do you think that the on-line shopping policies of major UK stores could be improved?*

Marketing information

An advertiser (marketer) who ignores marketing research is as guilty as a general who ignores the decodes of enemy signals.

David Ogilvy

INTRODUCTION

The objectives of this chapter are to define marketing information, show how it can be relevant to decisions throughout an organisation, and in particular to those functions which are specifically concerned with marketing. It will cover 'information' in its widest sense and the value of a marketing information system.

The overriding theme in this book, and every book on the subject of marketing, is that successful organisations meet the needs of their customers. It follows that managers are more likely to make good (rather than bad) marketing decisions if they understand the effect these decisions are likely to have on their customers: they can do this only if they understand who their customers are, the needs of these customers, and how these customers might respond to different marketing activities.

The importance of asking the question, 'who are our customers?' has been mentioned in earlier chapters. Generally, it is an easy question to ask, but a difficult one to answer with any degree of precision. For example, a manufacturer of small cars might say that its customers are 'mostly young people who can only afford a small car'. This may be true, but is not very helpful in the marketing context. To be useful such information needs to classify these customers in more definite terms. This could be with regard to their occupation, the type of newspapers/magazines they read or any of the other segmentation variables discussed in Chapter 8. It would also be useful to know how large these groups are, what proportion of the group are existing customers, and what proportion are buying competitive products.

This is likely to be very important especially if different strategies are needed for existing customers who already own or use your product, and potential customers, who have yet to buy your product. Clearly the more we know about our existing and potential customers and how they feel about the products and services they buy, the better our marketing decisions will be.

THE NATURE OF ORGANISATIONAL INFORMATION

Before considering marketing information specifically it is useful to discuss organisational information generally and to establish marketing information as a part of it. This involves appreciating that there are two distinct categories and three different types of organisational information. The two categories are labelled *tangible* and *intangible* and the three types are identified as *direct operational*, *indirect operational* and *marketing*.

Tangible and intangible organisational information

Evidence of tangible information can be seen throughout all types of organisation stored in filing cabinets, desk drawers, cardboard boxes in archives and on computer files. It is often classified by business function. Hence there will be files containing accounting information, personnel information, operational/production information, design information, marketing research studies and so on. It is classified as 'tangible information' as it can be seen and moved or downloaded from electronic files.

The tangible information within most organisations is impressive in terms of the space it occupies. However, this is because most of it is the stored record of past activities which has to be kept to comply with legal and other regulations which apply to all organisations. Usually only a small proportion of the stored tangible information is actually needed for the regular day-to-day activities of the organisation. Much of it is historical business records, but it will probably also include a statement of the procedures a company needs in order to operate effectively. By establishing a learning culture, organisations are able to benefit from the experience gained through past successes and avoid repeating past mistakes, both operational and marketing.

There is also an entirely different type of information which cannot be separated from the individuals who use it. This is because it involves their individual skills, the approach these individuals have to their work and the relationships between them. Since such information cannot be seen or moved it is called 'intangible information'. Whilst intangible information is a feature of all organisations, its importance varies between organisations and between functional departments within organisations. A lot of marketing 'know-how' is intangible, in particular there is the instinctive 'feel' a successful marketing manager has for the market in which he or she operates. However few successful marketers rely on intangible sources, there is always a role for marketing research and for re-visiting relevant past reports in order to take better marketing decisions.

TYPES OF ORGANISATIONAL INFORMATION

It is not only important to appreciate the difference between tangible and intangible information, it is also essential to appreciate the fundamentally different characteristics of the three different types of organisational information.

Direct operational information

Direct operational information is the information or knowledge an organisation needs to provide a service or manufacture a product. For example, it would be essential for a business set-up who trade over the Internet to have staff with programming skills and a knowledge of computing. This is the direct operational information for a dotcom company. Essentially, it would be the personal knowledge and skills of the staff who work for the company so would be intangible direct operational information. The company is likely to want to maintain records of the customers who contact it and the items bought and prices paid. This will probably involve setting up a database that can be used for accounting and stock control purposes. This is an example of tangible direct operational information. Of course such a database can also provide much useful marketing information, but very often there is a tension between the operational needs of a business and the information required for the planning of future marketing.

For a manufacturing organisation such as a major car manufacturer there are clearly more examples of tangible direct operational information than there is for a dotcom company. The type of intangible direct operational information will also be very different. There are nevertheless two common characteristics that are important in all cases:

- First, both tangible and intangible direct operational information is very specific to the service or product being offered.
- Second, direct operation information has to be complete even though it may be tangible, intangible or a combination of both.

For example a dotcom company would not be able to offer a complete service if, for instance, none of its staff had any knowledge of designing a website. The situation is even worse for a car manufacturer as in the following example.

Example

To assemble a motor car requires people who have knowledge of design, sources for the supply of components, and the appropriate information and skill to manufacture a product. In the case of a car it must be remembered that it has many thousands of components with especially complex mechanical and electrical features. The knowledge of these issues are part of the direct operational information that is critical to the efficient running of a car assembly plant. The scope of the operational information required is obviously far greater than that required for an Internet retailer. Clearly if any aspect of this information is missing the organisation would not be able to produce any cars. It is also necessary to employ people who understand such indirect operational issues as quality control and cost accountancy.

There is no doubting the importance of operational information, but it does nothing to ensure that any of the cars are sold after they are produced, therefore operational information is only part of what is needed for the company to be profitable. Commercial success requires quite different information to ensure that the *right* products are built, at the *right* time, and are the ones that can be sold at the *right* price. As Lee Laccoca, former boss of Chrysler said, when describing the company at the time he took charge: 'The manufacturing guys would build cars without even checking with the sales guys. They just built them, stuck them in the yard and hoped somebody would take them out of there. We ended up with huge inventory and a financial nightmare.'

Indirect operational information

Being effective as an organisation involves more than simply manufacturing a product or providing a service. Most physical items manufactured have to be packed and shipped to the customer who ordered them. Furthermore, information is required not only to deliver these items but also to keep track of them. Thus, in addition to actually manufacturing, an organisation has to offer a service and produce delivery notes and invoices. Similar issues involve companies that are solely service providers. Information, again usually in the form of routines and procedures, is also needed to process orders received from customers, to place orders with suppliers, pay accounts, pay wages, meet the requirements for dealing with Value Added Tax (VAT), and similar tasks. There could be a requirement to produce monthly statements for each customer, and there is generally a need to measure the financial standing of the supply organisation. This is just as essential as the direct operational information but is essentially common to all businesses. For this reason it is classified as indirect operational information.

Like direct operational information it can be either tangible or intangible and has to be complete for the organisation to function. Hence if for some reason the organisation did not have the information needed to determine the deductions which need to be made from employees' wages to cover income tax and National Insurance contributions its future would quickly be threatened. Unlike direct operational information, indirect operational information is not specific to the product or service being offered. Thus a wages clerk who knows how to calculate tax and National Insurance contributions could work for either a dotcom company or a large car manufacturer.

MARKETING INFORMATION

In addition to direct and indirect operational information, organisations need a third type of information. This is the information which ensures the organisation actually produces and promotes products or services which are required by sufficient customers (or clients) to make the organisation viable. This is called marketing information. This can be defined as any information relevant to, or that affects, the *profitable exchange of a product/service between an organisation and its customers*. It includes information on the market environment; customers and potential customers; direct and indirect competitors; the features required in a 'total product offering'; distributors; and all aspects of promotion.

For a manufacturer of *street clothes* the essential marketing information required to trade successfully might include a knowledge of customers' fashion trends, forecasts of future demand and perhaps information about other manufacturers who could be considered competitors. Similar marketing information might also be required by a new internet retailer specialising in street clothes. However the retailer would use the information in a slightly different way. It would want to guide its merchandising and promotions policy, whereas the manufacturer would need the information to ensure it was manufacturing the *right* products.

There is an essential difference between operational information and marketing information. In order to accomplish the tasks for which an organisation exists it must have *"All"* of the direct and indirect operational information required. This is not the case with marketing information. Indeed all organisations have to operate with incomplete marketing information, although that information is actually required in order to make decisions regarding future activities in dynamic markets. What is important is that an organisation has *relevant* marketing information as this is essential for it to continue to meet the needs of its customers.

Example

If the company manufacturing street fashion wear received an enquiry from overseas asking them to quote for supplying 300 jackets in mixed sizes, and *standard* colour, they may well quote their usual price. If, when the order is received, it is clear that the required mix of sizes in this *new* market is different from that in the home market, the lack of this information about the norms in a different market place could have resulted in a bad marketing decision being made. The required mix of sizes for the overseas market is a form of marketing information.

For production the problem is different. If an order for jackets is accepted without having patterns for some of the required sizes, they cannot be produced immediately. For production this information is essential.

Exercise

> It was suggested in Chapter 1 that marketing could be seen as providing the right product, in the right place, at the right price and at the right time. Can you suggest what marketing information might be required to enable a dotcom fashion retailer to achieve this?

Like other types of organisational information, marketing information can be either tangible or intangible. In many organisations there is little evidence of tangible marketing information. Furthermore, unlike tangible operational information, tangible marketing information is often dispersed within an organisation. Departments such as sales, design or advertising may have formal files. In addition, many managers are likely to have their own file labelled 'Competition', containing catalogues collected at an exhibition or other similar event.

Marketing information is also extremely *time-dependent* – it is useful only when it is relevant and current but it can easily go out-of-date as markets evolve. Therefore it is often discarded when it is out of date since there is no legal requirement to store it. This can make it extremely difficult or even impossible to collate the information needed to show, for instance, long-term trends in market preferences.

Marketing as a business activity has developed as a result of recognising that the success of an organisation depends upon creating and retaining customers. In the short term these decisions are likely to be concerned with meeting the needs of future customers efficiently. In the longer term they are likely to focus more on the organisation's need to respond to the ever-changing expectations of the users of its products and/or services.

Example

The problems suffered by Marks & Spencer as it attempts to re-invent itself have been analysed in great depth. The company that is now facing the challenges of the 21st century is very different from the one that faltered in the last few years of the 1990s. There have been small, yet visible initiatives such as the acceptance of credit cards, but the real changes have still to appear. In the glory years for M&S, marketing of any sort was considered rather alien to the company. It exhibited 'well-produced' merchandise from UK manufacturers and backed up the produce with a no-quibble 'returns' policy that was the envy of many competitors. This formula worked as long as the market did not move too far away. The problem was that M&S was tightly controlled from its offices in Baker Street, London and it did not gather relevant marketing information from its customers. Store managers had virtually no say in the range of products stocked in their branches even though they were close to the customers and should have been able to report on the changing trends.

The problem was that these customers just deserted in large numbers and M&S did not realise until sales levels were well below the budgeted level. Profits fell by 53% in 1999!

This has now been changed. A new management team has been recruited, and the company has been re-organised into business units with executives responsible for the profitability of their own unit. The company is considering new products, even mobile phones. It is experimenting with new layouts for stores, and it is attempting to update its image through a rebranding exercise.

It is too early to comment on the success or failure of the changes. Some have been hasty responses to a critical situation. The best use of marketing information relies on continuous tracking of the market and evolutionary changes taking place as and when required. Big changes, especially ones that are rather hurried, can be very risky but if, like M&S, the impetus for change comes from a crisis then it is obvious that revolutionary actions must be taken.

The key marketing question is whether M&S can regain its position offering a broad range of merchandise, and appealing to all ages. There are a number of more focused competitors such as Gap: is there also room for a new M&S?

On another level the term 'getting close to the customer' can be a very sophisticated operation. Organisations in direct contact with their customers such as many 'business-to-business' (B2B) companies and direct retail operators have gained considerable competitive advantage by developing comprehensive customer databases. These are used to improve their understanding of consumer needs, and to support the development and marketing of new products. The mail order company Grattan gathers information on the personal characteristics and buying patterns of customers, as well as more general information on non-customers. They use this information to select "prospects" for sample mailings and to analyse the response and to identify the specific characteristics of those who purchased. They then use the analysis to identify other customers with similar characteristics for a more general and usually very successful direct marketing offer.

Exercise	Consider an enterprise with which you are familiar and itemise: (a) the operational knowledge likely to be necessary to produce the product or provide the service, and (b) the marketing information necessary to implement this production knowledge successfully.

Example	As a result of market analysis, the marketing department of a major car manufacturer found that they were selling a lower proportion of 4-door cars, and therefore a higher proportion of 2 or 3-door cars, than their competition. Should they wish to investigate this further, they would need to look at the sales of this type of vehicle in terms of: the level of trim, e.g. L, GL, GTi, and so on; the size of engine; the type of gearbox; and even perhaps by colour. They might also want to know whether there were any regional variations in demand.
	Although it might be expected that production would have records from which such information could be easily obtained, in practice their records may not show the detail required. For production purposes the information would be required in a different form. It could well show that of every 100 vehicles built, 50 have 1300cc engines, 30 have 1600cc engines and 20 have 1800cc engines, and 50 have 2 doors, 30 have 4 doors and 20 are estates with 5 doors. From these components any combination of vehicle could be built and any minor variations in demand would be allowed for by adjusting the next batch accordingly. There is no reason why any records should be kept of how many 4-door cars have 1600cc engines against either of the alternatives. Nor is there any reason for knowing whether the overall mix changes according to geographic region, or season or other factor. Thus, obtaining the information wanted by the marketing department would involve either having a separate system designed specifically to provide this information or analysing individual customer orders, invoices or shipping notes, which would inevitably be a tedious and error-prone process.

Indeed, it is because such data is often effectively unobtainable that many marketing decisions have to be made without adequate information or based on incorrect assumptions. For instance, it may be logical to assume that since the estate version of the vehicle looks larger than any of the other models, most estates sold would have the larger engines. Equally, this could be entirely wrong since buyers of the estate model might consider it a utility vehicle and so rate its performance as relatively unimportant.

This example illustrates another important aspect of marketing information: its sheer *volume*. Most internal marketing information involves the collation of data from production or finance departments. This data must be measured against the tests of currency and relevance to the marketing decision being made. It is also very important that the data can be analysed in a way that is useful when making marketing decisions.

Marketing as a function can be critically dependent on information generated within the other functional areas within the organisation. Karmarkar (1996) develops a persuasive case for marketing information and research activities to be more closely integrated with parallel efforts in operations management, in the interests of cross-functional co-ordination and the analysis necessary for developing business strategy. Similarly, Ratnatunga, Hooley and Pike (1992) review the practice of information integration between the marketing and finance functions, and the degree to which information exchange is affected by organisational factors. At a more strategic level, Bondro and Davis (1996) argue that the marketing function should seek to improve its own performance, and augment its strategic role through a more active and deliberate involvement in the organisation's management information system.

RAW DATA AND INFORMATION

It is important to distinguish between *data*, the facts collected about a situation, and *information* that is based on an analysis of that data. Most systems set out to capture data but, taken on its own, this is just the raw material for analysis. The gathering of required data is an essential first step but it must then be evaluated and combined with other data in order to create the marketing information that can be used for making marketing decisions. The data comprises the *facts* and other collected details from which things can be deduced, whereas the marketing information is the synthesis of that raw data. A fact is a measurement of anything that actually exists or has existed. An example of a fact is that our company sold 4,000 units last month (tangible fact), or 8 out of 10 cat owners say that their cats prefer Whiskas Cat Food (intangible).

Much marketing information will comprise issues other than basic facts because, for marketing decisions, it is likely that a company could need information on:

- what people know, true or false (*knowledge*)
- how customers perceive our product/service and other relevant attitudes or beliefs (*opinions*)
- what consumers intend to do, and the strength of those *intentions* and
- why people behave as they do (*motives*).

SOURCES OF MARKETING INFORMATION

The information an organisation has about its market comes to it in a variety of ways, both formally and informally. All organisations have a fund of '*internal*' knowledge available both from the people who work for it and in the records accumulated over many years. For example, any member of staff when reading through a technical magazine could notice an article about developments at a competitor's plant. Maybe this is to allow for a new product or to improve efficiency. If this information is passed to the appropriate department within the organisation it could be very useful. Although there can be a problem of an excess of such information, the most important issue is that all employees should know where to send such information. It would then be the responsibility of that department, usually marketing, to decide what to keep, what to check out properly, and what to ignore.

Example	**A failure to inform**

A supplier of electrical components had noticed a sudden drop in the sales of one product. The marketing manager decided that he should consider reducing the price or increase the promotional activity to revive the line. He was supported in this by the sales director who was concerned by the effect the loss of sales was having on the commission earned by the sales team. Before deciding which action to take, the marketing manager decided to phone up a major customer to see if he could get any clue as to the reason for the lower sales. He was surprised by the customer telling him that a competitor had introduced a product of higher quality yet lower price some three months earlier. No one in the sales team had thought to report this, and the marketing manager admitted that for more than two months he had been working on the company's long-term plan so had not been out meeting customers. Why had the marketing manager not been informed about the launch of such a significant competitive product? A number of reasons were suggested by members of the sales force, such as:

'I'm already working 12 hours a day trying to make a decent salary, I don't have time to pass on every bit of gossip.'

'I used to tell my boss everything, but the information was just ignored. My target was increased and I got no thanks for ringing in with information.'

'I phoned my Area Sales Manager, but he wasn't in so I left a message with his wife. Maybe she forgot to tell him.'

'I thought the Head Office always knew these things. That is the impression they give when you meet them.'

They obviously all got it wrong, and these comments show the company also has other problems. The serious one for the Marketing Department is the failure to have a proper system for capturing relevant information, and to reward those supplying it. A 'thank you' is usually sufficient – it does not have to be a financial incentive.

No organisation has complete knowledge about its markets, customers or competitors. At best it is like a mosaic or jigsaw, where the picture can still be clear, even though a large number of pieces are missing. It is quite common for past information to be merged with more recent input in a form of *marketing intelligence system*. This can then be interrogated whenever any future marketing initiative is being considered. Sometimes it would be helpful to acquire more information to make the picture clearer. However, information is often expensive so is only worth acquiring if it is likely to improve future marketing decisions. It must also be remembered that marketing information does not replace decision taking – it is at best an aid to help take better decisions. Therefore the purpose and value of information gathering must always be set against the cost of obtaining and processing that information.

Generally, the knowledge provided by marketing information changes over time. Thus, returning to our analogy of a mosaic, the colours of some of the pieces will fade over time. To revive the pattern, these pieces must be replaced as new ones become available. This is why it is important to update any marketing intelligence system (see end of chapter) on a regular basis. When information is used for marketing, it must be current: out-of-date information is likely to result in bad decisions. Again, like the pieces used to make a mosaic, marketing information has to be obtained from different sources and whenever possible alternative sources should be used to improve the overall reliability of the information collected. It is very easy to download masses of data from a search on the world wide web (www), and this is becoming increasingly common. However this can lead to disaster if insufficient attention is paid to the *quality* of such data.

Sources of marketing data

Useful marketing information can be obtained from any of the following sources:

- **Undirected observation**. Informal, unstructured collection of information from any source. It includes casual reading of magazines and newspapers, meetings with contacts, TV reports and many other chance events.
- **Conditioned viewing.** Formal searching but sometimes with unstructured collection whereby a comprehensive search is made covering a specified range of publications. This can be done using an on-line database or a CD-ROM, maybe searching for some key word. It could involve setting up a specific department to scan publications and extract interesting articles to circulate within the marketing management team.
- **Informal searching**. A structured way of capturing vital information, such as a system of receiving sales force reports. The information might present itself in an informal way but the system to ensure it reaches the relevant managers is structured.
- **Formal searching**. This utilises formalised marketing research techniques. It is a specific study undertaken to fill in some of the gaps in the mosaic of information available. It involves the collation, analysis and presentation of appropriate, available and required data.

Research can be defined as the use of investigative techniques to discover non-trivial facts and insights that lead to an *extension of knowledge*.

There are well-established techniques for undertaking marketing research as a formal business activity and these are described in many specialist texts. Some of the more common are discussed in Chapter 21 and Appendices 4 and 5 at the end of this book.

QUALITY OF DATA AND INFORMATION

It will already be apparent that information must be accurate and up to date (current), but there are other criteria that are equally important when considering the quality of data. The analogy of a mosaic can still be applied and while the mosaic is unlikely to be complete, a certain number of critical pieces are essential for the picture to be seen. Similarly it is essential to have the specific data needed to support any marketing decision. This means the information must be directly relevant, which is not always as easy as it sounds. For instance, government statistics often cover a large category of products, but if the decision relates only to one small specific subsegment it may not be possible to separate this accurately from the total data, which could be misleading or irrelevant. It is essential that all data used is both valid and reliable.

Reliability is associated with data being consistent although coming from a number of independent sources or repeated measurements. When either different sources or measurements disagree, which often happens, the differences need to be evaluated to establish which information source should be used.

Validity is often an issue where data is obtained using a small sample in a formal market research survey. It refers to the extent to which the survey findings are in line with the research problem or hypothesis. Usually it is a measure of whether the findings can be extended to the whole population or the market being considered. This involves using appropriate statistical theory to establish confidence levels and is covered in most standard marketing research texts.

While there is no direct link between good decisions and good quality data, there is a real risk of poor decisions being taken if the information fails to be:

- reliable (accurate)
- valid
- relevant
- sufficient
- current (up-to-date).

There has been a massive increase in the data available to marketers in the last few years. Access to data stored on the world wide web is relatively easy when utilising one of the many available search engines (e.g. <copernic.com>); the Internet has changed data collection forever. However, it is as well to post a warning regarding the ease of collection and the apparent quality of data available:

- First there is a problem of volume, the huge volume of data available. This can lead to what one commentator called *'paralysis by analysis'*, or maybe the quantity available could just overwhelm the recipients so that no analysis takes place.
- Second there is often no way of checking on the original sources for much of the data. It is possible that the some of the data is not very reliable. The real problem is that there is no way of knowing because little is known about the methods by which such data was *obtained before it was posted on the Net*.

It is very easy to be impressed by the *quantity* of data, but good marketing decisions rely on the *quality* of the information obtained as a result of a data search. Good analysts know when to stop searching and to start trying to understand the impact of any issues discovered. They are then able to produce *quality* information that will, hopefully, lead on to quality marketing decisions.

CATEGORIES OF MARKETING INFORMATION

It is useful to classify marketing information in terms of the five main categories mentioned earlier. These, respectively, relate to:

1 The environment and market in which the product or service is produced, provided, supplied and used (termed the wider environment (level 4) in Chapter 3). This includes the technological environment.
2 The target customers, clients, or users served by an organisation (and other key stakeholders).
3 Competitor information (see Chapter 4).
4 The product or service being provided.
5 How that product/service is communicated to the target customers.

The marketing environment

In Chapter 3 the various aspects of the marketing environment have been identified and discussed. Often, events which are likely to have an impact on an enterprise are seen, in the first instance, within the wider marketing or macroenvironment which comprises social, cultural, technological, economic, political and legal aspects.

Example	Reports forecasting the macroenvironment are regularly published, both for individual countries and for groups of countries such as the members of European Union. While many are expensive, often an adequate summary can be obtained from a library or a report in the business or trade press. Many are also available through computerised business data services such as McCarthy's in the UK. These commercial reports are a good way of monitoring the wider environment but they should always be used with caution as their conclusions often appear to disagree significantly. Because of this it is important to understand the origin of any report used, and of the data used. If possible try to compare the conclusions from a number of different sources and note the following warnings:

- Many forecasts cover entire countries or industries and are not necessarily specific to the smaller sector or industry you may be studying.
- Forecasts are based on historical data and specific assumptions, so they can have a wide margin for error.
- Forecasts that conflict with 'common sense' should be carefully reviewed.
- Forecasts will always be wrong.

The last warning in the example above is one of the 'fundamental laws' suggested by Flores and Whymark (1985) who also advise that:

We should not forecast things that don't need to be forecast.

and

The average of several simple methods often works best.

There are many specialist textbooks that cover the analysis of the marketing environment. Some are basic economics texts, but more specialist marketing references can be found in Palmer and Worthington (1992).

Over the last fifteen years, the use of *scenarios* has become an accepted method of evaluating the macroenvironment. A scenario is a qualitative description of the future and the approach involves developing a range of different scenarios each based on defined assumptions. Usually these include a 'most-likely' scenario and a 'worst-case' scenario. The use of scenarios was developed by the Royal Dutch Shell Company after the dramatic oil price movements in 1978. This technique has helped Shell and other organisations to study the likely effect of future plans in various different future situations.

Customer information

Customer information is central to the concept of marketing. Many existing businesses, especially those providing services, have direct contact with the people who use their service. For instance, hairdressers can judge from this direct contact whether their clientele is getting older or younger, as well as more prosperous or less prosperous. By consciously recognising such trends, hairdressers can maintain the future of their businesses either by ensuring that the service offered is changed to match the changing needs of the clientele or to attract another category of clientele. Customer information obtained through direct contact, although intangible, is likely to be the best available.

The management of larger organisations, even those who essentially provide services such as banks, can easily lose direct contact with their customers. To avoid this, managers need adequate tangible marketing information such as up-to-date customer satisfaction surveys. Without it, they will have no option but to make decisions based on the information, perhaps now out of date, they gained prior to becoming managers. The problem is even worse for the manufacturers of products. Very often these are sold through wholesale and retail intermediaries which means that managers could be making decisions without having any contact with their final customers and users.

Customer information can be either qualitative or quantitative. Qualitative information might involve opinions or reasons for a particular action. This can be as useful in the context of marketing decisions as quantitative facts such as that 8 out of 10 people buy a particular brand of cat food.

Information can be obtained as a one-off (ad hoc) study. It can also be tracked over a period of time, perhaps using a consumer panel to measure changes in behaviour.

An interesting and radical new approach to customer information and analysis, *virtual shopping*, has become available through ongoing development in computer modelling. Though methodologies can vary, a typical virtual shopping (or 'virtual store') experiment might involve having target consumers track their way, on screen, through a virtual shopping environment, or floor area, select products to buy, examine displays, record levels of interest and so forth. The virtual approach has obvious value in product development and testing settings. Research specialists and agencies, especially in the USA, are developing more comprehensive and integrated programmes (e.g. wish advertising exposure), and more dedicated applications such as for car showrooms and travel agencies. The results of two US validation studies on virtual shopping are discussed in detail in an informative article in the *Harvard Business Review* (March–April 1996).

At a more theoretical level, the whole field of computer modelling in marketing, and the related topic of market-based expert systems, is comprehensively covered within the authoritative text produced by Moutinho et al. (1996).

Competitor information

It is important to appreciate that the success of a product is dependent as much upon the alternatives available to a potential customer as upon the product itself. It is the appreciation of these alternatives, and the impact that they are likely to have on the acceptability of a product/service to the potential customer, which often requires specific marketing information.

Most successful organisations will continually update a comparative profile of all their direct competitors. This will include what those competitors are doing, what products they are offering, as well as when, why and how they are performing and any other relevant information. It will often include some form of *SWOT analysis* that can highlight the strengths and weaknesses of those competitors.

It should again be stressed that marketing is related to the future activities of an organisation and therefore it is important to develop a feel for what competitors are likely to do in the future. In his book *Managing for Marketing Excellence*, Ian Chaston suggests that:

> Even in their analysis of existing competition, some marketers make insufficient use of information sources outside of standard market research studies. Marketeers could learn a valuable lesson from the financial community on the benefits of studying annual accounts and shareholder reports as a basis for appraising the capabilities of companies.
>
> Financial analysts also exploit other sources of information to gain a more complete picture of the future prospects for a company. These include the perspectives of supplier/intermediaries,

publicity releases, announcement of capital investment programmes and recruitment advertising programmes. Given such a range of information it should be a danger signal to management if the marketing department only presents conclusions based on market share and customer surveys.

There have always been some highly questionable methods of obtaining information on competitors. Many years ago there was an interesting article under the heading 'How to snoop on your competitors' (*Fortune*, 14 May 1984) that provided a real insight into the lengths to which some organisations go to get such data. Whether or not you approve of such practices they do go on, and they affect the whole image of marketing research. The article less controversially also suggests that:

> Competitive intelligence is a bits and pieces business ... much information you will find is inaccurate, irrelevant or stale and you must search hard to find golden nuggets. But, once you have 80% of the puzzle, you see things you didn't see when you had 20%.

Product/services information

Marketing information on products or services cannot be isolated from customers or competitors. Specifications can be compared but it is the degree to which an offering matches the future needs/wants of the customers which is of major importance to a marketer. This can be considered under the headings of acceptability, affordability, and availability.

Acceptability

Whilst it may be necessary to conduct a new product research study using blind (unbranded) tests it is essential that as far as possible the tests are applicable to the branded product to which the actual marketing decisions apply. Existing products can, of course, be assessed in direct comparative situations to evaluate how a product or service offering is perceived alongside competitive offerings with respect, for instance, to its acceptability in a specific situation. Indirect competition tends to be much more difficult to forecast. But very often it is not actually recognised until identified as a result of research initiated, for instance, as a result of significantly reduced sales of a product or group of products.

The development of the Sony Walkman as a new product is an interesting example of a product which, at least for a time, affected the market for some apparently unrelated products. One example was the market for good quality pens. Both Walkmans and quality pens were similarly priced gift items for young people and were therefore competitors in the gift market. This is referred to, in Chapter 5, as *indirect competition*.

Exercise	Consider what impact the trend from hot to cold beverages is likely to have in the future. Are there any associated products that are likely to be affected by these changes?

Affordability

Within this category of study will come the price of an offering. The determination of what a supplier can charge for a product depends on many external variables. Issues regarding value require a study of the actual prices charged for comparative products. This is an area where the facts can be obtained quite easily in consumer markets although it is sometimes more difficult to get information in some industrial markets.

In some markets there is an indirect distribution channel so products are first sold to an intermediary who then resells to the final consumer. Data about the differences between retail prices charged to final consumers and the trade prices will lead to important information about distributors' margins.

Price has many associations with quality, image, and value-for-money. Price as evaluated by a customer is at the heart of any consideration of affordability and it is therefore critical to establish a feel for the range of possibility for price. However, price is a very difficult topic to research in situations when customers are not actually buying a product. Thus the establishment of price elasticity, that is how many customers will buy at each different price point, is often impossible because the data relies on customer's stated intentions and not on the *actual behaviour* in a competitive market place.

Availability

Channels of distribution are described in Chapter 13. Since some products go through several intermediaries on their way to the final consumer, it is obviously important to learn as much as possible about the various intermediaries. Each is a customer of a supply organisation and has a key role in the promotion of products en route to the final consumers.

Decisions on distribution channels are critical to success and, once set up, require careful monitoring. This area of trade research is often carried out as part of a continuous study by major research agencies such as the A. C. Neilsen organisation.

In terms of physical distribution across the entire supply chain, Wheatley (1996) illustrates the increasing role of sophisticated IT-based logistics systems and software solutions. These utilise technical developments such as those associated with barcoding, electronic point-of-sale (EPOS) and electronic data interchange (EDI). In short, growing competition, on the demand side, and technology developments, on the supply side, have encouraged manufacturers to focus on the competitive advantage which can be gained through improved delivery, response and service levels, whilst maintaining cost, productivity and quality targets.

The biggest change in terms of reaching customers in the 21st century is the Internet. Many companies are trying to decide the advantages of using this new channel. Setting up a website is not difficult but marketing managers must monitor the advantages and disadvantages of such a channel both with respect to their own company and for competitors. As technology allows for better interactions between suppliers and customers, with more reactive user friendly sites being developed, basic facts are continually being revised and customer reactions monitored to ensure any information is really up-to-date.

Advertising and promotional information

The origins of marketing research are closely linked with those of advertising research. Perhaps because so much money is spent on consumer advertising this is still a key area of study. Most media providers have extensive information on readers/viewers. This allows careful targeting of marketing communications to a chosen segment. The information is usually made available to all potential advertisers. The effectiveness of advertisements is also studied in detail with most advertising agencies having good in-house research departments.

The value of good research when studying promotional effectiveness is well established, and especially important when it comes to pretesting a multi-million-pound advertising campaign. Gathering the data could involve the use of some quite elaborate devices such as the pupilo-meter, which records how the eye moves when an advert is being read. There are many other ways of evaluating advertising both before and during a campaign. Data is obtained on many aspects, but the most important information relates to how a promotion affects a customer's buying behaviour. Relating the cause and effect in advertising is very difficult as it cannot be considered in isolation from other market influences.

Data such as awareness of product names and opportunities to see a particular advertisement are relatively easy to study. The problem arises in trying to relate these to *sales volume changes*. This is what prompted the now famous comment, sometimes attributed to Lord Leverhulme, 'I know half my advertising is wasted, but I don't know which half' (see also Chapter 15) – maybe information should be sought to establish which half! This is possible with respect to any direct response marketing initiatives. The redemption rate for coupons, the characteristics of customers who purchase as a result of a directly mailed offer and facts about the success or failure of other promotions can prove very useful for planning future marketing campaigns.

MARKETING INFORMATION SYSTEMS

All companies need to establish suitable processes that organise and analyse the accumulation of data and provide a flow of appropriate information to those who require it. Marketing information systems are really the frameworks used for managing and accessing this data, and processing it into valuable information. They can be a simple way of sharing information manually between key departments, but are more likely to be some form of integrated system using available computer technology. Even in quite small companies there can be large quantities of data. A logical solution to the problem of extensive data is to use IT, developing a system that not only stores and integrates the relevant data but helps to create useful information. Access to that information can then be given to those who are involved in the planning of marketing activities. The important issue is that the information from such a system is presented in a way that is useful for making marketing decisions.

The term 'marketing information system', or MkIS, is used to describe such a system. Such systems are generally discussed in the context of marketing information or marketing research. (It should be noted that the term MIS is commonly used for the somewhat more far-reaching 'management information system'). Whilst it is essential for organisations to have systems by which marketing information can be stored, processed and accessed, it should be clear from the points made regarding the nature of information in general, and marketing information in particular, that such systems have fundamental limitations. At best the system can only handle such tangible and intangible information as is made available to it. There are three basic components of a good marketing information system:

1 Information acquired via market intelligence
2 Information from operating data, often in database form
3 Information library.

What an MkIS does is integrate the data from many different sources, usually into a computerised database. If structured appropriately, this should allow interrogation and linking of data accessed from a wide variety of sources. It is important for such systems to be basically designed by marketers rather than computer specialists as the form of the output can be critical to good decisions. In order for a marketing manager to perform his or her role effectively it is necessary to use information that has been updated, brought together and then retrieved from all parts of the MkIS. This includes all forms of market intelligence, marketing research and internal operational records.

There is a tendency nowadays for managers to carry out searches of data bases from their computer (via the www), but then to consider the data accessed as information. This is wrong. There is no substitute for analysis of relevant data, and a properly constructed system for undertaking this, as well as merging data from various sources, is the best way to create information.

Market intelligence can come from many external sources, some of which have already been mentioned in this chapter. Internal data will be acquired from operational and accounting records, external data may have been acquired formally or informally, internal facts are usually derived from formal structured data records. All data, especially from external sources, should be checked for reliability before it is entered into an MkIS.

With advances in software design and IT generally, the development and use of both integrated and specialist databases has become increasingly commonplace. Networking and systems integration facilities allow companies to exchange, merge and cross-analyse data from databases within specialist functions (e.g. accounting and purchasing, or distribution/logistics and marketing), or to develop databases for common use within the organisation (e.g. on customers or suppliers). Equally, there has been a

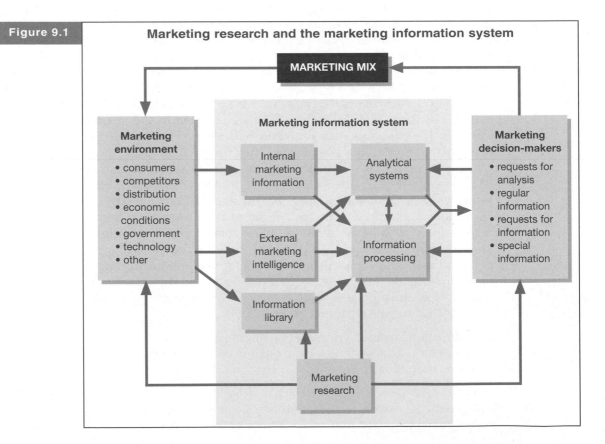

Figure 9.1 Marketing research and the marketing information system

rapid expansion in the availability and use of on-line databases, capable of providing (by subscription, or usage fee) up-to-date facts on a range of issues, from market aggregate statistics to target segment profiles and listings. This is the raw material for most market analyses.

Information from operating data, such as production or accounts, has been covered under the heading of 'operational information'. It is usually different from marketing information as it is collected for very different reasons. Nevertheless, there is likely to be some marketing relevance in this data and that must be input into the MkIS. It could perhaps contain the details of car production, 2-door versus 4-door, or various engine sizes ordered, as in the earlier example. Certainly sales information drawn from invoices is very important and yet this needs to be presented in a way that might categorise customers by relevant market segment, or might show products purchased in as much detail as possible. Most organisations have computerised databases, in some cases very sophisticated ones, such as those originally developed by major service companies for mail-order business or airline reservations. Computerisation has increased the speed and scope of data collection, analysis and dissemination, but it must be properly planned to ensure the output offered is usable information.

The *information library* is a collection of all the formal research gathered by an organisation that is still relevant and up to date. It might also include research surveys carried out by trade associations or by associated companies, as such reports are sometimes available and they do add to knowledge. Thus the MkIS will contain a comprehensive collection of all relevant information which could help achieve better marketing decisions (see Figure 9.1).

Computer-based systems are particularly useful for handling numerical information, but can provide only limited assistance when handling qualitative information based on descriptions and ideas. The need to address this problem has been recognised, and much work has been done to develop 'decision support systems' designed to provide the information needed for marketing decisions. No doubt the number of companies developing and using such systems will increase. The main benefit offered by such systems is likely to be the facilities they offer for accessing the available information. Because of the volume, complexity and time-dependent nature of marketing information, the provision of marketing information will continue to be the specialist marketing activity of marketing research.

CONCLUSION

Marketing, no less than other functions, depends for its efficiency on the availability and utilisation of internal and external information. Information internal to the organisation may range far beyond data on marketing activities proper, and will include central and dispersed sources on operational tasks, procedures and routines throughout the company. In particular, information on production processes and stages may be critical to marketing success, as it will guide managers on the quality and capacity limitations of the organisation, product specifications and current commitments. Equally, the marketing information collected from customers and others in the market place will be critical as an input to the design and production functions. Any decision on what products are to be produced by an organisation must be made on the basis of customer considerations. It is the role of marketing in any organisation to ensure that this information is effectively disseminated within that organisation.

It is crucial to distinguish between data and information. The '*information super high-way*' has rarely produced useful marketing information specific to a current problem, but it does allow easy and fast access to masses of relevant and irrelevant data. By *surfing the Net* it is possible to capture almost any amount of such data. The requirement for marketing, as with other business decisions, is to choose the right data, collect it but don't risk excessive amounts, check it for validity and reliability, then use it effectively to produce information required in planning activities for the future.

QUESTIONS

1 '*Information is power.*' Discuss this in relation to the cross-functional information flows necessary for good customer service.

2 Taking as an example any commercial product, consider the information sources that would shed light on changes in its market and economic environment.

3 Outline what you consider to be the characteristics of an effective marketing information system, and consider the means by which it might be designed and maintained.

4 Discuss how it might be possible to ensure that data gathered via the Internet can be relevant and valid, and not be so overwhelming that analysis is impossible because of the sheer volume of data available.

FURTHER READING

Besson, J. (1993) *Riding the Marketing Information Wave*. HBR S/O.

Bondro, J. and Davis, T.R. (1996) 'Marketing's role in cross-functional information management', *Industrial Marketing Management*, 25(3), May, pp. 187–95.

Chaston, I. (1990) *Managing for Marketing Excellence*. McGraw-Hill.

Flores, B. and Whymark, D. (1985) 'Forecasting "laws" for management', *Business Horizon*, 28(4), July. *Harvard Business Review*, (1996); 74(2), March–April 128–134.

Karmarkar, Uday S. (1996) 'Integrative research in marketing and operations management', *Journal of Marketing Research*, 33(2), May pp. 125–131.

Palmer, A. and Worthington, I. (1992) *The Business and Marketing Environment*. McGraw-Hill.

Wack, P. (1985) 'Scenarios: shooting the rapids', *Harvard Business Review*, November–December.

Wheatley, Malcolm (1996) 'IT drives the chain', *Management Today*, November, pp. 102–118.

Wright, L.T. and Crimp, M. (2000) *The Marketing Research Process*. FT Prentice-Hall.

Home shopping for groceries

Over the last few years there has been increasing interest in the opportunities for customers to use the Internet in order to shop on-line. There are some products that are particularly suitable to this channel and others that are more difficult. Recently the major supermarket groups have investigated the possibilities and have set up websites linked to home delivery for food products. The time has come to evaluate the advantages and disadvantages of these operations when set against the traditional supermarket where customers visit and where they make their selection from the actual products on the shelves.

Visit the websites of the major grocers such as Tesco <www.tesco.com>, and J Sainsbury <www.sainsburys.co.uk>, and see what is currently on offer. Then gather as much data as you think is appropriate about the market for home delivery of food products ordered over the net. Don't restrict your data collection to the Internet, as you will find many other sources. Analyse the data and produce a short report regarding your views as to the future of such operations. Perhaps you could assume you are a market analyst who has been asked to recommend whether or not a new entrant, say a major European food retailer, could enter the UK market by utilising the Internet to reach customers.

Critically evaluate the data that you gathered. In particular, suggest how easy it was to confirm the *validity* and *reliability* of the data. Then describe how this data was turned into useful information that could assist a company in assessing the future of this type of food shopping.

The marketing offering – the fundamental link between a supplier and its customers

INTRODUCTION

Chapters 1–2 of this book have described the competitive environment in which marketing operates. Chapters 3 and 4 have covered those uncontrollable factors that can affect the exchange between a buyer and a seller and that must be understood if good marketing decisions are to be made. Of course some of the most uncontrollable elements are the decisions made by customers, hence the need to study customer behaviour and to introduce activities which close the gap between a supplier and their chosen customers (see Chapters 6 and 7). Market segmentation (Chapter 8) is at best a compromise which enables a focus on an homogeneous group of customers with a uniform offering. The analysis and understanding of the competitive environment (see Chapter 5) is important, but only if it helps to make *better decisions* in the marketing of a particular product or service.

The next section of this book (Chapters 10–19)looks at those elements over which organisations have control and the tools that are used to try to influence customers to choose the products offered by one particular organisation in preference to another. These are generally termed the 'marketing mix'. This description, which conjures up images of mixing together all the things that have a bearing on the 'supplier–customer' relationship, was first published almost 40 years ago by Neil Borden. His original marketing mix did include four *'external'* variables (customer behaviour, distributors, competitors' position and behaviour, and government regulations) which we have already covered. It is the *'internal'* factors that make up the actual offering which are considered in this next section. Drucker once suggested that the whole purpose of any organisation is *to create and retain a customer*: this is a useful definition of business purpose because it is obvious that if you have no customers you have no business.

In Chapter 1, the basic concept behind marketing was introduced. The aim is to achieve a profitable, mutually beneficial, exchange between a buyer and a supplier. Both must be satisfied otherwise there will be little chance of further exchanges (repeat business). Obviously if the seller is dissatisfied with an exchange, maybe it fails to make a profit, then it is likely that the product being offered will be withdrawn from the market place. If it is the buyer who is dissatisfied then it is unlikely that they will make the same mistake again because they won't buy that product in the future. More damaging is the fact that there is a good chance the dissatisfied buyer will tell friends, who in turn will be less willing to buy from that supplier in the future. This can be critical since 'word of mouth' comment from someone you respect or trust has a significant influence on attitudes and hence affects future actions. Thus, positive comments can be far more beneficial than a series of TV commercials and negative ones can undo the effects of a brilliant promotional campaign. This will be discussed more fully in Chapters 15 and 18.

In this chapter the concentration will be on four key issues:

- *First* – the consideration of those markets within which an organisation chooses to operate
- *Second* – the offering as viewed by a customer, and considered in terms of the benefits received and satisfaction gained
- *Third* – the elements that make up the total marketing offering as made to a potential customer
- *Fourth* – the way the offering can be positioned in a market, and the resulting image, including some aspects of the benefits from achieving a strong brand identity.

WHAT MARKET ARE WE IN?

A market was defined in Chapter 1 in its traditional sense as a meeting place for making exchanges. It can be considered, therefore, as:

- *either* a collection of individuals/organisations that could be potential purchasers of a product
- *or* as the set of competitive offerings that are being offered to those purchasers.

The risk of defining a market in terms of the products offered is that it tends to focus too heavily on the tangible features of an offering. Whilst it is necessary to consider these features and to compare them with those offered by competitive products when exploring the boundaries of any market place, it is important that markets are not defined too narrowly otherwise major competitors could be excluded, nor too widely making them difficult to understand.

The question of 'what is a business?', as well as 'what business are we in?' was the subject of a classic article, published in 1960, by Theodore Levitt, then a lecturer at the Harvard Business School. He gave examples of organisations that had failed to understand the benefits their customers derived from the products offered.

Example	**Marketing myopia (from the classic article by Levitt)**

In the case of the American railroads Levitt argued:

'The railroads did not stop growing because the need for passengers and freight transportation declined. That grew. The railroads are in trouble today, not because the need was filled by others (cars, trucks, airplanes and even telephones), but because it was not filled by the railroads themselves. They let others take customers away from them because they assumed themselves to be in the railroad business rather than in the transportation business. The reason they defined their industry incorrectly was because they were railroad-orientated; they were product-oriented not customer-orientated'.

The message is that every organisation should consider, and define its market in terms of the benefits which customers are seeking and not in terms of the technical features of the products being produced. Levitt's achievement was to get individual businesses to look at themselves from the customer's viewpoint and assess their total offerings in terms of the benefits that are perceived by their customers.

Exercise

1   Consider the changes in book retailing at the start of the 21st century. New companies such as Amazon.com have established themselves in a strong position. What are the more traditional, established book retailers such as Waterstones doing to defend their business?

2   There are now many ways to manage your money through a bank account. Many new providers such as Egg and Smile have been very successful in attracting customers. Of course, the need for banking has not reduced so this has affected Barclays, Lloyds and NatWest. They have reacted. Can you explore their reactions and suggest if, in your opinion, they really understand the fundamental link between supplier and customer?

The total marketing offering will be discussed later in this chapter, but from a customer perspective the item purchased includes the *basic product* as well as *all the added features and services* that together make up the '*total product offering*'. This offering is therefore a combination of goods and services which could include both 'good' and 'bad' features, some tangible whilst others will be intangible, such as the image or the attitude of the sales staff.

PRODUCTS AND SERVICES

In the context of marketing the word 'product' is used as a general term which covers any output from a supplier. Products and services are in this context considered interchangeable, since a service is only a product without a tangible core. We do not want to stray too far into jargon, so the difference between products and services is best illustrated by the following example.

Example

I own a car. This obviously is a product, very tangible: I can touch it, wash and polish it and put petrol into it. I am very happy if it is reliable. I use it to get to work, and of course it is important that I get to work on time. One day I could not start my car so I took a taxi to work. This made use of a service. I know I could also touch the taxi, but it is not the same as my own car. There is no tangible 'product' for me, and yet I derived the same benefit, getting to work on time, albeit that in this case the service was rather more expensive.

Of course there are many reasons for owning a car, but I do not own it to leave it sitting on the drive for my neighbours to see. I own it to enable me to travel easily to work, to see friends, to do the shopping and many other things. Some people do not own cars but they have the same needs. They probably do not use taxis on a regular basis – although I know one elderly person who does. Most use other means of transport: buses, trains, bicycles, even walking. Figure 10.1 neatly summarises this.

This example shows that the essential differences between a product and a service are *ownership* and *tangibility*. There are other aspects of services that are covered in Chapter 11. However these factors are only important if they affect the basic benefits received by customers, such as the pride in ownership of a car.

Even if we are able to answer Levitt's question, and we understand that airlines are substitutes for trains, and trains or taxis for private cars, we still only understand one facet of the marketing role. The orientation of a business was introduced in Chapter 1 and it is the need to concentrate on satisfying customers rather than producing products which should be paramount when defining which market an organisation chooses to compete in. Further issues regarding both products and services are discussed in Chapter 11.

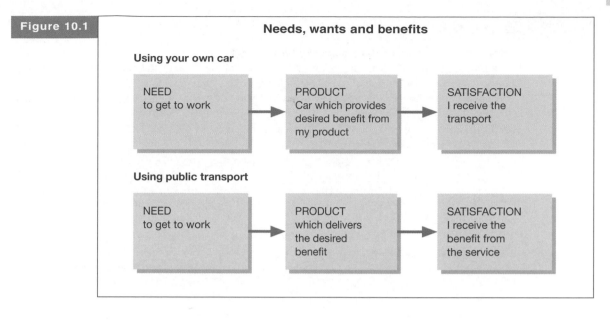

Figure 10.1

Needs, wants and benefits

Using your own car

| NEED to get to work | → | PRODUCT Car which provides desired benefit from my product | → | SATISFACTION I receive the transport |

Using public transport

| NEED to get to work | → | PRODUCT which delivers the desired benefit | → | SATISFACTION I receive the benefit from the service |

THINK BENEFITS

Marketing provides the interface between organisations and their customers. To do this it is essential that marketers *think like customers* so they can promote the needs of those customers to others within their organisation. Of course marketing still has the responsibility to promote the company and its products to potential customers. In order to achieve both these roles a key marketing task is to identify customer needs and wants, expressing these first in terms of the benefits required by buyers. The next step is to translate them into the specifications for product/service offerings that can be provided by a supplier. You could say that this role can be undertaken by a sales-person, and you could be right. Marketing, however, is not selling. Peter Drucker suggested that 'The aim of marketing is to make selling superfluous', implying that if marketing is successful in identifying needs and providing appropriate product/service offerings then the selling task is made much easier. Whilst marketing has a prime responsibility in identifying the future needs of customers, it also has a wider scope encompassing advertising, PR, packaging, product development, marketing research and many other related areas. All of these factors contribute to developing

the right product at the right price, available in the right place at the right time.

This one-line definition of marketing can be split into three elements, each concerned with meeting a separate part of the needs of a customer:

- First, an offering must be **acceptable** to customers. (the **RIGHT PRODUCT**)
- Second, it must be **affordable** to them. (the **RIGHT PRICE**)
- Third, it must be **available** where and when it's wanted. (the **RIGHT PLACE AND TIME**)

These three tests are used regularly by the Coca-Cola Company when considering their marketing plans. Only those marketing activities that increases the **acceptability**, **affordability** or the **availability** of an offering are considered as worthwhile actions.

Example	## The 4As

Acceptability – Visitor take-up at the Millennium Dome

In April 2000, Pierre-Yves Gerbeau, chief executive of the £758 m Millennium Dome attraction, was trying to decide whether to call on the government for extra financial support following disappointing attendances at the Dome over the Easter weekend. Gerbeau said the Easter period should have been buoyant but had fallen short of expectations, leaving the summer and the last few months of the year – which would be a 'last chance' to see the Dome – as two remaining critical periods for attendances.

Gerbeau suggested that it would be a 'challenging' task to attract the break-even target of 10m paying visitors this year. The original 12m target was lowered after fewer than the required number of visitors came in the first few weeks; this led to the appointment of the former Disneyland Paris executive, who was given the task of improving attendances. Some industry commentators doubt that even the 10m figure is attainable, suggesting a 'worst-case' scenario as low as 6m!

Gerbeau said the attraction was 'sparkling, everything is working, there are no queues and it is very clean'. He blamed the strength of the pound, an exodus of British holidaymakers and poor weather for the disappointing Easter weekend's attendances but said sales for the rest of the month and May were looking good.

Source <FT.com> 26 April 2000. (Copyright © The Financial Times Limited.)

Note: If the Dome were an entirely private venture, without the benefit of government support it is likely that it would be bankrupt already. By the time this book is published the real total visitor figures will be known.

Question: *Do you agree with Gerbeau, or do you think that the Dome is just unacceptable as an attraction for 10 million people? (Of course products that are completely unacceptable to one customer may be acceptable to another.)*

Affordability – Millennium night out

Many tourist attractions and clubs raised their prices in anticipation of a real bonanza event on New Year's Eve 1999–2000. The general view early in 1999 was that there would be a huge boom in demand, and most of the hype was aimed at getting people to book early. To be fair to hoteliers and club owners they knew they would have to pay bonuses to persuade staff to work, but that was not the main reason behind the premium rates. It is also fair to consider that when it came to deciding prices, nobody had any precedent to give a benchmark for a price that balanced the costs, demand and potential for profit.

As the big date approached it was obvious that demand was not as strong as expected. In fact, bookings were often below those in any normal year. In many places customers were being put off by the high prices, with many people opting to organise their own celebrations in a more affordable manner.

There were also similar problems with bookings for holidays abroad over the New Year period being below forecast. A survey carried out by ABTA (the Association of British Travel Agents) showed a large number of potential travellers were planning something 'out-of-the-ordinary' but at a later time in 2000, after prices had come down from the high levels. Others were prepared to wait for bargains.

The moral is that customers are not fools: they don't want to feel ripped off, and even for a once-in-a-lifetime event they still require affordable prices and value for money.

Affordability – Cheap and expensive jewellery

A Cartier diamond necklace will cost many thousands of pounds. Only a few can afford it. On the other hand many can afford a simple gold-plated chain from H. Samuel jewellers. Affordability is also a comparative measure, depending on financial circumstances. It is also an important measure because controlling the pricing level for a product is critical to managing demand. This issue will be discussed further in Chapter 14.

> **Availability – Grocery shopping in a town centre**
> In a recent survey of students at Coventry University it was found that over 60 per cent shopped at the local Sainsbury store in the city centre. When asked why the general answer was that it was convenient and local because few of the students in the group surveyed had access to a car. The competitive supermarkets are all a little distance away from the centre making them unavailable to these students. The choice of products in a small 10,000 square foot store is considerably less than in the superstores outside the city which are five or six times larger. Therefore any product not stocked in the city centre store is practically unavailable to those students.

In Coventry, as well as the Sainsbury branch mentioned above, there is also a city centre branch of Marks & Spencer. When asked why students did not shop there the replies suggested three reasons:

- M&S is too expensive for many students (i.e. products are not *Affordable*)
- Most products in M&S were not suitable for student needs (i.e. not *Acceptable)*
- Several comments were made saying that M&S was 'full of older people' (another way in which something can be viewed as not *Acceptable*!).

The last point illustrates how an organisation must understand its specific customers and prepare its offering to appeal to those customers it wants, being prepared to forego other customers who have different needs. Without the customer focus resulting from being marketing-orientated, organisations inevitably tend to concentrate on developing a product, usually by maximising its features and quality while minimising the price. This is not necessarily what some groups of customer actually require, therefore M&S can concentrate on food products which are affordable to their chosen customers but also offer a level of variety and interest not available in the same way elsewhere.

THINK EXPECTATIONS AND SATISFACTION

Benefits are what customers receive; product/service offerings are what suppliers offer. But the ultimate judge of any offering, with the power to buy or not to buy, is the customer. The customer's measure of satisfaction will be based on a perception of how well an offering delivers the specific desired benefits within an affordable level of costs.

There is a critical difference between the **needs** of customers and their **expectations** regarding a product offering. '**Needs**' can be defined as a condition where something necessary or desirable is lacking – e.g. the 'necessary' **need** for a drink, or the 'desirable' **need** to be entertained. '**Expectations**' describe what a customer hopes to receive from a specific purchase. Whilst it is the finding and filling of the underlying **need** that is the goal of marketing, in many cases customers cannot identify a perfect product for their complex **needs** and therefore they make compromise decisions, choosing a product or service that offers the most acceptable and affordable benefits. The **expectations** of a chosen product prior to a purchase, and it is these which are then compared to its performance after buying. This then determines the customer's level of *satisfaction*. At its simplest, satisfaction will result when the benefits received match, or exceed, the expectations of what is being offered: but, if expectations are higher than the resulting benefits, the customer will be dissatisfied.

Consider a person's need to travel. There is a logical progression from the examination of the various means of travel onto a decision to use a train. Then the specific service will be selected, such as the 9.10 from London to Birmingham, although this is just one individual 'product' offered to satisfy a potential demand. But when evaluating the options there will also be an expectation regarding the time that the train will arrive at the destination. If it fails to arrive on time and this means you are late for an important meeting the effect on the satisfaction will be enormous. If the arrival time is not critical then the specific expectation would be different and the effect of a late arrival not so annoying.

Customers will evaluate the offering using the tests of the '3 As' (acceptability – affordability – availability) introduced earlier. These factors are discussed individually in more detail in Chapters 11–14. However, it must be remembered that a customer will evaluate the offer mix as a *total package*, trading off one element against another in making a buy/no-buy decision.

Exercise	■ Think of a purchase you have made recently and note down the reasons why you bought the item under the '3 As' mentioned above ■ Did it match your 'expectations', and did it also meet your 'needs'? ■ When you have done that, think of an item or service that you did not buy, and evaluate why you did not buy it, utilising the '3 As' model.

Marketing is usually dealing with products/services that already exist and are on sale, and for these there will be a perception in the minds of potential customers as to the degree of **acceptability, affordability and availability** that they offer. For existing products the requirement is to develop sales and keep the product up-to-date. Of course if any of the key dimensions are changed it is the responsibility of the marketer to inform customers. Occasionally marketing will be involved with a new product that must be developed and launched successfully. In this situation the role of marketing is to make customers aware of the new offering and develop expectations. For both new and existing products there are three stages of marketing:

■ **Pre-purchase**, when the goal is to create or manage expectations
■ **The actual purchase**, with an aim of delivering customer satisfaction
■ **Post-purchase**, where the aim is to reinforce satisfaction or resolve problems.

The last stage can be much broader, with activities to maintain or develop a relationship with chosen customers, as well as trying to ensure positive reports and future repeat sales.

Example	**Satisfaction** From an Indian train timetable: The times shown on this timetable are not the times when the trains will leave: rather they are the times before which the trains will not leave.

The above quotation is an excellent example of managing the expectation of customers. The message ensures that the benefits offered can actually be achieved. Of course it doesn't go as far as claiming anything regarding arrival times but all passengers can be sure of catching a train if they turn up in time.

A spokesperson for Virgin Trains told a marketing seminar that the critical issue in running a train service is to keep the public informed and not to raise their expecta-

Exercise

Since the privatisation of train services in the UK, companies that have purchased the franchises now provide the services. All of these companies have passengers' charters that are generally based on the one originally introduced by British Rail on 3 May 1992. These charters are statements of the companies' commitment to provide a high-quality service for all customers. They offer customers:

– safe, punctual, and reliable train services
– clean stations and clean trains
– friendly and efficient service
– clear and up-to-date information
– fair and satisfactory responses when things go wrong.

In the light of recent major rail disasters (both in the UK and India), it is instructive to look at the issue of what benefits customers really desire. Are these related to safety or to some other benefit?

■ Compare the benefits offered by railway franchise companies in the UK with the expectations you have of their services.
■ Then speculate about the expectations of train passengers in India.

tions too high with unachievable promises. A comparative study of the way resources are deployed by the different franchise companies might show how to avoid creating dissatisfied customers.

It is important that any product or service offered satisfies its customers by fulfilling their specific needs. However, it is equally important that there is no confusion regarding the benefits offered. The Indian train service may not fulfil all needs of train passengers in India; in fact it will disappoint all those for whom arrival time is critical. But, importantly, it is very clear what is not being offered, so customers do not have hopes raised unrealistically. The best promotion in the world rarely sells a bad product twice.

There are many examples of companies who fail to satisfy their customers, but most are consigned to history as those companies have failed to survive.

Example

The curse of the 'Phantom Menace' has struck again

FT

Three months after Dorling Kindersley (DK) announced a £25m loss caused by poor sales of Star Wars books, a similar fate has hit Character Group, the toys' distributor. Shares in the group fell dramatically after it warned that it too had been left with large quantities of unsold 'Star Wars' goods and would make a 'significant' loss in the first half as a result.

Richard King, chairman, said the group had expected bumper sales of Star Wars products following 'four years of hype' in advance of the film Phantom Menace – Episode One, which was released last year. But he admitted the toy industry was fooled by 'phantom expectations and phantom figures' after the film and its associated merchandise left critics and the public unimpressed. Mr King blamed part of Character's troubles on George Lucas, Star Wars' creator:

'Everyone expected Lucas to rekindle the magic of the original films, but special effects have progressed so much in the past 20 years that it looked no different to other films' said Mr King.

However, strong sales of Toy Story products and Pokémon stationery are expected to fight off the Phantom Menace, reducing losses in the full-year trading to 31 August 2000.

Character's over-exposure to Star Wars was not quite on the scale of Dorling Kindersley's. The publishing group sold only 3m of the 13m books it printed. For DK, the slump cost it its independence when, earlier this month, Pearson, the media group that owns the *Financial Times*, bought the DK publishing group.

Mr King admitted that Character could also fall prey to a financial predator, but said it was not looking for a white knight – or, for that matter, a Jedi Knight.

THE TOTAL PRODUCT CONCEPT

Earlier in this chapter a 'marketing' or 'total product' offering was defined as a combination of goods and services which could include both 'good' and 'bad' features, some tangible whilst others are intangible. Simply stated, a marketer must view the 'product' as a multidimensional offering, a mix of physical features together with other non-physical attributes usually including an element of service, bundled around a basic or core benefit. Gummesson explains the situation as follows:

> Customers do not buy goods or services in the traditional sense. They buy an offering and the value may consist of many components, some of them being activities (services) and some being things (goods). As a consequence, the traditional division between goods and services is long outdated.

What is relevant is that the basic product can be viewed only as the *core of any offering*. It is then 'augmented' by additional features, both activities and things that are of value to customers. In this book we call these levels of additions the *'real product'* and the *'marketing offering'* (or *'total product'*) to emphasise that it is the supplier who through investment and by using marketing skills can add value to the *'basic product'*. This multi-layered view of the product is illustrated in Figure 10.2.

At the centre of *'the total product offering'* is the *'basic product'*, which represents the *essential benefit on offer to the customer*. This should be expressed in a tangible form, e.g. an easily applied scuff-resistant shoe polish for children's shoes or, if it is a service, described through the intangible benefits it offers, such as the repairs carried out on a broken machine.

But almost every 'product' has an additional 'layer' of tangible features that make up the listed product or service – e.g. design and colour, packaging, quality specification, brand name. The *'real product'* is the term used to describe this greater mix of product features.

The *'total product'* will then add to the *'real product'* a number of intangible extras that augment the offering by adding utility through services (e.g. delivery, customer service), and perhaps subtle qualities and assurances of distinctive value to the customer.

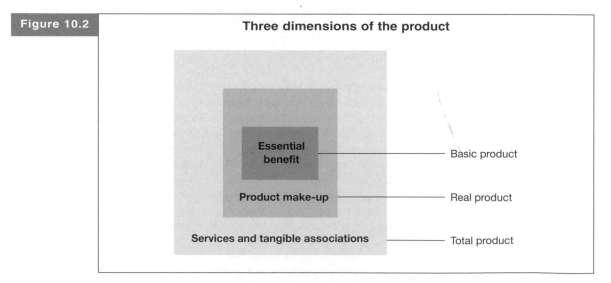

Figure 10.2

Three dimensions of the product

Essential benefit ———————————— Basic product

Product make-up ———————————— Real product

Services and tangible associations ———————— Total product

It is probably worth noting that, in an era of increasing buyer sophistication and market competitiveness, marketing success is more likely to be achieved by those companies that manage to develop competitive advantage through creative service offerings and combinations associated with the 'penumbra' of the total product: all offerings have the potential for development and differentiation. Alternatively stated, the critical part of the value chain has shifted from the base product and the production process, to the wider product and the extended organisation that supports it.

Example

Consider the example of a farmer growing a seasonal crop, say potatoes.

A customer's decision to purchase potatoes will involve a choice based on experience and information gained from many sources.

At one level there could be a choice between a 50 kg sack of unwashed potatoes from the farm shop; or delivery at home from a mobile greengrocer with a van; or maybe a 5 kg bag of presorted and cleaned potatoes from a local supermarket.

Each comes with a different level of added features and the acceptability of the purchase is likely to depend on the customer's particular requirement for such features, as well as all the other elements in the total product offering. Some of these elements the farmer can control others he can't. He certainly cannot control the actions of a customer who is fed up with peeling potatoes and deciding to purchase frozen chips instead!

This should illustrate the difficulty of separating the product from the product offering, a problem that is even greater when considering well-known branded manufactured products.

One obvious way of making an offer more acceptable is by the addition of *service features* to the core product. Service companies have always been able to achieve a level of 'customisation' in an offering because the production and the delivery of the service can easily be personalised at every delivery occasion. The delivered service is of course liable to variations, depending on who actually delivers the service. This is why service organisations such as McDonald's pay so much attention to the achievement of *consistency* in the quality of service given. This also introduces the requirement for all employees to value customers, which is discussed in the section on internal marketing in Chapters 12 and 23.

It might be appropriate here to consider another view of the levels of an offering. Figure 10.2 considered the different levels of a product offering. Figure 10.3 is another way of representing the total product. It illustrates how a product can be developed away from a commodity. The relative importance of all these factors will vary and depend both on the type of product and the particular customer involved. It is always a good discipline for marketers to try to put themselves in the position of a customer and try to see how a total offer can be assessed.

It is obviously an important aspect of competition that an 'offering' should be differentiated from other competitive offerings, by additional features or better service or greater availability perhaps. In his article 'Marketing success through the differentiation – of anything' (1980), Theodore Levitt wrote:

There is no such thing as a commodity. All goods and services can be differentiated and usually are . . . Everybody – whether producer, fabricator, seller, broker, agent, merchant – engages in a constant effort to distinguish his offering in his favour from all others.

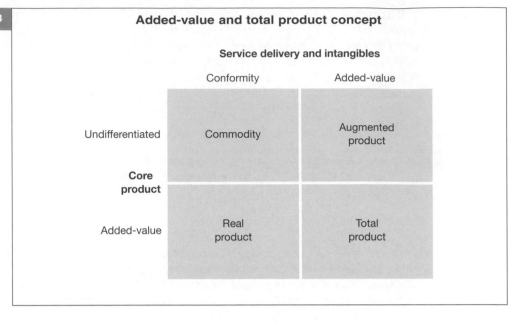

Figure 10.3 Added-value and total product concept

PRODUCT DIFFERENTIATION AS A FUNDAMENTAL MARKETING CONCEPT

Theodore Levitt's famous quote was used in his article about differentiation as a means of gaining competitive advantage. In this article he refines the three-level concept of a product to explore those areas where advantage is possible. In particular, he uses the term 'expected product' to describe the minimum expectation of customers for a particular class of product. This is the basic product plus those other additions that are necessary to even be considered within the customer's evoked set. The expected product will, therefore, include some features in both the real and total product categories discussed earlier.

There are two further categories that are critical to marketing success. First the *augmented* product which an organisation offers to its customers, in the hope that the additional features, tangible and intangible, will be sufficient to achieve sales in a competitive market place. Levitt's augmented product is therefore the same as the total product offered by a supplier.

The second additional category is the *potential* product 'which consists of everything potentially feasible to attract and hold customers'. So while the total augmented product is the total of everything currently being offered, the potential product is only limited by a company's imagination. This category embraces anything that could be done both now and in the future as new technologies or other opportunities arise.

As already discussed, marketing takes place in a dynamic and ever-changing environment. It is therefore necessary to consider how a total product must change its formation over time to remain competitive. Raymond Corey in his classic book on industrial marketing said: 'the form of a product is a variable, not a given, when developing market strategy. Products are planned and developed to serve markets.' This is especially true in the changing conditions in many markets. There is a continual migration between the various categories of the total and potential product.

One reason for this is that customers become accustomed to a particular level of added value and therefore increase their expectations over time. This is possible as competitors see the augmentation of one company and move to copy it. For instance, there was a time when no UK banks were open on Saturday. However, it was seen first that building societies were benefiting from Saturday opening so the NatWest Bank started opening at these times. Now the branches of most banks have some form of operation at a time convenient to many personal customers. This is an example of the move from augmented to expected in considering the 'product' offered by a bank.

But banks are now reviewing their provision of physical branches as more convenient links through 24-hour telephone banking and internet services are developed. There are also the Automatic Cash Dispenser (ATM) machines that make some banking services accessible outside normal bank hours. For many customers the services available through the use of technology is more than sufficient to meet their regular needs. The implications on employment in the banking sector are dramatic, with thousands of redundancies and many branch closures. However, it is the service to the customers rather than justification of traditional operations that is critical.

Sometimes a company gets things wrong and suffers a customer backlash and much damaging adverse publicity. This happened to Barclays Bank in April 2000 when a decision to close 10 per cent of their branches, whilst not providing alternative services, caused a major debate. The problem Barclays faced was the need to look after

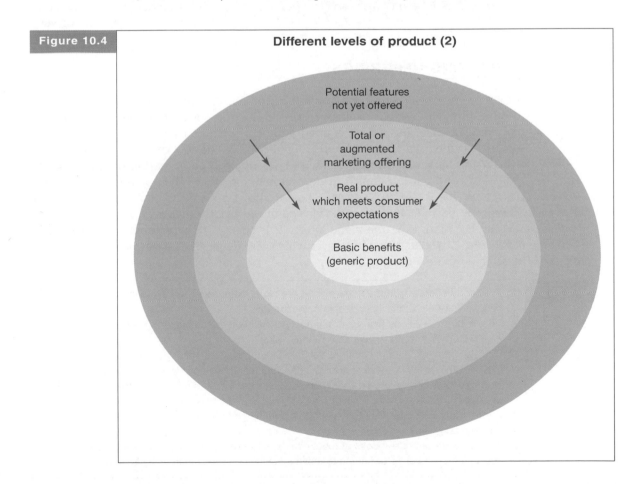

Figure 10.4

Different levels of product (2)

Potential features
not yet offered

Total or
augmented
marketing offering

Real product
which meets consumer
expectations

Basic benefits
(generic product)

existing loyal customers, often older people in rural areas, whilst also changing to reflect the new needs of new customers, and the need to match the new initiatives of other providers of banking services.

Of course, as competitors copy those features which once gave a single supplier a competitive advantage, then more has to be added to the total product to maintain an advantage in the market place. This involves drawing from the category of the potential product to provide future augmentation. It is for this reason that Figure 10.4 has arrows from the outer rings pointing in. These indicate that elements originally in one of the outer rings might easily move in as the features that are expected by customers, and therefore necessary for competitive advantage, change over time. Also those which are offered as part of the total product are further augmented to retain an advantage over competition.

Example   ### Häagen-Dazs

The Häagen-Dazs plants in France and the USA certainly produce ice cream efficiently and operate with minimal workforce and carefully controlled overheads. That is the style of a company owned by Grand Metropolitan plc. However the thrust of the Häagen-Dazs developments is not to lower prices. On the contrary, since Grand Metropolitan acquired Pillsbury, which included Häagen-Dazs – a luxury brand of ice cream sold in New York since the mid-1960s – their efforts have been directed at enhancing its quality with luxurious and indulgent ingredients. A few cents of Almond Crunch can put half a dollar on the list price. Now sold in more than twenty major markets in Europe, Asia and the Americas, it is an example of creativity in developing markets and widening margins.

MARKETING OFFERINGS

A total product will be successful only if customers are willing to buy it in preference to other products. For this to happen the product obviously must be acceptable, but must also be available when required and at a price considered affordable by customers. The idea of a complete marketing offering is a development of the *total product* – the term 'marketing offering' is used to describe this combination of total product, availability and price. It aims to focus a supplier on what is being offered to a specific customer. This is a useful concept since it allows all aspects of different marketing offerings to be compared from the viewpoint of the customer.

Using the marketing offering as a focus it is possible to explain why so many products succeed in spite of having prices which are higher than their main rivals. This is illustrated by the following exercises.

Exercise

1 Fruit and vegetables in the supermarket are more expensive than my local market. Is it convenience of location that people pay extra for?

2 People hire televisions when it is 'cheaper' to buy. Is it the convenient way of spreading expenditure or the after-sales service they value?

3 Company car purchasers buy from the Ford Motor Company and pay extra for 'Fordsure Cover'. Why do they pay the extra? Is it peace of mind they purchase with the extra warranty, or is perhaps the warranty an additional product that adds value to the basic product?

4 A local carpet supplier is not the cheapest, but they offer free fitting. Is this the reason they attract customers?

5 Amazon.com can offer books at reduced prices to internet shoppers. However bookshops selling full-price books still seem to thrive in town-centre locations. Why is this?

Perhaps you can think of other examples.

It is the total marketing offering made to a potential customer that critically determines whether an exchange takes place or if that customer is lost. The components of the marketing offering can be seen to correlate with the Form, Place and Time components of value in its widest sense. This was previously described as

the right product at the right price, available in the right place at the right time.

The actual offer that an organisation makes to its customers is called the *offer mix*. Thus, a marketing offering comprises all elements of the mix as below:

- the total product and/or service offered
- the price including all discounts and deals and
- the level of availability of the offering.

It would be naive to assume that marketing communication in the form of advertising and promotion does not play a significant role in making products seem acceptable. It obviously does, but this is in addition to and separate from the actual offer. It is, of course, possible to change how customers behave and their attitudes towards an offering by use of specific communications and promotions. The perception customers have of a total offer is the critical test of that offering. There are three major roles of communication, and different elements of the so-called 'promotional mix', and each can play a different part in achieving the best results regarding:

- creating awareness of the offering
- a stimulus to purchase which can affect how an offer is evaluated
- post-transactional reassurance.

It can be seen that these mirror the three stages of marketing. Chapter 15 explores the process of communication and Chapters 16–19 explore the four traditional elements of the promotional mix: paid advertising; direct marketing; sales promotion; and personal selling.

The basis of the marketing concept is that organisations should match their marketing offerings to the *environment* in which they are operating. Effectiveness measures marketing relevance, it derives from meeting customer needs with the total product offered. Efficiency is a financial measure based on internal operations and the way

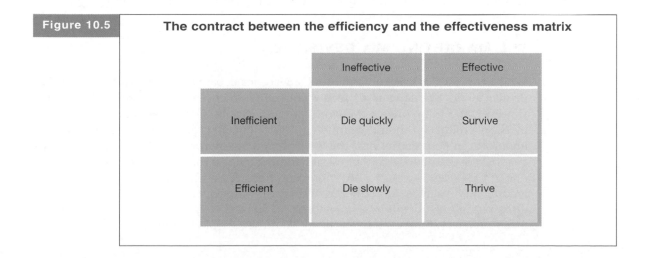

Figure 10.5 The contract between the efficiency and the effectiveness matrix

	Ineffective	Effective
Inefficient	Die quickly	Survive
Efficient	Die slowly	Thrive

resources are utilised. Even a relatively inefficient company, which is effective at creating and keeping customers, can survive. Companies who fail to satisfy customers are basically ineffective, and they will not survive however efficient their operations (Figure 10.5).

THE ORIGINAL MARKETING MIX

The term 'marketing mix' has been used for almost 50 years to describe that mix of factors over which an organisation has some specific control. It affects far more than the basic product, embracing not only aspects of the *'total product'*, but everything that can be considered as part of the *'total marketing offering'*. The first attempt to list these factors was made by Neil Borden (1964) although the actual term was in use in the early 1950s. Borden suggested 12 internal variables as part of the 'mix'. (See Box below).

Internal factors in the original marketing mix

Borden's list of controllable internal variables had 12 specific factors:

- Product policy
- Servicing
- Packaging
- Display

- Promotions
- Branding
- Personal Selling
- Advertising

- Pricing
- Channels of Distribution
- Physical Handling
- Fact finding and Analysis

This list is not easy to remember and it should be obvious why Jerome McCarthy condensed the 12 items in Borden's original marketing mix into four major categories, popularised as the '4 Ps'.

The internal variables are therefore loosely grouped together under the headings of:

- **Product**
- **Price**   } = The offer mix
- **Place**
- **Promotion**   = The promotional mix

You will note the distinction between what is offered, product price and place, and the promotion of that offer. This will be expanded in future chapters.

THE MARKETING MIX REVISITED

Whilst the '4 Ps' is a useful framework, a vigorous debate has taken place over the last decade about the dangers of seeing marketing solely as the control of the '4 Ps'. However, the full scope of the word 'product' can be seen to embrace more than a physical product, it should definitely include servicing. This wider definition is very important in considering how the '4 Ps' should be interpreted. 'Place' should include channels of distribution and physical handling but, on too many occasions, it ignores one or the other. The '4 Ps' also ignores another key element of the original mix – Fact Finding and Analysis. But criticism of the basic '4 Ps' runs deeper. These issues will be discussed in more detail in later chapters. In fact the '4 Ps' can be a trap that tends to make suppliers think exclusively about what they should be doing. It is easy to forget the needs of customers, as well as the importance of a mutually beneficial exchange, but it is very dangerous to do so.

Because there is an attraction to the letter 'P', some authors on service marketing have suggested the addition of three other Ps which are critical to the achievement of customer satisfaction. These additional P's reflect how an offer, especially a service offer, is received (see Chapter 11).

The additions suggested are:

- **People**
- **Processes**
- **Physical evidence.**

All of these additional factors could be defined as 'controllable variables', which can be determined by a supplier. These and many others all have a good claim to be included but it does not matter how many elements are included in the marketing mix. Neither is it important that all categories start with the letter 'P'. What is important is that these controllable factors are what the customers see. They must be consistent one with another, and together they form the *'promise'* of an offering being made to customers. The concept of a promise made by suppliers as a result of the various components of the marketing mix is perhaps the critical aspect of the marketing offering. Customers then evaluate what they perceive as the claims and benefits that comprise this 'promise', deciding how to behave in the light of all the aspects of the total offering.

This brings us to the simple and obvious fact that a product/service will not be purchased by a prospect or potential customer unless they are comfortable with the promises perceived in the marketing offering. For the customer to reach this situation they must know:

(a) that it exists
(b) where it can be purchased
(c) that it is affordable – and, most important
(d) that it is likely to meet the need for which it is required.

This introduces what within marketing can be referred to as the '4 As':

- **Awareness**
- **Availability**
- **Affordability**
- **Acceptability**.

As previously mentioned, the Coca-Cola Company has been using 'Availability, Affordability and Acceptability' as their test of strategy for many years. Of course Coca-Cola are clearly confident that most of the world is already aware of their product. Indeed, at the start of the new millennium it was the second best-known brand in the world.

It follows that a supplier cannot expect to sell a product to a potential new customer until the following four conditions have been met. The supplier must thus ensure that the potential customer:

(a) is aware of the product's existence
(b) finds the product to be available when it is needed
(c) can afford to buy the product and
(d) has belief in, or is willing to test, its acceptability.

It further follows that the possibility of a sale is likely to be increased by any action taken by a supplier to improve the awareness, availability, affordability or acceptability of a product. All of this is involved in the task of marketing. But how can this be accomplished? Returning to the original categories listed by Borden it is obvious.

Awareness is affected by:	*Availability* is affected by:	*Affordability* is affected by:	*Acceptability* is affected by:
Advertising	Channels of distribution	Pricing	Product policy
Promotions	Physical handling		Packaging
Branding			Servicing
Display			
Personal selling			

It will further be seen that each of these groups of variables can be conveniently summarised using McCarthy's four categories: Product, Place, Price and Promotion, (the '4 Ps'). Of course it can easily be seen that the '4 Ps' completely mirror the '4 As' introduced earlier. Thus:

- Awareness is developed by Promotion in all its various forms
- Availability, by Place (used as a generic term for distribution), also processes
- Affordability is a function of Price – or, more accurately value and quality
- Acceptability is of course determined by both the 'total' Product and the Service.

These '4 Ps' act as a reminder of the major components of the marketing mix, and are referred to as such in many marketing textbooks. Usually their order is reversed to rank them as the supplier (see Figure 10.6) might approach them. That is:

Product, Price, Place and Promotion.

But marketers should consider all issues from a customer viewpoint. Consumers do not approach these factors in this order, so it is necessary to consider the consumer ordering, who is most likely to start with Awareness/Promotion when using these categories for functional marketing. In this way suppliers can fully understand the effect that each of these variables can have on the potential customer. Each of the components will be considered in detail in subsequent chapters.

It is equally important that the concept of a marketing mix is *never seen in isolation*. Its validity as a concept depends upon it always being considered in context. This

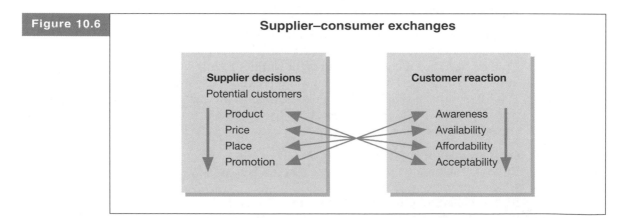

Figure 10.6 — **Supplier–consumer exchanges**

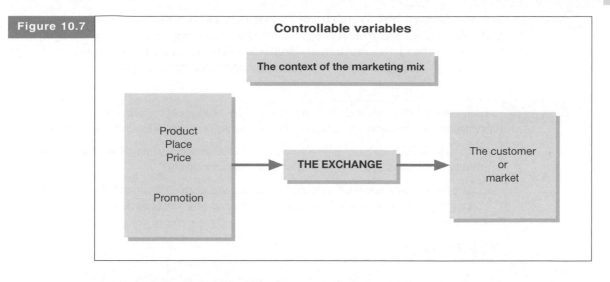

Figure 10.7

means ensuring that every discussion of any element of the marketing mix 'product, price, place or promotion' is always done within the context of a clearly defined exchange and a customer or market segment (see Figure 10.7) as well as being evaluated relative to competitive offerings.

The variables a supplier can change are the '4 Ps' of their marketing mix which define the promises made. Those they have to monitor are the '4 As' of their customers

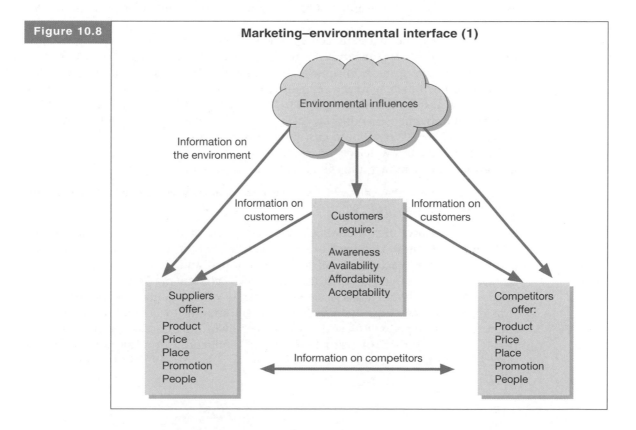

Figure 10.8

and the '4 Ps' of their competition (see Figure 10.8). Competitors have an important influence on how customers respond to the marketing mix selected by a supplier. Customers are in the position to decide between competitive offerings, hence the importance of the question: **'Why should customers buy from us?'**

Exercise	Newly established competitors can often benefit from changes in the environment, such as new technologies or new attitudes, by offering modified products before existing companies:

1 'Why did Body Shop have such a success with environmentally friendly products when major competitors such as Boots failed to see the opportunity?'

2 'Why were quartz/electronic watches from companies such as Casio able to take such a large share of the market before the Swiss watch industry fought back with Swatch?'

POSITIONING

The next consideration after the marketing offer is what is termed the positioning of a product or service. Positioning can be a confusing concept as there are two distinct approaches within marketing. One is market *positioning* which is an *'a priori'* activity (based on what is known before). In this context it refers to the 'placing' of a product in that part of the market where it will be able to compete favourably with competitors' products. The other is based on the perception of customers regarding the product. It is the place a *'product'* actually occupies in a given market, as perceived by the relevant group of customers. This can be seen as a *post hoc* activity.

As can be seen the first approach considers the decisions taken by an organisation in putting together a competitive marketing mix, making *promises* to customers. It could be that an organisation chooses to adopt a premium position or, maybe, a low-cost position within its market. Competitive positioning demands that an organisation considers what it is offering compared to its competitors for the same target customer segment. It must choose a position which enables the organisation to answer the question posed earlier, **'Why should customers buy from us?'**

The quotation below relates to the second approach, emphasising that the most important issue is, in fact, the *effect upon a chosen potential customer*:

> **Positioning is not what you do to a product; positioning is what you do to the mind of the prospect.** (Ries and Trout, 1981)

So the other aspect of positioning is the perception of the offer as evaluated by a customer. Customers often have to decide between two or more offerings from competing companies. Each offer will be communicated and promoted with the *promises* made to the target group being based on a chosen marketing mix. This will include all the relevant aspects of what is being offered (Total Product, Price and Availability). All the organisations involved will attempt to achieve a position, but the actual customers will view this from their own, different perspective. To complicate things further the situation can be influenced by the uncontrollable, macroenvironmental factors (PEST) discussed in Chapter 3. This is illustrated by Figure 10.9.

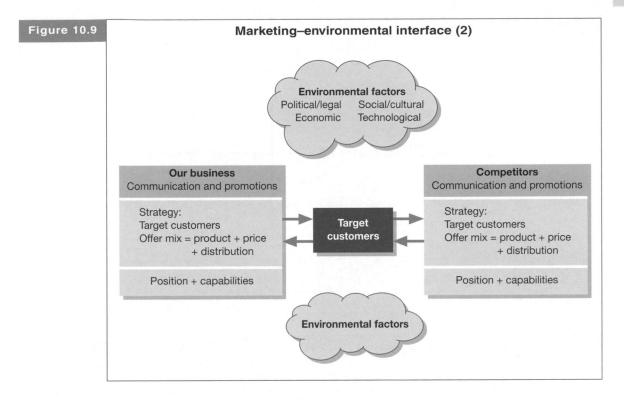

Figure 10.9 Marketing–environmental interface (2)

Example

The boycott of French products

In 2000 debate was still raging in Europe about the safety of British beef following the BSE problems. Although a group of European vets had given the all clear, there were still problems and the French government had not yet approved it for sale. The UK Minister for Agriculture, Nick Brown, announced that he intended to personally stop buying products from France until the ban was lifted. This was followed by a media campaign, and a number of supermarkets started removing French products from their shelves.

For an importer of French cheeses it did not matter that their product was of the highest quality, nor that they offered the widest range of speciality cheeses, what affected the position of the offering was the way the external, uncontrollable variables affected the situation.

Note: Speculating on the future, the authors of this book suggest that the situation could be resolved by the time this book is published. Students should consider the after-effect of this situation and the effect, if any, on the customer's perception of products such as French cheese.

Whilst environmental factors are uncontrollable, and therefore unpredictable, it is necessary for marketers to consider those attributes of the total offering which they can control, the aim being to do the maximum possible to ensure that a product is perceived as acceptable, affordable and available by all the target customers. It should be possible to identify those factors which potential customers see as desirable. There may be many such factors or only a few. But it is usually possible to plot them on a simple perceptual/positioning map (see Figure 10.10 and Figure 10.11) in two dimensions as long as it is realised there may be other key dimensions that customers value. Of course the importance of different factors varies, but this can also be accommodated.

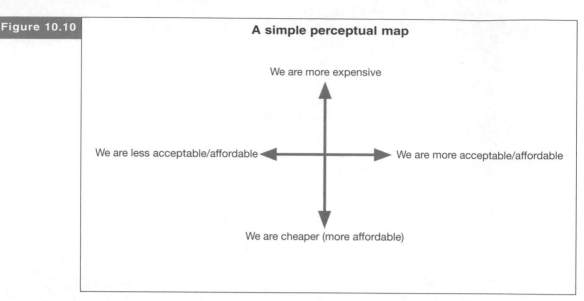

Figure 10.10

A simple perceptual map

Example

A study of compact discs found factors such as: gives out a very good sound, enjoyable to play and will not scratch, were rated much higher than: easy to store and can programme the selections. This study was not aimed at specifically identifying attributes, but rather at seeking consistency in the information from respondents. Reliable and consistent methodology is a technical matter, but vital when developing attributes for use in positioning studies and gap analysis. It was possible to plot the sound and enjoyment dimensions on a map and to compare different offerings in the compact disc market.

A positioning map for the US car market was published in the *Wall Street Journal* in the mid-1980s. The axes are reproduced in Figure 10.11. You will see that they amalgamate several factors to enable a two-dimensional perceptual map to be produced. It will come as no surprise that Chrysler Motor Corporation research found customers placed BMW and Porsche in the top right quadrant; Toyota, Nissan and Volkswagen in the bottom right; with Cadillac and Mercedes in top left. Perhaps the surprise is that these positions have been retained for so long in the dynamic market place for cars. Ford was considered as a single entity in bottom left in this report, but bringing it up to date if you considered the different models now sold in Europe, it is likely the XR3i would be in a different place from the Focus.

But even considering the three dimensions of acceptability, affordability, and availability it can be seen that a two-dimensional map could be constricting. In these cases where a large number of factors are involved it is only by harnessing the power of computers that a three-dimensional, or even a multi-dimensional model, of the issues can be constructed.

For each segment, a number of ideal positions and desired levels of attributes will emerge. There will also be specific positions identified for competing brands. If you

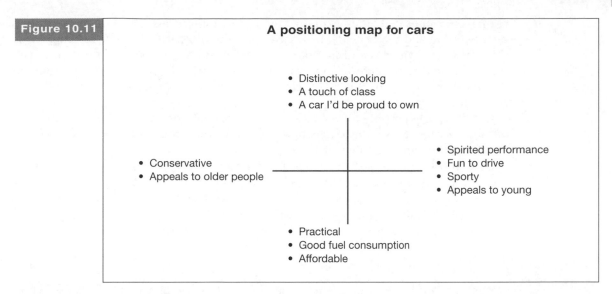

Figure 10.11

A positioning map for cars

- Distinctive looking
- A touch of class
- A car I'd be proud to own

- Conservative
- Appeals to older people

- Spirited performance
- Fun to drive
- Sporty
- Appeals to young

- Practical
- Good fuel consumption
- Affordable

Exercise

You could suggest where to place some other car models with which you are familiar, but remember it is not your opinion that counts – it is the opinion of the customers in a particular target segment that is crucially important.

were designing a new product then the closer it is to the ideal mix of attributes, the better the chance of success. For an existing product it may be a strategy is necessary to try to change its position as perceived by potential customers.

When evaluating positioning it is the attributes of an offering as interpreted by the

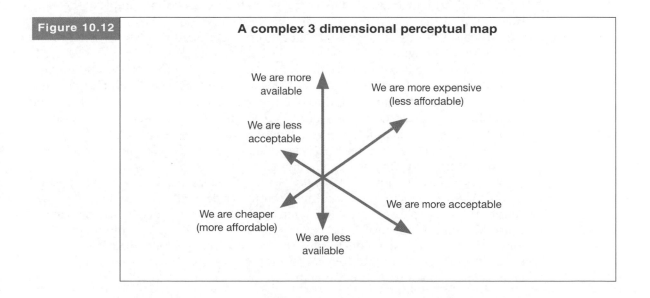

Figure 10.12

A complex 3 dimensional perceptual map

We are more available

We are more expensive (less affordable)

We are less acceptable

We are cheaper (more affordable)

We are more acceptable

We are less available

chosen customers that are used in the buying decision process. These include rating of quality, value and the benefits those customer thinks a particular product offers. It is this perception which is critical, not the organisation's view of what it is offering. The role of marketing is to create a consistency between the offering and the appropriate customer perception. In this task there is a high degree of managing the expectations of the customer.

It is obviously possible to lose customers if a competitor makes a superior offering, but it is possible to win customers by positioning your product so that it is perceived to offer particularly desirable attributes.

US advertising men Ries and Trout describe this as repositioning your competitors. This actually means looking for a weakness in the competition's offering when compared with customer demands, and then to see if your strengths can be used to find an opening. If it is done in an effective way it could not only create awareness for your offering, but also develop a strong position for your product in its market.

Example	One of the examples cited by Ries and Trout (1981) is from the US market for vodka. Pepsico ran an advertisement for their brand of imported vodka headed:

Most American Vodkas seem Russian

Samovar: made in Schenley, Pennsylvania

Smirnoff: made in Harford, Connecticut

Wolfschmidt: made in Lawrenceburg, Indiana

Stolichnaya is different. It is Russian.

Made in Leningrad, Russia.

This advertisement assumed the real thing was Russian-made vodka and it exposed the other brands with their pseudo-Russian names as frauds – a classic example of the repositioning of a brand and depositioning of the competition. (*Note*: In the past the English vodka, Vladivar, made a virtue of its origins, it used to advertise itself as the 'Vodka from Varrington'.)

This has now changed as, over the years, the whole play on 'Russia-ness' became irrelevant to potential customers, in comparison with other more important differentiators in the market. Smirnoff in the UK is the brand leader 'the sophisticated one' the establishment. However, vodka is drunk predominantly by under 25s, so Vladivar repositioned itself to appeal to the young with a cheeky, irreverent style.

Repositioning is also possible by trying to change the image customers have regarding an offering from your own organisation.

All these examples involve changing the consumer's perception of an existing product for which there was a continuing customer demand. In every case what was considered acceptable or affordable was changed. This involved making changes to the controllable aspects of the marketing offering and thereby changes the basis of customer evaluation of the product. Interestingly most changes were made to the product or its promotion, for these examples price was less relevant. 'Place' as an element of geographic location of Torbay is static but 'place' as one of the four marketing 'Ps'

| Example | Another example of repositioning, is the way the holiday resort of Torbay (Torquay, Brixham and Paignton) halted the decline in visitors by rebranding the resort as the 'English Riviera'. South Devon has Britain's best climate in terms of sunshine hours and temperature, but ten years ago it was attracting a decreasing number of visitors. Visitors came primarily from northern England and were disproportionately from the lower socio-economic groups. The rebranding has created a new image of the area. It has had to be backed up by product improvements, as indicated in this quote from Maggie Corke, assistant Director of Torbay Tourist Board: 'If you call yourself a Riviera, you have to live up to it.' |

This has meant redevelopment and new amenities. It is, however, the new position of the 'English Riviera' that is credited with the change in perception of the area and the halting of the decline in tourists.

| Example | A further example of repositioning an old product was the new image for the British Labour Party. The new position did not attract a sufficient number of voters to win the 1992 General Election. But there is no doubt that a change in the perception of the party has been achieved. The result of the 1997 election, and the overwhelming victory by the New Labour Party illustrates that it works. However there are now many tensions in the party in government and it will be interesting to see how the customers (voters) consider the position of the Labour party at the next general election. |

(Note that this might have taken place before this book is published!)

actually refers to channels between supplier and customer. It can be seen from these examples that 'place' is not a particularly controllable variable, especially outside the area of consumer and industrial products. In fact physical evidence, as mentioned earlier, is more important for Torbay, as this certainly shapes perception, while with a political party the 'people element' is vital.

When a specific product achieves a strong position in the mind of a customer then that product itself develops a personality, and it can be considered as a *'brand'*. Brands are the outcome of a relationship between a customer and a product. They require effective and consistent input from the supply company complemented by the development of similar attitudes from the consumer. This 'relationship' is explored more closely in Chapter 12.

THE PRODUCT LIFE CYCLE

It is necessary at this point to consider how products and markets might change over time. This involves introducing the concept of the product life cycle, which lays the foundation for a more detailed examination of key issues within product policy, which will be covered later in Chapter 20. The basic principle suggests that every product and all markets are subject to an unavoidable life cycle, this was first introduced in Chapter 1. This idea is particularly relevant when considering the effect of tactical marketing activities that take place in short cycles of weeks or months. They may be aimed at only one component of a 'total product', maybe increasing the benefit in terms of *availability*. Alternatively it could increase customer satisfaction by adding something that makes the product more *acceptable*. These short-term activities can affect the

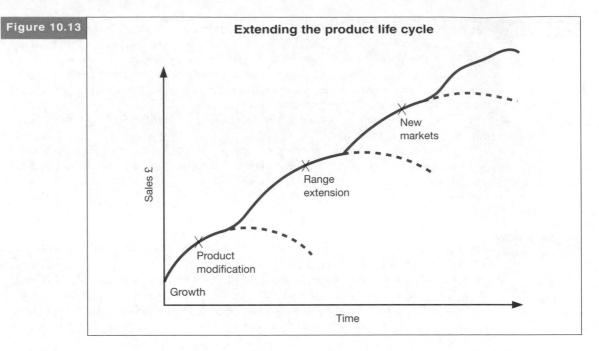

Figure 10.13

Extending the product life cycle

mature phase of a product or brand's life cycle and this is measured in years, and it is itself part of the overall life cycle of actual consumer needs which has an even greater longevity.

The result of marketing actions that prolong the actual competitive life of a product is illustrated in Figure 10.13. This shows clearly that changes to the marketing offering need to be introduced sequentially to maintain the success of a specific product or brand. There are products that continue to satisfy an on-going underlying need such as toothpaste, for cleaning teeth, or shampoo for hair cleanliness, and many brands in each category. The effectiveness of the marketing activity can be measured in terms of how well the specific brand performs in the mature stage of its life cycle. This is very difficult to achieve over long periods as may be judged by how few products have maintained a leading market position for really long periods of time.

Furthermore even brands which have maintained leading market positions through effective marketing cannot avoid being affected by fundamental market changes. An example of this would be the falling popularity of the Levis brand of jeans when these became associated with the middle-aged rather than the young as more casual products and styles emerged. Another example could be the market for many of the traditional products offered by Marks & Spencer that has also been affected by changes in fashion and customer perceptions.

Exercise

Make two lists:

■ One of brands or products which you believe have stood the test of time.
■ A second of brands or products which are clearly less important than they were.

Can you identify any differences or similarities between the products/brands in each list?

CONCLUSION

This chapter sets out to investigate four key marketing issues:

1 The markets that an organisation chooses for its operations.
2 The marketing offering as perceived by a customer in terms of the benefits received and satisfaction gained.
3 The elements that make up the total marketing offering.
4 The positioning of that offering, and the resulting image in the mind of a potential customer.

Each of these issues is of crucial importance to marketing managers; however, there are only a limited number of controllable variables that can be used to try to gain an advantage over competitors. In all respects the customer is right, they can decide what to buy, when to buy and where to buy. They can also decide *what not to buy*. Supply organisations can decide which markets to tackle and they can also put together a combination package of goods and services in order to tempt a customer, but they cannot make that customer actually purchase an offering. The best marketing decisions take account of the external environment when choosing which market to tackle and they also try to understand the motivations and other behaviour of customers when putting together a *'total marketing offering'*. In particular good marketers understand that customers require some form of benefit from any purchase, and, although this is not necessarily a financial benefit, it must reflect a greater value than alternative products and any sacrifice necessary to obtain the offering.

A marketing offering has to meet three criteria in order to be considered by a customer. It must be:

1 **Available**
2 **Affordable** and
3 **Acceptable** to the customers.

In a first application of these tests it will be seen whether an offering is able to be considered by a customer, entering their 'evoked set' of potential purchases (see Chapter 5). A further comparative look at these issues, comparing the acceptability and the other 'As' with competitive offerings will determine if a product is likely to be bought. But it is not the supplier who applies this comparison, it is the customer. Since a *'total product'* has several dimensions the customer will be able to offset one feature offered by one supplier against another feature, or maybe greater affordability, offered by someone else. However this is only possible if the 'basic' product is able to satisfy the underlying needs of the customer.

The marketing role is to try to ensure that the benefits offered by one supplier are those that really are valued by the chosen customers, and to continually review the product with this in mind. In this a supplier might be assisted by the strong position a product has in the mind of a customer. There is of course a downside when the position is rather weak, and changing the perception of customer to a poor image takes a great deal of time and money: this is a lesson that Volkswagen is finding with the attempt to change attitudes towards the Skoda range of cars. Intangible issues, such as the image of a product can be the critical factor in a purchase situation. They certainly are part of the bond between a customer and a product offering. Their value should never be underestimated and this issue will be taken further in Chapter 11.

Perhaps the most important marketing role involves the way a *'total product'* is perceived by customers. Whilst no marketer can dictate to a customer, there are many ways of putting pressure on someone to buy. This is not unethical, rather it comes from presenting the product as a complex combination of benefits rather than as a form of commodity. Once products become identical, commodity-like, the only determination will be the price. Understanding the complexity of behaviour related to **acceptability**, **affordability** and **availability** enables a good marketer to forge a strong link with certain customers, and this leads to actual purchases, and profit.

QUESTIONS

1 *There is a market for last-minute holidays, sold via High Street travel agents or over the Internet [lastminute.com]. Do you think this is the same 'market' as the offering of annual family holidays to be booked in advance, and required at a time to fit in with school holidays and the times when it is possible to get time off work?*

2 *What is the total product offered by McDonald's hamburgers? How does this give them an advantage over their competitors?*

3 *Select an advertisement that describes 'benefits' rather than product features. Comment upon its effectiveness.*

4 *Suggest some ways in which a bank offering student accounts could add to its offering to provide a more attractive 'total' offering. Do you believe it would be cost effective to enhance the offering in this way?*

5 *Using the matrix in Figure 10.11, position six cars according to your perception. Compare this with the matrix produced by another student, and explain any differences.*

6 *Consider a purchase that you have made recently. Write a list of those features that made it acceptable, affordable and available to you. Then identify any features that are unacceptable and suggest how the offer might be improved.*

FURTHER READING

Booms, B. and Bitner, M. J. (1981) 'Marketing strategies and organisation structures for service firms', in J. Donelly and W. George (eds), *The Marketing of Services*. American Marketing Association, pp. 47–51.

Borden, N. (1964) 'The concept of the marketing mix', *Journal of Advertising Research*,.

British Rail Passengers' Charter, (May 1992).

Corey, E. R. (1991) *Industrial Marketing*, 4th edn. Prentice-Hall.

Drucker, P. F. (1973) *Management Tasks, Responsibilities and Practicalities*. Harper & Row.

Grönroos, C. (1979) 'Marketing orientated strategies in service businesses', *Finnish Journal of Business*, 4.

Gummesson, E. (1991) 'Service quality: a holistic view', in S. Brown *et al.*, (eds), *Service Quality: Multidisciplinary and Multinational Perspective*. Lexington Books.

Levitt, T. (1960) 'Marketing myopia', *Harvard Business Review*, March–April.

Levitt, T. (1980) 'Marketing success through the differentiation of anything', *Harvard Business Review*, January–February.

McCarthy, E. J. and Perrault, W. D. (1990) *Basic Marketing*. Irwin.

Palmer, A. (1997) *Principles of Services Marketing*, **2nd** edition. McGraw-Hill.

Piercy, N. (1998) *Marketing-led Strategic Change*. Butterworth Heinemann.

Ries, A. and Trout, J. (1981) *Positioning the Battle for Your Mind*. McGraw-Hill.

Rock band attacks web piracy

Metallica, the heavy metal band, has begun to use the power of its celebrity to try and discredit Napster, the Internet service that enables users to swap songs on-line.

The rock group, which is suing Napster for promoting on-line music piracy, said on Tuesday it had identified more than 300 000 people who were said to be sharing the band's songs on-line in violation of copyright laws. Metallica also said it would hold an on-line forum to discuss the piracy problem directly with fans.

Napster, based in Silicon Valley USA, has developed software that allows computer users to go on-line and download music files from the hard drives of other people using the Napster system. It has become the focus of the high-tech development that most concerns the established record industry – digital piracy.

The company, which has been accused of building a 'business based on large-scale piracy', faces litigation on three fronts. The Recording Industry Association of America has filed a multi-million dollar lawsuit against Napster and a preliminary court ruling is expected imminently.

Metallica, as well as the rap artist Dr Dre, have also launched legal action against the company. The heavy metal band filed a copyright infringement and racketeering suit in the federal court in Los Angeles against the song-swapping service last month.

The on-line music delivery industry received its sharpest rebuke to date from the US legal system last week, when a New York federal judge ruled that MP3.com, the web music service, had violated copyright laws by allowing customers remote access to music through the website.

Yesterday, Metallica took its case to its fans, saying in a statement: 'We recognise that this is a very complicated issue with larger implications that our fans may not completely understand.'

Not all musicians are opposed to Napster. Limp Bizkit, the rock group, announced it was launching a tour sponsored by the software maker. Fred Durst, the band's singer, said: 'We couldn't care less about the older generation's need to keep doing business as usual. We care more about what our fans want, and our fans want music on the Internet.' Chuck D, the rapper, has also sought to highlight the 'positive aspects that Napster has to offer artists'.

James Harding

(Copyright © The Financial Times Limited, 2 May 2000)

Comment: Obviously if music is free via the net, the recording industry and record shops will lose a great deal of their business.

Question

What are the long-term implications of this, especially with respect to the link between a band and its public (fans), and the link between a record store group (say the Virgin Mega Store group) and its buying customers?

Products and services – the acceptability factor in marketing

INTRODUCTION

In Chapter 10 the concept of a total marketing offering was introduced and discussed. Three dimensions of the offering were proposed, considering it from a customer perspective.

- First, an offering must be **acceptable** to customers (the **right product**).
- Second, it must be **affordable** to them (the **right price**).
- Third, it must be **available** where and when it's wanted (the **right place and time**).

In this chapter it is the dimension of Acceptability that will be studied in more detail. There are specific issues relating to both products and services that require particular understanding although the three levels of the *'total'* product' concept have already been described in Chapter 9. The first level, the *'basic'* product, is the framework around which all the other elements of the marketing offering are clustered, therefore decisions regarding this reach to the very centre of marketing strategy and management. At the second and third levels, the *'real'* and *'total'* products will be an obvious focus of attention for all customers, and should also be the central issue for all the staff within every marketing company. They will also, of course, be objects of interest to leading competitors, suppliers, potential customers, intermediaries and many others. It has been said that the product determines the upper limit of a supplier's profitability. The quality of the remaining components of the marketing mix determines the extent to which that potential is achieved.

It is necessary to remember that the *'basic'* product is that part of the marketing mix which satisfies the fundamental customer need, but it is easy to confuse the *'basic'* product with the *'total'* product offering. While customers select from different *'total'* product offerings rather than simply *'basic'* products, it is the basic product element that meets the underlying needs of customers and delivers the core benefit as introduced in Chapter 10.

It has often been said that the 'quality of a product is remembered long after the price has been forgotten'. The point of this statement is that a product is purchased for a *specific purpose* and to meet a *particular need*. It is this *product/service* that will be judged over time, and the evaluation will be centred on how well it continues to perform the required functions, even over a long time after the actual purchase.

Example	Perhaps you own a calculator bought several years ago. Can you remember how much you paid for it? Even if you can, do you really think of the value for money aspect of the calculator? For many people the important issue is that you want to know it will continue to perform all the calculations you require. Is this your view?

WHAT IS A PRODUCT?

While the question is almost rhetorical, it is necessary to see the product from a customer perspective, rather than in solely physical or company-centred terms – a mistake often made by production-dominated companies.

The term 'product' applies not only to physical products, but also to services and other intangibles including causes and ideas, as has been described in Chapter 10. For example, the major charity organisations such as Oxfam and Save The Children are actively involved in marketing *'product offerings'* in a very similar way to the ubiquitous widget manufacturer in the West Midlands! Even in the case of an everyday physical product such as washing-up liquid, there will be intangible extras and associations that are offered in addition to the basic product such as the quality assurance of a known brand name and manufacturer source. With a charity it is the 'feel-good' aspects of making a donation.

These aspects are certainly reflected in one of the most useful definitions of a product proposed by the American Marketing Association:

Anything that can be offered to a market for attention, acquisition or consumption including physical objects, services, personalities, organisations and desires.

Our definition is more focused on what the customer perceives a product to be, so that a working definition might be:

Everything that the customer receives that is of value in terms of a perceived want, need or problem.

This second definition allows for those aspects of an offering both acceptable and unacceptable, the latter being elements which actually reduce the perceived value to a customer. Though rather broad and vague, this definition also allows that different customers will vary in their perception of their needs, wants and problems. Simply stated, the marketer needs to view the product as a multidimensional offering, a mix of tangible features and intangible attributes, good and bad, together with an element of services, bundled around a basic or core benefit.

It is obvious that some products might appear to customers as better value or more attractive, for various reasons almost irrespective of producer intentions or objective measures of quality or product input. The result is that a few will gain commanding market shares as 'brand leaders' in their markets. Others may survive and continue to be marketed although in low volume and not necessarily producing many profits (so-called 'weaker' or 'marginal' products), whilst some product offerings will not be accepted by enough customers, and will fail commercially.

Although most of the accepted definitions of a product were probably intended to refer to the need-satisfying object or service component part of the *'basic'* product, in practice it will be seen that they apply equally to a product offering. Therefore the use of the word 'product' to cover the core or *'basic'* product, or perhaps the *'real'* product, or even the *'total'* product offering (see Figure 10.2), does mean that marketers must be extremely careful when using the term. It is critical that they should ensure under-standing of the appropriate meaning of the word 'product' relevant to a specific given situation.

Example	**A 'total' product**

A Mars Bar is a good example of a product widely accepted and as popular now as it ever was. The 1999 ingredient panel states that it contains:

> MILK CHOCOLATE, GLUCOSE SYRUP, SUGAR, HYDROGENATED VEGETABLE FAT, SKIMMED MILK POWDER, FAT-REDUCED COCOA, MILK FAT, MALT EXTRACT, FULL CREAM MILK POWDER, SALT, LACTOSE, WHEY POWDER, EGG WHITE, MILK PROTEIN, FLAVOURING.

These are the ingredients we consume when we eat a Mars Bar. We are not told the actual pro-portion of chocolate to milk fat, but a clever food scientist could make an acceptable analysis, and, further, could probably make a good copy of a Mars Bar.

The copy should offer a similar degree of enjoyment to anyone eating the product. Some 20 years ago a rival confectionery firm (Cadbury's) did in fact develop a product called 'Aztec', which marketing research showed to be comparable to Mars in many ways. The product was launched, and as Cadbury's is a large company with a good reputation it was easily able to per-suade retail shops to buy the product. The trouble was, that not enough consumers (members of the public) bought it from the retailers to make it a success then.

You may have heard of Aztec although Cadbury's stopped making it after only a short time. This is because it was relaunched in 1999 as Aztec Limited edition 2000. At this moment we don't know if Aztec 2000 is selling well, nor if it will be discontinued in the year 2000 . . . but con-sider the events 20 years ago and suggest why the original Aztec failed against Mars in what is after all a very large market?

- It was not the *'basic'* product – they were very similar
- Nor was it the price or availability
- It was the other features: brand name, packaging styling, quality, and – most importantly – image.

We don't know if Mars can *'make it* happen' – the slogan currently in use, but there are cer-tainly some psychological features which are part of a Mars Bar which give it a real advantage over the competitor from Cadbury's.

TYPES OF 'PRODUCT'

There are a number of useful ways of classifying products. One of the most basic was introduced in Chapter 10, see Figure 10.2, in the discussion regarding the different ways of making a journey. This referred to the ownership and tangibility of an offer-ing, contrasting the hard issue of the physical control of the means of delivery with the possibility of receiving the same benefit from a service provider. The example covered several different ways to receive a specific benefit including travelling in a car owned by the traveller, in a hired car, and by train, bus or plane. It was clear from this that a journey could be made by using purchased physical objects (i.e. the car, petrol and so on), or by purchasing the service offered by the car hire company or one of the organisations providing one of the alternative modes of transport.

This is an interesting example since although the use of a hire car or other transport provider involves purchasing a service, the use of the traveller's own car involves pur-chasing the essential physical objects (car and petrol) and in addition at least two

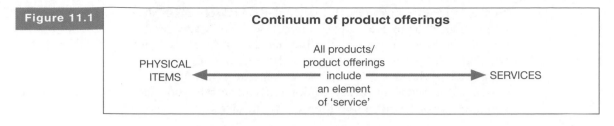

Figure 11.1 — Continuum of product offerings

mandatory service products. The first of these is vehicle insurance and the second is that offered by the Vehicle Licensing Authority who collects the Road Fund License Fee on behalf of the government and issues the tax disc. In addition, the car user will usually require other services such as those offered by garages that supply and service cars, sell petrol, carry out MOT tests and even provide toilet facilities.

Thus, while it would at first sight seem possible to separate products or product offerings into physical objects and services, in practice very few 'products' are purely 100 per cent service or 100 per cent tangible product. Usually they involve a mix of the two. It is useful to see the specific product offering as a continuum, ranging from a pure service through a combination of a service and a physical object to a tangible offering (see Figure 11.1). This reflects Kotler's four categories of 'products':

- a pure service
- a major service with accompanying minor goods and services
- a tangible good with accompanying service
- a pure tangible product.

Irrespective of where a product/service offering is located on this continuum, it is the way that the basic offering *satisfies a customer* that is important in evaluating the overall acceptability. Perhaps levels of satisfaction can also be used as a measure of product/service quality, a topic that will be covered later in this chapter.

In Chapter 10 the added value matrix (Figure 10.3) was introduced, linking products and services in order to provide a unique offering. The next section will look at the specific issues of making the service element acceptable.

SERVICE PRODUCTS

Whilst the continuum above and the four categories of offerings are important the service element is sometimes divided into just two classifications – **service products** and **product services**.

1 **'Service products'** are those pure services, or major service components, directly offered to customers, such as hairdressing, health care, transportation, education and insurance.
2 **'Product services'** are those service elements associated with a physical object such as car repairs, property repairs and plumbing services, each involving tangible goods.

These distinctions apply equally to consumer markets and industrial and business markets. In the consumer market, internet shopping and telephone banking are both fast-growing areas. In the 'business-to-business' (B2B) sector service products might include specialist services such as market research, advertising, or perhaps financial advice, but they range through to such peripheral services as cleaners and the catering contractors who provide canteen services. Some 'pure services' have been built on new technological developments, creating new industrial markets for advisory services in specialist fields such as expert-systems software development.

Product services are often used to *enhance the benefit* offered by a tangible product. For instance, servicing of key equipment and installations such as photocopiers or computers is often integral to the supply contract for that equipment.

Example

Service product and product service

'Service product'

One very high-profile 'service product' is Microsoft's Internet Explorer. First launched free as part of Windows 95, it quickly became the leading software in this market. It has recently been at the centre of the US anti-trust lawsuit against Microsoft, but that has not stopped it being an excellent example of a service product that provides real, intangible benefits to users. Whilst many 'services' rely on human involvement from the supplier, this example shows that it is not always necessary.

'Product service'

When purchasing computer hardware, it almost always happens that an extended warranty, or a service/repair contract will be offered as an add-on extra. This is an example of a product service.

Exercise

'Service product' or 'product service'?

Some industrial service companies provide an essentially financial benefit, as, for instance, the contract car leasing companies who are often the legal owners of the cars provided by employers to their employees. Such companies have developed the service offered so that for their customer organisations it is significantly cheaper to lease these cars than it would be to own them. It also allows the trading organisation to concentrate on its own core area of business, leaving the car leasing in the hands of a specialist company.

Like vehicle leasing, haulage and distribution services are also likely to involve contract arrangements, so which category of services would these be?

Earlier in this chapter products and services were placed in a continuum. This can be illustrated more effectively by considering the proportion of an offering that is tangible compared with the elements that are intangible (see Figure 11.2.).

The key issue is to understand that any of the elements in the total product offered to customers can be a vital ingredient to gain advantage over competition. Therefore achieving an effective combination, and making an offering more acceptable, is a necessary role of marketing.

The question that has to be asked here is whether the marketing of a service product, or a product which is a major service with accompanying minor goods, is different from the marketing of tangible physical goods? The best answer will refer back to the basic idea of a mutually beneficial exchange, and the requirements for the proper application of the marketing concept as discussed in Chapter 1. It will be seen that the basic principles of marketing apply in all situations.

Figure 11.2

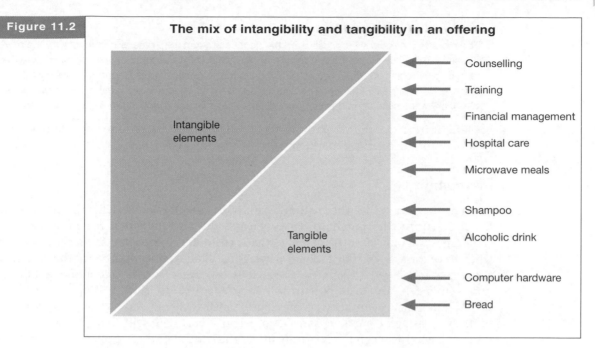

The mix of intangibility and tangibility in an offering

Intangible elements

Tangible elements

← Counselling

← Training

← Financial management

← Hospital care

← Microwave meals

← Shampoo

← Alcoholic drink

← Computer hardware

← Bread

MARKETING SERVICES

Kotler (1997) defines a service as: 'Any act or performance that one party can offer to another that is essentially intangible and does not result in the ownership of anything. Its production may or may not be tied to a physical product.' This definition emphasises two key elements of a service:

1 **Intangibility**. The service being offered cannot be experienced *in advance of the purchase*. It can of course be tested by prior experience but could suffer from variability (see below).
2 **Lack of ownership.** There is no aspect of ownership in a pure service or service component. However there are three other distinctive features that must also be considered:
   - **Inseparability**. The fact that the production of a service takes place *at the same time as its* delivery.
   - **Perishability**. Services cannot be *stored or kept in a warehouse*. Time is part of services and once that time has not been used then the service opportunity has gone.
   - **Variability**. Because each delivery is unique there is *no standardisation of output*. The product and delivery depend on the two parties involved at the time of delivery (see inseparability above).

Because of these issues there are likely to be some different actions and different emphases present when marketing a service product or the service elements of a total offering. However, as many total products have both a service component and a physical core the actions required to market a service successfully are likely to be similar to those required to market any total offering.

Levitt (1976) observed that:

> The more technologically sophisticated the generic product (e.g. cars and computers), the more dependant are its sales on the quality and availability of its accompanying customer services (e.g. display rooms, delivery, repairs and maintenance, application aids, operator training, installation advice, warranty fulfilment). In this sense, General Motors is probably more service intensive than manufacturing intensive. Without its service, its sales would shrivel.

Looking at the factors above in more detail will help to highlight the important actions necessary for good service marketing.

Intangibility

Intangibility means that the customer cannot be sure of what benefits he/she is going to receive until after purchase. This increases the uncertainty of the purchase, and sometimes it is only after the purchase that a customer realises that the service was not what was expected. Of course, there are ways of reducing uncertainty; for the customer these come in three areas. First is previous experience or the recommendation of others; this can play an important role in any buyer's decision. A supplier can assist this by encouraging contact with previously satisfied clients. But if there is no direct or indirect measure of previous satisfaction then a customer will look for other, more indirect cues. The second area is fully under the control of the supplier. It includes the attitudes of the people representing a potential supplier and the way they go about their business, maybe the ambience of the surroundings such as the state of the supplier's premises, or perhaps the speed of producing a quotation. If these factors are perceived as positive then the uncertainty is reduced, but it can never be removed altogether because of the other issues such as the risk of variability (see page 191). The third issue is to attempt to give some degree of tangibility to a service offering. This is also important in overcoming the problems of lack of ownership. An obvious approach is to add some physical extra to the intangible product. Examples could be guarantees for work performed by a mechanic added to a 'car service' product, or perhaps textbooks supplied as part of a college course of study, or the more recent facility to print out your own tickets after booking rail travel over the Internet. All of these 'tangibles' will help to overcome the problems of intangibility.

Lack of ownership

The next area that can cause concern is the fact that a pure service cannot be owned. All that can be acquired is the access to that specific service for a period of time. Of course such an exposure to the service should confer a benefit on the recipient. For instance, a rail journey is experienced from the point of departure to the destination and the benefit is arriving at a chosen location. But, after handing in the ticket, no tangible item remains. Similarly a student will receive knowledge from their teachers or from a search across a website. This can be given an aura of tangibility by the handouts given or printouts of material, but these are not the education and it is impossible to touch or feel the actual knowledge. For instance providing a tangible component such as a degree certificate for a successful student could help. These examples can give a clue as to the problem of the lack of ownership and some of the marketing activities that can be used to overcome them. But a distinction must be made between the ownership of a physical symbol giving a right to receive a service and the service itself. A season ticket for your favourite football club gives you the right to attend all home matches and always sit in the same seat, however it gives no additional benefits and while you might enjoy the football you do not own the team. In the same way being given a password might give access to a restricted website, enabling a student to acquire new knowledge, but you do not own the contents of the site.

Inseparability

The intangible product benefit in the case of a football match is the enjoyment and entertainment experienced by watching the match actually take place. This leads on to the third important feature of any service product, i.e. the production of the service cannot be separated from the receipt – they take place at the same time and in the same place. There is an involvement between the provider and the recipient of the service so that the production and delivery cannot be separated. This opens up the question of how the quality of a service is judged at the time of delivery, and what a supplier can do to try to achieve a positive response for their total offering.

It is the way the service is presented by the providers, and the environment within which it is provided that are critical. This includes the comfort and cleanliness of a train, the attitude of employees who are in contact with the passengers and other issues that make a train journey a pleasure rather than something to be endured. These considerations also affect the issue of intangibility.

Example   When conducting an on-line search for a specific item you might wish to purchase, it is the search engine you chose to use, and the keywords you select, that determine the outcome of the search.

Thus your activities, together with the prompts and layout of the sites, are inseparable, each contributing to the eventual success or failure.

A service encounter occurs every time a customer interacts with a supply organisation. These encounters could be person-to-person or, as in the case of on-line encounters, could be impersonal.

In most encounters the most vivid impression of a service occurs in the first few minutes of the encounter, meeting an employee of the supplier or accessing a website. Jan Carlzon, former Chief Executive Officer at Scandinavian Airways (SAS), described personal 'moments of truth'.

SAS is not a collection of material assets but it is the quality of the contact between an individual customer and the SAS (front line) employee who serves that customer directly.

Carlzon goes on to explain that each of SAS' 10 million customers come into contact with approximately five SAS employees. So there are 50 million contacts, yet each contact was averaging only 15 seconds at a time. He goes on to say:

SAS is thus created 50 million times a year, 15 seconds at a time. These 50 million 'moments of truth' are the moments that ultimately determine whether SAS will succeed or fail as a company. They are the moments when SAS must prove itself to its customers that it is the best alternative.

The training of staff and encouraging all contact employees to listen to customers, and act appropriately are vital for success. These issues will be discussed again with regards to the importance of personal contact in marketing. The same 'moment of truth' concept could be extended to non-physical contact encounters. If there is too much complexity involved in any encounter, the customer will not feel comfortable, if the site visited is clear, well laid out and inviting then a better encounter will ensue. Try visiting different websites to evaluate how inviting they seem.

Example	(*Actual experience of one of the authors*)

In a Safeway supermarket the person in front of the checkout queue was wearing a Safeway uniform and obviously knew the till operator. They were chatting about common interests while the three customers behind had to wait to be served. Even though the encounter only took a few minutes it was obvious that other queues were moving while this one was not.

Question

What will be the effect on the others in that queue, and does it really matter that staff are seen to be served in front of other customers?

Perishability

The next issue that separates services and tangible goods is that while goods can be produced ahead of the time required and stored until needed, this is impossible with a service. They cannot be prepared in advance for later exchanging with customers. This does not matter when demand can be controlled to take place at a constant rate, but it affects services where demand fluctuates.

Such changes can be accommodated when demand for tangible goods varies, for instance a UK company making chocolate creme eggs used to make them throughout the year putting many into cold storage until the start of the Easter season when this product is much in demand. A service cannot be stored in this way so peaks of demand can be met only if additional staff are employed at the peak times. This is why supermarket checkouts are not fully staffed at periods of low business, but fully manned at busy times. But there have to be sufficient checkouts in the first place, and, therefore it is necessary to supplement the people with the necessary facilities for them to cope with the demand. Provision of these facilities is expensive and organisations have to decide the levels they are prepared to make available. The provision of extra facilities and staff during peak periods is a supply-driven strategy of the sort which operation specialists will need to develop to deal with the problem.

It is also possible to try to reduce the extremes of high and low activity by marketing initiatives aimed at modifying demand, for instance the use of differential pricing. An example of this are the discounts offered to encourage rail users to use off-peak periods for travel. These are never more than partially successful. It is sometimes more appropriate to accept the problems and then try to benefit out of the situation by modifying the total product. For example, the famous London wax works museum Madame Tussauds expects long queues in the peak summer periods. To make the long waits more acceptable they hire entertainers such as jugglers and clowns to perform for those waiting. This has become as much a part of a visit to Tussauds as the museum itself. Another example is a hotel that offers an automatic checkout to approved business customers. This increases the benefit to those customers and reduces the demand on busy cashier staff at the peak period around 8.00 a.m. when many guests want to settle the accounts and leave the hotel. There are innumerable creative marketing solutions to problems of uneven demand. However, the fact still remains that the time period over which a service is offered is the same time as when it is received: if a service is ready for a customer and no customer can be found then the *service opportunity perishes for ever*.

Example

Museums that don't attract enough visitors are 'perishable' products   FT

In 1996, the Royal Armouries moved some of its choicest objects, including Henry VIII's personal armour, from its traditional home in the Tower of London, to its new base in Leeds. The prospects looked pleasing for the first public–private finance initiative, and companies such as Yorkshire Electricity were happy to invest in this brave merging of the academic and the commercial. Research suggested that 1m people a year would visit the museum that was built on a potentially dynamic canal site not far from the centre of a city that was transforming itself into the shopping capital of the north.

Three years later, with debts of £20m, the venture was up. Paying visitors collapsed to less than 300,000 as the admission charge rose to £7.95. Commercialising the museum, to the extent of inviting in a dinosaur show, failed to stop the rot. The Royal Armouries has now reclaimed exclusive control of the museum. It has cut prices – a season ticket costs just £6.50; invested again in displays and events, such as an all-weather tilt yard; and stressed cultural values. The Royal Armouries now believes it has turned a corner.

It is certainly nearer stability than the National Centre for Popular Music at Sheffield. Here again forecasts of visitor numbers – 400,000 a year – proved hopelessly optimistic, and with just 100,000 coming in the first nine months the centre had run up debts of £1m. Staff numbers were cut and managers came and went. With £11m of lottery money invested in the project it has just been re-launched with fresh management, lower ticket prices, and more live music.

Anthony Thorncroft

Source: Extracted from *Financial Times* 24 April 2000. (© Copyright The Financial Times)

Variability

The final key difference to be considered by anyone involved in the marketing of a service, or a product with a service component, derives from the repetition of the service, i.e. it being a new production every time. Services can perhaps be likened to the performance of a play in the theatre. Each time it is performed there will be a different audience and the actors will have different feelings and moods with which to contend. So the services can vary at each performance, yet to those who receive the service, the people providing it on a specific occasion are the service.

On the supply side, organisations often look for systems to control the quality of a service, and sometimes try to find alternatives that are less dependent on people. Examples of this are Automatic Teller Machines (ATM) in banks, or the use of barcodes on grocery products, so the supermarket operator does not have to enter prices into the till. Levitt (1976) called this development the 'industrialisation of services', and his article gives further examples. However, it is as true today as when Levitt wrote his article that inconsistent service exists, and when that service falls below the standards acceptable to customers, those customers either complain – or, more likely, do not return. Marketing should encourage customers to complain about poor service, as studies show that where a customer contacts the organisation and gets a satisfactory response, that customer is far more likely to use the service again. Most customers know that mistakes happen because no one is perfect, and they are often prepared to forgive organisations that they perceive as helpful.

A COMPLETE MARKETING MIX

While there are many factors which separate activities (services) from tangible products the principles of marketing are unchanged. The objective is to gain profitable business by satisfying customers.

A study of the factors considered above would show why the traditional marketing mix (Product, Price, Place and Promotion) was considered too restrictive for the planning of service delivery. Perhaps the key difference where there is a large service element in an offering is the close contact between individual employees from supplier organisations and the individual customers. This leads to a re-evaluation of the traditional mix, and in particular the definition of product acceptability. The role of the people who participate in the delivery of the service is obviously vital, but so is the way a service is provided and the actual environment in which it is received. This is why Mary Jo Bitner with Bernard Booms has suggested an addition to the '4 Ps' of the traditional mix by the inclusion of *People, Process* and *Physical evidence*. Bitner argues that these three 'new' elements should be included as separate parts of the marketing mix because they are within the control of the supply organisation in the same way as the original factors. These additional 'Ps' certainly highlight areas that can make an offering both more acceptable and more available.

THE IMPORTANCE OF PEOPLE TO DELIVERING AN ACCEPTABLE OFFERING

The nature of most service encounters requires direct personal contact. This leads to the view, that in many offerings the *people providing the service are the service*. This dependence was neatly described by one of the great advertising men, Leo Burnett, who said 'All our assets go down the elevator every evening.' It is the people who make the difference between good and bad service, and yet in many industries they are badly rewarded. This was highlighted by Schlessinger and Hesketh (1991) who found that average real wages fell in the service sector in the USA in the period 1979–89, and further commented that 'for the most part these jobs are poorly paid, lead nowhere, and provide little if anything in the way of health, pension, or other benefits'. They concluded that in restaurants, hotels, grocery, department stores, building services, supply and personnel over 90 per cent of all jobs can be classified as 'truly dead-end jobs'. Drucker highlighted this in his article 'The new productivity challenge' where he suggests that the 'most pressing social challenge developed countries face is to raise the productivity of service workers'. It is the motivation and training of people which is crucial in service delivery, but their importance must be put into perspective. A simple mapping of the involvement of people against the relative cost of those people can be useful (see Figure 11.3).

This map can be used to highlight those areas where attention must be focused. For offerings in the top right quadrant such as hairdressing, or teaching, the emphasis is on the human resource activities. At the opposite side there are remote encounters and offerings where service plays a small part. Here the people are less important but can still make a difference during moment-of-truth encounters. This could be true when an aggressive bus driver tries to hurry passengers and drives off before some travellers have sat down. It could also be a situation when the receptionist answers a telephone call to a company. Robert Townsend in his classic book *Up the Organisation* gives the

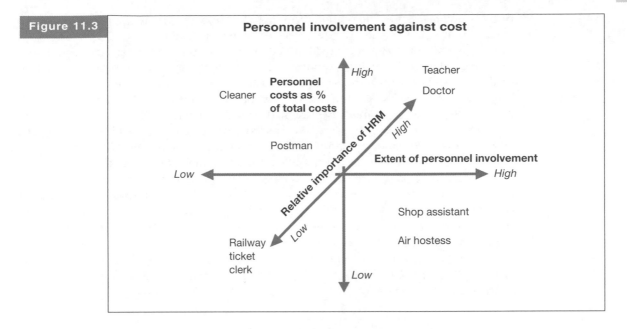

Figure 11.3

Personnel involvement against cost

advice 'Call yourself up – when off on a business trip or a vacation, pretend you're a customer. Telephone some part of your organisation and ask for help. You'll run into some real horror shows. Don't blow up and ask for name, rank, and serial number – you're trying to correct, not punish . . . Then try calling yourself up and see what indignities you've built into your own defences.'

In addition to the two dimensions in Figure 11.3, another factor that should be considered is the level of skill required by the person giving the service. Most of the jobs highlighted by Hesketh are low-skill activities, however there are a number of skilled and complex services that are very different in nature. The role of a doctor or a lawyer is a good example. In these professional services there is a high degree of specific training but this tends to be related to the operation of that particular role rather than any training in how to interact with customers. It is often difficult to persuade a highly qualified professional that they need to respond to patients and clients as customers, but there is competition in these areas as much as in other services and the way contact with customers is managed is equally important.

It is possible to split human resource management (HRM) into 'hard' and 'soft' categories. 'Hard' is measured in terms of efficiency and worker productivity, and is concerned with costs and financial measures. 'Soft' emphasises the role of employees as essential assets who must be encouraged and motivated in their jobs. It is these 'softer' qualitative issues which are reflected in the way customer contact is performed.

THE PROCESS OF PRODUCT/SERVICE DELIVERY

To complement the people who deliver a product or a service it is necessary to also consider the actual procedures and mechanisms involved in the delivery. Drucker was sceptical as to whether 'capital' could replace people in service delivery. He concludes that in service work, the people are the 'tools' of production. However a quick study of the way new technologies are developing will show that there are opportunities to reduce human involvement if the processes are well planned.

There are all sorts of operational issues that directly affect customer's perception and level of satisfaction regarding a service. This could be the speed of an order being delivered in a fast-food restaurant or, in an industrial setting, perhaps the ease of paying a bill, or any other issue regarding the way the offering is transferred to the customer. Of course, where remote contact is present the process is paramount, but most services have some procedures that can make that service more or less acceptable to customers. When these procedures are unnecessarily complex and customers do not see any reason for the bureaucracy, then there is a natural tendency to reject the offering.

Some complex procedures have developed over time and, in some industries all the organisations offering that service seem to follow the same methods. It can take an outside entrant into the market to find a way of providing the service which is easier for and more acceptable to customers and thus develop an advantage for the new competitor over more established companies.

The food and clothing retailer, Marks & Spencer, have tried to capitalise on this by entering the pensions business. The extract from their publicity leaflet gives some idea of the claims they make:

To live life to the full when you retire you need to take the right steps now. And all too often it is easier to put things off – even though the sooner you arrange a pension plan, the sooner you can start looking forward to a prosperous retirement.

So, what if you could choose a pension designed to be simple, easy to understand and from a name you can trust?

We have taken a new look at pensions, and cut out the jargon and the complicated forms, the salesmen and the pressure – making it easier for you to reach your own decision.

Source: Marks & Spencer Life Assurance Ltd

As mentioned above technological developments are another factor that have also been utilised to make it easier for customers to make purchase decisions. For instance computerised ticketing and reservation systems used by airlines, or the use of credit cards to purchase from remote locations.

Example   ## Net tickets poised for take-off   **FT**

E-commerce could fundamentally change the way airlines deal with big corporate clients writes Amon Cohen.

The combination of vast amounts of fast-changing data and no other physical product than a ticket makes travel the ideal sector to sell through the Internet. Indeed, it ranks alongside computer peripherals and software as a commercial category on the web.

However, the Internet procurement revolution has yet to happen for large corporate buyers of travel. According to Jupiter Communications, 3 per cent of on-line air bookings are made by managed business travellers from big companies, compared with 60 per cent made by leisure travellers, and 37 per cent by unmanaged business travellers (those not guided by a corporate travel policy, usually self-employed). Figures for hotel and car hire purchases are similar.

There are several reasons why this sector is not yet booking on-line. One is that installing relevant programs into companies' data systems has proved harder than expected. Another is that self-service reservations only make sense for simple there-and-back journeys. So far, a trained human travel agent can organise a complex itinerary more swiftly and often find a better fare.

In the USA, where the preponderance of simpler, domestic travel has made on-line booking easier to introduce, one benefit reported by early adopters is that the average cost of a ticket drops by about 20 per cent. Travellers, when presented with a range of fares from which they must choose with a mouse-click, feel more obliged to select the cheapest option.

As on-line booking starts to catch on, strategists are examining whether e-commerce will fundamentally alter the way airlines conduct business with their leading corporate clients.

One likely benefit is that airlines will finally yield to demands from multinationals for a single worldwide-negotiated deal. Carriers have been reluctant in the past because they felt both they and their clients were unable to consolidate reliable purchasing information. 'This will lead to globalisation of air deals,' says Simon Parks-Smith, head of British Airways' new business-to-business e-commerce division. 'E-commerce provides a much more transparent flow of information.'

Travel managers are looking at ways of linking software to their on-line reservations systems so that the restrictions on which carriers can be booked are changed automatically and speedily as the company strives for the best returns.

Many new ideas are still being tested and no one is sure how they will work in practice. What is clear, however, is that the increasing focus on price threatens to transform airline seats from carefully branded products to negotiable commodities. 'E-commerce potentially commoditises air travel,' admits Mr Parks-Smith. 'Our challenge is to create real value to ensure it is not just a commodity, such as by striving to be Europe's most punctual airline.'

(© Copyright The Financial Times)

Source: <FT.com>, 23 April 2000.

Payne (1993) suggests two areas where processes should be given attention:

- As structural elements that help to achieve a position
- As a way of achieving synergy between marketing and operations management in delivering a service.

The first involves issues such as the complexity of the process and the amount of individuality allowed to the person actually delivering the service.

The second ensures the actual operations are consistent with the claims and promises made to customers. In this second sense, the process of delivering a service can therefore be considered equivalent to the category of physical handling of a tangible good as in the original marketing mix presented by Borden.

Exercise   Consider the purchase of rail tickets via the net. What are the advantages and disadvantages for passengers, and how can companies such as Virgin Trains install systems to make the process more customer-friendly?

PHYSICAL EVIDENCE

This category is the third of the additions proposed by Bitner for inclusion into a total marketing mix. She defines it as 'The environment in which the service is delivered and where the firm and customer interact, and any tangible components that facilitate performance or communication of the service'. Payne (1993) agrees on the two separate components of the category but suggests they are better considered under the more traditional heading of 'Product'. This perhaps says more about the restrictive nature of some interpretations of the marketing mix than any dispute over these controllable issues. There is agreement that the physical evidence must be consistent with the other elements in the mix and can greatly affect a customer's perception of the service offering.

Environmental factors

These are the locations in which a service is offered and consumed. The *feel of the surroundings* is particularly relevant when a customer visits a supplier's premises such as a bank, restaurant, or sports club. If the environment is unacceptable then this affects the total offering in an adverse way.

Banks have traditionally used solid, large buildings that are supposed to reinforce the feeling of security for your money, although now such symbols are becoming increasingly old-fashioned as internet banking develops. For the Net the environmental factors relate to the web environment, and this must be judged in a very different way. Fast-food outlets are known to favour colour schemes that include red and yellow to give an impression of speed. Both colours and designs are also visible in the uniforms worn by employees. These complement the surroundings, and well-dressed staff are said to enhance images of efficiency with colours chosen to add to the message. It is really a form of *packaging*, but interpreted as intangible offerings, and aimed at enhancing the acceptability of the total offering.

Environmental elements can be used in many ways, in fact they can affect any of the customer's senses, including smell or sound, as well as sight. In retail supermarkets, the smell of freshly baked bread is promoted to enhance the environment, whereas the odour of fish is eliminated. Clothing stores aimed at young people play appropriate music, and also organise shops so that the target customers feel welcome. All these are examples of environmental evidence.

Physical clues

Two categories of services were introduced earlier – a pure service, and a service with accompanying minor goods. In fact to overcome some of the problems of intangibility and lack of ownership, it is quite common for providers of services to add some tangible features to the basic service. These could be a railway ticket, an insurance policy document, a holiday brochure, or a restaurant menu, none of which have much independent value by themselves. The use of the word 'clues' is important, as customers are often looking for information about the scope of the service and quality of the offering. A fully illustrated travel brochure with pictures, temperature/climate information is useful, but this could be the expected product. Some tour companies enhance the offering by additional information based on customer comments and unambiguous fair trading promises. All these are clues presented in a way which could be considered as physical evidence; all are designed to reduce uncertainty. Since the objective of marketing is a satisfactory exchange then it is vital that these clues are used as part of the management of customer expectations. It is, of course, the actual offering which will be judged against these expectations. If it is perceived to meet, or better, expectations then the result is a satisfied customer. If not . . . the customer could be lost.

Exercise

Many products can now be booked using the Internet. However a lot of offers made over the Net concentrate on the price of the item rather than its additional features. It is very easy to use a website to enhance a product by giving technical details, supplying a picture, or even allowing a potential customer to click onto an image of the product in use.

However many customers trying to buy a music system, or a computer, or a camera still go to a local retail store to see and handle the product before revisiting the Net to find the best price.

Can you think of other ways in which a customer might be offered more tangible clues regarding a durable product that they could wish to purchase? In particular, consider the customer's need to feel involved in the purchase, and the fact that this type of product is often quite expensive and there are usually several alternatives that should be seriously considered.

PRODUCT AND SERVICE PROMISES

Promises is another word beginning with 'P', and it could be considered the totality of the marketing mix encompassing all the claims made and benefits offered. The promise made to customers has a great influence on the acceptability of an offering prior to purchase. Every element of the mix adds up to a *total promise regarding the offering*. Promises are obviously important in all categories of products, but in service industries the promises are critical because of the inseparability of the delivery of the service to customers. It is therefore critical to ensure that the promises made are realistic and that all employees involved in the delivery of a service are aware of those promises. If changes have to be made then the supplier should not hide such facts from customers, but they should keep customers informed of the situation and the implications discussed. It is not enough just to say 'sorry'. If a delivery is going to be late, tell customers as this defuses the anger and allows a strong relationship to develop. Of course, too many *broken promises* equals lost customers.

THE QUALITY OF PRODUCTS AND SERVICES

We cannot consider marketing without studying the topic of quality. 'Quality' is one of those issues that everyone agrees is important but many find difficult to define. Quality measures need to be applied to the products or services offered as well as all the aspects of the exchange and the relationship with a customer. The problem comes in *defining quality*. For instance a car or a piece of industrial equipment could come with very high technical specifications, or perhaps many added value benefits, or maybe some top of the range characteristics, usually also at a premium price. However, quality does not have to be viewed in this way. A supermarket like Tesco offers far less in terms of personal service and ambience when compared to the Food Hall at Harrods in London. Nevertheless within the chosen parameters both offer quality. In fact, quality has more to do with the *expectation of customers* than with the features a supplier might define as important.

One useful approach to the issue of quality is to consider a product against the eight dimensions of quality proposed by David Garvin in his 1987 article in the *Harvard Business Review*:

■ *Performance* – a product's primary operating characteristic.

- *Features* – the 'bells and whistles', those characteristics that supplement basic functioning.
- *Conformance* – the degree to which design of operating characteristics meets established standards.
- *Serviceability* – relating to the ease of maintenance.
- *Reliability* – the probability of a product malfunctioning during a specified time period.
- *Durability* – a measure of product life with both economic and technical dimensions.
- *Aesthetics* – how a product looks, feels, sounds, tastes or smells.
- *Perceived quality* – personal judgement comes in with both the last categories.

As consumers do not always have complete information to judge a product or service (amateur buyer), perception of quality, reputation or other intangibles are important in judging how customers rate your offering in their value equation.

It will be noticeable that Garvin's list progresses from the tangible characteristics and features of a product through the way a product performs to the perceived attributes that depend on customers making a value judgement.

These dimensions are a good starting point when considering the basis on which quality can be judged; a challenge for marketers is to reduce the dimensions to a manageable set selected as being relevant to the chosen customers. It will then be possible to achieve a better match between a supplier's offer and customer's requirements.

Quality can also be studied from the service perspective. Berry et al. (1991) revised their widely accepted SERVQUAL© model of service quality to reduce the issues down to the five key determinants that are:

- **Reliability**
- **Responsiveness**
- **Assurance**
- **Empathy**
- **Tangibility.**

Whilst these obviously apply directly to service aspects of an offering, it is necessary for the total offering to be seen as reliable and offering assurance alongside the overall perceived quality as judged by customers.

Quality relationships are built on confidence and trust, but cannot exist without quality being present in all aspects of the offering. Where such quality is found then there is a greater probability that high levels of loyalty regarding the offering will also exist. That, after all, is a major aim of all marketing programmes.

Exercise	Visit a retail web site of your choice. Consider the offering made and evaluate the marketing against the quality criteria above. Do you think the offer meets the requirement of a customer for a 'quality' product/service?
	If you can't find a site then visit <qxl.com> the auction web site. The information below was on the site in May 2000, you will find more information when you visit the site. Do you think that QXL provide the necessary reassurance to customers wishing to purchase products via their site? Are there any other issues relating to quality that worry you?

We take security seriously at QXL. Please read our policies thoroughly to become familiar with our principles and practices. To find out about our policies check:

- Terms & Conditions
- Privacy Policy
- Fraud & Piracy Policy
- QXL guarantees

Frequently asked questions about security and privacy

- I'm worried about sending my credit-card number over the Internet. Need I be?
- Can I phone or fax my credit-card details instead of using the Web?
- Will you sell my email address to other people who will send me junk mail?
- I've signed up for your Bargain Alert e-mail service. How do I unsubscribe?

ANOTHER WAY TO CONSIDER PRODUCTS – CONSUMER AND INDUSTRIAL

It might be helpful to consider product and service offerings in another way in order to assist marketing decisions. This is to classify them by the type of customer and the way customers use particular products.

The different purchase behaviours of consumer and industrial customers have been discussed in Chapters 5 and 6. These differences must be accommodated in any marketing initiative. Some products such as heavy machinery, packaging machines, lorries, consultancy services and security are, with few exceptions, exclusively purchased by industrial organisations after consideration by employees on behalf of their organisation. Such products can then be classified as 'industrial products'. Other products such as shoes, tea, visits to the cinema, cans of soft drink and so on, are usually purchased by individuals for their own use. These products are accordingly generally classified as 'consumer products'.

Whilst few industrial products are purchased by individuals, many consumer products are also purchased for use within organisations. Thus hotels need to buy essentially the same food and household products as are purchased for use in the home. The difference is the quantities in which these products are typically purchased. For instance, whereas toilet tissue might be purchased in packets of one to nine rolls for use in the home they could well be purchased by the 100 or 1000 rolls for a hotel or hotel chain. In a purely pedantic way a bulk purchase of a product from a catering supplier could be seen as very different from the same basic product bought singly in a convenience store.

It will be seen from Figure 11.4 that products can be classified as consumer or industrial, as well as consumable or durable, the first classification based on the *type of customer*, the second on the *characteristics of the products themselves*.

Consumables are those products that are used up in the process of satisfying the need for which they were purchased. Thus, a thirsty person who buys a bottle of Coca-Cola needs to drink the contents to benefit from that purchase, or a company buying stationery uses the paper and envelopes in the course of business.

Durables are purchased for the benefit they provide to customers who will use them

A classification of products

over a (long) period of time. Thus a bicycle purchased to take part in the London to Brighton cycle ride will, providing there are no mishaps, be essentially the same at the end of the journey as it was at the beginning or at any stage in between. Providing it is looked after, it could be used year after year for the same purpose. Over time it will suffer from use until eventually it will need to be overhauled or discarded and replaced. It may then be considered to have come to the end of its useful life. Similarly a packaging machine bought by a food manufacturer will be used to pack products for the organisation, and will be depreciated as an asset in the company accounts, but would be expected to last for several years. It can be seen that the type of buyer, and how a product is likely to be used by the purchaser, can make a considerable difference to the way it should be offered to a potential customer.

Consumer products

Consumables

There are two main types of consumer consumables: *convenience* and *speciality* goods/services.

Convenience goods/services

These represent the majority of frequently purchased consumer goods, bought with little effort or deliberation, e.g. newspapers, breakfast cereals, coffee, soap, cosmetics, and services such as dry cleaning. The list includes all the classic mass-market products that can be purchased from any supermarket or corner shop. Much of the early development of marketing theory was aimed at the needs of these, so-called fmcg (fast-moving consumer goods) products.

It is often useful to further differentiate products within this category using the sub-categories staples, impulse, and emergency:

- Staples are those products that are usually bought as part of an everyday shopping-list.

■ Impulse goods are those purchased on sight without being considered previously, e.g. special offers or the chocolates, sweets and magazines sold at supermarket checkouts.

■ Emergency goods are those consumable products for which buyers are likely to make a special visit to the shops when supplies run out or are low. Disposable nappies, milk, and cigarettes are all products that might come within this category on occasions.

Speciality goods/services

These are consumable products which can only be purchased from specialist retailers and which consumers select deliberately. In these cases, there is a greater need to ensure that the contact with a potential customer is informative and products are made available through appropriate channels. Examples are prescription medicines or private health care, alcoholic beverages and hobby consumables including DIY products such as paint, photographic processing chemicals and artists' supplies. In a second category would be food products purchased for a special occasion such as a dinner party, goods bought as a gift and many cosmetics and personal care products.

Durables

Consumer durable products can be further divided into three categories. It will be obvious that some products or services can be placed in more than one category depending on the context and purpose for which they were purchased. This is quite acceptable providing those responsible for the marketing decisions realise the differences and develop different marketing mixes for each category.

Shopping goods/services

These are those products that are usually selected after 'shopping around' to compare price, quality, specifications, design or colour. Clothes, white goods (washing machines, refrigerators, etc.), brown goods (television, stereo systems, etc.), furniture and motor vehicles are typical of products in this category. Services could include long-term warranty contracts for electrical repairs or maintenance of a gas central heating system.

Shopping goods are purchases made after considering the options available, and are often products where value for money is as important as the features themselves. Buyers generally exhibit dissonance-reducing buying behaviour when purchasing this type of product. The marketing issues are obvious.

Speciality goods and services can be viewed as a subset of shopping goods. These are generally products that are available from only a limited number of outlets. Car spares, textbooks, foreign maps, specialist tools, lampshades and musical instruments are examples of products in this category. For such products the full marketing offering will include an element of well planned selective availability, and all aspects of the marketing mix must be consistent in supporting the special nature of the product.

Emergency durable goods/services

These are those products/services which buyers are likely to need without delay. Typical of this category would be replacement windscreens, exhausts and tyres. In certain circumstances the hire of a taxi to get home when your car fails to start is also an emergency purchase.

Industrial products and services

Industrial products, sometimes termed 'business-to-business' (B2B) products, are products bought by organisations manufacturing or supplying products or providing services. Unlike consumer goods, they are bought not for their own sake or for personal consumption, but in order to contribute to an organisational objective of the purchaser business. However there are the same two basic categories, consumables and durables.

Industrial consumables

Industrial consumables are the intermediate products or other goods/service inputs that are necessary to carry out some operation for the buyer. This means that the demand for this type of product will ultimately depend upon that of the final market being served by the organisation. Economists use the term 'derived demand' to describe this link. For this reason the markets for most types of industrial products (goods or services) are subject to greater fluctuations in demand and periodic cycles of activity than is usual for consumer products.

Materials (raw and processed) and components

Materials and components are the physical inputs to a customer's production process and are items included within the final product. Therefore they are often specified in some detail as the supplier has to be the one with the required skills in supplying against a rigorous specification. It is also crucial that these items are delivered at the required time and that they always meet the required quality levels. Therefore materials and components are often bought as habitual re-buys from long-standing reliable suppliers (producers or intermediaries). Whether the item is a component such as a nut, valve, or a switch, or a more specialist customised material, or perhaps a particular chemical formulation, if a failure occurs it could have serious implications for the customer.

If the volume justifies a long-term contractual arrangement then that is often the best way to ensure continuity of supply and the appropriate quality standards. Promotional elements rarely feature heavily in the marketing of materials, whereas close relationships which involve increasing collaboration between customer and supplier are common. Following practices pioneered in Japan, this increasing collaboration can include implementing JIT (just-in-time) systems, quality vetting programmes and single-sourcing agreements. All of these have implications for the successful marketing of materials and components.

Supplies (consumables)

Unlike materials and components that form part of the finished product produced by the customer organisation, supplies are those products and services that are used within the production process, or in other supporting activities. These include materials such as lubricants, abrasives and cleaning materials; services such as maintenance and quality inspection; office sundries such as paperclips and note pads; and a whole miscellany of other items needed for various functions within the organisation. Generally these are standard, easily substituted, items purchased through intermediaries who often compete as much on the basis of the service provided as on price. Although there is often promotional activity, it is the service component of the marketing offering that is often a critical factor in achieving a sale.

Such items are not major cost items and are usually replenished regularly without much consideration of alternative products. They generally fall into categories based on usage such as **m**aintenance, **r**epair, and **o**perational items. This leads to the mnemonic *MRO items*, which in some organisations is also the term for **m**onthly **r**e-**o**rder. This is why these items can become habitual re-buys and that is a strong position for an organisation that is able to establish itself as a competent supplier.

Industrial durables – capital plant and equipment

As with the other industrial categories above, it will be seen that a great deal depends upon the relationship between the producer company and the purchaser company. Organisations buying capital plant tend to be extremely knowledgeable regarding their requirements. These requirements will thus normally be specified very precisely and suppliers will be expected to comply with these specifications. These products normally involve carefully prepared production plans, design investigations and trials, and protracted discussions and negotiations. Marketing such products involves direct links with prospective purchasers, specialist-to-specialist technical contacts, presale service, and often contractual relationships extending far beyond the installation and commissioning stage.

In marketing terms, the capital equipment markets will be characterised by the number of competing manufacturers who deal directly with their major corporate customers and specialist stockholding dealers who serve the market at large. Purchase decisions for capital items usually involve all the aspects of decision making, and influencing considered in Chapter 6, organisational buying behaviour.

The importance of understanding product classifications

The earlier part of this chapter considered the make up of a total product. This is a combination of goods and service features, and it is necessary to explore the characteristics of the individual elements when deciding on marketing actions. However it is equally crucial to consider the way a product fits into a customer's activity cycle. That is the way a total product is used by the customer, and its importance for that customer, alongside all the other products that the same customer also buys. Thus the difference between consumables and durables, emergency goods and regular purchases and other differences will directly affect any decision about marketing. It might be that **acceptability** of an offering is not enough as, for instance an emergency product must be easily **available** at the time when the need occurs.

CONCLUSION

The total product and the marketing offering are often the logical starting point for any marketing analysis since it can be as useful to define customers and markets in terms of the type of products they buy. In turn, many product definitions depend upon the customer. However, the objective of marketing programmes is to achieve some measure of success in a given market place and in this, the aim is to differentiate one offering from another and thus win the competitive battle. Although the whole of the marketing mix is relevant at the time of most purchase decisions, it is the product itself, together with the service elements and added features, which is at the centre of the exchange. It is the basic product or service that is critical in satisfying the needs of customers. This is why we suggest that the **acceptability** of products and services is crucial to the fundamental marketing offering.

Products must be seen as complex combinations with many facets, and some of these have been explored in this chapter. Through the understanding of the various categories of products it is possible to understand more accurately how a customer might approach the purchase of that type of product. Also by appreciating the scope for changing total products it should stimulate creative thinking about the potential that the total product could achieve in a competitive context. The greater the **acceptability** of a product or service the more likely it is that an exchange will occur in the market place.

QUESTIONS

1 *Suggest ways in which a computer manufacturer could add to his product offering to provide a more **acceptable** 'total product'.*

2 *What do you think is the 'total product' offered by McDonald's hamburgers? How does this give them a comparative advantage over their direct competitors?*

3 *How could a* tradesman, *such as a plumber or an electrician, offering a service to local house-holders, demonstrate that their service meets the relevant quality levels?*

4 *Which dimensions of quality are most likely to be most important to a serious amateur marathon runner when seeking to purchase an **acceptable** new pair of running shoes?*

5 *Which dimensions of quality are most likely to be most important to a large industrial firm when seeking to purchase an **acceptable** item of new 'capital equipment' to increase the efficiency of the production operations?*

6 *Which dimensions of quality are most likely to be most important to a motorist who has suffered a puncture in one of his/her car tyres when looking for an **acceptable** replacement so that they can continue on a journey?*

FURTHER READING

Drucker, P. F. (1989) 'The new productivity challenge'.

Drucker, P. F. (1973) *Management Tasks, Responsibilities and Practicalities*. Harper & Row.

Garvin, D. A. (1987) 'Competing on the eight dimensions of quality', *Harvard Business Review*, November–December, pp. 101–9.

Levitt, T. (1980) 'Marketing success through the differentiation of anything', *Harvard Business Review*, January–February.

Palmer, A. (1994) *Principles of Services Marketing*. McGraw-Hill.

Payne, A. (1993) *The Essence of Services Marketing*. Prentice-Hall.

Peters, T. and Waterman, R. (1982) *In Search of Excellence: Lessons from America's Best Run Companies*. Harper & Row.

Townshend, R. (1990) *Up the organisation*.

Boo(m) or bust in fashion retailing

Would you pay £150 for a pair of Paul Smith shoes without even trying them on? That is the dilemma facing customers buying footwear, or clothing and other fashion items over the Internet. The collapse of boo.com in May 2000 brought to an end the 18 months of trading by the high-profile internet retailer. The boo.com website combined impressive graphics with video images and included interactive functions to help customers to chose the right product. However it is one thing to see a picture of an item of clothing it is quite another to actually see and feel it.

This is also a problem for the more traditional mail order companies. As one Director said 'you can make a dress look a thousand dollars in a photograph, but when the customer receives it they might not like the feel of the material or the stitching or the cut. That is why all mail order houses have to run efficient returns departments'.

On the same day as boo.com went bust, the High Street retailer Debenhams was holding a '12 hour sale spectacular' – a promotional event that was designed to get the tills ringing. Of course it is possible to buy Debenham's products over the Net *<www.debenhams.co.uk>* and the company also runs its own mail order catalogues. Also most other mail order operators are now developing retail websites to run alongside their catalogues. So the important question all retailers must ask is what makes a fashion item such as clothing or footwear *acceptable* to a customer?

The answer could be different for every individual customer. For some, the fun of internet buying is part of the 'total product', and perhaps there is no requirement to 'feel' the quality of the actual product before buying. That is perhaps why boo.com might be back in business by the time this book is published, the receivers claim to have received a large number of offers to buy the company within the first 24 hours following the bankruptcy. In fact there was nothing wrong with the basic fashion products being offered by boo.com, and it should be remembered that the Italian clothing group Benetton were one of the original backers of the company. However there are many commentators who believe that the Net is best used when offering different sorts of products such as music, videos, books and branded electrical goods.

Acceptability is a complex dimension, especially when it comes to fashion items. These products have to look good, feel good, and meet the high personal needs of customers (see Maslow's hierarchy of needs in Chapter 6). In order to satisfy their purchasers it is necessary for the suppliers to understand the needs of the potential customers and to ensure that these are fully met. The Managing Director of Homedirectory.com stated that 'the average dot.com sees as much as 70% of their money spent on promotion – we're keeping it to less than half that. The right way to make money is to have the best product and then do your (promotional) marketing'.

Task

Consider the different ways of purchasing a fashion item – internet, mail order, and various types of physical, 'bricks and mortar' stores. What are the factors that could make an item, say a pair of shoes acceptable to (1) a student, (2) a middle-aged consumer in full-time work who is unable to get to the shops regularly and (3) an old-aged pensioner. Which channel is likely to offer the most acceptable combination of goods and service to each customer group?

12 Branding and building relationships with customers

INTRODUCTION

This chapter will consider three issues, which have been the focus of much marketing attention in recent times. These are the development of a strong brand image in the minds of customers, the building of long-term relationships with those customers and the internal marketing issues that can affect the achievement of a satisfactory offering. There have already been a number of references to these issues in previous chapters such as the description of 'Mickey Mouse' marketing and the wider aspects of the exchange process in Chapter 1, the discussion on benefits in Chapter 10, the service component of the total product concept in Chapter 11, and various sections on customer behaviour and keeping customers in other chapters. All these references will indicate that the topics are not confined to a discrete area of marketing, nor are they really new. The problem is that as markets have grown and the organisations that serve them have become more complex, the issues which were once instinctive have been partially overlooked.

Before the industrial revolution, most trade was based on the understanding and direct interaction with customers. Because much of the business was direct and personal between a local supplier and customers, there was an obvious need to develop good ongoing relationships as an adjunct to the sale of such products as food, clothing, medicines and other items which required repeat orders. Most activity was at a local level and concentrated on individuals. The 'brand' did not exist as we now know it, but the image and reputation of each individual supplier was crucial. These local markets changed dramatically with the development of mass markets, growth in manufacturing scale, mass communication and mass distribution channels. Marketing is a response to the *increases in the scope of trading activities*, and the early marketing theory was indeed based on mass markets. Now with the rapid growth of e-commerce new marketing skills are required, and the role of a brand as a reassurance for customers is more critical than ever.

However, the element of personal contact in business exchanges will continue to be important, especially in the direct selling function and in industrial marketing. Organisations are just collections of individuals and in spite of work roles there are many individuals who meet, service, and in other ways interact with the customers of their organisation. When such dealings have been positive an ongoing relationship has developed between the employees of the supply organisation and the individuals with whom they do business.

The only difference from the local traders of the eighteenth century is that many of these 'personal' messages today can be delivered through high tech information exchanges utilising computers, the Internet, fax machines or even the (old-fashioned) telephone. There are countless opportunities for returning to personalised marketing, but many of the future exchanges will be through the use of modern systems, perhaps the Internet, rather than direct personal contact.

Nevertheless, personal contact remains of the utmost importance, both in how the exchange is performed and in the environment in which it takes place. The latter being very important as it represents the space where the customer actually meets a supplier. Close contact between the two parties brings both problems and opportunities, but the objective remains that of achieving an exchange through an offering that is **acceptable**, **affordable** and **available**. Therefore the specific nature of *interactive marketing* must be studied and a wider interpretation of the traditional components of product and place must be found.

There can be three types of marketing, and each requires full attention to ensure that customers receive a satisfactory offering from within a satisfactory exchange relationship.

- **External** marketing is the traditional focus of activity. It refers to the direct link between a supply organisation and its customers. The traditional tools of marketing – *product, price, distribution channels and communication* are part of external marketing. Branding can also be seen developing within this link, but this relies on both supplier and customer input.
- **Interactive** marketing focuses on the specific contacts between the people within a supply organisation and the processes used, both of which can affect relationships in a positive or a negative way. The perceived level of customer care is usually determined during these interactive encounters. The development of strong relationships between customers and suppliers are dependant on these interactive links.

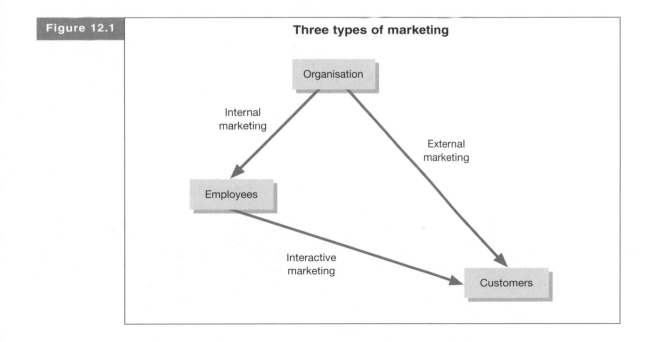

Figure 12.1

Three types of marketing

■ The third type of marketing looks at the interplay between a supplier and its own employees. The way an organisation treats and informs its own staff reflects through into the way those staff interact with external customers. Whilst there are many aspects of general management and specific issues from human resource management involved there is a contribution that marketing can make. Using marketing skills and techniques specifically aimed at internal staff is called *internal* marketing. (See Figure 12.1.)

Since the marketing activities of a company will be judged by the results achieved with customers, it is essential that all three types of marketing are considered important, and efforts are made to ensure consistency in all aspects of customer contact.

BRANDING

An introduction to branding

In the introduction to Chapter 10 reference was made to the famous quote from Peter Drucker that the 'whole purpose of any organisation is to create and retain a customer'. This is, of course, the objective of most marketing activities, and some of the relevant issues have been covered in Chapters 10 and 11. Kotler (1999) is more specific suggesting that the 'Art of marketing is largely the art of brand building. When something is not a brand, it will probably be viewed as a commodity.' If an offer is perceived to be the same as those from competitors then it is the price that counts because it is highly likely that consumers will choose the most affordable or the most easily available. When a supplier is forced to compete on price alone there is little chance of making satisfactory profit. Therefore it is important to move an offering away from being considered a basic commodity. Doyle (1997) described this as 'de-commoditizing a company's offering'. He suggests that 'Brands are at the heart of Marketing ... because successful brands create wealth by attracting and retaining customers.' This reflects Drucker's view as to the purpose of an organisation.

Branding has a long history, and is probably most commonly associated with the makers' stamps and hallmarks used by artisans through the ages. From a marketing perspective, branding has become more commonplace since 1900, developing alongside the emergence of marketing itself. Adcock (2000) suggests that

> a brand is not a product that just happens to have high awareness, nor is it just a recognisable name or logo, although both these are often present. It is so much more, it is a powerful stimulus that conjures up a complex image and level of expectation about itself and what it can do for a consumer.

But 'brands' are a paradox, they don't have a physical presence or any objective existence but they do provide a mass of values and promises that act as powerful stimuli for consumer decisions leading them to buy or perhaps not to buy.

Brands develop in a holistic way, fuelled by the messages put out by suppliers. However, brand personalities develop in the minds of consumers as the multitude of messages are interpreted in a very subjective manner. If these images are positive the brand become a major element in the development of a relationship between a supplier and a customer, but there are other issues that are also relevant in achieving a strong bond with customers and developing the *purchase loyalty* which is the ultimate goal.

An important result of the way customers perceive an offering is the recognition of that offering as a brand. This is a substantive endorsement of all the activity that stems from the marketing offering, and is a distinct image that differentiates one offering from another. A brand can be either an asset or a liability depending on the attitude of the customer towards it. The strength of a brand is reflected in four ways:

- **Brand awareness** – how many potential customers 'know', or are familiar with the brand.
- **Brand beliefs** – qualities attributed to a brand as perceived by potential customers, perhaps concerning the reliability or the efficacy of the brand. Such beliefs can be developed through effective promotion as much as through experience, use and knowledge.
- **Brand associations** – this is anything that is directly or indirectly linked to the brand in the mind of the customer. For instance the type of people who are seen using an item could enhance its brand image.
- **Brand loyalty** – the critical issue is how many customers remain loyal to a brand, resisting incentives to change to a competitive offering.

Branding usually develops from a distinctive identification – usually a name, symbol or design – given to a product or range of products, and through usage and promotion this image becomes established in the market place. Products or product lines so identified are termed 'brands', and are the focus of marketing activity that is often referred to as 'brand strategy'. Branding issues have recently become more popular within industrial markets; however, the most well-known brands are still almost exclusively among consumer goods and service markets.

Dimensions of successful branding

Companies build brands by the consistent marketing outputs they deliver, this determines the way an offering is made to the market place. However the actual brand is created and measured by the reaction of customers to the specific offering. The result is that in many markets, brands and brand names are used by buyers as convenient signposts during search and shopping behaviour, where favoured brands are mentally ranked at the top of a 'evoked set' of **acceptable** contenders.

Successful brands offer three distinct benefits to customers:

- Fast recognition of an offering, thus acting as a shortcut in purchase situations
- Assurance as to the quality and performance of the offering which is derived from the beliefs held regarding it
- Emotional benefits which add meaning or feeling to an offering and give a buyer additional, sometimes intangible benefits.

All of the above dimensions of a brand can be seen to be important in a purchase situation. The objective of brand marketing activity is to attract a group of customers who are 'brand loyal', in other words they purchase the brand regularly and resist switching to other competing brands. Marketers will be concerned to maintain and develop such brand loyalty. A strong brand and a strategy based on such strength is likely to prove very difficult for competitors to copy, and hence lead to a real advantage over other offerings.

Research studies employing 'blind' product tests, comparing branded versus unbranded goods and control products, repeatedly show respondents to have preferences for the branded products. They are also willing to pay more for them. Doyle (1997) suggested the tangible evidence of the real commercial value of a brand can be seen in the facts that:

- Strong brands usually obtain price premiums from customers
- Strong brands obtain higher market share
- Successful brands have loyal customers and this generates more stable, and less risky earnings
- Successful brands offer avenues for future growth.

Exercise

1 Retailers' own brands

- Visit your local supermarket and find a product that is offered both as a manufacturer's brand (e.g. Kelloggs, Maxwell House, Radox) and as a store's 'own label' product. Compare the product in every detail, design, pack size, price, image and value for money.
- It is possible the 'own label' product offers a more cost-efficient, and in some cases a more effective option. But the other products must sell regularly or they would not be given shelf space. Why do you think there are still so many customers who buy these 'branded' products?
- What characteristics do you think describes:
  a. Purchasers of 'retailer's own label' products?
  b. Purchasers of manufacturers 'branded' products?

2 Branding and Internet shopping

- Internet shopping is growing at a staggering rate. In 1999 it increased by over 500 per cent. The book and 'CD' music category is one of the most important, but many other products are also sold on the net.
- Consider someone who wishes to purchase a camera; visit an appropriate web site and obtain details of those on offer. Then assess the importance of the brand name in providing reassurance to the prospective purchaser in making a decision to buy/not to buy.
- Is it most likely that a purchaser would buy a camera with an established brand name?
- If a product was offered where the manufacturer was unknown would it be more likely that a purchaser might want to see it in a retail shop before purchase?

Brand names

Perhaps the most obvious manifestation of a brand is the name and this is then the trigger for all the *associations related to the brand*. Brand names give products an identity among customers and intermediaries alike, distinguishing them from standard commodities, and particularly from competitor products. Brand names are adopted by customers as a shorthand identification of the product, and taken as an assurance of the general quality and characteristics of the product.

It takes a long time to create a distinctive name to which consumers relate positively. Once established, a brand name becomes a valuable asset to the owner. Indeed the value is now sufficiently tangible for it to be included as a balance sheet item. It is not surprising, therefore, that those companies nowadays assign asset values to brand names. For legal purposes, brands and brand names have to be protected from unauthorised use by the use of a trademark, and the owners of famous brand names such as Rolls Royce or Coca-Cola go to great lengths to defend their brand names, almost regardless of the legal costs involved. An equivalent legal safeguard for less tangible properties such as literary and artistic works is the establishment of a *copyright*.

Although brand success is most often measured by short-term business ratios such as profitability, it is the longer-term customer-based criteria that really matter. These include issues such as perceived added value, differential advantage and positive associations. Though distinctive symbols, corporate logos and packaging may accompany the brand, it will usually be most readily identified through a brand name. The brand value is inevitably enhanced when there is a suitable visible focus for customers and the brand name provides this in the most accessible way. Generally the best names are distinctive as well as being:

- Easy to remember
- Easy to spell
- Easy to pronounce (ideally regardless of language).

Clearly names such as: Ford, Tesco, McDonald's, and Coca-Cola conform to these requirements. However some brands have proved very successful in spite of failing one of these tests, for instance Häagen-Dazs might be distinctive and memorable but it is not so easy in other ways.

The adoption of a suitable name for a product can have a profound effect on the product's long-term success. The Japanese founders of Sony made up the name Sony on the basis of the English word sound as they initially saw their business in this sector of the electronics industry. Compaq, the computer company also adopted a carefully crafted brand name to epitomise the major feature of their original product: its relative compactness and portability. Clearly in both of these examples the name selected has outlasted the limited product orientation involved in the name's creation.

Exercise

Consider the names used by new internet banking companies such as egg.com (Prudential Group) and smile.com (Co-operative Bank). Why have these well-established companies sought to utilise such brand names that seem to have nothing to do with the product offered?

Do you think new names, Egg and Smile, have advantages over the more established name of the organisation?

Brand values and brand extensions

The term 'brand' in the marketing context refers to more than a readily recognisable name. It involves a *product and a set of values*. The product is the visible symbol but it is the hidden imagery enshrined in the '*values*' which is the real determinant of a brand's strength. Values usually relate to the perceived quality of the product or to its value for money. Ford as a brand could be said to represent value for money whereas Ghia within the Ford range of products is intended to represent extra quality.

It is clear from this example that within the concept of brands there is a number of levels. At the highest level is the organisation, for example Ford, McDonald's or Coca-Cola. This is sometimes called the 'Umbrella' brand. At the second level there is what might be referred to as the sub-brand. Within this level would be names such as the Focus, Big Mac or Diet Coke.

In choosing brand names and developing a branding strategy, suppliers with a range of products may opt for:

1 **Individual brand names**. These are used when a company wishes to separate its products and does not think there are any benefits from joint associations. This practice is commonly seen in consumer good sectors such as biscuits, detergents,

and cigarettes, where companies field a variety of products that are often individually developed, targeted at different segments or designed for particular uses or occasions. Examples of this type of branding are Snickers (from Mars), Persil (from Lever Brothers), and Silk Cut cigarettes. In other instances, less through design than circumstance, large manufacturer groups will find themselves with an extensive mix of competing brands, taken on board through a series of corporate acquisitions.

2 **Multiproduct brands, or 'umbrella' or 'family' brands**. Where the company uses one standard brand name, often the company name, for all its products, e.g. Heinz, Walkers, Cadbury's, or Tesco, this is then linked to the sub-brand that could be a simple description such as Heinz Baked Beans, Cadbury's Dairy Milk or Tesco fruit juice. *Multiproduct branding* can offer marketing economies where a strong favourable brand name carries across a whole product assortment, to the benefit of otherwise weaker products, and assisting in the acceptance of new products by consumers and intermediaries alike. Equally, a problem or failure in one product could work to the detriment of the whole brand 'family'. Companies do not have to restrict themselves to one strategy for branding, as can be seen by reference to Heinz and Ford below.

3 **Multi-branding of products**. This occurs when a manufacturer uses an umbrella brand together with a different sub-brand name for its various product offerings. Examples such as Ford Focus, Walkers Dorritoes and Heinz Weight Watchers show this type of multi-branding. Care has to be taken to ensure that each of the individual names *supports*, and is *consistent with*, the overall umbrella name.

The issue of umbrella brands or individual names is best considered within a matrix which compares the target customer groups and the values associated with specific brand names. Where there is a common target group and common values, then multiproduct branding is best. If only one of these is similar then multiproduct branding still could be acceptable but multibranding is a viable alternative. Where both the target group and the brand values differ then an umbrella strategy is inappropriate and individual brand names should be used (Figure 12.2).

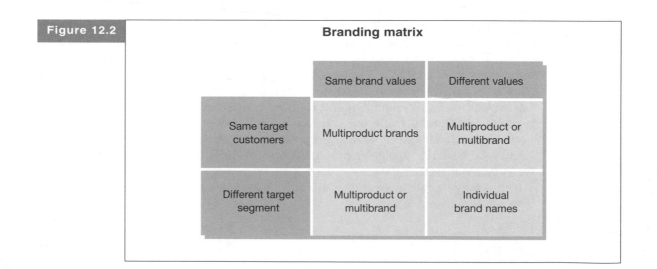

Figure 12.2

Branding matrix

	Same brand values	Different values
Same target customers	Multiproduct brands	Multiproduct or multibrand
Different target segment	Multiproduct or multibrand	Individual brand names

Exercise

Obtain the report from a large diverse manufacturing company such as Unilever, or Cadbury Schweppes. Consider the brand names utilised by that company and decide if their strategy regarding the use of multibranding or individual brand names is appropriate. What reasons do you have for your views?

Note: There are specific issues of concern to those manufacturers who undertake the production of *own-brand merchandise for retailers*, e.g. for supermarkets such as Tesco or Sainsbury. These supply contracts are useful in order to obtain extra sales, and typically they involve pre-planned volumes and specific delivery dates. They offer production economies, with little promotional outlay, and they can be useful in achieving entry into segments otherwise closed to the manufacture, or perhaps supplied by one of their competitors. However, the cost of such business may be strict adherence to contract terms that include quality inspections, production vetting and no-question returns policies, at prices that demand strict cost controls for often thin margins. The manufacturer has no contact with the final consumer, and there is no opportunity to develop any brand value from such business. Even worse, the supplier can easily be rejected, as the much-publicised suppliers to Marks & Spencer found to their cost in 1999. In fact leading retail groups have, through concentration, become so powerful that they have had to consider their brand strength and in some cases have developed sub-brands to reflect the enormous spread of their retail operation.

The importance of customers in brand development

All brands are developed in the minds of prospective customers. In fact it is possible to consider a brand as a sort of 'emotional link' that represents the relationship between a customer and a product offering. Of course, every customer is influenced by the marketing activity undertaken by the brand owner, but the customer alone supplies the 'added value' dimension of a brand based entirely on the perception they have as to the benefits they might receive from it. So whilst the marketing activities of suppliers offer cues to customers it is the customer who ultimately decides on the attributes associated with a brand, and the strength of that brand.

A key difference between the markets for many consumer goods and, say, industrial products is that there is little opportunity for close personal contact between the supplier and the buyer of consummables. Grönroos (1990) says that 'Consumer markets are traditionally characterised by a prevalence of low value, low involvement purchases by a large number of anonymous customers'. This does not mean that there is no opportunity for suppliers to build up a database containing some personal details of consumers. In fact many consumer goods' companies put a lot of effort into such activity by finding ways of communicating directly with potential customers, and then, where appropriate, retaining the names and addresses for future marketing purposes. For example Heinz is able to target new mothers through its 'Baby Club'. Such activities are usually driven by the suppliers and controlled by the terms of the Data Protection Act, as well as by social fears regarding unwelcome intrusion and privacy.

The reality in many consumer markets is that there is a stronger relationship between the customer and the specific 'product' they purchase than between the customer and the supply organisation. The attitudes of customers regarding a brand offering will increase over time as they gain more experience of it. Thus as the relationship between customer and product grows, more additions to enhance the brand image will become apparent. It is as though the customer is adding layers of paint onto a picture with each new brush stroke giving a further covering over the original blank canvas – or the 'naked product'. This gives rise to an ever-changing image and thus brand development must be seen as a continuous and ever-developing activity – crucially an activity that is reliant on the perception of customers regarding an offering, in which a supplier cannot be certain how the marketing messages it is sending out are being received.

If the customer perceptions develop in a positive way the result will be a *strong brand link*. The process will then be characterised by strong positive feelings about a particular brand, increased trust in the benefits offered by that brand and greater commitment regarding that brand in future purchase situations. This is why it is important to consider a brand in terms of an emotional relationship that can develop between a customer and a product.

This relationship represents an *intangible bond* between a customer and an offering. It reflects both the brand beliefs and the brand associations and it is a measure of the strength of the brand. Whilst a brand is not a person it can have a personality derived from the beliefs and associations held by customers. The 'brand personality' can be seen as the reflection of the stereotype of the people most likely to purchase that particular brand.

Exercise	What type of person might own each of the cars below:
	(a) BMW?
	(b) Renault Clio?
	(c) Proton?
	How do these stereotypes reflect the personality of each brand?

Brand loyalty

Successful brands are those that *customers want to buy*. For some product classes a single purchase is all that might occur, for instance most people require only one barbarcue set! There are other types of product where repeat purchase is important, in fact the supplier rarely makes any profit from the first sale of these items but they do profit by achieving repeat purchases. The level of *exclusive* repeat purchase is measured by the loyalty exhibited by a customer with respect to a specific brand. But loyalty is a complex issue. It represents more than regular purchasing as it can also be seen in positive attitudes towards a brand. This is important for single-purchase items. For instance if you had just bought a computer you would be unlikely to require another one in a hurry. But a strong advocacy in favour of one model is a valuable expression of loyalty and it is possible this could influence other potential purchasers to buy the same offering.

There are, of course situations, maybe involving a regularly purchased item, where a customer might not wish to be restricted to a single brand. The idea that a customer should be loyal to only one specific offering is very restrictive, there could be many reasons for using two or more brands. For instance many industrial buyers utilise two suppliers to ensure reliability and as a way of comparing price trends. Another common situation is where consumers move to a different brand for a short period to provide variety, so-called 'change of pace', before returning to the original one. Some customers show loyalty to a restricted group of products from within their evoked set, accepting any one as a good substitute for any other. Whatever the reason, marketers must respect the actions of customers whilst trying to provide incentives to alter such behaviour and increase the level of brand loyalty. The marketing initiatives usually include activities to strengthen the desired brand image. This is assisted by a consistent approach to all communications, as well as promotional schemes that benefit loyal customers, and, where possible, direct mailings sent to past purchasers in the hope of encouraging repeat purchase.

Where loyalty results in high patronage then the relationship between the brand and customer is really apparent. The most obvious advantage is that a supplier can charge a premium price for a strong brand. This can be seen in many markets. However suppliers must guard against excessive exploitation of customers, because if the prices become too high sales will reduce and the brand image will be damaged. A less obvious benefit is that well-known brands are not only chosen more frequently but they are to be found in more evoked sets than lesser-known brands.

Example

In a town there are two competing restaurants. One is known by everyone, the other by only 60% of the potential customers. When it comes to choice, 40% visit the only place they know, but research shows that even those who know both outlets are more likely to choose the better known one. The result is:

	Restaurant 'A'	Restaurant 'B'
40% who only know 'A'	40%	0%
60% who know both	35% (say)	25% (say)
Total	75%	25%

Whilst these are illustrative figures it can be seen that the real benefit in terms of business is 75/25 rather than the actual loyalty ratio. This is sometimes called the 'double jeopardy effect' on the lesser-known product.

The building of brand loyalty will lead to many benefits deriving from ever-closer relationships with customers. Brand-building involves consistency in all marketing actions over a period of time, brand loyalty results from positive customer attitudes. Loyalty can be measured by the 'depth' of repeat business that occurs, that is how frequently a customer buys and how much they spend as a proportion of the total spend in a given category of product.

Brands as a business asset

Strong brands lead to higher levels of profit for organisations. There are three main reasons for this:

- First – higher-volume sales, owing to high loyalty and high market share.
- Second – strong brands can sustain a higher price, and avoid excessive discounts.
- Third – a strong brand equity can be extended into other markets, thus further exploiting the brand name.

It is important for a strong brand to dominate its market space. But it is not important for a strong brand to be in a large market. In financial terms it is better to be a big brand in a small, niche market, than to be a small brand in a large market.

Building strong brands takes time, investment, consistency and a little luck. It is an investment that can yield high returns as has been shown by a number of expensive take-overs launched in order to buy the owners of major brands. However there is a continuous debate inside companies regarding marketing investment in brand-building. Unlike most fixed capital investments, the benefits of marketing investments are uncertain so the traditional cost/benefit analysis cannot be undertaken. Therefore there are many managers who question the costs involved, even though they appreciate the value of a strong brand when they own it.

Many organisations want to find ways of quantifying their brands as financial assets. There is a general belief that if the asset value of a strong brand is not shown on the balance sheet then the company could be undervalued by investors. Also, since it is possible to sell or licence a brand name, the balance sheet value can provide a useful benchmark.

There are several methods of brand-asset valuation in use but all are, at best, just good estimates of the future earnings that can be expected from a particular brand. Various accounting conventions are involved in order to arrive at an approximate valuation. But whatever financial method is utilised, it is important for marketers to remember that brands are valuable assets only if they contribute to *competitive advantage and customer loyalty*. These, in turn, will generate future sales, future profit, and greater return to shareholders.

BUILDING RELATIONSHIPS WITH EXTERNAL CUSTOMERS

In today's highly competitive business environment there is an extensive range of products and services leading to increasing choice for customers. The result of this is that it is increasingly difficult for a company to keep customers. Many companies now realise that their success in the market place is largely dependent on the relationships they establish with external customers, and how many of those customers they retain. Relationship marketing is not new but it does require a new way of thinking about and acting towards customers. It is a concept that complements the building of brands and enables the link with loyal customers to be continued into the future well after current products have become outdated. Grönroos (1990) defined relationship marketing as:

> **To establish, maintain and enhance long-term customer relationships at a profit, so that the objectives of the parties are met. This is done by the mutual exchange and fulfillment of promises.**

The real benefit of building a long-term relationship with a customer comes in the added-value experienced by both parties. If one party, either supplier or customer, does not feel some additional benefit from being in a relationship then there is no reason for that party to remain constrained by any loyalty to the other.

Customers as a business asset

Whilst brands are now valued and placed on a company's balance sheet, this is, perhaps, approaching the issue from the wrong angle. All the marketing effort, both in terms of analysing markets for opportunities and planning a competitive mix, are aimed at *creating customers*. Loyal customers are valuable because they represent a future stream of profitable business, and the brand is important only because of the potential it offers for that future trade. Therefore the real business assets are the regular, loyal customers, or advocates, who will purchase again in the future. At a time when many companies are valuing their brands as assets and incorporating these values into their balance sheets, it is a pity that no way can be found to put a value on loyal customers and include this also among the organisation's intangible assets. Of course the accountants do not treat customers as assets because most buyer–seller relationships are not contractual in a formal manner, but rely on the informal relationship between the two parties. However, it would be positive thinking for organisations to value their customer relationships even more than they value their other assets, and to devise strategies to ensure they retain these valuable customers.

Earlier it was suggested that the purpose of an organisation is to 'create and retain' a customer. This is sometimes referred to as 'customer winning and customer keeping'. The traditional marketing emphasis has been on the creation of an exchange rather than the retention of customers for future business. However, the first exchange with a particular customer might not be profitable because it could cost so much to find that customer and achieve the initial sale. In addition, as further business progresses, future exchanges will be more profitable, primarily because of the fewer up-front costs but also because exchanges with existing customers can benefit from past experiences.

However, it is important not to lose any customer. Every lost customer costs money (profit) because in addition to the lost profit from future sales there is the cost of recruiting new replacement customers and the unquantifiable loss owing to the failure to benefit from word-of-mouth recommendations from satisfied customers. Estimates vary, but there is general agreement that it can cost five times as much to get an initial order as it does to obtain a repeat order from an established customer.

A useful analogy would be to consider a bucket full of water that has a small hole through which some of the liquid escapes. To keep the bucket full involves constant topping up. But the bigger the hole, the greater the loss of water, which in turn requires more effort and cost, and if it is too big then maybe it might lead to a total loss.

Research in America suggests that recruiting a new customer by credit card providers can cost up to $50. This initial outlay will not be recovered until the customer has held the card for some 15 months. Sasser (1978) suggests that retaining just 5 per cent more customers than normal can double profits. MBNA, an American credit card company, collected information from every lost customer. As a result they revised their offerings, amended their processes and enhanced their services. Their defection rate is one of the lowest in the industry and their profitability one of the highest.

Many organisations are now trying to calculate the lifetime value of their customers. It has been estimated that a new baby will require over £1000 of disposable nappies in the first year. Anyone who buys a newspaper every day could spend £10 000 in a lifetime, and most students will earn £1 million in their working life. These figures show the benefit that can derive from long-term relationships.

Winning customers

Before an organisation can think of retaining a customer, they have to create (win) that customer. Winning customers is not as simple as a game of chance that you sometimes win and sometimes lose. A continuum can be constructed illustrating the different

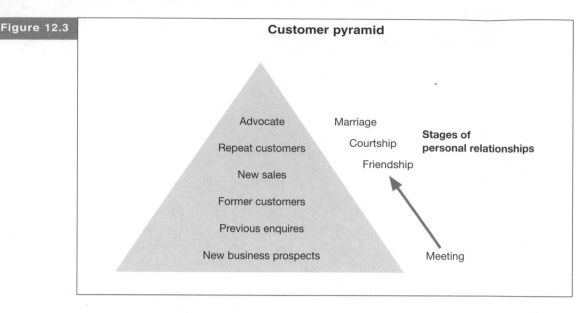

Figure 12.3

stages of development for each potential customer, as shown in Figure 12.3. It is inappropriate to offer the same marketing mix to all groups. The *promise* to an existing customer will be interpreted in a very different way compared to the incentive required to attract a new customer. The new business prospects are at a *pre-transactional stage*, which describes the period before any exchange takes place. These customers have to be persuaded about an intended purchase from a new supplier, and require reassurance that the offering is right for them.

There are various estimates about the cost of attracting new customers, but it is probably true that it costs on average up to five times more than the cost of retaining an existing customer. New business is the most expensive because it usually has to be won from a competitor. New customers, for whatever type of product, need to receive a disproportionate level of marketing input, which could include product design, promotion, personal selling or any other element from within the marketing mix.

At the other end there are repeat sales either to loyal or occasional users, where the *post-transactional stage* exists. Strategies for customer retention are discussed later in this chapter.

Sustainable advantage must be judged against the criteria of *acceptability, affordability* and *availability*. It comes from all elements of the marketing mix and to win a customer there has to be some element of *perceived added value* when compared to competitive offerings. Competitive advantage is an ever-changing condition as in a dynamic market new initiatives are always being introduced. Writing on sustainable advantage, Pankaj Ghemawat said:

> All of your competitors may be stupid some of the time but you cannot count on them being stupid all of the time.

The difficulty with winning customers from competitors is that your competitors do not like it, and will probably fight back.

Example	A successful move to win customers directly from a competitor was the promotion by Diners Club when it offered free membership to anyone sending them a cut-up American Express card. Not only did this take out the competition, it also freed Diners Club from the effort and expense of doing a credit check on applicants. They decided that anyone with an Amex card would also be likely to qualify for Diners Club. The result was a boost for Diners Club membership.
	Diners Club did not gain any long-term sustainable advantage from their promotion as American Express hit back to recover its lost customers.

Once having gained a customer it is just as important to hang on to that customer and to trade with them on a regular basis.

Long-term relationships

The rationale for a supplier building relationships with external customers is based on the long-term financial benefits that can accrue. It depends upon two economic facts:

1 It is more expensive to obtain a new customer than to retain an existing customer.
2 The longer the period of the relationship, the more profitable the relationship becomes.

Building strong relationships with chosen customers requires a level of commitment which goes beyond that required for a simple, 'one-off' exchange transaction. The benefits of a long-term relationship come when both parties derive added-value from working together. For some customers there are real advantages in being loyal to a particular supplier. In other cases, such behaviour can be viewed as too restrictive.

Example	Product categories where strong relationships could offer benefits to both parties:
	■ Automotive components supplied as original equipment
	■ Personal banking services
	■ Regular daily newspaper sales
	■ Grocery supermarket.
	Product categories where relationships might fail to offer added benefits over time:
	■ New car purchase
	■ Undifferentiated stationery needs (pads of paper, ballpoint pens, etc.)
	■ Single-purchase category (no repeat, such as the purchase of a portable barbeque)

It is not always the case that long-term relationships are profitable. There are investments to be made in order to build good relationships and these must be evaluated against the benefits expected. It is possible to study the needs of customers and the style of relationship, plotting these along a continuum (Figure 12.4). At one end there are customers constantly purchasing a particular category of product, but with low switching costs so it is relatively easy to change suppliers. Under these conditions there are few benefits to the supplier from investing in relationship marketing strategies. At the other end real advantages are possible, but often there are high costs involved in switching suppliers so customers have a real incentive to remain loyal and hence the conditions favour close relationships. In such circumstances changing partners is more difficult and will happen less often. Barbara Bund Jackson called the first 'always a share' and the second 'lost for good'.

'Always a share' customers can have multiple suppliers and they have a short time

Figure 12.4	**Continuum of exchange opportunities**

Always a chance
to get a share of
any business

High switching costs
so if sales lost they
are 'lost for good'

⟷

Transactional marketing

– Basic commodities
– Regular tenders for contracts
– Occasional purchases
– Products where loyalty is
  not an issue

Relationship marketing

– Computer systems
– Capital equipment + servicing
– Regular reorder products
– Products with high brand
  loyalty

horizon in relationships. Suppliers can always hope to get business and the established methods of transactional exchange marketing are appropriate. Marketers practising relationship marketing will try to move customers along to the other extreme by increasing switching costs. The risk is that if such an account is lost, it is lost for good along with the investment made in trying to develop the business. Of course, sometimes customers get tired of their regular brands and move to an alternative for a brief change. Such actions are perfectly understandable within a relationship and should not be a problem in most cases. Remember a business relationship is not like a marriage with a single partner, rather there are many appropriate models for business, but both parties in any close relationship must understand the limitations of the bond otherwise trust will be destroyed.

The quote below from a major retailer illustrates how a chosen supplier could obtain continuous business and be very hard to dislodge in a well ordered *'manufacturer–retailer'* relationship:

> We are not looking for new suppliers in any of our existing product areas. We have the suppliers we want and, unless something goes wrong with the relationship, we will not search for new suppliers.

Strategies for customer retention

Building and maintaining long-term customer relationships involves a number of stages, in part these reflect, and extend the development of customers, as shown in Figure 12.3. These can be likened to the same stages in personal friendships, meetings, courtships, adjustments and advancement. These mirror the stages of brand development as emotional bonds develop between the customer and the offering.

Perhaps the most important issue in retaining customers is to refocus the marketing effort away from a single exchange onto the activities that will achieve a strong relationship with mutual added-value benefits for both parties. The customers may also require confirmation that their purchase was right, and perhaps some tangible encouragement to buy again. Repeat customers who become strong advocates also act as a source of new business, because satisfied customers tell others and such endorsements are worth more than any advertisement.

The issues in relationship marketing show how important it is to consider both the actual transaction and the period after the sale when the relationship can be strengthened. As time goes on, the benefits from any relationship can increase if both parties approach the interaction in a positive way. However, it is the perception of the advantages that is also important. Both the reality and the perception are reinforced by the ongoing contact between the parties based on some form of two-way communication.

Building good relationships concentrates on the softer issues of partnerships, more than the increasing of physical barriers to switching by customers. The latter are often resented. Strong relationships are ones that both parties enter into voluntarily, rather than because they have no choice. Enduring relationships provide a unique and sustained competitive advantage. It is difficult in a general book to give a full list of actual activities as there are many different individual contexts where relationships are developed. Buttle (1996) considers a dozen areas in more detail. These are:

- principal–agent
- manufacturer–retailer
- business-to-business
- financial adviser–client
- advertising agency–client
- charities–donors
- airlines–passengers
- retail banking–personal customers
- corporate banking–customers
- credit card operators
- hospitality
- internal company links.

To these we could add many others such as Heinz customer clubs, Morgan Cars owners club, University alumni associations and supermarket loyalty cards. In any specific situation there will be issues particular to that relationship.

Grönroos suggests that marketing can be considered as revolving around relationships, some of which are like single transactions, narrow in scope and not involving much or any social relationship (e.g. marketing soap or breakfast cereals). Other relationships, on the other hand, are broader in scope and may involve even substantial social contacts and be continuous and enduring in nature (e.g. marketing hospitality or financial services).

The common issues in achieving strong relationships are:

- Concern for the welfare of customers
- Adding benefits in the longer term
- Ongoing communications and
- Building trust and commitment between the parties.

The issues above are easy to appreciate when there are few dramatic changes in the marketing environment but they are severely tested when major changes occur. These might be new technological initiatives, such as the advent of internet shopping.

Table 12.1   Differences between transactional and relationship marketing

Exchange marketing	Relationship marketing
Importance of single sale	Importance of customer retention
Importance of product features	Importance of customer benefits
Short time scale	Longer time scale
Less emphasis on service	High customer service
Quality is concern of production	Quality is concern of all
Competitive commitment	High customer commitment
Persuasive communication	Regular customer communication

Discussion question

Why should someone booking a holiday remain loyal to their friendly local travel agent when there are many deals advertised daily on Ceefax as well as on the net?

Alternatively there might be a major change in the customers' personal circumstances. If a person retires from work then they are bound to reassess their total purchase activities in the light of having more time but probably less disposable income than before. Another example is given below. These changes in the environment and customer activity give rise to *'strategic windows of opportunity'* when it is easier for competitors to win over customers. Unless the relationship is strong, and the supplier takes action to retain the customer, then it is possible the relationship will be terminated. It is as well to remember what O'Malley et al. said:

> Customers aren't stupid – if they feel that the relationship exists simply to make another sale, then they will seek to 'dissolve' it!

Example

Most students have a bank account. When it is opened, several incentives are offered, and during the time as a student costly facilities such as free overdrafts are allowed. Research by a student at Coventry University suggests that it takes between five and nine years for the bank to recover the cost of this type of account. However many students are not very loyal to their original bank, with up to 40 per cent switching to another in the three years following graduation.

Unless the banks take action to build strong relationships with students this situation will continue. The result will be heavy losses on student accounts and this is obviously very bad business for those banks who cannot retain customers.

CUSTOMERS AND CONSUMERS

In this chapter the term 'customer' has been used to indicate the recipient of a product. In fact as the following example shows there can be more than one customer for such an offering.

Example

Consider a manufacturer of chocolate confectionery countlines such as Mars Bars. This company needs, at the very least, to have individual product offerings that specifically address:

- the needs of the wholesaler who receives the product in bulk from the factory
- those of the retailer who displays the product to potential customers and
- the consumer who buys the product as a snack or treat.

Each of these is a kind of customer but each requires a different package of benefits. The final consumer will focus on an enjoyable, widely available and reasonably priced product. The retailer wants a product that will attract people into the shop, look attractive when displayed and give a good profit margin. It is also probable that supermarkets might need a different balance in their total offering from that required by a wholesaler supplying a corner newsagent or station kiosk. One example of these different needs is that manufacturers of chocolate confectionery countlines have introduced multipacks, which are more relevant to the needs of grocery customers.

Therefore it can be seen that the closest customer links for a confectionery manufacturer is with the retailer or wholesaler. It is likely that the manufacturer will attempt to build a strong relationship with these direct customers, investing in additional services and other benefits to enhance the interactions. Whilst the brand is still important to the retailer, this importance lies more in the level of demand from the final consumer who will purchase it from the shops. The manufacturer has a responsibility to both the immediate customers and the final consumer. It is necessary for them to consider the separate needs of the different parties and attempt to satisfy both customer and consumer.

In addition to these separate requirements there is also a need to co-ordinate activities along a distribution chain. For instance, television is an important tool in the promotion of this product. For a TV campaign to have maximum impact it is essential that the wholesaler be informed in time to ensure that adequate stocks are available, and the retailer perhaps given a special point-of-sale display to reinforce the television message.

The above example applies to a manufacturer who has decided to supply several different channels of distribution in order to gain the maximum sale of a product. However, such decisions also cost money. A smaller organisation than Mars might be faced with a choice between a number of different ways of reaching the final consumer.

Every contact between the supplier's organisation and their customers adds to the relationship. Where a supplier is addressing both direct customers (e.g. retailers) and consumers they must ensure that there are no inconsistencies in these different operations. These contacts can be trading exchanges, or exchanges of information, or social exchanges. What is important is that all contacts should be *mutually supporting*. All should incorporate the best practice in marketing so that the offering is *acceptable, affordable and available* as and when required. It is likely that companies will need to monitor and plan all contact exchanges across the whole organisation. This leads onto the need for effective *interactive marketing*, as well as the necessary efforts to support the staff who interface with customers.

Interactive marketing and customer care

Customers will initially assess an offering by the way it satisfies the substantive need for the core benefit they desire. This might be the requirement to be entertained by a football match, or the basic need to carry out some numerical calculations accurately which could involve some electronic aid, or the core benefit of travelling to another town which might be provided by a train journey. However there are secondary attributes which are just as important to customers when evaluating any offering. The best exchanges occur when customers feel that a supplier really cares about their satisfaction. It is possible to identify some of the key attributes that determine a caring supplier and therefore make a product/service offering more *acceptable*. The attributes below, suggested by Sasser (1978), extend the components of an *acceptable* quality offering that were discussed in Chapter 11.

- Security (safety of the customer and his/her property)
- Consistency
- Completeness
- Condition

■ Availability
■ Timing.

Most suppliers put a great deal of effort into the core benefit and the basic product, so there is rarely an opportunity for any real differentiation in this respect. Therefore real competitive advantage often derives from the ability to meet the *secondary needs* of a customer better than the competitors. The elements involved are the augmented features of the total offering discussed in Chapters 9 and 10. These attributes are often intangible service features and it is possible to see the importance of them in respect to the interactive way an offering is presented. Remember the *'moments of truth'* that occur whenever a customer interacts with a supplier.

Interactive marketing extends beyond the area of direct personal contact into all relevant encounters. Shostack suggested there are three types of encounters which can be experienced:

1 Face-to-face encounters
2 Telephone encounters
3 Remote encounters.

Remote encounters take place without any direct human contact, such as with an Automatic Teller Machine (ATM). With these it is the quality of the *process* or *systems* that is used to judge the quality of the interaction. But even when judging a process, and more specifically when reflecting on telephone or face-to-face encounters, it is the perception of the customer as to what was received, evaluated against what was expected, that is the critical measure of quality and satisfaction. This perception could distort what was actually received as it depends on the value judgement of the customer.

Another issue that can affect an interaction is the *environment* within which it is provided. For a train journey this could include the comfort and cleanliness of the train, the information provided at the station, the 'reassuring' state of repairs of the carriages, and other issues that make a train journey a pleasure rather than something to be endured. It must not be forgotten that Levitt's *Marketing Myopia* (1959) focused on the core benefits of travel when defining what business a company is in. Nevertheless the secondary features play a major role when it comes to assessing customer satisfaction.

Referring to Sasser's list above, the issues of *consistency* and *completeness* are the most important. These are relevant every time an encounter occurs. It is necessary to focus on good staff training and motivation in order to ensure really satisfying *'moments of truth'* for customers. Marketing can play a part here both with ways of improving internal communications and by providing feedback from the market place on how customers react to particular offerings. However, Levitt (1981) suggested that: 'No matter how well trained or motivated, people make mistakes, forget, commit indiscretions, at times get hard to handle'. The fact is that many interactions usually depend on people – or more often, specifically on a single person who has the responsibility for delivering the service. This is as true in a McDonald's fast-food outlet as in a highly-trained dentist's surgery.

Complaints are also a very valuable source of marketing information about any offering. They represent the *negative perception of an offering* as evaluated by the customer. Therefore complaints provide an excellent source of information about those issues that require attention. Complaints are unsolicited, and surveys suggest that only

one out of every **ten** dissatisfied customer actually complains. The rest just walk away and are lost permanently. The golden rule of complaints is to actually welcome them and encourage any feedback from customers. This could be made easy by providing a freephone number or a customer comment form where possible.

To support the complaints process the organisation must respond as quickly as possible in every case, and must always keep the communication with the customer open so that there are no misunderstandings. It is necessary to think about the *cost of a problem to the customer* rather than the inconvenience to the company. Responses ought to reflect whatever is required to retain the customer rather than a straight replacement. Of course action can be initiated to remedy the underlying cause of the problem, but this should never precede the attention to the customer.

Example	Imagine you've bought something from a store in your local High Street, maybe some clothing, on getting home you realise that the stitching is coming undone. What do you do?
	Maybe you take the item back to the store and they immediately replace the item with a perfect one. Are you satisfied?
	Well, you've had the inconvenience of a return visit to the store, maybe having to take additional time off. You've had the cost of getting there, maybe a bus fare or car parking charge. You've had the initial disappointment regarding the item. You've also had your confidence in the quality of products supplied by the store challenged.
	A straight replacement does not compensate for all these, maybe the rule should be replace PLUS. That is replace, apologise, and offer a small extra item to win back the goodwill and go some way to recognising the additional costs suffered by the customer.
	What do you think?

In too many organisations the complaints department is controlled by the operations function or by some aspect of quality control. This is wrong – the responsibility should be with the marketing function. This is because marketing must undertake responsibility for customer satisfaction in all its aspects. There should not be any blame attached to complaints, rather they should be viewed as an opportunity to learn from the people who really matter, the customers.

INTERACTIVE AND INTERNAL MARKETING

In the introduction to this chapter the direct link between an organisation and its customers was termed *external* marketing. The actual delivery of this, involving people, employees of the organisation, and their direct relationship with customers, is *interactive* marketing. To complete the link there is the way that a firm treats, as well as how it motivates, its employees. It is possible to consider employees as internal 'customers' of their company. If this happens there are opportunities for using marketing techniques in order to improve the link between a company and its employees. The marketing activity affecting these internal relationships is called *internal* marketing. (see Figure 12.1). If all aspects of Figure 12.1 are positive, the organisation will offer excellent customer service. The opposite could be as a result of the following vicious circle:

- **Company**: *The staff treat customers like rabble. 'They need a good talking to.'*
- **Employees**: *'If the company does not care about me, why should I bother?'*
- **Customer**: *'I'm not coming back.'*

It is obvious that the way an offering is supplied to a customer is as much a part of the product offering as the product itself. The issues regarding the service components of a 'total offering' were discussed in Chapter 11. Marketing must consider all the interactive factors and get involved with internal marketing, otherwise all the other efforts in designing a competitive offering will be wasted.

Internal marketing

Internal marketing has been defined by Christian Grönroos as:

> **To create an internal environment which supports customer-consciousness and sales-mindedness amongst all personnel within an organisation.**

If an organisation is to be 'marketing orientated' then there must be an attitude amongst staff that regards customer satisfaction as paramount. As shown above, the individual employees who are in contact with customers are absolutely crucial to the *'moments of truth'* interactions. But those same employees are also 'customers' of their employer's organisation. If they feel dissatisfied in any way then this could affect their attitude to the 'external' customers. Also if the internal employees do not know what an organisation is trying to achieve with regards to its customers, then there could be confusion and inappropriate actions. A marketing orientation was described in Chapter 2 together with a definition of *part-time marketing*.

Internal marketing is the use of marketing skills and techniques to identify the needs of all internal 'customers' (especially the part-time marketers) and to communicate with them in a form of marketing activity. The aim is to enhance and clarify the relationship between employees and their company. This being undertaken for the mutual benefit of both parties.

Internal marketing also involves other functional disciplines, in particular HRM. Marketing specialists, however, should have both the research skills to identify employee needs and wants as internal customers of the organisation and the communication skills to assist in meeting these needs effectively. The role of internal marketing will be discussed further in Chapter 22.

CONCLUSION

This chapter has explored the links that develop between a supplier and their customers. Good marketing is a lot more than the achieving of a single exchange transaction. It should be obvious that if repeat business does occur then both parties – supplier and customer – are likely to be even more satisfied with each other. This is of benefit to the supplier because the costs of acquiring new customers are much higher than the costs of retaining existing ones. It also assists the customer, offering the reassurance that comes from experience, as well as other intangible benefits based on the emotional bonds that develop. There can also be tangible benefits in terms of reduced costs, not necessarily in the actual price paid but in the cost of finding a suitable product or service, and any cost involved in using the product.

Supplier ↔ customer links can be explored in two different ways. Both are important, and each of the links must be consistent with the other. First is the bond that can develop between a customer and the actual marketing offering, product or service. The second is the relationship between the customer and the supply organisation. The first is a relationship with an inanimate object, the other is with a corporate entity and the people who work for it. It is not necessary for each of these to develop in parallel as each will depend on market conditions and different market inputs. It is possible for there to be a strong brand equity but little relationship with the supplier as in many consumer markets; alternatively there can be a strong interactive relationship between the two organisations but no need for a brand, as in industrial services.

Nevertheless both *brands* and *relationships* develop, over a period of time, because of the increasing confidence of customers, and in response to the consistent marketing activities of suppliers. Both exist only if the customer really accepts the situation – if a customer feels exploited, or just disinterested or uninvolved in the series of exchanges, then the emotional links fail to develop. It does not matter how many messages a supplier puts out, nor how many other activities they undertake, if a customer does not engage emotionally then no *brand personality* and no *interactive relationship* will evolve.

If, however, a relationship does develop, either with the marketing offering – a *brand* – or with the supply organisation, then the increasing mutual dependency can bring benefits to both sides. The *brand* will take on a personality that gives value to the customer and can be exploited further by the brand owner. And the *interactive relationship* between the supplier and customer should lead to a more efficient series of exchanges. *Branding* and *relationship marketing* can both, therefore, be seen as closely related concepts. Understanding both requires a marketing manager to distinguish between a discrete transaction, one that has a distinct beginning, short duration and sharp end (the sale), and a series of exchanges, longer in duration and involving many interactions. The desirability of either depends on market conditions and an appreciation of the additional time and cost involved in fostering the development.

It must never be forgotten that a customer *will not commit to any relationship they do not value*. However, it takes more than marketing activities to develop interactive relationships. That is why the topic of *internal marketing* was raised at the end of this chapter. Customers experience *everything* a supplier offers to them – some good experiences that satisfy needs, other less satisfying elements of a 'total offering'. Philip Kotler, the guru of American marketing, once said: 'Customers are attracted through promises, and retained through satisfaction. Marketing can deliver the promises, but only the **whole** company can ensure satisfaction.' Therefore anything marketers can do to their internal organisation to encourage a culture of *customer-consciousness* can be helpful. Marketing should not get involved with those roles that are specifically 'human resource management' (HRM), but there are ways in which marketing can help. This is a topic that goes far further than this text, but the ideas are highlighted here because of their importance in the building of strong, satisfying relationships with customers

QUESTIONS

1 *'The brand is more important than the product'. Discuss this statement.*

2 *What is the role of the customer in the development of a* brand*?*

3 *Suggest a situation where investing in long-term relationships would not be the best choice.*

4 *How can the interactive contact between two individual people representing buyer and seller affect the delivery of a marketing offering?*

FURTHER READING

Aaker, D. (1991) *Managing Brand Equity*. Free Press.

Adcock, D. (2000) *Marketing Strategy for Competitive Advantage,* Wiley.

Buttle, F. (1996) *Relationship Marketing – Theory and Practice*. Paul Chapman.

Carlzon, J. (1987) *Moments of Truth*. Ballinger.

De Chernatony, L. and McDonald, M. (1998) *Creating Powerful Brands,* 2nd edn. Butterworth Heinemann.

Cram, T. (1994) *The Power of Relationship Marketing*. Pitman.

Doyle, P. (1997) *Marketing Management and Strategy,* 2nd edn., Prentice Hall.

Ford, D. (ed). (1998), *Managing Business Relationships*. Wiley.

Ghemawat, P. (1986) 'Sustainable Advantage', *Harvard Business Review*, Sept/Oct.

Grönroos, C. (1979) 'Marketing orientated strategies in service businesses', *Finnish Journal of Business*, 4.

Grönroos, C. (1990) 'Relationship approach to the marketing function in service context: the marketing organisation interface', *Journal of Business Research*, 20, pp. 3–11.

Grönroos, C. (1994) 'From marketing mix to relationship marketing: towards a paradigm shift in marketing', *Management Decisions*, 29(1), pp. 7–13.

Gummesson, E. (1999) *Total Relationship Marketing*. Butterworth Heinemann.

Jackson, B. B. (1985) 'Build customer relationships that last', *Harvard Business Review*, November–December.

Kotler, P. (1999) *On Marketing*, Free Press.

Levitt, T. (1958) *Marketing Myopia*.

Levitt, T. (1983) *The Marketing Imagination*, Free Press.

O'Malley, S., Paterson, M. and Evans, M. (1997). 'Intimacy or Intrusion, The Privacy Dilemma for Relationships Marketing', *Journal of Marketing Management*, Vol. 13.

Pearson, S. (1996) *Building Brands Directly*. Macmillan.

CASE STUDY

Manchester United – football team, brand, or total emotional experience?

As a football club, Manchester United needs few introductions. It is of course the world's richest football club, and in March 2000 its market capitalisation (value of its shares) exceeded £1 billion. However ManUtd are much more than a football club as they have a range of business activities that go well beyond the field of play.

Some of these are directly related to footballing facilities, for instance MUcatering which offers an impressive complex of function suites of varying sizes available for business and social usage. The publicity states 'whatever the requirement, Manchester United has options to suit'. Other activities are overt extensions of the brand name. The club Megastore offers club replica kit, children's clothing, toys and games, adult clothing, bedroom items, luxury goods, clocks/watches, videos, books and music. These are all possible because of the way the club has marketed its image, and developed its relationship with its fan base. Of course the presence of such a large following is one reason why sponsors are prepared to pay so much for the privilege of advertising on the team shirts. There is also the MUTV, the media channel run in association with Sky Digital. This shows many highlights, interviews, and other programmes on subscription in the UK and parts of Europe.

A visit to the web site, manutd.com, will reveal the full range of businesses that are now part of this successful company. The web site receives a staggering 8 million hits every month, and will soon be offering video highlights of club games. However as one analyst said 'the company's future growth potential is still to be realised. There will be a number of internet winners and the ones with the best content will be the ones that win – Manchester United has fantastic content potential'. The club has a huge worldwide following, especially in Asia, and that adds more scope to the extension of activities.

Task

Evaluate the 'Manchester United' brand and the way the club is building a relationship with its various customer segments. How much further do you think they can go in extending the brand?

Also with respect to the web site, suggest how you believe it can be utilised to further enhance the both the ManUtd brand and the relationship with customers?

Making products available

If you build a better mousetrap the world will beat a path to your door.

Ralph Waldo Emerson

INTRODUCTION

The quote above, by an American philosopher, is far from the truth in markets where supply exceeds demand. Obviously it is important to communicate with potential customers about your products, and the key benefits they offer. There are only a few products which customers will make the effort to seek out, although now, with the development of e-commerce, it is possible to stumble across them by utilising effective search engines. In general a customer will search hard for an offer if they have a really strong desire for a particular need to be met.

If the product required is specialised, or maybe one that needs to be made to an individual design as is common in industrial markets, then a purchaser might use all their skills to locate a potential supplier with the necessary abilities. Here they might 'beat a path to your door'. But this is unusual and this search is not necessarily going to find all organisations that can fulfil the requirements. It will be more likely to find those organisations that take positive action to develop channels linking them to potential customers.

In reality, there are very few products where customers will beat a path to your door. It is therefore very important that products are made easily available to customers. This involves thinking about the specific customers and about the probable ways in which they might search for a product offering, then ensuring that it is more than 'chance' that your offering is found. This could involve a decision to use an internet site, maybe in conjunction with a physical location, but whatever the decision, the better the 'signposts' guiding a customer to the offering the more likely it is that a sale will occur. Marketing has already been described as 'making it easier for your customers to say yes'. Certainly any purchase decision made by a customer can be helped by making products available *where potential buyers can find them*.

In some cases a product will be offered 'direct' to the final customer, with no intermediary between producer and recipient, in other instances it is more efficient to use a chain of distributor(s) in order to reach the eventual consumer. The problem of channel choice is not restricted to physical products alone, but can just as easily apply to a service (Figure 13.1). Consider a student insurance policy made available through an insurance broker, such as Endsleigh Insurance. It is covered in the '4 Ps' of marketing by the word 'place', but 'place' really does not describe all the elements involved in the task of making products easily available to customers. These include:

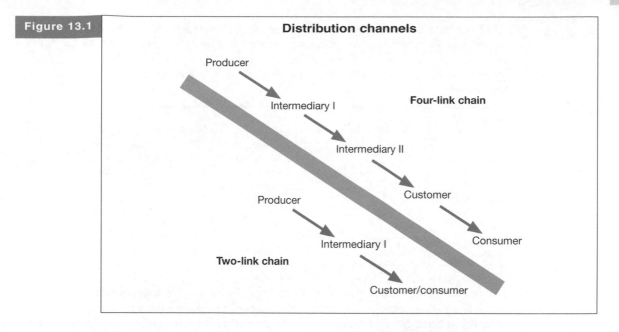

Figure 13.1

Distribution channels

1 Bringing customers into contact with offered products/services
2 Offering a sufficient choice to meet customers' needs
3 Persuading customers to develop a favourable attitude to a particular product
4 Maintaining adequate levels of sales both for your organisation – and, if appropriate, for the intermediaries
5 Providing appropriate services and information to help purchase decisions, especially when indirect channels are used
6 Maintaining an acceptable final price, taking into account the profit requirements of those intermediaries in the distribution channel.

The key decisions for an intermediary organisation regarding which goods to purchase will be taken to meet both the objectives of the final consumer as well as those of the intermediary. You might consider the role of a buyer for the Sainsbury supermarket group responsible for jams and marmalade, and how his or her actions would affect both a major supplier and a customer for this product.

The above example considers how to make products easily available to the final customers, and it might suggest a sales-based solution for the manufacture. It also highlights the fact that while Sainsbury's are a potential customer for Baxters they have chosen not to buy. But the final consumer who is, in fact, a customer of the retailer, has not had a chance to take this decision. The term 'trade marketing' is used regarding that part of the exchange process between supplier and intermediary. It is as important a marketing job as dealing with final consumers. The specific role of the intermediary will be discussed later in this chapter. This example also highlights what are called *distribution channels* (see Figure 13.1), which are the links connecting (marketing) organisations and through which goods or services are transferred from the original producer to the final consumer.

The task of 'making products available' to the final consumer involves consideration of how to ensure the *right* goods are found, at the *right* time, in the *correct* quantities and at the *right* price. Not every product benefits from wide distribution. A specialised

Example

Let's say that you were trying to purchase a jar of jam. You may go to your local grocer's shop. In the price list published by The *Grocer* magazine there are 11 suppliers of jam shown. But no supermarket has enough shelf space to stock every brand. Within a couple of miles there are medium size branches of Asda, Tesco and J Sainsbury. A visit in May 2000 showed the following brands in stock:

ASDA	TESCO	J SAINSBURY
—	Robertsons	Robertsons
Hartleys	Hartleys	Hartleys
St Dalfour	St Dalfour	St Dalfour
Streamline	Streamline	
Bonne Maman	Bonne Maman	Bonne Maman
—	Duerrs	Duerrs
Baxters	—	—
Clarks Wham Bam (A cheap product @ 33p)	—	—
Asda own label	Tesco own label	Sainsbury own label

This offers a good choice in any one store. But in the case of the Baxter's product this is not available in either Tesco or Sainsbury. Shoppers don't tend to change supermarkets just to buy a particular brand of jam. The problem for Baxters is therefore how to reach potential customers, especially those who did most of their shopping at Tesco or Sainsbury's. Certainly few, if any, of these potential customers would have tried to visit the Baxter's factory in Scotland. So if Baxters fail to change the decisions of Tesco and Sainsbury's regarding the brands to be stocked, and cannot find an alternative way of getting close to potential customers, they will miss approximately two out of every three shoppers. Of course things might change as better offers are made to the retailers, but it will be interesting to see how things change in this very competitive market.

item of photographic equipment might be better supplied through special outlets with appropriately trained staff. This is why not every product is suitable for sale on the Internet. It is one thing to buy a familiar item, perhaps with a known brand name, but if more reassurance is required then another type of distribution outlet could be *right*! In other circumstances, where the product is an exclusive designer dress, for example, it might be that no-one else could possibly get the item that is important, so in this case a form of *exclusive availability* could be more important to the customer. It is therefore necessary to consider the characteristics of the particular offering to decide if it requires:

- Intensive
- Specialist or
- Exclusive distribution.

These decisions will be taken as a result of fully understanding the purchase drive of customers.

Distribution, when considered by a marketer, is not really concerned with physical distribution. It is more concerned with making the products available in the *right way*. The decisions, once taken, require careful setting up, but they then become fixed for a long period of time. For this reason, great care must be taken when considering the distribution channels to be used. The prime decisions cover:

- The choice of channel structure – direct or indirect

- Decisions on whether to use a single channel or several different (complementary) ones
- Decisions on how to make those channels actually connect with consumers.

SELECTION OF CHANNELS

The prime aim of any marketing decision relating to distribution channels is how to reach the relevant customers. This must be in the most appropriate way, given the following four major considerations:

1 Potential customers' requirements
2 Your organisational resources
3 Competitors' and distributors' actions
4 Legal constraints.

Peter Chisnall wrote in his book, *Strategic Business Marketing*:

> Among the decisions then to be taken is the important one of how products will reach customers. Unless the channels of distribution are appropriate for the type of product and are efficiently operated, even intrinsically good products can end up as failures . . . it is worth spending a considerable amount of time and effort in evaluating alternative ways of ensuring that the channel eventually selected will make its full contribution to the marketing mix. Carelessly chosen methods of distribution may seriously damage the reputation of suppliers and also involve them in expensive litigation, if they seek to terminate agreements with distributors.

Established firms have well-defined channels. These channels often establish the norm for that particular market. While such channels will clearly differ from market to market, the channels themselves develop from the exchange between suppliers and customers. They then come to fit the needs of many customers and again become the expected norm. Such arrangements are usually of a long-term nature, and can prove a challenge to new entrants trying to break into the market.

Of course, this is an area where innovative new channels can sometimes alter the whole market and provide opportunities for new suppliers. Today this is happening with the Internet, in the past development of large out-of-town retail parks also changed the way we shop.

Customer requirements

The choice of efficient distribution channels relies on knowledge of a particular market. But, more specifically, it relies on the *needs and wants of customers*. It may not be possible to satisfy everything a particular customer wants, but that customer's decision is likely to be based on issues such as cost, convenience and availability. Look at the different ways in which varying types of food retailer offer a particular food item for sale.

Example

An out-of-town hypermarket might offer two different brands at a good price (especially if one is its own brand). The hypermarket will support it by long opening hours, including most outlets being open on Sundays. In fact, the term 'place' does not just refer to the location as might be imagined, it also refers to such issues as opening hours, which are equally critical to availability and, therefore, to customer decisions.

▶

The problems facing most customers are (a) travel to the hypermarket which could be difficult without a car, and (b) the queues at the checkout if you visit it at a peak period.

A town-centre store such as Marks & Spencer will offer only its own brand, but it is likely to be slightly more expensive. Marks & Spencer trade on their quality position and not their price. The store might be more convenient to a customer shopping in a town centre, but that is not always so. Also, in some locations Marks & Spencer is not open especially late and some of their stores are not open on a Sunday.

A neighbourhood store, owner managed, but perhaps a member of a buying group like Spar, will have limited choice. They may stock just one branded product, offered for sale at its recommended retail price. Such a store could be near urban housing, and is likely to be open for even longer hours than the hypermarket.

The decision facing potential customers is how they rate the different elements of cost and convenience. The supplier of the food product will perhaps see no conflict in supplying all three types of retailers. The attempt by the supplier to obtain maximum coverage is termed 'intensive distribution'. This is the strategy of giving the product the maximum exposure possible, so that it has the best chance of being found by a customer. However, the supplier is likely to put greatest effort into trying to develop the channel that offers the greatest return. In supplying a hypermarket it is likely that a direct approach will be used. But to supply the neighbourhood store they will probably work in an indirect way via a wholesaler or Cash and Carry.

Opening times are relevant to the availability decision of customers, especially for such diverse organisations as public libraries and supermarkets. The restrictions on local authority budgets has been blamed for shorter library opening hours, as well as a more limited 'product' owing to less spending on new books. However, the visible result is fewer books are being borrowed. It is possible to argue that the reason also has something to do with the ever-increasing presence of substitute products such as TV or video. While marketing is not a term used by many in the library service, the need to satisfy customers is still a key requirement. The use of mobile libraries over many years was one way libraries found of increasing availability. The reduction of opening hours in some towns is the opposite.

One of the advantages of shopping on the Internet is that it is open all hours. The problem is that the products once bought have to be sent to the customer in the same way as a mail order purchase. There is a delay before the product is actually seen, and before it can be checked as being fully satisfactory. Purchasing from a local store means there is immediacy in obtaining the goods but there is the time and trouble of visiting the outlet, and probably the cost is higher than the Internet price. All customers make a *trade-off* between time, trouble and other factors, and this means that e-commerce is particularly suitable to products such as holidays, records and books. Direct sales work well for car insurance, whereas physical locations still offer a great deal when it comes to regular grocery orders.

Exercise

1 Draw up a list of products and services that are, in your opinion, more appropriate for distribution via the Internet. Set out the reasons for your decisions.

2 Then repeat the exercise, but find products and services suitable for direct marketing such as telephone sales.

3 Finally suggest some products or services that still benefit from traditional 'bricks and mortar' stores offering a physical location rather than a remote 'virtual market space'.

Some students may be aware that Tesco and other supermarkets are experimenting with internet retailing. The maximum availability of food products, via all chosen channels, is desirable for the food supplier. If the product is not on sale when required then potential customers could buy an alternative (competitor's) food item. Here there could be an alternative for the customer but the supplier loses a sale. Perhaps one advantage of ordering via the Net is that the intermediary can use a central warehouse and thus reduce the risk of an item being out-of-stock when required. This could influence future customer behaviour and hence the decisions regarding channels of distribution for consumer products.

The needs of industrial customers are often different from those of individual consumers. For example, a specialist component may be required by a manufacturer, whose production line could be brought to a halt if that component is not available when required. In the past, firms invested working capital in buffer stocks, but such costs are increasingly being reduced as companies change to sophisticated supply-chain systems such as JIT (just-in-time). This type of supply chain can work only if there is a close partnership between supplier and customer. E-commerce has its role here as there are many ways of linking the scheduling computers of the supplier and customer so that a re-order is triggered automatically when required. Issues of convenience and availability would determine decisions by the customer on whether to source locally, or perhaps import cheaper components. Such a situation provides an interesting challenge for the marketing department of a potential supplying company. For this reason knowledge of customers' behaviour is critical to decisions on suitable channels of distribution.

Fictitious example

Offline sites favoured by new shoppers

There's a 'new kid on the block', it's called p-commerce. This novel concept is catching on fast as news of an innovative way of shopping is being spread around by personal communication, sometimes termed 'word of mouth'. It offers everything a customer wants in terms of availability and acceptability.

We can reveal that in these new 'shops' customers simply walk in off the street into a range of different sized buildings with glass fronts and attractive displays, and choose from a range of items available for sale. It has none of the frustration of the current e-commerce trading and is becoming increasingly popular with the *'cash-rich'*, *'time-poor'* generation of new consumers. These shoppers simply don't have the time to download graphics onto their computer to view fashion gear and trainers and then wait five days for them to be delivered with the risk that the item might not fit anyway. They don't want the problems, and have not got time to get involved with returns.

P-shoppers (personal shoppers) actually like talking to service staff, enjoy trying on the clothes and prefer to complete the transaction in real time, paying cash and then walking away with the goods. P-shoppers can have the goods when they want them, a real advance in availability. This is far better than the problems experienced when something ordered cannot be delivered as the customer is out, and to get the item requires a frustrating trip to an industrial distribution centre in another part of town.

There are advantages for the shops as well. They are being clustered together in something called a High Street. The delivery is direct in bulk to the shop and there is no messing around with collections from fickle customers.

Whilst this is a spoof, adapted from Rupert Steiner of the *Sunday Times* who found a similar item on the Internet, it does illustrate the importance of understanding customers, the requirement to undertake a trade-off between acceptability, availability and affordability, and not getting carried away by new technology.

Organisational resources

The choice of channels has to be consistent with the needs and capabilities of the organisation as well as meeting the needs of customers. It might be considered necessary for a qualified person to install a more technical product such as a gas fire or a heavy-duty machine. In this case suitable channels might be restricted to those where such a service is available. The producer could, of course, set up a network of wholly-owned outlets. This option is very expensive, it may be beyond the resources of a producer and it could also be an inefficient way of achieving the objectives.

For some complex products a manufacturer might set up their own website with a view to giving information to potential customers. However this is more akin to advertising than distribution. But if there is a possibility of using the Internet, either through a company-owned site or via a retail site such as Amazon.com there is still the need to ensure that resources are well deployed as many sites are not particularly user-friendly. In addition, the supply organisation has to consider if their customers are actually able to interact, as not every customer has access to the net.

Therefore the first consideration for a supply organisation will normally be to identify the *market segments* to which they want to offer their product, and the way such customers might seek out purchases. As has already been discussed, there is likely to be an ongoing need for relevant market information to be fed back to the manufacturer/supplier. In view of this, it could be decided to work with a particular type of channel that will facilitate the process. Many companies admit they are better off working through intermediaries because they can provide the resources to cover all the potential customers in a cost-effective way. In fact this is another reason why food manufacturers market via retailers rather than directly. In other cases intermediaries are in an excellent position with regards to customers. This is why certain life insurance and pension companies operate via solicitors, accountants or banks rather than recruiting large direct sales forces. The intermediary gives credibility to the product. In fact the issue of credibility is crucial when considering the reputation of an internet link.

Imported products can also benefit from indirect channels, which is why French mineral water, Perrier, although owned by Nestlé, is distributed in the UK by Coca-Cola Schweppes beverages (CCSB). Both organisations benefit: Perrier from an efficient transport system and CCSB's large professional sales force, CCSB by being able to include a very desirable product in their portfolio.

One problem arising from the use of intermediaries is that it almost invariably leads to some form of loss of control over the way markets are served. Obviously, it also involves lower margins, but this needs to be set against the costs of direct distribution, and the breadth of potential customers that any channel can achieve. Of course, if a manufacturer wants to reach regular customers of Marks & Spencer he cannot do it without losing his identity and control because he would have to supply an own-brand product. This now gives Marks & Spencer a very powerful position in part of the supply chain. Companies who work successfully with them, can gain very large sales by co-operating in this way. But, as has recently been shown, the retailer can change products and suppliers, hence it could be dangerous for a company such as William Baird who were heavily reliant on M&S to distribute their goods.

Market considerations

The example above is also relevant when considering which channels are (a) suitable for customers, (b) acceptable to the organisation and (c) feasible in light of existing market conditions. Control of the distributive channels is a very effective barrier to entry in many markets. Even if it is possible to gain access to a general distributor alongside competitive products, it will not be enough if the distributor constantly recommends a competitor's product rather than yours.

An interesting phenomenon is that brands with small market shares suffer, in what A. Ehrenburg calls, the 'double jeopardy effect'. This describes how the customers buying lesser-known brands are also less loyal to that brand in regular purchases, hence emphasising the poor sales. This effect makes it very difficult for minor brands to compete effectively.

Example

Opportunities do exist to develop sales in any market, as the example of Canon photocopiers shows. Rank Xerox used to dominate the UK photocopier market. They offered a range to meet almost every need. They supported this with a very large direct sales force and a national service network.

Canon broke this dominance by a strategy of producing reliable standardised machines that, although not as sophisticated, initially were cheaper. Canon offered their range through independent distributors who could undertake their own service requirements – a much cheaper operation than the Xerox sales and service teams.

Of course Rank Xerox have fought back and Canon have developed from their initial strategy. However, the role of alternative channels in Canon's market entry strategy was vital.

Another case where the use of alternative distribution channels was introduced to avoid direct competition with established products is the way Avon cosmetics use thousands of direct sales agents rather than selling via retail outlets. Avon have a large turnover in the UK and make an excellent profit on their business.

The difference between a company like Avon with its proactive approach through commission agents calling on customers, and using the Internet is the *hit rate*. the Net is essentially a passive location waiting for customers to come, as such it can get overlooked, missed by potential purchasers.

Avon use a very *intensive* channel of distribution, recruiting a large number of agents and contacting as many customers as possible. Another example of intensive cover is the attempt by confectionery company Cadbury's to get its chocolate bars into as many outlets as possible – shops, cinemas, garages, vending machines, etc. This is because the product can be an impulse purchase – 'see it and buy it'. The alternatives of selective and exclusive are described in the next section. The decision as to the best type of channel will be heavily influenced by product and market factors.

Legal issues

The legal environment is important. There are obvious issues such as product liability laws, which affect all offerings, and these restrictions vary from country to country. It is equally important to appreciate legal issues when developing channels for distribution. Key legislation such as the UK Sale of Goods Act puts responsibilities on UK retailers. In structuring the channels support must be given to the retailers (your customers) even if they are not the final consumers. Policies on returned stock and replacing faulty goods are a key element of distribution policy and customer service. One current concern with e-commerce is that the supplier might be in a different country altogether. The legislation will be different, and this has led to some complex problems and unresolved legal problems.

There are many laws restricting business. The legal environment relating to the customers (and the customers' customers) is part of the environment that must be considered when making products/services available.

TYPES OF DISTRIBUTION CHANNEL

Channels can be long or short, single or multiple (hybrid), and can achieve intensive, selective or exclusive distribution. The length of channel could have any number of intermediaries or be direct to customers (see Figure 13.2). This figure considers the options open to a farmer trying to get his fruit to the eventual consumers.

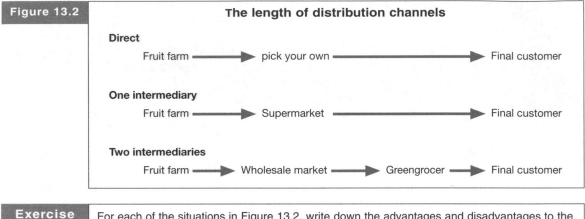

Figure 13.2 — The length of distribution channels

Direct

Fruit farm ⟶ pick your own ⟶ Final customer

One intermediary

Fruit farm ⟶ Supermarket ⟶ Final customer

Two intermediaries

Fruit farm ⟶ Wholesale market ⟶ Greengrocer ⟶ Final customer

Exercise For each of the situations in Figure 13.2, write down the advantages and disadvantages to the fruit farmer. The issues you are likely to consider are ones of control, cost, feedback, customer service and how likely it is that the supplier will achieve particular objectives.

Direct channels

A direct channel is said to exist when there are *no intermediaries between the supply organisation and its customers*. Such contacts could be very direct, face-to-face with a representative of the supplier, or more remote, such as through a catalogue or web page.

Such an arrangement could be:

Face-to-face contact:

Insurance company	→	own sales team	→	customers
Clothing manufacturer	→	party plan	→	customers
Library service	→	mobile library	→	customers
Small bakery	→	own retail outlet	→	customers

The last is an example of vertical integration of the intermediary.

Remote contact:

General trader	→	mail order catalogue	→	customers
Holiday company	→	company Web page	→	customers
Garden bulb supplier	→	direct mail leaflet	→	customers.

Figure 13.3

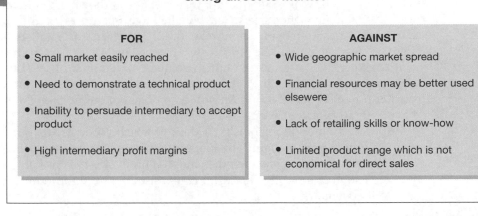

'Going direct to market'

FOR	AGAINST
• Small market easily reached	• Wide geographic market spread
• Need to demonstrate a technical product	• Financial resources may be better used elsewere
• Inability to persuade intermediary to accept product	• Lack of retailing skills or know-how
• High intermediary profit margins	• Limited product range which is not economical for direct sales

In these examples the supplier will decide all aspects of the contact with the customer. This could include how often the salesperson should contact the customer, or how frequently to send out a catalogue. In this type of direct channel there is no doubt who has control of the many decisions regarding the exchange. The situation is more complicated in indirect channels. There are many reasons for using direct channels, but equally there are a number of reasons why such channels are not always used. Some of these are listed in Figure 13.3.

Indirect channels

The conventional channel structure is shown in Figure 13.4. The roles of wholesaler and retailer could be filled by any of the intermediaries relevant to a particular market.

The links are important, with a marketing exchange taking place at each stage. The link provided by negotiation is not necessarily formal, but it certainly takes place in the legal sense of an offer and acceptance.

It is important to realise the effect of the nature of the channel, and the supply pipeline, on these indirect channels. One well-known British company launched its

Figure 13.4

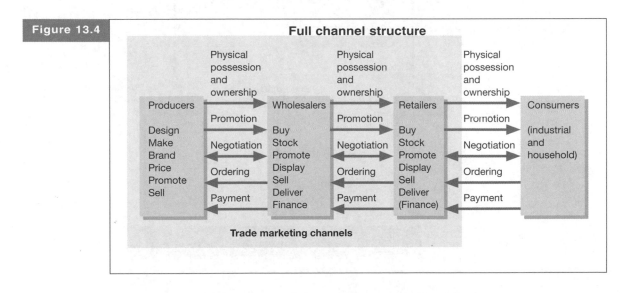

Full channel structure

product into the USA with apparently great success. It more than met the year 1 estimates of sales. In year 2 sales did not increase, in fact they fell. On investigation it was found that many wholesalers had bought large quantities in the first year, being encouraged by attractive promotional deals. However, the retailers and consumers were not buying, and so the pipeline was blocked by large stocks of the old product. It was an expensive lesson as the British company attempted to sort out the problems. This example shows the importance of *information* and *feedback* from all parts of the distribution channel. It also illustrates the problem of *loss of control* that a supplier can have with an indirect channel.

Another common problem is the extent to which products are 'out of stock' at one level in a distribution chain. The longer the channel, the more difficult it is to cope with the variations of consumer demand. If a product is not available when required, it could lead to a lost sale. This again emphasises the need for monitoring all levels of any indirect channel.

Hybrid channels

There is no reason why a supplier should stay with a single channel. Educational toy supplier, Early Learning, started with most sales via its mail order catalogue. It carefully monitored sales in large areas of population and, when it considered the time was appropriate, a retail outlet was opened in a secondary shopping area. Note that these areas were not in the prime High Street sites: it was considered that customers would

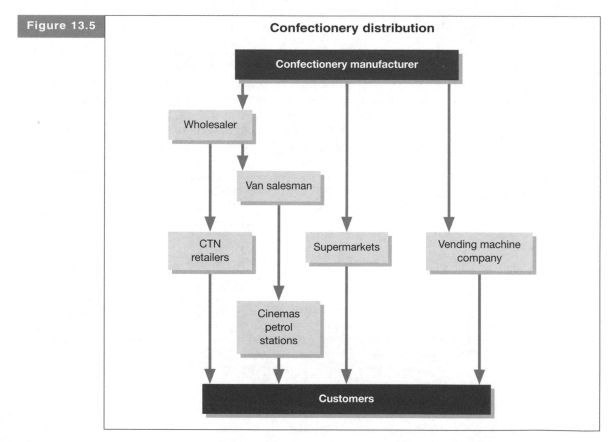

Figure 13.5   Confectionery distribution

be prepared to seek out an Early Learning outlet because the company felt they offered a unique type of product. So it was decided there was no point in paying the highest retail rents for prime High Street sites. The catalogue still continued and sales justified both channels running alongside each other. Demand for the products offered has been such that some High Street sites have been opened in busy locations.

Figure 13.5 represents the channels used by a well-known UK confectionery company where maximum distribution (intensive) is vital for sales of impulse purchase items.

There can be problems with mixed channels, as the following example illustrates.

Example

Wang Computers tried to base its distribution activities on a combination of its direct sales force, in conjunction with dealers.

In 1985 the company lowered the sales commission rates of its sales force for sales made jointly with dealers. Consequently, the rates for these sales were below those for sales made directly by the sales force without involving dealers. Inevitably Wang's own sales representatives began to compete with, rather than co-operate with, their resellers (retailers) – some Wang dealers even filed lawsuits because of this policy. Apparently it is now difficult for the company to re-establish its channel relationships as a residue of ill-will remains with the dealers towards the Wang direct sales operation. Obviously Wang failed to manage a workable hybrid channel strategy.

Note: In August 1992, Wang filed for protection from bankruptcy in the USA.

Exercise

Find out which channels are used by airlines to sell their tickets – you may be surprised by the diversity of outlets. In particular, you will find that the Internet is available and you should try to visit the website for companies such as easyJet <easyjet.com> and Go. There are also retailers of tickets, intermediaries, such as <expedia.com> who offer a search service based on the cheapest price.

Intensive, selective and exclusive distribution

- Intensive distribution involves *maximising the number of outlets where a product is available*. This wide exposure means more opportunities to buy. It is typified by confectionery, soft drinks and other fmcgs (fast-moving consumer goods).
- Selective distribution is used where the choice of outlet or service offered is *specifically relevant to the buying situation*. Examples are electrical or photographic specialists who can offer professional advice, or plumbers who can install purchases. However, this type of restricted distribution is becoming less common, with supermarkets and chemists, as well as department stores, offering ever-wider ranges of household and electrical goods.
- Exclusive distribution is much more restrictive. In this case there is often only *one exclusive company in any one geographic area*. The major main dealers for motor cars come into this category but, in addition to sales, they offer service, repair and warranty facilities. They receive the benefit of exclusivity that reduces competition. It is likely that the relationship will be formalised with a legal contract including targets, and obligations on the distributor. In return for acting as the local distributor for Ford or BMW or Rover, the distributor could receive promotional help.

It is interesting to note that Daewoo Cars, relative newcomers to the British market, have chosen a different distribution strategy. Daewoo have chosen direct selling, hassle-free showrooms where customers are shown courtesy and are free to browse in peace. This approach, combined with their aim of being the UK's most friendly and customer-focused car company, appears to be paying dividends in that, instead of meeting targets of gaining 1 per cent of the market within three years, they sold 18,000 cars in the first year, giving a market share of 0.92 per cent, a very successful launch indeed. As yet other car manufacturers have not followed this lead.

THE ROLE OF INTERMEDIARIES

Many markets are subject to dynamic change and in some the functions of channel members are being modified. Nevertheless, the common roles of the intermediary remain important. The most basic role is to reach customers at a *lower cost per unit than the supplier can achieve directly*. Perhaps the role could include reaching the target in a more effective way, given the buying habits of customers. This could be achieved by simply buying in bulk from the supplier and selling individual items on to the customers. The supplier concentrates on production, and delivers in quantity to the intermediary who becomes the supplier's customer. The intermediary will obviously take a share of the profit from a product/service, but it might still benefit the supplier because the intermediary could well be responsible for:

- Stockholding costs
- Transport and delivery to final customers
- Breaking bulk and consolidation of orders
- Providing local services such as display or after-sales service.

It is also possible that the supplier would be paid more quickly by the intermediary

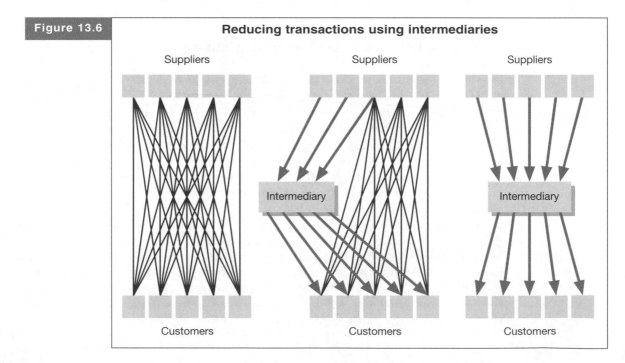

Figure 13.6   **Reducing transactions using intermediaries**

rather than the final customers. Certainly, use of intermediaries can reduce the number of transactions involved in reaching customers (see Figure 13.6). If the decision is taken to use an intermediary then it is essential that the upstream supplier considers the issues below with great care:

■ Building relationships with, and training intermediaries
■ The ownership of the intermediaries, and the proper level of investment within the channel.

There are many different types of intermediary, such as those listed below. One key difference that should be noticed is whether the intermediary takes ownership for the products in transit as a merchant, rather than acting as an agent who just puts buyer and seller in contact:

1 *Agent* – primarily concerned in the identification, conduct and negotiation of sale of goods either direct or through intermediaries. Agents do not take title or ownership of goods, nor do they often become involved in the physical handling of goods.
2 *Merchant* – takes title (buys) and resells merchandise. Wholesalers and retailers are the two main types of merchant.
3 *Wholesaler* – buys and resells products to retailers and to major industrial institutions and commercial companies. Normally sells little directly to the consumer.
4 *Retailer* – a merchant dealing primarily with the final consumer.
5 *Dealer* – buys and resells merchandise at wholesale, retail or both. Thus dealers take ownership, are involved with stock and usually have close market contacts within a particular area.
6 *Distributor* – often confused with dealer. More precisely, distributors are closer to the wholesaler role, often controlling independent dealers for retail distribution.
7 *Jobber* – a term widely used to designate a distributor or wholesaler. In the UK it usually carries the connotation of specialist knowledge or franchise with a particular market sector.
8 *Franchisee* – basically a licensing system under which the owner of a product or service grants an independent local operator the right to trade under the umbrella of the brand owner's name, offering the brand owner's product.

Recently much has been written about the power of food supermarket buyers in the selection of products. They are offered hundreds of new products every year and have room for only a small proportion on their shelves. Therefore the power of the buyer for the retail outlets is vital in deciding which products should be added to the range, which products should be delisted (deleted), and which will never be bought by that retailer, thus never becoming available to the customers of the shop. In these decisions a *strong brand name* can be an extremely powerful lever to persuade a major supermarket to stock a product. Once a relationship is formed it can be a long-term partnership. An article by Knox and White (1991) on the subject of fresh produce concluded:

> We have observed that these relationships are both highly interdependent and concentrated. Because of the increasing volume of high quality produce required by the retailer, they are obliged to work with a limited number of large suppliers who are capable of producing sufficient volume to meet these needs. As a consequence, there appears to be a reluctance to make rash changes in either supplier or retailer affiliation. Consequently, the average duration of a buyer–supplier relationship in the horticultural market was found to be about eight years.

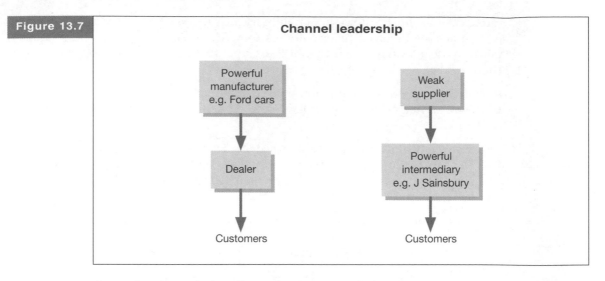

Figure 13.7

Channel leadership

Certainly channel choices are long-term and the interdependence of the parties is obvious. But in some markets the intermediary may lead the marketing and promotional effort; in others it is the supplier (see Figure 13.7).

The model of powerful suppliers or intermediaries competing for control of a distribution channel is now being challenged by what is termed 'vertical marketing systems' (VMS). Certainly conflict can arise in a channel where channel members have their own distinct objectives which may not complement those of other channel members. Figure 13.8 suggests these differences.

The companies in Figure 13.8 represent separate businesses, and each is seeking to maximise its own profits. The problem is that conflicting actions could reduce the effectiveness of the total system. But the companies are also interdependent, as the Knox and White study showed. Hence it is really not sufficient to count intermediaries and measure/monitor members' performance. Not all channel systems have members

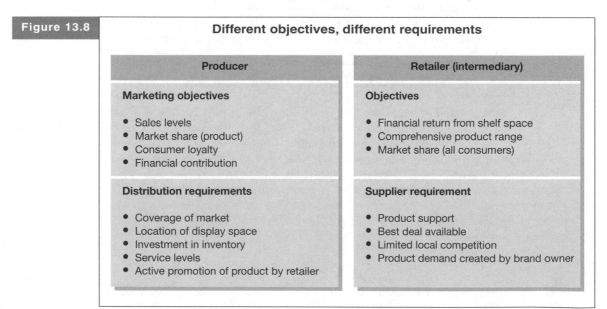

Figure 13.8

Different objectives, different requirements

Producer	Retailer (intermediary)
Marketing objectives	**Objectives**
• Sales levels • Market share (product) • Consumer loyalty • Financial contribution	• Financial return from shelf space • Comprehensive product range • Market share (all consumers)
Distribution requirements	**Supplier requirement**
• Coverage of market • Location of display space • Investment in inventory • Service levels • Active promotion of product by retailer	• Product support • Best deal available • Limited local competition • Product demand created by brand owner

Figure 13.9	Vertical marketing system

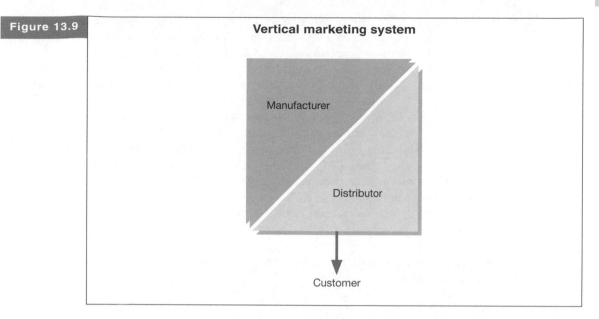

who see themselves as part of a system. This does little to enhance the quality and effectiveness of service. The idea of a VMS is that producers and intermediaries make a serious attempt to co-ordinate the channel of which they form a part, and to eliminate conflict between individual members (see Figure 13.9).

A survey of such relationships by Dawson and Shaw (1989) used a structured survey of 42 large British multiples and 60 suppliers in four very different product areas. Findings indicated that there are many examples of retailers and suppliers entering into long-term arrangements to do business together. Both parties invest heavily in the development of the relationship. It is interesting that 43 per cent of the retailers and 92 per cent of the manufacturers agreed that they preferred to remain with the same supplier/customer from year to year whenever possible. Factors acting to increase the stability of relationships included:

- A need for consistent quality
- A need for a flexible response
- Joint product development work
- Specific delivery requirements.

Even if no formal VMS is developed it is still important to build strong relationships between channel members:

- Any manufacturer that can appeal to the *channel partners' self-interest* will find its influence over distributors or retailers probably higher than if its programmes are totally self-interested. This is providing benefits – the basis of marketing. For example, Levi-Strauss jointly developed a computerised order processing-inventory management system with its retailers, the advantage of this being that retailers found themselves in a more favourable position in terms of profit. However, these information systems require closer partnerships. This has proved to be very well accepted by Levi wearers as well as retailers, as there is an added benefit, a custom-made pair of jeans to fit perfectly can now be ordered – the information sent directly from the retailer to the manufacturer.

- Knowledge about the *actual balance of power* may be helpful to prevent wrong decisions with serious consequences. Attempts to drop the dealer network in order to sell directly from company-owned sales branches may end in a situation where former dealers join with competitors and successfully work against a manufacturer.
- Furthermore, channel arrangements should be based on *adequate compensation*. A distributor's response to a margin squeeze may be to cut back stocking levels to shift inventory-holding costs back to the manufacturer's side. In the long term, this can have only negative effects on both parties.
- Manufacturers should be sensitive to the possibility of *horizontal channel conflicts*. These may be caused by increasing the number of outlets/intermediaries in an attempt to intensify distribution. Increased margins, for example, may be helpful to prevent such a conflict.
- The manufacturer's *own sales* force is a vital link to distributors. Training the sales force to support the distributors' sales forces may improve the overall channel performance.
- As a general guideline manufacturers should treat their channels of distribution as *strategic assets*.

VERTICAL INTEGRATION AND FRANCHISING

It will be apparent that there are two themes running through the subject of channel choice. First is the different operational roles of channel members at different levels in the system; the other is the co-operation and control of these different members within a total system.

To overcome the problems of control, the most obvious solution is for an organisation to combine the different levels in the distribution channel under a single ownership. Such an arrangement is usually called 'vertical integration', although now

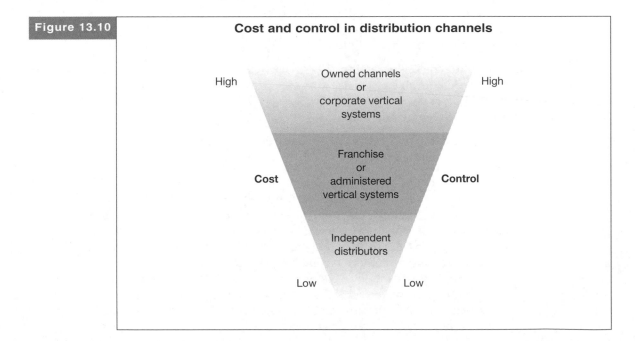

Figure 13.10   Cost and control in distribution channels

sometimes termed a 'corporate vertical marketing system'. It is more costly for the supplier, but this can be offset by the higher revenue from not having to fund distributors' margins. Costs and control of distribution channels are illustrated in Figure 13.10. Examples of this are the development of manufacturing units by the Cooperative Wholesale Society (CWS), or the way Laura Ashley, which started as a design and production operation, developed its own retail outlets.

An even longer integration was the Union International group run by the Vestey family. They combined companies to supply the Dewhurst Butchers chain that they owned. These included Weddel Meat Wholesalers, The British Beef Company (which also imported meat via the wholly owned Blue Star Shipping line), Thornhills Poultry (sold in 1987), Union Cold Storage (UCS) and many other related companies. For several decades the advantages were of great value. Now the increasing trend by consumers to buy less in traditional butchers and more in supermarkets and the general decrease in demand for beef has led to problems of such integrated companies which are difficult to solve. In fact none of the three companies have been particularly successful recently, although when they first developed vertically there were real advantages such as:

- economies of scale
- savings in transaction costs
- close supplier relationships
- barriers to entry
- efficiency.

For a time, all companies performed very well. The problems have come with a dynamic, changing competitive world. The lack of flexibility, the stifling of competitive forces and the lack of focus by the organisations have been reflected in performance. Laura Ashley Plc has completely altered its business to concentrate on design and retailing, dramatically reducing its manufacturing operations in mid-Wales. CWS has been losing share to other food operations for many years; and Union International have been on the financial pages, although property was partly to blame for their problems.

Management guru, Tom Peters, advises companies to stick to the basic business that they are good at ('stick to the knitting'). This would suggest that companies who try to both manufacture and retail products could be spreading their activities too broadly.

One way of obtaining the advantages without all the problems is to use a *franchise arrangement*. It is often believed that franchising started in the USA; however, the concept is a development of the tied-house arrangement used by many British brewers, which has lasted for over 200 years. This tied-house arrangement was challenged as restrictive by the 1989 Monopolies Commission report on Beer and Brewing. At the same time as this report restricted the franchises available in beer retailing (public houses), other franchise arrangements covering such companies as Body Shop, Prontaprint, DynoRod and Benetton have been on the increase.

A franchise has a proven greater survival rate than other small businesses. It is therefore usually a better option for a small business person than starting a new business in an untried area. This is because the franchisor should have been through all the learning processes and expensive mistakes that can affect a new business. Franchisees find it easier to raise the necessary capital and they take on a tested formula. The advantage to the franchisor is that they can expand business with lower capital commitment, and yet gain highly motivated franchisees keen to benefit, and sharing both risks and rewards.

DISTRIBUTOR QUALITY AND SERVICE

Most intermediaries offer a level of service to add to the original supplier's product. Service organisations are dependent on people and processes, as considered earlier. The major problem is the level of commitment from employees in such service industries: a survey in the USA has suggested that over 80 per cent of employees in service industries are really in dead-end jobs. (The problem that suppliers have in ensuring that the quality and service levels offered by their intermediaries is of a sufficiently high level is therefore a key element in channel decisions.) We have already seen such solutions as franchising where the intermediary uses an agreed retail format controlled by the supplier, but this is not always a possible route. It is always very important for the supplier to find ways of achieving the right level of support for their product. When a distributor is offering their product as well as some competitor's products, then the supplier may have to offer incentives to the distributor's staff to get them to promote the supplier's offering. This can become a costly ever-increasing spiral. It is an area that will be of vital interest to the sales force responsible for ensuring that products are sold *through the distributor* rather than just *to the distributor*.

The issue of customer service is also important when the Internet provides the distributive link. In fact most remote links suffer because of the worries over service levels. It is a major challenge facing the .com e-tailers who are now becoming very influential intermediaries in many markets. It is sometimes not enough for a customer to get the lowest possible price when the quality, after-sales service and even the true availability could be in doubt.

GETTING PRODUCTS INTO DISTRIBUTION – THE PUSH–PULL METHODS

There are two ways products get into a distribution channel. The first is through the efforts of a sales team to convince distributors/intermediaries to stock a product. Here a product is being pushed into the distribution channel. A good salesperson will not overload distributors with products, but will try to ensure the right level of product is available to meet requirements of the distributors' customers. To do this successfully a partnership needs to be created between salesperson and buyer. In some organisations the use of increasingly sophisticated electronic data and control systems could mean a product will not be purchased until it has been entered into a computer. The use of barcodes (article numbers seen on many products) means that purchases and sales can be tracked efficiently, and in some cases re-ordering of products is automatically controlled.

There is no point 'pushing' products into distribution if they do not move on to the final consumer. The customers can create demand, pulling products along a distribution chain. Perhaps you have wanted to buy a particular book, but found it not available in your local bookshop. By ordering it you create 'demand pull'. However, before you can initiate such a chain of events you will need to be aware of the existence of the required book. Perhaps your awareness came from advertising or a recommendation from one of your lecturers.

In practice most markets have a mixture of both 'push' and 'pull' techniques acting on the distribution chain. They are both necessary to keep the flow of products and services moving. At different stages in a product's life cycle there will be different emphasis on the balance between 'push' and 'pull'. You might like to consider the following examples in this context.

- A well-known national confectionery manufacturer such as Cadbury's when they launch a new product.
- The launch of Daewoo Cars into the British market using direct selling.
- Insurance policies specially designed for protection of students' possessions while in college/university halls of residence.

THE ROLE OF OVERSEAS AGENTS AND DISTRIBUTORS

The basic role of agents and distributors does not change in overseas markets; however, they are usually given more detailed consideration. Market entry is vital and the distances involved, together with cultural differences, mean that a local intermediary is often beneficial. It is possible to set up a wholly-owned channel, but agents and distributors are the most common in terms of numbers of exporters, although not always with larger volumes of goods. When volume gets high enough a supplier will be tempted to replace the agent with a corporate representation. However, to be fair to agents, and to get the best from their efforts, the partnership must be developed in an honest and open way.

An alternative arrangement, which is always worth consideration, is the joint venture – or, even further, a strategic alliance. Such arrangements can be immensely beneficial, not only in one overseas market but, if well constructed, for the mutual development of both organisations.

PHYSICAL DISTRIBUTION MANAGEMENT

This chapter has described the vital role played by choice of effective distribution channels. However, this could all be wasted if the physical distribution of a product is not organised as efficiently as possible. It is also vital that the right level of customer service is achieved, hence the need to consider what an organisation is really capable of achieving: it is not subsidiary to the task of selling, nor is it purely a cost to be borne by an organisation. It is a key element in creating satisfied customers.

Peter Drucker (1973) suggested the difference between efficiency and effectiveness was that the former was 'doing things right' and the latter 'doing the right things'. If for the sake of efficiency you do not dispatch a delivery vehicle unless it has a 100 per cent full load, it could save costs. The delays involved with customers receiving the product late could lose sales and materially affect future business. The choice of levels and quality of service will be influenced by both what customers expect, and by what competitors are prepared to offer.

Physical distribution management is concerned with transportation, materials handling, packaging, warehousing (and locations of depots), inventory policy, stock control and order processing. It is not the role of this book to discuss such issues in depth. However, it is essential to understand how added-value can be achieved through distribution policies and appreciate the necessity for a marketer to understand the role of logistics and physical distribution in the total product.

CONCLUSION

There are many ways of making a product available to potential customers. The marketing role is to identify the target market and to understand how a target customer might make a purchase decision. This can then be translated into an 'availability' strategy that matches these requirements. It is never enough just to post offers onto a company website and then hope that customers find it.

The decisions on channels are long-term. They can involve direct links with consumers or be indirect, through intermediaries. If intermediaries are used, then the relationships developed between suppliers and distributors can be critical to the effectiveness of the channel.

It is the effectiveness of the availability strategy that should be the prime concern of marketers. That is why new options such as internet links should be evaluated alongside other alternatives and the most appropriate one selected based on organisational, product, customer and market considerations. Within this strategy, channel decisions can give a competitive edge, with one organisation reaching customers and gaining sales because its products reach customers in a more appropriate way than those from competitors. An example of this is Coca-Cola – the product is an impulse purchase product and, by being available in more outlets, Coke is able to outsell Pepsi.

Other types of products require different distribution strategies. For some a selective or exclusive pattern might be best. It might be sensible to utilise several different links, such as the Internet, direct mail and selling via an intermediary. If this is done the different channels must work in harmony and not conflict. What may be a suitable strategy for an industrial product may not be suitable for a consumer durable.

The one certainty is that it is unlikely that customers will 'beat a path to your door'. In a market with excess demand, availability strategies play a vital part.

QUESTIONS

1   *Why might an organisation choose not to use an intermediary in its efforts to reach its customers?*

2   *What are the advantages and the disadvantages for a clothing manufacturer in making products available via their own website, or a mail order catalogue sent to known customers, or offering their product to High Street stores?*

3   *Suggest three products that might benefit from intensive distribution, and explain how this might be achieved.*

4   *When using an intermediary it is possible to set up a franchise distribution network. How might this be preferable when compared to other distribution intermediaries (wholly owned or fully independent)?*

FURTHER READING

Chisnall, P. (1995) *Strategic Business Marketing*. Prentice-Hall.

Dawson, J. A. and Shaw, S. A. (1989) 'The move to administered vertical marketing systems by British retailers', *European Journal of Marketing*, 23.

Drucker, P. (1973) *Management Tasks, Responsibilities and Practices*. Harper & Row.

Ehrenberg, A. S. C., Goodhardt, G. J. and Barwise, T. P. (1990) 'Double jeopardy revisited', *Journal of Marketing*, July.

Knox, S. D. and White, H. F. (1991) 'Retail buyers and their fresh produce suppliers', *European Journal of Marketing*, 25.

Marketing, IPA Advertising Effectiveness Awards 1996 Category One: New Launches.

Narus, J. A. and Anderson, J. C. (1996) 'Rethinking distribution', *Harvard Business Review*, July–August.

Saunders, M. (1997) *Strategic Purchasing and Supply Chain Management*. Pitman.

Stern, L. W. and El Ansary, A. (1996) *Marketing Channels*, 5th edn, Prentice-Hall.

CASE STUDY

South Devon holiday cottage

A friend of your family owns a holiday cottage in South Devon. For the last few years this has been offered for let using the services of an intermediary. The 'Cottage Agency' act on behalf of a large number of cottage owners, and traditionally have taken a small percentage commission for every successful letting. However if the cottage was let to family friends or returning visitors who booked direct with the owners, then no commission was paid.

This year the 'Cottage Agency' have changed their terms of business and demanded a flat fee based on a full year of letting fees, and have offered no rebate should the property remain empty. They also demand that all family lets are placed through their books.

This means a very large increase in costs for your friends, and they are also furious that 'family lets' cannot be excluded from the terms. They have therefore decided to end the arrangement with the 'Cottage Agency'.

Knowing that you are studying marketing they have asked you to suggest if it might be a good idea to create a web site and use that in order to reach potential customers. They still expect a few returning customers from past years and of course the family lets. But unless they can get customers for the whole of the Easter to September period they will worry about the financial viability of their cottage.

■ *Your first task is to advise of the benefits and risks of using the Net in order to reach potential customers.*

However there are other ways of 'making the cottage available to potential customers'. Maybe you can suggest some alternative channels of distribution that could be considered. Remember a holiday cottage is a product, even if it is not a traditional type of product. It requires marketing decisions to be made and these are more than pure advertising. It could be that other intermediaries could be found, for instance the South Devon Tourist Board. Direct marketing without intermediaries does not mean it has to be the net, but as the owners found out when they asked the *Sunday Times* about advertising costs, whilst it would be good to back every possible way of reaching customers they cannot afford to fund too many initiatives.

■ *Now draw up a list of the alternate options with their benefits, problems and some evaluation of the costs [high or low] and other risks involved.*

14 Affordable offerings – price and value

There is hardly anything in the World that some men cannot make a little worse and sell a little cheaper.

John Ruskin (1819–1900)

INTRODUCTION

The economic environment was discussed in Chapter 3. Even a cursory glance at the relative exchange rates or a study of inflation will show that the economic balance changes over time. In the first year of the 21st century the UK pound is strong against the new 'Euro' currency operating in much of Europe. This means that many products from those other parts of Europe seem more affordable than ones produced in Britain. Of course, this situation could change. However, from a marketing perspective customers compare prices and then decide which offering seems to be the best value when measured against the tests of **acceptability** and **affordability**.

During the 1990s the inflation rate in Peru reached 1400 per cent per annum. In the UK, we cannot contemplate prices doubling every month, but we can appreciate the problems it causes for both suppliers and customers. In some areas of Peru, people have so little faith in money that they rely on exchange of goods, such as chickens for clothes, and eggs for firewood. Their exchanges are dictated by the *desirability of what is offered by the two parties*, they have little to do with the cost of production. What is important is the relative values that each of the parties participating in an exchange give to the products involved. It might seem strange now, but some 300 years ago a Dutchman exchanged his house in Amsterdam for one of the first tulip bulbs. He obviously valued that bulb extremely highly and decided the exchange was worthwhile.

In this chapter we will look at the whole aspect of *price*, *value* and *cost*. There are different strategies where price can be used effectively within the marketing mix. These can vary, as new products require different strategies from those appropriate to existing products. Also, different strategies are necessary for different market conditions, and at different stages of the product life cycle. There is no doubt that pricing decisions are vital for every organisation – after all it is the only element within the marketing mix that creates revenue for your organisation. Many companies are now finding that pricing lower than competitors is not the way to succeed, it generally leads to an eroding of profit levels and an inability to fund future growth projects. A balance must be struck, the price must reflect the added value, and many companies now find that when they want to put prices up they must also change the product or service very slightly to help justify the increase and thus make it more **acceptable** to customers.

When it comes to low price as a strategy, it is as well to remember that anyone can give money away. Anyone can cut the price of a product, but price rarely offers a sustainable competitive advantage. If your competitor loses sales owing to your price cut, then a similar price reduction redresses the balance. Of course, the customer gains in a price war at the expense of company profit. However, this can continue only while profit is still possible.

Exercise

> If you live outside London, examine ways of travelling to London (if you live in London consider a journey to Birmingham). Write down five ways of travelling and find out the cost* of a return journey. Then explain the advantages and disadvantages of each type of journey and explain why they are all used by different groups of travellers. For example:
>
> ■ coach
> ■ train (peak time)
> ■ train (off-peak saver travel)
> ■ hire car
> ■ own car.
>
> *Note: Cost to you is the price charged by the supplier.

COMPONENTS OF A PRICE

It will be clear from the exercise above that price has more components than the money actually charged. For instance, if you pay for your ticket by credit card rather than by cash, you have an extra few weeks before paying the account. This could benefit you in a number of ways, although the rail operator pays the credit card company a small fee, which adds to its operating costs. If you decide to drive to London you will have to include petrol and perhaps car parking charges, not to mention the problem of apportioning depreciation and tax/insurance. Alternatively, if you use a student travel card you get discount on your coach or train travel. There are other pricing situations where other components are involved. For instance, in many industrial situations the parties negotiate stage payments, and also additional benefits such as service levels, as part of the contract.

In deciding between alternatives, we should also cost the time required during the search for suitable products. In assessing benefits, time is also important. Compare the different times experienced in delivery. In our travel example, for instance, trains are faster than coaches; air freight is quicker than sea for overseas orders. A fleet car purchase manager will probably look at a lowest total cost model when deciding what to purchase. This could include: manufacturer's recommended price; discount offered; payment terms (when payments due); additional features offered (service deals or radio cassettes fitted free, for example); delivery terms; cost of use (routine maintenance and running costs); convenience; reliability; lifespan; and resale value of cars at the end of use by the fleet. In addition to the **affordability** issues, there are, of course, aspects of **acceptability** such as the image of the car and other psychological issues to be considered.

It will be apparent from these various examples that it is almost impossible to list all the elements that will be considered by a purchaser.

Exercise

> Think of a recent purchase, and write down all the costs incurred by you in the total purchase. The following headings might help:
>
> ■ Cost of searching for the right product (including cost of time involved)

▶

- Costs involved in ensuring it would meet your needs.
- Deposit paid
- Actual price paid at time of sale
- Deferred payments perhaps due to credit arrangements
- Cost of extended warranty and guarantees
- Charges for delivery, installation, etc.
- Cost of regular maintenance
- Cost to use
- Depreciation

There could be more elements depending on the product involved.

From a marketer's point of view, it is vital to understand the way that a potential buyer is likely to behave with regards to all the different types of expenditure. If this is understood then a supplier can offer the right deal to attract purchasers for their product. Pricing a marketing offering should be thought of as an inexact science, one where the customer does not always fully understand the supplier's costs, and usually does not care. The customer is looking at the *affordability of a purchase* from his or her own individual standpoint.

Example   A mobile phone hand set actually costs over £100 if it is bought direct and as a sole purchase (this might be required if you lose your handset!). If you go into the local phone shop and look at the package deals available you will see that the charge for the handset is much lower, and sometimes they are offered free. This is because the retailers and networks understand a high initial capital charge might deter customers. The phone is not really free, it is just that a customer will consider the 'total marketing offering' as a complete package rather than assessing the individual costs of every item. The cost of the phone in an initial purchase is heavily subsidised by the network. The actual cost of the handset will be recovered over time as a customer pays the regular charges and uses the phone. Subsidising the cost of a phone makes an initial 'total' purchase affordable.

THE ECONOMIST'S PRICE

In an economist's view of the market place, price is seen as the major factor determining the level of sales of a product. The theory suggests that demand for a product will rise dramatically if its price is reduced. The actual amount of change in demand is a factor of the 'elasticity' of the product (see Figure 14.1).

The demand for a product is said to be 'inelastic' if the quantity sold hardly varies in spite of a substantial price change. This can be the case where there are few substitutes available. Such a product is heating oil for an oil-fired central heating system. It is too expensive to replace the system with gas, and, in cold weather, heat is required for the home. Hence the heating oil is purchased when required in the cold weather. Price is less important than the actual winter temperature in assessing the volume of oil to be sold in the UK. However a study by a major oil company showed that in Germany, where they have installed larger domestic storage tanks, householders were very good at studying the oil market and buying when prices were low. In the UK, consumers generally purchase when the tank is nearly empty whatever the price, even

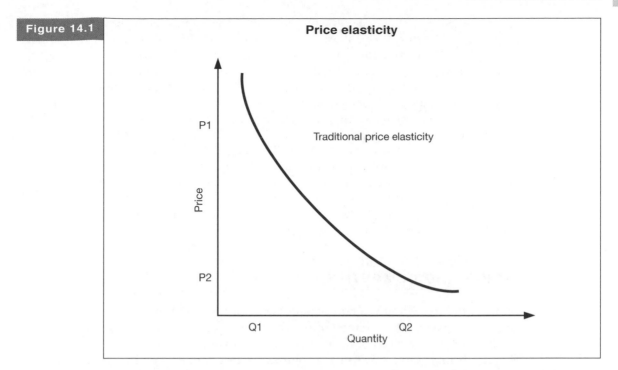

Figure 14.1

Price elasticity

Traditional price elasticity

though the difference of 1p/litre could mean £10 on a typical bill. So the UK market is more inelastic than the German market.

An 'elastic' demand certainly occurs where a price rise is likely to frighten off a large number of customers, who either do not buy at all or purchase a substitute product.

$$\text{Price elasticity of demand} = \frac{\text{\% change in quantity demanded}}{\text{\% change in price}}$$

Of course, there are products that do not follow the basic economist's model. These are often products that appeal to the highest level of needs in Maslow's hierarchy (see Chapter 6). Perfume is an example – the more expensive a perfume is, the more it is generally desired. Another prestige product is a Rolex watch, which is in demand because of the exclusivity enhanced by the high price and prestigious distribution outlets. There has been a recent advertising campaign for a range of personal products from L'Oréal that justified the expenditure by using the advertising strap line 'because

Exercise

■ Chose a product and consider its price.

■ Would volume increase if price was reduced or would consumers believe quality had also declined? More importantly, as profit is a multiplication of volume and margin, would total profit increase or reduce?

I'm worth it'. Certainly these prices have more to do with personal value than basic economic utility.

As times change so companies must adapt to the changing customer perception of products. The debate over 'rip-off' Britain (see example on page 257) was particularly aimed at prices for clothes, cars and food, all of which are found cheaper in some other countries. In grocery retailing the take-over at Asda by Wal-Mart has focused a lot of attention onto pricing issues: the promotional activity involved is starting to affect all the competitor stores. This illustrates the obvious fact that price is of crucial importance in most purchase decisions. However it is the **comparative price**, set against direct competition and considered in the light of the affordability of a product to the customer, that is important. The careful wording of government minister Stephen Byers stressed 'the need for a *fair deal for consumers* in particular markets that appear to lack price competition'. From a marketing perspective this is absolutely right but, of course, it is sometimes possible to reduce the level of direct competition by constructing a unique offering that customers really value.

Traditional economists claim that prices should be set to maximise 'short-term' profits. This is said to be when 'marginal revenue', the increase in revenue for one extra unit of sale, is equivalent to 'marginal cost' of one extra unit of production. However, while this has a mathematical integrity, it fails to understand the role of price as a marketing tool in a competitive market place.

PRICE AND COMPETITION

One reason for changes in both volume and price is action by competitors. The basic demand curve assumes that all other facts remain constant, in reality they rarely do. At its simplest there can be a vicious circle as shown in Figure 14.2.

It can easily be seen that such a competitive reaction, leading to a price war, would have a disastrous effect on an organisation. However, if you consider the situation

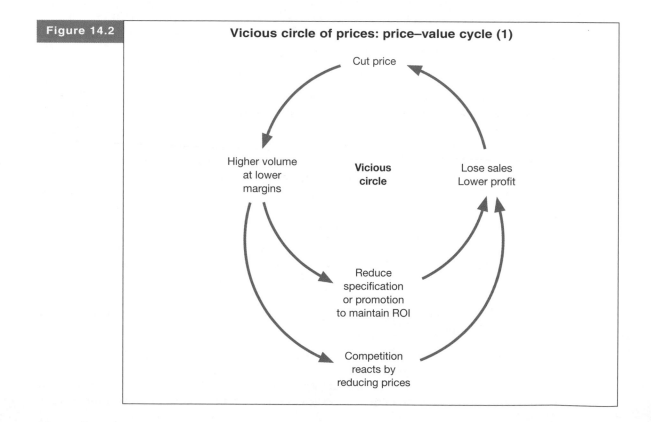

Figure 14.2   Vicious circle of prices: price–value cycle (1)

from the point of view of one of your competitors, they do not want to lose sales because of your price cut. From your customers' position it all depends upon how they perceive value. This can be considered in the framework of buyer behaviour which is discussed in Chapters 6 and 7.

Example

In 1999 there was a great deal of publicity regarding the high prices of products in the UK as opposed to other countries. The term rip-off Britain was coined and featured in many press articles, although subsequently a more muted approach was taken. However there was a dramatic effect in the car market as the purchase levels for new cars fell and manufacturers ran into serious financial difficulties.

The Consumers' Association warned car manufacturers and dealers that it was time to stop selling cheaply in Europe whilst maintaining high prices in the UK. They gave the example of a Rover 414 priced at £11 379 in Birmingham, the city in which it is made. The price was said to be only £7951 in Portugal, some 43% below the UK level.

On 2 December 1999 the *Financial Times* reported:

MITSUBISHI UK CUTS CAR PRICES BY 10%

Mitsubishi Corp UK announced an average 10% retail price cut for its four main models sold in the UK as of 4 December.

In a statement, the company said sales were brought 'virtually to a standstill' by the so-called 'rip-off Britain' campaign and delay in the government's competition report on UK new vehicle prices. As other models were introduced to the UK during 2000, their prices were harmonised with those in mainland Europe, the company added.

It is important that pricing decisions are made within the overall context of the marketing mix. Products rarely offer directly equivalent features – and, in fact, it is one of the roles of marketers to find ways of differentiating their product. This could be achieved through offering additional levels of service, so the customer can decide to place a value on the total offering, rather than directly comparing identical products. In the customer's decision process, the perceived value is a function of required features, and the price paid. The object is to achieve a *virtuous circle* (see Figure 14.3).

The level of competition varies from one product market to another. Some will have a large number of competing firms, others relatively few. Where there are many competitors, price (and other marketing) competition will be very severe. The other extreme is a monopoly, and perhaps that single supplier can fix his own price. The price set by a monopoly is, of course, modified by legislation and the Monopolies Commission.

In some competitive markets, one or two companies emerge as leaders: the level of prices they charge can become the norm for the market. Smaller firms take their lead from these larger organisations without direct collusion, but most move price only when the leaders change. A study of the price of petrol will show how such a market operates.

To show that a competitive price does not always ensure a sale we could perhaps look at the fmcg (fast-moving consumer goods) market for a product such as instant coffee. Some shoppers search for low-priced brands, or own-label products, while others remain loyal to premium brands, such as Maxwell House or Nescafé. This could be because some consumers think these branded products to be better than the shop's own-label brands. However, they are not necessarily better, as companies such

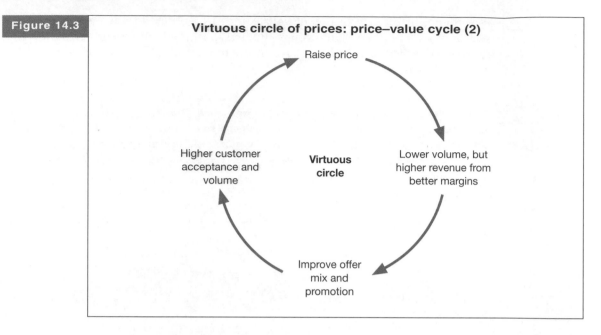

Figure 14.3

Virtuous circle of prices: price–value cycle (2)

Raise price

Higher customer acceptance and volume

Virtuous circle

Lower volume, but higher revenue from better margins

Improve offer mix and promotion

as Marks & Spencer or Sainsbury have very high quality standards which they impose on suppliers of their products, including instant coffee. There is no doubt about the good quality of Nescafé and other major brands of instant coffee, but even Nescafé offers different blends at different prices. Of course, another reason for the success of Nescafé is the marketing strength of the actual brand name. This will be discussed elsewhere, but the value of a brand name is being recognised by some companies who are valuing brand names and including the valuation on their balance sheets. The major accounting bodies also now realise the marketing value of brand names as an asset to a company. It is surprising, therefore, that in relation to the offering to the customers there is still a blinkered view in many companies that prices must be based on costs.

PRICE, QUALITY AND VALUE

The reality of pricing in competitive markets is that it is customers rather than competitors who do the most to influence what is an **affordable** price. The buying decision process involves a great many factors being considered, but crucial to the prospective purchaser are the questions:

- Can I afford it?
- Does it offer good value for money?
- How does it compare to other offerings?

The affordability of an offering will be based on a measure of disposable income set against the importance of the purchase. Some products are discretionary buys, ones where there is a great deal of personal choice regarding whether to treat yourself or not with regards to a non-essential purchase. Others are more important, basic needs such as food and other products needed to survive. It is up to a marketing manager to understand the degree of importance of an offering and to establish a price that reflects the circumstances of the customer. Failure to do this effectively will lead to low sales and marketing failure.

It is necessary to go a little further and to offer real value to a customer. The customer will undertake a personal equation, comparing the sacrifice they have to make to obtain the offering against the benefits from actually owning it. As shown already in respect of the components of a price, there are many factors involved. There are also many different ways in which a customer might evaluate the benefits and the value derived from a purchase. Benefits can be both psychological and economic, and in all cases it is the *perception* of the customer as to the actual value received that is the key issue. Understanding this requires appreciation of customer behaviour and in particular the ways a customer actually uses a specific purchase. Some purchases might be valued for their use characteristics, while others, such as designer clothing, are valued for more emotional reasons.

Exercise	■ Do you know anyone who has bought a pair of branded trainers, such as Nike?
	■ Find out if they paid more for the Nike shoes than for an alternative brand. If this is the case, what do you evaluate are the additional psychological benefits of the Nike shoes when compared to a cheaper option?
	■ Do you think these additional benefits are worth it?

The comparison of total **value** received against actual **price** paid will be part of a customer's evaluation of satisfaction. If a purchaser feels they paid too much they will be dissatisfied and are likely to tell their friends and family. Such negative publicity is detrimental to future sales, so every effort must be made to achieve a satisfied customer.

All the qualities of a Mercedes-Benz for £5670

Hard to believe, isn't it? Fabled Mercedes-Benz refinement and peace of mind for the price of a run-of-the-mill volume car.

And the good news doesn't end there . . .

Source: Adapted from an advertisement for Mercedes-Benz seen in a local paper, March 1992. Too good to be true but actually a misprint.

Customers also use *price levels* to help determine the likely *quality* of a purchase, goods or services. High prices typically indicate high quality to a buyer looking for clues when considering options. A low price might cause a potential customer to worry whether the product was really up to the job. In general the adherence to the dimensions of quality discussed in Chapter 11 certainly add value to a product and assist a customer in evaluating price and value. You might offer your own measures of quality and how they help to add value to an offering. These dimensions, however, are a good basis for such discussions. Figure 14.4 shows a balance between quality of offerings and the benefits for an organisation.

There is a *trade-off between price and quality* at the basic level. To add features can add to the costs of the supplier, and this is not always recovered in profit in sales. However, the relationship is not that simple, and programmes such as zero defects are often very

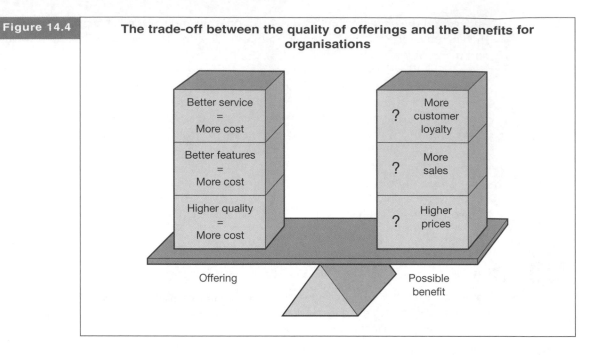

Figure 14.4

The trade-off between the quality of offerings and the benefits for organisations

positive when assessing costs. But price should not be dependent on costs, but on customers' evaluation of value. Of course, some aspects of quality can increase this evaluation, others will not do so. The balance between quality and price should be considered in the context of profit, level of sales and organisational positioning. It is not an easy equation but it is vital in an integrated marketing offering.

However whilst price, quality and value are intertwined at the point of purchase, it is only experience when using a product that really reveals the true quality. There is a very perceptive adage that 'the quality of a product is remembered long after the price is forgotten'. This of course refers specifically to the **acceptability** of a purchase over time, but the link between price, value and quality cannot be ignored.

PRICE AND COSTS

Decisions on price are of crucial importance to all organisations since, as stated already, it is the only element in the marketing mix that brings an input to the company. It is too important for price to be decided on some automatic formula based solely on cost; it is also too important to be left to accountants, or salespeople, or even marketing managers in isolation. Charles Dickens gave good Victorian advice when Mr Micawber, having been through a debtors' prison, says to David Copperfield:

> Annual income twenty pounds, annual expenditure nineteen shillings and six pence, result happiness. Annual income twenty pounds, expenditure twenty pounds and six pence, result misery . . . and in short you are forever floored.

A variety of cost-based formulas have been developed by organisations. The simplest version is to calculate the total cost, including all overheads, and add a set percentage for profit. This is known as 'cost-plus' pricing, and is usually justified on the basis that a satisfactory profit can always be achieved. This method of pricing seems very straightforward, but it does reflect the ways costs are calculated in an organisation. It also includes all the costs, even the excess costs of inefficient operations that might exist. The more this method of pricing is examined, the more it seems a long way away from the issues of importance to a customer, and away from the concept of value that is part of the buying decision process. Perhaps the biggest problem linking costs and prices lies with allocating overheads since the basis for this allocation is, at best, arbitrary.

Cost-plus pricing should be challenged by anyone working in marketing. The most obvious reason being that:

- Costs are about **production**
- Prices are about **value.**

Of course, costs must be used to set a bottom line below which prices cannot go without some counter-balancing profit elsewhere. There can be a case for including a loss leader in a range, or giving away a mobile phone handset, as in our earlier example. Where one part of the offering is sold at below cost in order to encourage custom, then it is necessary for the firm to recover any loss and make its profit on the other items or services sold. The use of portfolio planning to ensure an overall profit for the company will be considered later.

Example

Many retailers base their prices on the variable cost of each item they buy in. This is possible because they are in fact re-sellers of goods and services. So a typical clothing retailer might double the buy-in price and so arrive at a selling price. In this case the *'mark-up'* is said to be 100%, and the *gross margin* 50%. However sometimes the retailer actually starts with the price they want to sell at and then works back. This is more market-driven, although it is sometimes difficult for the supplier. For instance, suppose a retailer wishes to make a margin of 30 % and also wishes to sell a product at no more than 99 pence, then in this instance they might tell a supplier that they will pay no more than 69 pence for the item. They are able to achieve this because of the strength of the large supermarkets when compared to some smaller companies who supply them.

However as Marks & Spencer found it is not enough to use sensible price points of £9.99 and £14.99, nor is it enough to ensure that every item in the store is priced at a given level of gross profit. There must also be sufficient shoppers in the store, and enough items sold to cover the costs of operating a retail group. One way of attracting shoppers is by offering some products at 'bargain prices', even making a loss on some sales but hoping to sell other items at the same time in order to achieve an overall profit.

Exercise

Visit your local supermarket and try to identify the 'loss leaders' (products sold below or near to cost) that are offered to encourage shoppers into the store.

Sometimes a new product might be offered at a low price in order to encourage customers to try it. If the intention is to raise price later, then this situation is similar to a price-cut promotion. It is not enough for a company to assess the high level of development costs and set out to recover them quickly by charging a high price, because every action affecting the price of a product also affects the sales levels and the attitude of customers towards that product.

One important calculation relating cost, prices, and volume is the calculation of the so-called *break-even point* for a product. This can be explored in standard accounting

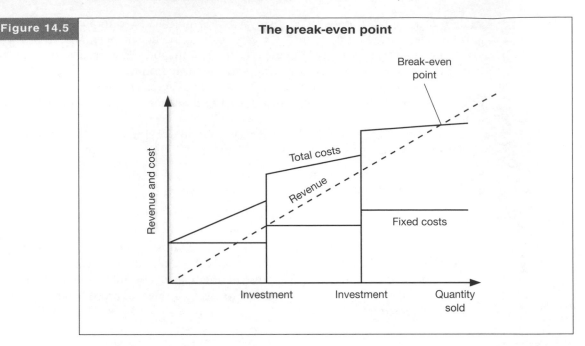

Figure 14.5

The break-even point

texts and we will look at a sample break-even calculation here. Figure 14.5 illustrates the break-even point.

The break-even point is the level at which the cost of producing a product or service equals the revenue from selling it. Assume a manufacturer has fixed costs of £1million, they sell their products at £3 each and the variable costs of manufacture and sale are £2. They will make £1 (£3 *less* £2) on every product sold. To 'break even', covering all the fixed cost, they will have to sell 1 million units.

To use break-even analysis effectively, it is necessary to calculate break-even levels of volume for several alternative prices. However, great care must be taken in using break-even analysis as it does assume inelastic demand. This might be a fair assumption over a small change in price, but not over a large variation.

The calculation of break-even allows us to look at another cost-based pricing method called 'marginal cost pricing'. The marginal cost, or variable cost, of a product is the extra cost an organisation suffers in producing one more unit of that product – in our example above, £2 per unit. We could decide to add an agreed mark-up to this to determine our price. So if we suggest a 50 per cent mark-up then, given a £2 marginal cost, the mark-up will be £1, and the final price £3:

$$(£2 + (50\% @ £2) = £2 + £1 = £3)$$

Marginal price deals are sometimes done, with selected customers, to stimulate demand, or to develop business with those chosen customers. The problem with marginal costing is that it guarantees only a gross profit per unit, it does not guarantee a net profit from total sales.

John Winkler, a noted authority on pricing, states that if 'cost-plus pricing will generally keep you in business, marginal costing can easily put you out of it'. He goes on to suggest:

- 'Never do it if it will set a precedent for the long run with your biggest customers'
- 'Never do it if news of low price deals will spread in the market'
- 'Never do it if it commits you to extra capital cost in the short run, or long run'
- 'Never do it if it uses up scarce resources you need elsewhere'
- 'Never do it if you have to sacrifice some full profit business to fit it in'
- 'Never delegate discretion on marginal pricing decisions down the line. Anyone can give products away, the aim of marketing is profitable business.'

Another perhaps dispiriting fact that John Winkler emphasises is that in today's highly competitive, economic climate it is extremely difficult to win any type of price increase. Customers are resistant to too many price increases, in fact a significant rise in a price often stimulates a customer to re-evaluate that purchase item.

Although reducing prices can stimulate demand, it must be handled very carefully. Remembering the advice from Mr Micawber – say a car is priced at £10 000 and the manufacturer makes a gross profit of 18 per cent and net profit before tax of 7 per cent. If price is reduced by £1000 (just 10 per cent of reduction in price) we get the following effect:

Revenue	£10 000	£9 000
Cost of goods	£8 200	£8 200
Gross profit	£1 800 (18%)	£800 (8.9%)
Other costs	£1 100	£1 100
Net profit before tax	£700 (7%)	(£300) (loss of 3%)

It can be seen that a reduction of 10 per cent in price turns a healthy profit into a loss.

Example	In the early months of 2000, Rover Cars reduced the price of all models and stimulated increases in the volume of car sales just prior to time when the company itself was sold by BMW to a British consortium. It was never clear if the significant losses incurred by BMW were as a result of a high number of unsold cars when the price of Rover cars was considered too high, or the low margins after the price was reduced. By the time this book is published it will be possible to evaluate how Rover is performing under the new management, and to compare the price of a Rover with other makes of cars trying to attract similar buyers.

To conclude this section on costs, it should be clear that costs have a role in the determining of price. However, costs alone should not determine selling prices. The costs provide a bottom line to guide the pricing decision, but as previously stated the *customer perception of price and comparative value* is the crucial factor in decisions about whether to buy or not.

PRICE AND ORGANISATIONAL OBJECTIVES

Marketing decisions must be consistent with the total organisational objectives. Pricing decisions are just one of the marketing decisions. Obviously, if the organisation has a target return on investment, you can see the link to pricing. However, organisational objectives could be: 'Pile it high and sell it cheap', the phrase coined by the founder of Tesco, Sir John Cohen. If your organisation has this latter objective all its operations must be designed to supply volume at low prices.

Example

In the 1980s Tesco changed its philosophy to reduce the emphasis on price and focused efforts on improving the quality of its service and product range. During this period Tesco became the market leader. In the past few years price wars have again broken out as all supermarkets continue to compete for customers, and new low priced competitors such as Aldi and Netto have entered the market. Tesco had to slash prices in the run-up to Christmas 1996, and have subsequently kept their offering very competitive. Sainsbury's position has been encapsulated in the line, 'Good food costs less at Sainsbury's', a slogan that includes both price and quality in a statement of value directly related to customers. The major price threat has come from Asda, now owned by the giant US Wal-Mart group, where price has become the most visible component of the company's marketing.

Exercise

Pricing a service

Two former secretaries have set up a secretarial and book-keeping service on a local trading estate. It offers basic services to the small companies on the estate. The major expense is the salaries of the two partners, and one employee, a word processing operator. Overheads include office rent and rates, and the maintenance of office equipment such as computers, fax machine, answerphone, etc. There is also the interest on the bank loan used to buy equipment. The organisation is really offering 'time', carrying out routine tasks. They calculate the overheads are £15 200 per annum, the employee is paid £6000 (including employee-related costs) and the two partners draw £1000 per month each. Total running costs for stationery, telephone bills, postage are a further £10 000, giving a total £55 200 per annum.

There are 230 working days per year if we eliminate weekends and holidays. But no one works at 100 per cent; 80 per cent is still good, so if we assume days each (80% × 230) for the three productive workers there are 552 working days each year. To just break even they need to charge £100 per working day. What do you think they should charge clients?

PRICING STRATEGIES

Figure 14.6 links the price to the quality of an offered product or service. Quality is a very difficult factor to measure. However, you should now realise that other elements of the marketing mix add to the 'quality' of value of the offering. It is useful to remind ourselves that: 'quality is remembered long after the price is forgotten.'

Premium pricing

A 'premium strategy' uses a high price, but gives good product/service in exchange. It is fair to customers, and, more importantly, customers see it as fair. This could include food bought from Fortnum & Mason (in London), or designer clothes, or a Jaguar car. We should remember that customers for consumer goods are often amateurs, they do not really know how to judge value. They build up a perception of such value, and sometimes use price to help establish levels of 'quality'. If you see a new Jaguar car on offer at your local garage with a sign saying 'half-price offer' you might be suspicious about what you are being offered. If the offer were a Zil, which is a Russian luxury limousine, you might perhaps have less scepticism if it were offered at half price. But then you would worry about servicing and reliability.

An industrial buyer could have more knowledge of the technical characteristics of

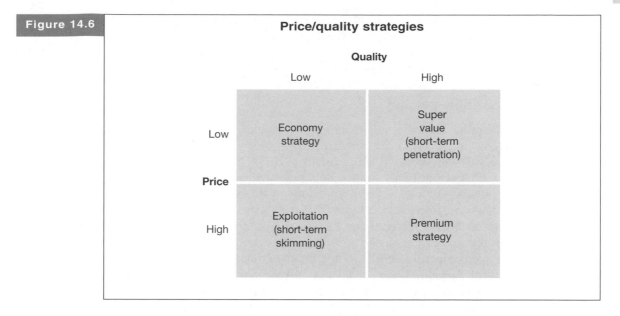

Figure 14.6

Price/quality strategies

Quality

	Low	High
Low	Economy strategy	Super value (short-term penetration)
High	Exploitation (short-term skimming)	Premium strategy

Price

his purchases. In many cases, tight specifications on the performance of machinery are used for buying in this area. But not all industrial purchases are professionally assessed, although no one should underestimate the ability of customers to assess value. Nevertheless, sometimes the benefits of a product need to be presented in a way that will help a buyer to make a buying decision. Remember, marketing is about making it easier for the customer to say 'yes'.

In considering which car a company should use for its sales force, the car fleet manager mentioned at the beginning of this chapter might consider the lowest total cost over the life of 70 000 miles. It might be the resale value of a Ford Mondeo that gained it a superior rating to an equivalent car from another supplier. The car fleet buyer might be a professional, but might still require help to appreciate the total value of what is offered to him.

Even when evaluating relatively inexpensive products such as wood glue, some people view a higher price as a measure of the quality to expect from the product.

Penetration pricing

'Penetration' pricing is the name given to a strategy that deliberately starts offering 'super value'. This is done to gain a foothold in a market, using price as a major weapon. It could be because other products are already well established in the market, maybe at high prices. Alternatively, penetration pricing could be used as an attempt to gain a major share of a new market. It can also deter competitors who see no profit in the market. As time goes on and the product is established, prices can be raised nearer market levels. Alternatively, the supplier's cost could come down as volume increases. In this case, the consumer benefits by a continuation of the low prices.

Penetration pricing must be used carefully as it is very difficult to raise prices to catch up with the market levels. There are many examples of products launched at a low price which lost significant sales volume when prices rose. It is sometimes possible to offer customers an initial discount to gain business provided you make it clear that prices will rise later. Building societies have been offering discounted mortgages to first-time buyers at reduced rates for the first 12 months; after that, they rise to commercial rates and there is often a hefty penalty to repay should the borrower try to move the mortgage to another lender, or even make a lump-sum repayment over and above that required for the monthly payment.

Economy pricing

'Economy' pricing is a deliberate strategy of low pricing. It could be that you are offering a 'no frills' product/service, with a price reflecting this. However, before such a product is launched, it is important to decide the position it will have in the market place. That position is how you want your customers to perceive it. A product that competes purely on price is vulnerable to attack from more established products.

This has happened with low-cost airlines such as RyanAir and Easy Jet. Competitors such as British Airways, Aer Lingus and others, reduced some of their prices. More importantly British Airways has set up its own low cost operator 'Go', with the objective of competing effectively for those customers who require low prices and accept 'no-frills' products. It is not always the case that low cost is best; there have been many attempts to set up low-cost airlines in the past, and the companies concerned have failed to survive and are now consigned to history. It is perhaps not surprising, therefore, that Richard Branson of Virgin Airlines has decided to compete on customer service rather than low price, and has thereby attracted a loyal segment of customers in spite of tough competition from British Airways.

The Victorian philosopher John Ruskin (1819–1900) once said:

> It is unwise to pay too much, but it is unwise to pay too little. When you pay too much, you lose a little money, that is all. When you pay too little, you sometimes lose everything, because the thing you bought was incapable of doing the thing you bought it to do.
>
> The common law of Business Balance prohibits paying a little and getting a lot. It can't be done. If you deal with the lowest bidder, it is as well to add something for the risk you run. And if you do that, you will have enough to pay for something better.

Example   In order to enter the book retail market using the new opportunities now possible through the Internet, <amazon.com> and <barnesandnoble.com> have both tried to follow an economy pricing strategy. In fact Barnes & Noble were already a well-known US bookshop famed for low prices before they entered the world of internet marketing.

It would be interesting to compare the price of books offered by these companies with the price in a local bookshop such as Waterstones. In some cases there are significant differences, but in other cases there are no savings through the web-based sellers. The low price in these cases is only in the *perception of the customers*.

Of course, there is legislation, such as the Sale of Goods Act, which demands that a product must be fit for the purpose for which it is sold. Nevertheless, Ruskin's point is sensible from a customer's position, and all suppliers would do well to take heed of it.

Price skimming

We do not need to discuss 'exploitation' in detail. *Customers won't pay if they don't think they are getting value*. However there are times when high prices and large margins are appropriate. It is certainly easier to reduce prices than to raise them. A policy of 'price-skimming' is often used for products at the introductory stage. Here, the price is initially pitched high, which gives a good early cash flow to offset high development costs. If the product is new, and competition has not appeared, then customers might well pay a premium to acquire a product that is offering excellent features. The launch of many home computers showed this pattern. As competitors came into the market, and these new entrants added new features, prices dropped for all products. Another market with high margins is the drug market. The prescription drug market uses fairly cheap basic ingredients. The cost of developing medicines is high, and made even higher by the cost of testing and then gaining approval from the regulatory bodies. The prices are high when new drugs are launched and patents protect the manufacturers from competition. When the patent runs out, a 'generic' drug will often be launched to compete and so prices fall. The official monopoly, based on the legal protection of a patent, is a reflection of the unique effort in developing a new drug. It is certainly justified by the costs involved.

Psychological pricing

'Psychological' pricing is designed to get customers to respond on an *emotional*, rather than rational, basis. It is most frequently seen in consumer markets, having less applicability in industrial markets. The most common is the use of prices such as 99 pence or £9.95 which can be seen in many retail outlets. We all know that 99 pence is £1.00 less 1 penny, and £9.95 is £10 less 5 pence. In recent years some companies such as Marks & Spencer have been phasing out this practice, although it still remains widespread. You might like to consider why such prices are used.

In some markets companies are oversensitive about price levels. Cadbury's were conscious of this with their chocolate bars. To maintain prices, as raw material costs rose, they reduced the thickness of the chocolate blocks. The result was thin chocolate bars. Rowntrees spotted this and decided that Cadbury's had gone too far. Rowntrees saw an opportunity for a chunky product, and so the Yorkie Bar was launched, with great success.

Product-line pricing

'Product-line' pricing is a strategy that involves all the products offered by a supplier. There may be a range of normal price points in a market. A supplier might decide to design a product suitable for all price levels, offering opportunities for a range of purchases. For instance, in May 2000 a basic Mars bar retailed for about 26p, a multipack of five full size bars £1.09p and a multipack of eight-snack size Mars bars at £1.45: the price points are 26p, £1.09p and £1.45. (These prices were correct in the summer of 2000, and were almost identical to the price 3 years earlier. You should check the prices now, and see how each price level fits into the range of Mars products available.) Mars also offer a 346gram bag of fun-size bars for around £1.75 but these are aimed at a different market.

Pricing variations

'Off-peak' pricing and other variants, such as early booking discount, stand-by prices and group discounts are used in particular circumstances. They are all well known in the travel trade but it is also appropriate to use different prices such as these in other industries. You could argue that an off-peak journey, say a rail journey to London one Tuesday afternoon, is not the same 'product' as one during the morning rush period. In the customer's eyes, it is a different product. If you have to be in London by 9.00 a.m. you cannot travel in the afternoon. Certainly, 'stand-by' prices represent a different product as there is no guarantee of travel. The opposite is an early booking price that not only ensures travel is reserved, but can offer the supplier a guarantee of the known demand.

PRICING IN INDUSTRIAL MARKETS

Industrial products can be ones purchased for resale, or they can be raw materials that are incorporated into manufactured products. Alternatively, they can be installations or consumables used in industrial operations. When dealing in this market, there are other considerations affecting all aspects of the marketing mix, including pricing strategies.

Consumables are the convenience goods of the industrial market. However, there is no need for fancy packaging to attract shoppers as in a supermarket. They therefore tend to have basic packing for protection, and can often be supplied in multiple packs. The price will reflect this. In addition, there may be a quantity discount, although this is more usual with raw materials. Certainly the business is usually done on credit, but it is common to offer discounts to customers who pay their invoice within (say) 10 days.

Installations are more likely to be negotiated, with all the requirements costed to give a price specific to the customer's requirement. There is no role for psychological pricing, but it is common for the sales negotiators to be given some freedom in the price to be charged. In these types of negotiated situations the sales force can be rewarded according to profit achieved, and they certainly need to know the limits within which they can negotiate.

Raw materials will be regular purchases, and it is probably more important that suppliers are reliable. Customers will be prepared to pay a little extra to a known, and trusted, supplier rather than risk supply problems. Of course, a customer may operate a policy of dual sourcing so as to compare competition prices. If the supplier builds up a strong relationship with the customer, then a good exchange of information takes place, and prices are continually discussed along with other issues. There may be an annual contract between supplier and customer that confirms price for the whole year. The contract might have a rebate clause that allows for a discount if volume exceeds an agreed figure. As industrial markets are distinguished by smaller numbers of partners and larger orders, many of their contracts are individually negotiated and overriding discounts are built into the agreement.

Many of the above pricing methods are possible because industrial markets have much more direct contact between supplier and customer through the wide use of direct personal selling in these markets.

There is one very difficult area of industrial marketing where direct selling is not a factor. This is when suppliers are invited to submit a tender, or to bid for a contract offered by a large customer, who may be a local authority or a government department. In this situation, the customer specifies what they want, and asks a number of suppliers to submit a bid. In such a case it is necessary not only to carry out detailed costing on what is required, but also to have an appreciation of who else is bidding for the work. Here, a pricing strategy can be based on the knowledge of the competition, as well as how badly your organisation wants the contract. The final price is therefore a *marketing decision*, and not based solely on costs. This situation is common in the oil and gas industry with competitors bidding for the exploration rights to designated geographical blocks.

DISTRIBUTOR PRICING

Many producers are not in direct contact with their customers. They will use indirect channels of distribution, perhaps via wholesalers or other intermediaries. No product is finally sold until it reaches the eventual consumer. So it is the final price to the final purchaser that is the measure of value.

Example

You might have recently bought a birthday card for one of your friends, maybe paying, say, £1.49 in a card shop. This might seem expensive for a small piece of printed cardboard, and an envelope. Even if you understand that 17½ per cent is VAT charged by the government, it might still seem a lot. But remember the printing company will probably have sold the card at 63p (excluding VAT) and the card shop will usually wish to double the price. In this business 100 per cent mark-ups are usual, and can be seen in the light of the relatively low turnover of individual designs, and the high fixed costs of running a shop.

However it is the customer who makes the purchase decision. If they think the price is too high they won't buy, but they might consider it in relation to a more expensive present, and maybe the price could be considered both **affordable** and **acceptable** in spite of the retailer mark-up.

However it might be that the customer has a suitable graphics package on a computer and can now make a personalised card for just the input of his or her own effort. If the final selling price becomes too high customers will used alternatives and the companies concerned, both manufacturer and retailer, will lose volume.

The problem many producers face is how to control the eventual selling price of their product. At one time it was possible to insist on the final selling price, but now this is not possible in most industries. Producers may suggest a recommended retail price (RRP) but that is all it is, a recommendation. Each member of the distribution chain will want to make some money from handling the product. It is therefore important for producers to understand the way distributors add margins so that they can judge the effect on the final selling price of any action taken further up the distributive chain.

PRICING AND ITS RELATION TO THE MARKETING MIX

In this chapter price has not been considered in isolation but as one key part of the marketing mix. The word 'affordability' was used at an earlier point, but although this introduced the customer view it does not encompass the full area of value. The price is what is paid as part of the *exchange process* (see Figure 14.7), being passed from customer to supplier either as money or in kind. What is received by the customer is the composite of the other elements of the marketing mix. This is an acceptable product, conveniently available so that the customer feels it is well worth the price asked. It is therefore essential that price is put into the wider context of the total marketing mix.

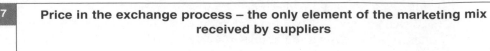

Price in the exchange process – the only element of the marketing mix received by suppliers

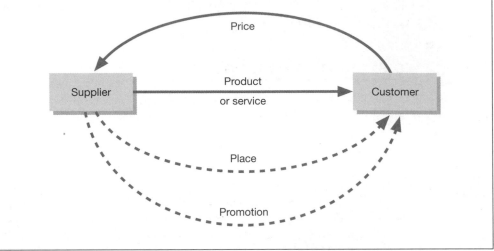

If a product is made more attractive (added-value by additional features), it makes that product more valuable to customers. Similarly, a service could be made more readily available and thus more valuable to customers. In this case it might be possible to raise prices to reflect the increase in value. Alternatively the enhanced value could lead to additional sales. The decision about additional features must be taken by managers who realise the way consumers measure value, and not simply by saying the additional features have increased costs hence prices must rise.

Accountants are used to cost–benefit analysis in other parts of their work, but where price is concerned it is essential to do a cost–benefit analysis for the customer – cost to the customer being price from the supplier; benefit to the customer a measure of the quality of the offering.

PRICE AND THE PRODUCT LIFE CYCLE

In Chapter 2 you were introduced to the concept that a product develops through a 'product life cycle'. At different stages of this life cycle there are different competitive pressures, and differences in the way customers evaluate a product/service. For a new product (the first in the market) a 'skimming' policy could be appropriate. However, in a competitive, declining market with a mature product a different strategy is relevant.

Exercise

- Select a product you have bought in the last month. Decide where it is in its product life cycle.
- What is the range of prices for competitive products and where does the product you bought fit in?
- Why do you think this is so?
- What pricing strategy do you think the supplier is pursuing?

This advertisement illustrates the powerful use of visual imagery in advertising.

Reproduced with permission from Bartle Bogle & Hegartly.

subliminal advertising experiment

fcuk

This poster for French Connection challenges the myth of subliminal advertising and won best 96 sheet poster, best fashion, beauty, healthcare and toiletries poster and best use of typography poster at Campaign Poster 1999.

Reproduced with permission from TBWA GGT Simons Palmer Limited, London.

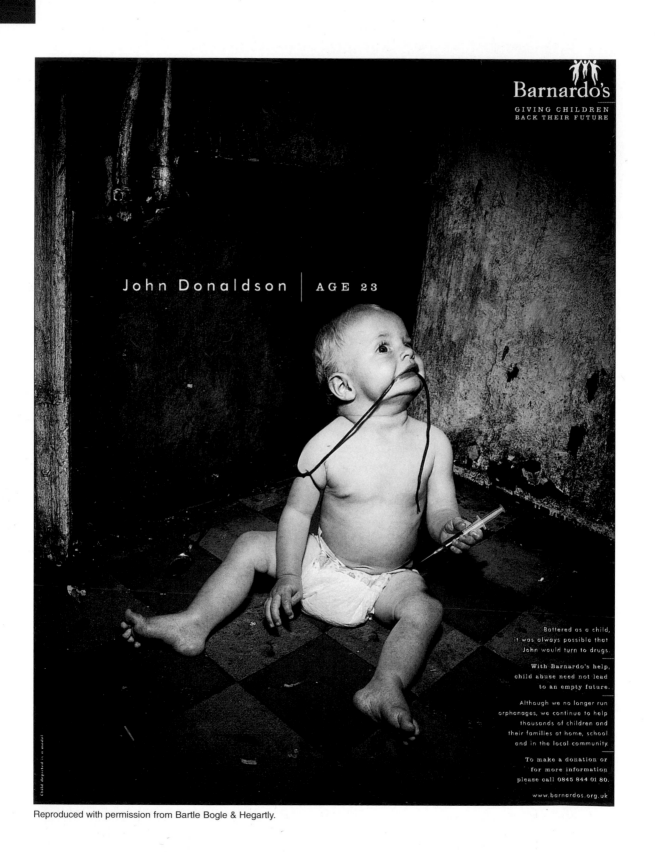

Reproduced with permission from Bartle Bogle & Hegartly.

BARNARDO'S: A BRIEF CASE HISTORY

PROBLEM (UK 1999)

- Barnardo's is the UK's largest children's charity. Its strong heritage had earned both the trust and respect of the British public.
- However it has witnessed its perceived 'deservedness' erode relative to other charities.
  - A particular issue amongst 'younger' people, as over 50% of existing donors are aged 70+ and not enough new, younger donors are coming in.
- Why? Because there is an enormous disconnect between what people think the charity does and what they actually do.
  - Despite having ceased running homes for orphans over 30 years ago, the majority of the public still think that's what Barnardo's is all about.
  - In reality, Barnardo's is a pioneer in diverse fields of modern childcare research and practice.

SOLUTION

- Over-write the culturally imprinted association with homes and replace it with something that reflects the Barnardo's brand truth today.
- In a market defined by short-term action, rescue and crisis relief, focus on Barnardo's key differentiator: the *long-term perspective* they take.
- Tightly focused press campaign in broadsheets and Mail, talking to our core target audience: 'open minded' adults, aged 30-54.
  - Quality positions and full page executions to build credibility and stature.
  - Weekends only to build regular, extended dialogue with core audience.

GIVING CHILDREN BACK THEIR FUTURE

RESULTS

- Brand entered the 'premier charity league' and began challenging the NSPCC's dominance.
- 'Deservedness' increased by 19%.
- Share of all charitable donations over 6 months estimated to have increased by 66%.
- Image improved, notably the contemporisation of the charity and no longer running homes.
- Web-site traffic rose from 684 visits in wk. 1 of campaign to an average of 2,050 visits per week at the end of the campaign – c. 300% increase.
- The core target (30-54/ABC1 with children) accounted for a higher proportion of donors post-campaign (34%) than pre-campaign (19%).
- The controversy over the 'Heroin Baby' ad generated £630,000 worth of media coverage.

'The Audi A6 is a breakthrough design for us. Its unconventional form shakes up the traditional "executive saloon" car shape. Follow the roof-line and you'll see that it gives more interior passenger space with greater headroom. We've also added ultra lightweight front suspension for superior handling. And for those of you wondering, yes, the coat hooks are fluid damped for smooth operation.

If you happen to find yourself driving around Seville head for the giant harp in the distance. The Alamillo bridge doesn't look or work like your average bridge. We like the design because it ingeniously combines form and function. The weight of a massive, inclined steel pylon counterbalances the deck. The spine cleverly serves as an elevated footpath, bisecting the traffic lanes below. And best of all, it glows in the dark.'

Reproduced with permission from Audi UK.

THERE'S ALWAYS ROOM FOR MURPHY'S

IN CORK WE ALWAYS DRINK MURPHY'S

These posters for Murphy's bitter show that it is possible to run an advertising campaign using contrasting imagery, such as the winter sport activity and traditional craft skills shown in these posters.

The 'Nipples' advertisement dramatises the powerful experience of the PlayStation brand and in a subversive and coded way. It won the Grand Prix at Cannes '99 for world's Best Poster and Gold and two Silvers at Campaign Press Awards '99 for Poster of the Year. This high profile brand is also strongly advertised on the web. Students should visit this site (www.playstation.com) to evaluate the way this reinforces the advertising message.

Reproduced with permission from TBWA GGT Simons Palmer Limited, London.

Web sites are becoming more relevant every day. The important issue is how the site increases the acceptability and accessability of a product offering. Students can evaluate sites for themselves.

Top: www.louisvuitton.com
Centre: www.virgin.com
Right: ww.mercedes.com

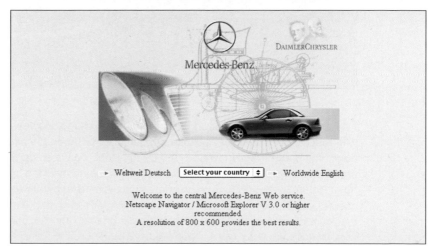

Packaging is critical to support a strong brand message. However, there is a problem with respect to Budweiser because the dominant US brand is being challenged by the traditional brand from Budweis in the Czech Republic which can claim to have been around for a considerable time. There is great debate over the 'real' brand in this case, but it is certain that both have an interesting claim. Brands are valuable marketing assets, and the result of long term investment, for every marketing led business and therefore companies will defend their brands against 'me too' competition.

Reproduced with permission from Anheuser-Busch Companies, Inc.

CONCLUSION – THE ART OF PRICING

Pricing is a management decision with a large marketing input, it also involves accountants, salespeople and probably the Managing Director. The objectives for the organisation will influence management policy. All organisations need to establish a framework within which to operate and this will provide the limits for their decisions. Figure 13.8 is quite useful in this respect.

The actual limits for the high and low points are still a matter of judgement, but the key points of competitors' prices can often be established to give reference points. But it is not always possible to establish the real price competitors charge as the 'price-list price' tells only part of the story. Winkler lists ten ways to 'increase' prices without increasing prices:

1 Revise the discount structure
2 Change the minimum order size
3 Charge for delivery and special services
4 Invoice for repairs on purchased equipment
5 Charge for engineering, installation, and supervision
6 Make customers pay for overtime required to prepare rush orders
7 Collect interest on overdue accounts
8 Produce less of the lower margin models in the product line
9 Write escalator clauses into contracts
10 Change the physical characteristics of the product.

Obviously not all these are available in every market. However, the fact that such a list is possible shows how involved pricing decisions really are.

QUESTIONS

1 *Some companies price a product at £9.99 or £19.99. What are the advantages and disadvantages of such prices?*

2 *Why do customers sometimes believe high prices indicate high-quality products?*

3 *Explain the reasons behind 'off-peak pricing'.*

4 *What are the drawbacks to using penetration pricing as the main strategy in entering a new market?*

CASE STUDY

The mobile phones' price war

In November 1999 it was reported that Richard Branson was to get involved in the UK's mobile phone market. He claimed he was 'the *white knight* riding to the rescue of Britain's *chattering classes*. The market being an example of *rip-off* Britain'. In fact this was just one way of announcing the launch of Virgin mobile as a 50–50 joint venture with network provider One2One. Nevertheless the opportunity for a new entrant was made possible by the confusion over the perceived price levels, and the reality of high price contracts for mobiles.

The UK market is an oligopoly, comprised of four rival networks – Vodaphone, Cellnet, One2One and Orange. These networks do have some wholly-owned retail outlets, but much of the business is done through agents such as the Carphone Warehouse. What is it that a customer is buying from these outlets? Primarily the ability to talk on the phone wherever and when ever they want. This is the basic benefit.

The actual product has several components:

- The phone itself (offering talk time and stand by time, and requiring recharging time)
- The network connection (with different levels of coverage and call quality)
- The features (e.g. voice only, or text capacity, or e-mail)
- Additional add-on services (e.g. call waiting or voice mail)
- The method of payment
- Useful options such as itemised billing.

The price is made up from a number of components: the basic up-front fixed price for phone and connection, the regular annual or monthly or pay-as-you-go fixed price for remaining connected and making calls (including perhaps some free minutes and other benefits); the variable cost of calls additional to those already covered; the cost of additional services (including insurance).

When deciding which package to purchase it is important to consider all the requirements that a customer might have. For instance an international business user requires very different facilities from a student, but also different from a local builder working in a defined area. Affordability will be a feature of individual situations, and this has prompted the development of 'pay-as-you-go' options to be set alongside 'Pre-pay' packages and other schemes.

The tariffs can vary with plans for heavy users, off peak only, and many other arrangements. In fact there seems to be a price package to suit every group and every need.

Task

1 *Consider the plethora of packages available. Try to decide which segment is likely to be attracted by each package. Suggest if there is really any confusion for customers and if the pricing deals seem appropriate given the long-term and short-term objectives of the providers.*

2 *Find out the level of penetration of potential users? Identify the non-users and suggest if they are deterred by the basic cost, the complexity of pricing options, or the fact that they just do not want to purchase a mobile phone.*

Communications and promotional planning

I know that half of what I spend on advertising is wasted; but the trouble is I don't know which half.

INTRODUCTION

The above quote has been variously attributed to Lord Leverhulme, the first Chairman of Unilever, and John Wannamaker, the famous Philadelphia retailing magnate. While the comment was made specifically on advertising, it could just as easily apply to the wider field of marketing communications, where precise answers and predictable results are as elusive as within advertising itself. Notwithstanding this, companies and organisations have come to recognise the importance of communications as a means to achieving and making known their corporate objectives. Indeed, without good communications, both internally and externally, no organisation would be able to operate effectively.

This chapter considers the role of communications in marketing, within what is often referred to as the company's *communications mix*. There can be many objectives in marketing, such as launching a new product, promoting a brand or product range, or informing about the whole of a company's activities. In all of these there is a need to utilise some forms of communication. Basically, marketing communication involves enhancing or achieving awareness, better understanding, shared beliefs and meaning, and positive associations, attitudes and predispositions . . . in favour of the product, service or organisation that is being marketed.

While all business functions depend on some dissemination of information and communication with others, marketing activities are perhaps more people-centred than most, and are certainly more directly involved with key stakeholder groups such as customers, trade bodies, media commentators and the like. Obviously, relations with these stakeholder groups require a carefully planned and executed communications programme. Furthermore, as marketing effectiveness depends at least partly on non-marketing functions within a company, it follows that marketing communications may be affected by any of the company's dealings with the outside world. In reality, therefore, practically everything a company does will communicate something to its market place and its stakeholders. In turn, certain stakeholders such as distributors, contractors and service agents will need to be brought in as collaborators within a company's marketing communications activities.

A company's reputation and market standing may well be expressed through accounting convention as a 'goodwill' item within financial statements. In practice, the true worth of its reputation and image will be the outcome of how the company relates to and communicates with its various publics. A company's communications strategy is therefore of major significance to its survival and prosperity. This should be reflected in a co-ordinated programme of activities that presents a consistent picture to the world at large, while still accommodating the particular or local communication requirements of certain specialist groups or market sectors.

THE COMMUNICATION PROCESS

The communication process is the foundation of any relationship whether in the commercial or personal field, and it is on this that the success or failure of any relationship depends. A typical definition of communication would be:

The act of making known; intercourse by speech, correspondence, and messages.

Communication is more than a message being sent. For communication to have taken place, it is necessary for the message that is received to have been *understood in the way it was intended*. This means that the sender of a message has to have a measure of response reaction to know whether communication has taken place. The response or feedback enables the sender to develop the message thereby ensuring that it is understood by the receiver. Communication is therefore a 'two-way' rather than a 'one-way' process.

It will be seen from the two-way communications process shown in Figure 15.1 that the transfer of a message from a sender to a receiver involves a number of distinct stages. Each of these provides an opportunity for the message to be altered from that originally intended. Furthermore, at each stage of the communication process the message can be affected by 'noise', a term used to identify any extraneous factor which can affect the transfer of a message. This can even be extended to the effect of external factors on a consumers' attitude to spending.

It is perhaps easier to understand the communications process by considering how we as individuals respond when meeting someone for the first time. Generally, we are able to respond to the person appropriately without being aware of our response. We

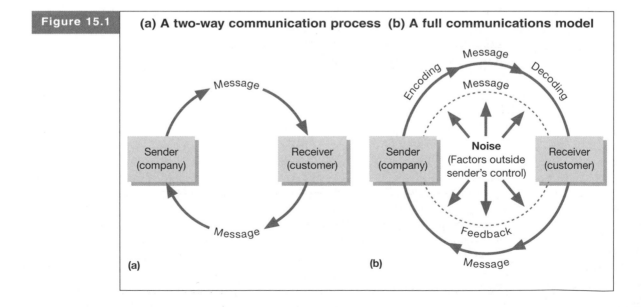

Figure 15.1 **(a) A two-way communication process (b) A full communications model**

automatically note aspects of the person and assimilate unconsciously the information provided. For example, we note posture, gestures, facial expressions, eye movements, eye contact, the style and quality of clothing and perhaps status symbols, such as jewellery. Such *non-verbal messages* are just as important in the communications process as the spoken message itself.

Usually when a person speaks, what they say is in keeping with the impression we have formed about them. Occasionally when this does not happen, such as when someone dressed casually speaks with unexpected authority, we are taken by surprise and as a result completely miss what was said. This is an example where the non-verbal messages can be considered to be 'noise' since they have affected the transfer of the message. Noise can thus take many forms, all of which have the effect of drowning, distorting or distracting from the message being communicated.

The messages could also be distorted directly as a result of the processes involved in transmitting it from the sender to the receiver. The problem could lie with the sender, for instance:

1 The message may be incomplete because the sender may not have the full information that should be included in the message
2 It may be vague because the sender may not know the precise words that should be used in some aspect of the message
3 The sender may choose the wrong medium for sending the message: the telephone is used when a letter is needed.

These are examples where the message is distorted by the sender. It can also be distorted by the receiver. If a drawing is used to send the message the receiver will need to be able to interpret it. If words are used, the receiver will need to know what they mean.

In direct person-to-person communications the problems which arise as a result of the message not being heard or being distorted can easily be corrected as the communication progresses because the sender is able to revise the message according to the receiver's responses. In indirect communications it is not so easy as there is usually a time delay before feedback is received and thus before any clarification or revision is possible.

THE DYNAMICS OF MARKETING COMMUNICATIONS

Let us imagine that a message is to be sent to a potential group of customers and television is selected as the communication channel. For the message to be sent via television it must be first encoded in the form of words, pictures and images; it must then be broadcast as television signals. Those signals will be received by every television tuned to that channel. The message will not, however, be the same on every television as the quality of the image and sound vary according to TV quality and area reception. As a result some of the people watching the television will receive essentially the original message, while others will receive something quite different. Those who decode the message may then either react to the message or just store it for future reference.

It is important to remember that each one of us is different. People differ psychologically and physiologically. They vary in intelligence, education, religious beliefs, social background and experience. These differences mean that different people receive and decode messages in different ways. As perception is known to be selective, individuals will perceive different messages. Further, situational factors (e.g. individual needs, lifestyle) may make the received messages either more or less relevant to the recipient.

COMMUNICATION OBJECTIVES

In general, the objectives of communication will be derived from one of the three categories below:

- **Informing** – giving information, building awareness that a product/service exists, what the product does, where it can be obtained
- **Persuading** – creating a favourable attitude, providing a stimulus to favour one brand over another, or one point of view against another
- **Reinforcing** – dispelling doubts about an action already taken, building support/loyalty to a point of view or purchase, ensuring a good climate for future sales.

An equation can be developed, as shown in Figure 15.2.

The equation must be followed through before the implementation of communication plans are decided. The overall objectives can cover any of the main categories of informing, persuading or reassuring. The gap is the *perceived difference with the actual situation*. It is only by setting clear goals in this area, as in other parts of business, that successful execution can be assessed. One of the key studies in covering both objectives and assessment is the DAGMAR work by Russell Colley. This study was undertaken for the Advertising Research Foundation and an obvious but key conclusion was that in order to know how successful your advertising is you must start with clear communication objectives. DAGMAR stands for 'Defining Advertising Goals for Measured Advertising Results'. However, in Colley's study he lists over 50 possible advertising objectives. Further coverage of feedback in marketing communications is included later in the chapter.

MARKETING COMMUNICATIONS MEDIA

One of the basics of communications is the *selection of media* to be used to transmit the intended message to the target group. In general, media can be split into two categories:

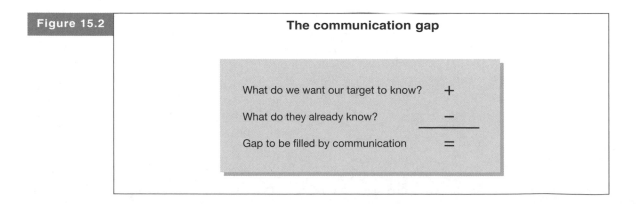

Figure 15.2

The communication gap

What do we want our target to know?   +

What do they already know?   −

Gap to be filled by communication   =

personal and non-personal. Very often it happens that several different media need to be used in conjunction with each other in order to convey the message effectively.

Again, *repetition of messages* is often necessary in communicating information, though it is important to know when the receivers of your message have heard enough. Some advertisements really irritate when seen for the twentieth or thirtieth time.

PERSONAL CHANNELS

The term 'personal channels' refers to those marketing communications involving an element of personal contact. A key advantage of this type of communication is that it is possible to tailor the content of the message to each recipient. Also, the communicator might be able to gauge the reaction of the recipient and, in some circumstances, modify the message in the light of any feedback. This may increase the likelihood that the content of the message will be properly received and interpreted.

Personal channels for marketing communications range from telephone selling to office memos. The major areas of personal communications are:

- internal company communications
- personal selling
- personalised marketing – telesales/telemarketing, the Internet and direct mail
- trade fairs and exhibitions.

Internal communication

Though many see 'communications' as largely referring to interactions with external actors, communications may also be *internal to the organisation*. Most internal communication is of a personal nature, i.e. letters, memos, telephone calls, face-to-face meetings, presentations. Indeed, perhaps the most effective method of communication is word of mouth, whereby colleagues, friends or family make personal recommendations. The desired result is to produce an offering that is acceptable to external customers. In this situation, internal marketing may be necessary. Some authors propose that every employee is a potential part-time marketer so that they should have as deep a knowledge about the product as possible. In this respect, the quality of internal communication will have a direct input on the effectiveness as well as the efficiency of an organisation and its marketing orientation.

Personal selling

The personal sales approach is the most direct and potent way of selling many products. It ranges from door-to-door insurance salespeople to assistants in your local department store. To be successful, salespeople must understand the use of body language, eye contact and asking questions, as well as being able to build a relationship with their clients. It is not about smart-talking salespeople who can talk their customers into submission. Rather, a good salesperson will use questions to discover customer needs and then show how their offerings fulfil those needs. Of course, atmosphere is important in creating the right conditions for a sale. Tupperware party-plan organisers, are aware of this and are very successful at developing a social gathering conducive to selling. However, personal selling can, at times, be a slow and expensive way of doing business. A less costly way is to adopt so-called 'personalised selling' which is a more customised form of selling. Chapter 19 covers selling in more detail.

NON-PERSONAL CHANNELS

Non-personal channels of communication cover those situations where there is no personal contact involved. The communication is completely external to the audience. Non-personal channels include the use of one or more of the following channels of communication: commercial television; the press and other print media; radio; cinema; outdoor media; point-of-sale displays; and packaging.

Within these channels, techniques of advertising, publicity (PR), sponsorship, and sales promotion can be used. These are considered in Chapters 16–18.

NEW MEDIA

There are always new ideas on possible media, both personal and impersonal, which can be used to communicate with customers. You might have seen ads set into carpets on cricket grounds and other public places and even ones on the walls of very unlikely places. David Pugh from poster company Mills & Allen suggests :

> Marketing Directors are finding themselves trapped in a vicious circle. On the one hand it is more and more difficult to keep abreast of all the changes in the media world, on the other hand the average marketer has less and less time to devote to the subject. These two pressures are pulling in opposite directions – while marketing departments are being compelled to improve on cost efficiency, the media choice continues to grow.

With the growth in media choice, the decisions on which media will achieve the communication objectives most effectively are becoming ever more difficult. Often media spending accounts for the greater part of the marketing budget, therefore, in an effort to get their communications to inform, reinforce and persuade, marketing managers should give serious consideration to both traditional and unconventional media.

Exercise   Think of recent communications from organisations that have attracted your attention and made you more aware of that organisation. How did they do it?

PROMOTIONAL PLANNING

Promotional planning can be viewed as a sequential process aimed at deciding the strategies and necessary action plans to achieve communication objectives. The four elements of the promotional (or communication) mix are:

Non-personal
1 **Advertising**
2 **Publicity**
3 **Sales promotion.**
Personal
4 **Personal selling.**

Figure 15.3

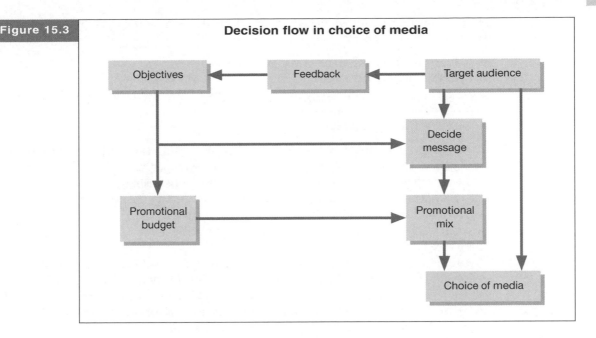

Decision flow in choice of media

Every company will use one, or perhaps a combination, of the elements of the promotion mix. This will happen irrespective of whether the organisation is production, product, selling or marketing orientated. The type of product or service offered by a company, as well as the available budget, will have a bearing upon which elements are used. The promotional mix decision process is shown in Figure 15.3.

The objectives of a promotion campaign represent the targets that a company will wish to achieve. Three possible groups of objectives can be identified:

- informing
- persuading
- reinforcing.

However, in the long run, the objective of promotions is not to inform but to encourage customers to purchase goods or to adopt ideas. Effective promotions are usually well researched. Some promotions may appeal at the subconscious level while, on other occasions, successful promotions may be more overt and eye-catching. Routine marketing research should be used to track sales levels and attitude patterns towards individual products.

It is only when the objectives have been analysed and decided upon that the company can set about deciding how best to achieve them. Objectives must be linked to the target audience – and, in particular, the stage they have reached in the purchase cycle. Informing is relevant to the pre-transactional stage (before a purchase), persuading equates to the transactional purchase period, and reinforcement may be necessary after a purchase (post-transactional).

Potential customers can pass through these stages in deciding on a purchase. However, communication objectives could also refer to any of the pre-transactional stages that a potential customer goes through before reaching the point of purchase. Effectiveness of communication can then be judged against the customer's stage of development. The AIDA model was developed in the first part of the 20th century and is based on the psychology of selling. It reflects the stages prospects move through in the purchase cycle above:

- **Attention** – gain attention of the audience
- **Interest** – kindle interest in the product/service on offer
- **Desire** – arouse desire for your product above any desire for your competitor's product
- **Action** – the customer buys the product.

The utility of this model has been questioned in recent years. Other models such as Lavidge and Steiner (see Figure 15.4) have been developed and it is now evident that AIDA is not robust when considering the success of advertising with all types of products. It will be possible in many instances for a product to create interest, perhaps by the very nature of the advertisement, but this in itself is not enough to create *desire*. Also AIDA does not cover the important post-transactional stage when repeat purchases are considered.

The more inexpensive and frequently bought products do not always require purchasers to go through all the stages of the model. For this type of repeat-purchase product, advertising covers only the *reinforcement role* of keeping the customer permanently aware of the value of the brand. Top-of-mind awareness for brands such as Mars have been reinforced by slogans such as, 'A Mars a day helps you work, rest and play'. Shopping goods, which are more expensive and less frequently purchased, (e.g. dishwashers or televisions), usually require more stages in the purchase decision. They may demand all the stages of the AIDA model. Nevertheless, a communication may be considered a success if it moves a potential customer from attention to interest, or from interest to desire.

It is possible to see commonalities in most of the models which have been developed. In general, they can be classified under the three general headings of knowledge, attitudes and behaviour (see Figure 15.4). The second line represents the AIDA model, the third line the six stages of the Lavidge and Steiner model and the bottom line shows the four steps described in the Colley DAGMAR (Defining Advertising Goals for Measured Advertising Results) study. Other models might also be fitted into this progression. The starting point for products will differ so that the measure of effectiveness requires a clear statement of objectives within a specific context. At the pre-transactional stage, the need could be for information such as: announcing a new product;

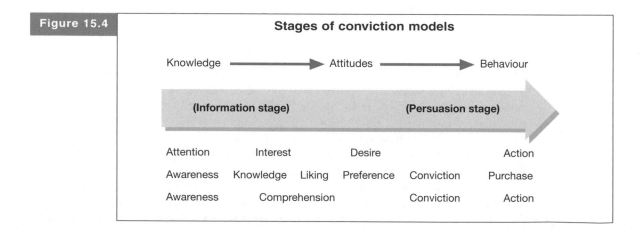

Figure 15.4

Stages of conviction models

Knowledge ⟶ Attitudes ⟶ Behaviour

(Information stage)   (Persuasion stage)

Attention	Interest	Desire	Action
Awareness	Knowledge	Liking	Preference	Conviction	Purchase
Awareness	Comprehension		Conviction	Action

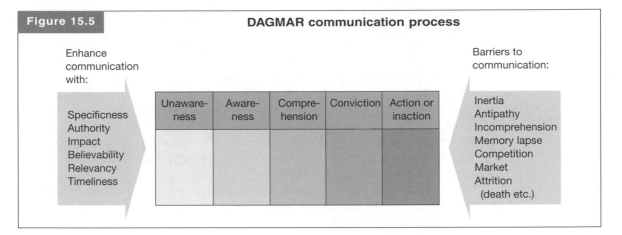

Figure 15.5   **DAGMAR communication process**

explaining product features; describing available services; suggesting new uses; correcting false ideas; and informing of a price change. Here potential customers would probably be at the awareness or interest stage on the AIDA scale.

The transaction might not be an actual purchase of a product. It could be just the acceptance of a sales call. However, at the stage leading to the transaction the element of desire has to be developed and then extended into action. Persuasion is most important here and objectives could be arranging a sales appointment; enhancing company image; changing perception of product; building brand loyalty; stimulating a purchase decision; or encouraging brand switching.

In the post-transactional period the need is obviously for reinforcement and reminders. Major objectives could be reassuring that the purchase was right; maintaining top-of-mind awareness; or encouraging recommendations to friends. Within these objectives it is essential that goals are set so results can be measured as in the DAGMAR process. In Figure 15.5 it can be seen that as people are moved through the spectrum of the DAGMAR communication process they are encouraged by the factors on the left of the diagram and inhibited by the variables on the right. Each of the factors can have varying degrees of impact on potential consumers, depending upon the particular situation.

INTEGRATED MARKETING COMMUNICATIONS (IMC)

This is an evolving body of theory and principles that has been met with mixed reactions among marketing academics and practitioners in recent years. While supporters of IMC argue vigorously that it represents a radical, holistic and strategic approach to communications planning, others hold that the 'innovative' claims made are not that new, and that marketing has always laid claim to integration across the communications mix. Kitchen (1999) provides a useful chapter that summarises the history and theoretical foundations of IMC, and considers empirical UK evidence on its acceptance among communications specialists.

Smith et al. (1997) define IMC as:

The strategic analysis, choice, implementation and control of all elements of marketing communications which efficiently, economically and effectively influence transactions between an organisation and its existing and potential customers, consumers and clients.

Variations on definitions obviously exist (see Shimp 1997; Brannan 1995), some laying emphasis on the need for consistency on *all* forms of communications, others stressing the key focus on recipients, and others on the creative commonality across communication forms.

As the field of IMC is relatively recent, and certainly more a debating issue in the USA than the UK or Europe, evidence on its merits, or its adoption, is still developing. Again, as a key element of communications activity usually involves advertising, the whole question of consistency of approach across media, and below-the-line and other activities, has become entangled within related planning and managerial questions about budget division, client control, inter-agency co-operation, multi-media creative execution and many other issues.

Notwithstanding this, interest in IMC, among both practitioners and researchers, continues to grow. For further specialist material on the subject, readers are advised to consult some of the authors cited above.

PROMOTION AS AN INVESTMENT

Clearly, promotional expenditure can have an important effect on the future of an organisation. Since promotions can, at times, lead to immediate returns, there is a tendency to view them as short-termist. Clearly, this overlooks the fact that communication represents an investment in the customers, helping to create positive attitudes towards an organisation or a product/service. Positioning has been described in the words of Ries and Trout as 'what happens in the mind of customers'. As professional advertising executives, these authors recognise how customer communication represents *investment in the development of customers attitudes and beliefs*.

In the same way as R&D and training, a great deal of promotional investment is future oriented. If an organisation understands the exchange process, then it should appreciate how both sides of the exchange can be influenced by marketing action.

THE TARGET AUDIENCE

A promotion strategy developed by a company will aim to accomplish an improvement in the way that the company and its goods/services, are perceived. In order to achieve this, some of the following stakeholder groups will be reached either directly or indirectly:

- Specific target customers
- The general public
- Present and potential distribution channel members
- Present and potential employees
- Suppliers of finance
- Present and potential shareholders.

It is probable that some communications will be viewed by stakeholders who are not necessarily the prime target. This fall-out must be appreciated when placing advertisements. In addition, competitors often learn from advertisements. However, all communications must be aimed primarily at those publics identified in the marketing and promotional objectives. Precise targeting of the communication can save money and ensure an effective response.

An audience of 10 million for a TV commercial could cost in excess of £150 000 for a single 30-second spot. This is £15 per 1000 viewers. For £42 000 you could buy the First mono full page appearing in all editions of the *Financial Times* with a circulation of over 300 000. This is £70 per 1000. On first sight, the TV is more expensive but better value (costs per thousand or CPT). Yet, if all *FT* readers were in the target group, but only 10 per cent of the TV audience were acceptable targets, the situation changes. Of course it is more complex than this. The TV programme may reach 1 million relevant people, which may be five times more than that reached by the *FT*. If the object is to get coverage of the greatest number of target customers, then the TV may represent excellent value. Therefore, value, CPT and coverage must be considered in the context of the most appropriate medium for the message. It is possible that neither television nor press are really suitable to carry the message: it could be that a direct mail shot offers a more appropriate medium, even if it is more expensive than either.

Example	Advertisers have always had to place their message in appropriate media. In an age of increasing leisure, a clear growth area in media terms has been the sports press. As a random example of the 'pull' of targeted sports coverage, the following advertisers are among those found within the sports supplements of two well-known Sunday newspapers in April 2000:

- Subaru (cars)
- Ladbrokes (betting)
- telme.com (match tickets)
- Jack Daniel's (whisky)
- Powergen (new telephone service)
- Fujitsu Siemens (computers)
- Vodafone (mobiles)
- Chello.com (broadband internet)
- William Hill (betting)
- eurobet.co.uk (betting website)
- Chevrolet (4 × 4 vehicles)
- Land Rover (4 × 4 vehicles)
- Marlboro (cigarettes)
- Lucozade (sports energy drink)

Therefore, marketers must start with a clear view of the target group. But, in particular, they must decide how *comprehensively the group is to be covered* ('coverage' is the percentage of total target who are able to see the communications), and what type of message and media is consistent with the communication objectives. Within the target group, it is imperative to understand the various roles of user, decider and influencer so that the message can be developed at the right level.

When considering promotion, there are two ways to create demand; products can be demanded by consumers who effectively 'pull' the product through the distribution chain; and products may be 'pushed' through distributors towards the customers (see Figure 15.9).

Pull strategy

A pull strategy is used by many companies. Basically, it is a strategy which by heavy use of advertising and promotion encourages consumers to demand the product. This strategy can be particularly successful when applied to goods which are sold through supermarkets or newsagents. Panini collector cards are an example at the start of the football season each year, as are British Airways' Air Miles; the frequent-flyer syndrome is part of airlines' marketing strategies to promote purchase of full and premium-priced tickets.

Occasionally there is a similar pull strategy when new magazines are launched, especially magazines of a specialist nature, such as *Do It Yourself* (DIY) or *Sewing and Knitting* which, by means of heavy advertising encourage consumers to demand that their local newsagents stock that particular magazine for them.

Push strategy

A push strategy works in the opposite direction to that of a pull strategy. It is the push from the producer to the distribution channel members and from them to the customer which increases demand for the product. Instead of aiming heavy advertising and promotional campaigns directly at the customer, the producer will specifically aim at the people and organisations selling the product to the final consumer. Examples of push strategy are very common in the industrial sector and also in the field of medicine. Medical sales representatives push products very strongly to doctors and back up this push with strong promotional measures. The doctors then prescribe the drugs to the patients who are ultimately the customer.

Avon, the cosmetics firm, is a well-known user of the push strategy. Salespeople call directly to the homes of customers to sell the products. Often companies will offer some kind of incentive to salespeople to push their product more than their competitors' products. This can occur with many different kinds of goods and services, from insurance to sports equipment.

It is difficult to measure the effect of either the push or pull strategy or to see how efficient they are. Many producers of goods and services do not want to take any chances and run both strategies simultaneously in order that they can reinforce any effect one or the other may be having. Figure 15.6 shows how the push strategy and the pull strategy differ.

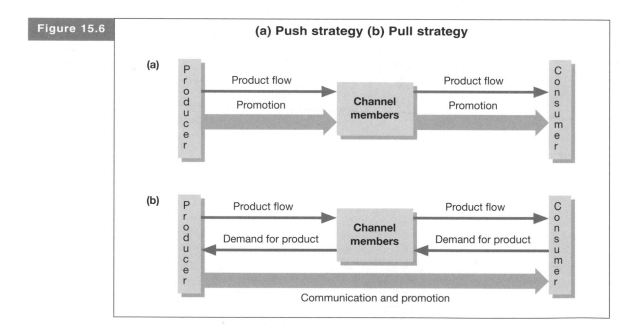

Figure 15.6   **(a) Push strategy (b) Pull strategy**

PROMOTION FUNDING

An economist might suggest that promotional expenditure should be raised to the point where the marginal return from additional spend matches the marginal cost of that spend. However, in practice, it is extremely difficult to determine the appropriate level of promotional funding. Moreover, the marginal costing method is inherently flawed as it overlooks the long-term effects of promotion. Given that the benefits of a sustained campaign may be long- and short-term in nature, a more suitable plan is to set the expenditure based on the objectives to be achieved and the task in hand.

Companies may adopt a number of methods to calculate their total promotional budgets:

1 The objective and task method (zero-based budgeting or ZBB)
2 The affordable method
3 The percentage of sales method
4 The competitive parity method.

It is noteworthy that Crosier (1999) cites a number of pre-1985 UK and US surveys showing 'executive judgement' to be the most popular method till then (just ahead of 'percentage of sales', though various post-1986 findings show the objective/task method in the lead, followed by the percentage of sales approach). However, Crosier points to the lack of coverage on this within UK texts on the field by respected sources (Cooper, 1997; Butterfield, 1997).

The objective and task method

The objective and task method, incorporating a zero-based approach, might be described as one of the most logical, yet time-consuming approaches to setting promotion budgets. According to this method, a company first determines its marketing communication objectives, then it identifies alternative ways of attaining its promotion goals. Subsequently, the tasks are costed and compared, and a decision is taken about which promotional tasks to undertake. Though systematic, this approach is not without its disadvantages:

1 It is very difficult to forecast the exact response to any particular promotional expenditure, and there is no guarantee that objectives will necessarily be met.
2 This method does not categorically consider the affordability of the chosen tasks. For instance, a company might be familiar with its promotional objectives, and perhaps how to attain them, yet it may be financially impeded from achieving them.

The affordable method

This method is easy to conceptualise and basically means that a company will spend on promotion that which it deems reasonable and can afford. It is often based on the previous year's promotional spend, or what is available once the forecast revenue and required profits have been determined. One significant advantage of this method is that it might prevent a company from overspending. Nevertheless, it is possible to identify a number of shortcomings relative to this approach:

■ Accurate long-range planning is almost impossible – a company cannot predict exactly the funds that will be available in the future to spend on promotion.

■ Ironically, in times of recession or company hardship, few funds will be available for promotion, thereby perpetuating the company's problems. On the other hand, when the economy is buoyant or when times are good for the company, more funds might be spent on promotion instead of on more worthwhile, long-term investments such as capital expenditure.

■ There is likely to be fierce internal competition for limited company funds, threatening loss of goodwill. Instead of aiming for a common goal, long-term company success, managers may strive to satisfy their own personal empire-building or departmental goals.

■ It is harder, by definition, to plan effective promotional campaigns because of the fluctuating level of funds.

The percentage of sales method

Perhaps the classical approach, this method is generally preferred by accountants as it is precise, easy to calculate and can be quickly monitored. A percentage of current yearly sales is determined and this amount is spent on the promotion mix. Again, a host of disadvantages can be listed:

1 There is no scientific basis to setting the percentage of sales – it is generally left to the discretion of management.

2 A fixed percentage provides a company with little opportunity to respond to competitor moves or environmental changes, possibly resulting in loss of market share.

3 It is impossible to calculate what sales can be attributed to promotional expenditure if the spend always relates solely to past or present sales figures.

4 Long-range planning for promotion is difficult to forecast. It is unlikely that the budget will remain at a similar level each year, unless the market place has remained fairly static.

The competitive parity method

With this approach, the amount spent on promotion is directly influenced by the levels spent by competitors. Therefore, such a method aims to achieve a 'share of voice' similar to the company's market share. In fact there is some evidence to suggest that market shares are roughly in line with long-term share of advertising spend in some industries.

In this respect, the amount spent on promotions almost constitutes an industrial norm since some organisations may feel uncomfortable being the odd one out. Again, one might cite a number of disadvantages with this approach:

1 All companies do not share the same goals; some have the sole objective to become market leader, while others may wish to become more profitable. Though these are not mutually exclusive objectives, it is rare to be able to achieve both simultaneously.

2 This method may reduce the likelihood of promotional wars as companies will align their spending patterns.

3 The comparative parity approach makes it less likely that a follower product could become a market leader since a challenger product is likely to require above parity promotional expenditure as part of its marketing mix.

PROMOTIONAL MIX DECISIONS

An organisation's choice of promotional mix tools (i.e. advertising, publicity, sales promotion and personal selling) is largely context-specific. For instance, where a company has a small number of customers, sales calls may prove more cost-effective, whilst mass-market products will almost certainly benefit from the adoption of mass media.

In short, each promotional mix tool has its own merits. By way of illustration, advertising is effective at creating awareness and interest. Though public relations can fulfil the same role as media advertising, there is nevertheless a loss of control over what is published. However, this can be countered by the apparent increased authority and credibility of an editorial item. Sales promotion might act both as an immediate stimulus that might provoke purchase and as a tool to encourage repeat purchase. Personal selling is particularly direct, yet is very expensive.

Depending on the type of product marketed, an organisation may choose to spend different amounts on the various promotional tools. For example, an industrial machinery producer might conclude that personal selling is most effective, whereas a toy manufacturer may concentrate on media advertising and sales promotion. In general, companies will focus on one element of the promotional mix and use the other tools in a consistent and co-ordinated way to reinforce the overall message.

In theory, the choice of promotional tools should be determined by the task to be achieved.

However, in practice, high mass-media costs might force organisations to look for alternative, more cost-effective ways of reaching the target audience. Sometimes corporate advertising is preferred over individual brand promotion. Similarly, experimentation with unconventional media has proved extremely successful.

Chapters 16–18 discuss the merits of the major promotional methods. It is obvious

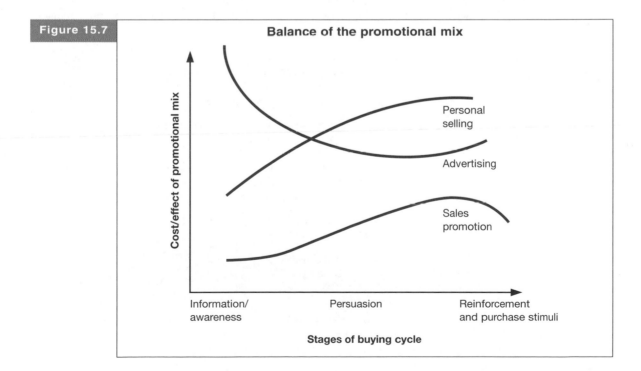

Figure 15.7

Balance of the promotional mix

that personal selling is a medium that offers direct customer contact. Non-personal promotional methods include advertising and publicity, involving indirect contact, as well as sales promotion, which supports in a complementary way.

As already stated, a company's mix of promotional tools should balance the push/pull requirements of reaching customers. Personal selling and sales promotion are effective 'push' techniques. The benefits of personal selling are that it is interactive, responsive and flexible but it can be very expensive. In addition to being a so-called 'push' technique, selling also plays a significant role in developing long-term customer relationships. Though a well-chosen sales promotion can reinforce a product or organisation's position and achieve significant short-term sales growth, care should be taken since money-off promotions may adversely affect a brand's image.

Advertising and publicity may be classified as longer-term investments. Though they might be indirect and non-personal, they can also be very intrusive if they succeed in reaching their target. The media is particularly overcrowded, and it has been suggested that consumers receive over 1000 media advertising messages every day. Nevertheless, consumers should be able to list a number of advertisements they remember well and these clearly represent the more successful ones.

The decision on how much to spend on each part of the promotional mix is obviously situation-specific, since it depends on a number of variables including, amongst others, marketing objectives and the promotional budget. As a company's overriding aim should be to deliver its message effectively, the budget allocation decision should be judged on the basis of achieving this.

Budget allocation problems may be more common when organisations do not use the 'objective and task' method of calculation. Indeed, this 'bottom-up' approach allows a mix of promotional methods to be considered in an ideal context. The alternative 'top-down' approaches inevitably require compromises in the mix allocation and the outcome of this is illustrated in Figure 15.7.

Where heavy advertising can increase the size of a market, an organisation may be faced

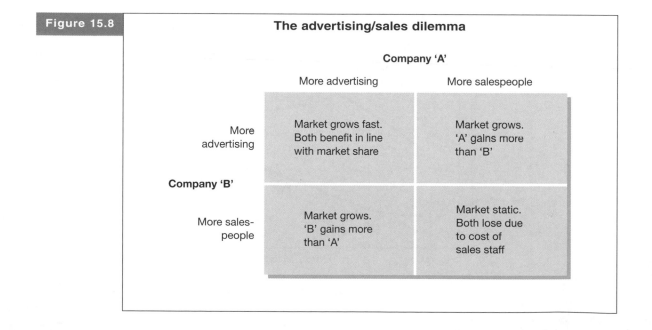

Figure 15.8

The advertising/sales dilemma

	Company 'A'	
	More advertising	More salespeople
Company 'B' More advertising	Market grows fast. Both benefit in line with market share	Market grows. 'A' gains more than 'B'
More sales-people	Market grows. 'B' gains more than 'A'	Market static. Both lose due to cost of sales staff

with a version of the marketer's dilemma; if your company 'A' increases advertising, will the increased demand also benefit your competitor 'B'? It certainly could benefit 'B' if company 'B' deploys extra salespeople. But if 'B' also advertises, the market could grow very fast so that both companies might benefit providing their products reach the customers. Two other scenarios are shown in the matrix in Figure 15.8. How would you approach this problem?

PROMOTION AND THE DEMAND CURVE

Demand curve shifting to the right

Chapter 14 looked at how price and quantity define the demand curve. However, price changes only move demand along the demand curve. By contrast, promotional activities can help to *shift the total demand curve*, as well as changing its shape. Hence, promotions can create a new environment in which buying decisions are made.

Clearly, organisations rarely have complete knowledge about their competitors' plans. Nevertheless, in spite of this environmental uncertainty, they need to make decisions for the future and aim to gain competitive advantage for their offerings. Companies cannot gain sustainable advantage simply by decreasing the price. If price elasticity of demand existed, then more of the product would be bought if the price was lower; if the price was increased, less of the product would be bought. This would only cause a movement along the same demand curve, and not a complete shift of the demand curve. Also, competitors would be able to imitate this, thereby creating the vicious circle described in Chapter 14.

It is possible to create or develop product differentiation through sustained promotional campaigns. This will produce a shift in the demand curve by changing the competitive situation. This might be easier to understand by looking at a few examples of products which have recently experienced a shift in their demand curves. One of the best British examples is the increase in healthy eating and organically produced food. Healthy eating has been promoted heavily on the back of government reports such as that of the Committee on the Medical Aspects of Health (COMA). Promotion has been supported by communications ranging from leaflets in doctors' surgery waiting rooms to articles in newspapers and TV

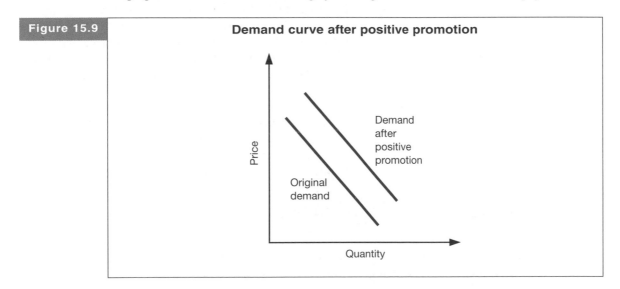

Figure 15.9   **Demand curve after positive promotion**

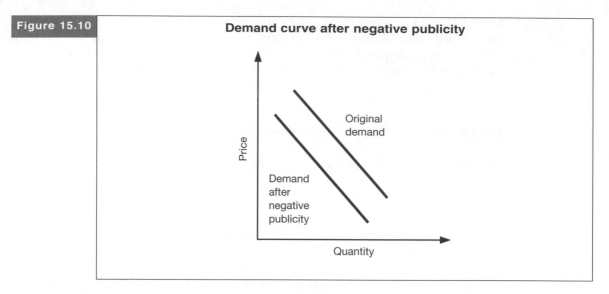

Figure 15.10

Demand curve after negative publicity

advertisements. The increased awareness of the issues has provoked a shift in the demand curve over a wide range of so-called 'healthy foods', including yoghurt, brown bread, muesli, and porridge. In England, porridge has become more popular, partly as a result of promotion. Sales of porridge oats have risen; the demand curve for porridge has shifted to the right as illustrated in Figure 15.9.

These examples illustrate how well-designed publicity can lead to a shift in the demand curve to the right. Of course, it can also move in the opposite direction as a result of bad publicity.

Demand curve shifting to the left

An example of a demand curve having a dramatic shift to the left can be seen by studying the demand for British beef. The problem follows the revelation that some cows had been infected with BSE or 'mad cow disease'. The situation became so serious that schools, colleges and hospitals removed beef from their menus. Prices dropped, and so did demand, some farmers faced financial ruin. The publicity about British 'mad cow disease' was so disturbing that the German government campaigned to get a ban on the export of British beef to the EU countries. A shift to the left is illustrated in Figure 15.10.

Negative demand effects do not always result from external events. There have been a number of cases where an organisation's promotional campaign has had an adverse effect on product perception, resulting in reduced sales. Some examples include, the Hoover free-flights promotion, the Fiat cars 'made by robots' promotion and Strand cigarettes 'if you are alone!'. It is important to recognise that most promotions may affect *customer expectations*, and that it is against these that customers judge how satisfied they are with any product offering.

MEASURING EFFECTIVENESS

In theory, all communications should be tested before their adoption. Likewise, companies should assess the effectiveness of the campaign and make any necessary modifications. This is imperative for two reasons in particular:

- to ensure that the money has been well spent
- to determine whether the promotion led to increased sales.

However, the fact remains that promotion is not directly related to sales in a one-to-one model. Though promotion is an investment in customers' perceptions of products, the return from such an investment is difficult to benchmark. Good promotion has an element of qualitative judgement about it, but the aim of feedback is to learn from experience rather than develop a 'feel-good' factor that the money was well spent.

In order to gauge the attitudes and behaviour of donors or customers it may be necessary to approach the customer. This is an action promoted by Tom Peters, who regards it as essential. He states that 'Marketers should be in the field at least 25 per cent and preferably 50 per cent of their time.' Peters suggests that all managers should go to the customer, look, listen and provide feedback. The need to listen is a necessary way of providing feedback on what has already been achieved. It is also a necessary preliminary to understanding what still needs to be achieved. Peters advocates going out with a 'naive' mind set to gauge customers' reactions. To communicate effectively, it is sometimes imperative to adopt the recipient's language and stage of development. Communication is the prime way of establishing customer relationships but, to be really effective, it should be bi-directional or two-way.

CONCLUSION

This chapter has considered the planning of communications and the different elements in what is termed the 'promotional mix'. Perhaps one of the most important lessons from the material presented is that communications act as a vital link between an organisation and its customers, both internal and external. In all cases, two-way communications are preferable and communication objectives should be well thought out.

It is important that a company is aware of the communication channels available, and that it utilises them effectively. The medium chosen to convey the message must be *appropriate*, and this depends on the product or service in question, as well as the target audience. If the product is of high value and aimed at the industrial market, a personal channel may be most effective. However, if the product is of low value and aimed at the consumer market, a non-personal channel may be more appropriate.

QUESTIONS

1 *Think of a recent communication from an organisation that has attracted your attention. Explain how this has affected your views about that organisation.*

2 *What is meant by encoding? How might an advertising agency or communications consultant help an organisation to encode its messages?*

3 *What are the advantages of personal communications over non-personal communications?*

4 *Why is packaging sometimes called the 'silent salesman'?*

5 *Why do large firms often use a combination of media in their advertising campaigns? Illustrate your answer with examples.*

FURTHER READING

Abraham, M. and Lodish, L. (1996) 'Getting the most out of advertising and promotion', *Harvard Business Review*, May–June.

Brannan, T. (1995) A *Practical Guide to Integrated Marketing Communications*. Kogan Page.

Butterfield, L. (1997) *Excellence in Advertising: IPA Guide to Best Practice*. Butterworth Heinemann.

Colley, R. H. (1961) *Defining Advertising Goals for Measured Advertising Results*. New York Association of Advertisers.

Cooper, A. (1997) *How to Plan Advertising*, 2nd edn. Cassell in association with The Account Planning Group.

Crosier, K. (1999), 'Promotion', in M. J. Baker (ed.), *The Marketing Book*. Butterworth Heinemann.

Fill, C. (1995) *Marketing Communications*. Prentice-Hall.

Gilchrist, S. (1994) 'Discounters unmoved by ceasefire in store wars', *The Times*, 21 September.

Kitchen, P. J. (1999) *Marketing Communications: Principles and Practice*. International Thompson Business Press.

Lavidge, R. and Steiner, A. (1961) 'A model for predictive measures of advertising effectiveness', *Journal of Marketing*, October.

Mueller, B. (1996) *International Advertising – Communicating across Cultures*. Wadsworth Publishing/Thomson.

Peters, T. (1988) *Thriving on Chaos*. McMillan.

Rees, A., and Trout, J. (1981) *Positioning the Battle for Your Mind*. McGraw-Hill.

Rowell, R. (1994) 'Flattering to deceive', *Marketing Business*, September.

Shimp, T. A. (1993) *Promotional Management and Marketing Communications*, 3rd Edn. Dryden Press.

Shimp, T. A. (1997), *Advertising, Promotion and Supplemental Aspects of Integrated Marketing Communications*. Dryden Press, pp. 10–12.

Smith, P. R. (1993) *Marketing Communications*. Kogan Page.

Smith, P., Berry, C. and Pulford, A. (1997) *Strategic Marketing Communications*. Kogan Page.

Carborundum – launching a new band

> Formed one year ago and all five members based in London, Carborundum have brought together a variety of different influences to create their own unique and energetic sound. The band are regularly receiving recommendations in *Time Out* for their gigs at The Garage, Bull & Gate and The Monarch and have always had a great response from the audience.
>
> Please listen to their first demo tape and find enclosed some photocopies of photos taken during and after their most recent gig at The Garage.

This is a publicity letter sent by the band Carborundum – launching a new band to record companies and the music press. The band play Industrial Rock, writing all their own numbers. They see their music as similar to such bands as Limp Bizkit, Ministry, and Tool. The publicity package they use is similar to most bands, comprising :

- publicity letter
- tickets for future concerts
- photos of the band
- demo tape.

As yet, they have had little reaction from this publicity mail shot, although Island Records, Epic and Skint have telephoned to register receipt of the material. The music press such as *New Musical Express* and *Melody Maker* (both owned by the same publisher), and specialist magazines like *Kerrang* and *Metal Hammer* have given no reviews.

Getting known in the music business is very tough. There are a large number of bands playing regularly in London, but those without a recording contract can do no more than break even at most events, as will be seen below.

Typically the band produces fliers (publicity leaflets) for gigs and, after expenses at the venue, receive no more than 50 per cent of the takings from customers showing the flier at the door. Carborundum's first appearance at The Rock Garden netted only £200 owing to a large number of friends who attended. More recently audiences of over 250 have yielded some £500+ between the five band members, though these engagements are not frequent enough to represent useful earnings, and not firm enough to build up a regular live audience following or radio station interest.

They would like to make a CD to support the publicity and to sell at their concerts but the costs are high with a run of 500 likely to cost:

$$\text{CD} \quad 1000 \times £2.30 = £2300$$
$$\text{Sleeve} \quad 1000 \times £0.45 - £450$$
$$\text{Box} \quad 1000 \times £0.30 = £300$$

Even if they do their own art work this is over £3000, which they will struggle to find. The influencers who could really enhance their music careers, and help them to get profitable gigs, are the record labels, particularly the more specialist labels, and the music press. The important thing is to stand out from all the other publicity on new bands, yet to achieve this within an affordable budget.

(*Note*: The name of the band in this case has been changed from the real name to avoid confusion. To our knowledge no band named Carborundum exists, but should one be using this name the authors confirm the above case is not referring to that band.)

Question

How would you suggest that Carborundum should attempt to communicate with these key influencers?

16 Advertising

The great art of writing advertisements is the finding out a proper method to catch the reader's eye; without which a good thing may pass over unobserved, or be lost among commissions of bankrupt.

Addison, *The Tatler*, No. 224

INTRODUCTION

Advertising is still often referred to as 'above-the-line' expenditure, a term which derives from the historical way advertising expenditure was treated in marketing budgets. Main media expenditure was shown 'above the line' because it represented actual expenditure, as opposed to sales promotion which was shown 'below the line', because much of the cost of such items came from a reduction in revenue, e.g. price cuts. Most advertisements run on behalf of a commercial organisation will be placed by an agency, who buy the space and pay the media owners. The agency then receives a commission from the media owners, but charges the full cost to the advertiser. It is not the same as placing a classified advertisement in your local newspaper where you would pay the media owner yourself. 'Above-the-line' is no longer specifically related to the accounting conventions, but the term is still widely used to encompass money spent on media coverage.

THE SCOPE OF ADVERTISING

Advertising has a very wide scope. When someone places a card in the local newsagent's window with an item for sale, it is an advertisement. This can be contrasted with a major company's commercial shown on television. Each of these examples may be successful if they achieve their objectives – namely, moving potential customers *closer to the point of purchase* for a particular product or service.

Advertising is perhaps the first thing that people think about when considering marketing. You will already know that it comes at the end of the marketing process after a great deal of effort to ensure that the marketing offer is worth promoting. However, it can be the most visible part of the marketing process. Main media advertising with multimillion budgets is undertaken by major consumer goods companies. These are only a small number of the total organisations who use advertising to communicate with their publics. For the major companies large amounts of money are involved, and the impact of their advertising creates strong recall.

Advertising is a major part of their activities. For instance, Guinness have traditionally been high spenders. Guinness state that the reason for their spending is the need to promote their product more than other major brewers, as they do not own any pubs, unlike Ansells, Bass or Whitbread. So we can already see a relationship with other parts of the marketing mix, in this case the channels of distribution. Other high spenders that will immediately come to mind are companies like Procter & Gamble, Coca-Cola, Pepsi Cola and Cadbury's. Their expenditures on advertising are important in maintaining a high profile for the various brands, thus keeping them firmly in the minds of consumers.

Other high spenders include financial institutions such as banks and insurance companies, as well as major High Street retailers like Boots, Debenhams and J Sainsbury. This reflects both the competition faced by these companies and the way retailers have taken the lead in many markets. Another major advertiser has been the government, particularly in promoting the various new share issues, as state industries were sold to the general public. Promotional budgets of up to £10 million were allocated to individual privatisation campaigns. The result was not only the successful sales of shares, but also an increased awareness of share-owning in general among a wide spectrum of the British public.

It should be realised that advertising covers more than the persuading of a consumer to buy something. It is also a means of trying to *influence behaviour and beliefs*. This is the case with the following types of organisations:

- political parties
- local authorities
- charities
- churches
- pressure groups, such as Greenpeace.

Each of these organisations has a 'product' that they want to 'sell'. The advertising of their 'products', which could be their policies and beliefs, is how these organisations hope to influence and gain the support of the general public.

You will remember that the objectives of communication fall into the three categories:

- Informing
- Persuading
- Reinforcing.

In general, media advertising is most effective when introducing new brands, or announcing modifications to existing brands. The research of Abraham and Lodish indicated that 59 per cent of new products received a positive impact from advertising, compared with 44 per cent of existing brands. The exact figures are not important, but advertising is much more effective at an early stage in the purchase cycle. When a product has lost its novelty factor, having been on the market for some time, consumers will have had time to make a balanced judgement about it. It is always difficult to change firmly held opinions and the advertising task therefore becomes more difficult. The objective of communication may change to one of trying to attract customers from different market segments, or perhaps introducing a new, improved version of the original product. Examples of changes to existing brands include a springfresh variant to Fairy Excel Plus, Right Guard launching an antiperspirant deodorant gel, and HP Bulmer launching Strongbow Smooth to the take-home market.

| **Exercise** | Over the period of a few days make a note of any new products, or modifications to existing products, the advertising for which has been in magazines or on the television. |

The stage of the product's life cycle will have a marked effect on the type of advertising and promotion that is carried out for a product. At the introductory stages of the product's life, advertisements are designed to create an awareness of the product. After the product has moved into the growth stage of the life cycle, building interest will be of paramount importance. Later, when competition becomes more intense, the benefits of the product, against those of competitors' products, will be stressed, and perhaps the emphasis will switch to other types of promotion, maybe sales promotion.

ADVERTISING CONSIDERATIONS

There are many factors which should be considered before advertising is undertaken. Advertisements should first be considered as part of the *total communication process*. The objectives, message and likely budget could well have been determined. Decisions now have to be taken on the role of advertising as part of the promotional mix. Primarily it revolves around the balance between advertising and personal selling, as these are usually the elements where most money is committed. Often decisions will be taken on the basis of the previous year, rather than a proper objective and task evaluation. It is not easy to switch between personal selling and advertising, as salespeople are usually employees, with consequent rights. Even if an organisation does not employ a salesforce but uses commission agents, there is still the human problem of reductions. However, the cost-effectiveness of advertising reduces as customers move through the stages of the purchase cycle. This is also carried into a similar relationship with the stages of the product life cycle mentioned above. Advertising is more important at the early stages. Nevertheless, it is not advisable to stop all advertising in a competitive market place, as customers soon move on to new products.

Because salesforce costs are less directly variable than expenditure on advertising and other direct promotion, there tends to be more unplanned fluctuations in advertising budgets. Keith Crosier suggested that 65 per cent of promotional budgets were based on either the percentage of sales or the affordable methods. Both these methods are subject to fluctuations, and so when cuts come they fall on advertising rather than sales costs. This makes the effect even more pronounced.

To plan an advertising campaign, the following must be considered:

1 The type of product or service offered
2 The key benefit offered (why that product should be bought ahead of its competitors)
3 The objectives of the communication
4 Who the target market consists of
5 The advertising message and how it relates to other communication messages
6 The amount to be spent on advertising within the context of the total communication spend
7 The media chosen to carry the advertisement
8 The prevailing marketing environment.

ADVERTISING CAMPAIGNS

The campaign planners will already know the answer as to who the target market is and what message is required. They need to decide when, where and how they can reach that target in media terms. When, because timing is a key variable and advertising must be co-ordinated with other communication plans. Also, other marketing plans need integration, as there is no point in advertising heavily if there are not sufficient extra stocks available with distributors. Where and how is the media choice linked to the message. If the organisation is using a major advertising agency, they will have access to a wealth of statistics linking media to target groups, as defined by segmentation variables.

In organising for advertising very few organisations design their own advertisements. If they do, media facts are available from media owners, but these do not give comparative facts, nor are they able to link together a campaign using several media to calculate the total coverage. However, the range of skills required for advertising are better bought in from a specialist agency. You might be able to put together a good internal team with the necessary skills and, of course, doing it in-house can be seen as reducing costs, but does it really work out cheaper when considering the opportunity costs of staff time and the other risks involved in this specialist area? Another benefit from using a professional agency is that they are able to stand back and review your communications plans in an objective way. If you do not like the agency you are working with you can always change them. But agencies offer a service, and, as in all service marketing, interactions and the building up of personal relationships can be rewarding. Advertising agencies should become an extension of an organisation's own marketing department.

It is still important to have someone responsible for briefing the agency and approving plans. In small companies, dealing with local agencies, this can be done by the overworked marketing manager, who is trying to carry out all the marketing roles himself. Larger companies might use more than one agency and maybe even a specialist media buying service. These companies tend to have large advertising departments, not to produce advertising but to compare the different agency performances. Sometimes they get involved in media buying to ensure that the buying power of a major company like Cadbury Schweppes can be used to get good discounts across all its brand advertising.

The prima donnas of advertising agencies are rightly the creative talent. This is the key reason for using an agency, because an 'everyday product' has to be presented in a way that takes the target market through all its stages of attention, interest, desire and action. The very best agencies combine creative talent with first-rate business planning.

Advertising is not a function where a budget is stretched as much as possible and therefore a good brief and clear objectives are the most important issues. There will be a type of interactive process where media choice, message type and budget availability are continually studied against the coverage of the chosen target group. However, it is sometimes better to reduce coverage but present a full message with the preferred number of opportunities to see (OTS) for those reached, than to reduce OTS yet still try to reach everyone in the target.

The agency will try to answer the 'when, where and how' questions through a mixture of message presentation and media selection. The two are inextricably linked, as reflected in the saying that 'the medium is the message'.

ADVERTISING MESSAGES

Having decided on the communication objectives and the target audience, the next decision is the *content* of an effective message. This is necessary before deciding upon the balance of the promotional mix. The message has two components: content and mood. The content will reflect the requirement to communicate some particular information or relevant encouragement. This will be what the communicator hopes the receiver will do or consider following receipt of the message. The mood refers to the way the appeal is made to the target audience. Some moods are more appropriate than others for different types of message. Sometimes the mood is modified further when the medium is chosen and even when professional creative teams start to work on the actual advertisement. Relevant moods could be: rational, emotional, nostalgic, inquisitive, humorous and so forth.

The AIDA sequence is critical here (see Chapter 15). The types of headlines which can grab attention must be consistent with the progression of the message. As already mentioned, it may not be necessary to take the target audience through all AIDA stages for a repeat purchase decision, but for the communication itself all stages are relevant. The communication must:

- grab **attention**
- excite **interest**
- create **desire**
- prompt **action.**

In terms of the total content the rule KISS (keep it simple – keep it short) is good to remember. Adding too many messages into one brief communication generally dilutes the effectiveness of the primary content. Do not let detail get in the way of a good strong message.

Pre-testing of messages using specialised marketing research techniques is highly recommended. The research might study the format/layout of the advertisement. For instance, one technique tracks the movement of an eye across the page when reading an advertisement. This can be used to ensure the key messages are correctly positioned in the copy. However, the simplest techniques are just as important. Show the proposed advertisements, perhaps in rough form, to a sample of your audience and ask them what they make of the message.

The message will usually emphasise the key facts that an advertiser wants to communicate. This is part of the content described in Chapter 15. Sometimes there will be an attempt to find a unique selling proposition (USP) – something tangible or intangible that the brand can claim as its own. In some advertisements it is sufficient just to get over the brand name. This is sometimes forgotten in the creative enthusiasm. There have been some notable occasions when the recall of an advertisement was high, and the contribution of the actors involved was well received, but the recall of the brand was minimal. This does a lot for the actors but gives little return on the advertising investment. There have been a number of brands that have succeeded in gaining brand recall without using brand names. Cigarettes such as Silk Cut and Benson and Hedges Gold have achieved it, while in the past, Cadbury Smash ran successful advertisements without names. Where these succeeded was in the receiver having to work hard to understand the advertisement. Having worked out that the cut piece of purple silk represented the cigarette brand, the recall was stronger than if the brand name had been given and the receiver had not had to work it out. This is a clever approach to receivers but one that few brands dare risk. Another effective no-mention advertisement was just three words: 'Beanz meanz WHO?' No prizes for guessing which brand.

It is often said that to be effective an advertisement must be read, understood, believed, remembered and finally acted upon. This is a good list when developing and testing a suitable message. It is another variant of the AIDA progression already mentioned on several occasions. It leads into the question of repetition of messages. Do you remember a message on the first hearing, or does it take several repeats to really understand? For an advertiser, there is no firm rule. Some messages for some audiences require a number of opportunities to see (OTS), others are remembered on the first showing. But the requirement needs to be established before the media planning stage, so the media schedule neither undershows nor overexposes an advertisement.

An issue in campaign planning that is often ignored is the need for *consistency* in the messages offered. It is important for a brand to gain a suitable position in its market. The communication is part of the development of this position. Also, it is very difficult to change opinions held about a mature brand. It is, however, very easy to confuse customers through inconsistent messages. Sometimes a new marketing manager is appointed, and to create activity he/she changes the advertising. This might bring a new, fresh image to the product. It is acceptable if it is part of a well-thought-out campaign, but all too often it is confusing. If a new campaign ignores past messages and is inconsistent when placed alongside them, it has to work that much harder to achieve the desired result. A recent example is:

> Allied Domecq relaunched its flagging sherry brand Harveys Luncheon Dry across the globe to woo a younger and more up-market customer. The dry sherry was renamed Dune and repackaged in an elegant bottle to build up distribution in fashionable restaurant and retail outlets. The brand was also made less dry.
>
> (*Source: Marketing*, 10 April 1997)

One final point regarding the advertising message is its role in reinforcing a buying decision. If a customer has just bought a major product, then interest in that product category continues beyond the actual time of purchase. Advertisements featuring both the model purchased and competitive models will be studied with interest. Even if the real purpose of an advertisement is to persuade rather than reinforce, the high probability that recent purchasers will see it must be considered. The key benefits need to appeal to this group as well, as they can also influence future sales by their word-of-mouth endorsement of the product – a very useful addition to any marketing communication programme.

It is impossible to select word-of-mouth as a communication medium, although it is a very effective medium, and a supplier can hope everything else in the offer is sufficiently attractive to ensure good personal recommendation.

ADVERTISING MEDIA

In most developed countries there will be a range of advertising media available, from TV and radio to press, posters and other media. International differences in media availability and provision do exist, though, through factors such as advertising controls (e.g. on commercial TV in Sweden), or technology development, or for economic, cultural or historical reasons (e.g. compare the USA with markets such as India or New Zealand).

Table 16.1   Major UK advertising media and 1998 advertising expenditures

Media type	1998 Advertising expenditure (£m)	No. of titles/stations/sites
Television	4029	13 regional companies, plus GMTV, Channels 4 & 5, satellite and cable
National newspapers	1793	14 daily and 11 Sunday titles
Regional newspapers	2389	Includes morning, evening and Sunday regional titles
Consumer magazines	710	Over 3500 titles
Business and professional journals	1209	Over 6300 titles
Outdoor/transport	563	Includes 82 000 poster panels
Radio	463	241 commercial stations
Cinema	97	2680 screens (many multiplex)

Note: This does not include directories, press production costs or direct mail expenditures.

Source : Information Centre, The Advertising Association <http://www.adassoc.org.uk>

Total 1998 UK advertising expenditure amounted to £14 307 million. Of this, more than 80 per cent was spent on display advertising in the press, broadcast, print and outdoor media. The remainder was accounted for by classified advertising (small ads), financial, legal and corporate notices, recruitment ads and business/professional press advertisements (*Source*: The Advertising Association). Table 16.1 presents a summary of UK advertising by media.

Advertising revenue forms a large proportion of the income for most media owners, so they have to 'market' their 'product' to potential customers, agencies and advertisers. The benefit offered by the media is access to the relevant target customers – that is, the one the advertiser is trying to reach. To help identify the relevant groups the media owners supply *very detailed profiles* of their readers/viewers. The matching of these groups with the target audience has been greatly increased by the use of computers, and media planning is now a highly specialised business.

Several years ago most advertising agencies offered a full service of account handling, research, planning, creative and media. Over the last 15 years more specialists have developed, concentrating on just one of these functions. The more successful are creative hot-houses and media planning specialists. If a company wished to do its own creative work it could still use a specialist agency to buy the media.

Decisions on media buying cover the right medium for the message, and then the interrelated question of frequency versus coverage – that is, how many opportunities to see against the percentage of the target market reached (covered) by the advertisement. The figures produced by the media planning packages are usually the averages. If an average OTS is 10 then that inevitably means some people see it on more occasions and some less. The ideal is never obtained. Also a highly concentrated campaign where there is an OTS of 10 over a period of a week or two will have a different result to one where the 10 OTS are spread out at one per month.

The vehicle for advertising is mass media. Each insertion of an advertisement in the chosen media is likely to be directed at a group of people and not an individual. As it is also one-way communication, there is an inevitable lag before any feedback can be obtained. Therefore there is rarely any opportunity to modify a campaign after it has been launched. Pre-testing must involve both the message and the media as the two are inseparable in the actual campaign. Indeed, advertising commentators such as Marquis (1998), have stressed the need for media choice, and media strategies generally, to be guided by careful consideration of brand equity and history.

Figure 16.1

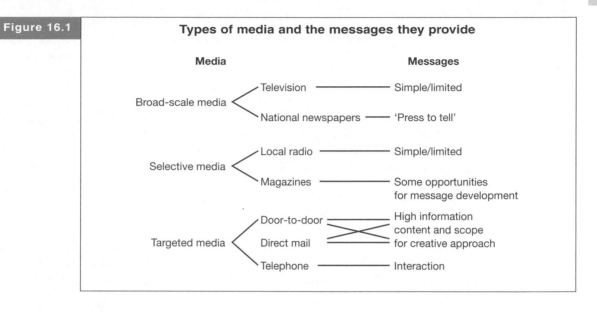

Types of media and the messages they provide

The choice between the different media will be taken based on the different strengths of each: that is, not only the ability to reach the target group efficiently, but the effective way in which that message is delivered. The issue of cost per thousand (CPT, a measure of media cost divided by audience) is relevant only when comparing two media of equal effectiveness. For TV, press and other media, actual space costs will vary around the published 'rate-card' prices, with higher rates for prime positions (in print media) or spots (broadcast media), and discounts available for less popular positions and 'package' deals. The choice is therefore both the media used and the relevance of the timing or position in that media.

Lead-times are also important. Newspaper advertisements are quick to produce and so can be very topical. Lead-times for monthly magazines tend to be quite long, while weekly Sunday newspaper colour supplements tend to be booked early. Television also cannot be rushed, although the use of video has helped here. Although all these aspects are relevant, the key decision still is the one concerning 'the right media for the message' (Figure 16.1).

Commercial television

This is the most important non-personal communication channel with very wide coverage to its audience. How many people come home from a day's work, have something to eat and then sit watching television for the remainder of the evening? If they watch a commercial television station they will be subjected, during the course of an evening, to many commercial breaks, in which a large variety of products will be advertised. There may also be some exposure of products on the non-commercial channels, especially with sponsored sports events.

The television stations research in great detail the type of audience expected to watch each of their programmes. Similar detailed research is also carried out with regard to the other non-personal media and their audiences. For television, it is to be expected that toys will be advertised during the period when children's programmes are screened, whereas products like cars might be featured in the evening, say around news bulletins.

Television does not offer lasting images, but it does combine sound and moving pictures in a very powerful way. Advertising, using television as the medium of communication, is considered one of the quickest ways of ensuring that your product is known to a wide audience. The technical terms coverage and OTS (opportunities to see) are used in advertising. Coverage is the percentage of the potential audience that is reached, OTS is the number of chances they have to see a particular advertisement.

In Britain 97 per cent of homes have a television set, and 50 per cent have two or more sets. The figures vary slightly for different European countries. In Norway 99 per cent of homes have television, whereas in Greece only 78 per cent do. Major 'soap' serials get regular audiences of 10–20 million viewers in Britain, although specialist programmes such as 'gardening' are more relevant for particular products. The UK commercial television stations are regional. It is therefore possible to use geographic segmentation, as well as including other demographic and psychographic segmentation features related to programmes, when timing commercials.

In recent years satellite television has gained in popularity in Britain as the price of receiving equipment has fallen. The cable networks have increasingly drawn on the products of the satellite companies and the actual ownership of satellite dishes is increasing steadily.

An extension of television advertising is *product placement*. This is where the company pays the broadcaster a fee to ensure regular exposure of its product within the context of a specified programme. Any such exposure is felt to be beneficial. Television is such a powerful medium for images and associations that a saying has emerged in the industry: 'Television to sell, newspapers to tell.' This, of course, links to the objectives of a communication campaign.

The press

The press includes all forms of the following: newspapers both local and national; magazines; directories; and year books. If it is 'press to tell' the fact that twice as much is spent on newspaper and magazine advertising compared with commercial television will show the importance of the printed media.

Newspapers

The advertisements carried will obviously depend on whether the newspaper has national or local distribution. With local papers there is always a large section of classified advertisements. There are usually so many advertisements placed by the general public and small local firms that they are split up into different categories and displayed in groups.

Exercise	Find out how much it costs to advertise in your local newspapers. Is it much less than in a national newspaper?

There are a wide variety of daily newspapers on sale in Britain and the newspapers in general portray a wide spectrum of political views. To some extent it is possible to divide their readers into broad political and socio-economic groups. Most readers have a brand loyalty to the paper of their choice and will buy it each day. However, the loyalties may be changing as newspapers regularly use price promotions to increase sales. Other promotion tools being used include free papers, vouchers on Saturday for

Sunday papers and other tempting offers. The competition between newspapers is an example of aggressive marketing and it would be a good exercise to monitor the effect on circulation, readership and profit. Generally, however, it is possible to segment the readership and target specific groups with certain advertisements. Many newspapers have developed a strategy where specific days of the week are used regularly to advertise certain things on a larger scale, sometimes jobs, sometimes cars or perhaps property.

Almost 90 per cent of the population has access to a newspaper, but in order for the same advertisement to reach this population, a tremendous number of advertisements would have to be placed; that is why knowledge of the readership is so important. As a medium for target marketing it is very powerful. There is a great deal of flexibility in newspaper advertising where the size of the advertisement, appearance, and colour, are a few of the variables available.

In general, the public have a greater propensity to believe the written word. Certainly a lot of information can be given in a newspaper advertisement. A disadvantage with placing an advertisement in a newspaper is that it is likely to have a very short lifespan as newspapers tend to be read on the day they are published, and then are soon discarded.

Magazines

There are a great many magazines covering subjects which range from those covering topics of general interest to ones on highly specialist subjects. For practically any hobby or interest, it is possible to find some magazine which caters for enthusiasts. There is an obvious link between a magazine and the lifestyle of its reader. It is therefore much easier for advertisers to be more selective by segmenting and targeting their audience through the use of magazines. For example, someone buying *Prima* magazine is likely to be interested in fashion, craft, knitting and beauty, and have far different interests from someone buying the *New Musical Express*, unless of course they have interest in both subjects.

Magazines do not suffer from the disadvantage of being discarded on the day they are published. Many are saved for several years by the people who buy them and are used as a source of reference. They may be passed from friend to friend until the copy is battered and torn, or they may be stacked in doctors' or dentists' waiting rooms. They are normally read and digested at a more leisurely pace than newspapers. *Vogue* claims that every copy is read by an average of eight people, so a circulation of 180 000 means a readership of almost 1.5 million people.

Exercise	List places where old copies of magazines are placed. Do many people have access to them? Are they read?

Many products can be enhanced by good-quality colour advertisements and in magazines most advertisements for food products would fall into this category. High quality does mean high production costs but the results can be worth the expense.

Exercise	Find out the cost of advertising in your favourite magazine.

Directories and year books

Directories and year books range from the *Yellow Pages* directory to the *Daily Mail Year Book*, and would even include diaries promoted by a professional organisation. They include a tremendous amount of information and promote many different fields of interest. Despite being relatively inexpensive as a vehicle of communication, they can be highly effective. A local plumber having a large entry in the local *Yellow Pages* directory can win many customers. If the advertisement is good, and the plumber then proves to be a reliable worker for the customer who chose him from the directory, the plumber will be recommended to others and thus expand his business.

> **Exercise** Examine your local *Yellow Pages* directory. What size and kind of advertisements gain most attention?

Radio

Radios are a major communication media for some more 'captive' audiences, reaching car drivers as well as factory audio systems, while they are often just turned on as background sound in the home.

Radio commercials are much less expensive to produce than television commercials, but do not have the same advantages: there is no visual presentation, so only the aural senses are assailed. However, the medium is used by both local and national companies. Local organisations are able to target their message very precisely and at very reasonable costs. Programme sponsorship has become popular in recent years.

Radio messages are usually short-lived and they do not have the impact of television. Radio is sometimes described as 'noisy wallpaper'. Radio accounts for only just under 3 per cent of all advertising spending. Repetition is often necessary to create attention.

Cinema

As a vehicle of communication, cinema has had a chequered past in that its popularity has moved with the times. In Britain the cinema was very popular in the 1940s and 1950s, but its popularity waned in the 1960s and 1970s when audiences fell to an all-time low. There was a recovery in audience figures in the 1990s with the advent of multiplex screens. Advertising in the cinema has many of the same advantages of sound and moving pictures as television. Perhaps the cinema audience is slightly more captive – the majority of cinema goers tend to be in the age range 15–34 and it is therefore possible for precise target marketing to take place. As an advertising medium, cinema is popular with local businesses such as restaurants that are in relatively close proximity to the cinema.

> **Exercise** Next time you are at a cinema, note the type of advertising that is shown. Would the advertising vary from screen to screen if one was showing a Walt Disney film and another an Arnold Schwarzenegger film?

Outdoor media

Outdoor advertising can be a very effective channel of communication, and it is also one of the cheapest, in terms of cost per thousand (CPT) of the adult population reached. Most of the adult population have the opportunity to see (OTS) posters every day. For this reason, posters tend to offer an ideal form of reminder advertising, often as a back-up to a mainstream TV or press campaign. Message content in outdoor advertising is often necessarily short and simple, though this by no means reduces its effectiveness, and commentators such as Fry (1999) have stressed that outdoor advertising can demonstrate its own unique opportunities for creativity. Not only does outdoor media include large posters, but also outdoor features such as parking meters and litter bins can act as host sites to advertisements. Every year more host sites seem to be discovered: carpark tickets are one example, with McDonald's using the back of carpark tickets to offer special prices on meals. More exotic outdoor vehicles include tethered balloons and aerial advertising, though these can be expensive.

Exercise What outdoor media other than posters are you aware of? How effective as channels of communication are they?

Transport advertising on the sides of buses has become very popular, and other commercial vehicles advertise company names and telephone numbers. However, advertising is not limited to the sides of larger vehicles. Taxis always have their telephone number displayed prominently, and now are often painted in the livery of a major advertiser.

Exercise Study the advertisements on as many modes of transport as possible. Compare the variety of products which are advertised. Is there a common theme?

Passengers in transit, in planes, trains, taxis, buses or underground trains are effectively a captive audience for the various types of advertisements to which they are exposed. Transport termini such as airports, bus and railway stations are also obvious sites for poster advertising.

Exercise Next time you are at a railway station or bus station, note the *number*, *location*, *size* and *subject* of poster advertisements. Are there any common factors within the examples that you note? Are there any differences between these and posters to be seen at city centre and roadside locations?

The size of the posters also varies, but there has been a concentrated effort by the advertising agencies to standardise the size of posters to ninety-six, forty-eight and six sheet size which increases impact and reduces production costs. There is also a move to increase poster illumination as they need to work after dark as well as during daylight. Mechanised posters which change picture are also on the increase.

The sites chosen to display posters are of paramount importance, the aim being for as many people as possible to see them. Sporting events are popular sites, especially if they are in areas which may be televised – such as Premier League football grounds. Competition for good sites is fierce and there is much creativity in discovering unusual sites where there could be an increasing impact from the advertisement. The use of electric scoreboards is an example of an unusual medium that is being used with success.

ADVERTISING AGENCIES

An advertising agency should be an extension of an organisation's marketing department. It can bring specific skills to the partnership, and these should enhance the ability of a company to get the most from its advertising. Agencies can be large, London-based, high-profile operations with international connections, or small, local but equally professional set-ups. The skills they have are related to communication in media. Since no two advertising problems are alike, each needs to be considered separately and in detail. Agencies can be what is termed 'full-service', offering all services to their clients. However, there is an increasing number of specialist agencies, concentrating on just one function.

As in any rewarding relationship, honesty and trust are needed to work towards the best solution. The agency skills are in projecting messages either visually or in words. The main functions in a full-service agency usually consist of the following:

1 A selection of creative teams comprising an art director and a copywriter, each team specialising in particular media. Agency reputations are often built on their creativity. These groups work closely with the production groups who translate approved creative ideas into finished commercials.

2 The account supervisor/director function, really a key account manager who builds and maintains the relationship in the same way as a sales manager might in another organisation. They also get involved with specialist areas such as advertising research, and other services directly relevant to the client relationship.

3 The media planning and buying function which contributes in this vital area.

The clients work directly with the account team, but there is no reason why they should not meet and help brief the other functions. However, clients should not try to do the agency's job. The way to be a good client is to give a clear brief and, when evaluating work, to do so fairly but as a total package.

It must be remembered, however, that agencies are in business, and sometimes are very profitable. They started as agents for the media owners and that is the basis of the commission payments they receive when booking space. The Institute of Practitioners in Advertising (IPA) recommend that contracts from full-service agencies should allow a 15 per cent net (17.65 per cent gross) margin on media. Even after the Office of Fair Trading (OFT) ruling that the fixed 15 per cent standard rate commission represents a restrictive practice, many agencies still benefit from increased media spend by their clients. There are other elements of the promotional and marketing mix which compete for marketing investment, and sometimes agencies forget this. Some agencies do offer a range of additional marketing services alongside the advertising role. These could include marketing research, marketing planning, precision marketing/direct mail, publicity/PR and sales promotion. At times these will be offered from the main agency, and sometimes from a separate agency in the same group. As with the basic agency relationship, a lot will depend on the interaction between the marketing manager for the client and the account supervisor in the agency. One client might feel comfortable with various services from a single group, others might use separate researchers or promotional groups.

The idea that a full-service agency can save the Marketing Director time has rightly been challenged. Certainly such one-stop-shop agencies should be able to offer a more integrated approach to client needs. But not all clients (advertisers) need to achieve this by buying from a single source. However well the agency is briefed, it is still an agency. The advertiser knows the product intimately and can assess the requirements. The different services can all be bought separately, but increasingly it is the media buying function which is being placed with a specialist. Figure 16.2 shows a traditional advertising agency structure.

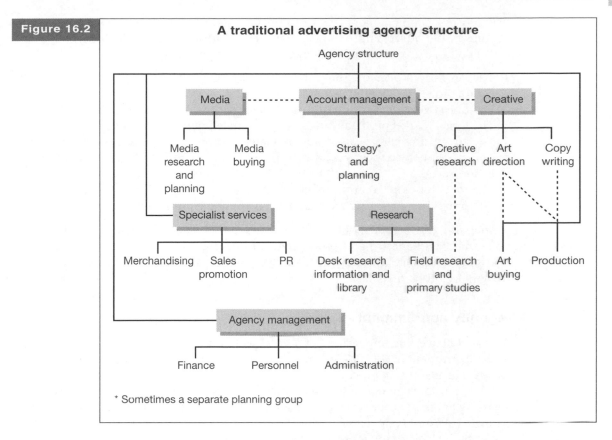

Figure 16.2 A traditional advertising agency structure

For other elements of the promotional mix such as direct marketing, publicity or sales promotion, there are both separate, independent agencies and members of large communications groups. The structure of creative, account handling and delivery of message are still present in these agencies. They need to be judged as any supplier on the basis of their abilities. If an organisation decides to use an agency, then a proper briefing is appropriate.

Briefing an agency

This section refers primarily to briefing a specialist advertising agency. However, the issues can easily be adapted to cover any agency retained to advise on part or all of the communications mix.

Before appointing an agency, it is necessary to go through a *selection process*. This can involve a competitive pitch, where several agencies are given the same brief and asked to present their plans. These presentations can be very elaborate and expensive for the participating agencies. Sometimes the client offers a payment to subsidise the agency costs, but for very large accounts many agencies are prepared to invest, in the hope of landing a profitable account. As the process of agency appointment is somewhat different to briefing *per se*, a separate section is devoted to it below.

When briefing a new agency an advertiser has to give rather more background information than would be given to an incumbent agency which would already have the basic data. Mercer (1992) gives an excellent study on the process of developing advertising from a good brief and lays stress on the extent to which the proposed advertising meets the advertising objectives within it. Although the list below repeats some earlier points, it gives the key headings necessary for a good brief:

1 The key benefit offered – the USP (why that product should be bought ahead of its competitors)
2 The objectives of the communication mix and the advertising role within it
3 The target market profiled using the appropriate segmentation data
4 The advertising message, and how it relates to other communication messages
5 The amount to be spent on advertising within the context of the total communication spend
6 The media chosen to carry the advertising
7 The prevailing marketing environment, including competition.

A brief will give details about all these issues and should also include any historical issue that could affect the responsiveness of the target group. It is also important to share any up-to-date and relevant research data with the agency to ensure they are able to work as full partners.

Agency appointment

As noted above, the importance of a good working relationship makes the selection and appointment of the advertising agency an important precondition for success in the overall advertising process.

While a number of researchers have presented insights into the criteria employed in selecting advertising agencies (e.g. Crosier, 1999; Mahoney, 1995), no really definitive listing exists, and there may be wide variations from company to company. Table 16.2 presents a collage of some of the more oft-cited selection factors.

Some of the factors cited in Table 16.2 are rather self-evident and require little elaboration – e.g. creativity demonstrated (in its presentation) by the agency, and its overall track record and reputation. Other factors might merit further comment. Under the 'people' dimension, clients would obviously form impressions about whether the general approach and culture of an agency was sufficiently people-centred, and particularly, whether the proposed 'account team' performed and integrated well (i.e. at the 'pitch' presentation). In more advertising-related terms, judgements on agency marketing analysis are obviously quite relevant, while many clients would be interested in the level of service responsiveness of the agency and its overall business efficiency.

While such factors are commonly cited as agency choice criteria, the reportings of a number of researchers (e.g. Lace, 1998; Ghosh and Taylor, 1999) indicate that they continue to be prime ingredients in client views on what makes for positive agency performance, and what constitutes a good client–agency relationship.

Table 16.2 Some common selection factors behind choice of advertising agency

■ Creativity	■ Business efficiency	■ Size and location	■ People chemistry
■ Marketing aspects	■ Agency record	■ Service responsiveness	■ Account team make-up

Table 16.3   Advertising effectiveness

Relative ad/sales compared to direct competitors	Average share of market (%)
Much less	14
Less	20
Equal	25
More	26
Much more	32

ADVERTISING EFFECTIVENESS

The subject of advertising effectiveness has been a contentious issue for a very long time. One study, undertaken by advertising man Alex Biel using the substantial PIMS database of over 3000 companies in USA and Europe, looked at comparative advertising to sales ratios related to market share. The results are shown in Table 16.3.

While these results could simply reflect the fact that major brands can afford to spend more on advertising than minor brands, the numbers and diversity of the firms investigated would suggest a correlation between advertising expenditure and market share. These results must be seen against research by Abraham and Lodish who concluded that only 46 per cent of the established brands they studied received a positive sales impact from advertising.

Exercise

> Think of television advertisements which you have seen recently that have encouraged you or anyone in your household to take action by doing something or purchasing a particular product. What was it in the advertisement that really stimulated action? Was there already some prior knowledge or propensity to that action? What part did the advertisement play in the process?

Usually some form of *attitudinal research* or a *continuous tracking* study is carried out. Certainly 'benchmarks' can be established for targets such as level of unprompted awareness, level of message recall, stated brand preference and knowledge of facts included in the advertisement. These measures are mainly to do with measuring the effect of the communication. Even brand preference, as measured following a campaign, does not link precisely into actual sales. For many businesses the bottom line from any of their promotional investment is increased sales, though there are many problems in attempting advertising reviews based on sales effects. For one thing, sales data correlations may well exist, but indicate nothing about the direction of causality. Equally, as many authors point out (e.g. White, 1997), advertising is but one contributor to communications objectives, much less sales objectives, so that logic would indicate a more holistic approach to effectiveness research.

Exercise

> For the UK government Health Education programme different objectives apply. These could be changing people's behaviour because of the risk of AIDS. The research carried out following a major AIDS campaign showed that the awareness of AIDS had exceeded the targets set. The worry was that few people said they had changed or were about to change their behaviour in spite of the new knowledge. If you look at the anti-smoking campaigns over many years it will be seen that behavioural changes happened very slowly, even though levels of knowledge had changed.

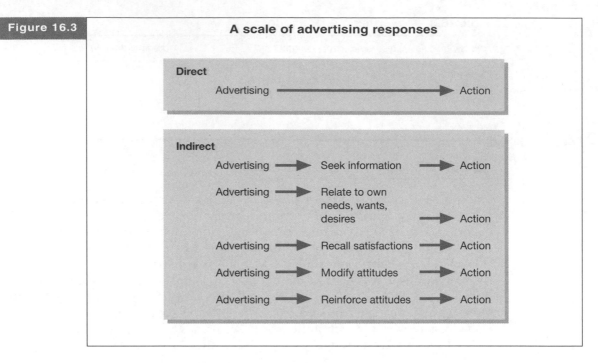

Figure 16.3

A scale of advertising responses

The problem is not how to give information, but how to persuade the target audience to *act*. Because of this, it is usually inappropriate to measure the desired actions. It is more appropriate to measure against objectives related to the message. There are occasions where direct response is obvious. Say a charity advertises for donations to meet a particularly severe problem of malnutrition in Somalia; they can immediately measure donations and they do not worry if these are new gifts of money or donations which would otherwise have been made to an alternative charity. The short-term effect is easily quantified. There is also a long-term effect, for although the effect of a particular communication reduces with time, there will be some lasting subconscious residue which could mean you donate to 'Save the Children' again next time. This long-term shift is not so easily measured.

Work by Stephen King (1975) showed the gap between the desired action and the various ways of measuring advertising effectiveness. He suggested a scale of responses dependent on the task to be undertaken, as illustrated in Figure 16.3.

QUESTIONS

1 *Explain the reason why it is said 'TV to sell, Press to tell'?*

2 *Why should an advertiser use an agency to create and place advertising?*

3 *What problems can be caused by trying to include a complex message in an advertisement?*

4 *Why might an attention-grabbing advertisement fail to achieve its objectives?*

5 *Suggest a suitable situation for a 'pull' as opposed to a 'push' strategy.*

FURTHER READING

Aakers, D. A. and Myers, J. G. (1987) *Advertising Management*, 3rd edn. Prentice-Hall.

Abraham, M. and Lodish, L. (1996), 'Getting the most out of advertising and promotion', *Harvard Business Review*. May–June.

Beil, A. L. (1990),'Strong brand – high spend', *Admap*, November.

Boyd, P. (1992), 'Data protection', *Marketing Business*, May.

Brannan, T. (1995) *A Practical Guide to Integrated Marketing Communications*. Kogan Page.

Colley, R. H. (1961) *Defining Advertising Goals for Measured Advertising Results*. New York Association of Advertisers.

Corstjens, J. (1990) *Strategic Advertising: A Practitioner's Handbook*. Heinemann.

Crosier, K. (1999) 'Promotion', in M. J. Baker (ed.), *The Marketing Book*. 4th edn. Butterworth Heinemann.

Doyle, P. (1994) *Marketing Management and Strategy*. Prentice-Hall International.

Engel, J. F., Warshaw, M. R. and Kinnear, T. C. (1994) *Promotional Strategy*, 8th edn. Irwin.

Fill, C. (1995) *Marketing Communications*. Prentice-Hall.

Fry, A. (1999), 'A leap in outdoor creativity', *Marketing*, 23 September, p. 19.

Ghosh, B. C. and Taylor, D. (1999), 'Switching advertising agency – a cross-country analysis', *Marketing Intelligence and Planning*, 17(3).

Hart, N. (1995) *The Practice of Advertising*, 4th edn. Heinemann/CIM.

King, S. (1975) 'Practical progress from a theory of advertising', *Admap*, October.

Lace, J. M. (1998), 'Evaluating advertising agency performance: actions to enhance the client/agency relationship', *Management Research News*, 27(7/8), pp. 47–59.

Lavidge, R. and Steiner, A. (1961) 'A model for predictive measurement of advertisement effectiveness', *Journal of Marketing*, October.

Mahoney, L. (1995) 'Choosing an advertising agency', *Bank Marketing*, 27(12).

Marquis, S. (1998) 'Media strategies must be built on a brand foundation', *Marketing*, 3 September.

McNulty, W. K. (1985) UK Change Through a Wide Angle Lens. Futures.

Mercer, D. (1992) *Marketing*. Blackwell.

Miles, L. (1992) 'Going solo', *Marketing Business*, June.

Mueller, B. (1996) *International Advertising – Communicating Across Cultures*. Wadsworth Publishing/Thomson.

Peters, T. (1988) *Thriving on Chaos*. Macmillan.

Ries, A. and Trout, J. (1981) *Positioning the Battle for Your Mind*. McGraw-Hill.

White, R. (1997) 'Shouldn't we be assessing the effectiveness of total communications campaigns rather than individual techniques?', *International Journal of Advertising*, 16(2), p. 118.

CASE STUDY

Cavendish Hair Studios

Cavendish Hair Studios is a medium-sized hair salon based in a busy market town in North East Leicestershire. It was originally a 'unisex' hairdresser, established by Brian Cavendish some 26 years ago, and now run by son Darren and his wife Julie, both qualified hair stylists.

There are now separate 'studios' for male and female customers, though demarcation of staff across the two sides, or of the joint proprietors, is by no means absolute, mostly for efficiency and flexibility reasons.

Additional to the hairdressing business, which accounts for some 90 per cent of business turnover, there is a modest ground floor beauty shop on-site which retails designer skin, hair and female beauty products, and which is supervised by Julie.

Darren Cavendish has recently become concerned about a downturn in business, which he ascribes to the opening during the last year of three well-appointed competitor salons in the town – two of them better located than Cavendish. These newcomers are all-female salons, which leads Darren to correlate this with his own revenue fall (of some 15 per cent over the year, mostly on the female hair side).

In an effort to analyse the problem better, he has recently hired the services of a TEC consultant, who has helped install a customer database, founded on the manual appointment books of the last 18 months. This indicates some 3000 female customers in all, though analysis of the dormant ratio has not been done. (Male customers, who account for 30 per cent of hair trade, do not usually make appointments, so there are few records.)

Darren estimates that his regular female customers come on average once every 4–6 weeks, and spend on average £20–25 (though some more expensive highlight and other treatments cost £451). He feels that his prices are reasonable, and comparable with others and does not anyway want to trade on the basis of price discounting (he has never been keen on concession prices, even for OAPs, and anyway would consider too old a customer profile as bad).

As he feels his downturn is a function of increased competition, he reckons he must promote the business more aggressively, and possibly reach a wider catchment area – he has customer addresses and telephone numbers for maybe half his female clientele.

His TEC consultant contact has mentioned the possibility of a door-to-door leaflet drop, through a local firm, but Darren feels this would cheapen his image. Instead, he is seriously considering contacting a design specialist, to produce artwork for local weekly newspaper advertising, which he understands would cost some £250 per week for a postcard-size ad. What he is less certain about is the amount and timing to decide on for his advertising, and whether to consider other publications, local radio or even posters.

Questions

1 *Do you consider that Darren has diagnosed his business problem?*

2 *What further analysis could be done to aid problem-solving?*

3 *Assuming an identified need for advertising, what course of action do you think appropriate?*

Direct and on-line marketing

INTRODUCTION

Direct marketing is the use of direct media to reach a target. There have always been opportunities to use direct mail, door-to-door and telephone communications. The actual media choices are rather wider than these but the growth in direct marketing has come about because of the:

■ development of database marketing
■ proliferation of new products
■ multiplication of distribution channels
■ demassification of markets
■ decrease in the 'efficiency' of mass media.

These subjects are discussed in the excellent book by Rapps and Collins (1987) which used the term 'maxi-marketing'. Maxi-marketing is the requirement of marketing to achieve:

■ maximum efficient reach to target customers
■ maximum chance of marketing sales
■ maximum opportunity to develop relationships.

Direct marketing is much more personal than mass advertising, and so it can be a key part of the development of relationships with customers. In 1983 Levitt suggested that:

> the future will be a future of more and more intensified relationships, especially in industrial marketing, but also increasingly even in frequently purchased consumer goods.

Now, of course, relationship marketing is a reality.

Technology is developing fast in the area of communications, but so is the skill base to use it effectively. Jane Bird suggests that in the next five years there will be two types of company: those that use the computer as a marketing tool and those that face bankruptcy. This might be an overexaggeration, but harnessing the skills of 'database marketing' to the 'direct marketing media' is producing 'precision marketing'. The distinction between 'direct marketing' and 'database marketing' is well discussed by Keith Fletcher and his colleagues. They suggest Shaw and Stone's definition of database marketing as:

> an interactive approach to marketing communication, which uses individually addressable communications media (such as mail, telephone and the sales force) to: extend help to a company's target audience; stimulate their demand; and stay close to them by recording and keeping an

electronic database memory of customers, prospects and all communications and commercial contacts, to help all future contacts.

The high-quality, computerised database must then be linked to direct response media, which includes everything from the so-called 'junk mail' to statement stuffers and electronic media. The advantages are:

- better targeting
- powerful personal communications
- flexibility
- creative opportunities
- controlled timing
- controlled input.

Jane Bird describes a mailing to thousands of customers of the Nationwide Anglia Building Society. Obviously each letter is personalised to a named recipient. The additional element is that each letter offers a personalised offer based on detailed segmentation and geo-demographics. The mailing is therefore designed to give a *different message to each different segment*, so that this should be of much greater relevance than a circular sent to all customers.

The key to success in any communication is access to the audience, reaching the chosen target. However good the message, if it fails to reach its target recipient, it is wasted. It used to be thought that a poor message reaching the right target could do some good – witness the general circulars and junk mail still in use. However, the wrong message can leave the relationship with the receiver if not neutral then actually harmed. The retaining of customers, and building of deep, profitable relationships can be achieved only if customers believe you know them and their needs. David Jones, formerly of Grattan Mail Order, said: 'You don't send a gardening catalogue to someone living in a high rise flat.' All mail order companies are developing sophisticated databases – and, most importantly, they are continually refining them to keep them up to date. The precision that direct marketing now offers is luring large firms such as Heinz and Lever Brothers, the UK arm of the Anglo–Dutch giant Unilever. Both firms see direct marketing as a more precise way to target individual consumers and have allocated large portions of their advertising budget to it.

The action of these two large companies is consistent with the view that manufacturers must become more aware of how important it is to strike a good balance between the advertising media they use. It has become obvious that television will be used more to build up brand awareness and company knowledge while direct marketing can be used to accurately pinpoint targeted consumers and gain immediate response.

Apart from the absolute precision afforded by direct marketing, other reasons why it is gaining in popularity, especially in America, is that the cost of advertising on television is very expensive, coupled with the fact that it is hard to calculate the cost-effectiveness of such television advertising. One solution is that an increasing number of firms are now experimenting with a form of direct marketing on television where advertisements are shown along with a freephone number that viewers can call to place orders for the product. In Britain on satellite/cable television such adverts are becoming commonplace: products advertised in this way include jewellery, kitchen knives and car polish.

When assessing media cost the role of 10 × applies. The following rule is a rough guide to costs:

1 Television can cost as little as £10 per 1000.
2 Magazines vary greatly but maybe cost £50 per 1000 (5p each).
3 Direct mail is again 10 times more expensive – £500 per 1000 (50p per contact).
4 Telemarketing costs £5000 per 1000 (£5 each contact).
5 Personal direct selling can be in excess of £50 per call.

However, it is not the cost that counts but the *effectiveness*. A telesales operation replacing regular weekly sales calls could save £45 per customer per call. But the sales call still produces more business so it is a real saving. On the other hand, if a well-targeted direct mail shot sent to a well-chosen segment brings more enquiries than from a magazine with a much larger circulation, there is a real gain. The gains are much greater and every reply adds information to the database, and can be used next time to improve the performance yet further. It is this constant development which really brings long-term gains in effective communications.

TARGETED MEDIA

Direct mail

The director of the European Direct Marketing Association (EDMA), Alena Hola, quoted in *Marketing Business*, said: 'Some postal authorities do not seem to have grasped the fact that companies will only use direct mail if it is the most cost-effective, efficient and reliable tool available to sell their products.'

Technological change has become a threat to European postal authorities – the most lucrative customers have been seeking alternative ways of having their goods delivered. Private carriers have been gaining in popularity at the expense of the postal service. They have seen the opportunity to gain customers by offering extra services at no extra cost.

Some postal monopolies in Europe are being abolished in an effort to create a more efficient system. Sweden, whose postal monopoly was abolished in 1993, now has the most liberal postal system in Europe, with only 5 per cent of her mail sourced from individuals, the other 95 per cent coming either from business or direct mail.

Direct mail, despite having competition, has become more popular, with over 2.6 billion items a year sent in the UK, and an expenditure of £1666 million. In Britain the average household will receive about seven items of direct mail every month, but in other European countries this figure varies.

Mailing lists can come from various sources, for example:

■ Electoral register – geodemographic selection
■ Named subscribers to business magazines
■ Companies classified by SIC code.

It is now possible to classify households by town, region, television area, type of property, lifestyle, income, spending habits, the drive time from retail outlets and even the number of pets, babies and plants in the house. This information revolution has led to direct marketing gaining customers, as targeting can be very sophisticated. Whether this popularity will continue remains to be seen, but there is much ground to be covered by direct mail before much of Europe reaches the same levels of usage as the USA.

Direct mail

When direct mail is sent using the names of the target customer personally, then it moves into the realm of a personalised communication. The ability to use a more personalised approach has come about owing to the advanced technology afforded by computers.

Many people claim they are not influenced by 'junk mail'. However, a response rate of a few percentage points is often enough for a mailing to be considered a success. The economics of direct mail depend on the complexity of the actual item mailed, and the postage (which can be up to a third of the cost). The address list must be relevant to the offer, and the mailing itself must create attention. One company sent a mailing from Moscow. This not only dramatically reduced postage costs, but the letters from Russia created interest among recipients to the benefit of the sender. It is important, however, to ensure that the correct name/title of the proposed recipient is used, otherwise offence can be engendered and a potential customer lost.

The direct mail industry has set up a service, the Mailing Preference Service which offers consumers the possibility of either increasing or decreasing the volume of direct mail they receive.

Exercise	Over the period of about one month note any direct mail correspondence that is sent direct to a named person within the household. Make a note of the accuracy of the printed name and address, and any code numbers that might indicate their source. Note also any immediate or likely response to the mailings. How effective did they prove?

Telemarketing

As head of Direct Marketing and Sales Promotion at BT, Phil Mounsey, has been quoted as saying: 'Telemarketing is the systematic use of the telephone to achieve business objectives in sales, customer care, market growth, promotions, market research, database building and cash flow management.'

One advantage of telesales or telemarketing is that it is a much cheaper way of reaching the target audience than sending a salesperson to call and has been defined as 'the systematic use of the telephone as a communications channel between a company and its customers'. Such communications are common in industrial and other business-to-business situations (B2B), in particular those concerning regular repeat orders. For example, in the bakery trade it is common for the flour supplier to telephone the bakery: the order can then be noted and dispatched very quickly. A representative from the flour company would then be required to call only at infrequent intervals in order to maintain good customer relations.

For teleselling to succeed, the companies involved must try to make the approach as personal as possible. Normally the target market is well researched, even if it is only to make note of their prospective customers' names from the telephone directory. Using someone's name, even as a potential customer, makes the telephone call seem more friendly. It is thus more difficult to disregard immediately. If a company relies entirely on telesales there is a problem in that the salesperson rarely establishes a close personal relationship with the customer. However, skilled telemarketers are able to project their personalities over the telephone. The medium has to be used with care as some people view unsolicited telephone calls as intrusive. This subject is discussed further in Chapter 19.

The last few years have witnessed a tremendous growth in the use of the Internet as an effective media for communication. In some cases it is personalised and therefore direct, in other uses it falls into the category of indirect media. Internet marketing is dealt with in more detail below. In one sense, of course, the Internet is no more than another direct medium, to be added to the direct marketer's toolkit. In another sense, though, the whole raft of linking technologies that it overlaps with represents a radically new scenario for marketers, and business managers generally.

THE INTERNET AND MARKETING

In the last few years the use and potential of the Internet has grown to the extent that it has become a necessary feature of everyday communications for millions of people within the developed world, and arguably the most revolutionary step ever made in communications technology. The scale of the technical revolution that it represents is testified by the fact that the estimated adoption period of internet/world wide web communications (based on achieving a benchmark of 50 million users) has been some four years, an adoption curve markedly shorter than previous technologies such as personal computers (16 years), TV (13 years) or radio (38 years). Further, it is estimated that traffic on the Internet is doubling every 100 days, indicating that both user population and intensity of usage are expanding geometrically.

The ever-growing influence and presence of the Internet has reached all sectors of social and commercial life, to the degree that it is difficult to read the newspapers or watch TV without seeing references to 'cyberspace', 'virtual technology' or 'e-commerce', and without encountering standard references to e-mail addresses and websites for individuals, public and private sector organisations alike.

Indeed, it is easy to forget that in the span of 25 years what started life as a US defence information tool had progressed to an academic and research mechanism, and more recently developed into a major business tool for the business community and society at large. Stroud (1996) argues that, while the various information retrieval and communications services related to the Internet were originally academic or research-related, their adoption and further development owes much to the growth of applications within the commercial sector. Within commercial applications, marketing usage has become increasingly significant.

Exercise	Identify a company website on the Internet. What is the purpose of the site? Is it more likely to be found by casual surfers or are potential customers guided to it?

In terms of both marketing and business transactions generally, the Internet is being integrated as a vital strategic tool, and certainly in marketing circles it is now commonplace to see company executives developing 'internet strategies' as key elements of corporate and marketing strategy.

Cronin (1996) has proposed that the marketing value of the Internet will be a function of customer connectivity, external competition, and network capabilities and access. Cronin sees four key competitive benefits:

- Cost/efficiency savings through substituting the Internet for other links with vendors, information providers and partners
- Performance improvement through internal usage of internet technology (e.g. intranets) to integrate resources, people and information

- Market penetration supported by high customer connectivity, including websites and on-line support services
- Product transformation, including the development of internet-driven products and services that re-map the company's strategic positioning.

Walters and Lancaster (1999) argue that appropriate use of the Internet can enhance value from product conception through to every link in the value chain. The critical links that the Internet gives to customers, vendors and suppliers facilitates all business processes, from commercial transactions and payment systems, to information transfer and two-way feedback. The strengthening of relationships across the whole supply chain has been furthered.

INTERNET MARKETING

The marketing applications of the Internet have arisen so recently and so rapidly that there has not yet developed a strict convention on what exact terminology to use for the field in general, or specific elements of it. Like many new developments, it will doubtless fall to popular usage to determine a clear classification of terms. To illustrate this potentially confusing situation, Table 17.1 lists a number of competing contenders for the 'name claim', though it can be seen that some of the terms are overlapping rather than exact equivalents in meaning.

For the purposes of this chapter, the term '*internet marketing*' will be used to refer to *all* applications of internet technology and facilities to all aspects of marketing.

'*On-line marketing*' is used here to denote the use of the Internet as a vehicle for direct marketing (as opposed to direct mail, telesales, etc.) though, again, it should be noted that usage varies, and certainly such direct marketing applications are but a minority of the growing uses of the Internet in marketing.

Figure 17.1 presents an overview of the various applications of the Internet in marketing, though the divisions are by no means watertight or exclusive.

Customer research and market information

As emphasized by Brooks (1999), the Internet is an incomparable source of marketing and market information, often free or through registration (log-on) procedures. Key market survey and specialist research sources (e.g. Mintel) are also available, regularly updated, through subscription; whilst vast quantities of government, publisher and media data are accessible on-line. Strauss and Frost (1999) stress the usefulness of internet information that is both detailed and up-to-date, while digital format reduces the cost of manual data entry.

Table 17.1   Internet marketing: alternative titles

■ Internet marketing	■ On-line marketing
■ Cybermarketing	■ Digital marketing
■ Web marketing	■ e-business
■ Net-marketing	■ e-commerce
■ Net shopping	■ e-tailing
■ Web-retailing	■ On-line retailing
■ Virtual shopping	■ Digital commerce

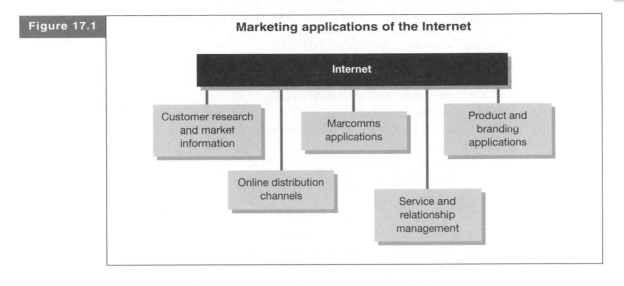

Figure 17.1

Marketing applications of the Internet

With increased internet usage, by customers, suppliers and other stakeholders, companies are finding it more practicable to conduct on-line primary research, through feedback web pages or customised questionnaires, or by e-mail or web conferencing and on-line discussions. Again, server software is now sophisticated enough to track and analyse visitor enquiries and search sequences and collect key (data-mining) information on customer classifications, on-line behaviour and order characteristics.

'MARCOMMS' APPLICATIONS

the Internet has firmly established itself as an up-and-coming marketing communications and promotion tool that offers many advantages over non-digital vehicles. It is cheap, fast, independent of time differences (asynchronous), and offers global access to a growing number and variety of users. As Evans and Wurster (1997) comment, traditional communication channels suffer from a pervasive trade-off between audience reach (= size and variety) and message richness (= detail, customisation). Interestingly, the Internet is not so affected by these constraints, and potentially offers the best of both worlds in this respect.

In many ways, of course, the Internet can be used in just the same way as other communications media, and it certainly is the case that marketers, advertising, promotion and publicity specialists are increasingly including internet advertising and promotional activity as part of their multi-media campaigns.

As with more traditional media, internet advertising is no less subject to the need for good planning, pre-research, target audience profiling, communications creativity and effectiveness monitoring. Given the increasing 'noise' and competitiveness in internet advertising (e.g. through often a clutter of rival small ads, or 'banner advertisements'), on-line advertising is becoming more demanding in terms of creative treatments such as colour blends, animation and movement, music and sound effects, contests and 'freebies' offers, customised links to other product web sites and so forth.

Table 17.2 presents a summary of the variety of 'marcomms' applications that might be served by a dedicated company web site. It should be noted, though, that a web site should

Table 17.2   Marcomms' applications served by a website

Present general company information, and FAQs

Present on-line product range catalogue, detailed specs

Generate customer enquiries and requests

Inform/educate on new products, developments

Promotional information, special offers

Invite communications feedback, monitor effectiveness

Reinforce customer loyalty

Integrate with other promotional media

Communicate with/customise messages for specific groups or buyers

Support PR and image-building

not be treated as a stand-alone communications vehicle, but should support and integrate with other marcomms activities by the company.

Most of the applications within Table 17.2 are self-explanatory, though the list does illustrate the scope for on-line activity as part of an overall marcomms programme. Equally, this at least indirectly underlines the need for more traditional activities (e.g. sales promotion, PR), to accommodate and even actively exploit the new on-line vehicle.

On-line distribution channel

The term 'channel' has conventionally been used to describe the unidirectional flow of a product from its source to an end-user via a number of intermediaries (e.g. wholesaler; retailer). However, in recent years, developments in information technology (IT) have revolutionised channels of distribution by offering suppliers and retailers alike the possibility of closer customer relationships through the creation of combined marketing/distribution channels. the Internet, with its increasing reach, its speed and flexibility, offers suppliers and retailer/intermediary companies, whether in the business-to-business or business-to-consumer field, the opportunity to simplify, shorten or extend their channels of distribution and customer service.

Of equal relevance, even well before the popularisation of the Internet, there had developed among companies (through other media such as telephone) a major trend towards dealing direct with customers, e.g. tele-banking, direct-phone insurance, mortgages etc. Interestingly, Hagel (1997) proposes that a consequence of 'interactive' retail channels might be a shift towards a bi-directional retailer/consumer relationship, in which more power accrues to the consumer.

In assessing the utility of the Internet as an alternative distribution channel, it would seem necessary to explore the advantages and disadvantages associated with this interactive medium:

Advantages

- Accessibility – the use of the Internet is forecast to expand exponentially in parallel with increased PC ownership
- Direct communications – enabling more customised targeting and segmentation opportunities
- Cost savings – resulting from fewer store overheads

- New markets – the Internet ultimately offers access to the global market place
- Ubiquity – almost any product and service can be purchased over the Internet.

Disadvantages

- Buyers cannot examine goods before purchase
- Difficult to create a 'store' environment
- Less interaction, especially interpersonal
- Satisfactory service level difficult to achieve, requires planning and experimentation
- Delivery and fulfilment costs and resources
- On-line access requirement, and related level of 'techno-sophistication' may limit profile of buyers, though this is becoming less of a factor
- Some continuing concerns about security issues – e.g. payment, confidentiality, computer viruses.

Among retailers, even some of the more conservative and traditional operators are currently undertaking limited trials of on-line shopping, while other retailers have gone beyond this to become committed 'pioneers' of the cyberspace retail format.

If distribution channels were to be identified (Peterson et al. 1997) with the three key roles of (1) physical distribution, (2) transaction/deal completion and (3) communications, then the Internet would have differing levels of service across these three criteria. For example, while it excels in distributing digital assets such as software and text, its limitations with physical assets means it requires well-managed processing and delivery facilities as a back-up to ensure efficient fulfilment. In other respects, too, extra order handling, versatile logistics operations, inventory control systems and information processing (McNutt 1998) must all be managed efficiently, for both timely and reliable delivery and – increasingly important – for feedback through customer service on order progress.

| Example | **Federal Express: A model of efficiency and customer service** |

Federal Express has for long been an enthusiastic innovator across a range of technologies relevant to its worldwide delivery operations. An early user of toll-free telephone hot-lines and fax facilities for customer service, it has established itself as a pioneer in electronic commerce and customer service back-up systems.

With a worldwide delivery throughput of over 2.5 million packages per day, across over 200 countries, the company has an obvious interest in staying at the cutting edge of any technology that supports its customer service vision.

While the company still offers customers the ability to track delivery progress by phone or fax, it is finding that more and more tracking requests (over 900 000 per month), are coming on-line via 5000 websites linked to its customised tracking network Fedex InterNetShip. Of course, with a 99 per cent on-time delivery record, the majority of its customers have no pressing need to reassure themselves about delivery timing!
<www.fedex.com>

Product and branding applications

Net features of product range and individual products obviously help marketers in terms of market positioning *vis-à-vis* competition – in distribution/market 'cover' terms the Internet is a level playing field, so that all products are equally 'in stock' and equally visible and accessible.

In simple product description and display terms, product information and features can be instantly updated on the Net. More interestingly, net technology can be harnessed as a valuable aid in developing flexible product designs, through the encouragement and maintenance of customer participation – input and feedback – in the design process (Lansanti and MacCormack 1997).

Again, mass customisation has become a reality through Internet technology, so that products can now more readily be tailor-made to customer requirements.

In terms of branding, companies using the Internet or developing websites need to consider what domain names to use and whether to use existing brand names – existing brand domain names may prove expensive if pre-empted by others, though these costs may still be worthwhile to ease customer web-searching. As for brand name 'stretch' and versatility, it could be that Internet site-linking technology will facilitate brand extension and even cross-product synergies.

On-line competition can prove difficult even for established 'off-line' brands, since the on-line setting presents new learning challenges for companies. Conversely, solely on-line brands (e.g. Amazon.com) often appear to adjust better to the off-line scene (e.g. by using traditional media to generate web site traffic).

Service and relationship management

While the more everyday aspects of service back-up can be expected to be met by on-line delivery processes, there remains the more critical and strategic role of service within ongoing commercial relationships. If relationship marketing is about regular communications with customers, structural solutions to their problems and generally the establishment and enhancement of customer relationships through product fulfilment (see Grönroos 1990; Berry and Parasuraman 1991), then certainly the Internet has much to offer. As the first fully interactive and precision-target low cost multimedia channel (Strauss and Frost, 1999), the Internet is the ultimate one-to-one marketing tool, and a potent communications link with stakeholders generally. In this wider mission, parallel to the Internet, intranets and extranets can help to widen and strengthen stakeholder relationships. As Table 17.3 implies, the digital era spells radical changes for the way companies manage themselves and their stakeholder relations.

As Taylor (1999) reports, the high-performing businesses of the Internet era – new or newly-reinvented businesses such as Oracle (software), Cisco (network equipment) and Dell (computers) – have effectively become 'extended' or 'virtual' enterprises by electronically linking key stakeholders (clients, suppliers, joint venture partners) across organisational and market frontiers, to serve a common business purpose. Taylor continues:

Table 17.3   Business transformations in the digital era

Sector	Pre-digital era	Digital era
Business organisations	Internally driven	Extended 'virtual' companies
Customers	Limited contact with manufacturers	Direct continuity contact with manufacturers
Suppliers	Restricted relationships	Digital relationships
Intermediaries	Independent	Interdependent 'info-mediaries'
Employees	Hierarchical, task management	Multi-functional team management

Source: Adapted from Taylor (1999).

At the same time the Internet makes it easier for companies to focus on what they do best – their core activity – and spin off or contract out other operations to their 'wired' partners.

He concludes that for some of these businesses the logical extension of this is to create virtual electronic 'consortium' companies that join forces on a project-by-project basis, but otherwise retain their own distinct identities. Obviously, the advent of this scenario has major implications for markets, marketers and corporate management teams generally.

QUESTIONS

1 *What do you think would be the key steps involved in planning a direct mail promotion?*

2 *For any product field, compare examples of direct and on-line marketing.*

3 *Assess the relevance of on-line marketing to a charity organisation.*

4 *Collect samples of direct mail material across two market sectors (e.g. credit cards, cars) and compare their approaches and effectiveness.*

FURTHER READING

Berry, L. and Parasuraman, A. (1991) *Marketing Services: Competing through Quality*. Free Press.

Bird, J. (1992) 'Pinpoint accuracy', *Marketing Business*, April.

Boyd, P. (1992) 'Data protection', *Marketing Business*, May.

Brooks, K. (1999) *New Marketing in a New World*. Bardo Internet Marketing.

Coad, T. (1994) 'Can the EC deliver postal harmony?', *Marketing Business*, February.

Cronin, M. J. (1996) *the Internet Strategy Handbook: Lessons from the New Frontier of Business*. Harvard Business School Press.

Evans, P. and Wurster, T. (1997) 'Strategy and the new economics of information', *Harvard Business Review*, September–October, pp. 71–82.

Fletcher, K, Wheeler, C. and Wright, J. (1990) 'The role and status of UK database marketing', *Quarterly Review of Marketing*, Autumn.

Grönroos, C. (1990) 'Relationship approach to marketing in service contexts: the marketing and organisational behaviour interface', *Journal of Business Research*, 20, pp. 3–11.

Hagel, J. (1997) *Net Gain: Expanding Markets through Virtual Communities*. Harvard Business School Press.

Lansanti, M. and MacCormack, A. (1997) 'Developing products on internet time', *Harvard Business Review*, September–October.

Levitt, T. (1983) *The Marketing Imagination*. The Free Press.

McNutt, B. (1998) 'A matter of priority', *Precision Marketing*, 21 December, p. 16.

Peterson, R. A., Balasubramanian, S. and Bronnenburg, B. J. (1997) 'Exploring the implications of the Internet for consumer marketing', *Journal of the Academy of Marketing Science*, 25, pp. 329–48.

Rapps, S. and Collins, T. (1987) *Maxi-marketing*. McGraw-Hill.

Shaw, R. and Stone, M. (1987) 'Database marketing for competitive advantage', *Long Range Planning*.

Stewart, A. (2000), 'UK supermarket on-line: diverging routes to the on-line buyer's heart', *Financial Times*, 15 March.

Strauss, J. and Frost, R. (1999) *Marketing on the Internet (Principles of On-line Marketing)*. Prentice-Hall.

Stroud, D. (1996) *Internet Strategies: A Guide to Exploring the Internet*. Macmillan Press.

Taylor, P. (1999) 'On-line revolution set to overthrow many established practices', *Financial Times*, 19 July.

Walters, D. and Lancaster, G. (1999) 'Using the Internet as a channel for commerce', *MCB Management Decision*, 37(10).

Wilson, R. F. (1999), 'Laws of web marketing', *Web Marketing Today*, 1 April.

CASE STUDY

UK supermarketers.com

Leading UK supermarket groups are becoming locked in an intensive race to establish leadership within the on-line grocery market, which in the UK is tipped to achieve growth rates higher than the USA, the originator of on-line retailing.

Against an increasingly difficult and dynamic competitive backcloth within the grocery market itself, supermarket groups are keen to leave no stone unturned in what appears sometimes as a desperate struggle for marginal business and market share points. This is in spite of the fact that on-line grocery shopping has yet to prove itself as profitable and worth the investments and organisational procedures necessary for entry into the sector.

Some of the key factors affecting both profits and operational efficiencies include:

- Identification of target customers, and their location
- Level of service to offer – e.g. range of products, delivery frequency
- Price of delivery/overall service
- Market coverage – countrywide, in prime store sites only, regionally?
- Order reception methods – e.g. internet only, phone etc.
- Fulfilment systems – their resourcing, staffing and operation, how dedicated or separate?
- How to target and promote for market on-line uptake?

Among the leading supermarket groups, responses to these issues are varied, and are often still fluid and experimental, since there appears to be no consensus view on where the viability benchmarks of on-line grocery ordering and home delivery will be. By way of illustration:

Tesco – UK supermarket leader, uses 100 of its existing stores, mainly in the South East of England, and picks orders across its whole store range of 20–25 000 items. It has no plans to establish dedicated and separate on-line food centres.

Sainsbury – the No. 2 food retailer in the UK, summer 2000 open a warehouse facility in Park Royal, North London, dedicated to picking on-line orders against a limited range of 5000 items. The facility will cover the M enclave and will take orders by phone, fax and on-line.

Asda – the No. 3 supermarket in the UK, now part of Wal-Mart, operates its Asda@Home service from picking centres in Croydon and Watford, with two more London-based centres opening by December 2000. In line with Wal-Mart strategy, 11 more centres will be added nationwide in the next three–five years.

Safeway – the supermarket in the number 4 position, is completely different to other supermarkets. It operates a telephone/fax order system, from eight stores across the country, whereby customers subsequently collect their order (i.e. no home delivery). Buying across its full 22 000 line range is possible at its Basingstoke store and Hayes HQ through palm-top computers programmed with 'Easi-Order' software.

Somerfield – operates 24-hour phone ('24–7') and fax order lines, now supplemented by Open satellite interactive TV links. Additionally, it operates two on-line picking centres in London and Bristol, serving allocated postcodes.

Iceland – In October 1999, the group was the first supermarket to offer on-line ordering (of 2750 items) with free home delivery across the UK, subject to a minimum spend of £40. (*Note*: most competitors charge between £3.50–£5.00.) The company makes about 100 000 deliveries per week, from across all of its stores. It accepts orders by phone, on-line and in-store.

Waitrose – Has no plans for home delivery, but offers delivery across a 10 000 + product range, to the workplace car park, through its 'Waitrose at Work' scheme.

Clearly, with such variations in company policies, set against a rapid growth in digital 'connectivity' across the UK (e.g. an estimated 1 million new internet users logged on in March–April 2000 alone), it is difficult to predict the future picture in on-line food retailing. A point of agreement that is emerging, though, is that the on-line market, far from offering easy profits, may conceal grave pitfalls for the unwary.

Source: Adapted from Stewart (2000).

Questions

1 *What are the possible benefits to supermarkets of on-line grocery shopping?*

2 *Can you identify any potential downside to on-line service operations?*

3 *Using case evidence, assess the relative service provision of the leading supermarket chains.*

4 *What factors are likely to 'drive' the demand for on-line ordering and home delivery?*

5 *What 'grave pitfalls' may await the unwary within this market?*

6 *Through on-line searching and library research, provide an update on the details of the current on-line grocery shopping scene.*

18 Sales promotion, PR and related activities

In every field of human endeavour, he that is first must perpetually live in the white light of publicity.

Theodore F. MacManus, 'The Penalty of Leadership', (*Saturday Evening Post*, 2 Jan 1915)

INTRODUCTION

This chapter brings together a number of specialist elements of promotion. Public Relations (PR) and sales promotion can form a key part of the traditional promotional mix. Sponsorship is a form of promotion which must be viewed as an opportunity for publicity as well as a type of sales promotion. The expenditure on sponsorship has risen dramatically over the last decade but now organisations are trying to evaluate the return. Finally, point-of-sale display, packaging, and exhibitions are briefly covered as logical links with the sales promotion field.

All of these forms of promotion are seen as effective but perhaps not excessively expensive. They are more difficult to evaluate and yet many case studies exist to show the substantial benefits that can accrue when they are used appropriately and as part of a well-co-ordinated communications programme.

PUBLIC RELATIONS (PR) AND PUBLICITY

Public relations (PR) represents a specific element of a company's communications activities that is designed to project the company and its interests in a positive way. PR has been succinctly defined as:

> **The deliberate, planned and sustained effort to establish and maintain mutual understanding between an organisation and its publics.**
>
> Institute of Public Relations

In a business setting, then, PR is about managing in a proactive way the communications and relations that a company has with the various groups that have an interest or influence in its activities. These groups, representing the company's various *publics*, may range from the general public to formal representatives of the public (e.g. government, local authorities), and parties with particular interests (e.g. employees, shareholders, suppliers, customers). These publics are illustrated in Figure 18.1.

The array of interested publics shown in Figure 18.1 demonstrates that PR has very much a corporate brief, much wider than marketing issues alone, and it would be inaccurate to subsume the broader field of PR within the marketing mix.

While some of the 'publics' that PR addresses will clearly be of prime interest in marketing terms (e.g. customers, distributors), other groups may have no direct trading or

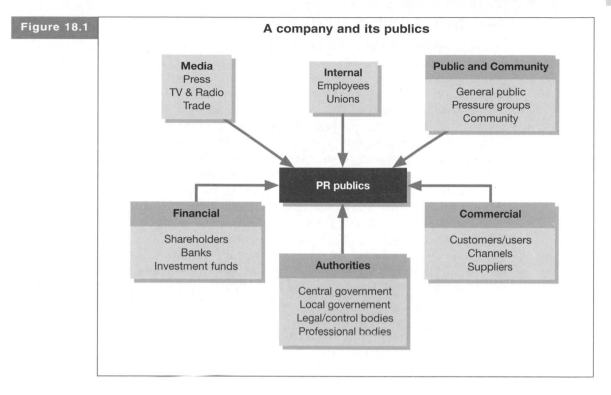

Figure 18.1

A company and its publics

market relationship with the company, but nevertheless possess key influence on corporate success (e.g. government bodies, community groups, financial institutions). A brief review of the scope of public relations may serve to illustrate this.

The scope of PR

As the brief of PR is broadly about dialogue and understanding with the company's various publics, the scope of PR is far-ranging, embracing matters such as:

■ Promoting products and services through media publicity
■ Enhancing public awareness of the company and its reputation (corporate identity and status)
■ Projecting the company's mission and philosophy
■ Portrayal of the organisation as a good corporate citizen (e.g. through charitable and community-based projects)
■ Creating a climate of co-operation and interest with the media (media relations), in order to obtain positive news coverage of company achievements and to receive sympathetic reporting on company problems
■ Promoting relations with officialdom, formal law-making and control bodies, both locally, nationally and internationally
■ Protecting the company's reputation, e.g. through correcting media or public misconceptions
■ Promoting the company within its trade or industry
■ Projecting the organisation as a source of opportunities e.g. for investors, prospective partners and high-calibre staff applicants.

The place of marketing PR

As demonstrated above, the scope of PR is much wider than marketing itself, since much of a company's PR will be carried out on a corporate level that transcends functional boundaries. For the same reason, publicity will tend to vary in its functional scope, and it would be incorrect to see it as the 'sole property' of marketing.

To counter a number of common misconceptions on this, marketing writers and practitioners have in recent years adopted the term 'Marketing PR' (abbreviated to MPR in the USA) to identify those PR activities that work to specific marketing objectives (e.g. brand building, product launches), or with publics (e.g. consumers, distributors) of direct concern to marketing (see Kitchen and Papasolomon 1997).

In parallel with this, terms identifying other (non-marketing) fields of PR have gained common currency e.g. *Corporate PR, Community PR* and *Financial PR.*

Financial PR deserves separate mention because it is a major area of importance to public 'quoted' companies. The share price of companies, and their financial credibility, cannot be separated from an organisation's trading success. The key measure with financial backers is *confidence* – the confidence the 'money markets' have in the management of an organisation. This includes institutional investors, professional financial advisers and the financial media. It is naive to suggest an organisation is judged by its published performance.

The role of financial PR is to directly influence the relevant individuals and institutions, and to develop good relationships with them. The media used are highly specialised, including the use of screen-based electronic news such as the CNS (company news service) established by the Stock Exchange.

Publicity

Publicity represents a key end-product of public relations. It might be defined as any publication or news coverage about an organisation, issue or product that is independently provided by the media.

Whether a company's PR activities are handled through a specialist PR agency, or in-house by a PR department or (as is still to be found in some firms) a 'publicity section', a major preoccupation will be to obtain in the media *positive publicity about the company and its business.*

Unlike advertising, which is also transmitted by the media, publicity involves no media costs and so there is no direct payment link with a client. In turn, this lack of a commercial link can make publicity appear more objective and believable than its paid-for advertising counterpart. A summary of the relative advantages and disadvantages of publicity is presented in Table 18.1.

Table 18.1 The relative advantages and disadvantages of publicity

Advantages	Disadvantages
Greater credibility	Uncertainty of media take-up
Greater readership	Message distortion
More information content	No repetition
Cost benefits	No timing control
Speed and flexibility	
Great potential impact	

The advantages and disadvantages of publicity

Advantages

Publicity should be an important but subtle part of the promotional mix, not just an adjunct to advertising. The most important advantages to be gained are:

- **Credibility**. If the public are made aware of the benefits to be gained from a company's products from an independent source, and that source is not being paid by the company in question, then the credibility factor is that much greater.
- **Greater readership**. When glancing through a newspaper it is seldom that a great deal of attention is primarily paid to advertisements. Much more attention is given to editorial or news sections. Similarly, people are more likely to divert attention from the television to do other things while the advertisements are being shown.
- **Contain more information**. Publicity is able to impart more information to the public than advertisements can. A glance is all that is usually given to an advertisement, whereas publicity, when presented as news, is given more attention and is therefore able to contain much more detailed information.
- **Cost benefits**. No direct payments are made to the media for publicity. There are obviously costs involved, but PR budgets are far less than those for advertising.
- **Speed**. Publicity has an advantage of speed. Information on a major development can often be issued and reported in a short space of time. Publicity can also be flexible and reactive.

Disadvantages

Publicity is generally looked upon as being of benefit, but sometimes both companies, and famous personalities, wish that they could avoid it. If there is a major accident on the premises of a company, or an oil leak from one of the oil companies' installations offshore, that company will be on the receiving end of some very bad publicity. They can try to minimise this by breaking the news to the media themselves, and being as helpful as possible, but damage to their reputation will still be incurred.

- **Message distortion**. A company has no control over what the media report about them. A press release, which a company hopes is reported in full, may in fact not be used at all, or may have only a small portion of it reported. If the publicity given is untrue or libellous, of course, the organisation will have recourse through the judicial system, but such action is expensive, and creates a difficult situation for the future. With good relations, and a good understanding of the type of release required, the risk of distortion can be dramatically reduced.
- **Repetition**. With advertisements a company can ensure that there is frequency of the message. Publicity does not have this advantage and the message may only be given once, if at all.

The tools of public relations

Subject to the objectives served in any PR campaign, its scale and target audience(s), there will be a number of 'tools' or approaches that can be used to effect (See Figure 18.2 below). Often these tools will be used together for increased impact.

Media relations

Media relations involve taking news to the editors, taking editors to the news, creating

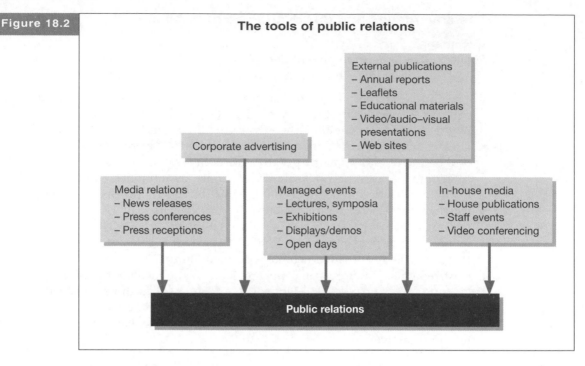

Figure 18.2

The tools of public relations

relevant news stories and managing the news. Building good relationships with the media is obviously a benefit. The personal contact with editors is covered in the first two tasks above. The other two relate to the need to produce a regular supply of news items as part of the deliberate, planned and sustained publicity effort.

Editorial and broadcast material

Editorial and broadcast material is the 'product' of public relations. It covers press conferences, news releases, personal interviews, feature writing, case histories, press visits and journalist briefings. News releases and press conferences are the most commonly used methods of gaining publicity, but as you can see, there are many other techniques which can be used.

Press conferences

A press conference is held in order to brief members of the media about a major news event. You may be familiar with these conferences being used by a political figure, or maybe by the police during an enquiry into a serious crime. The technique is equally applicable to PR for a company or product. Editors and feature writers receive many invitations to such events. They are, therefore, selective about which press conferences they choose to attend. The subject has to be particularly interesting or topical, or maybe the conference/presentation is attractive because it is held in an interesting location. The cider makers, H. P. Bulmer, used to own the steam engine, King George V; they used steam-train runs as a location for press conferences, and always found a willing audience.

News releases

A news release is an item circulated to the media in the hope of getting it placed in a publication. It is the mainstay of publicity and, if published, can be of considerable value. Editorial matter is seen and read by more people than advertising in the same magazine or newspaper. The contents of an article also gain credibility by having the implied support of the publication. Whereas advertisements are seen for what they are, editorial comment is often considered objective and unbiased. The drawback of relying on publicity is that the editors decide what will be published and when it will appear. If a news release is set out in a way that is unsuitable for the publication, then it might be modified before insertion. This modification could change the balance and meaning of the release. The release could, of course, be rejected. Rejection is more likely with a major publication which is inundated with releases. Specialist journals, however, are often pleased to receive items about product successes, new contracts, innovations, export achievements or people in the industry. In some cases the specialist journals could be the best media to reach your target.

News releases are a 'one-way' communication, which do not give an opportunity for questions. Press conferences do give an opportunity for 'two-way' exchanges but only with the media editors, not with the eventual target audience. They are often used to support a news release where it is felt the story could be enhanced by contact.

External publications

Controlled communications is the area of publicity material for company use. It includes annual reports, educational material, leaflets, audio–visual presentations, and any material that could be successfully placed to support organisational objectives. This low-cost material is a luxury for some organisations because of the time required to plan and prepare it. The benefits are even more difficult to measure than advertising or other main-media publicity. But such channels should not be ignored. The less usual ways of reaching consumers could prove effective just because they offer a different approach.

Managed events

These include other ways of reaching the chosen audience direct. Conferences, displays, lectures, shopping centre events, demonstrations, open days, public visits are examples of activities used to facilitate contact. The environment for such contact is a key ingredient. Then the event has to be structured to give the right level of interest, linked to the communication message, for the event to be considered worthwhile.

Exhibitions are an excellent way to present an organisation to its customers. They can be expensive, but can also be a simple, low-cost 'shell' construction. Whatever the cost, it is important to ensure that an exhibition is as effective as possible. This means being proactive in inviting visitors to your exhibition stand, rather than reactive, waiting for visitors to appear. The role of PR, as well as direct mail, in attracting visitors must not be ignored. The cost of such an exercise is only a small proportion of the cost of the exhibition as a whole, and usually is money well spent.

In-house or agency?

The decision on whether to handle PR internally, or to appoint an agency, can depend on the way PR is perceived. In a small organisation it is often the Managing Director who takes control, but there are three other options: to train an existing manager to handle PR; to appoint professional PR staff; and to use an external agency. It is always possible to use a combination of these options to deal with the planned programme. However, there are always the unplanned events which have to be handled in-house.

Just as every member of staff is a part-time marketer, so are they also all part-time PR people – anyone can accept an incoming enquiry from the media. In some 'sensitive' industries, for instance Nuclear Electric, there are nominated executives who are trained in dealing with tough media reporters, and all incoming enquiries are routed to these selected managers.

For the basic decision on in-house or agency PR the trade-off is between intimate knowledge of the company, its products and services and the wide range of experience and objective advice from a PR consultancy. A compromise is often used whereby a small PR department, or just one nominated individual, works with an external agency, the agency being paid a retainer related to the task required.

It goes without saying that *monitoring effectiveness* is a key role to play. With a direct link to effectiveness and evaluation, reports Gray (1999), PR trade bodies are beginning to develop agreed standards for measuring the communications effectiveness of PR, at both a practical and a strategic level.

SALES PROMOTION

Most marketing commentators would agree that sales promotion grew in importance during the 1990s. In part, this has been a reaction to the ever-increasing cost of media advertising (higher than the rate of inflation); in part, it has been a reflection of the effectiveness of sales promotions in creating additional sales in a very direct manner. The Advertising Standards Authority's (ASA) Code of Sales Promotion defines sales promotion as:

> **those marketing techniques which are used, usually on a temporary basis, to make goods and services more attractive to the consumer by providing some additional benefit whether in cash or in kind.**

The code covers such forms of promotions as: premium offers of all kinds; reduced-price and free offers; the distribution of vouchers, coupons, and samples; personality promotions; charity-linked promotions; and prize promotions of all types. In fact, almost any promotion that is not main-media advertising or publicity can be grouped under the general heading of 'sales promotion'.

The term 'below the line' is applied to sales promotion as opposed to 'above the line' for advertising. However, both sales promotion and advertising are key parts of the promotions mix. There was a time when advertising agencies were critical of the use of promotions. Now 'below-the-line' techniques have become increasingly sophisticated and effective; they are seen as an important complement to advertising. In fact, many companies use advertising to support promotions, while sales promotions are often chosen to develop and support brand positioning.

There is a difference between promotions that really do benefit the promotional message and those that just bring forward sales to an earlier period. The latter outcome is described by Neilsen, the market research company, as 'mortgaging' future sales. This occurs if no overall sales increase is achieved – that is, the increase during the promotion is lost by lower-than-expected sales in following periods. Another criticism of 'promotions' is that they can be easily copied by competitors. In this case a vicious circle, similar to a price war, can occur.

Companies such as Unilever have been reported (Jones, 1990) to be particularly wary of the risks involved in such a spiral, which is illustrated in Figure 18.3.

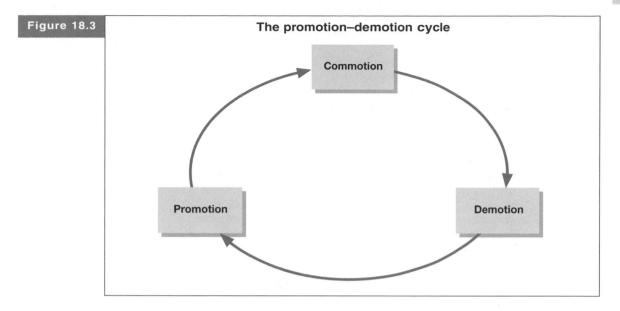

Figure 18.3   The promotion–demotion cycle

Commotion

Promotion

Demotion

However, Jones proposes that, in slow-growth or declining markets, sales promotion might be a cost-effective way of diluting, or even eliminating, costly theme advertising outlays.

Example   ## Business promotion

The Institute of Sales Promotion awarded a Gold Winner Prize to the Trade/Business Promotion 'Operation X' devised by MX Promotions for manufacturer LG Electronics Ltd. The £30 000 promotion was designed to return LG to sales growth and to achieve sell-out over a three-month period by motivating all sales staff in distributors.

The promotion involved assessing sales results for staff to qualify for 100 places at a special sports event (Operation X). Over the period of the promotion, company sales increased by 37 per cent.

The identification of long-term profitability as a key aim is fine, though other objectives such as brand loyalty and market share may be important. However, when products reach the later stages of their life cycles, the suggestion that some mature products should receive minimal support is consistent from a marketing strategy perspective. Viewed strategically, good sales promotion, rather than poorly thought-out short-term offers, does give an extra dimension. The problem is how to choose the right mix of promotions to meet the needs of varying marketing circumstances. With this in mind, it would make sense to categorise sales promotions according to their intended 'recipient' or target markets, as follows:

- consumer promotions
- industrial and trade promotions
- sales staff incentives.

Consumer promotions

Most sales promotions make one of the three popular appeals: Save! Win! Free! There are also several secondary appeals: Give! Now! Fun! Reassurance! The motivations appear to lie deep in the human psyche, and show themselves in many forms in our society:

- Most people like a bargain
- Most people will jump at something for nothing
- Most people like to indulge some skill, or 'have a flutter'.

This was how Chris Petersen, a prominent sales promotion consultant, started a chapter of his much-praised book, *Sales Promotion in Action*. Of course, Petersen is talking here about the various themes used in promotions. For a promotion to be suitable it must be consistent with the overall marketing objectives of an organisation. These are often listed as:

1 **Extra sales volume** The original aim of sales promotion, it is usually short-term, but extra profitable sales represent the key aim of most commercial organisations.
2 **Point-of-sale impact** Linked to increased volume, this objective is to gain maximum exposure at the time of purchase and at the point of deciding on whether and what to buy. The joint tasks of persuasion and reinforcement can be enhanced by effective point-of-sale promotion.
3 **Repeat purchase** The role of marketing as described in this book is to build satisfying exchanges with customers. These will, hopefully, lead to increased levels of repeat purchase as well as gaining product advocates who will recommend a particular brand. Techniques such as collector schemes, which build ongoing repeat business, can reinforce loyalty and habitual buying.
4 **Sample purchase or product trial** One of the most difficult marketing objectives is to get people to try a new product. If a potential customer tries a product then at least they can evaluate the product properly. They might like it, or consider it is not as good as their current product. But trial is far superior as a basis of consumer judgement to ill-informed prejudice.

Example	Among the promotional offers made by leading magazines during Spring 2000, the following are typical examples:

- *Slimming* – Free *1 Calorie Cookbook*
- *Practical parenting* – Free *Babies R Us Catalogue*
- *Amateur gardening* – Free *seeds*
- *Good food* – Free *kitchen herb collection*

Note : While one of the objectives of the promotion is clearly to increase circulation within competitive markets, another objective is likely to be reward loyal readers. Of course, all these promotions could be judged to be highly appropriate to their target groups.

In a hard-hitting critique of the state of sales promotion practices at retailer level, Lucas (1996) argues that manufacturers should concentrate on promotional effectiveness beyond short-term sales effects, and that they should weigh carefully the real benefits of promotion relative to more radical activities such as product innovation and brand development.

Malcolm McDonald suggested a structured classification of consumer promotions based on direct versus indirect appeal, and whether the offer was based on money, goods or services (see Table 18.2).

Table 18.2   A classification of the direct and indirect appeal of promotional materials

	Direct	Indirect
Money	Price reduction	Coupons, Money equivalent, Competitions
Goods	Free goods, Premium goods, Free gifts, Trade-in-offers	Stamps, Coupons, Vouchers, Money equivalents, Competitions
Services	Guarantees, Group participation and events, Special exhibitions and displays	Cooperative advertising, Stamps, Vouchers for services, Event admission, Competition

Money-based consumer promotions

Money is the most widely acceptable type of offer but it suffers from the criticism of short-termism described by Jones. For instance, goods might not appeal, as not every purchaser wants the item offered. But, by offering 'money off' the purchasers are presumed to make a saving. They can, therefore, decide what to do with that saving, while the value of the product is enhanced. Money can be offered: directly as a price cut; indirectly as a coupon linked to a product purchase; or as a money prize in a competition where proof of product purchase is required.

However, there are problems with both coupons and competitions. Some supermarket groups will accept coupons without the customer purchasing the relevant item. This negates much of the benefit from a coupon promotion. Competitions are controlled by the Lotteries and Amusement Act (1976), one of a number of legislative controls affecting sales promotions. Such laws can cause problems for ill-informed companies.

The four major problems of 'money-off' promotions are:

1 They are expensive, with the reduction in revenue coming directly from profit
2 A significant proportion of customers are 'price-off' buyers who buy only during the reductions
3 Regular price reductions can damage the quality image of a product or company
4 'Money-off' promotions are easily copied by competitors.

However, in a competitive market place, it can be difficult to resist competitive pressure. For example Marks & Spencer for many years refused to run 'money-off' sales. With the problems of retail volume they now compete with other major department stores running sales events.

Example   **You will not bogof**

In Brussels, an Expert Group within the European Commission is currently examining the nature and effect of sales promotion techniques across Europe. Informal feedback on the deliberations to date indicate that the Expert Group is looking favourably on adopting the competitive stance on sales promotion that is taken by Germany, a country known to be highly restrictive and conservative generally in terms of competition law.

If this is proved to be the case, there would probably be an end to BOGOF (buy one get one free) offers and similar premiums, loyalty schemes, free draws, instant wins and many other promotion schemes that have proved popular outside of Germany.

Source: Institute of Sales Promotion website, <www.isp.org.uk> 26 April 2000

'Money-off' schemes are appropriate in many situations, such as to create sampling of products. In launching a new food product the first requirement is to get potential customers to try it. A coupon or reduced price will help to achieve this. These offers can also encourage possible multiple purchases. Another use of 'money off' is to bring purchases forward – for example, an early booking discount for holiday booking.

'Money-off' promotions are widely used, but perhaps, given the risks and problems they involve, they should be used more selectively, and certainly not be an automatic first-choice method.

Goods- or merchandise-based consumer offers

Value can be offered by goods and merchandise, without the same risk of damaging brand images. For example, free product (500 grammes extra free) costs relatively little to producers, and certainly does not change pricing structures. Also, merchandise can be bought in bulk at very heavy discounts. Consequently, excellent offers can be made either free or by so-called 'self-liquidating' offers (i.e. at cost). By linking to purchases of the main brand, then, promotions can build brand loyalty and repeat purchase in a very direct way.

| Example | The garden fertilisers division of a major international chemical company used to encourage early purchase by offering an early purchase discount every year. Fertiliser is used by gardeners primarily in the spring when it has maximum effect. One year sales were lagging so much that, in spite of the springtime price promotion for early orders, the company subsequently dropped its prices further during the summer. Early purchasers were in fact worse off. Next year, the early promotion was a disaster as regular customers had lost confidence in the company and its quality image. The fertiliser division never recovered from this mishap. |

It was suggested earlier that goods/merchandise might not appeal because the item offered might not be desired by the target customers. This is a risk, although it is possible to offer a range of items. One example of this is a choice from a catalogue offered by a major petrol company. The mechanics of the promotion is that sales are recorded in the form of points recorded on a swipe card. The points are then exchanged for a wide range of products, from a catalogue. This is just one attempt to offer value, and also to reduce the problem of restricted choice.

In considering how promotional offers influence behaviour, ask your student friends why they chose to open a bank account at a particular bank. It might be the convenient location of the branches, the overdraft limit, the fact that their families use that bank, or the promotional offer made. It could be that more than one of these issues influenced the decision, but it would be interesting to find out the role of the promotional offer.

| Exercise | All major banks in Britain make offers to encourage students to open an account. Check the offers from leading banks. Do banks in other countries offer similar inducements? Ask a group of students to see what offers they value most. How do these offers affect bank selection? How many of the students questioned have two or more accounts, and for what reasons? Do similar promotional and other factors affect adoption patterns for credit cards? |

The offers made by banks to attract students are often well chosen and very relevant to the needs of this group. The choice of offers is very important to the success of any promotion. You will be able to find evidence of this in many of your local retail outlets. However, sometimes the promotional offer can give problems which reflect badly on the product being promoted. Some years ago a brand of table jelly offered a 'free goldfish' as a promotion. Major problems resulted in dead fish being delivered to customers, and the resultant complaints affected the brand concerned. The Code of Sales Promotion Practice is particular on the subject of suitability of promotional products:

> Promoters shall not offer promotional products which are of a nature likely to cause offence, or products which, in the context of the promotion, may reasonably be considered to be socially undesirable.

Particular care should be taken in the distribution of free samples to ensure that children or other particularly vulnerable groups are not harmed.

Consumers should not be led to overestimate the quality or desirability of promotional products. Particular care should be exercised where the recipient has no opportunity to examine goods before taking delivery.

It might be interesting to find some current promotions, and see how they adhere to the code.

Services as promotion

Promotions of this type are very varied: a guarantee, or a 'no-quibble' exchange are excellent in building strong positions in markets. New retail store openings, often featuring a showbiz personality, can create high initial awareness; famous authors signing their books can draw large crowds; while charity-linked promotions can show a brand as caring (for example, by a link with the Save the Children Fund). The scope is enormous. Events and sponsorship might be covered in part under this heading, although they could equally come under publicity. The subject of sponsorship cuts across all three areas of consumer, trade and sales force promotion and so has been included in a separate section later in the chapter.

Services promotions, then, usually provide additional and specific benefits (added-value) such as point-of-sale impact and enhanced product personalities. In many cases the benefits are qualitative and difficult to measure. But the effect they can have will usually last for longer than a short-term 'money-off' deal.

Industrial and trade promotions

This sector of business-to-business promotion can be subdivided into:

1 Industrial customers who are users of a product
2 Trade intermediaries who sell the product on.

The first group will be receptive to some of the techniques discussed above under 'Consumer promotions'. However, in industrial companies, the person who raises the

---

Example

- An executive collects 'Air-miles' from her company travel trips. Should she use the benefits for company business or her next holiday?
- A purchasing manager has placed a series of good orders with your organisation. You give that purchasing manager an expensive personal organiser featuring your organisation logo. Is this good promotion?
- A purchasing manager has placed a series of good orders with your organisation. You are offering a free case of whisky for large orders. Should the purchasing manager receive the whisky for his personal consumption?

sales order is not always the end user, nor necessarily the influencer of the purchase decision. It is therefore very important to understand the role and position of the person who could receive the promotional benefit. There is often a problem of deciding what is fair promotion and what is bribery!

The dilemma that these examples have in common is that the expenditure and purchase order is from the customer company, but the promotion is offered to one employee of that company. The Code of Sales Promotion practice states:

> No trade incentive which is directed towards employees should be such as to cause any conflict with their duty to their employer, or their obligations to give honest advice to the consumer.

Similar dilemmas are faced with respect to trade intermediaries. But where do you classify a meal purchased by a sales representative, who invites a buyer to that person's favourite (expensive) restaurant as a 'reward' for a particularly large order?

The ethical issues are brought into sharp focus because of the clash of people and their employing organisations. It is worth considering the type of promotional objectives a supplier organisation might have with respect to trade buyers. Writing about the promotion of durable products, Quelch et al. (1987) suggested that objectives might be:

1 To persuade existing outlets to:
   – maintain existing floor/shelf space
   – stock additional models or promotional versions
   – provide additional floor/shelf space
   – provide special displays and features
   – increase inventories of a specific brand
2 To persuade new outlets to stock a brand
3 To insulate the trade from consumer-price negotiations at the point of purchase
4 To insulate the trade from a temporary sales reduction that might be caused by an increase in price
5 To compensate the trade when customary retail margins have been eroded by price competition
6 To identify which items in a product range the dealer should push during particular periods.

While Quelch et al.'s focus was on durable products, this list could equally well apply to non-durable products, and to promoting to retailers generally, where certainly issues such as ongoing stockist interest and support, sufficiency of stock 'cover' and promotional aids to increase sales rates are everyday concerns.

All of these objectives can be satisfied by the type of 'push' techniques which typify many sales promotions. Again, the types of promotion aimed at an industrial or trade buyer can vary from money-based to goods/merchandise-based and services-based schemes.

Tailored promotions

Many organisations sell to a mix of different intermediaries. A 'tailored promotion' is a promotional offer that is made to a particular intermediary. It is a highly focused strategy, chosen to apply to a single outlet type or market segment. The promotion is designed to meet the specific objectives the supplier might have towards that particular segment.

Example ## Corporate support for a good cause

The Sunshine for Children Appeal (April 2000) promoted by the Institute of Sales Promotion (ISP), provides a good example of corporate support appropriately applied to a worthy cause. Under this scheme, ISP members are invited to donate excess stocks of promotional goods such as toys and games, books, tapes and CDs, to the Variety Club Children's Charity, ensuring that they get to children who will appreciate them, and are not sitting uselessly in stock-rooms or being sold by unauthorised outlets. Collections and co-ordination of donations was handled by ISP member Frazier International.

Source: <www.isp.org.uk> 26 April 2000.

'Tailored promotions' are most relevant to major outlets, or ones that could be significant. For such outlets, a promotion specifically designed for that outlet has a strong appeal. The use of techniques which are wider than 'money-off' promotions with a particular intermediary has a definite appeal. For instance, a drinks company will run special events with individual public houses to promote new products. Alternatively, a cosmetics company could offer the services of a trained beauty consultant to a particular department store in return for extra stock levels.

SPONSORSHIP

A workable definition of sponsorship might be:

> A commercial exchange between a provider of finance, or other resources, and a corporate or legal entity (e.g. an organisation, person or event) which allows the sponsor contractual associations that may be used for promotional purposes

Cornwell and Maignan (1998) provide some interesting data and insights on the increasingly international sponsorship field, and comment on the dynamics and workings of the business relationships involved in sponsorship ties.

Example ## Growth in the sponsorship field

On a worldwide scale, sponsorship has in recent years grown to a multi-billion dollar promotional field, displaying annual growth rates in some sectors (e.g. sports) of over 10 per cent. Worldwide expenditures of some $18.5 billion were projected for 1999, supporting forecasts that the global market would effectively reach $20 billion during Y2K. On a geographical basis, the 1999 figures divide into roughly one-third in the USA, with the balance dominated by Europe and Pacific-Asia. (*Note*: such estimates are difficult, as some expenditures and activity areas, such as sports, have become more global.)

On a comparable scale, UK sponsorship has also grown vigorously, projected to reach official figures equivalent to $1 billion in 1999 (c. £630 million+), within which roughly 65 per cent is expected to be in sports, and approximately 15 per cent each on the arts and broadcast sponsorship.

It is worthwhile making a distinction between *sponsorship* and *charitable donations*, which amounts to corporate gift-giving, usually but not exclusively as money, to charitable causes (e.g. registered charities such as Oxfam, or local or temporary fund-raising events such as school fêtes). In the latter, the major difference is that no commercial 'strings' or influence will accrue or be on offer (tax-exemption conditions will also probably vary from the costs involved in sponsorship).

Table 18.3   Factors underlying the growth of sponsorship

- Ability to avoid overcrowding and clutter in advertising media
- Spiralling media costs forced adspend rethinking
- Helps companies gain attention and approval of key stakeholders
- Helps achieve multiple corporate objectives (e.g. corporate citizenship)
- Sponsorship market growth fuelled by early adopters (e.g. tobacco companies)
- Offers alternative contact during periods of changing media habits
- Enables access to certain segments e.g. youth market
- Offers opportunities to outpace competitors
- Increasingly global reach of sponsorship (e.g. satellite TV).

In sponsorship, by contrast, there is at least an implied aim to generate positive image-building and favourable attitudes by association of the sponsor's name with the sponsorship recipient. The recipient might be a sport, an artistic event or institution, a particular cause (e.g. wildlife preservation), an individual (e.g. an up-and-coming sports or showbiz personality), or a broadcast TV programme or series. Indeed, the vast majority of sponsorship expenditures divide between these categories.

Table 18.3 outlines in summary form the factors underlying the growth in sponsorship over the last 10-15 years. Clearly, it is difficult to be specific or to overgeneralise across what is now such a broad field of activities. One factor that has become significant recently is that both parties to the sponsorship process – sponsors and recipients – have become more experienced, successful and confident in managing their mutual relationships, and their individual objectives – in short, sponsorship has attained a maturity and credibility. As a product of this maturity, it is possible to support the proposition, advanced by Erdogan and Kitchen (1998), that sponsorship has potentially developed a symbiotic relationship with advertising and other marcomms elements.

An interesting variation on sponsorship occurred in Lillehammer, Norway, in preparation for the 1994 Winter 1994 Olympics. The Olympic Committee were faced with preparing all that would be required to ensure that everything would be in place and working in time. The first step the Olympic Committee took was to prepare a detailed budget for the infrastructure and then to invite companies with environmental concerns to bid for the work.

There were two ways in which the companies could join this select group:

1 Donate a large amount of cash which then gave the company the right to use the Olympic logo
2 Supply at budget level (or less) the infrastructure required – e.g. arenas (the balance between the company's bid and the budgeted amount in effect being the donation).

The companies who were successful gained the following advantages:

- The use of the Olympic logo for a four-year period
- The status of being a successful company capable of completing a job on time and to a high standard
- The right to invite 'guests' to the Olympics where transport was by accredited bus and hospitality was provided by the company in special accredited VIP tents with excellent facilities.

The high profile and reputation the 'sponsoring' companies gained from this would hold them in good stead with customers for many years. Customers would remember the special event and hospitality received and hopefully repay the company by placing orders with them in the future.

A good illustration of a well-integrated programme of Arts sponsorship is provided by Amex Canada, who in April–May 2000 sponsored the 'Monet at Giverny' exhibition at the Montreal Museum of Fine Arts. The integrated programme included travel savings (by Air Canada and Via Rail) and entertainment and accommodation discount tie-ins, while privileged rates at Montreal restaurants were available through an 'American Express Monet International Card'.

Sponsorship benefits

When considering sponsorship as part of a promotional campaign an organisation must assess the benefit they receive for the money spent. First must be the 'extra dimension' gained by association with a person or an event. The very act of sponsoring says something about a sponsor in a way no advertisement can. However, there are other positive advantages. Sponsorship can offer real opportunities for advertising or PR. In fact, one rule of thumb suggests a company shall spend as much again on publicity as they commit to the basic sponsorship. But the chance to gain publicity at a pre-arranged time can be very valuable. Media coverage, especially television, can be gained for products. This is only a small part of sponsorship, although it might be the area with which most people are familiar.

Sponsoring an event could give a company publicity but could also give them an opportunity to link to corporate hospitality. Inviting major customers to 'the company event' is much stronger than other events. Special ticket allowances are common practice. Promotional opportunities featuring the sponsor link can extend to merchandise (e.g. golf umbrellas). It will certainly be featured on event-related material. The link could go further so that key personalities meet customers or visit employees. Employee interest can also be enhanced if they have a team or event to follow. Again tickets can be used very effectively.

The key to successful sponsorship is to make it fun for all concerned; also to view sponsorship as a *partnership* which can yield benefits for a significant period of time, as was the case with the 1994 Norwegian Olympic Games.

The benefits from any sponsorship deal should be *quantifiable*. IBM sponsored the Atlanta Olympics, and is reported to have spent $40 million (£26 million) over a four-year period in almost 200 countries; the payback was that it sold $540 million (£346 million) of product because of that spend.

The real future for successful sponsorship is for companies to undertake it only when they are able to integrate it into the marketing mix; without this, the chances of a good payback to the sponsoring firm are very slim.

Sponsorship and promotional planning

An interesting and highly informative review of the marketing role of sponsorship is provided by Crimmins and Horn (1996), who lay stress on the objectivity, business analysis and planning necessary to make sponsorship a promotional success. Sponsorship should not be considered as a cheap alternative to media advertising. In most cases it is not done as a way to circumvent advertising restrictions. Sponsorship is not something to be offered to the first interesting project you consider.

The first thing in all areas of promotion and communication is to sort out clear *objectives*. Sponsorship can become a link between all the elements of the promotion mix – advertising, publicity, sales promotion and selling. It provides a theme which can be exploited in many ways. However, sponsorship is expensive in terms of time, money and people. To benefit fully, an organisation must clearly know what it is trying to achieve and where it is now. If the aim is to enhance the corporate image, then first explore what is the current perception of your organisation and, also, of the intended sponsee. Then follow up by exploring if the link is credible. In fact some large companies, such as Siemens in Germany and Elf in France, take a more strategic long-term view with regard to sponsorship and have fully structured foundations in place to fund cultural, scientific or humanitarian works, enabling them to blaze a philanthropic trail in foreign markets.

One issue often forgotten is the effect of *ending a sponsorship deal*. The end can receive as much publicity as the commencement. The announcement that your company has decided not to renew a sponsorship needs to be handled well or the negative publicity could undo all the positive benefits previously achieved. But perhaps the biggest risk with sponsorship is that it is a very difficult area to predict; it is difficult to forecast the level of media coverage; it is difficult to forecast the way an event or a personality will interact with a company or brand name; it is difficult to know if the target audience will see, and respond, to the sponsors. Nevertheless many organisations are prepared to take this 'risk' because the 'return' from successful sponsorship can be substantial.

POINT-OF-SALE DISPLAYS

Advertising at or close to the 'point-of-sale' (POS) can prove to be a very effective vehicle of communication helping to influence a purchase decision at the precise point where and when decisions between product alternatives are being made. Often the material for point-of-sale displays is not only supplied by the producer of the products, but is also placed in position and restocked and generally looked after by a regular salesperson. But this is becoming much harder in the major supermarkets as they use their powerful position to control activities of suppliers, preferring instead to use their own material designed to be consistent with the store layout and colour schemes.

Point-of-sale material can include all or only a selection of the following: shelf edging; dummy packs; display packs; display stands; mobiles; and posters.

Exercise   In your local supermarket note the different kinds of point-of-sale material used.

PACKAGING

Packaging, which is sometimes called the 'silent salesman', is the ultimate point-of-sale communication tool. It is a non-personal channel of communication, which has become an increasingly important part of the communications mix. Most grocery products are now purchased from a self-service supermarket, and so the need for good packaging has increased with the growth of self-selection. The packaging of a product involves the following functions:

1 Give protection

2 Contain the product
3 Be convenient
4 Give information
5 Have display advantages
6 Convey any brand image.

Give protection – contain the product – be convenient

In order for the product to reach the consumer in perfect condition the packaging must offer basic protection. Protection is especially important when the product is very fragile (e.g. eggs). The protection must also safeguard against damage from rain, heat, cold – in fact, against all the elements of the environment. This function relates more to the total product concept and quality of the offering rather than communications. However, just as a person's appearance is one of the initial communications in a personal situation, so the appearance of a package is an *initial communication regarding a product*.

As well as providing protection the packaging must contain the product – whether it is a bag of sugar or a bottle of wine or an aerosol deodorant. It would have been possible in the 1950s and 1960s to purchase four small nails loose from an ironmonger; today's consumer is more likely to find nails at the local DIY superstore and they are sold prepacked in 10s. There are many different kinds of containers for products – e.g. toothpaste can be in either a tube or a pump dispenser. You might consider if this is really meeting the needs of the customers. Remember that the convenience of the packaging is important but it is the overall value to the customer that is paramount. Some products such as multipacks of drinks have been improved by having a ready-made handle attached, making it easier for the consumer to carry the product home. Product tampering has become a threat, as happened with baby foods a few years ago where it was discovered that glass had been put into the food. The manufacturers' reaction was quickly to change the design of the baby food containers, so that it would be obvious if a jar of baby food had been opened. Manufacturers have spent much money and time in designing tamper-proof containers.

Other product factors could be the size of the package – it may be a carton of pot noodle or even individual tea bags or a small one-person portion of custard. Is the size of the package right for the consumer? Giant family packs of cereal or washing powder can be useful when large amounts of the product are used, but they are not so convenient if they don't fit on any of the shelves in the customer's kitchen. The product packaging should also be suitable for shelf display at the relevant retail outlet.

Packaging that is *reusable* has increased in importance with the growth of the 'green revolution'. Many products are now being designed so that when the original container is empty it can be filled again. This is common with many of the Body Shop products. With fabric conditioner it is also possible to buy refill packs. The original container for the fabric conditioner may be plastic and would cause a pollution problem when disposed of, whereas the carton container with the refill can be disposed of with much less harm to the environment.

Give information – have display advantages – convey brand images

Packaging now gives much more information about the product than was given a decade ago. It is now expected that the following information will be given as standard on food: ingredients, country of origin, sell-by date, calorific values and a barcode, which can be used as both a stock control and a pricing mechanism. However, much of the information on packaging is to attract customers, even if some of it is to meet legal requirements.

Packaging should have display advantages, especially if it is to be sold via intermediaries. It should be sufficiently attractive and eye-catching to interest the consumer as well as serve the needs of the members of the distribution chain.

One of the most important features of packaging is that it can convey the *brand image*. This has become easier with the advent of new processes and materials within the packaging industry, as more and more products are capable of being packaged: the last 20 years has seen an almost revolutionary change in packaging and distribution across many product ranges.

Exercise	Name five products of which the brands are easily recognised by the colour or shape of the packaging alone.

Packaging can be very important when a company is portraying a *corporate image*. They can use the same or similar designs and colours for all products and the packaging is constant over the whole product range.

Although packaging can carry out functions of protection, the communication and promotional aspects are of tremendous importance. It would be very dull indeed to go shopping and not be assailed by all the different colours, shapes and sizes of products in their various packaging. One of the reasons why Radion washing powder was so successful after its launch in Britain was that the packaging colours were so noticeable, being orange and lime green. This factor alongside the abysmal, old-fashioned television advertisements, assured it was noticed in the market place, and from this it became a successful product. However, it is not recommended that other companies follow this route to success with their products, as it is a very dubious one.

TRADE FAIRS AND EXHIBITIONS

It has been said that if a salesperson visits a customer they have gone to sell. If the customer visits the supplier they have come to buy. The latter is a much stronger position for the supplier. A half-way situation is a trade fair or an exhibition. The advantage is that suppliers meet customers on neutral ground away from the formal office environment. The shows are generally industry- or trade-specific. Examples are the Smithfield Show and the Royal Show which are mainly for the farming and agricultural industries. However, the Royal Show, which is held annually, is more than a show for farmers. In June 1997 the Royal Show aimed at providing a family day out with such attractions as ostriches, a working bakery, the Royal Marines' freefall parachute team and the latest in jeeps and Jaguars alongside the tractors and combine harvesters. The advantage of such exhibitions is that the relaxed atmosphere can be very conducive to business. There are now many large exhibition centres throughout Britain, Europe and the rest of the world, which attract a large number of exhibitors, both home-based and from overseas, to regular events.

Exhibitions and trade shows give organisations the chance to show how they compare with their competitors, who are often present at the same event. The budget required to participate in such events can be substantial, so any involvement must be well planned, and probably communicated to potential customers in advance. Salespeople will always be in attendance to give advice, explain any complicated features, as well as trying to sell the product. New products are not only seen, but also tried and tested and compared to other similar products; but competitors are doing the same. Companies often use major exhibitions as an opportunity to launch new products. It can be important for a company to attend the major exhibitions in their product area so as to show all potential customers that it is still thriving in this particular market. In Britain, major exhibition centres include Earls Court, Olympia and the National Exhibition Centre. On a very much smaller and more localised scale this category could also include local craft fairs and perhaps could be extended to the popular 'car boot sale'.

Exercise

Through a trade publication or via your favourite web search engine, identify a specialist trade show and assemble brief details on its timing, exhibitor listing and product range, venue etc. Make a preliminary assessment of the promotional value it offers to appropriate exhibitors, and the benefits it might offer to visitors.

CONCLUSION

Advertising is not the only way to promote a company or its products. All techniques need to be considered together in order to deliver a sustained and regular series of planned messages to target audiences. The objective of the communication element in a general marketing decision is derived from the overall marketing objectives. The delivery of the messages is a specialised function requiring highly skilled functional people. There are so many messages being broadcast that it is difficult to stand out from other communications. Creativity is needed to deliver a message that grabs attention and leads to action. Therefore no organisation should fail to consider the rich variety available with publicity, promotion and sponsorship.

QUESTIONS

1 *How does corporate PR differ from publicity for a product?*

2 *What are the advantages and disadvantages of price-based sales promotions?*

3 *How might an organisation evaluate the success of a sales promotion?*

4 *Choose a successful sponsorship, and explain why you consider it to be successful.*

5 *In what ways can the ending of a sponsorship affected the organisation?*

6 *Consider the ethical and economic trade-offs involved in efforts to prohibit sports sponsorship by tobacco companies.*

FURTHER READING

Bend, D. (1994) 'Sponsors' sporting chance', *Marketing*, 7 July.

Cornwell, T. B. and Maignan, I. (1998) 'An international review of sponsorship research', *Journal of Advertising*, 27(11).

Crimmins, J. and Horn, M. (1996) 'Sponsorship: from management ego trip to marketing success', *Journal of Advertising Research*, 36, pp. 11–21.

Curtis, J. (1997) 'Fear of the unknown', *Marketing*, 6 February.

Erdogan, B. Z. and Kitchen, P. J. (1998) 'Managerial mindsets and the symbiotic relationship between sponsorship and advertising', *Marketing Intelligence and Planning*, 16(6).

Gray, R. (1999), 'Strategic Planning gives a whole new dimension to PR', *Marketing,* June 8.

Howerd, W. (1988) *The Practice of Public Relations*, 3rd edn. Heinemann.

Jones, J. P. (1990) 'The double jeopardy of sales promotion', *Harvard Business Review*, September–October.

Kitchen, P. J. and Papasolomou, I. C. (1997) 'Marketing public relations – conceptual legitimacy or window dressing?', *Marketing Intelligence and Planning*, 15(2).

Lucas, A. (1996) 'In-store trade promotions – profit or loss?', *Journal of Consumer Marketing*, 13(2), pp. 48–50.

McDonald, M. (1984), *Marketing Plans*. Heinemann.

Miles, L. (1992), 'Going solo', *Marketing Business*, June.

Petersen, C. (1979), *Sales Promotion in Action*, Associated Business Press.

Quelch, J. A., Neslin, S. A. and Olson, L. B. (1987) 'Opportunities and risks of durable goods promotion', *Sloan Management Review*, Winter.

CASE STUDY

Troy Wright Communications

Troy Wright Communications (TWC) is a fast-growing PR and communications company, the product of a merger between Troy Corporate Relations and Wright Cyber Communications, formerly independent PR firms founded respectively by Alan Troy and Jenny Wright, now the joint Managing Directors of TWC. While each 'half' of the new company has markedly different competences – Jenny Wright's specialism is internet-enabled PR and on-line promotion, while Alan Troy's is corporate and financial PR – the 'urge to merge' came via a chance meeting of the two directors through an advertising agency event they attended in Central London. A few follow-up discussions convinced both parties of the case for combining forces, opening new joint business opportunities (e.g. with high-growth companies) while also enabling operational cost savings and, importantly, an upgrade in office location and facilities.

Now, one year on, TWC has roughly doubled both its gross revenues and its staffing, and is in negotiations with a leading venture capital fund for a financial restructuring package designed to support a still higher-gear growth programme.

A key element of the venture fund finance stake in the company is the expectation that high growth will be achieved, annually, over the next 3–4 years, and that contingent on this a market-flotation is then achieved, through the offices of the venture fund.

While Alan Troy and Jenny Wright have no problem in principle with this – they could become multi-millionaires if the growth and flotation programme succeeds – they need to formulate clear objectives.

In addition to redoubling efforts on core activities – on the one side integrated web communications and web design and on the other ongoing financial publicity and merger-related PR – the directors feel that they need to find 'concentric' growth paths in related fields that have potential.

Jenny Wright is already aware of the realignments taking place in the PR and Communications industry generally, with the advent of new media (e.g. satellite and digital TV, WWW) and of re-groupings among leading industry players (e.g. joint advertising and PR groups, and strategic success stories such as Incepta and Cordiant). Further, through contacts she has in the USA, she has watched with interest the sensational growth of dedicated hi-tech and technology PR Consultancy firms such as Text 100, Alexander Ogilvy PR and the Hoffman Agency, serving technology clients at science park locations such as Silicon Valley, Seattle, Boston and elsewhere. She feels that in the UK, in spite of some investor disenchantment with .com companies (which

TWC have avoided), there is a US-style growth market for Technology PR, possibly even linked with Alan Troy's Financial PR side of the business.

Meanwhile, Alan Troy has been reflecting on the opportunities that might drive growth if TWC went into the international PR field, possibly in Europe or even further afield (Central Europe, India?). Certainly, he is aware, from his own financial 'side' of TWC work, that both PR clients and their investor/financial briefs (e.g. the Telecom Italia transfer, or the Vodafone – Mannesman takeover) are becoming much more international.

Questions

1 *How might 'realignments' within the PR–Communications industry offer TWC opportunities?*

2 *Do you think TWC has been right in avoiding the .com phenomenon, or have they missed opportunities here?*

3 *What do you think is involved in technology PR work? What technology PR opportunities might exist in the UK market?*

4 *What activities do you think might be involved in international PR? Could you consider segmenting this potential market? Are there particular segments that might offer potential for TWC?*

5 *How would you propose that TWC move into either, or both, of the growth sectors (i.e. technology, international PR) identified?*

19 Selling

I have heard of a man who had a mind to sell his house, and therefore carried a piece of brick in his pocket, which he showed as a pattern to encourage purchasers.

Jonathan Swift (1667–1745)

INTRODUCTION

It is often easy to confuse *selling* and *marketing*. This is because the two disciplines are linked in many companies and sales marketing functions are easily found. But selling is not the same as marketing. It is, however, a key part of the marketing role and many of the skills of a good salesperson in understanding customers are required by good marketers.

The publicity material for a national sales training roadshow suggests that, 'No matter what business you are in, there are people out there waiting to buy. Lots of them. All you have to do is to find them before your competitors do.' There is nothing wrong with this statement if it is then developed into a range of activities consistent with a marketing approach. That is:

- identify target customers
- discover needs
- develop ways of fulfilling those needs.

Selling involves more of a micro-relationship than does marketing. The product is often given and restrictions on price and distribution can exist. The salesperson has less flexibility with the offer, and has to get sales now. But immediate sales are often made possible by existing relationships. What a salesperson must do is build on these personal relationships. They can do this by:

- augmenting product delivery in an appropriate way
- creating a more receptive attitude from potential customers by using a combination of information and persuasion.

The idea of a sales orientation was introduced in Chapter 1. Personal selling is a widely used way of reaching individual customers and can be defined as:

> **The process of identifying potential customers, informing them of a company's offer mix, and finding a match between the benefits offered and customers' needs through personal communication.**

Selling is very much part of the communication mix. It is *two-way and personal*. This means that salespeople have the maximum opportunity to find the connection between benefits and needs, and so to persuade the customer to change needs into wants.

Sales representatives are company advocates to the customer. But they can also be customer advocates whose detailed knowledge can be fed back to their company regarding future opportunities. Therefore, while selling is not marketing, it is wholly consistent with marketing. It is simply that part of marketing which deals with individual contacts with customers, and short-term achievement of sales with an existing offer mix.

TYPES OF SALES POSITIONS

To illustrate the major variations to be found within the sales occupation, Montcrief (1988) identified five distinct categories of industrial sales jobs, differing in terms of industrial setting and technical complexity, sales relationships and seniority. Taking a still wider perspective of the sales field, Lidstone (1994) proposed nine categories of sales position, ranging from inside order-takers in retail outlets to, 'missionary salespeople' undertaking more indirect sales-building duties, and technical salespeople selling industrial components and equipment. Figure 19.1 presents a simplified categorisation of sales positions broadly derived from the subdivisions proposed by Lidstone. Some brief comments will now be made on these categories of sales positions.

Order-takers

These sales staff perform a largely passive or reactive role in, literally, taking or collecting orders from customers who are either regular purchasers, or at least predisposed to buy.

Internal order-takers are typified by retail sales assistants, whose role may involve persuasively presenting, demonstrating or explaining products, but who often do little more than taking payment in exchange for wrapping and handing over the goods.

Another variation on internal order-taking, increasingly common in both manufacturing and service sectors, involves *telesales*, where sales assistants receive and process

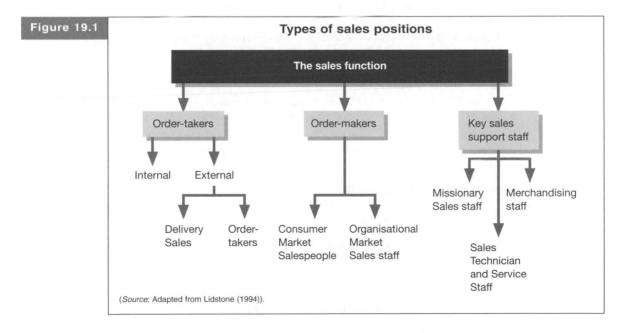

Figure 19.1   Types of sales positions

(*Source:* Adapted from Lidstone (1994)).

telephone orders from customers, or ring customer accounts at regular intervals to invite or receive new orders (see Overell 1998).

External order-takers involve sales personnel travelling to customers, either on request or at regular intervals, to collect orders, and maybe deal with associated paperwork and account queries. While many of these staff are still termed sales representatives, and some persuasion and presentation tasks may be called for (e.g. to 'push' special offers), the role is still largely passive, and is increasingly being replaced by telesales or tele-marketing operations.

Delivery salespeople are concerned largely with product delivery, often of perishable fast-moving products (e.g. bread deliveries to retail outlets), where the 'sale' involves little more than a standard replacement order of the same products. In household markets, perishable products such as newspapers and milk are still delivered to house-holders – though certainly milkround delivery sales continue to lose ground to super-market 'jumbo-pack' purchases made within the weekly food-shopping trip.

Order-makers

These positions are more proactive front-line sales jobs that require persuasive presentation, negotiation and customer-handling skills, often in highly competitive markets where, by definition, buyers can choose between alternative suppliers and products/services.

The sales representatives, or sales executives, that undertake such roles are likely to be well-trained specialist professionals whose duties include selling and advising on both existing and new products, to existing and new customers.

Consumer market salespeople undertake selling to individuals or households more complex or higher-value products (e.g. cars, cavity insulation, insurance) that require detailed explanation and technical advice, effective presentation, custom-ordering or price negotiation.

Organisational market sales staff undertake proactive selling to various organisational customers (e.g. commercial organisations, manufacturing firms, public sector bodies). While the products/services sold will obviously vary in technical sophistication (e.g. computer systems v. office stationery), the common factor in this role will be the service standards and professional commitment involved in developing and maintaining a business relationship with designated buyers and key 'influencers' at various levels within client organisations.

Depending on the market and product requirements, technical sophistication and issues of commercial viability, sales representatives in some organisational markets may operate as part of a team or 'account group' , involving support staff such as sales technicians or engineers, service staff, financing advisors and other specialists.

Key sales support staff

Within this catch-all grouping may be found various specialists undertaking important supporting roles.

Sales technicians and service staff may operate as team members alongside assigned sales representatives, or service product and client requirements at critical times (e.g. product installation, repairs) or by regular service visits.

Missionary sales staff are to be found in a number of markets (e.g. proprietary drugs, academic publishing) where the 'specifiers' that they visit (e.g. doctors, university lecturers) do not directly buy the product, but instead play a key role in prescribing or recommending it. Obviously, in such situations the 'sales' task is more indirect, involving up-to-date information provision and more subtle forms of recommendation.

The scope of selling

Notwithstanding the diversity that exists in the selling occupation, it is likely that most proactive sales positions are likely to have in common the following key activities:

- Prospecting or cold calling
- Customer interaction
- Account maintenance and development.

Prospecting or cold calling

The role of these prospectors is to seek out new customers, establish contacts and determine needs. They also need to identify the decision-makers and influencers who must be convinced if a sale is to be made. These salespeople work in the early *pre-transactional stage* with a new customer.

The skills required in finding potential new customers are very different from building relationships with existing customers. It is much harder to persuade a customer to buy for the first time than to get a repeat order from a satisfied customer. This is because it involves an element of the unknown.

Even if the customer knows the company or product, they may have to be convinced to change from a competitive product. Prospectors have to deal with customers who say they are not interested. They have to move these potential customers into making a first appointment. Having achieved this, they must remember that they never get a second chance to make a first impression. This is why one group of potential customers – lapsed users and former customers – can be even more difficult to win back. Former customers already know your company and its products but have decided to trade with your competitors. It may be a simple evaluation of product features and price which a new offer mix would change. It may, however, be that your company let the customer down, gave poor service or somehow upset the relationship. Undoing the past can be much more difficult than starting from a situation where nothing is known.

Perhaps the most powerful weapon a prospector can use is personal recommendation. When contacting a new customer it can help if you can say that an existing customer suggested the contact. In some industries, such as life assurance, the salespeople are trained to follow up with existing customers to get recommendations to new prospects. Life assurance is a product that is not purchased regularly, so salespeople are always trying to find suitable new prospects who have reached the right stage in their life cycles to require the product.

Customer interaction

This is the *transactional stage*. A customer could be:

- a 'hot prospect' – someone who is close to making a first purchase decision with your organisation
- an occasional customer, who conducts limited business with you
- a regular repeat customer or

■ an advocate who goes out of his or her way to trade with you.

The transactional stage is the most important as far as current performance is concerned because *current sales* are what keeps the organisation going. The process of making a sale is discussed later, because it is not solely the application of persuasive skills.

In some situations the customer comes to buy, for instance in a retail outlet or a visit to a manufacturer's factory. Here the salesperson has an advantage in that they are working in a familiar location. The disadvantage for retail sales staff is that they often have no knowledge of the potential customer, the customer background, or any previous history of a transaction with that particular customer. The salesperson has to find this out by suitable questioning.

In other situations, the sales representative or sales engineer can be visiting the customer. The seller will have researched the customer, have some knowledge of the customer needs and the previous history of transactions. But the customer will be on home territory. The salesperson has gone to sell. Issues such as the salespersons' attitudes, their beliefs in their products as well as their negotiation or persuasion skills are relevant in achieving success when selling. Chapter 2 included a short case study on the day of a travelling salesman. It will be apparent from this that the time spent actually face to face with a customer is comparatively short – sometimes less than 10 per cent of the salesperson's day. There are many other roles, like administration, that a salesperson needs to do. The need to make the contact time most effective is a critical role of a professional seller.

A good salesperson will have objectives for each individual customer. These objectives will lead to an individual strategy for the sales contact period with the customer. Such objectives could be:

■ For a *new customer/hot prospect* – an objection that has to be overcome
■ For an *occasional user* – to discover why they are not regular customers and find ways of increasing sales frequency
■ For a *regular customer* – to introduce an additional product line to complement existing purchases.

The objectives and strategy should be thought out in advance, but the very nature of personal selling means that issues will be raised during a meeting that will require the plan to be modified. In this situation, salespeople are on their own. They are the representatives of their organisation to the customer. They cannot continually refer back to Head Office for instructions, and so must fully understand the flexibility that they may have to vary the offer mix. They must beware that they do not make promises that cannot be kept, such as priority delivery dates. Of course they can make offers and promises that are possible. It is in this situation that a salesperson can be said to be at the sharp end of a company's operations.

Account maintenance and development

The building of relationships with customers is the key to *future profitable sales*. Therefore the process does not normally finish with a successful sale. Post-transactional activities start with successful, on time, delivery, but move through to many activities which forge strong relationships for the future. These could go as far as using computerised marketing and even distribution data to track relationships. Such benefits can be part of what is now called 'direct marketing.' It could mean establishing

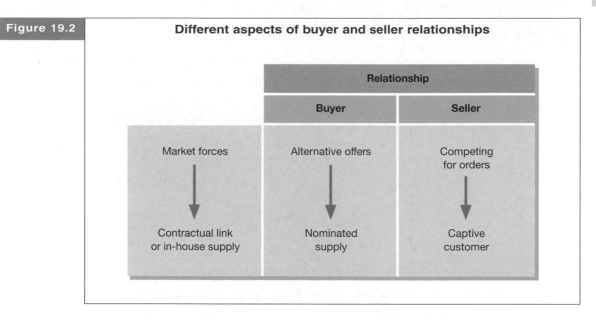

Figure 19.2

Different aspects of buyer and seller relationships

The elements of the figure show a continuum. Under **Relationship** are two columns: **Buyer** and **Seller**.

Market forces	Alternative offers	Competing for orders
↓	↓	↓
Contractual link or in-house supply	Nominated supply	Captive customer

electronic links for future re-ordering such as that which links the production planning department of JCB excavators to its suppliers, to really produce 'just-in-time' (JIT) ordering; or it could mean a simple note in a diary for a follow-up meeting. Figure 19.2 shows the continuum from a sale taken in a competitive market through to a close relationship, contractual link or dealing with an in-house supplier.

Losing customers is much easier than winning customers. The consulting firm Bain and Company has researched the situation, and concluded an increase of 2 per cent in the retention rate has the same effect on profits as cutting costs by 10 per cent – a worthwhile target. In cruder terms, *Business Week* suggested:

> Smart selling means building relationships with customers, not just slam-dunking them on a single sale.

The elements of what is sometimes called 'relationship marketing' were given by Christopher, Payne and Ballantyne (1991) as:

- Focus on customer retention
- Orientation on product benefits
- Long timescale
- High customer service emphasis
- High customer commitment
- High customer contact
- Quality as the concern of all.

It can be seen that in the building of strong relationships there is a key role for personal salespeople.

THE PRINCIPLES OF SELLING

The role of a salesperson is often that of a solitary representative of an organisation who visits other organisations. There are occasions and industries where team selling

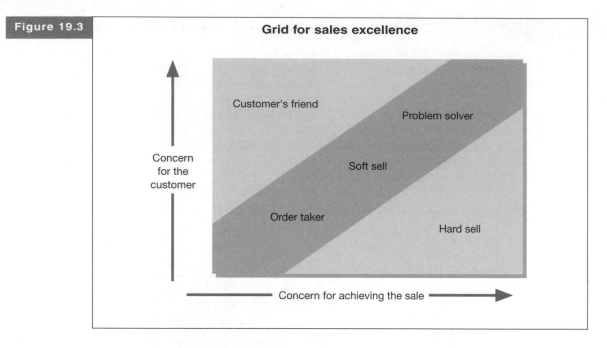

Figure 19.3

Grid for sales excellence

is appropriate (and, of course, there is the related issue of sales management), but many of the half-million UK salespeople work alone. The different roles of selling were discussed in the previous section but, for all groups, the principal role is to be an effective link between a *supplier organisation* and a *potential customer*.

The stereotype salesperson, depicted by Arthur Miller in his play *Death of a Salesman*, is a back-slapping, joke-telling individual who drops in each season to present products. This is still a reality in some industries and can be a relevant way of doing business in some instances. But, at a cost in excess of £50 for each sales call, it is a very expensive way of communicating with customers. There are many other ways of bringing products to customers' notice.

The principle of personal selling is that personal contact is a very powerful way of communicating. Blake and Mouton, who are best known for their work on management and leadership styles, produced a grid for the two elements of the selling role – concern for the customer and concern for achieving the sale (see Figure 19.3). Salespeople can fill all these roles. The relevant one for any particular situation is the one that matches the *buying style of the customer*.

The idea of a customer's friend could be: 'I want to understand the customer and respond to his feelings and interests so that he will like me.' It is the personal bond that leads him to purchase from me. This takes relationship marketing too far. However, it has more long-term opportunities than the hard sell: 'I'm in charge of the relationship and will pile on the pressure to get the customer to buy.' The hard-sell approach may seem appropriate to a commission salesperson who gets paid only when a sale is made, but it can go against the basic principle of identifying a customer's needs and satisfying them.

Neither of these positions really reflect the principles of modern selling. The better positions lie along the shaded diagonal in Figure 19.3, the actual position varying for different selling roles.

THE SELLING PROCESS

Selling is best thought of as a staged process of interaction with customers and prospects. Figure 19.4 presents the selling process in terms of a 7-stage sequence that broadly involves preparatory activity (Stages 1–2 in Figure 19.4), face-to-face contact and negotiation (Stages 3–6), and follow-up work (Stage 7). It should be noted that the 'sequence' depicted in Figure 19.4 is very much a simplification, and that in practice certainly the dynamics of the customer contact and negotiation stages may involve much to-and-fro exploratory discussion and tactical movement on the part of both parties.

Research

The research stage involves obtaining information on four key elements:

1 The product/offer mix
2 Competitors', products/offer mixes
3 The customers
4 The relationship between the organisation and the customer.

The first item seems obvious but it relies on proper *internal communications* in an organisation, so that the salesperson fully understands what is being offered. There have

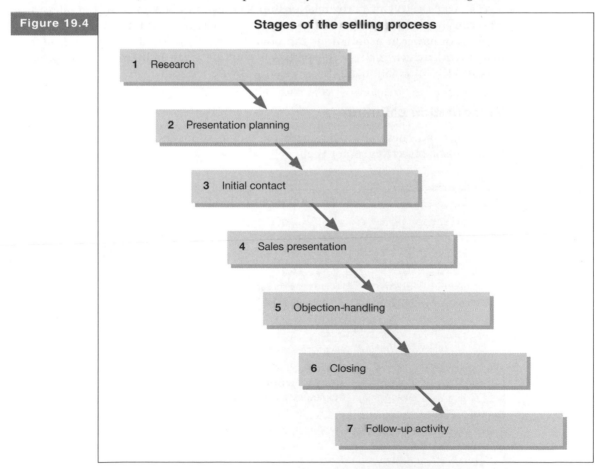

Figure 19.4

Stages of the selling process

1 Research

2 Presentation planning

3 Initial contact

4 Sales presentation

5 Objection-handling

6 Closing

7 Follow-up activity

been times when a customer has seen details of a new product, maybe in a trade journal, before the salesperson. You can imagine the embarrassment this can cause when a customer tells you your own business. It is also important for salespeople to know the constraints on how far they can negotiate. Buyers are well informed and this must not be underestimated. But the object is a win–win deal when both buyer and seller are satisfied. The limits need to be established well before negotiations start, hence the need for consistent and clear information.

Individual salespeople often learn a lot about their competitors and the directly competitive offerings being made, but employer organisations should not believe that all their salespeople will have full information on all issues in their market place. Collection and dissemination of information on competitors to all salespeople can be linked to suggestions on how to *counter the claims* that competitors could be making.

The third element is again obvious but necessary. It is the studying of the *prospect organisation*, and this helps to reveal opportunities and threats which could arise. The customers will obviously know their own organisation better than the salesperson, but if there are plans for expansion, or contraction, or other developments, then prior knowledge can help in setting objectives, and in the actual face-to-face situation.

Prior 'account' knowledge is equally necessary for maintaining the relationship between supplier and customer. Maybe there have been problems in the past, or perhaps there are reasons above normal trading that bind the organisations together. All *previous contacts* will affect the relationship, so they must be known by the salesperson who can then decide a negotiating strategy with regard to such information.

Issues of power in negotiations can often be directly referred to the *quality of information* with which each of the parties is working – research efforts to improve or update such information are therefore critically important.

Presentation planning

Experience indicates that, to be successful, presentations should be carefully planned, with realistic objectives set for them.

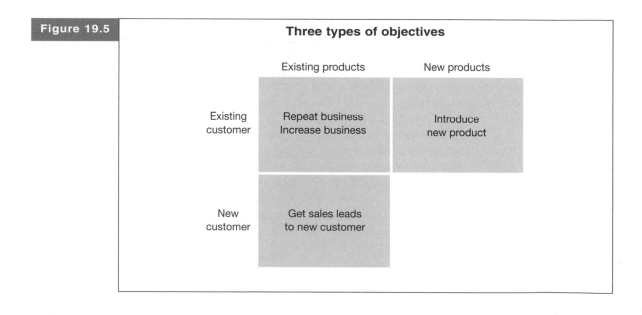

Figure 19.5

Three types of objectives

	Existing products	New products
Existing customer	Repeat business Increase business	Introduce new product
New customer	Get sales leads to new customer	

Setting objectives is necessary for businesses as a whole, and for individual sales calls. A strategy for a meeting with a customer will have objectives – let's say, for example, to get an order for 500 items, or to get machine X in the customer's plant for a test period, or to increase prices by 10 per cent and keep the business – but objectives must not be so rigid that they allow the customer no room for discussion or negotiation.

The requirement in setting objectives is to have an acceptable 'fall-back' position of alternatives which could be offered; not just price but perhaps payment terms, or special after-sales service, or free merchandising help. Such alternatives can be introduced during the negotiation, if appropriate, with a view to making an offer that is acceptable to the customer. There will be other objectives for a meeting, such as to introduce a new product to an existing customer, or even to discover the names of potential new customers for existing products. These objectives are illustrated in Figure 19.5 (derived from Ansoff's matrix).

Initial contact

No matter how enthusiastic or well-prepared the salesperson, the actual sales call must proceed in step with the *customer's schedule* and at the *customer's speed*, and all aspects of the sales presentation and discussion must be subject to the customer's ultimate sanction. The initial stages of customer contract – prior to the 'getting down to business' stages of the sales presentation onwards – are usually quite significant in terms of setting the scene and establishing a rapport with the customer. This may in various subtle ways go much beyond the standard social niceties such as greetings, introduction (necessary for cold-calling) or small talk, though it is interesting that some customers may value these conventions more than others. It is also likely that in international selling contexts the protocol of initial contacts may be heavily influenced by cultural factors, so that, for example, in many Far Eastern markets the rituals of introductions are taken very seriously and are certainly not to be hurried or treated lightly.

At the very least, it may be necessary for the salesperson to briefly justify the sales call, or its timing, to perhaps allow a mutual 'recap' of the current business or contract situation, and to lead in to the main business at hand, the sales presentation.

Sales presentation

Basically, the sales presentation represents a key part of the sales meeting or sales call, where the salesperson persuasively 'presents' to the buyer the product/service offering of the supplier organisation.

Successful sales outcomes usually depend on more than a 'canned presentation', the well-rehearsed script recital associated with the stereotype 'sales rep' – nowadays such repetitive messages are more likely to be conveyed by direct mail or telesales than by face-to-face contact.

To succeed, sales presentations, however well-prepared, must have some flexibility to allow for differences in customer requirements, or for any recent changes in needs or usage circumstances experienced by individual customers. To incorporate this flexibility, and so 'customise' the presentation, professional salespeople will usually devote the early part of their presentation to establishing, or confirming, the *particular needs of the buyer*. This will usually be done through a skilful, if seemingly casual, questioning process.

Questions need to be *open-ended* to allow customers to respond and to volunteer information that can be used in the subsequent presentation. Open questions are typically ones such as:

> 'In what way does this machine fail to meet your requirements?'
> 'What are the main reasons for your interest in this service?'

Closed questions, such as the ones below, do not give opportunities for enlargement:

> 'Does your company use a three-tonne press?'
> 'Who currently supplies this service?'

Questions can be used to identify problems, which in turn may indicate sales opportunities. But, during a sales meeting questions can also be used as a way of keeping control of the situation by dictating the agenda. A key aim of questioning, though, will be to define and refine buyer needs and problems, so that these in turn can feature a part of a customised offer that is expressed in terms of *benefits* that matter to the customer.

An offer must be: **acceptable**, **affordable** and **available**. Since the customers are the judges of these factors, it is preferable to present the customers with benefits they can understand, not technical features that could confuse. Benefits can be described at two levels:

- the benefits offered by a particular product or service
- the benefit of dealing with the salesperson's organisation.

The way to describe the benefits will come direct from questioning customers, and will often use the customer's own language, something all successful salespeople are able to do. In the earlier questioning stage, the benefits required will be probed. Later in the meeting, any objections and other issues would be dealt with.

Objection-handling

Objections are a natural part of the sales process. They can come during the initial approach for a meeting right up to the point when the salesperson is trying to close the sale. If no objections are raised, even an experienced salesperson will worry that something unknown is wrong. Objections are not usually excuses but genuine statements of interest. Some objections can highlight issues of key importance to a buyer, though others can be trivial or even false. In these cases the salesperson has to dig for the real problem. When handling objections it is essential that the salesperson does not take any objection personally. It is not a personal rejection and, if considered to be so, could be demoralising. Objections can be countered. Objections such as, 'I'm too busy to see you' can be countered by saying: 'Of course, I appreciate you are a busy person, but what I'd like to show you will only take ten minutes of your time.' This technique agrees with the prospect but then counters with a reasonable suggestion.

It is vital to respect the customer during negotiations. Do not interrupt and certainly do not argue with a prospect/customer: if there is an argument and the customer wins, the sale is probably lost; if the salesperson wins the argument, then the sale is most likely lost.

Closing

'Closing' is a word from sales jargon. It relates to the key requirement of closing the sale, getting the order, or meeting the objectives of the sales contact. To close, finish, bring to an end, conclude or complete is the last stage of a sales negotiation. But this is not a sudden action, at some pre-arranged time. It is a logical development that can take place at any time. Skilled salespeople look for signs, called *buying signals*, that the customer is ready to close. The body language is important in a personal sales situation, and it is often said that the whole period of contact is an attempt to bring the situation to a satisfactory close.

There are all sorts of devices for forcing a close, and successful salespeople have an instinct as to when they should use these. They know when to ask for an order, and then the golden rule is to shut up. By doing this, they do not talk themselves out of an order after the event. The use of silence is powerful in forcing customers to either accept the proposal or raise another objection. If a new objection is raised following an attempt to close (get an order), then the process of dealing with that objection, such as offering compensating benefits, is repeated. And then, perhaps, a new close can be attempted. A successful close might be the end of a particular sales contact but it is only the start of the next important stage – the follow-up.

Follow-up activity

It will come as no surprise to readers of this book that after-sales service is stressed as a key ingredient of follow-up activity. Of course, some delivery issues might be in the control of another department but, even if they let the customer down, it is the salesperson who has to visit the customer again next period. The salesperson is the real point of contact, and good after-sales service can mean increased business. It can also lead to contacts with new prospects. Poor service is likely to do the opposite.

Six things to avoid

Salespeople must carry out the various elements in the sales process effectively. However, there are six major mistakes that can be made even by successful salespeople:

1 Not following up quotations, enquiries or other promises quickly enough
2 Making unrealistic promises to customers
3 Overestimating their own ability to get a sale, and underestimating the competitor's ability
4 Exaggerating the probability, size and profitability of future orders
5 Underestimating a customer's potential
6 Overselling a customer, so that the customer buys more than is really required.

The first two factors are ones where there is no excuse. A good salesperson knows what is possible, and then deals with customers on that basis. The next two are more difficult. They stem from the necessary optimism and self-confidence required by a salesperson. In compiling sales forecasts from the estimates of sales forces, a usual precaution is to reduce such predictions by a little to allow for excess claims. The final two factors, underestimating potential and overselling, are major errors. It is difficult to identify when underestimating happens, but it obviously represents a lost opportunity. It is cheaper to get increased business from existing customers than from new customers, and hence the full potential of existing customers must be considered. But overselling is perhaps a worse mistake. In the continuous contact between supplier and customer, this represents an abuse. It will not help the building of trust that is so necessary in a good relationship.

SALES MANAGEMENT

To produce cost-effective results, and to fit in with overall marketing plans and strategies, personal selling activities need to be organised and managed. While sales management is a broad field, and company approaches to it may vary in practice, most commentators would agree that, like the general field of management itself, it covers both longer-term tasks (forecasting, budgeting, planning, strategy formulation) and day-to-day activities (e.g. monitoring, staff motivation and control).

Figure 19.6 presents a simplified breakdown of the different aspects of sales management. While this is based on an 'average' company with its sales force, it is worth noting that some companies (e.g. smaller firms) may not have any full-time salespeople, while by contrast very large companies may require many managerial subdivisions not reflected in diagram (e.g. regional sales managers, telesales sections, area sales offices, and Head Office-based salespeople such as key account personnel and sales administration managers).

Strategic sales planning

A planned sales effort, often formally expressed in a *sales plan*, needs to be consistent with the company's marketing plan, and in turn with the overall corporate or business plan.

Logically, the marketing plan will heavily influence the significance and role of sales activity (v. other 'mix' elements such as direct mail or advertising), and it will indicate key targets for sales management to follow, such as:

■ Sales volume (unit and value $)
■ Profitability (various measures)
■ Market share (% by market or segment)
■ Resource constraints (e.g. staffing and expenditure budgets).

Again, the marketing plan will effectively give the lead on which sales objectives sales managers should follow (e.g. build market share, maintain distribution coverage, find new customers, promote new products etc.). In turn, these overall sales objectives will help sales managers to determine targets or quotes for individual sales representatives (e.g. numbers of new accounts opened, percentage of customers taking new product A, volume of orders for 'special' promotion offer B).

Sales force design

This involves the twin decisions on what size sales force to have, and how it should be organised (or structured). While, obviously, in a dynamic market setting some changes in sales team size and organisation may be quite common (e.g. for staff turnover), it will only be infrequently that wholesale re-organisation-reconfiguration decisions are made.

Figure 19.6

The tasks of sales management

Strategic sales planning

Sales force design
(i) Sales force size   (ii) Sales force organisation

Sales force management
• Recruitment and selection
• Training
• Motivation and compensation
• Evaluation and control

Sales monitoring and marketing co-ordination

Sales force size

The sales force is an expensive resource, but the cost is not the prime consideration in determining size. The question must be: 'What is appropriate for the task to be tackled?' Two approaches are commonly used to indicate appropriate sales force size:

1 The workload approach
2 The productivity approach.

The *workload* approach recognises that there is only so much work any individual can tackle. If it is possible to calculate the number of customers, and frequency of calls, then this can be related to the workload and hence the required size of sales force. But this may not be appropriate to develop new customers. The *productivity* approach looks at sales potential and costs to work out when the marginal return matches costs.

Often sales forces are well established, which makes it difficult to suddenly increase or reduce the numbers employed. It does take time to train new salespeople, but this must be provided for as salespeople are mobile in their careers. In any company up to 10 per cent of the sales force could leave every year. Hence, the level of investment in the sales force needs to be continually reviewed, and modifications accommodated as part of regular staff turnover.

Sales force structure

The effectiveness of a sales force will be related to both the individual skills of the salespeople and the structure chosen. For instance, it would be difficult to continually change sales territories if it is accepted that a key role of selling is to build good relationships with customers. Historically, field sales forces have been subdivided into geographical territories. Sometimes the division goes further, with salespeople specialising by groups of products, or by a particular type of customer.

Geographical territories

Dividing the sales force into geographical territories allows a salesperson to become responsible for a certain geographical area. The territories should be organised in a way which makes the possible workload as similar as possible in each territory. The size of the territory should be such that little time is wasted in excessive travelling. A key advantage of a territorial design is *continuity of service,* so that customers can get to know and trust the salesperson. Also, administration and expenses can be more easily controlled.

Division by product

When the sales force is divided by product speciality, some salespeople are responsible for one group of products while others are responsible for different products. The main advantage of this method of organisation is that the salespeople can develop deeper and more specialist product knowledge. A disadvantage is that costs may be duplicated if customers buy more than one of the firm's products, since this would entail visits by more than one salesperson.

Division by type of outlet

By using this type of organisation of a sales force, a supplier hopes to take advantage of the different skills that may be required when servicing different industries. This is quite common in the industrial sector where engineering firms may make components which can be used in several large industries. The salesperson will then try to become an expert in selling to one particular type of industry, by building up knowledge about the needs of that industry.

There is no universally right answer to sales force organisation. There can be intensive coverage and selective coverage in sales, just as in the case of channels of distribution. Life insurance salespeople could claim to be part of both the communications mix and distribution. A large national life insurance company could use intensive coverage even if it meant occasional conflicts when two salespeople contacted the same prospect. However, for the multiproduct company, organisation by products and customers meant some customers received multiple visits from sales representatives from the same company.

This example shows how sales organisation links to distribution for physical goods. In fact the whole marketing mix is interrelated, so any decision on a sales force or its organisation must be part of a *totally integrated marketing plan*, and not taken solely for sales convenience.

Example At one time a survey by Cadbury Schweppes showed a single wholesaler received visits from Cadbury Confectionery, Cadbury Foods (Marvel, Smash, Biscuits), Typhoo Tea, Chivers-Hartley jam and marmalade, Cadbury-Typhoo Catering Foods, Schweppes drinks, Jeyes disinfectants and Kenco coffee. Some of these calls were every week, some every month, but with eight separate representatives involved, then eight different relationships were being established. This situation has now changed as Cadbury Schweppes have sold several of these subsidiaries, but at the time the distribution of four of the companies was handled by a single delivery operation. Often this meant four separate deliveries, each week, to the same customer: clearly a costly operation.

Sales force management

This involves direct management of salespeople (i.e. the sales force) and will usually represent the main responsibilities of sales management, though it is worth noting

Table 19.1   The sales recruitment and selection process

Stage I	Outline job description
Stage II	Develop person specification
Stage III	Advertise/communicate vacant sales position
Stage IV	Receive and shortlist applications
Stage V	Interview and/or other selection methods
Stage VI	Job offer: (a) Unconditional – immediate start
	(b) Conditional – subject to successful training and/or trial selling period

that many sales support activities and personnel (e.g. sales administration, technical support, contract documentation, invoicing etc.) will also come within the scope of sales management. Core elements of sales force management, though, will range from sales recruitment to training, motivation and evaluation.

Recruitment and selection

As with all aspects of organisation, ultimate success in sales depends critically on the quality and capability of staff. The importance of recruiting salespeople of the right quality cannot be overstated.

Within companies that find themselves regularly recruiting sales staff – perhaps through business growth or more likely staff turnover – recruitment usually follows an established sequence, as outlined in Table 19.1 and briefly explained below.

In Stage I the job description is written up, in terms of job title (e.g. Sales Executive, Tertiary Sales Specialist), main duties, location (e.g. regionally or sales office-based), reporting relationships etc.

In turn, this allows the profiling of a person specification (Stage II), written in terms of the personal qualities applicants must have – e.g. qualifications, industry background, selling experience, specialist attributes (e.g. higher-level negotiating experience, specific software capabilities, etc.).

The job advertisement (Stage III) will contain summary points from both job description and person specification, and will probably appear in regional or national newspapers, or suitable trade/industry publications. (*Note*: With larger companies that frequently recruit sales representatives, and particularly for more senior sales positions, specialist recruitment agencies may be used, either at certain stages e.g. Stages III and IV – or through all stages of the process).

The shortlisting process (Stage IV) is likely to be made by screening applicants against the criteria laid out in the person specification, though other factors may be relevant (e.g. present salary or applicant expectations, stated willingness to relocate, etc.).

In Stage V, whether selection is made solely through interview(s) or other means (e.g. selling demonstrations, role-play), candidates must state requirements, perhaps through possession of key personal qualities held to be correlates of high sales performance. Unfortunately, there is little consensus on what personal qualities are sought from sales applicants. Table 19.2 presents a general listing of salesperson qualities commonly cited positively by customers. While such a profile has much intuitive appeal, it is unlikely to be exhaustive or practically useful, and may represent little more than 'accepted wisdom'.

It is somewhat disappointing, though, that across a 30-year spread of formal research studies within this area (see, for example, Garfield 1989; McMurry 1961) there is little more to show than a succession of *differing* (sometimes conflicting) *trait listings*, usually

Table 19.2   Salesperson qualities rated positively by customers

- Self-organisation, good preparation
- Sincerity and honesty
- Conscientious and thorough
- Technical expertise
- Market and competitor knowledge
- Detailed product knowledge
- Positive problem-solving attitude
- Courtesy and tact
- Assertive and confident
- Customer sensitivity

with no indication of weightings, or how in practice to measure or test (sales applicants) for these qualities.

Unsurprisingly, therefore, selection methods and criteria vary somewhat across companies. For some companies, intensive (or multiple) interviews are favoured, while 'selection centres' (group dynamics sessions), mock sales interviews and role plays, personality or aptitude tests are favoured by the recruiters. Lorge (1999) reports on the application of user-friendly selection tests to aid sales recruitment within a US software company.

Again, given the uncertainties of the appointments process – paralleled by an increasing mobility among salespeople and competitive 'poaching' of prospective high-fliers – it is not uncommon to find the terms of job offers (salary start, commission rates, allowances and other benefits) to be conditional on successful training or a probationary period.

Training

Training is important for all new sales recruits, whether they are new to selling or experienced salespeople transferring in to the company. For the latter, at least some *induction training* (e.g. in company products, procedures, reporting contacts) will be needed.

Obviously, for new sales 'trainee' recruits a more comprehensive sales training programme is called for, which may take from a few weeks to many months. The elements of such sales training are likely to include skills development and knowledge in:

- Company products, policies and procedures
- Competitor products, competitor suppliers, market trends and analysis
- Company organisation, policies and procedures
- Client/customer needs, user problems, customer profiles
- Sales skills and competencies, e.g. negotiation, closing techniques
- Practical advice on self-organisation, territory analysis, call planning.

Various approaches and media are used in sales training, and certainly large companies with sizeable sales forces may have dedicated trainers, perhaps headed by a Sales Training Manager, who operates both standardised training courses (e.g. for new recruit training and induction) and customised courses (e.g. for new product launch programmes, for newly promoted sales staff).

Training aids and media can vary from discussions and specialist subject presentations to case studies, videos and live recordings-playback sessions, guest speakers etc. Increasingly, also, sales representatives are being issued self-tuition or distance-learning training aids such as training videos, dedicated literature and CD-ROM-driven interactive programmes. Even in the absence of specialist in-house training resources, sales management can call on a growing number of outside consultants, professional bodies and sales trainers, for both standard sales-marketing courses and for more specific customised training programmes. Additional to such formalised programmes, more continuous, if less structured approach to sales training involves *on the job training*, whereby salespeople literally learn as they go.

Sales recruits, after some initial formal training, would typically commence regular sales duties in their assigned territory, initially accompanied by a trainer but progressively learning-by-doing and 'going solo'. Such field sales training may also feature as part of continuing development and refresher training for all sales representatives, and will usually be effected through periodic field visits (or accompaniment) by the sales representative's sales manager.

Control ratios

The decision to use a sales force to communicate with customers is an expensive one. Even a small sales team can cost several million pounds every year. Therefore the expenditure should be treated as an investment, in just the same way as an investment in other communication media, or an investment in plant or equipment. There are alternative ways of reaching customers, but if the sales force is the way chosen, the sales performance must be controlled.

An investment needs to be monitored to ensure it is giving an adequate return; in this case the return will be measured in terms of *sales made*. However, there is no way of guaranteeing sales, and, in many organisations, salespeople do overestimate the probability of getting future orders. Unfortunately, when these orders are not forthcoming, it is often too late for the manager to take action to generate the required level of business. While sales orders are obviously required as an output, the measurement of sales level as the control is only one way to gauge selling success. In fact, sales levels are a resultant effect of the total selling operation. For instance, there should be a mixture of sales calls that produce the desired results, and some that do not. To assume all sales calls will produce orders is a mistake. Therefore it is important to measure elements of selling which can be considered the cause rather than the effect of sales performance.

In this context there are *three key control ratios* which could indicate how the business is developing:

1 Call effectiveness
2 Strike rate
3 Prospecting success.

Call effectiveness measures the *average return from a successful sales visit*. It can be average sales revenue per order, or profit per order. Since the cost of a call is not very different (whether the order received is large or small), this measure can be used to show if too many small, perhaps unprofitable, calls are being made. Of course, it is also important to maintain the level of successful calls.

'Strike rate' measures the *ratio of orders received to calls made*, or sometimes orders received to quotations issued. It measures the productive level of the salesperson.

The third key measure involves *new business prospecting success*, which obviously comes from new customers/prospects. If the customer group is not being renewed, there is a problem when an existing customer ceases to order. The measure can be expressed as numbers of new customers (who order for the first time) as a proportion of all prospect calls (where no order has yet been received). This measure reflects the difficulty in converting prospects into customers. It sometimes includes a measure of total calls as well.

These three ratios need to be linked to the *total call rate* to give a good measure of the effectiveness of individual salespeople. There are other ratios suggested in sales textbooks, but the controls covering how many calls a salesperson makes and how successful they are, on average, in each call, actually get closer to the cause of sales performance than the output of sales revenue.

Motivation

The management function is widely researched and many theories of motivation have been suggested. Motivation is particularly important with a sales force because of the scattered locations which could be involved, and the individual natures of most salespeople. This book is not the place to discuss the theories of human resource management (HRM) and psychology, but a few relevant points can be made. Salespeople often work alone – regular, scheduled sales meetings, bringing people together, say once a month, can motivate individuals by group recognition and support. Salespeople tend to have a strong driving force. Stick-and-carrot techniques do not necessarily work well in this situation. The use of monetary rewards such as bonus payments and commission systems can prove effective means of directing supplementary efforts and acknowledging achievements, though the design and operation of such schemes is fraught with administrative difficulties and potential inequity. McAdams (1987) provides a useful review of reward systems, while in a similar vein, Murphy and Sohi (1995) propose a more informed approach to the use of one-off rewards and incentives such as sales contests. Of increased significance within a context of relationship marketing, the mutual benefits and motivations of teamwork have been re-examined by Cespedes *et al.* (1989), while Cron *et al.* (1988) stress the career-related aspects of motivation at the individual level.

Figure 19.7 presents a basic theoretical model of motivation, though clearly the issue is highly conditional and dynamic, requiring great care and sensitivity on the part of sales managers and corporate management alike.

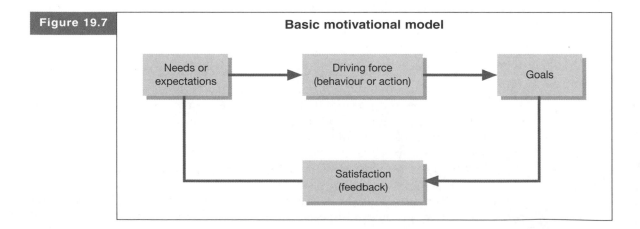

Figure 19.7

Basic motivational model

FUTURE TRENDS IN SELLING

When thinking of salespeople, there is a general image of company car, lunch allowance, stopping at good hotels, in fact a good life. But in practice the car doubles as an office, the lunch is often a rushed sandwich between calls and hotels are just boring. But selling can be a good life for those who enjoy meeting people. The problem is that much time is spent doing administration, driving, waiting and sorting out problems caused elsewhere in the organisation. Three trends need to be considered to conclude this section on selling:

1 Can new technology be used to make salespeople more effective in their profession?
2 Are there situations where direct personal selling is no longer cost-effective, and what happens in this case?
3 Are there changes in the structure of industries that mean the sales role must be redefined?

Selling is about meeting people, establishing relationships and communication. This cannot be replaced by modern technology but it can be helped by such developments. The aim is to improve effectiveness. For instance, mobile phones can keep salespeople in contact with their base. Entering orders into a laptop is faster than writing an order. The orders can be downloaded automatically via telephone lines and directly input into the delivery schedule with minimal delay. Word processors can produce standard quotations twice as fast. Direct marketing databases can store much more information than a handwritten record card, and the information in the database can be analysed to help a salesperson target a customer more precisely. Increasingly, technology advances are making for greater speed, accuracy and administrative efficiency in both the core sales role and at the level of sales management and planning.

In terms of software, recent developments have made quite commonplace the provision of tailored sales territory maps and routing systems, customer account and office administration systems, forecasting and modelling packages, and sophisticated customer relationship management and direct marketing software. Overlapping such developments, rapid improvements in multi-media and communications technology have made themselves felt in state-of-the-art audio-visual facilities for sales presentations and business meetings, in interactive communications and research through the Internet and intranet, and in a span of other innovations ranging from voice-activated foreign language translation software to multi-size video conferencing networks. Commenting on the extent to which such technological aids have been harnessed within the sales field, Rines (1995) has suggested that the art of selling is becoming more interface than face-to-face. Anderson (1996) sees the selling and sales management field moving generally to greater professionalism.

Many uses are being made of modern technology to improve preparation and the following up of sales calls. Even during the call a salesperson could show a video or use a small printer to print a personalised quotation. Generally, there is a growing interest and investment in sales force automation (see Parthasarathy and Sohi 1997; Keiller et al., 1997).

A direct call by a salesperson could be replaced by a telephone call. This could save 90 per cent of the cost of the direct call. The loss of contact might not be critical, although there is evidence of both a reduction in sales received and more especially of information required for the future. Sometimes a successful hybrid system can be used, combining fewer sales visits with regular telesales contact. Another development mentioned earlier is direct computer-to-computer re-ordering links between customer and supplier. These can again be supplemented with periodic direct sales contact.

In some organisations, and in some industries, suppliers have decided that the cost of sales staff is greater than the benefits (see Brown-Humes 1997; Howard 1998). These are areas where the supplier lets customers choose for themselves. In the past this has happened with self-service retail stores replacing traditional service, self-service petrol-stations, cash and carry wholesalers replacing delivered wholesalers and direct (mail order) insurance companies challenging traditional insurance brokers. The sensible rule is to reassess continually the investment in a sales force against the benefits received.

In some industries, it is the customers and their needs that are changing. Not many years ago sales forces for major food manufacturers had several hundred people, each calling on a number of outlets. Now buying is centralised and a team approach is used with perhaps a senior sales account manager meeting a buying director, then account managers liaising with regional managers who control a number of stores, and, finally, maybe a part-time merchandiser visiting an individual outlet. In this situation, there is a need to ensure excellent teamwork. Good communications between the various members of the sales team and an appropriate contact with the customer are essential.

Example	Donaldson (1998) gives an informative account of how Kraft General Foods radically restructured its sales operations, reducing the sales force from a headcount of almost 300 to 24 key account managers. This change reflected changes in buying centralisation among major food retailers, increasing costs of servicing smaller independent retailers and the need to have a more senior, strategic and flexible representation format with key accounts.

The major sales force may not be used, but the senior account manager could have a role to negotiate sales. The account manager might ensure orders are placed and influence deliveries either direct to stores or to the retailer's central warehouse. The merchandiser is not a salesperson but efforts to improve product displays can ensure the product sells through the intermediary on to the eventual consumer. This type of multi-level contact can build very strong relationships, each at a relevant level. It is an example of assessing the task and answering the question, 'What is appropriate for the task?' The answer should cover all elements of marketing, but there is no reason that it must require a direct sales organisation.

CONCLUSION

This chapter has demonstrated the key role of personal selling as one way of reaching customers. While most selling activities are more immediate, or short-term, the marketing skills of understanding customer needs are equally necessary. There are many levels to building personal relationships with customers and a successful salesperson will usually understand all of these. Selling is not just the actual customer contact. It includes a great deal of preparation and follow-up. In these activities sales and marketing are closely related, and the people concerned need to work together.

Marketing managers have been described as representing the environment within the company as well as projecting the organisation out into its environment. To do this involves meeting customers. Salespeople are doing this all the time and can be a key part of such information channels. However, marketers must not leave it all to the sales force who have a key task of getting the sales required now to keep the company in business. In many companies the marketing or product managers will plan to accompany a sales visit or attend a sales meeting at least once a month. But more than this, marketing must ensure the sales force are always informed of key decisions that could affect sales prospects and outcomes.

QUESTIONS

1 *What is the difference between a salesperson involved in prospecting and a salesperson concentrating on account maintenance? Do you think these involve different skills?*

2 *Suggest some simple ways a salesperson can build a strong relationship with all customers, even if that salesperson regularly contacts 500 of them.*

3 *Why is preparation so important in the selling process?*

4 *How should a salesperson deal with objections raised by customers during a sales presentation?*

FURTHER READING

Anderson, R. E. (1996) 'Personal selling and sales management in the new millennium', *Journal of Personal Selling and Sales Management*, 16(4).

Blake, R. and Mouton, J. (1970) *Grid for Sales Excellence*. McGraw-Hill.

Brown-Humes, C. (1997) 'Staff to go as Eagle Star disband direct sales team', *Financial Times*, 13 November, p. 10.

Cespedes, F. V., Doyle, S. and Freedman, R. J. I. (1989) 'Teamwork for today's selling', *Harvard Business Review*, March–April.

Christopher, M., Payne, A. and Ballantyne, D. (1991) *Relationship Marketing*. Heinemann.

Cron, W. L. et al. (1988) 'The influence of career stages on components of salesperson motivation', *Journal of Marketing*, 52.

Donaldson, B. (1998) *Sales Management: Theory and Practice*, 2nd edn. Macmillan.

Garfield, C. (1989) 'What makes a top performer?', *Sales & Marketing Management*, May.

Howard, L. (1998) 'UK direct sales force held to be "uneconomic"', *National Underwaiter*, 15 June, pp. 23–8.

Keiller, B. D., Bashaw, R. E. and Pettijohn C. E. (1997) 'Salesforce automation issues prior to implementation', *Journal of Business and Industrial Marketing*, 12(3–4).

Lidstone, J. (1994) in M. J. Baker (ed.), *The Marketing Book*, 3rd edn. Butterworth Heinemann.

Lorge, S. (1999) 'Recruiting the right rep', *Sales and Marketing Management*, November.

McAdams, J. (1987) 'Rewarding sales and marketing performance', *Management Review*, April, pp. 33–8.

McCall, J. B. and Warrington, J. B. (1984) *Marketing by Agreement*. Wiley.

McMurray, R. N. (1961) 'The mystique of super-salesmanship', *Harvard Business Review*, March–April.

Meredith, S. (1997) 'We have the technology', *Marketing Business*, Chartered Institute of Marketing.

Miller, A. (1949) *Death of a Salesman*. Penguin.

Moncrief, W. C. (1988) 'Five types of industrial sales jobs', *Industrial Marketing Management*, 17, pp. 161–7.

Mullins, L. J. (1989) *Management and Organisational Behaviour*, 2nd edn. Pitman.

Murphy, W. H. and Sohi, R. S. (1995) 'Salespersons' perceptions about sales contests: towards a greater understanding', *European Journal of Marketing*, 29(13), pp. 42–67.

Oliver, J. (1996) 'New improved salesforce', *Management Today*, December, p. 82.

Overell, S. (1998) 'On-call targets bring back the mill', *Sunday Telegraph*, 12 July, p. A6.

Parthasarathy, M., Sohi, R. S. (1997) 'Salesforce automation and the adoption of technological innovations by salespeople: theory and implications', *Journal of Business and Industrial Marketing*, 12(3–4).

Power, C. and Driscoll, L. (1992) 'Smart selling', *Business Week*, 3 August.

Rines, S. (1995) 'Forcing change', *Marketing Week*, March.

Stafford, J. and Grant, C. (1986) *Effective Sales Management*. Heinemann.

Whitford, D. (1998) 'Another good day for a Dell sales whiz', *Fortune*, 20 July, pp. 146.

CASE STUDY

Debbie Harris, candidate no. 2: key account executive post

Debbie Harris, a 25-year-old marketing graduate from a well-known Midlands-based new University business school, has just been shortlisted for the final round of appointment interviews to the post of key account executive at Giftworld Ltd. In the four years since her graduation, Debbie worked for a year in a commission-only sales job with a local newspaper, followed by a successful three-year stint as a full-time sales representative with a London-based importer and distributor of sports equipment and accessories.

During her three years as a sales representative, she considers that she has gained valuable experience and achieved sales success in a stereotypically male-dominated environment. Keen to move up the career ladder, possibly into marketing or promotion management, she felt that the key account executive vacancy at Giftworld Ltd would fit her experience, offer new challenges and move her nearer towards her career goal. As a candidate for the job, she was very pleased to be one of three (of a field of nine) to successfully come through a day filled out by two first-stage interviews and a series of psychometric tests. She has just received a letter from Brian Slattery, sales director of Giftworld Ltd, inviting her to attend the final selection stage for the post in 8 days time.

Giftworld Ltd are manufacturers of silverplated gifts and importers of other items to enlarge the range of products available to a wide mix of customers. These customers range from a large supplier of thermal underwear who this year offered a small silverplated tray with their direct mailshots, through to many organisations who order items to use as gifts for clients. In these latter cases, Giftworld often used an in-house engraving facility to add the customer's name or logo to the gift so that it could be used as a key part of that customer's promotional plans.

Many regular customers place large orders at key occasions such as Christmas, when over 60 per cent of all Giftworld's sales are made. Every February the company exhibits at the Birmingham International Spring Fair, held at the NEC, which attracts over 90 000 trade visitors. This exhibition, together with advertisements in *Promotion and Incentive Magazine*, are the source of most new customer enquiries. However, many of the new customers want only gifts for Christmas, so there is an increasing problem of maintaining the level of work for the rest of the year.

Over the last few years a silverplated 'Mother's Day' tray engraved 'For Mother' has been advertised in a number of consumer magazines, which has proved successful in sales volume terms and has filled the post-Christmas slack time, Mothering Sunday being in March. This product was the idea of one employee who remembered the immensely successful 'Coronation' tray, though unfortunately such high-profile events occur infrequently. Giftworld have also tried to market a 'wedding day' tray but this has proved less successful as weddings are not confined to one part of the year and the number of weddings has fallen to an all-time low.

The problem Giftworld have is how to ensure they use their silverplating capacity to its full at the other times of the year. It is believed the mailshot by the thermal company will not be renewed in future years and so from March, when the Mother's Day trays finish, to September when production starts for Christmas orders, there is the prospect of very little work, except low-value subcontracting orders.

Faced with the prospect of a permanent sales trough for at least half of the year, the company finally decided to bite the bullet and create a dedicated sales position to develop key sales openings to fill the gap, and to improve sales profitability generally.

While the company already has two salesmen, one covering the Midlands, and the other the North of England, these have largely reactive order-taker roles, and report weekly to the Sales Office Manager at the company's main office in Bradford. With a general brief responsible for sales policy and development, exhibitions and PR, Brian Slattery, the sales director, has a natural interest in the new key account sales post, and is of the view that the appointee should combine hard-hitting sales skills with creative ideas on new business development.

With this in mind, he has personally written to the three final candidates, informing them of their individual schedule on the selection day. In addition to a 30-minute tour of the factory and a 45-minute final interview (with the managing director and Slattery himself), candidates will be expected to give a 30-minute presentation based on the theme 'Key Sales Development Prospects at Giftworld Ltd – A preliminary assessment' , followed by 10–15 minutes of questions.

Questions

1 *Consider the preparations that you would advise Debbie Harris to make for the selection day.*

2 *What would you advise in terms of structure and general content for her presentation?*

Product policy and new product development

He that will not apply new remedies must expect new evils; for time is the greatest innovator.

Francis Bacon

INTRODUCTION

Product policy is of fundamental strategic importance in marketing. At its most basic, it involves an organisation in a commitment to a deliberate policy on which markets it is to serve, with which products/services and marketing offerings. Though such a policy will doubtless change over time to reflect market dynamics, it should be robust enough to provide a guide for key commercial decisions across an organisation. It therefore needs to be based on sound analysis of an organisation's capabilities and standing within its chosen markets. An effective product policy should ensure an organisation is able to match its objectives to market requirements by ensuring it is able to provide the products and services needed to do this.

As it is an organisation's product/service offerings that provide the most enduring link with its customers, it is essential that this aspect of the marketing offering matches the expectations of customers. Other elements of the marketing mix can alter a customer's expectations but cannot compensate for a product failing to meet these (revised) expectations. The actual product or service offered is the obvious focus of attention for all customers, and for all staff and service functions within the company. It will also, of course, be an object of interest to leading competitors, suppliers, potential customers, intermediaries and many others.

THE ESSENTIALS OF PRODUCT POLICY

A company's product policy may not explicitly appear in any one policy document or statement, but should significantly influence all major decisions involving corporate and marketing strategy that may affect product planning, future development and innovation. Product policy will therefore integrate closely with the organisation's mission statement and any ongoing re-evaluation of 'what business are we in?' Essentially, product policy will be concerned with:

1 Developing strategic guidelines relevant to both the marketing of existing products/services and the development of new products. While these guidelines will be associated with company-wide objectives such as profitability and growth-market share potential, they will also reflect corporate policy in respect of what is a desirable mix of product and service features to be offered. These guidelines will deter-

mine the overall strategic direction of the company in terms of product-market development, and will be the concern of senior management and marketing decision-makers.

2 Translating these general guidelines into operational performance at the level of both individual product and service features as well as the wider product mix. Specifically:

(a) For existing products/services, this will involve managing and monitoring the marketing of these offerings in respect of markets served, quality-performance indicators such as profitability and image, sales targets and competitive standing. These tasks will be the core of day-to-day marketing at the product level. While companies will vary in the way in which they staff and organise these ongoing activities, it is not uncommon in larger companies to find a division of marketing responsibilities according to product lines or brands, by the employment of specialist brand managers or product managers, within the marketing department. (Though a more detailed examination of marketing organisation approaches will be made later, for present purposes it is enough to understand that each brand or product manager looks after the marketing and competitive 'health' of an allocated number of the company's brand ranges or offerings.) Managing products and services and developing brands represents the most obvious marketing tasks of the company on a day-by-day basis. While for many existing products there will be a comfortable and familiar job to be done in maintaining an established position within the chosen market place, there will occasionally be the need to engage in more radical changes in marketing plans, and in the very offering itself. The dynamics of customer tastes, or the cut-and-thrust nature of competitive marketing or new product activity, may sometimes make it necessary to change fundamentally the marketing of certain products, to redesign and re-present them, perhaps for a different market, or even to delete them from the range.

(b) In due course new products could be added to a product range, and occasionally new offerings could be substituted for withdrawn products. The reasons could relate to extraneous factors such as competition or market change, or perhaps the need to achieve corporate growth or diversification objectives. While the arguments for a market-centred approach to new product development are nowadays accepted by most companies, the successful development and launch of new products and services involves the commitment of marketing resources to an integrated company-wide innovation effort. As with comparable activities such as product modification and relaunch, new introductions and their marketing involve effectively rebalancing the total product range, and should reflect decisions on product policy made at the corporate level. Within such a market-centred approach to new product development the role of the marketer will be to advise, inform and initiate product change, and to participate in a cross-disciplinary teamwork approach to development and commercialisation.

Product policy thus represents an important aspect of corporate and operational decision-making involving:

1 Managing and marketing existing products and services.
2 Effecting ongoing modifications to ensure the marketing of the current product range meets new market requirements.
3 Developing and commercialising new products and services, as part of a total corporate plan.

THE PRODUCT LIFE CYCLE

The idea that product and marketing offerings are subject to a kind of life cycle was first introduced in Chapter 1 and reinforced in Chapter 9. The 'product life cycle' concept is an accepted aspect of marketing theory and it provides a potentially valuable way of considering a product and its marketing needs. For this reason it is now appropriate to discuss this concept in greater detail. The basic life cycle pattern borrows heavily from the biological model of successive life stages, from gestation and birth, through adolescence, to maturity and eventual demise. The marketing translation of this progression is illustrated in simple form in Figure 20.1.

Introduction	In the immediate post-launch period sales build rather slowly, while financially the product has not recouped the resources put into its development, during what is strictly speaking a prior stage, gestation.
Growth	The product 'takes off', attracting an early majority of buyers, encouraging repeat purchase, and gaining volume and market share. Profits start to increase.
Maturity	For many products this is the longest period, beginning at the end of the growth phases with few new customers entering the market. Buying behaviour and competitor activity are more predictable and eventually market stability/saturation approaches. Profits are initially good but could dip later in this period, as marketing outlays are stepped up to counter new innovative entrants.
Decline	Sales may fall drastically as new products replace obsolete offerings. Some products may linger unhealthily for some time. Profits fall appreciably, giving way to losses that are sometimes heavy.

The generic product life cycle (PLC) model is commonly depicted as a bell-shaped curve, though variations are sometimes introduced to illustrate special cases. These could be, for example, the inverted V-shape of a short-lived fad or novelty product, or

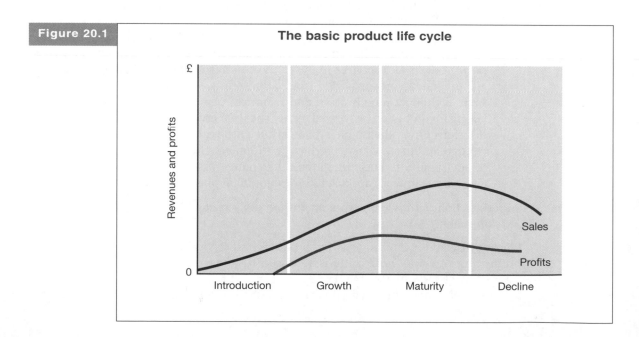

Figure 20.1

The basic product life cycle

the scalloped shape that might be associated with a fashion product adopted by 'waves' of followers. Individual products are accepted as each having a unique pattern, in terms of sales-profits volume, gradient, shape and duration. Long-standing brand-leader products are likely to show an extended 'maturity section' with variations both up and down, reflecting market trends, competitor activity and company marketing successes. In practice, of course, most veteran brands will have to undergo major changes in their product/service features and marketing over the years, if only in order to survive!

It is dangerous to assume that the product life cycle is an inevitable progression. Some products become prematurely obsolete when a better substitute is introduced. It is interesting to speculate whether the ability to download music from the Internet will put the compact disc market into such a decline. Other products seem to go on forever – see the Persil example on page 377.

Over the course of the product life cycle, changes are likely to be registered in terms of market size and growth, customer types, and the dynamic interactions between company marketing strategies and those of competitors. These differences may both reflect and partly determine the successive stages within the cycle.

A different marketing strategy is required for each stage of the product life cycle:

- In the earlier period the focus needs to be on creating customers and market development.
- In the growth stage strategy should become more offensive, developing repeat business and strong positions.
- In the maturity stage defensive strategies predominate, and maintaining good relationships with loyal customers becomes crucial. It is at this stage that modifications or new offerings are best introduced.
- As markets decline there will be more consolidation and activity aimed at making the best of current product offerings while establishing new ones (if its not too late).

A more detailed outline of strategy changes over the PLC has been presented by Doyle (1976), and appears in summary form in Figure 20.2. The reader would benefit

Figure 20.2	**Marketing implications of the product life cycle**			
	Introduction	**Growth**	**Maturity**	**Decline**
Characteristics				
Sales	Low	Fast growth	Slow growth	Decline
Profits	Negligible	Peak levels	Declining	Low or zero
Cash flow	Negative	Moderate	High	Low
Customers	Innovative	Mass market	Mass market	Laggards
Competitors	Few	Growth	Numerous	Fewer
Responses				
Strategic focus	Expand market	Market penetration	Defend share	Productivity
Marketing expenditure	High	High (declining %)	Falling	Low
Marketing emphasis	Product awareness	Brand preference	Brand loyalty	Selective
Distribution	Patchy	Intensive	Intensive	Selective
Price	High	Lower	Lowest	Rising
Product	Basic	Improved	Differentiated	Rationalised

by reading the complete article, which has become a landmark in the literature (see Further Reading on page 399).

DEVELOPMENT OF PRODUCT LIFE CYCLE ANALYSIS

From the earliest interest in the generalised 'product' life cycle research has moved on to distinguish at least three distinct levels of aggregation: that for the product class (e.g. breakfast cereals), the product form (e.g. health-conscious cereals), and the specific product or brand (e.g. Nestlé Cheerios). Working at an analysis of three levels of market sales, it is possible to more realistically locate the position and prospects of one particular product or brand, and make strategic decisions in the light of market and sector trends, competition and general performance indicators.

Figure 20.3 illustrates such a three-level analysis, showing a scenario with three marketing offerings. It will be seen that the product class has recently shown signs of growth and the product form has started to decline at a faster rate. In spite of this each of the individual marketing offerings are continuing to follow the pattern of a normal product life cycle.

USES OF PRODUCT LIFE CYCLE ANALYSIS

Used carefully and with the support of appropriate research, the PLC provides valuable insights regarding total products and markets. Mapping the path of both company and competitor brands, product form and general market sales assists the company in reaching decisions about new product development or product modification, as shown in Figure 20.3. Across the life of a product or service the study of its life cycle characteristics (growth, stability or decline) might enable a company to exploit untapped potential, and to avoid problems by reacting with well-timed strategy changes. Such a

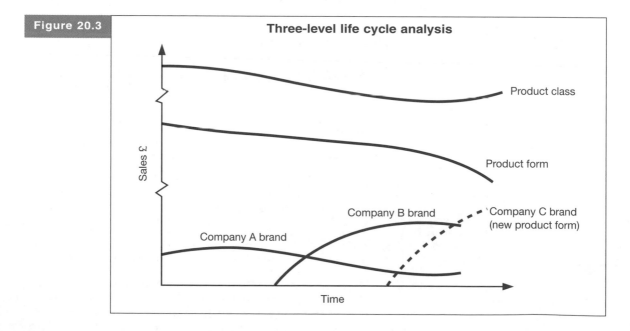

Figure 20.3   **Three-level life cycle analysis**

Figure 20.4

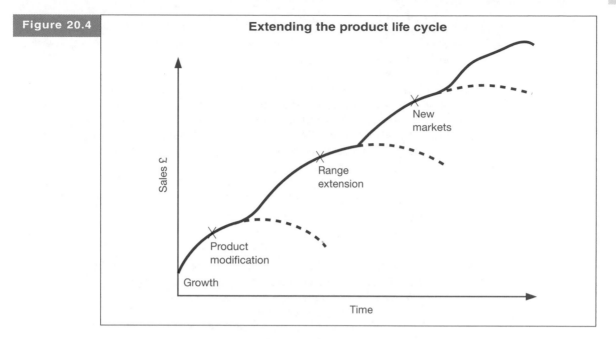

Extending the product life cycle

situation is illustrated in Figure 20.4, where the company has avoided losing sales by changing the product offering to meet competition and the changing market conditions.

There are differences in the opportunities at different stages of the PLC. Because of this those organisations that correctly appreciate their position can achieve a level of competitive advantage. In the growth stage there are likely to be fewer competitors, and the emphasis will be on growing the total market whilst also continuing to make customers' aware of a specific offering. By the time the market growth has slowed and maturity has been reached there will be more competitors and the emphasis will be on retaining customers and increasing the perceived *'added-value'* benefits offered by each competing brand.

Example   **Extending the product life cycle — the example of Persil**

'Whatever the washing need, there is a type of Persil to suit, be it conventional or concentrated; powder or liquid; biological or non-biological; specially formulated for colour fabrics; for use in a top-loading or front-loading washing machine.'

Lever Brothers Ltd Product information sheet

Persil was developed in 1909 by two Stuttgart professors, the name derived from Perborate and Silicate, two chemicals in the initial formula that enabled the product to be described as *'the amazing oxygen cleaner'*.

The original Persil was a soap incorporating a bleaching agent. It was soon offered in powder form but this needed to be stirred into a paste before adding to the washing. This 'new' way of washing was advertised as *'soap powder that would do away with the dolly rub and washboard and the labour of rubbing clothes'*. Of course the whole method of washing was very different then to the automatic washing machines of today.

The actual formulation has changed regularly over the years, although for 70 years Persil has

▶

remained purely a soap-based product in spite of new competition from different types of detergents developed from 1950. The long-running slogan '*Persil washes whiter*' helps to create a powerful position in the minds of consumers.

By 1968 the trend to front-loading washing machines had given rise to a need for low-lathering washing powders. Although biological powders were being launched in the UK the new product, Persil Automatic, was still soap based and it was marketed alongside the traditional product.

Persil did not add biological enzymes until 1983, relaunching as 'New System Persil'. However in 1984 they relaunched 'Original non-biological Persil' alongside the New System product. This illustrates the problems of moving too far away from the core values of an established product.

The last 14 years have seen many changes in this mature product as it utilised changes in available technology and sought to keep the offering competitive in a demanding market place.

1987   Persil available as a liquid
1990   Persil soap powder reformulated
1991   Concentrated Persil powders and liquid launched
1992   Further concentration as Persil Micro and launch of Persil Colour
1993   Launch of Persil Colour Liquid also Persil Eco-bag and tin
1994   Persil Power, Pure and Colour new concentrated format
1995   Persil Finesse, and New Generation Persil
1996   Whole range reformulated and relaunched in new packaging.
1998   Tablet versions of Persil Performance and Colour Care products launched.

Having initially been a single product, Persil is now a range of more than 12 different products in the UK, each targeted at a specific customer segment or requirement. These include product range extensions such as washing-up liquids and product variations such as standard, concentrated, liquid and tablet versions of Persil Colour Care. This approach provides significant opportunities for mutually supportive advertising programmes but makes doing this effectively more difficult due to the problem of defining so many market segments.

In 1996 Persil UK sales were estimated as £185 million, with an advertising spend of £26.8 million, giving it one of the highest advertising to sales ratios of any major product. Further study of this trend and of the activities of competitors with their product offerings will show how important it is to actively manage the total marketing mix at all stages of the product life cycle.

Note: Persil is marketed by Unilever in France and the UK. In Germany and much of the rest of Europe the brand is owned by Henkel. Such split ownership can cause problems in brand development.

PRODUCT RANGE ANALYSIS

The product range, sometimes called the product portfolio or product mix, is the assortment of different products and services offered for sale by a single company. Most established companies are multiproduct organisations offering a range of different products or services. This is the result of new products having been introduced together with the addition of variations based on existing successful products/services. Some of these will be to cater for new or different customer groups (new users or new usage). Others could be justified by the need to expand sales and profits, or to become a more competitive and credible supplier in the market, or to spread commercial risk over a wider product mix. Growth in the product range may well be the chosen instrument of corporate growth, though the size (or length) of the mix will not guarantee

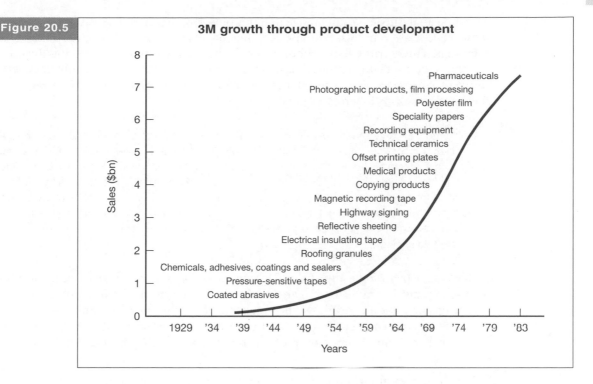

Figure 20.5

3M growth through product development

success, and two similarly sized companies in the same market may have major differences in the number of products that they offer. Figure 20.5 illustrates graphically the way in which 3M has grown over the years through product development.

The four main issues relevant to product range analysis are product line, width, depth and consistency.

- **Product line** A number of products that are related by being targeted to similar markets or for similar uses, or sold through similar outlets or on comparable terms, e.g. Procter & Gamble has a number of product offerings within its line of detergents, including famous names such as Tide, Bold and Dreft. A company's product mix can be measured in terms of size or length – the total number of products in the mix.
- **Width** The number of different product lines within the product mix. Thus, in addition to a sizeable detergent product line, Procter & Gamble also has toothpaste, shampoo, toilet soap and many other product lines.
- **Depth** The number of different versions offered within each product in a product line, e.g. a Procter & Gamble toilet soap may be offered in two sizes (regular, family) and three colours (pink, blue, white), giving the product line a depth measure of six. Obviously, depth will vary by product line, so for example a newly introduced soap may only be offered in one regular size and one fragrance.
- **Consistency** This refers to the closeness of various product lines across the mix, in terms of production methods and materials, target markets, common distribution outlets and so on. It may not always be obvious how or why a company has an apparently disparate mix of products, e.g. 3M introduced Scotch masking tape after its abrasives customers in the motor trade voiced the need for such a product.

While analysing a product range in terms of width, depth and consistency is normal practice it is often necessary to use the same basic approach with regard to marketing offerings. This is particularly important when marketing offerings involving the use of e-commerce are being introduced. It is tempting to try to meet the assumed expectations of customers using the Internet by offering lower prices rather than providing better value at possibly higher prices.

Example	Within the USA and Canada the Internet is regularly used to purchase a wide range of leisure activities. Among the many organisations offering motorhomes for hire in Canada is one that prices their product in terms of how many they have left for hire in any particular week. Thus the price is lower if you wish to book a motorhome for a week when there are ten available than it would be for a week in which only four are still available for hire. Thus those who book early save money while those who do not have this option may still be able to get what they want, although this means paying a higher price. Can you think of other products or services that could use this approach to pricing?

Both as a basis for longer-term decisions and for day-to-day marketing purposes companies need to monitor and analyse key performance indicators across their product range. Of critical concern will be indicators of product-market match, performance vis-à-vis leading competitors, identification of market opportunities and challenges, and some ongoing diagnosis/projection of each product's performance in terms of

| Figure 20.6 | Accounting and resource measures of product performance |

Measure	Measurements
Sales	Volume (units) Revenue (£000) Percentage of total (%) Ranking (1–n) Sales growth (% ± 12 months)
Profits	Total (£000) Gross margin % ROCE % Percentage of company profits (%) Ranking (1–n) Profits growth (% ± 12 months)
Costs	Total (£000) Unit cost £ Overhead allocation (£000) Fixed v variable cost (x:y)
Others	Investment (£000) Capital spending and recovery CASH flow (£000) Plant use Budget X Functions e.g. marketing, transport, service

profitability, growth and resource usage. Such analysis will therefore range from the holistic (i.e. total range) level to a detailed focus on individual product items, pack sizes and individual product variants.

To undertake such analysis will require data from accounting and costing records and other internal control data, company market research findings and other information that may be accessed through a marketing information system (MkIS). Accounting measures such as sales and profits allow the within- and across-range comparisons of product performance vital to product planning and strategy development. Figure 20.6 illustrates a more comprehensive list of measures by which a company might conduct an internal product audit, product by product.

By comparing product performance anomalies and problems can be identified, examined and addressed. Often a profit and loss account and balance sheet is prepared for each major product to determine their relative financial performance. As a result many larger companies will treat leading products as separate profit centres, and organise these within product divisions or strategic business units.

An important aspect of marketing planning is the need to recognise and exploit the extent to which products support each other, with respect to marketing, resourcing or other factors. Often overall company performance depends on the product range and management of the resources used to support the range as a whole.

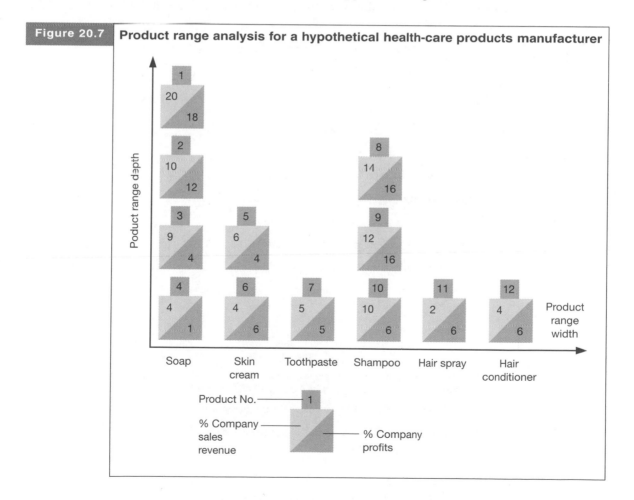

Figure 20.7 **Product range analysis for a hypothetical health-care products manufacturer**

Figure 20.7 presents a simplified product range analysis for a hypothetical manufacturer of healthcare products. Though simplistic and generalised, the analysis gives some insight into the strategic and managerial issues involved in product policy. In marketing terms, the company is fielding a spread of product lines (i.e. width), offering differing line choices (i.e. depth) to consumers. The sales and profits percentage figures indicate that the product lines make different contributions to company performance, while individual products within the lines themselves differ in their sales/profit profile. It is interesting to note that, even with a limited portfolio of 12 products, sales revenue contribution of individual products ranges from 20 to 1 per cent, while that for profits varies from 18 to 1 per cent of the total.

Even with only two yardsticks, profits and sales, it is clear that some products are performing better than others. While this will always be the case, especially within extensive product ranges, companies need to understand why and how performance varies, as part of the overall product management and marketing process. For example, in Figure 20.7, Product No. 4 may be facing severe market competition and production difficulties, while Product No. 11 may be a recent addition that has great profit potential, once it is established.

The above analysis is internal to an organisation. For a thorough marketing analysis of products, financial information must be supplemented by external measures of how products perform within the competitive market place. Figure 20.8 illustrates the vari-

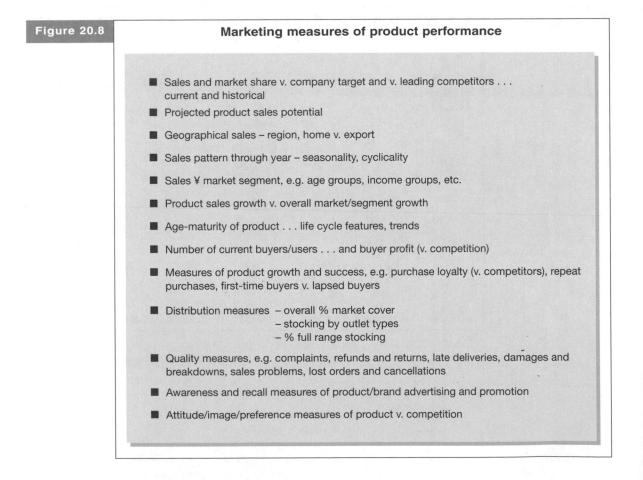

Figure 20.8

Marketing measures of product performance

- Sales and market share v. company target and v. leading competitors . . . current and historical
- Projected product sales potential
- Geographical sales – region, home v. export
- Sales pattern through year – seasonality, cyclicality
- Sales ¥ market segment, e.g. age groups, income groups, etc.
- Product sales growth v. overall market/segment growth
- Age-maturity of product . . . life cycle features, trends
- Number of current buyers/users . . . and buyer profit (v. competition)
- Measures of product growth and success, e.g. purchase loyalty (v. competitors), repeat purchases, first-time buyers v. lapsed buyers
- Distribution measures – overall % market cover
   – stocking by outlet types
   – % full range stocking
- Quality measures, e.g. complaints, refunds and returns, late deliveries, damages and breakdowns, sales problems, lost orders and cancellations
- Awareness and recall measures of product/brand advertising and promotion
- Attitude/image/preference measures of product v. competition

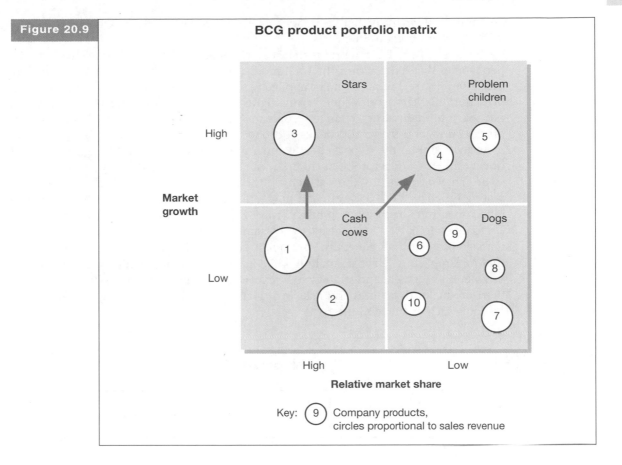

Figure 20.9

BCG product portfolio matrix

ous measures of marketing performance that might be applied to products and product lines.

Various techniques of product range/portfolio analysis have been developed to assist this, usually based on a matrix (or grid) representation of the products/product divisions within the firm. One of the best known is the Boston Consulting Group (BCG) matrix which provides a means of comparing competitive strengths and uses memorable terms such as Cash cow, Star, Problem child and Dog to differentiate between the various categories of performance. Figure 20.9 illustrates this approach.

The BCG matrix is based on two principal dimensions: relative market share (i.e. related to the nearest major competitors); and market growth (a proxy for life cycle development, and subject to interpretation). To apply the matrix, a company would plot its major products in the appropriate cells, positioning them, as in Figure 20.9, by circles proportional to current (or projected) sales income. (*Note*: the technique makes reference to cash generation, which is a basic and definitive resource, rather than the possibly more nominal and conditional values that might measure profitability.) The analysis therefore attempts to describe the basic resource interdependencies of products within the portfolio. However, this matrix should be used with great care as it has major limitations due to its reliance on market share and market growth as the only two dimensions in constructing it. Some high growth markets are really quite unattractive or very risky, e.g. the current personal computer hardware market, and there are some stable markets that are financially viable even when the relative market share is low. Perhaps you can identify some?

The value of the BCG matrix is that it gives some insight into the resource interdependencies that exist within the total product range, or within any mix of company initiatives (the technique could be applied to some effect in analysing a company's mix of export markets worldwide). It highlights in general terms the policy decisions necessary to maintain or change a company's position in respect of both individual product lines and the total product portfolio.

As an example, the hypothetical company in Figure 20.9 would need to consider how Products 4 and 5 (problem children) can be promoted leftward by gaining market share. They also need to know which are the loss-makers and which the cash-earners among Products 6 to 10 (dogs), and how long Product 1 (the major cash cow) can be relied on to fund a possibly top-heavy array of less productive investments. Indeed, the company might well be advised to re-examine the criteria it uses to develop and manage product lines generally. As a qualification to the above, it should be stressed that no simple 2 × 2 matrix analysis will cope with the complexities and dynamics of product management and strategy to be expected in a large company setting. Certainly there are major difficulties and risks in applying and over-interpreting formal analytical tools such as the BCG matrix.

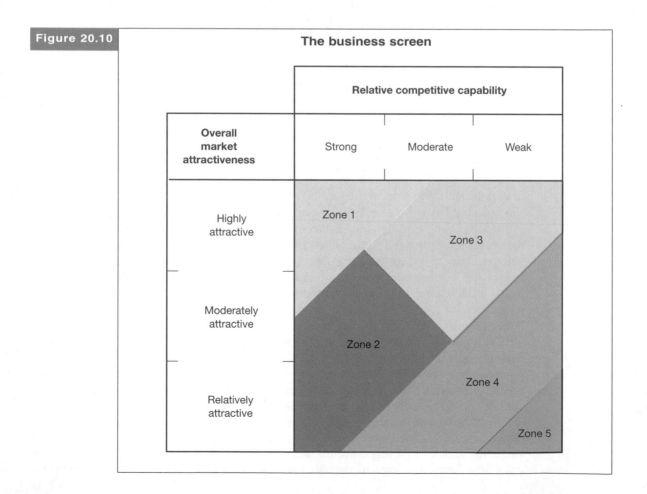

Figure 20.10

The business screen

Large multi market companies such as General Electric and Shell International have developed alternative and more complex matrix approaches in recent years. However the same advice applies: the basic merit of these techniques lies in the analytical skills and insight in producing the categories, rather than the development of standard prescriptions or panaceas. Other matrices have been proposed, such as the Directional Policy Matrix championed by McDonald (1993) and a development of the Hofer and Schendel matrix described by Rick Brown. This debate is beyond the scope of this book, but Brown's business screen is shown in Figure 20.10.

This screen uses more dimensions than the Boston matrix in assessing market attractiveness and competitive capability. It is very helpful in considering options that an organisation might follow. These are discussed further in the strategy section later in this chapter. The decisions that could be available are:

■ build for growth (Zone 1);
■ hold position and use cash generated for new developments (Zone 2);
■ harvest for cash recognising share decline (Zone 4);
■ termination of real 'dogs' (Zone 5).

The most interesting products fall into the question mark Zone 3 where the market is attractive but the organisation lacks real competitive strength. Here resolving the marketing direction depends on many factors but it is the area where marketing decisions to build, hold or harvest are most crucial.

THE CASE FOR NEW PRODUCT DEVELOPMENT

New product development is a vital part of marketing policy for all companies and organisations. It represents one of the key means by which corporate renewal is achieved, and a future secured. As it is a future-directed activity it affects the whole company and should support corporate objectives and strategy. It will therefore involve much corporate deliberation and decision-making, and in most well-managed companies it will be the focus of a planned development programme.

Marketers have a major role to play in new product development, for a number of reasons. First, product development is itself a material part of marketing strategy, and a route to both increased competitiveness and customer satisfaction. Second, marketers are, perhaps uniquely, in the position to direct and assist the development effort, through their market knowledge and research capability. Furthermore, it will be the role of the marketing function to launch and successfully commercialise the new products, once readied for market.

The most obvious case for product development is the strategic need to innovate and change in response to, or preferably somewhat ahead of, market change. While companies will innovate at different speeds, and with varying success, some will appear more competitive and forward-thinking in their product development activities and others more reactive and conservative. As in business generally, product development is an undertaking concerned with opportunity-seeking, but beset by risks – statistics vary, though conservative estimates would indicate that at least 50 per cent, and possibly up to 70 per cent, of new products fail within their launch year. Furthermore, a high proportion of the remainder never become major successes. However risk, and risk-taking, are necessary ingredients of the innovation process, as summarised in the adage: 'The biggest risk of all is to take no risks.'

Example	Sony's new HiFD disk

The question is whether the new HiFD disk from Sony will provide sufficient new benefits for consumers – if it doesn't it will be a real *floppy*!

The new disk has 140 times the capacity of a standard floppy, and it is 20 times faster. However it costs over £10 compared to a basic floppy at 50 pence. But is this the right comparison? What market is the HiFD aimed at?

When compared to a CD (compact disc) the new disk offers much less. CDs are cheaper (around £1.50) and are available in both 'write-once' and 'rewritable' formats; CDs can hold three times as much data as the HiFD; and CD drives are similar in price to HiFD drives. CD drives are also becoming faster and so there seems to be no real advantage in favour of the HiFD. Yet Sony is a major company with excellent marketing skills, and Sony decided to launch the product. It must have something to persuade the company to invest in it.

Consider the market for the HiFD and the competitive offerings already available. Then assess whether, in your opinion, Sony have a potential winner with their new product, or whether they have made an expensive mistake.

In simple terms, one of the most telling implications of the product life cycle model is that a company must ensure that a succession of new products is coming on-stream, to cover the commercial ground lost through the demise of older products at the other end of the life cycle. Certainly the prospects would be rather weak for a company with a product range hemmed within the later stages of the life cycle. Appropriate to the biological analogy of the life cycle model itself, new product development can therefore be viewed as a form of plough-back, an investment for the future.

E-commerce is forcing many organisations to develop new marketing offerings. In particular the major banks are having to respond to significantly increased competition from new e-commerce initiatives. Abbey National's new stand-alone Internet bank, called 'Cahoot', is expected to have 1 million customers by the end of its first year in operation and 5 million within four years. To facilitate this rate of development it has set up an on-line service that allows customers to switch current accounts with all the associated debits and credits with just two signatures being required.

The growing body of research on new product development has shown that the rationale for product development will vary among companies, depending on factors such as market conditions and company performance. Among the strategic objectives that companies follow in their innovation programmes, the following are perhaps the most common:

- To increase or defend market share. Given the evidence that market share has a strong association with profitability, due to experience and production economies.
- To develop or enter a future new market or segment, perhaps as a pre-emptive strategy to outpace competition.
- To maintain a lead position as an innovator. While this objective is competition-related, those companies that operate in fast-changing technology fields, such as electronics, will find themselves almost carried along by a constant stream of product and process innovations.
- To diversify into new product markets, as a strategic hedge against over-dependence on a limited product range: the classical 'third leg' strategy.
- To exploit distribution strengths, to stimulate distribution channels, or to cement a firmer trading relationship with intermediaries.

- To make productive use of slack resources, e.g. in sales or production capacity, or perhaps to remedy seasonal or cyclical dips in activity.
- To exploit company experience in working with a new technology or new materials, or otherwise to commercialise spin-offs and by-products of the company's primary endeavours.

Whatever local policy guidelines companies set for themselves in product development terms, it has become a commonplace observation that dependence on new products for sales and profits growth is increasing steadily over time. Innovation-watchers might argue that the rate of change is multiplicative, making for a continual growth in product innovation. Reference to factors such as the dismantling of trade barriers and the globalisation process, the convergence of technologies (e.g. telecommunications and computing), and the growing sophistication and *'innovativeness'* of customers could certainly support such a view generally.

TYPES OF NEW PRODUCTS

Product development represents a wide spectrum of activity, spanned at one end by the painstaking development of products and technologies through basic research programmes, and at the other extreme by the countless variations and improvements to existing products that are everyday features of rapidly evolving markets such as grocery products.

'Newness' is a relative term, and most products introduced to the market place are developments or variations on existing product formats. The norms for most markets will likely be a constant drip-feed of incremental product changes, with the occasional major product innovation that regroups the market and redirects technological development. In line with such a process, most major companies will subscribe to both ongoing product improvement and longer-term programmes of fundamental research. The variety of 'new' products to be met with will therefore encompass the following broad types.

- **Major innovations.** Products involving radical new combinations of technology, formulation or user benefits, with the potential to form entirely new markets and even whole industries – television, X-ray, the microprocessor and VCR technology would typify such innovations. By definition, such innovations are rare gems and not without major development and commercialisation risks. For example the build-up of a customer base can itself be a key issue, as instanced by the multi billion dollar failure in March 2000 of the Iridium satellite telephone system. The company was unable to compete with GSM (Global System for Mobile Communications) roaming, a more recently developed digital terrestrial cellular mobile telephone technology with a developed customer base.
- **Product improvements.** At one end of the scale these products may represent major innovations in existing markets, with the potential to marginalise other competitors. A good example would be the succession of 'system' products that have effectively created new segments in markets as diverse as writing instruments, wet-shaving products, cameras and lawnmowers. In these and other markets (e.g. cars, washing machines) it is possible to trace a thread of development through to second- and third-generation products that consolidate updates in design and technology.

At the other end of this category would be the more everyday, marginal improve-ments and modifications that are regularly incorporated through features such as product redesign, repackaging, and formula and ingredient changes. A particular marketing variant on the improved product is the repositioned product, an existing product that can be retargeted, often unchanged, to a new market or segment.

■ **Product additions.** Products without major claims to innovation or novelty, usually imitations of current market leaders, or simply line extensions of product ranges that a company already markets successfully. Certainly below the brand leadership 'skyline' in the market place, most product entrants are likely to fall within this cat-egory. Not surprisingly, most product failures occur within the ranks of these 'me too' products. However, exceptionally it may happen that a largely imitative prod-uct lacking distinctive features, perhaps entered as a diversification move by an established company from another market, assumes market leadership through better marketing.

Note: A key point to make about new products is that 'newness', like beauty, is in the eye of the beholder – in marketing terms customer perception is the ultimate judge of whether a product is new or not.

THE PRODUCT DEVELOPMENT PROCESS

The corporate setting

The development of any new product, or service, is usually a lengthy, costly and risky process. While some successful new products seem to be the result of good luck these are very much the exception to the general rule: 'success comes from 1 per cent inspi-ration and 99 per cent perspiration'!

Most companies will seek to maximise their chance of success by adopting a disci-plined, commercially directed programme of new product development that follows key corporate objectives (market share, growth, profitability), and is consistent with whatever product policy guidelines these imply (as discussed in Chapter 11). Such a programme will depend for its success on the following prerequisites:

■ An up-to-date summary, or shared understanding, of key corporate priorities for development.

■ Shared knowledge of company resources, capabilities and limitations.

■ Market, competitor and other external knowledge and information sources, e.g. for checking the commercial potential of projects.

■ Commitment to a base level of specialist resourcing, projected forward against target activities and projects.

■ A known and agreed set of procedures and decision criteria against which to assess and progress development projects.

To emphasise the importance of these many companies have incorporated some of these elements in their corporate mission statements, annual plans and product policy guidelines, or more specifically in product development or research and devel-opment plans. While over-formalisation may hinder rather than help, what is important is that at the appropriate levels in the company informed decisions are made and strategic criteria followed in respect of assessing and advancing develop-ment initiatives.

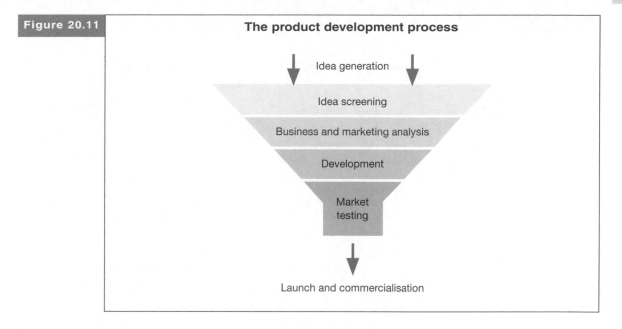

Figure 20.11

The product development process

Idea generation

Idea screening

Business and marketing analysis

Development

Market testing

Launch and commercialisation

Stages in the product development process

While the time necessary to develop a new product will vary according to factors such as technological complexity, resource availability and corporate priorities there is a generally accepted sequence for the development process. Figure 20.11 illustrates this simple 'funnel' model of the process, in which new product ideas are initiated, screened, commercially assessed and progressed further, rejected or set aside for later reworking. The product development stages outlined in the model are examined in some detail below.

Idea generation

This stage, the logical beginning of product development, represents for most companies a continuing process of accumulating and generating development ideas, rather than this being a discrete occasional activity. As worthwhile ideas are at a premium this continuing approach is essential to the creativity of all possible sources.

The number of ideas necessary to support successful product development has been illustrated by research studies conducted by the US consulting firm Booz-Allen, Hamilton. In a landmark 1968 survey among American manufacturers it was estimated that 58 ideas were necessary to sustain a successful new product launch. This figure had been reduced to seven when the consultants conducted a duplicate survey in 1981, indicating that manufacturers had improved their development performance through stricter management and investment procedures. Even so, the research indicates that most product ideas fail to 'run the gauntlet' of successive stages and filters within the development process. Moreover, as no company can claim any monopoly on creativity, it would make sense to consider potential product ideas from a variety of sources.

Figure 20.12 presents a summary of idea sources available to a typical company. In most companies product ideas will come from both internal and external sources, though certainly in technology or science-led fields such as pharmaceuticals or elec-

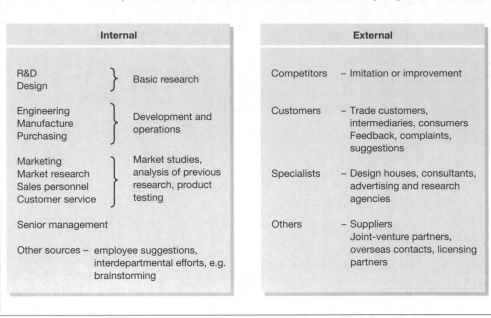

Figure 20.12

New product idea sources available to a company

Internal		External	
R&D Design	} Basic research	Competitors	– Imitation or improvement
Engineering Manufacture Purchasing	} Development and operations	Customers	– Trade customers, intermediaries, consumers Feedback, complaints, suggestions
Marketing Market research Sales personnel Customer service	} Market studies, analysis of previous research, product testing	Specialists	– Design houses, consultants, advertising and research agencies
Senior management		Others	– Suppliers Joint-venture partners, overseas contacts, licensing partners
Other sources –	employee suggestions, interdepartmental efforts, e.g. brainstorming		

tronics there will at any time be a feedstock of ideas and formula alternatives that stem directly from ongoing research programmes. Even in these cases, though, there is a strong case for drawing on problem 'cues' from users and customers, trade channels, competitor intelligence and sales force feedback. Without such market direction there is a danger that development efforts lose their focus and become directed solely by the forces of 'technology push'.

Whatever the product field, ideas for new products, and product improvements, can come from anywhere within the value chain, inside or outside the company. Within the company, multidisciplinary efforts, drawing on specialists from a number of departments, may prove especially effective. The logic of these approaches is that a more balanced spread of ideas may be generated, and that political or inter departmental rivalry is reduced by eliminating the NIH ('not invented here') syndrome. Such teamwork efforts may take many forms, from the regular employment of creative techniques such as brainstorming, group problem solving and discussion sessions, to more permanent organisational mechanisms such as venture teams, 'think tanks' and new product committees.

Idea screening

Given a number of development ideas, it is necessary to put them through a standard screening method to select only those with apparent business and development prospects. This first-level screening will usually rate and compare ideas across a number of key factors held to be important in terms of company/product fit, such as compatibility with company technology and manufacturing capability, marketing resources, distribution channels, research/design capability and so on.

Figure 20.13 presents a simplified example of a rating sheet that might be used for comparing development ideas across such a screen of weighted factors. The score pro-

Figure 20.13

Development idea rating screen

Product selection criteria	(A) Weighting	(B) Criterion rating 1 2 3 4 5 6 7 8 9 10	Weighted idea score (A ¥ B)
Corporate objectives	4	9 ★	36
Financial capability	4	9 ★	36
Marketing compatibility (including export)	4	8 ★	32
Relation to present products	3	8 ★	24
R & D/Engineering	2	7 ★	14
Manufacturing	2	9 ★	18
Suppliers/sourcing	1	9 ★	9
	20		169

Weighted key score: 0 – 89 poor; 90 – 139 fair: 140 + good.

file illustrated in the figure is quite encouraging, though in practice most development ideas would score quite modestly, while still others would be rejected as too middle-of-the-road to justify retention, too high a 'pass-rate' might dilute development resources and prejudice the real potential winners. While the shortlist criteria and their weightings will vary from company to company, and over time, the important consideration is that a consistent and agreed set of benchmarks is used from the outset.

Business and market analysis
The development ideas that survive the initial screening illustrated in Figure 20.13 will effectively enter a more rigorous series of checks and analysis within the next filter, as it is after this stage that 'green light' decisions will be made to authorise and commit costly resources to development projects.

The business and market analysis stage is concerned with establishing a viable commercial rationale for development products, as both a guide for development work and a first-level business planning statement. The assessments made will involve market and marketing investigations, financial projections and costing/scheduling estimates. These investigations are likely to be carried out by separate departmental specialists, though the final business assessment will depend on some information interchange between parties, e.g. sales forecasts will be required to assess revenue/profit calculations.

The marketing information required within the business analysis will likely come from a combination of existing market data and previous research findings, frequently supplemented by specific qualitative research exercises designed to validate the market attractiveness of shortlisted product ideas. Usually the ideas will need to be translated into alternative product concepts, i.e. succinct statements of the essential dimensions, attributes and rationale of the proposed product, expressed in customer language. The most common means of concept testing is via group discussions, where a small number of potential customers are exposed to alternative concepts, sometimes supported by pack mock-ups or models, asked questions and led in discussion on issues such as concept acceptability, apparent uses and benefits, advantages over existing products, etc. The findings of such research, though highly tentative, give some early insight into customer reactions and perceptions, and usually a means of selecting the more viable concepts, together with the benefits to incorporate into their further development. Alongside existing market data, and information on matters such as buying and switching behaviour, it should be possible to estimate preliminary market and sales forecasts, as an input to financial assessment work.

The marketing assessment of a successful product concept is commonly summarised in an outline marketing rationale, which will include overall comment on market volume, target segments and product positioning, together with specific guidelines on product attributes and qualities, indicative price-bands, and performance targets versus likely competition. These latter details will serve as an early product specification and a development brief to be followed by the research and development team.

Business analysis of product ideas is likely to be expressed through financial reports, which will combine aggregates such as sales forecasts, investment requirements, functional outlays and costings, and profit projections. These broad indicators in turn may

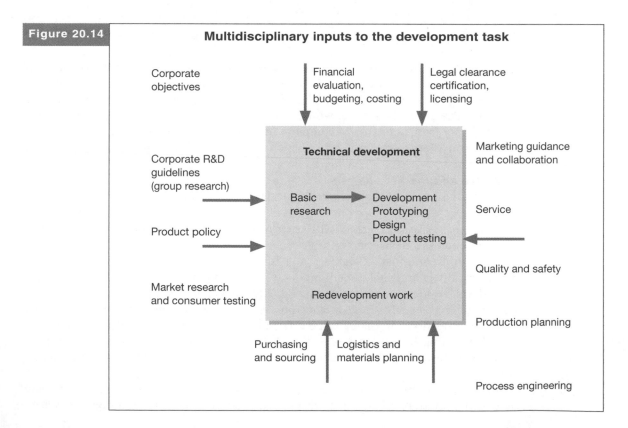

Figure 20.14   **Multidisciplinary inputs to the development task**

break down into detailed components such as investment appraisal/payback sum-maries over an assumed product life or depreciation period, direct-indirect cost struc-tures and departmental estimates, pricing and break-even calculations, and other financial arithmetic necessary to compare the viability of alternative product proposals.

Development

The development stage proper is really a succession of overlapping activities, orches-trated as a team effort. While in most companies the responsibility for development work will be located within the R&D department, or an equivalent function such as design or product engineering, in practice a variety of inputs are needed from other functions in order to ensure that the final product or service is both marketable and commercially viable. Figure 20.14 illustrates the complexity of interfunctional working within the development stage.

In scientific sectors such as medicines, the development stage will be lengthy, and usually divided into sub-phases, starting with pure research in pursuit of chemical/physiological reactions, leading to a development stage proper, itself divided into lab-oratory and clinical phases. In other science-led or high technology fields such as aero-space and electronics, development may be equally complex, speculative and costly. The scale of resourcing and effort at risk within the development stage therefore makes clear the case for co-ordinated teamwork, planning and controls.

In the interests of co-ordination many companies have adopted particular forms of organisation for product development. As previously stated, marketers have a particu-lar guidance role to play in product development, if only to ensure that customer real-ities remain a focus of the development task. The experience of many marketers is that R&D personnel, unsupported by market guidance, fall prey to a 'technology myopia', an interest in the (research) chase itself rather than the (market place) end product. During the development stage, therefore, marketers need to stay close to development staff, by ensuring for instance that prototypes are developed to market guidelines and assessed through customer research, and by generally advising on the maintenance of deadlines, cost, quality and design guidelines.

During the development period a succession of product tests will be made on a number of product formulations or prototypes in order to develop an acceptable fin-ished product ready for ultimate production and launch. For manufacturing planning purposes alone, varying tests will be made among alternatives associated with, for example: materials specifications, design-performance configurations, production-assembly approaches and cost estimates, quality and safety assessments, and supplier selection. Logically, marketing specialists will need to stay abreast of these activities, and where necessary offer comment and advice on commercial and market place aspects of the decisions to be made.

Parallel to these 'internal' tests, there will usually be the need to subject successive product designs to customer tests, in order to check on market acceptability, decide on yet unresolved issues of product attributes (e.g. colour, materials, user controls, design aesthetics, minor design changes), or to make performance comparisons through in-use tests or trial placements.

A marketing-centred approach to development is therefore an iterative process, involving a dialogue with outside parties, primarily potential customers, and internally with various functional specialists within the organisation. It is worth stressing that both external and internal sides of the dialogue are critical. Furthermore, in today's competitive climate they are also interdependent. The increased zeal with which companies now embrace initiatives centred on total quality improvement, just-in-time (JIT), design for assembly (DFA), and simultaneous engineering – to name but a few approaches that have gained a deserved respect within manufacturing and engineering – demonstrates that real market advantages can be won through internal improvements in production efficiency, quality and accelerated development.

Market testing

After the various product performance, functional and customer preference tests of the development phase, most companies will subject the, by now market-ready, product to a final assessment under market conditions, prior to full-scale launch. The objectives of doing this will be to reduce commercial risk by uncovering unforeseen product problems, fine-tuning the marketing and distribution programme, and making more accurate projections of sales, market performance and profitability.

The ultimate form of market test will be to conduct a formal test-marketing operation, usually in some test-market area(s) or town(s) chosen as representative of the total market area. Tests in TV regions, urban areas (e.g. London) and provincial cities are quite common for consumer goods. Test marketing would be undertaken as a scaled-down version of the intended national launch, involving similar advertising media and campaigns, distribution and sales cover, promotion and pricing elements of the marketing mix. Sometimes variations (e.g. in price, advertising intensity) may be tested in different test locations, in order to optimise the launch marketing mix, and to more accurately project sales volumes, purchaser profiles, buying volumes, first-time and repeat purchases. While marketing activity 'on the ground' will be most obvious in sales and advertising terms, the value of the test market will rest as firmly on the research conducted at trade and household level, through retail consumer audits, sales-force feedback and other sources. It may be necessary to buy in research for a control area outside the test market to determine sales effects on competitor products, and to eliminate market-wide variations. Of particular interest to the marketer will be the recorded incidence of initial sales (penetration) and repeat sales (repurchase), that, together with purchase size, will indicate the likely success of the eventual full launch.

Though generalised, the trial-repeat patterns set out in Table 20.1 would indicate varying degrees of success.

Limited market testing may be conducted instead of a full test-marketing operation, perhaps where:

1 Product and production variables have to be finalised well in advance, e.g. with cars and other durable manufactures.
2 The product does not represent a major launch or commercial risk, e.g. as with a range addition or minor variation on a trusted formula; or where extensive previous in-development research assures confidence.

Table 20.1 First-time and repeat sales combinations during test market

% Trial purchase	%Repeat purchase	Possible diagnosis
High	High	Marketing and product successful.
Low	High	Poor marketing threatens good product.
High	Low	Product unsatisfactory.
Low	Low	Both marketing and product unsatisfactory?

3 Competitive urgency may drive for an accelerated launch, or there may be the real risk of competitors spoiling test-market results (e.g. by underpricing, intensified sales and promotion), or the loss of competitive surprise, or even copycat products appearing.
4 There are other factors involved, such as budget constraints, or a need for marketing information limited to restricted areas, e.g. brand-switching patterns, promotional effectiveness.

Limited marketing testing might take various forms, for example 'mini' test markets involving selected stores or a regional chain, where test products are 'placed' by the company for a period of time. In other cases, commercial market and research test services will be used, perhaps involving panels of households that are recruits to a shopping circle involving catalogue choice or home delivery. Comparable, though less strictly commercial, are the simulated 'shopping laboratories' operated by a number of research companies.

Market testing industrial products is usually conducted on a more controlled basis, for example through trial installation with selected customers, or through invitation to demonstration events, company showroom and test facilities and so on. Arguably, heavy investment industrial products are more likely to be developed through continuing contact with prospective customers, so that many of the 'grey areas' covered by test marketing may already be resolved.

Finally, it is worth noting that, with growing internationalisation, large global companies are increasingly conducting test-market operations in selected countries prior to regional and international market launch operations.

Launch and commercialisation

This represents the end of the development process, and the full-scale introduction of the finished product to the market place. The resource costs and risks attending this stage are significant, as shown in the simple development-expenditure relationship outlined in Figure 20.15. The commercial risks riding on any major launch justify the careful analyses, tests and preparations involved in the development process, and also

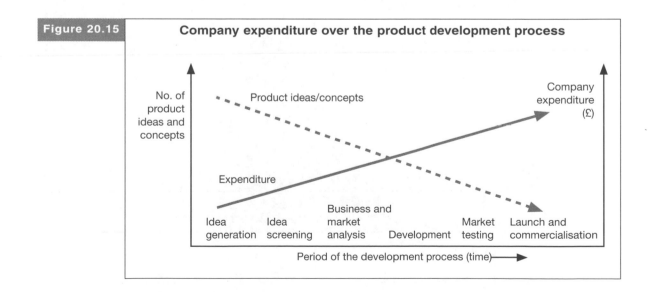

Figure 20.15 — **Company expenditure over the product development process**

the marketing professionalism required to support market entry. Competitive realities should ensure that the company makes objective decisions based on test-market results – even if the decision is to abort or delay product launch. Given a decision to proceed the company will still need to maximise the lessons of the test market and ensure that launch activity proceeds methodically to the marketing plan developed. Given that production volumes will require scaling-up from the pilot plant levels of the test market, many companies will decide on a gradual 'rolling' launch region by region, or compromise by stock build-up to shorten the release period and increase launch impact. Critical to the success of the launch will be the monitoring of market research indicators, and generally the quality of managerial decisions taken on the basis of the controls built into the launch marketing plan.

Product adoption and diffusion

Of direct relevance to the process of new product development, segmentation and target marketing is the issue of how products are received and adopted on release to the market place. There is a consensus that new products penetrate or diffuse into the market place at differing rates among different groups of buyers. The most notable theoretical contribution to this issue has been the work of the American researcher Everett Rogers who proposed that, at least in relative terms, first-time purchasers of new products could be classified according to the *'innovativeness'* of their adoption behaviour. Rogers presented the adoption behaviour of purchasers of a new product as a time-dependent phenomenon that could be plotted within a normal distribution curve, as illustrated in Figure 20.16.

The five adopter groupings statistically identified by this analysis might suggest that buyers vary somewhat in terms of innovativeness, openness to new propositions, conservatism, loyalty and related behaviourial dimensions. While there are a few research findings that indicate innovators to be younger, better educated, more cosmopolitan

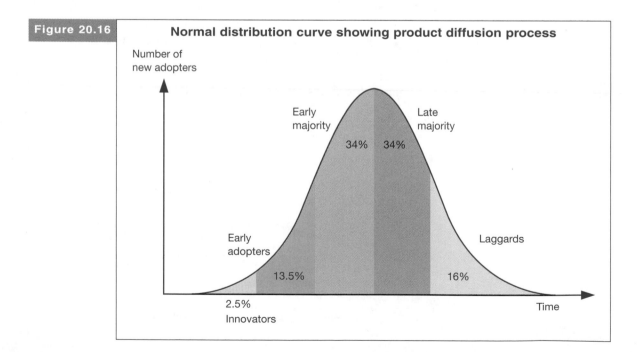

Figure 20.16   **Normal distribution curve showing product diffusion process**

and open-minded, there has yet to emerge any set of general findings, or any reliable and practical indicator of innovativeness, that might help marketers in the obvious interest that they have in identifying and targeting these innovation-prone buyers.

Exercise	Consider the development of the mobile phone market in the UK. Can you identify any characteristics of groups that might be described as:
	    innovators,
	    late majority, or
	    laggards?

ORGANISATION FOR NEW PRODUCT DEVELOPMENT

Of no small significance to the success of a company's innovation efforts will be the way in which it organises and manages the development effort. Research studies indicate that top management involvement and leadership are critical determinants of the 'entrepreneurship' shown by the whole organisation. Rigidity, bureaucratic rule-making, demarcation and inter departmental conflict are major obstacles to success in new product development. In order to avoid these problems and to encourage team-

Figure 20.17

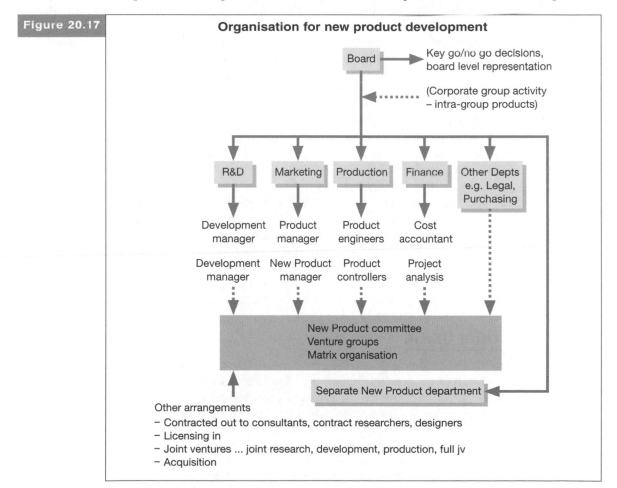

Organisation for new product development

work and co-ordination, progressive companies have evolved separate organisational arrangements for their innovation programmes. Figure 20.17 outlines a number of the more common organisational 'solutions', though it should be stressed that structural preferences vary from company to company.

The product manager system, commonly found in large consumer goods companies in particular, meets with mixed reports in terms of product development. The major reason for this is that product managers have enough pressing problems dealing with established products, so that, excepting more simple line extensions, new product development may suffer by comparison.

The new product manager position has evolved from the product manager system, specifically to allow the full-time efforts in innovation that product managers rarely manage.

New product committees are commonly used in large companies, usually for policy-making, review and product selection purposes, rather than full-time innovation management. Though composed of representatives of different functions, they may suffer the common committee malaise of bureaucracy, lethargy and political infighting.

The new product department represents a more visible and dedicated solution for development than a new product committee, and will usually be headed by a senior manager experienced in product development, supported by a multidisciplinary team of specialists. Properly managed and resourced, such departments can be the driving force of innovation throughout the company.

Venture groups or teams represent a multifunctional task force grouping assigned to particular projects, or ventures. The efficacy of such a teamwork approach has been confirmed by its major proponents, which include such large companies as Dow, Monsanto and 3M.

The matrix organisation represents a radical company – or division-wide restructuring of staff and management in order to 'kick-start' innovation through improved communications, integration and working relationships. In simple terms, staff and functions are reorganised so that dual reporting relations impose closer collaboration across departmental boundaries.

While all these structures represent internal organisational mechanisms for new product developments, there remain a number of external sourcing avenues that companies use, for reasons of cost, or time-saving, or in order to 'import' creativity and innovation. In high-cost research environments such as proprietary medicines, licensing-in is a supplementary means of staying abreast of developments, or of accelerated entry to new product sectors. Joint ventures and strategic alliances have the merit of risk-sharing and resource-pooling, and appear to be growing in popularity at the international level, especially in technology-led fields such as automobiles and aerospace.

CONCLUSION

The development of policies relevant to existing products and to new product development is of key strategic importance. These should ensure the organisation both fully benefits from the potential of its existing product and exploits its capabilities by introducing new products that strengthen its opportunities in the market place.

Products and services have to be relevant to the needs of customers in a dynamic competitive market place, and marketing must continually strive to achieve this. After a launch, a product/service will develop and grow as new users try it and satisfied customers buy again. However there will be a level of saturation, and when this is reached the product can be said to be mature. The actual life cycle will depend on many factors, but it is in the maturity phase that an offering is at its most profitable. By the time a product has reached maturity all the development and launch costs should have been recouped, and most customers will already be aware of it so marketing activity can be concentrated on retaining sales to existing customers. This will include modifications to the offering to keep ahead of market changes. As mature products are usually cash positive (*cash cows* in the BCG matrix), a company has an opportunity to reinvest some of the surplus in the development of the next generation of new offerings. This is prudent marketing management and must be considered in the light of the total product/service portfolio.

Logically, from a marketing viewpoint, new product development should start with the identification of the needs and problems of customers, and the means to offer them enhanced performance and improvements over competitive offerings. Commercially, the innovation process generally is both costly and risky. Companies therefore need to adopt a managed approach to product development, ensuring informed decision making, co-ordinated efforts and effective returns on the investments involved. The marketing function has an important part to play in the general development process, and in the successful commercialisation of new products.

QUESTIONS

1 *Consider the life cycle effect relating to a company operating within the service sector, and suggest how the offering might be modified to prolong the maturity phase of the service life.*

2 *Why do you think marketing people tend to get more excited by radical new products or services, in spite of the risk of failure, than by the task of improving existing offerings that could offer many years of continuing profitable trading?*

3 *Taking as your focus any recently launched new product, present in summary form a marketing rationale for its introduction, a broad view of its position relative to other products marketed by the company, and a brief listing of leading competitor products. (If you cannot think of a suitable product then consider the Sony HiFD mentioned in the text.)*

4 *Test marketing is wasteful, inconclusive and unnecessary – if a new product is going to succeed, it is in the real market that success will be achieved.' Discuss this view and explain the advantages and drawbacks of launching a new product in a small sector before rolling it out into the entire market.*

5 *The 'right' organisation is often argued to be a critical factor in a successful programme of innovation. Comment on this view and evaluate the alternative means by which the product development function could be organised in a company manufacturing domestic and industrial refrigeration equipment.*

FURTHER READING

Booz-Allen, Hamilton (1982) *New Products Management for the 1980s*. Booz-Allen, Hamilton Inc.

Cunningham, F. (1998), 'Cultures that bring new products to life', *Management Today*, June, p. 100.

Doyle, P. and Bridgewater, S. (1998) *Innovation in Marketing*. Butterworth Heinemann.

Kotler, P. (1999) *On Marketing – How to Create, Win and Dominate Markets*. The Free Press.

Rogers, Everett M. (1983) *Diffusion of Innovations*, 3rd edn. The Free Press.

Zeithaml, V. A. and Bitner, M. J. (2000) *Services Marketing*, 2nd International edn., McGraw-Hill.

CASE STUDY

Ford chief relaunches European branding strategy

Ford Motor Company is relaunching its European branding strategy after warning yesterday that its market share in the region could fall below 9 per cent this year, its lowest in almost a decade.

Nick Scheele, chairman of Ford's European arm, said the group had to redefine its brand after admitting Ford had lost 25 per cent of its market share in the past five years. This year its share is expected to be 8.7 per cent, down from 9.1 per cent in 1999. The company, which last month announced the end of car assembly at Dagenham – its largest UK plant – has failed to make a significant profit since 1990.

'It is clearly an untenable situation. The only way we're going to get out of it is to get product and costs under control, and we have to take a major look at our distribution system,' Mr Scheele said. Unveiling the strategy at the *Automotive News* annual congress, he said Ford needed to redefine itself as a durable brand that would underpin residual values on the 1.65m cars it sold in Europe yearly.

The branding drive will be launched at the Paris motor show in September, coinciding with the introduction of Ford's Mondeo replacement. It forms the latest stage of Ford's European restructuring, designed to return the group to profit.

Mr Scheele predicted that the restructuring would cut Ford's fixed costs in Europe by $2bn over the next three years. Future capital investment would be brought into line with the group's $1.2bn annual depreciation. Ford will still review its capacity utilisation in Europe, which at an average of 71 per cent is the lowest among the region's top five carmakers. Mr Scheele said moves to lift utilisation beyond the industry average of 82 per cent could mean further cost cuts.

He reiterated that the cost-cutting would be accompanied by increasing product launches to three a year for the next five years. That is expected to involve sports utility cars and at least three so-called 'segment busters' – emulating the success of models such as Renault's Megane Scenic.

Ford hopes to repeat the brand success of VW, which leads the market in customer perceptions of reliability. However, Ford is expected to remain loss-making this year, but return to profit in 2001.

Financial Times, 21 June 2000

Ford clearly have to plan for the future. It is one thing to get their costs under control and improve efficiency – but the marketing task is to reverse the declining levels of sales.

Ford have traditionally been admired for their product and segmentation strategies, which have offered key products – Ka, Focus, Escort, Mondeo and others in different specifications, each targeted at a different market segment. However it is now obvious that more marketing activity is required if Ford is ever to recover its once dominant position.

Tim Burt

Question

1 *Consider the problems facing Ford, and suggest how they might undertake a successful planning exercise aimed at achieving their objectives.*

21 Marketing planning

'Would you tell me, please, which way I ought to go from here?'
'That depends a good deal on where you want to get to,' said the Cat.

Lewis Carroll, *Alice's Adventures in Wonderland*

INTRODUCTION

While many organisations have gained significant competitive advantage by applying those aspects of marketing theory most critical to their specific product and market, long-term success in really competitive markets requires a more co-ordinated approach. This needs to involve all aspects of marketing and should provide a means by which an organisation can focus its resources to meet the needs of its chosen customers efficiently.

To do this it is essential to know in detail from where you are starting. It is also equally important to have a clearly stated objective with respect to specific time in the future. While it is inevitable that such objectives will need to be modified over time to reflect market dynamics, they should prove robust enough to guide key commercial decisions across the organisation, and should therefore be based on analysis and agreed by all those with relevant responsibilities within the organisation. These first two steps are obviously linked since the objectives need to be set relative to the starting position. In practice the objective should commit the organisation to a deliberate policy with respect to both product and service offerings, and markets.

The third step is to determine how to achieve the agreed objectives. This will involve developing both the overall approach to be followed (strategy) and the individual tasks needed to effectively implement each of the specific aspects of marketing: promotion, product policy, distribution and pricing.

As has been seen in earlier chapters, due to organisational factors product policy decisions often have very long-term effects. This usually limits the scope of many of the product policy decisions that might be needed to achieve the product-market match required to meet corporate objectives, especially in the near future. Any strategy will need to address these limitations by effectively targeting and positioning both current and future offerings.

To implement a strategy requires the acquisition and allocation of investment resources in particular for promotion in the short term and new product development in the long term. It will also involve co-ordinating marketing activity with the other functions of the organisation. Such activities need to be monitored to ensure consistent progress towards the specified objectives.

Stage 1	*Where are we starting from?*	The marketing audit. Product range analysis.
Stage 2	*Where do we want to be?*	Marketing objectives. Targeting and positioning.
Stage 3	*How do we get there?*	Evaluation of alternatives. Choice. Marketing mix strategies and resource allocation.
Stage 4	*How do we ensure we get there?*	Control and feedback.

THE MARKETING PLANNING PROCESS

The marketing planning process has evolved to provide a framework for all four of these activities. For small organisations this is a straightforward process involving well-established stages and, if required, the production of a document – 'The Marketing Plan'. Often this can be used as the basis for negotiations with organisations such as banks that can provide start-up finance for a new venture or the additional finance needed for expansion.

In many large organisations marketing planning has become an established formal procedure and part of the strategic planning process. In this context it is sometimes necessary to co-ordinate the marketing of a range of diverse products. This inevitably makes the process more complicated but potentially more beneficial. Also, in a number of organisations it has been found that the process itself has improved the level of co-operation between different business functions, and the co-operation of the managers involved.

One approach that has been adopted by many organisations is to set overall objectives in a mission statement. This sets out the general purpose of an organisation and the values to which it aspires while recognising the legitimate interests of other stakeholders such as customers, employees, suppliers and the communities in which the organisation operates. The mission statement is an important communication from an organisation and so it must also be seen as part of the overall marketing statement made by the company.

It is likely that planning will be an iterative, rather than a sequential process. When selecting a strategy to meet the chosen objectives there is a need to revisit those targets to assess both if they are really what is required and if they are likely to be met. As a result, the objectives could be modified, thereby requiring the strategy to be reconsidered. The process will be further complicated by the need to impose assumptions on both the objectives and strategy. These may involve estimates relating to data that is not available, the continuation or reversal of present trends, the timing of anticipated events and so on. The assumptions are often summarised as a forecast, which can be used to develop a provisional budget. The budget can then be used as the basis for subsequent stages of the planning process.

Example   ### The national music centre goes 'pop'!

As the Millennium Dome struggles to achieve its revised target of 6 million visitors – half the original estimate, the Museum of Popular Music in Sheffield closed its doors on 31 July 2000 after just 16 months in operation. The museum, housed in a building shaped like four giant steel drums, was expected to draw tourists from all over the world, and the original estimates were set at up to 400,000 visitors a year. It is another example of an organisation setting highly optimistic targets and then failing to achieve them. While the concept seemed well founded it attracted only a quarter of the visitor numbers required to meet targets and, despite £11 million of lottery funding and a recent rescue attempt, it has run into serious financial trouble.

In the original concept the major attractions were a number of interactive exhibits featuring state-of-the-art pop gadgetry, however these failed to attract visitors. In an effort to improve the crowds the museum tried to introduce traditional exhibits but it is not surprising that memorabilia such as an *autographed wobble board from Rolf Harris* failed to generate much enthusiasm!

Some analysts have blamed the museum's Sheffield location, for its failure, claiming that potential visitors might expect to find it in London, Liverpool or Manchester – cities more renowned for their pop history. But the targets were set in full knowledge of the location so such excuses are rather irrelevant.

It is essential that the assumptions upon which such a forecast is based are clearly stated, since it will allow the forecast to be amended as the assumptions are either confirmed or shown to be incorrect. The logic of this can easily be lost once the forecast has been buried within a carefully constructed budget and the outcome subjected to a variance analysis. While this is fundamental to the effective use of marketing budgets (we will return to it in the section on control), the impact resulting from having to revise assumptions can be minimised by the planning process (see Figure 21.1).

THE MARKETING AUDIT

All decisions in the planning process need to be made in the context of the skills and resources available to the organisation. This involves recognising what these are in comparison to the competition. While this is comparatively easy where the business is small, it is increasingly difficult as organisations become larger. The process is, however, the same and will cover the total organisation. Marketers are interested in those key elements of the wider business audit that involve marketing issues. This is usually termed the marketing audit.

A marketing audit has four major components that reflect the four levels of the marketing environment shown in Figure 3.2. They are:

- the wider external environment, which was discussed in Chapter 3;
- the company stakeholder system;
- the markets in which the company operates, and the performances of the products in these markets;
- the review of resources and skills that are available to the organisation, and the systems and structure to deliver them.

All should focus on any changes, either current or expected, that are likely to affect either an organisation or the markets that it serves.

The external part of the marketing audit focuses on the uncontrollable macro-environmental factors affecting the business. For many businesses the economic climate is of vital importance, so needs to be assessed critically. The technical and regulatory environments that affect the organisation, its markets and competitors also need to be at least discussed.

Figure 21.1

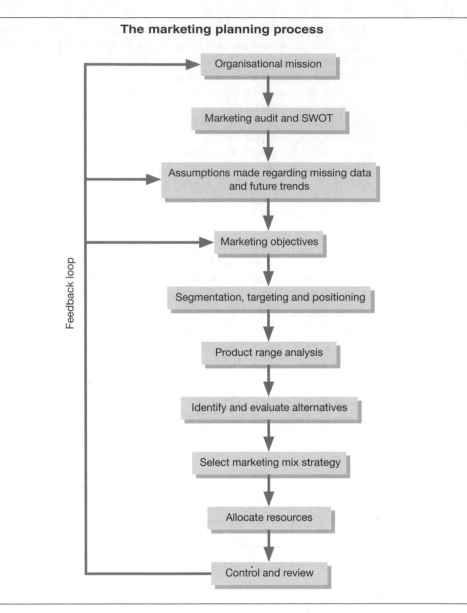

The marketing planning process

Organisational mission

Marketing audit and SWOT

Assumptions made regarding missing data and future trends

Marketing objectives

Segmentation, targeting and positioning

Product range analysis

Identify and evaluate alternatives

Select marketing mix strategy

Allocate resources

Control and review

Feedback loop

Example

EU plans food safety shake-up

FT

An example of a recent change that will have direct marketing implications is the new EU Food Safety Authority. Michela Wrong reported on July 17 2000 that:

The European Commission had unveiled a package of hygiene proposals which puts the burden of responsibility on farmers and food companies to ensure food safety from farmyard to dinner plate.

'We have learnt our lesson from the food crises of the 1990s,' said David Byrne, health and consumer protection commissioner, unveiling what was dubbed the most radical shake-up in food hygiene rules in 25 years.

The new legislation, first outlined in a white paper published in January, aims to harmonise and simplify overly complex hygiene requirements currently covered by 17 separate directives. It is one of over 80 initiatives promised by the Commission as part of Romano Prodi's drive to bring order to Europe's ramshackle food regulations, following a series of contamination scares.

The new legislation gives farmers primary responsibility for food safety through self-checking and record-keeping. Food businesses will be obliged to adopt a hazard analysis system and keep records of safety checks carried out. Heavy emphasis is placed on 'traceability'. The registration of all food businesses will become compulsory and every food business will have to be able to trace ingredients to source.

Extra hygiene rules for animal foodstuffs such as fish, meat and dairy product – the source of many food poisoning outbreaks – are included. But in a move certain to please British politicians who say soaring veterinary inspection costs are putting small abattoirs out of business, the legislation caters for greater flexibility over which personnel are qualified to conduct slaughterhouse checks.

The proposals are due to be discussed by the European Parliament and Council before being adopted by co-decision, meaning implementation could take up to 18 months. They look set to win the backing of consumer groups, although some food analysts questioned whether Mr Byrne and the Commission had taken on board the logical consequences of improved food hygiene.

'What really matters is how the regulations are going to be implemented,' said Tim Lang, Professor of food policy at Thames Valley University. 'Ultimately, is Byrne ready to get consumers to pay higher costs in exchange for food safety? Confidence in food does not come cheap.'

The audit should also include information that shows the size of the market in terms of both value and volume, and the trends in these. The position of the organisation should be compared with that of each significant competitor. The characteristics of the market should be defined and compared in terms of the range of products offered, their prices, distribution and promotion. In addition, the audit provides an opportunity for information gathered by the marketing research function, relevant to any aspect of the business, to be presented and its relevance assessed:

- Macro-factors:
  - Social and cultural influences
  - Technological influences   } (STEP)
  - Economic environment
  - Political and legal environment
- Micro-factors:
  - Customers
  - Competition
  - Suppliers
  - Other stakeholders.

The stakeholder audit covers the values and attitudes of those interest groups in this category. In particular it will concentrate on suppliers and customers.

The evaluation of all the product range in relation to customers and competitors is a key part of the audit. It covers both a wide look at the balance of the total product range offered and the individual elements of the marketing mix, concentrating on how these meet customer needs and wants in a competitive context:

- product/services
- price, quality, value
- distribution
- promotion and communication
- interactions (people contact and processes).

Product performance is usefully compared to previous periods to establish short- and long-term trends, and the analysis needs to be sufficiently detailed to highlight relevant differences.

The final part of the audit involves an appreciation of what an organisation is capable of achieving and the systems it uses. It will cover the current situation with regard to marketing research and information, personnel, planning and control systems and product development.

Both the external and internal elements of the audit should be sufficiently thorough to show clearly how they relate to the business environment and future trends.

MARKETING ANALYSIS AND ASSUMPTIONS

The *marketing audit* inevitably produces a great deal of data and information. The analysis process utilises this in order to give a good foundation for future strategies. It is at this stage that it is possible to identify gaps in the data and to take steps to evaluate issues that might otherwise be missed.

However it is important to remember that marketing decisions are made with respect to future strategy and therefore analysis of the past cannot be relied upon as a guide to the future. Because of this it is necessary to make assumptions as to the future and then make decisions based on these views of the future.

As has been seen by the earlier example of the Museum of Popular Music, it is easy to be over-optimistic regarding what is possible with new offerings in a market place. Analysis of the positive opportunities can sometimes result in poor assumptions as to the future. It is as well to understand that most consumers are already reasonably well catered for by existing offerings – they require a major stimulus to persuade them to change, or even to try something different. This is equally true when making changes to established products, the difficulty being how to attract new consumers while not alienating more established ones.

| Example | Marks & Spencer's problems have been well reported. They had been losing sales in the late 1990s and part of the problem seemed to be that they were not attracting new, younger customers. In an attempt to revive the store many radical changes were made to the range of clothes stocked. The dilemma facing M&S is whether the new merchandise will actually achieve this objective, and whether the changes can be made in a way that does not deter the remaining traditional shoppers. |

Critical application of sales/profits and marketing measures to the product range will enable a company to identify those products that perform well, and those that are patently under-performing. It can then make informed product policy decisions in respect of matters such as product improvement and modification, new product additions and replacements, and product withdrawals. It is probably no exaggeration to state that, even in the smallest of product ranges, products will differ in performance terms. Within larger product ranges, some products may have some common features that make for success or weakness in such a way that broad categories or types may be identifiable.

Peter Drucker, the well-known American management writer, proposed a broad typology of products that encompasses the following categories:

1 Today's breadwinners (cash cows).
2 Yesterday's breadwinners (dodos).
3 Tomorrow's breadwinners (stars?).
4 Others, referred to in such colourful terms as Cinderellas, also-rans, and investments in management ego (dogs and problem children).

While these descriptions are self-explanatory, if generalised they do indicate that company performance is closely linked to product offerings, and how these fare in a competitive market. There is also to be found in the writings of Drucker, and other management commentators, clear advice on how companies should plan and manage product policy through informed decision-making following strategic analysis. Too often, products are launched for the wrong reasons (Drucker's 'investments in managerial ego'), or for the wrong market (product-market mismatch), or managers proceed to squander resources on 'lost cause' products rather than those with real potential (the Cinderella syndrome). In fact it is now generally accepted that some two out of every three new products will fail to achieve their marketing objectives.

To plan effectively it is necessary to be very logical when analysing the data. An organisation must differentiate between those items that are likely to affect its performance significantly and those which will have little effect. Treating the internal audit data separately from the external data allows the significant data to be classified under four headings:

- **Strengths.** These are the internal factors that are likely to enhance performance, such as having a well-trained sales force, efficient production and high-quality products.
- **Weaknesses.** These are the internal factors likely to inhibit performance, such as excessive capacity (high fixed costs), obsolete designs and long delivery schedules.
- **Opportunities.** These are the external factors that favour the organisation, such as effective distributors, compliance with legislation, presence in growing market segments, security of supply of critical components or competitors being reorganised.
- **Threats.** These are the external factors likely to be to the organisation's disadvantage, such as strengthening currency making imported competition less expensive and exports more expensive, recently introduced competitive products, or substitutes able to offer comparable benefits to customers.

The selection of data in this way is known as a SWOT analysis, as these are the initial letters of the classifications used. Its purpose is to provide a framework within which the selected information can be compared, the strengths that can be developed to match the specific opportunities identified and those weaknesses for which there is a corresponding threat addressed. However a good SWOT analysis is not simply a listing of the key factors but a well-thought-out summary that clearly highlights the major strengths and weaknesses, that is those factors which are highly significant and of major importance within the chosen market place.

There are several ways of reviewing the factors, the easiest of which is to rank each on a scale of one (least important) to ten (most important). It is appropriate to

Figure 21.2

The tows matrix

	Major internal STRENGTHS of high importance	Key internal WEAKNESSES of high importance
Key external OPPORTUNITIES	**S O strategies** Build and grow	**W O strategies** e.g. acquire resources (if possible) to allow opportunities to be taken
Major external THREATS	**S T strategies** Reassess strengths in relation to threats	**W T strategies** Real problems

Internal factors / External factors

concentrate efforts on the more important factors when planning future activity for any organisation.

The use of a SWOT analysis should not stop at the evaluation of the major factors. What is often overlooked is that combinations of these factors could point to distinct strategic choices. To focus on this, a rearrangement of the headings into a TOWS (threats, opportunities, weaknesses and strengths) matrix is sometimes used. By highlighting the four strategy interactions below and allowing a time dimension the TOWS matrix helps both in the drawing up of marketing objectives and the formulation of strategy:

1 The WT strategy aimed to minimise both weaknesses and threats.
2 The WO strategy to minimise weaknesses and maximise opportunities.
3 The ST strategy based on the strengths of the organisation that can deal with threats from the environment.
4 The SO strategy, which shows insight into possible actions that will build on the advantages available.

The full TOWS matrix was originally presented by Heinz Weihrich in 1982 and you should refer to the fuller account of its use in his original paper (see Further Reading). The matrix is illustrated in Figure 21.2.

OBJECTIVES AND GOALS

From the SWOT/TOWS analysis it should be possible to develop marketing objectives that are consistent with the overall corporate objectives and the vision that might be set out in an organisation's mission statement. There will of course be financial and other operational objectives that also need to be internally consistent.

While a mission statement tends to state general objectives these need to be specific to the business. For instance the mission statement for a new retail clothes shop in a town where all the standard high street retailers had established branches should emphasise how this offering and shop will differ from these competitors to increase the possibility of success.

It is a fundamental precept of effective planning that there has to be a goal. A good analogy is that of a journey, since the route can be planned only if the starting point and the destination are both known. This does not go far enough since the real purpose of planning is to improve the effectiveness in achieving an agreed objective or task. Using the same analogy of a journey the objective might be to minimise the time taken to reach the destination. This would be the basis used to select the best route. The situation tends to be more complicated in the social or business context since many, apparently sensible, objectives are not fixed, as is a point on a map for example, but instead they are moving targets, such as being market leader. It is even more difficult to formulate useful objectives for business organisations where the basic aim is to increase asset value within acceptable levels of risk, and still more difficult for other types of organisation.

Exercise

In a town there are already two record stores. One is Virgin Records, centrally located and concentrating on chart music and videos. The other store has a preponderance of classical music and jazz but also carries the current top hits. What opportunities would exist for an independent record store to be run by two former group musicians? What objectives would you suggest are appropriate in this situation?

Alternatively, do you consider that there would be more opportunities for setting up an Internet site to sell specialised recordings? What objectives might the two musicians consider if this were to be achieved?

To be useful a marketing objective needs to have two basic components. The first is to specify what is to be achieved. This has to be realistic both in the light of present circumstances and of past performance. The second is to state the time by which the objective is to be achieved. The objective needs to be stated in absolute terms. It is not sufficient to specify it in terms of a market share or previous growth. This is essential since otherwise there can be no comparison between actual performance and the objective set month by month or week by week. If the objective is found for some reason to be unrealistic it should be amended, as otherwise it will have no value as a goal.

A useful way of remembering this is to have SMART objectives, i.e. objectives that are:

Specific
Measurable   } What is to be achieved
Achievable
Realistic

and
Time-based   }   When it is to be achieved.

The next stage is to specify how the stated objectives are to be achieved in general rather than specific terms. This is an important step since it provides the structure within which the detailed steps involved can be selected and implemented. It may be that the most appropriate strategy is to build market share, or it may be more suitable to harvest by withdrawing from a product or market. Many factors have to be taken into consideration, in particular the competitive strength of the organisation as compared with the main competitors. It is also important to consider how the different products/services offered by the organisation and its competitors support each other. Most companies will try to balance well-established and successful products with new products that need investment now in order to become the successes of the future.

GENERIC STRATEGIES – TARGETING AND POSITIONING

Twenty years ago Michael Porter made a significant contribution to the process of strategy development by identifying three generic strategies and suggesting that the management of every organisation must accept the need to select and follow one of these strategies to be effective within a competitive market. Porter's work has subsequently been refined and modified but it is still important to consider the original three ways of achieving success. These are:

1 By being cost efficient in operations,
2 By offering customers a real differential advantage,
3 By focusing specifically on the needs of a specific group of customers.

In the first of these generic strategies Porter suggested a drive for *cost leadership*. This involves developing more efficient processes and in practice usually having large-scale operations. In most markets it is a strategy that can only be adopted by organisations with a significant market share and in some markets it is therefore limited to the market leader. It can however be adopted by any organisation with access to sufficient investment resources in very fragmented markets with large numbers of competitors, none of which has a dominant share of the market. It is important to note that cost leadership does not mean or imply price leadership, and cost leadership is not a marketing orientation. The successful implementation of this strategic stance however usually allows using some of the cost advantage to add value to an offering through effective marketing and thereby enhancing the long-term profitability of the organisation.

Porter's second generic strategy is *differentiation*. This stresses the benefits in developing marketing offerings that are essentially different, and superior, from those of competitors. Usually this involves adding customer value through specific features or improvements, but it can be achieved by very effective marketing, often involving brand building. Organisations successfully following a differentiation strategy might be able to justify charging higher prices than their main competitors, but the real benefit of differentiation is that it separates one offering from another, making comparisons difficult. Compaq Computers is a classic example of a successful differentiation strategy. Compaq initially introduced a transportable personal computer. To do this they needed to develop more efficient electronics than those being used by the existing market leader IBM. Customers found that because Compaq computers had more efficient electronics they were significantly faster and it was this feature, rather than their transportability, that ultimately resulted in Compaq becoming the market leader. Since then other companies such as Dell have adopted other successful differentiation strategies for addressing the personal computer market. Another good example of an effective differentiation strategy is Subaru. All of their cars are differentiated from their main competitors by having four wheel-drive as a standard feature, and many have an unusual style of engine as well.

Organisations that successfully implement cost leadership strategies are often effectively challenged by competitors implementing a differentiation strategy. A classic example is the Ford Motor Company. The spectacular growth of Ford to become the first car industry market leader in the USA can be attributed largely to the successful implementation of a cost leadership strategy, the Model-T Ford as a standardised product. However in 1927 General Motors Corporation became the market leader in the USA by implementing a differentiation strategy. This resulted in such domination of the market that subsequently Ford were unable to compete successfully with General Motors using a cost leadership strategy.

Example

While cost leadership strategies tend to be associated with manufacturing organisations such as Ford or Texas Instruments the best recent examples come from the retailing sector. For many years the Sainsbury supermarket chain had the largest share of the grocery food market. Its relative size, compared with their main competitors, allowed them to adopt a cost leadership strategy whenever this was necessary to maintain their marketing position of 'good food costs less at Sainsbury', a position of providing better value. Tesco responded by repositioning their outlets and specifically focusing on a younger segment within the market.

The strategy worked and Tesco has grown to become significantly larger than Sainsbury, allowing Tesco to adopt a cost leadership strategy to support their marketing position of 'every little helps'. Sainsbury responded by unsuccessfully changing their approach to that of 'making life taste better'. To make the situation worse Asda was taken over by the US retailing giant Wal-Mart, providing them with both the resources and expertise to pursue a cost leadership strategy. As a result Sainsbury, together with the other significant groups, Somerfield and Safeway, are facing an increasingly uncertain future unless they can either differentiate their marketing offering by following the example of Waitrose or by combining their resources to match those of Tesco and Asda.

It is clear that to successfully implement either a cost leadership or differentiation strategy usually requires significant investment resources. This means that organisations without such resources have no option but to adopt the third of Porter's generic strategies – the focus strategy. This means selecting a clearly defined target market or a number of these and providing specific marketing offerings for these markets. Almost by definition any organisations that use price rather than value as a main feature of their marketing offering will have to accept that they need to adopt a focus strategy.

Discussion point

It is often difficult to differentiate between marketing offerings based on price and those based on value. The low-cost airlines offer basic transportation at fares that are significantly lower than those normally charged by the major international airlines. This should probably be classified as a marketing offering based on value. It is up to the passenger to decide whether the difference in price justifies the different level of service provided. Scheduled airlines however use a fare structure which means that a certain number of passengers on any flight would have been able to buy their ticket at below the normal fare by purchasing their ticket in advance. This again should probably be considered another marketing offering based on value, as such tickets normally involve accepting specific associated restrictions. Most airlines sell any tickets allocated to advanced sales but not sold in time to organisations that specialise in marketing tickets at short notice. Most of these so-called bucket shops have been able to sell these tickets profitably by using small advertisements in national daily and specialised newspapers. These sales are made strictly on price and this is clearly the basis of the marketing offering. More recently a number of organisations such as Last Minute.com have been offering these tickets through an Internet site. This would seem to be an ideal way of matching available seats with potential purchasers profitably. However in spite of the potential market using this approach being confirmed by the rapid growth of companies such as Last Minute.com it has yet to be matched by these ventures being shown to be profitable. Is this an example of a *'marketing offering'* being based on price rather than value? How could companies such as Last Minute.com provide a value-based marketing offering?

PRODUCT/MARKET STRATEGIES

Whether pursuing a cost leadership, differentiation or focus strategy it is essential that product and service policy are designed to ensure that the appropriate marketing offerings are positioned in the relevant chosen markets. This is especially important where a focus strategy is being followed in a specific niche market. Strategy implies purposeful, well-researched, well-planned and well-resourced activity. In product strategy terms, the research and planning foundation will depend heavily on the careful analysis and monitoring of the performance of existing products, on market research and forecasting, competitive analysis, and a firm understanding of company marketing and resource strengths and limitations. Product/market strategy can take many forms and variants, at a number of levels, depending on market circumstances, company practices and so on. For simplicity, the present treatment will deal with only the major, more generic, strategy alternatives. It should be stressed that product strategy does not operate by product dimension alone as certain market factors have to be considered in parallel.

Figure 21.3   **Strategy alternatives within the product-market vector**

(Key: ★ = indicative degree of risk in each strategy)

A useful perspective on product strategy that reflects this product-market focus is the product-market vector developed by Igor Ansoff, illustrated in Figure 21.3.

Four broad strategy alternatives are identified within this matrix:

1 **Market penetration.** Basically the company follows the advice of Peters and Waterman by 'sticking to its knitting', competing with the same product types in existing markets. This might involve increasing sales to existing customers, finding new users within present markets, or taking market share from competitors through more effective marketing. It is an area where it is important to retain existing customers by building barriers to prevent competitors taking sales. In this sector there is a need to emphasise the building of strong relationships with customers, driving down transaction costs and thus adding value to the exchange.

2 **Market development.** Here the company offers the same products to new markets or segments. A classic example of this strategy was the case of Johnson & Johnson's Baby Powder, which the company successfully targeted to women purchasers when facing a projected fall-off in demand in the primary babycare market. Companies building export markets would also exemplify this strategy.

3 **Product development.** This entails the introduction of new products, aimed at the same target market. Here the company is exploiting its basic marketing strengths and familiarity with customers in order to widen its product offerings.

4 **Diversification.** Here the company moves into both new markets and new product sectors, perhaps involving major changes in technology and marketing methods. As indicated in the risk star-rating (*) in Figure 21.3, this strategy involves the greatest risk of the four strategies outlined. For this reason, companies will often seek to contain or reduce their risks in some way, for example by licensing in technology or products, buying products and market share through acquisitions, or building on some familiar experience, e.g. in distribution channels or supplier links. By way of qualification, it should be pointed out that the rewards of risk-taking through diversification may be proportionately higher, while it is a truism that without risk-takers pursuing such strategies most really innovative products would never see the light of day.

Example   A diversification strategy can be as appropriate to survival as to growth. The Internet as an information source clearly has the potential to effectively eliminate an investment-intensive product such as the *Encyclopaedia Britannica*. Yet by using the strength of the *Encyclopaedia Britannica* brand as the attraction for an Internet website the organisation was able to make all 44 million words of information contained in the current version of the product available free of charge to users by selling associated advertising space. Such was the initial demand that immediately after opening the site access had to be increased significantly above that estimated. Thus by changing from being a publisher selling sets of books or compact discs to being a media organisation selling advertising space assured survival of the organisation to the benefit of both users and many of those who were employed by the organisation.

The Ansoff vector (Figure 21.3) as a decision tool is a very effective way of considering the various marketing options available. The direction an organisation might follow could include product development (see Chapter 20), market development, or possibly the risky business of diversification.

It is possible to modify the Ansoff matrix, and this can be beneficial when considering the issues of what is a product and what is a new product in more depth. Gary Hamel replaces the term 'product' with his concept of 'core competencies' which are the skills an organisation possesses. This considerably widens the basis of existing products and allows for a customer focus to be applied to solving customer problems, as opposed to the supplier focus on producing products. The category of new products also needs to be considered, as was discussed in Chapter 20. New products can be stretched even further away from the safety of existing products to the possible new products not based on existing skills. Even if offered to existing customers there is a major risk inherent in mastering the skills required to actually produce the new product.

Derek Abell has argued that when changes in the market are only incremental firms may successfully adapt themselves to each new situation. However, timing plays a vital role in all product and market modifications. There is only a limited window of opportunity between the market being receptive to a new development and the competitive activity or other changes that mean it is too late; this is especially true where market development involves major shifts in product offerings or in the target market. One of Abell's strategic windows is focused on the opportunity to use new technology to produce a new offering or modify a product. This can be seen in practice when studying the fast-moving consumer electronics market, where it is absolutely vital to get the timing right.

Abell's other strategic windows are based on either the customer *groups* to be served or the customer *needs* to be served. The most obvious one involves the move to market in new segments and the development of new primary demand. Alternatively new channels could be exploited, as in the move to out-of-town warehouses for companies such as 'Toys R Us'© which redefined their industry, and of course this is now happening again as e-commerce takes off.

Exercise	Visit the websites of <toysrus.co.uk> and <eToys.com> and evaluate the opportunities for companies to use the Internet to retail toys.

Both of these could be placed in the area of market modifications in the product/market matrix. Of more interest is the fourth category where Abell suggests that it is possible to redefine a market; 'frequently, as markets evolve, the fundamental definition of the market changes in ways that increasingly disqualify some competitors while providing opportunities for others. The trend towards marketing 'systems' of products as opposed to individual pieces of equipment provides many examples of this phenomenon.'

Again returning to the IT market, a system based on supplying both computer hardware and software is a good example.

PRODUCT/MARKET STRATEGIES – PRODUCT MIX DECISIONS

Decisions on the consistency and dimensions of the product mix will comprise key issues within a company's overall strategy, and will almost certainly involve senior management (i.e. corporate) decision-makers, as well as functional specialists in the marketing department. Corporate sales growth and profit objectives may be served by, for example, increasing the width of the product mix (i.e. adding new product lines) and capitalising on the company's reputation, or a leading brand name, in a horizontal move to adjacent product markets. For example, the recent introduction of Persil washing-up liquid exploited the strength of the Persil brand name in the laundry detergent sector.

Contributions to corporate growth objectives might equally be achieved through increasing the depth of the product mix, thereby gaining competitive advantage and market coverage, through reaching buyers with differing preferences, in other segments. For example, some time after the successful launch of Jif surface cleaner fluid, for bathrooms and kitchens, Lever introduced Lemon Jif, exploiting the favourable association of lemon-based ingredients with cleaning and grease-removing properties.

By the same token some companies will, through careful product policy guidelines, resolve that the product range must retain a consistency and logic that should not be diluted by straying into unrelated product areas. Other companies, after mixed experiences with diversification into other product fields, will tighten up their product policy by rationalisation, withdrawing or selling off products outside their reconsolidated product base. Such product policy moves will be difficult, and possibly costly, and will involve higher-level corporate deliberations and decisions. They will hopefully return to product policy a thrust and focus, and free resources to concentrate on product markets where the company has known strengths. For example, among the many companies to have withdrawn from the computer market in recent years, Honeywell Inc. appears to have little cause for regret, having successfully grown since through a well-managed concentration in fields such as electronic components, controls and instrumentation.

While most large companies have some variety in their product range they will usually seek consistency in their total offering, reflecting their key strengths and competencies. As an example, Figure 21.4 shows the product-market sales of Colgate-Palmolive, the US-controlled consumer products' manufacturer. This long-established company is probably best known for Colgate toothpaste and Palmolive soap, which are represented in the chart under the oral care and body care divisions respectively.

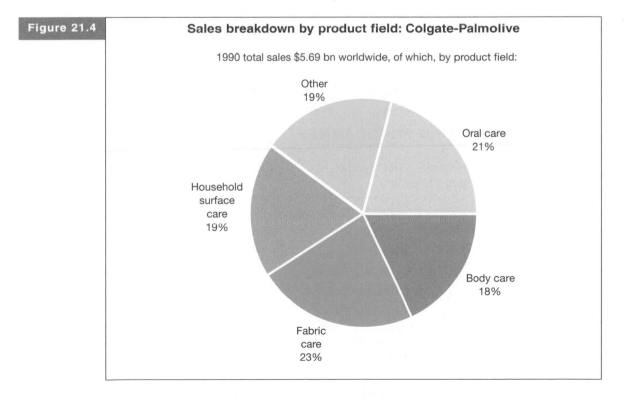

Figure 21.4

Sales breakdown by product field: Colgate-Palmolive

1990 total sales $5.69 bn worldwide, of which, by product field:

Other 19%

Oral care 21%

Household surface care 19%

Body care 18%

Fabric care 23%

While the company has 40 per cent of the world toothpaste market, it has a variety of product interests that range from household cleaners (e.g. Ajax) to mouthwash and other health care products.

EVALUATION OF ALTERNATIVES

With clearly defined objectives, a set of clearly defined assumptions about the future, and an appreciation of the different directions that might be followed in order to achieve the objectives, then the next stage of the marketing planning process is to evaluate the alternatives available.

In general this will involve trying to gauge the feasibility of success of a particular strategy, and ensuring that the organisation has sufficient resources and the willingness to pursue the chosen course. In some cases there will be an obvious direction to follow, but at other times there could be a number of feasible options. There may also be more opportunities than the organisation can afford to invest in. In this case some ranking is necessary and only those that can be properly resourced should be attempted. Every company will have its own way of evaluating alternatives, in many this will involve internal politics and decisions based on personal preference rather than objective assessments. Because the task is to decide the best strategy for the future, managers do not have the luxury of certainty in their deliberations.

One of the key factors involved in evaluation is the degree of risk an organisation is willing to chance. There is often room for a really speculative strategy in one area with a possibility of large returns, but a more certain programme in another market should balance it. There is no sense in risking the whole future of a company on one new product or service that could fail in a dynamic market.

A technique that is often utilised is to draw up scenarios regarding the future, incorporating the assumptions previously made about customers and competitors. Comparing the possible alternative strategies against the *most likely scenario* might suggest one specific way of proceeding, but then testing it against a *worst case scenario* could highlight a very different route forward.

MARKETING PROGRAMMES

Once the specific overall strategic direction and position has been decided it will be necessary to translate these into a set of clearly defined activities covering the controllable variables that must be included in the specific marketing programmes. The purpose of such programmes is to specify the actions, responsibility, resources and schedule needed to achieve the stated objectives via the selected strategy. They will cover both marketing actions and the interfaces between the marketing function and other parts of the organisation because these are essential to the achievement of the marketing task.

The simplest approach to programme development is to use all the components of the marketing mix as a framework. This involves more than the basic 4 Ps of *product, price, place* and *promotion*. It should certainly include the service dimensions of the offering and the *people* and *processes* necessary to ensure that all the essential tasks are covered and properly co-ordinated. A fuller study of the marketing mix is given in Chapter 10.

In order to ensure that the programmes are relevant to the chosen market segments, it is necessary to continually evaluate the content of the programmes against the tests of *acceptability, affordability* and *availability* that consider actions from the critical viewpoint of the customer.

It will usually be necessary to have a separate programme for each of the marketing mix elements that have been discussed in Chapters 11 to 19. There will also be programmes for the people and the processes that are required to deliver the offering effectively, but it is always necessary for the marketing manager to ensure that each of the separate programmes is complementary to all the others. It must form a coherent whole consistent with the overall strategy chosen.

Depending upon the strategy these may be extensive or simple. For instance, where the strategy involves new products or services the programmes will be significantly more involved than if only minor changes are considered necessary. Generally the introduction of new products/services will also necessitate a co-ordinated programme of both making that offering available and of promotion designed to create awareness among potential users. This, as a result, might be considered as a single programme and separate from the general promotion programme. Often the complexity of the promotion programme for a new product launch will justify having a separate sub-programme for each of the four elements of the communication mix (advertising, public relations, sales promotion, and a programme concerned with the personal selling aspects of promotion).

In spite of the attraction of new developments these are not the major focus of marketing planning. Most offerings are already in the market and therefore the majority of marketing programmes will relate to existing products and/or services. Marketing managers use a wide array of analytical tools such as the financial performance of each separate offering, study of where an offering fits in a portfolio or, perhaps, research studies such as the perceptual mapping exercise in Figures 10.11 and 10.12. These could highlight the need for a company to modify their range of offerings to a greater or lesser extent, or might indicate that things are best left alone in the short term.

If revision is indicated it may be that the offering itself meets the needs of customers but the positioning is inappropriate. Repositioning could require changing some part of the marketing programme, the advertising strategy, or the platform or proposition on which the product/service is presented. It might indicate that a redirection of the product to a new target group could work, or perhaps lead to new occasions for use.

Example	A now classic example of repositioning was the case of Lucozade, which was successfully re marketed from a remedial tonic drink to a leading 'soft' drink, targeted at younger health-conscious consumers.

Modification might take the form of other changes in marketing variables, such as a price reduction, or a change to the channels used in order to widen the coverage of potential customers and increase market share.

Example	Many organisations are now offering their products via the Internet as a way of reaching a greater potential market. Perhaps you can think of some?

More fundamental changes to the actual product or service might be indicated, however. These could take the form of design face-lifts, to improve the aesthetic appeal of a tangible product and achieve a more contemporary image. This commonly happens with 'white goods' such as cookers and refrigerators, where such cosmetic changes are necessary to stay abreast of fashion trends, but might go further and utilise some new technological development. More radical changes could involve a complete redesign of the total product or service (improving the benefits for customers) such as the provision of 24-hour on-line banking, which is likely to change forever the way we manage our money.

All of the above modifications and revisions could lead to the development of a new, second-generation or replacement product, but it is debatable, and somewhat irrelevant, which level of revision can actually be classified as leading to a new product/service. Most changes are minor, evolutionary in nature, but carried out to ensure an offering continues to be relevant to *tomorrow's* customers. There are, of course, radical changes leading to revolutionary new-to-the-world offerings but these are rare by comparison with the regular updating that is a critical outcome from good marketing planning.

A practical issue in both product modification and replacement activities is the timing of the new product and the phase-out of the old offering. Decisions have to be made about production plant, and stocks of any old model product, as well as the need to retain spares for some time into the future. This is more critical for tangible products than for services, as intangibles involve far less reliance on physical resources, but it is still necessary to consider the promotion and selling-in of any new offering and it will need to be handled carefully to ensure a co-ordinated operation. This is especially true if training is required for the actual service provision staff.

ALLOCATION OF RESOURCES

Once the programmes have been detailed the total resources required for their implementation can be determined. Almost inevitably this will exceed the resources allocated in the budget developed from the initial objectives, strategy and assumptions. This will require an iterative process to reconcile the cost of the required programmes with the available resources, providing the opportunity to optimise these two factors. In doing so it is necessary to estimate the impact on the objective of each programme. The effect of both increasing and reducing the expenditure should be considered.

> **Example** An organisation estimates that on the basis of existing data the most likely effect of reducing advertising expenditure is to make the overall situation worse, because of the corresponding reduction in sales revenue. An increase in advertising could improve sales but would be more risky as the level of sales growth, as well as the time before such sales are achieved, is uncertain. However, if both a promotional push and an increase in direct sales effort are combined then the increase is more certain. If the results of the revised programmes are thought to be better then this could be the option chosen. As part of the reconciliation process, the effect that changing the assumptions would have should also be investigated so that the final plan has less risk and more potential of achieving the agreed objectives than any of the alternatives.

In carrying out this process it is inevitable that the underlying assumptions will have been fully evaluated and some innovative approaches considered. Usually the final plan will deviate only to a limited extent from the approach followed previously. The planning process should, however, ensure that a radical plan could be adopted if justified. Volvo provides an example of a company that responded appropriately to changing market conditions even though this required a significant revision of existing plans. It had been predicted that without a replacement for the ageing 240 series vehicle by the early 1980s Volvo's market share would be severely affected. A new vehicle was designed and the investment in a new production facility completed when it became clear that demand for the traditional vehicle had revived. It was decided therefore to postpone the launch of the new vehicle in spite of the investment made. As a result, the 700 series vehicles were not launched for another two years, with a corresponding extension to the expected life cycle of this model range.

ALLOCATING RESOURCES TO MARGINAL PRODUCTS

One of the major lessons of both portfolio analysis and PLC monitoring is that there are dynamic resource interdependencies within a product range. An organisation cannot afford to have too many loss-making or marginal products in its range. Sooner or later radical action will be called for, in the interests of the company as a whole and to ensure that resources are targeted at those offerings most likely to give the best returns. This is not to deny that some marginal products or services may be knowingly maintained for a time in special circumstances. Such occasions could be a newly launched offering in a promising sector where future growth is predicted, or maybe an older product being used to perform a market-holding operation until a planned replacement offering is ready to be launched.

There are sometimes good arguments for an organisation to retain some products with specialist features, or ones with a strategic significance, perhaps among key customer groups. These may be kept in a range or given a period of grace in which to be managed back to solvency. In some cases 'special' products, whose importance can sometimes be vigorously defended by sales managers, might be repriced at 'special rates' in order to reflect their importance as part of a complete range. In other cases a concentration strategy might require the company to regroup its product-marketing activity and to focus on a particular segment, and this could involve the need to supply a full range in order to reduce the opportunities for competitors to get a 'foot in the door'.

Products identified through a portfolio analysis as cash-earning dogs ('cash dogs') will be left alone as long as they continue to produce positive returns. However loss-making 'dogs' require serious consideration. While loss-makers are known as drains on company resources it is often the case that the extent of their loss-making is under-recorded. This is because such products may give rise to continued quality and other problems that take disproportionate managerial time, thereby indirectly affecting the prospects of more healthy products. For some of these products it may be possible to engineer a temporary break-even or small profit, through drastic cut-backs in support, increased prices, or both. Exceptionally, if the product sector generally is depressed, this might buy extra time within which some competitors might pull out, effecting a further, if temporary, improvement.

Sooner or later, though, decisions will have to be made to cut out the 'deadwood' products and eliminate the clutter in the range. Though statistically unproven, there is a consensus that the 80:20 rule operates as forcefully within product policy as elsewhere: 80 per cent of the company's profits (or losses?) are attributable to 20 per cent of its products or services. The decision to delete an offering might take the form of an immediate discontinuation or, more commonly, a planned phase-out over a short period to complete order commitments. Occasionally a product, its brand name or associated production facilities may be successfully sold to other interests, perhaps smaller concerns more able to cope with diminished volumes and margins.

MARKETING CONTROL

Marketing is really very simple in concept. The ideal marketing offering (product or service) can be described as:

a combination of goods and services; unique and impossible for actual or potential competitors to match, that solves a problem for a customer in a way that no other combinations of goods and services can do as well; and which can thereby generate a revenue stream, discounted at the organisation's cost of capital, more than adequate to pay the costs of its development and provision.

In most organisations survival depends upon positive cash flow, but few are able to offer a perfect product. Good marketing is often the effective management of products and services that are far from perfect. Survival and future prospects can therefore depend upon the level of new business in the form of orders received. Accordingly, the level of new business is generally considered a critical measure of performance; unfortunately, it tends to be somewhat volatile. It is subject to seasonal variations, changes in the economic climate, and is affected by much talked about factors such as confidence. Because of such external factors it is usually difficult to attribute any changes to level of new business (sales) to marketing activity alone.

It is tempting, therefore, to simply compare the total of new business (sales) week by week or month by month with the figure shown on the budget and, providing there is no negative variance, to assume all is well. There are two serious and related problems with this approach. First, there is an underlying assumption that the budgeted figure, having been agreed or accepted, should be seen as a benchmark against which actual performance can be measured. In manufacturing businesses this is often viewed as realistic since production rates are seen to be also dependent upon assumptions being made. These, however, involve the reliability of the plant and equipment used, operator training, freedom from strikes and so on. Generally, deviations from an anticipated level of reliability can be traced back to a faulty repair or an incorrectly carried out maintenance procedure. The improvement in reliability depends upon these problems being identified and rectified. The marketing budget is very different, since the forecast is based on many more arbitrary factors. To consider it as a benchmark is akin to suggesting that the weather is unreliable because it is not as forecast.

The second problem is that opportunities will be missed unless performance, as measured by new business, is judged in terms of the current situation rather than with the assumptions used to develop the forecast and budget. For instance, if the new business is more than forecast and production is limited, profit can be increased by either reducing expenditure on advertising, for example, or by increasing prices. These are, however, short-term approaches. More often sales being above budget is an indication that the market is expanding more quickly than expected. This is serious, since if nothing is done to match this expansion market share will be lost. Many well-established companies have fallen into this trap. They have consistently exceeded their pessimistically set budgets while at the same time losing market share to competitors. This has two equally important implications. The first is that while production efficiency can be simply measured by output, new business cannot be used in the same way to measure marketing efficiency, unless it can be established that the assumptions, upon which the agreed budget was based, and the individual marketing programmes being implemented remain valid. There were periods when this may have been expected, but they were a long time ago. The modern experience is that situations can change rapidly and assumptions can become invalid just as quickly. The second implication is that to avoid these problems it is necessary to develop systems by which new business can be analysed in detail. The primary objective of the systems should be to discriminate between performance that can be attributed to factors external to the organisation and those which can be attributed to the implementation of the organisation's marketing programmes.

Example	To be successful <trainline.com>, the organisation set up to sell rail tickets via the Internet, clearly needs to develop ticket sales and turnover quickly in order to recover the start-up costs associated with providing this service. As advertising is likely to be an important component of these initial costs it is important to establish which media is reaching potential customers most effectively. One approach would be initially to use the main TV media, then Channel 4, then newspapers, then commercial radio, analysing both the use of the service by new customers and for repeat purchases. The advertising programme would then need to be optimised on the basis of this information.

THE IMPLEMENTATION OF MARKETING PLANNING

Within an organisation the marketing planning process requires individuals who have a sound understanding of the principles of marketing. In particular this has to be demonstrated by the commitment of senior management. Without this understanding the benefits of the planning process are perceived in terms of reducing uncertainty rather than, as it should be, of increasing the ability of the organisation to respond to uncertainty.

As should be evident from the preceding section on control, the marketing plan should be at the centre of the performance measurement process. It should also provide the starting point whenever there is a need to respond to changes in external or internal circumstances that could affect the organisation, its customers, or the relationship between these.

When economic and technical situations are stable, marketing planning might easily become an annual task. In the turbulent economic and technical environment in which organisations must now compete it has to be a continuing process. It should be stressed, however, that this does not mean that programmes are changed month by month. If the planning has been done effectively most, if not all, programmes will remain valid in spite of the assumptions upon which they were based. However, changing circumstances should be identified and analysed early enough to accommodate any needed modifications to the overall plan.

CONCLUSION

Marketing planning is the means by which well-organised companies bring their marketing activities into a concerted action plan, ready for the market. A logical sequence will usually be followed in marketing planning, commencing with information gathering and analysis, combined with a marketing audit exercise involving issues and influences both within and outside the company. From the audit stage will be developed the marketing objectives to be addressed, while these in turn will largely direct the strategies to follow within the plan. Key assumptions made during the planning exercise need to be made explicit, as these will have some bearing on the flexibility and scope of the plan itself. Finally, no marketing plan will be complete without some provision for implementation, supporting organisation and control.

QUESTIONS

1 *Taking any of the case studies in the text, develop a SWOT analysis to identify the major internal and external issues to be addressed.*

2 *What kind of market information would be necessary for marketing planning, and how might it be obtained?*

3 *Compare and contrast the marketing plan for an established product with that for a new product.*

4 *Consider the view that companies will derive as much benefit from the planning exercise as from the marketing plan itself.*

FURTHER READING

Aaker, D. A. and Adler, D. A. (1998) *Developing Business Strategies*, 5th edn, John Wiley & Sons.

Abell, D. (1978) 'Strategic windows', *Journal of Marketing*, vol. 42, no. 3, pp. 56–62.

Ansoff, I. (1989) *Corporate Strategy*, rev. edn, Penguin.

Boston Consulting Group (1971) 'The product portfolio', *Perspectives on Experience*, Boston.

Brown, R. (1991) 'Making the product portfolio a basis for action', *Long Range Planning*, vol. 24, no. 1.

Doyle, P .(1976) 'The realities of the product life cycle', *Quarterly Review of Marketing,* Summer.

Drucker, P. F. (1963) 'Managing for business effectiveness', *Harvard Business Review*, 41, May.

Fifield, P. (1998) *Marketing Strategy*, 2nd edn. CIM professional/Butterworth Heinemann.

Hamel, G. and Prahalad, C. K. (1994*) Competing for the Future*. Harvard Business Press.

Kotler, P. (1999*) Marketing Management: Analysis Planning and Control*, 10th edn (Millennium). Prentice-Hall.

McDonald, M. H. B. (1999) *Marketing Plans – and How to Use Them*, 4th edn, CIM Professional/Butterworth Heinemann.

McDonald, M. H. B. (1993) 'Portfolio analysis and marketing management', *Marketing Business*, May.

Peters, T. and Waterman, R. (1982) *In Search of Excellence: Lessons from America's Best Run Companies*. Harper & Row.

Piercy, N. F. (2000) *Market-led Strategic Change: Transforming the Process of Going to Market,* 2nd edn. Cim Professional.

Porter, M. (198X) *Competitive Strategy*. The Free Press.

Weihrich, H. (1982) 'The TOWS matrix – a tool for situational analysis', *Long Range Planning*, vol. 15, no. 2, pp. 54–66.

Direct Line

Direct Line was founded in 1984 and has revolutionised the private motor insurance market. The founders decided that traditional suppliers had lapsed into a culture of complacency typified by over-pricing and under-service. This opened an opportunity for a *new* service company that was focused on the consumer, bringing a *new* perspective to the industry, with *new* standards for simplicity, service and value for money.

The company has a simple philosophy that applies to all its offerings. Each of Direct Line's products is designed to give consumers a clear, straightforward, good value alternative to a product sold through traditional distribution channels – especially where those channels involve a 'middleman' who can be cut out to reduce costs. The company positions itself as customer-focused, innovative and pioneering, and through distinctive advertising and PR has achieved a 95 per cent level of customer awareness in the UK (1997, Millward Brown quoted on <directline.com>, the website).

The company suggests that the core elements of the Direct Line brand are that it is:

- Trustworthy
- straightforward
- human
- challenging.

As the company conducts the vast majority of its business using the telephone, customer service is at the centre of the Direct Line proposition. To ensure that standards are maintained the company provides all its staff with extensive customer care training and it re-engineers all of its processes to simplify things for customers, for instance insurance certificates are laser printed immediately and forwarded by first-class post to customers – usually arriving the following day. The company's automated call-handling systems are designed to ensure that the company's 15 million customer calls each year are quickly and effortlessly re routed between Direct Line's six different city centres to ensure the minimum wait for an available operator.

The first motor policy was sold over the telephone on 2nd April 1985. Although motor insurance volumes have remained static for the last five years they still account for 69 per cent of the company's business (1999 results, see the company website that contains much of relevant information). The website tells of the company's many achievements over the years, and as part of its growth strategy it has launched a number of new insurance products such as home insurance, pet insurance and travel insurance. In addition Direct Line customers can now purchase a wide range of other products such as credit cards, loans, savings and even mortgages over the phone. But Direct Line is still adding to its product range and has now entered the car breakdown market with its purchase of the Green Flag company. In September 1999 it launched <directline.com>, which allows customers to buy immediate insurance cover on-line.

It was reported in the *Financial Times* on 5 May 2000 under the heading:

INSURANCE GROUP TO PUSH AHEAD WITH MOTORING PORTAL PLAN

that:

Direct Line claims an almost 30 per cent share of the on-line insurance market in Britain since its web service was launched nine months ago.

Direct Line, which revolutionised the UK market in the 1980s by pioneering direct sales over the telephone, also said it had taken a 40 per cent share of the on-line car insurance market in the first quarter, well above its 15 per cent share of the total motor market. Citing industry

▶

research, the company estimated that about 8 per cent of its new motor insurance sales were coming from its Internet site, whereas the industry average was about 3 to 4 per cent.

'The growth of directline.com has been phenomenal,' said Oliver Prill, its Managing Director of e-commerce. 'Our target of selling 15 per cent of motor insurance on-line by 2003 looks within easy reach.'

Direct Line said it was issuing about 150,000 quotes a month over the site, with 40 per cent conducted outside call-centre hours. Mr Brill said that Direct Line would launch another marketing campaign to publicise the insurance site and would push ahead with previously announced plans to spend £50m on building a motoring 'portal' that will sell cars and provide motorists with a wide range of information and other services.

the Internet site for motorists <jamjar.com> is named after the Cockney rhyming slang for car. The aim is to sell popular models of cars at up to 30 per cent below list prices through a deal made with Dixon Motors. The service will also include an auction facility, insurance, loans and route planning. The fact that Direct Line is investing a great deal of resources in developing the service shows how committed the company is to it.

Tasks

1 Carry out a SWOT analysis on the motor insurance business of Direct Line, and suggest how the company might increase its level of business above the static level of 2.2 million policies that has been achieved every year from 1995 to 1999.

2 Consider the portfolio of products/services offered by Direct Line and evaluate the balance of the range, in particular the role of mature products and the need to invest in new offerings.

3 With regard to the new venture <jamjar.com> suggest where Direct Line might have an advantage over its competitors, and assess whether the company seems to be able to market this service as effectively as it has the other new offerings.

22 Research for marketing

Managers make decisions: a good manager is one who makes good decisions. The basis of good decisions is having appropriate information available and using it effectively.

Peter Jackson

INTRODUCTION

In Chapter 9 marketing information was defined in the context of organisational information and compared with operational information. Its importance to marketing decision making was introduced and this was shown to be an essential aspect on marketing planning in Chapter 20. This chapter introduces the formal approach to obtaining marketing information as a specific business activity or marketing function.

While as a marketing function this activity is generally known as marketing research there is no accepted definition of this term. This is in spite of many attempts having been made to define it both by the authors of the celebrated marketing textbooks and by the respected organisations involved in marketing. Of the many definitions offered one of the most straightforward is that originally proposed by the American Marketing Association. This defined marketing research as:

The systematic gathering, recording, and analyzing of data about problems relating to the marketing of goods and services.

While satisfactory with regard to the basics, this definition ignored the important problem-solving and reporting aspects of marketing research as a business function. It was for this reason considered unsatisfactory by many authors, including Kotler, who in 1987 proposed the following definition:

Marketing research uses information to identify and define marketing opportunities and problems; generate, refine and evaluate marketing actions; monitor marketing performance; and improve understanding of marketing as a process. It communicates findings and their implications.

This satisfies the main criticisms made of the earlier definition, but ignores the more fundamental point made by Buzzell in 1963. In an article in the *Harvard Business Review* he suggested it was the title 'marketing research' that was deceptive. In his opinion the function was in reality like military intelligence and the title 'marketing intelligence' would accordingly be more appropriate.

In spite of the logic of this argument the term marketing research continues to survive and, to confuse the situation further, is used by many authors interchangeably with the term 'market research'. This is unfortunate since, particularly in the UK, the term market research is accepted as that used to define the specialist activities involved in applying the observational, survey and experimental social research techniques for marketing research applications. Accordingly market research may be usefully considered a specialist activity that is within the scope of the marketing research function rather than an alternative name for it.

MARKETING RESEARCH AS AN AID TO MARKETING

While as a proportion of total marketing outlay the expenditure on market research has never been high – certainly nowhere near the levels of adspend budgets – most companies now appreciate the need for at least occasional marketing research inputs. Indeed, marketing research has gained recognition for the contribution it can make to marketing planning and strategy, and to the effective implementation of company marketing plans.

Basically, marketing research activities can be applied across two broad areas:

- *Market-based research* – literally market research, concerned with market measurement and description e.g. market size (by volume and value), buyer numbers and location, buying frequencies, market segmentation, market share breakdown.
- *Functional marketing research* – tactical and strategic research into the various activities within marketing, involving anything from new product testing to advertising 'tracking' studies, packaging research, corporate image studies and pricing research.

Certainly the boundaries of the marketing research field have grown appreciably in recent years, and advances in information technology and changes in marketing itself (e.g. e-commerce) have presented even further research and analysis possibilities.

In theory, though, almost any company could consider doing quite a bit of its own marketing research, utilising to the maximum its own resources and market contacts (e.g. service, sales and engineering staff out in the field, supplier feedback), and developing through experience its own marketing research competencies.

Where the need arises to use outside research suppliers such as market research agencies, this might be driven by particular factors such as:

- speed/urgency for quick results;
- cost factors, e.g. where outside multiclient surveys spread costs among clients;
- specialist expertise required, e.g. socio-psychological motivation research;
- large-scale research jobs, e.g. national and international surveys;
- 'outsider' objectivity required, perhaps to select between competing market scenarios.

In practice, it is likely that ongoing market intelligence, and the analysis of company-based data, will be addressed by internal staff, while more specialist and extensive research exercises are contracted out to dedicated market research agencies. Indeed, with the increasing costs and sophistication of market research in the field, all but the largest of companies are likely to find that having a full in-house market research department is simply not viable. A practical compromise is likely to be the retention of a small market research section, headed up by a qualified market research manager, to cover both internal information and market analysis needs and to manage the commissioning of special market research assignments to outside research contractors.

Commissioning research agencies

Obviously, the commissioning of research to market research agencies will involve the production and issuing of a formal research brief, which will form the basis of the research contract. Especially when using a market research agency for the first time, the marketer (i.e. the client) can face a picture of difficulty and confusion – even in terms of supplier choice; in the UK there are over 600 organisations that promote themselves as providers of market research services. However, where the client's research problem is more specialised, for example in researching children, or overseas markets, then the choice of qualified suppliers is more limited (i.e. 'horses for courses').

In terms of selection of a market research agency, directory and on-line sources (e.g. Market Research Society – *www.marketresearch.org.uk*) can help with initial contact and shortlisting, while the final choice of agency is likely to be made only after detailed discussion(s) with the client organisation. Clients concerned to make the right agency selection will likely have followed up references, undertaken their own checking on prospective agencies (e.g. with other agency clients), and perhaps viewed examples of previous agency research projects.

Baker (2000) proposes that those clients who are legitimately concerned with quality and professional standards in market research, rather than simply seeking lower fees, would be well advised to use only agencies that can evidence accreditation through acceptable quality 'kitemark' and registration schemes, such as those upheld by the BMRA (British Market Research Association) or MRQSA (Market Research Quality Standards Association).

TYPES OF MARKETING RESEARCH

There are four generally recognised approaches to classifying marketing research. The first of these relates to whether the research is routine, when it is known as continuous, or only undertaken when needed, when it is known as ad hoc. The second approach differentiates the three basic sources of data – secondary internal, secondary external and primary. These are discussed under 'Gather problem-specific data' later in the chapter. The third approach involves the essentially different types of data that might be obtained – quantitative or qualitative; and the fourth approach defines the different objectives for obtaining the information – exploratory, conclusive, descriptive or causal.

As will be seen in the paragraphs and sections that follow, these categories are interrelated rather than mutually exclusive, making the classification of marketing research activities in practice somewhat complicated.

Forms of research

Continuous marketing research

This involves collating marketing information, such as total sales by product variant or geographic region, on a routine basis so that it can be compared over time. This allows the performance of the marketing activities of an organisation to be monitored and, in particular, market trends determined. By definition, continuous marketing research is produced on a regular or periodic basis.

Ad hoc marketing research

When research is required for a non-recurring purpose it is generally referred to as 'ad hoc' research, as it is carried out only when actually required to assist a marketing decision. An example could be investigation of the viability of a new product, or the reasons behind a drop in sales. Usually the presentation of the research findings will be as a formal report. It is customary for such reports to be sufficiently comprehensive for the information presented to be of value to users who may have no relevant intangible marketing information on the subject. This is important since otherwise the value of the information provided is likely to depend more on the user's existing knowledge of the subject than on the quality of the marketing research.

In many organisations this type of research is seen as the main purpose of the marketing research department. However this is often misleading, since continuous research information presented routinely as a memo or newsletter may not be as impressive as a formal research report, it is often used as the basis upon which much of the ad hoc research has to depend. For this reason it is important that continuous research information is produced in a form that allows detailed analysis, whenever this might be required.

It is also inevitable that most marketing research textbooks focus mainly on ad hoc research. The reason for this is that ad hoc research involves a number of well-established stages and procedures. In contrast, since continuous research is a routine activity, most of these stages are only necessary when setting up the routine. In practice, most continuous research is, at least in part, subjected to the full research process from time to time as a result of being used in ad hoc research. In many organisations such research is also done when preparing the annual marketing planning reference document.

Types of data

Quantitative data

Any information that can be expressed using a numerical measure is considered quantitative. It includes not only numerical data, such as that obtained from internal sales and accounting records, but also the numerical aspects of other data, such as may be derived from questionnaires. It could also include studies of distribution levels, repeat purchase rates or even opinion polls regarding voting intentions. More than three-quarters of all marketing research data is classified as quantitative. Nearly all continuous marketing research comes within this category since usually it is undertaken to provide data for time series analysis.

Qualitative data

Qualitative research is concerned with information that is based on descriptions and shades of meaning rather than numerical analysis. It is commonly used in the early stages of ad hoc research studies. One popular source of qualitative data is that derived from small 'focus' group discussions. In general, it involves unstructured exploration or inductive problem-solving techniques that are beyond the scope of an introductory text such as this. Although in practice less than a quarter of the marketing research undertaken can be classified as qualitative, this category is much discussed both with regard to the methods used and resultant findings. It has resulted in the development of many concepts seen as useful in defining and categorising market segments, such as lifestyle.

Research objective

Exploratory marketing research

The purpose of exploratory research is to define the nature of a marketing problem and to identify what needs to be investigated or measured and how best to undertake a study. It is used to identify critical issues and to generate ideas or hypotheses. Since exploratory research is problem-orientated, it is always carried out as an ad hoc research study. Qualitative research techniques are often used in order to minimise the effect that the terms of reference might have on the research outcome.

Conclusive research

As has already been mentioned, research must be considered as an aid to marketing decisions and as such cannot replace this role. Conclusive research is aimed at providing the specific information needed by management to make a defined marketing decision. It might be used to test a hypothesis set up in advance of the data collection, but more likely it involves measuring the variables identified as relevant to a particular decision.

The deductive approach to problem-solving can only be applied to problems where it is possible and practical to obtain data that is appropriate and reliable. For other problems, the alternative inductive approach to problem-solving is generally more appropriate. The inductive approach involves establishing concepts by identifying repeated patterns in the behaviour being observed. The validity of the applicability of these patterns is then verified by repeated empirical studies. The results obtained are generally stated as paradigms rather than laws since their application is subject to exception. This is the normal approach used for psychological work involved in, for instance, buyer behaviour studies. It would have been the approach used by Maslow to develop his hierarchical theory of motivation. It is also the basis used for qualitative marketing research. The implementation of this approach to problem-solving requires specialist training and experience and is thus, like other qualitative research, beyond the scope of introductory texts such as this.

Descriptive marketing research

Descriptive research focuses on product performance, market size, trends, competitive strategies and market share. It is typically concerned with measuring or estimating variables and the frequency of their occurrence. Depending on the objective and context, this could be the result of either continuous or ad hoc research.

Causal marketing research

Causal research looks at the cause-and-effect relationships in an attempt to explain why things happen. For instance, whether loss of market share is due to the success of a direct competitor or the result of an indirect competitor's success in an associated market segment. Like exploratory research, causal research is usually undertaken on an ad hoc basis. It is usually more analytical than descriptive research and is intended to reveal the factors critical to the behaviour of consumers or, more generally, markets. It can thus involve using both quantitative and qualitative research techniques.

THE RESEARCH PROCESS

Marketing research was defined at the beginning of this chapter as the use of information, and the communication of findings and their implications. Much ongoing research is used to monitor situations, but, as stated earlier, there is an established, standard approach that can be termed the marketing research process. This comprises seven distinct stages. These are most obvious when setting up an ad hoc study, but are present in all studies. The relative importance of each stage will also vary according to the objective of the study. The seven stages are:

1 Define the problem.
2 Analyse the situation.
3 Establish objectives and agree cost–benefit parameters.
4 Gather problem-specific data.
5 Analyse the data to produce information relevant to the problem.
6 Prepare report.
7 Follow up to evaluate effectiveness of action taken.

In the following sections each of these stages is considered in detail.

Define the problem

Problem definition is often very difficult to complete objectively and, as the initial stage in the process, is all too easy to omit altogether. However, it is important both because it forces managers to think deeply about the reasons for collecting data, and to consider the value of information in the context of the decision to be made.

Analyse the situation

An important characteristic of marketing research is that it is very common for the person who is initiating the research to have considerably more information about the subject at the start of the research process than the person who is to carry out the research. This information is likely to be a combination of day-to-day experience resulting from being involved with a particular market over many years and from receiving information produced by continuous research procedures on a regular basis. This can create commonly unforeseen difficulties for managers commissioning research studies. For this reason marketing research briefs should include a comprehensive analysis of the current situation, especially when the work is to be done by a specialist outside organisation.

Establish objectives and agree cost–benefit parameters

It is important to establish objectives for the study to ensure that the research is properly focused, even when the problem has been adequately defined. Once the objectives for the study have been agreed the essential methodology can be determined, and the likely cost of the research in terms of time and resources estimated. This is essential since it is very easy to agree market research study objectives that cannot be completed within the time or budget available. Obviously decisions about the value of the information, and the expenditure limits placed on obtaining it, have implications for the scale and intensity of the research and for the budget to be spent on contracting outside research suppliers such as agencies.

Gather problem-specific data

This should be carried out by considering data sources in order of the cheapest, most readily available information first, and only later thinking about the more expensive, bespoke studies. There are three categories of data. These are defined by data source and discussed in the usual order in which they are accessed. While initially confusing it is important to remember that the first two of these are categories of secondary data, that is data from sources that already exist, whereas it is the third of these categories which is considered primary data.

Secondary internal data

Internal data is the information that is internal to an organisation and usually the starting point for data collection. It should provide a reliable source of up-to-date information immediately available within the organisation. It is thus essential it is fully utilised, and can be drawn from:

- sales records
- delivery and stock records
- prices and quotations
- sales promotion – price offers, etc.
- advertising – media and messages – size of budget
- sales personnel's call reports and assessments of their effectiveness
- past studies on marketing effectiveness.

In Chapter 9 the relevance of operating data was mentioned in the context of a marketing information system. Of particular interest in the context of marketing research is the time series data relating to orders received, products delivered, advertising expenditure, promotional campaigns, sales by customer or sales territory and so on. Sometimes the information required is available directly from routine reports giving continuous data. However, there are often occasions when it is insufficiently detailed in some way.

Much of the time series data will have been summarised, for instance as sales by day or week or month or even as quarterly or annual figures. Inevitably, detail is lost as the figures are summarised. Usually this is because the summaries are prepared primarily to provide managers with measures of financial efficiency. While such measures are essential in any business organisation they are likely to use conventions set by the accounting requirements rather than the needs of marketing.

Although one of the principal objectives of collating internal marketing data is to monitor the performance of the organisation, in practice this information is of little value for making marketing decisions unless it can be compared with the market as a whole. For long-term success, organisations need to grow faster than the market during periods of growth and decline less rapidly than the market during periods of decline. In order to make these comparisons it is necessary to use data obtained from outside sources.

Secondary external data

There is a plethora of external marketing data readily available if you know where to look for it. Some common sources are listed in Appendix 3. This section considers the use of secondary external data in detail since this is the main source of marketing data available to students.

Peter Jackson, in his excellent book *Desk Research*, states:

> many information needs can be met through desk research. This type of data collection is well within the practical scope of even a lone researcher and requires few additional, if any,

resources. Arguably, if more or more and better desk research was undertaken, less field research would be needed and research budgets would be more effectively and efficiently spent.

(Jackson, 1994)

The sources of secondary data available to desk researchers include newspapers, journals and magazines, directories of all sorts, on-line databases, government statistics and reports, company reports, surveys published by research organisations and others, including trade associations.

Many industries have established trade associations and some of these, such as the Society of Motor Manufacturers and Traders, have become the principal source of marketing information relating to their industry. This, of course, is only possible when the members of the organisation agree that it is in their individual best interest to provide information to the organisation and contribute to the cost of its collation. Very often the information produced is only circulated to those companies that have fulfilled their obligation to supply information to the collating organisation. Of course, the validity of the information produced depends upon the proportion of the industry willing to contribute to and buy such services.

In the absence of specially collated industry data more general data has to be used. Much of this is collated by government departments to measure the level of economic and industrial activity to determine the effectiveness of current economic policy. Some of these measures, such as the retail price index, have become newspaper headline news.

Wherever possible the accuracy of secondary external data should be checked. One approach is to find other sources for the same data. However, a word of warning: it is not sufficient simply to show that several sources agree, as sometimes this only shows that they all used the same original source. If it is not possible actually to check the accuracy of the information then an attempt should be made to put it into context.

Example

Suppose you are looking for information regarding the market for jeans in the UK and you find an article in which it is stated that in the UK 47 million pairs of jeans are sold each year and the value of the market is £650 million. If the population of the UK is approximately 55 million and 10 per cent are children there would be about 50 million adults. This data would suggest that adults buy on average about one pair of jeans per year. Is this reasonable? It is quite likely that some students buy two or more pairs of jeans per year; but then the average student's parents possibly only buy on average one pair per year and the average student's grandparents probably buy none. Taking all this into account, what at least can be said is that while 47 million may or may not be correct, it is clearly not obviously incorrect.

How about the value? This suggests that the average price of a pair of jeans is less than £14. Is this likely to be right? A walk round any town centre shops might show that there are jeans for sale at £14, but they are not branded, and most jeans actually being worn seem to be branded. What does this mean? Either the article was using information that was wrong, or out of date, or there was a printing error. There are other possible explanations – the figure could be based on ex-works prices rather than the retail selling price, or on some other cost basis such as the value at which the goods were imported. Whatever the reason it is clear that the figure needs to be treated with caution and, if it is used because it is the only information available, its apparent shortcomings should at least be discussed.

Generally speaking, when external secondary data is used within an organisation it can be compared with relevant internal secondary data such as sales to a specific market segment.

Different approaches have to be used by students and organisations that, not being involved in a market, do not have access to relevant internal data. This may involve estimating market size on the basis of likely usage and the total number of potential customers.

Another approach is to relate consumption to the population as a whole. Reliable population estimates are available for most developed countries since they are required as the basis for many government policies. Generally the population estimates are obtained by means of a census carried out every ten years.

The collation of relevant external data can involve continuously monitoring measures of national economic activity, such as the gross national product. Alternatively measures of business confidence, such as the Confederation of British Industry poll of investment intentions, can be used. Generally, as with internal data, only measures that over time have been shown to be relevant should be monitored on a continuous basis. Information required to respond to specific marketing problems need only be collated on an ad hoc basis.

Many marketing problems will only require analysis of either secondary external data or a combination of secondary external and internal data. In doing this it is always useful to try to check the validity of any external data used. In the jeans example this could involve at least a cursory visit to the shops to get some idea of the current price range of jeans. This simple example leads us to primary research, which is the third category of marketing research data.

On-line secondary data

With the rapid increase in internet connection and usage in recent years it is not surprising that on-line sourcing of research information has become both more popular and feasible. Increasingly, published sources of external data are being at least mirrored by on-line availability, usually through the web site addresses of the publishers and data sources themselves, e.g. government surveys and data are generally available, at least in summary form, on-line.

Again, as a standard form of service enhancement for members (or as a promotional invitation for prospective new members), business and trade associations are making at least edited compilations of data available through their web sites. From a data sourcing perspective, this offers major access advantages in the early stages of secondary data-gathering – the information collation is literally a form of desk research – and generally the information itself is recent or regularly updated.

Parallel to this, secondary data sourcing as a prelude to primary research (e.g. company listings by sector and address) is becoming easier through on-line directories, telephone listings, membership information, etc. Sourcing of market research contractors and consultants is obviously also furthered through on-line searching.

A major potential advantage of internet use for market research, of course, is the international scope of the medium – aside from the predictable density of US sources, European and global links and comparative sources are now becoming more widespread and user-friendly.

Again the valuable contribution to secondary sourcing made by libraries, universities and the media is, if anything, vastly increased through on-line access.

Generally it would be fair to say that on-line sourcing for secondary data offers advantages in terms of:

- speed of access

- multisource comparability
- downloading/copy facility
- up-to-date information.

While there are no major drawbacks to on-line sourcing, one limitation is that availability still varies somewhat, even for government sources. For commercial sources of data, on-line sourcing is by no means free, and will either be by subscription contract, by membership rights, or by direct on-line payment, though some data sampling may

Table 22.1   Some on-line secondary data sources

Site	URL	Comments
World Wide Web Virtual Library	http://W3.org	Multiple book, press and printed information sources
Brainstorm Business Forum	http://www.brainstorm.co.uk	CBI, Chambers of commerce, best practice
Europe Business Monitor	http://www.businessmonitor.co.uk	European Business information
UK National Statistics Office	http://www.statsbase.gov.uk	UK official economic and social statistics; databank of economic data (subscriber based)
US Census Data	www.census.gov	US social and economic census and survey information
Department of Trade and Industry, UK	http://www.DTI.gov.uk	Business, trade, economic, investment data and information; links to other EU and government sites
Business Link National	www.Businesslink.co.uk	Business link services, information and advice links – good for smaller businesses
University of Strathclyde	www.dis.swtrath.ac.uk	*Good* links through business information sources on the Internet section
Financial Times	http://www.usa.ft.com/	Topical comments and business analysis, links to other FT on-line sources
Institute of Export	http://www.export.co.uk	Leading professional bodies
American Marketing Association	http://www.ama.org/	
Chartered Institute of Marketing	http://www.cim.co.uk	
Market Research Society	www.marketresearch.org.uk	
The Economist	http://www.economist.com	Market and trade commentary, links to other sites
Europages	www.europages.com	European business directory – 500,000 companies listed in 30 European countries – search by sector/company
The Institute of Management	www.inst-mgt.org.uk	MICWEB information (by Gale Group) and other information sources on companies, products, markets – access by individual, corporate or student membership

be possible for web site visitors, or summary information made available 'free' via the web site home page. Table 22.1 lists a number of useful on-line sources of secondary research data.

Primary data sources

Primary research is often referred to as field research, in contrast to the term desk research, which is used to describe the collection of secondary data. Primary data is obtained by using one or more of the following market research approaches, which are briefly described below:

- observation
- surveys (interviews)
- projective techniques
- experimentation.

Observation

This involves observing, recording and subsequently analysing consumer or market behaviour in particular contexts. It can involve personal observation (e.g. store supervisors monitoring shopper traffic), or automatic recording of behaviour or events (e.g. monitoring electronically the direction of supermarket aisle traffic, digital check-out recording by EPOS (electronic point-of-sale) technology, video camera recordings, etc.).

Surveys

Conducting surveys means directing a series of questions at samples of customers/ users, either by personal interview (by an interviewer), by mail/postal survey (with a self-completion questionnaire), or by telephone. Each of these methods has its advantages and disadvantages, e.g. personal interviews can produce the most information but at a cost, while postal surveys are cheaper but tend to have lower response levels.

A more recent delivery mode is on-line questionnaire completion, through prior enlistment of on-line participants or, more informally, through user feedback via web site responses.

Omnibus surveys are periodic (e.g. every six weeks) questionnaire surveys with pre-recruited samples of consumers, using composite questionnaires that cover a differing mix of product fields each survey period. Each period, the market research agency operating the survey will (for a fee per question) 'sell' sections of the questionnaire to outside companies that are seeking relatively quick and low-cost answers to a limited number of questions involving their particular products and markets.

Focus groups are a kind of group interview, usually with six to eight people led by a discussion leader, with a broad focus on some particular market, product field or consumer decision situation. Usually audio- or video-recorded, focus groups are often used as exploratory research to develop a 'feel' for a market or issue, prior to more detailed research.

Projective techniques

These are forms of qualitative research that explore behavioural and psychological aspects of consumer choice such as perception, motivation, information processing and attitude formation. As these issues often involve subconscious or unconscious drives and influences, the investigative approaches used are often indirect and oblique (e.g. word association testing, story and dialogue completion, picture-matching, problem-solving) rather than direct questioning.

Experimentation

This involves a variety of 'action research' applications within marketing, where specific comparative tests or experiments are set up and the results monitored and analysed. Typical test situations might involve product tests (for new product development), packaging or display testing, price experiments, or testing alternative advertising treatments.

Note: While comprehensive coverage of the more specialised of these research techniques is beyond the scope of this book, Appendix 5 offers a detailed review of the practical aspects of questionnaire-based surveys in marketing research.

On-line market research

Computer technology has for some time been harnessed by market researchers, initially through analysis software programs (e.g. SPSS) and more recently through interactive data input at the 'research face' through developments such as CATI (computer-assisted telephone interviewing) and CAPI (computer-assisted personal interviewing). Technically, internet exploitation for survey work in market research is but a short step from such applications.

Indeed, the market research potential opening up through the Internet has attracted the attention of academics and practitioners alike, and an interesting cross-section of evaluative commentaries on on-line research is to be found in recent journal articles by Gray (2000), Pincott and Branthwaite (2000), Bradley (1999) and Johnston (1999).

In practice, though, it is only recently that on-line 'real-time' research has been practical, largely owing to the (still) varied connectivity across different respondent groups. Certainly the larger market research agencies are now developing on-line capabilities in primary data collection, especially in more technically advanced sectors such as financial services, computing and other high tech areas.

Interestingly, the more sophisticated 'client' users of market research may have opportunities through on-line technology to carry out their own research, albeit in specialist applications, e.g. as a by-product of an extended intranet network of a company's subsidiaries, suppliers and customer organisations. Such a development is a natural extension of relationship marketing, discussed elsewhere in this book.

Web site applications for market research purposes may therefore be quite feasible for at least feedback, monitoring or validation purposes, for:

- specialist business 'communities', e.g. scientific, high tech fields;
- business-to-business markets;
- special interest groups on-line, e.g. technically sophisticated consumer groups (such as computer 'buffs');
- high traffic websites (e.g. Virgin, Coca-Cola) that offer feedback and other ongoing contact links;
- e-mail conferencing and user discussion/feedback forums.

Smaller companies, or those undertaking feasibility or competitive scanning exercises, might undertake first-stage research by identifying (on-line) competitors and literally visiting and analysing their web sites. While the information potential of such approaches is limited, it is possible to make interesting on-line 'observations' about competitors, for example:

- Web site comprehensiveness – how detailed, how extensive, how many sections?
- Web site user-friendliness – how easy to navigate, speed of response, foreign language translation?
- How up to date/professional/well-designed?

Exercise	Select a product sector and identify four or five company web sites within it. Visit and explore each web site and 'score' each in terms of comprehensiveness and user-friendliness.

Market research companies themselves have actively used web sites as 'shop fronts' to promote their services, and as a means of getting closer to prospective clients. The corollary of this is that marketing client companies can now more easily access research agencies and organisations for commissioning purposes.

Table 22.2 lists a limited selection of research and consulting organisations.

The purpose of data analysis

In the context of marketing research it is important to appreciate that the purpose and objective of data analysis is to produce relevant information from the available data. Accordingly this aspect of data analysis will be discussed in this section rather than the specific techniques which may be used. One of the most important of these, the use of constant values for times series analysis, is introduced and explained in Appendix 4.

It needs to be stressed that the purpose of marketing research is to provide relevant information, not simply to present data. A primary necessity for useful information is that it can be understood without prior knowledge or interpretation. This involves analysing data and then putting it into context.

Table 22.2   Some leading research and consulting organisations

Site	URL	Comments
Frost and Sullivan Deloitte Consulting	www.frost.com/mec www.dc.com/deloitte	Engineering business research and consultancy Research and consultancy reports worldwide
Economist Intelligence Unit	www.eiu.com	Subscriber report and information service; some information available free to visitors
Esomar – World Association of Research Professionals	www.esomar.nl	Represents 1500 research organisations in 100 countries worldwide – all market research sectors included; useful practitioner directory source.
Millward Brown UK Ltd	www.millwardbrown.com	Leading market research agency with extensive international links
Mintel	www.mintel.com	Leading researcher and publisher of market surveys
The Gallup Organisation	www.gallup.com	Readership, opinion research, international research in many fields

The analysis of value data

Value data, whether collated from internal or external sources, is potentially an extremely valuable source of marketing research information. It allows expenditure on different types of product to be combined and trends over long periods to be compared with leading indicators to establish relationships that can be used for forecasting. This type of analysis, however, needs to be done on a constant value basis.

Thus, value data should be used on the basis of the following three points. First, trends should be considered in both value and volume terms. Second, monetary values should be considered in constant value terms and ideally using constant present-day values. Third, there are often trends that get hidden as figures are combined. It is thus usually necessary to fully analyse the detailed figures to reveal actual happenings in the market place.

Prepare report

Unless the information is properly presented it is unlikely to meet the requirements of the person who needs it. The report should show the objectives of the study, explain how the study was carried out, detail any assumptions made and present the findings of the study clearly. Data, whether directly applicable or as background information, are normally best presented in a series of separate appendices. Particular care needs to be taken with respect to the presentation of graphical information.

Follow-up implementation

This stage need not be formal but should be conscientiously carried out since it provides opportunities to understand how the methods used in the investigation of the issues and the presentation of the report could be improved on in future.

CONCLUSION

Marketing research means providing the information for decisions on marketing activities such as advertising, pricing and distribution. The approach used may vary in terms of research form (continuous versus ad hoc), data type (qualitative versus quantitative), or the research objectives (exploratory, conclusive, descriptive or causal), and the different data sources (secondary or primary).

Whatever the type of research, the demands of budget constraints, research rigour and timeliness will require a methodical, well-managed sequence to be followed, from the initial problem definition and objectives stage, through data collection and analysis to presentation and reporting of findings.

Marketing information must be reliable, accurate, valid, relevant, sufficient, and up to date. It must also be available at an affordable cost. Further, it needs to be presented and communicated to the user in an understandable format. Statistical information, in particular, needs to be carefully handled, and presented consistently in terms of time series, measures and values.

QUESTIONS

1 'A problem well defined is a problem half resolved.' Discuss.

2 Consider the distinctive advantages of continuous research, giving examples of the marketing questions that it might answer.

3 'Qualitative research has obvious value in the insights it can provide, but when overused it can be distinctly misleading'. Discuss.

4 Should primary research only be carried out after considering secondary sources and finding the data from such sources inadequate?

5 Taking as an example the manufacturer of any leading consumer product, illustrate the variety of marketing decisions that might be better supported through the effective use of marketing research.

6 Use the resources of your own library to find out the market shares and volume sales of the major soft drink brands. Look at the trends over several years and suggest if there could be an opportunity for a new brand to enter the market, and if so which segment would seem to be the most attractive.

FURTHER READING

Baker, T. (2000) 'Quality-assured research is well worth the price', *Marketing*, 3 Feb. p. 18.

Bradley, N. (1999) 'Sampling for internet surveys. An examination of respondent selection for internet research', *Journal of the Market Research Society*, Oct., vol. 41.

Burns, A. C. and Bush, R. F. (2000) *Marketing Research*. Prentice-Hall.

Chisnall, P. M. (1992) *Essentials of Marketing Research*. Prentice-Hall.

Gray, R. (2000) 'The relentless rise of on-line research', *Marketing*, 8 May, p. 41.

Jackson, P. (1994) *Desk Research*. Kogan Page.

Johnston, A. (1999) 'Welcome to the wired world', *Research*, Nov., pp. 22–25.

Kent, R. A. (1993) *Marketing Research in Action*. Routledge.

Malhotra, N. K. and Birks, D. F. (2000) *Marketing Research – An Applied Approach*. Pearson Education.

Moutinho, L. and Evans, M. (1992) *Applied Marketing Research*. Addison-Wesley.

Pincott, G. and Branthwaite, A. (2000) 'Nothing new under the sun?', *International Journal of Market Research*, Spring–Summer, vol. 42.

Proctor, T. (2000), *Essentials of Marketing Research*, Pearson Education.

Webb, J. R. (1992) *Understanding and Designing Marketing Research*. Academic Press.

CASE STUDY

Hairco GmbH

Hairco GmbH Corporation is a leading German producer of hair dryers, crimpers, curlers and other electrical hair-styling products with sales in several European countries. Tanya Schlecht was very pleased to be recruited as product manager for hair dryers immediately after completing her business qualification at a German university. She knew her ability to speak the three major European languages was a key factor in her appointment, but she also knew that the firm she had joined had a reputation for aggressive sales activity and the staff were judged by the results they achieved in meeting profit targets.

Hairco's current sales were around 500 000 hair dryers per year – all aimed at female buyers through department stores, discount electrical stores and beauty shops. Large retail groups were

▶

regularly offered special deals but it was not always clear how these were passed on to consumers. The promotional costs were just over 20 per cent of revenue, and this was spent on both main media and in support of in-store promotions. However there seemed to be little direct link between promotions and sales, and no attempt was made to test the effectiveness of different promotions. Tanya was also surprised to find very little data on the market for hair dryers, and only basic sales revenue data on outlets. Naturally Tanya knew the major competitors such as Braun, Philips and Pifco, but she had no idea how these companies were rated against Hairco by either retailers or consumers.

Tanya thought she could obtain some volume data quite cheaply from secondary sources, but she felt it was more important to understand why and when consumers bought hair dryers. She also hoped that if she could establish how they used the product she could influence product development for the future. She wanted to discover if consumers were loyal to a particular make or whether they bought mainly on price; also, were there any differences between German, French and British consumers?

She had considered buying a few questions on an omnibus study to ask:

- When did you buy your current hair dryer?
- What make/model is it?
- Why did you choose this model?
- When do you think you will change it?
- What features does your current dryer lack?

However she knew that some of these were open-ended questions and therefore difficult to handle in a general questionnaire, but in getting answers to these questions Tanya felt she could direct the promotional spend more effectively as well as communicating the most appropriate message to potential customers.

She therefore wondered what were the alternative ways to learn more about the product for which she had responsibility. She thought she could afford some 75 000 D-Marks from her current budget to obtain the much needed marketing information, so she asked a number of agencies to discuss with her what was possible. She now has to draw up a brief, prior to meeting with the agencies, giving details of what she hopes to achieve from the research.

Questions

1 *Identify the different types of marketing information mentioned in the case study, e.g. primary/secondary; quantitative/qualitative.*

2 *Rank the various information needs identified relative to their importance with respect to Tanya's stated objectives.*

3 *What sort of secondary sources could Tanya use in order to obtain general data on the total market, its sectoral breakdown, growth trends and so on?*

4 *Based on your understanding of Tanya's information needs:*
   (a) outline the information that could be provided by an omnibus survey;
   (b) consider how Tanya might select (from rival bidders) a market research agency to carry out the survey.

23 Organising marketing activities

We trained hard but it seems that every time we were beginning to form into teams we would be reorganised. I was to learn later in life that we tend to meet any new situation by reorganising, and a wonderful method it can be for creating an illusion of progress, whilst producing confusion, inefficiency and demoralisation.

Gaius Petronius (AD 57)

INTRODUCTION

As the nature and role of marketing will vary among companies, so too will the resources involved and the approach adopted to marketing organisation. Exerting a particular influence on the way marketing is organised will be company policy on organisational issues such as centralisation, formalisation and management reporting, while a fundamental factor will be the level of market orientation shown by the company. Production-orientated companies are still to be found in large numbers in some sectors, and coupled with this is a prevalence to financially driven management – this can bring with it strategic risks.

Marketing management and organisation will be affected by both the strategic requirements of the external environment and by a host of internal issues such as organisational culture, values and attitudes, management style, the company's own development pattern, ownership history and so on. Even within the same market, faced with similar problems, two similarly sized companies may therefore adopt totally different approaches to organising and resourcing their marketing function.

It should be stressed that the organisation chart itself can rarely be taken as an indicator of how serious or successful a company is in its marketing; some companies such as Dyson have built their success through entrepreneurial leadership rather than much publicised formal marketing appointments. Simply stated, a large marketing department bristling with specialists is not a sufficient nor, for some, a necessary condition for success. The organisation-wide imperative of the marketing message requires teamwork handling of customer issues across the company, so that functional specialisation without integration is unlikely to be successful.

An area where this is of paramount importance is in the supermarket arena. Firms such as Tesco, Sainsbury's, Asda and Safeway have been in a battle to win and retain customers. Research by the Carlson Marketing Group has found that the approach to organising marketing activities has been different across the board, but the quest for customers similar. The research findings showed the following were major determinants in how consumers are influenced.

These diverse elements, including good staff, better price and recognising needs, show the variety of activities that companies must try to excel at in order to win in today's competitive environment. This ultimately has to make companies aware of the need to merge some marketing activities, and at the same time highlight the differences in strategy implementation from company to company.

How consumers are influenced

Good staff	49%
Better price	31%
Easy to contact	23%
Trust	21%
Positive image	15%
Superior product	14%
Recognise needs	10%
Good loyalty points/Rewards	9%
Go extra mile	4%

Source: J. Hiscock (2000) Is loyalty past its sell-by? *Marketing*, 14 September 2000.

Strategy matters play an important part in discussions of organisation, since on the one hand good strategy implementation depends on organisation, while on the other hand strategy formulation should be free of structural tramlines – structure should follow strategy, not vice versa. In the sections that follow a brief examination will be made of the different approaches companies use in organising for marketing.

ORGANISATIONAL STRUCTURES

Organisational structures without a formalised marketing function

In many cases these will represent a less mature organisational form that predates the emergence and use of marketing departments. Commonly associated with traditional companies in stable markets, or with production-dominated organisations, this structure will likely follow a four-way functional division between the production, finance, personnel and sales departments, each with separate chains of command, each reporting at board level. Within such organisations those activities that might otherwise be undertaken by a marketing department are likely to be subsumed within the four functional pillars of the structure, e.g. market feedback through the sales department, forecasting and commercial analysis through financial planning, or a nominated director. While most market-related tasks may be covered, it is unlikely that these marketing activities will be co-ordinated to the standard achieved by marketing-led competitors. Of course, such an organisational approach may also be encountered within small developing companies where an enterprising founder and informal workings may make for success, even in the face of resource constraints.

In other circumstances, though more exceptionally, it may be that a well-established company has prospered without separately formalising the marketing activities that it does undertake, often to a high standard. It would therefore be inappropriate to style such a high-performing company as ineffective or lacking in market orientation.

The functional marketing structure

When a marketing function is initially incorporated into a formal organisational structure it is usually as a department with responsibility for market research advertising, promotion and sales support. Often this is structured in parallel to the sales department. Such arrangements are likely to result in rivalry, rather than co-operation, between sales and marketing. Indeed, there are many cases where long-established sales departments have hindered or thwarted the development of an effective marketing function.

The emergence and integration of marketing into one functional section or department is likely to come about as the level and complexity of previously dispersed activities increases, and as these new activities demand a co-ordination beyond the scope of previous organisational arrangements. The increase in marketing activities that prompts such a new structure will usually, in turn, be attributable to external changes such as increased competition or marketing maturity, internal factors such as increasing promotional activity or a need for more market research or marketing planning support. A typical functionally organised marketing department is illustrated in Figure 23.1. Essentially, the structure consists of an umbrella organisation that embraces both the sales function and the essential marketing activities such as market research, sales promotion and advertising. Significantly, in the example shown, marketing has achieved representation at board level through the installation of a marketing director, though generally it is more likely to be through a sales and marketing director. The problem is not the title but the entirely different priorities of the sales and marketing activities. Essentially, good sales managers focus on the present and immediate results whereas good marketing managers focus on the development of results in the future. It is difficult for a single manager to fulfil both of these roles successfully.

The major benefits of such a structure are that roles and reporting relationships are clearly defined, along conventional hierarchical lines, while specialisation is allowed without undue duplication or ambiguity. Activities requiring more horizontal integration can be accommodated by adding co-ordinator staff, e.g. new product development might demand such liaison between market research and product planning, and

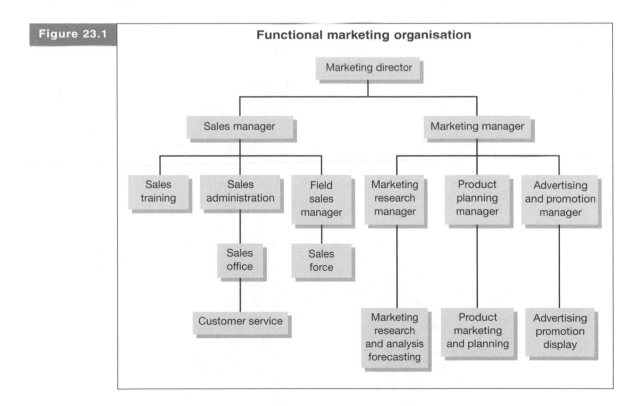

Figure 23.1 Functional marketing organisation

through other departments such as R&D and manufacturing. On the other hand, difficulties may arise if the organisation grows into a top-heavy hierarchy of specialists with strictly functional interests. Furthermore, frictions and inefficiencies may arise if increasing product and market diversification were to make heavily competing claims on the core specialisms. Such a structure is therefore more appropriate to everyday marketing support of a relatively narrow product range, or within more stable market settings.

Product-based organisation

Originally adopted en masse in the 1950s and 1960s by international fmcg (fast-moving consumer goods) companies, this structure has since spread to other sectors, such as industrial manufacturing, and more recently financial services. Essentially, a product marketing focus is introduced through the appointment of product (or brand) managers, responsible for the commercial health of some assigned product(s) or brand(s). Often seen as a mini general manager for product marketing, the typical product manager will be of relatively junior status with little line authority over specialists either in marketing or elsewhere. Effective working will rest heavily on persuasion and diplomacy, and hopefully the gradual assumption of expert power through demonstrated successes. Figure 23.2 depicts a typical product management organisation.

As shown in Figure 23.2, product managers will often be organised in groups, under the responsibility of respective product group managers, who are effectively marketing submanagers at the level of a group of related products. The product manager is mainly a liaison post, achieving for a specified product the necessary co-ordination of support

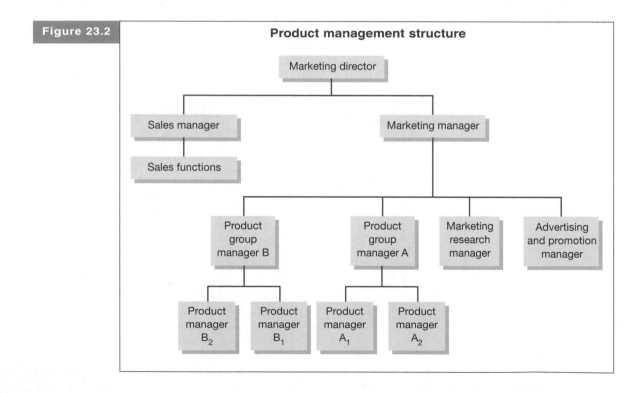

Figure 23.2   **Product management structure**

from marketing specialists (e.g. market research, advertising) and other functions alike. Product managers will usually be accountable for the financial and commercial health of their products, for product marketing planning and strategy, and for co-ordinating any necessary product development or modification activity.

Product management has a number of advantages as an organisational format. It ensures both a focus and specialisation of management expertise at the product/brand level, so that all the major products in the range get the benefit of a full-time champion dedicated solely to their well-being. In a multiproduct setting product management therefore ensures a level of management attention that would not be feasible under a functionally based structure. As the product manager position entails extensive company-wide co-ordination duties, it also offers an excellent training ground for management; a fact that is often recognised in the recruitment policies of major companies.

Product management has a number of potential drawbacks, however, and it is probably true to say that companies are nowadays more critical and pragmatic in their attitude to this structure. Problems can arise in terms of reporting relationships and decision-making authority, while the healthy rivalry shown among product managers may develop into unproductive competition and conflict. Some companies have rethought their organisations because of the overemphasis on product expertise at the expense of functional experience or even market focus. Again, product managers may become preoccupied with existing products, to the detriment of new product development: to remedy this some companies have introduced a hybrid position; the new product manager. In some markets, too, competitive conditions have demanded a change in orientation away from product strategy towards more operational issues, for example within trade marketing. Finally, it has been the experience of some companies that a product management system becomes increasingly costly and top-heavy, as new products are added and as original product appointments grow into teams through assistant managers, brand assistant positions, etc.

Market-based structures

The basic rationale for a market-based organisation is the need to give marketing attention to specific parts (e.g. groups, submarkets, segments) of the market. A popular version of this approach is the geographic division, where distinct regions or districts, or indeed countries or country blocs, are handled separately, perhaps even in separate locations. Industrial companies, for example, may have regional office bases that double as mini-headquarters, housing administration, sales, spares and service, marketing and showroom facilities. Where a product or service is actually provided at the local level, throughout the market, such regionalised organisation may be used for all functions, including marketing, e.g. utilities, retail chains, banking, franchise organisations. In some of these cases a regional organisation may exist alongside a central or corporate support organisation, even for specialist functions such as marketing.

The market focus on a geographic segment can have a major impact upon customers, and indeed upon the perception that customers have towards a company. The supermarket chain Safeway is aware of the power of this and is unveiling a new Scottish logo and brand identity, 'Safeway – Proud to Serve Scotland'. Not only will this logo and brand identity be used on shop signage, it will also feature on carrier bags and staff shirts.

Where companies offer the same product to different customer groups, trades or

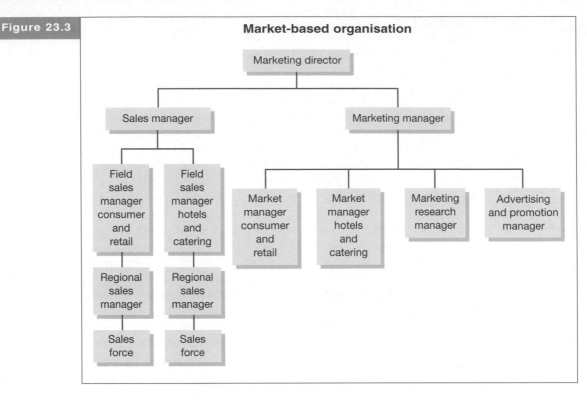

Figure 23.3 Market-based organisation

industries, there may be a need to organise their marketing around these groupings, through the installation of market managers, or perhaps industry marketing groups or sections. Figure 23.3 illustrates a market-based organisation for a hypothetical manufacturer of cooking utensils. This example shows a hybrid structure, where functions such as market research are shared by both market sectors. The sales function, though, has a regional or territory structure, commonly adopted in selling, whatever headquarters structure the company uses for its marketing base.

The major advantage of a market-based structure is the specific focus that it puts on customer requirements within different market sectors. This may even alter the flexibility and speed of response of the company. The major drawbacks of the structure centre on the resourcing issues of extra management layers, and the possible difficulties of co-ordination and communication associated with this. It may be worth noting that, while in principle the market-based structure is consistent with customer orientation, its practical value may be more difficult to calculate. It is interesting that in the example of Safeway in Scotland given above, the company intends to promote local suppliers and Scottish products. The resource issue will be met with the creation of 960 new jobs in the country.

Composite or matrix structures

A matrix organisation is a grid-like structure along two (or more) dimensions, typically a dual combination of functions with certain business areas known as programmes or missions. The structure is commonly applied to meet the complex marketing requirements of diverse products and markets, where a vigorous combination of functional,

Figure 23.4

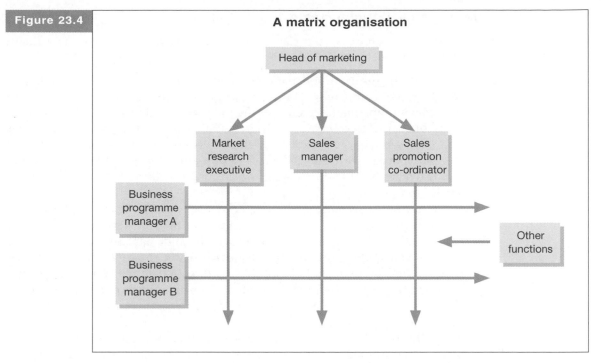

A matrix organisation

market and product expertise is required. As illustrated in Figure 23.4, co-ordination within the organisation will be achieved by designated programme (or project) managers drawing as necessary on the expertise of specialists in marketing and other departments. In managerial terms, the programme team members involved have two formal reporting relationships, one to the programme manager and one to their own department head.

Different companies are likely to produce their own variations with regard to structure. The *Financial Times* reported in September 2000 that KPMG, the professional services firm, is to launch a far-reaching restructuring that will transfer powers from national practices to three pan-regional bodies. The outcome of this is expected to be that the decision-making and governance responsibilities would be transferred to power bases representing the Americas, Asia and Europe, the Middle East and Africa. Other companies have not been so radical, and are likely to adopt modified versions of matrix structures, limited to perhaps strictly defined business units, or to particular activities such as new product development.

Having examined a number of organisational approaches to marketing, it should be emphasised that in reality organisation structures are adapted to effectively use existing skills as there is little merit in designing elegant structures for their own sake. To use existing skills to address new problems has resulted in many organisations developing a matrix structure with respect to the marketing function.

A number of managerial benefits have been claimed for the matrix form of organisation. It promises greater co-ordination in settings that demand functional interdependence and complex information and communications flows, while dual reporting allows more devolved decision-making, which should be faster and more flexible. The experience of some companies however suggests that matrix structures are no panacea, since they can create new problems in terms of resource costs, political arguments and other types of interdepartmental conflict.

Other organisational formats

Without attempting an exhaustive classification, the following organisational variants are worthy of brief mention:

■ **Key account organisation.** A variation on market-based structuring is common in consumer goods companies. Where major customers dominate a company's income, as with supermarket groups in the food sector, these are designated as key accounts or 'house' accounts and given special marketing support through key account managers or groups. As such business will depend critically on negotiations and regular contacts with the customer's headquarters buying office. Key account structures tend to be sales-dominated, and any associated marketing support sales-initiated.

■ **Divisionalisation.** This may take a number of forms, usually involving formal corporate restructuring, and even financial restructuring and devolution. Divisions may be based on broad product groups, geographical demarcation, or vertical divisions such as manufacturing trading. Though usually employed for higher level strategic reasons, divisionalisation will have a direct effect on marketing organisation. Often, separate divisions will operate their own marketing functions, though dependence on some centralised corporate advisory or planning support is not uncommon.

■ **Strategic Business Units (SBUs).** These are identifiable business areas within a company (usually product–market combinations) that are handled as separate profit centres. The treatment may be largely financial and strategic, though marketing and other functions are likely to be organised to service the SBUs. This format is therefore effectively a type of matrix organisation.

■ **Group marketing.** As with corporate marketing support within a divisionalised structure, a group of associated companies may draw on a common head office marketing service, with or without their own function at subsidiary level. In overseas markets, where local subsidiaries may have to be established as legal entities, local sales and service operations may be supplemented by marketing support at parent company level, although larger subsidiaries in major markets may warrant their own marketing departments staffed by country nationals.

Conflict and co-operation between marketing and other functions

It is obvious that the effectiveness of any individual function, and ultimately the whole company, will depend on co-operation among the specialist staff themselves and with their counterparts in other functions across the company. This is perhaps more necessary still for a function such as marketing, which by its nature tends to be more intrusive and integrative. Indeed, a rough indicator of marketing orientation could be the extent of effective interdisciplinary working on behalf of the customer.

In reality, many issues and influences may stand in the way of this ideal. As marketing is founded on a potent and purposeful philosophy, so other functions can claim their own professional standards and orientations, which may be at least partly at odds with a textbook marketing approach. Table 23.1 illustrates a number of issues that might present conflict or contention between marketing and other functions.

Many of these frictions will represent differences in attitude within different functions, and the apparently contrary aims to which they feel commitment. For example, the manufacturing – marketing relationship is often seen as an area where conflict is

Table 23.1   Potential conflicts between marketing and other functions

Function	Conflict source
Engineering	Marketers may request more customised components, while engineering prefers more standardisation.
R&D	Marketers may show interest in applied research and development work, or become frustrated with laboratory over-runs in time or budget. R&D specialists may emphasise basic or pure research.
Purchasing	Purchasing specialists may make decisions on component specifications, cost, purchase volumes and delivery times at variance with the preferences of (product) marketing specialists, or occasionally with no consultation.
Manufacturing	Manufacturing may insist on metric accuracy in sales forecasting for planning purposes – regarded by marketers as unrealistic. There may be differences on issues such as production lead-times, model or component changes, order scheduling, fabrication methods, etc.
Finance/Accounting	Potential differences may arise over prices and pricing methods, cost allocation, profitability targets, credit control, marketing budgets.

to be expected. Some of the difficulties stem from the inner versus outer orientations that might be ascribed, albeit as a generalisation, to manufacturing versus marketing. The following anecdote, by the well-known designer Kenneth Grange, provides a telling insight into the deep-seated hostility that can surface within the marketing–production relationship:

> One of my abiding memories is of a boardroom in a large company where the capital costs needed for a new product were under examination. On that day I sat among the product team; design, development and production men, their various interests represented by a brilliant, hard-pressed chief engineer.
>
> In the way those conversations go, a focus had been made on some detail; I think it was the value of prototype tooling. The fireworks started when the advertising director joined in. I then realised how deep was the contempt in which my production friend held that urbane, witty and elegant man. It seemed to me to point to a schism as serious as the management versus work-force, unions versus CBI that bedevils many industries.

Interdepartmental conflicts of another sort, and certainly grievances, can be attributed to issues of ownership or territory – where, within the organisation structure, certain functions should be located, and under whose authority. Within the broad marketing area, subfunctions such as public relations, customer service, packaging and distribution can often be the centre of ongoing border skirmishes between marketing and other functional claimants. Certainly in some companies the distribution area has recently witnessed such territorial rivalry, as it has merged with materials management to become an enhanced and independent logistics function.

Organisation structures should be robust enough to cope with such tensions, and to accommodate them at the everyday level through management control and co-ordination mechanisms, and ultimately through adaptation and evolution. In common with other functions, the marketing organisation should facilitate interfunctional co-ordination and conflict resolution through the following mechanisms:

- explicit, rather than vague, organisational responsibilities and relationships;
- adequate support systems in key areas such as planning and information processing;
- interdisciplinary liaison, planning, problem-solving and decision-making mechanisms such as meetings, committees, reports and audits;

■ staffing solutions through liaison and co-ordination posts, joint undertakings through venture groups or task force activity, and a wider role for training and staff development.

Implicit in the above is the understanding that good internal communications will be a major source of improvement in interdepartmental relations, and general company effectiveness.

Some commentators have in recent years isolated the communications field, and related behaviourial influences, as a key element of good management, within the company as well as outside. It is perhaps paradoxical that companies that spend literally millions on outside communications through their advertising agencies will sometimes balk at the thought of serious expenditures within the field of internal communications. A lesson for marketers here is that, as communicators, they, of all people, should be sensitive to the communications process involved in their interactions with other functions. In particular, marketers should promote their plans and activities to ensure greater co-ordination and effectiveness. This internal communication in many companies is improving with the increasing use of e-mail and other new technologies (see case study at end of the chapter) between departments, but there is still ground to be covered and much of this can be done through internal marketing.

INTERNAL MARKETING

As outlined by its major British proponent, Nigel Piercy, internal marketing is nothing more nor less than the employment of marketing activities and approaches within the organisation, in order to gain support and necessary co-operation from other functions, key decision-makers and general management, and all those contributing to the effective execution of marketing strategies. The emphasis given by Piercy is primarily on internal marketing in order to ensure success of a company's general marketing programme, though it is possible to see a wider role for internal marketing as an aid to any functional programme. Piercy argues that, both at the everyday level of marketing implementation, and to the end of a gradual culture change towards customer orientation, internal marketing has a contribution to make. He coins the general-purpose term Strategic Internal Marketing (SIM) to encompass all such endeavours. It is particularly instructive, and more appropriate, for marketers to follow an extract of this author's rationale for strategic internal marketing:

> It seems that in many organizations there is an explicit assumption that marketing plans and strategies will sell themselves to those in the company whose support and commitment are vital. When made explicit in this way, this is just as naive as making similar assumptions that, if they are good enough, our products will sell themselves to external customers. There are many issues that have to be dealt with regarding a company's customers and these include some of the following:
>
> ■ irrational behaviour by consumers and buyers;
> ■ the problems of managing power and conflict in the distribution channel;
> ■ the need to communicate to buyers through a mix of communications vehicles and media;
> ■ trying to outguess competitors.
>
> It is often overlooked that as we are dealing with people, many of these self same problems also occur within firms. The paradox is that we dismiss the better mousetrap syndrome for our exter-

nal markets, but adopt exactly this approach in expecting managers and operatives, whose support we need, to make a beaten path to the marketing planner's office.

(Piercy,1997)

Piercy's advice is that, within the company, marketers should recognise the internal market place for their products and programmes, and respond to it by developing an internal marketing programme to support their programmes for the external market place. The internal marketing programme itself, therefore, should be produced alongside the primary external programme, and might mirror the external plan in its structure – internal target groups, intelligence and information sources, internal product features and benefits, promotional mechanisms, internal marketing objectives and strategies. Care, attention and forethought are therefore important prerequisites to the actions taken that will require the support and enthusiasm of internal colleagues. With good organisation for marketing, both within a firm and when dealing with present and potential customers, the likelihood for success is much improved.

ORGANISATION IN AN ERA OF 'NEW MARKETING'

Since the mid-1990s key concerns have developed about the efficacy of what had become an organisational norm in the guise of 'marketing department marketing', and about some of its structural variants such as the product manager system. While some commentators question whether marketing had adapted sufficiently to issues such as buyer concentration, market competition and changes in marketing infrastructure, others point to the recovery of decision-making authority by parent companies, especially in parallel with trends towards globalisation and Euromarketing. Mitchell (1997) identifies also the influence of some of the managerial innovations of the early 1990s such as delayering, empowerment and multitask teamworking, and especially the application of (business) process re-engineering (BPR). Under such BPR approaches business functions, or departments, are subject to radical redesign, based on a fundamental review of their workings and interactions (i.e. process), and especially the scope for flexible and improved customer interfaces. As an example of the kinds of reorganisation and reshaping that might affect the marketing function, distinctions between subspecialisms such as advertising, sales promotion and direct marketing may disappear or be dispersed across the whole business, 'shared' within newly ordained processes such as customer relationship management, brand experience delivery, reputation management. The following article from the *Financial Times* of 2 August 2000 summarises nicely some of the latest developments.

| Example | ### Pioneer with a passion for delivering the goods | **FT** |

A young man from Idaho who saw how software systems could bring a greater understanding of customers' needs also launched the international bandwagon in customer relationship management.

Michael Dempsey interviews Brent Frei of Onyx Software

Companies that claim to be the first in a particular field of computer software are too numerous to count. But very occasionally the title of 'pioneer' is justified.

Onyx, the $700m software company that is synonymous with customer relationship management (CRM) programs, can boast that it launched the massive market in products that distribute pertinent information to 'customer-facing' employees. To be even more accurate, the CRM bandwagon started with one man, Onyx founder and chief executive, 34-year-old Brent Frei.

Meeting Mr Frei is an interesting experience. The exuberant 6ft 8in former college football player makes an immediate impression. He is brimming with anecdotes about the early days of Onyx. After three years at Microsoft he left to found Onyx in 1994, starting out in the basement of a house in Seattle with eight people and two dogs for company. His friends wrote software. The dogs ran around pulling the connections from the backs of PCs.

It is a homely picture, one that fits in with Mr Frei's very American image as 'a boy made good' from the Midwest. But the same man who still drives a pick-up truck and claims to have little interest in material goods is worth $60m and spoke as a 'Technology Pioneer' at this year's World Economic Forum in Davos.

Mr Frei is a contradiction. His build and appearance mark him out as a natural for a contact sport such as American football. But the native of Idaho did not spend his football days at the state university. Mr Frei went to the East Coast and took an engineering degree at Ivy League Dartmouth College.

He is quick to play down his achievement in winning a place at Dartmouth. 'I was probably the dumbest guy in the college,' he says. But even in his late teens Mr Frei understood the value of having a talented team of associates. 'I met the smartest people at Dartmouth, the most interesting people.'

Observation is Mr Frei's strong point. Working at Microsoft he became aware of a significant weakness in most large organisations. 'There was too much inertia. We needed something to manage product information for customers.' He had spotted the niche that would be occupied by CRM.

The tidal wave of marketing that accompanied the adoption of CRM technology over the last five years has made much of 'understanding the customer'. But Mr Frei swears that his whole ethos revolves around giving the Onyx customer appropriate service. 'I never want to look at a customer and find they are employing anything I would be ashamed of,' he says.

With software being notorious for delivering little of what it promises, Mr Frei's declaration of principle could sound hollow. But he obviously keeps sufficient control of his 425 employees for it to ring true. The IT industry produces disgruntled and disillusioned customers in industrial quantities. His early travels around software users confirmed the wide gap between promise and delivery in IT. 'I went into prospective customers and found that what they had been sold to fill the CRM space was a "turkey" – software that could never perform that function.'

Mr Frei recognises that buzzwords and vogue terms such as 'quality assurance' (QA) often stand for nothing more than marketing trends. His passion is for 'solid products ... our QA department ships software, not marketing'. He talks seriously of 'ethical software' and takes a great deal of time to secure long-term relationships with customers.

At a recent Onyx customer conference in Florida he spoke to 250 individuals over three days. With 225 Onyx customers represented at the event he succeeded in meeting a fair chunk of

Onyx's 500-strong customer base. 'They appreciated our interest in helping them to succeed, they all had issues for us, such as how they could get their salesforce to use the software more effectively.'

These customers are under siege from Onyx's rivals. So Mr Frei knows he either stays in step with their wishes – or Onyx will lose badly in an extremely competitive sector. This is where customer loyalty becomes real and urgent. And it puts the farmer's son's adherence to homespun values into perspective.

He comes from Grangeville, a 3,600-strong community occupied with farming and logging. Friends and neighbours from the small Idaho town invested in Onyx back in the early days. Today, one friend of his mother owns $3m worth of Onyx stock. His original investment was $10,000.

And Mr Frei still banks in Grangeville. His bank kept him in funds when he went overdrawn while starting off Onyx. Today, he repays that loyalty with his continued custom. Onyx is guided by the knowledge that a small bank branch in Idaho can teach the concept of CRM.

Mr Frei knows that he is on to a winner with the vogue for customer relationship management. 'CRM will be fashionable for at least the next five years,' he predicts. But there are new technology models out there. The idea of an application service provider (ASP), renting out the functions of a large computer program for relatively small sums, is the latest trend to sweep through the IT world. Onyx is well placed to exploit this emerging market.

Mr Frei has just returned from Asia where an Onyx customer, Singapore Telecom, is studying the potential of letting out software via the ASP route. The Australian PTT Telstra is targeting a market of 50,000 small and medium-sized businesses, using Onyx's ASP offering. It will charge a subscription of $1,000 to very small operations that will be able to pull down and exploit customer data held on a large Onyx system at Telstra.

Back at Onyx's headquarters in Seattle, a company team lead by Mr Frei has taken seventh place in a gruelling relay race that involves covering 195 miles of mountainous terrain using a 12-strong team running 'legs' of five miles at a time. One glance at the towering ex-football player tells you he does not have the perfect build for long-distance running. But he participates in this event because he enjoys it.

A revealing insight into Mr Frei's character and values lies not in the founding of Onyx, or its 1999 IPO. Three years ago, he was involved in a serious road accident. Driving alone, his vehicle was struck by a heavy lorry on a remote stretch of road. A passing family laid him out in the back of their station wagon and raced to the nearest hospital. He remembers their children staring at the badly injured man behind them and inquiring innocently: 'Is he going to die?'.

This brush with death in 1997 reminded him how much being alive matters. It accounts for his relaxed attitude to material success. And it lends Onyx a head start in a market that has to supply systems that fit into the real world of walking, talking, breathing customers.

Source: Financial Times, 2 August 2000. (Copyright © The Financial Times Limited)

It can be concluded from the above article that the marketing function must change in response to the changes that are affecting organisations generally. It is clear that the environment is changing at a fast pace.

CONCLUSION

Marketing, no less than any other business function, needs to be managed, controlled and appropriately resourced. The organisation structure adopted for the marketing function will need to reflect and serve these managerial processes. Needless to say it will also need to facilitate the effective execution of those marketing strategies required by the company's competitive position, and the general demands of the market place. As companies vary in terms of resource strengths, market position and general policies on matters of management and planning, the approach taken to organising marketing will vary somewhat in practice.

Of perhaps equal importance will be the internal, social and political aspects of the company as an organisation, and the related need for internal marketing.

Suffice to say marketers need to be aware of the dynamic and behavioural interactions that beset them within the organisation. As noted in numerous research studies, the people dimensions of the informal organisation may well become more significant than the line geometry of the formal organisation chart.

A major factor that could have a dramatic effect upon the way in which companies organise for marketing is of course e-commerce. Much of the technology available has not yet been adopted by many companies, especially those within the small and medium-sized sector. There are firms, however, that have firmly embraced the new technology and the changes and improvements that it offers. The next few years is likely to see many strategy shifts within slow-changing companies, as they see for themselves the benefits to be reaped. This may become more evident as other firms overtake them by implementing changes made possible with technology input, and they see the time for change is ripe. However, major diversions within firms take time and money, so the way forward for them may as yet be unclear, it will be interesting to view what happens next.

QUESTIONS

1 'The key ingredients of success are surely strategy and execution. Organisation changes amount to little more than rearranging the furniture.' Comment.

2 Argue the commercial case for a closer working relationship between marketing and the following specialisms:
   – purchasing
   – accounting
   – design
   – credit control.

3 Consider the implications for marketing organisations of continuing growth in a company's overseas business.

FURTHER READING

Chartered Institute of Marketing UK (CIM) (1996) *The Status of UK Product and Brand Management in the 1990s.*

Doyle, P. (1997) 'Go for robust growth', *Marketing Business*, April 1997.

Gummesson, Evert (1987) 'The new marketing–development long-term interactive relationships', *Long Range Planning*, vol. 20, no.4, pp. 10–20.

Mitchell, Alan (1997) 'Speeding up the process', *Marketing Business*, March, pp. 18–21.

Peel, M. (2000) 'KPMG shake up to put power in regions', *Financial Times*, 18 September.

Piercy, N. (1997) *Market-led Strategic Change: Transforming the Process of Going to Market.* Butterworth-Heinemann.

Wilson, I. (1994) *Marketing Interfaces*, Pitman Publishing.

More business applications needed: research to extend Wap services

Improved software will expand the range of professional applications, something that could convert Wap from mere consumer gizmo to essential corporate technology. Is Wap just the latest gizmo or something genuinely useful? MagiWap software, which lets business travellers call up files left in the office, is one example of a new breed of Wireless application protocol (Wap) services designed to solve real-life problems.

'Lots of solutions are also being developed to connect mobile workers with information on the corporate intranet – an in-house version of the Internet,' according to Margaret Rice-Jones, managing director of Psion Computer.

Even that age-old problem of how to send and receive e-mails on the move without carrying a back-breaking laptop, is starting to be solved.

But for the busy businessperson separated from their files, MagiWap can solve an all too common problem. If you are about to start work on a report but the file you need is on your office PC or you are in the office and it is sitting on your laptop at home, software from UK-based Tadpole Technology can help.

It effectively turns your Wap mobile into a remote control device that switches files from one computer to another. For example, you could switch a file from your office machine to the laptop in your hotel. Or, if you did not have the laptop with you, you could just send the file to the hotel fax.

To use the system, your Wap mobile needs to be loaded with MagiWap software, which can be downloaded free from the Net by using the Wap browser in the phone to connect to *www.magi.endeavors.org.*

The system works by making all the computer-based devices you use behave like secure computer servers on the Internet. So the mobile is effectively transferring files at the user's request between one internet site and another.

MagiWap software will also need to be downloaded on to the various computer devices to make them resemble servers on the Internet. This is also available free from the website, but Tadpole will be selling related workflow software to companies which want to include mobile workers in their work processes.

For example, your boss could, in theory, sign off your expenses from a mobile while playing golf with a supplier.

The software, developed by California-based Endeavors Technology, acquired by Tadpole in March, grew out of research carried out at the University of California into the world wide web and its use across mobile workforces and multiple organisations.

Bernard Hulme, group chief executive at Tadpole, says: 'Instead of just using Wap phones to read public broadcast information, such as stock prices, weather, business news and sports scores, our software allows phone users to obtain "private broadcast information" – business plans, price lists, research documents – as well as those of colleagues within a trusted workgroup. The mobile user can read, edit, e-mail, fax or print documents, such as Microsoft Office 2000 documents, from a Wap mobile.'

It is also possible to retrieve files through a computer firewall, software many corporate networks have in place to prevent hackers getting in. The only drawback of the system is that the computer devices you want to retrieve files from have to be left switched on and connected to a modem or network.

Mr Hulme says: 'So far, the computer industry has not really succeeded in developing software that brings mobile workers into company processes.'

One company that is trying to is personal organiser company, Psion. The new Revo makes it much easier to connect to the Internet and use e-mail than its previous organiser. So long as you have an infrared mobile, the Nokia 7110 Wap phone for example, you simply line up the phone with the Revo's infrared port, click on a few commands on the organiser, and hey presto (plus the usual Wap wait), you are connected to Psion's Wap site.

It is also easy, using the Revo's Opera browser, to connect to non-Psion Wap sites such as *www.wap.yahoo.com* and, because an e-mail ID is built into the Psion, you can send and receive messages.

It is a shame, however, that a mobile phone is not built into the new Revo, as lining up devices while on the move could be tedious. However, Ms Rice-Jones says: 'We really think General Packet Radio Service (a higher-speed mobile data technology) will have a significant impact on mobile data and we're waiting for that to be widely available before launching an integrated device.'

Yet even with the limitations of today's technology, it is possible to see how a portable device such as this could help companies come up with solutions to real-life problems.

For example, field engineers could connect to the company intranet via Wap to get information on how to fix an obscure problem.

In Finland, service personnel working on site for Helsinki Energy will have access to a vast company database using Nokia Wap services over a Tetra mobile radio network. The services have been developed in conjunction with Helsinki Energy and another Finnish company, Tekla Corporation, a software business.

Kari Suneli, senior vice-president, professional mobile radio at Nokia Networks, believes Wap over Tetra technology, which reduces Wap waiting time, will help open up the market for professional Wap services.

With better software becoming available and the sheer portability of Wap devices, Wap could be moving closer to becoming genuinely useful.

Joia Shillingford

Source: Survey – *FT* Telecomms, *Financial Times*, 20 September, 2000. (Copyright © The Financial Times Limited)

Question

Outline the ways in which the above technology can be used in a company of your choice, and the impact that it will have on the way that the business is organised.

24 Consumerism, ethics and social responsibility

Right and wrong exist in the nature of things. Things are not right because they are commanded, nor wrong because they are prohibited.

R.G. Ingersoll, *The Ghosts*.

INTRODUCTION

This chapter introduces some of the ethical issues inherent in the application of marketing principles and practice. It does this first by considering how these have been promoted as issues through co-ordinated consumer action, often referred to as consumerism. Some wider ethical issues are then identified and the need for organisations increasingly to demonstrate 'social responsibility' is discussed. While all three of these issues are relevant to marketing in general their relative importance will vary from culture to culture and from country to country. In each, this relative importance will depend upon factors such as the level of industrialisation, prosperity, education and the effect of legislation. Accordingly the purpose of this chapter is to introduce some of these issues so that their importance can be appreciated by anyone who is working in an organisation and involved with marketing.

There is an obvious starting point for marketing and general behaviour, which is the need to obey the law. However, this is not always easy, as legislation varies between countries and what is acceptable in one situation is illegal in another. Going further and linking legal constraints to consumer sovereignty is not enough. Questions are raised about marketing techniques themselves. It is often suggested that these techniques artificially stimulate consumption, so people buy and continue to buy products that are unwanted, provide little benefit to the purchaser, or both. Marketing has to justify itself against these charges of encouraging materialism and the waste of scarce resources.

CONSUMERISM

There is no single, agreed definition of consumerism. It is generally accepted as being any organised group pressure on behalf of customers or users of a product or service. This may be specific to an individual organisation such as a 'user group' or aimed at protecting consumers in general from organisations with which there can be exchange relationships. The objective of both is to influence organisational behaviour to the benefit of the consumer.

In exchanges with organisations individuals have little power. Consumerism is one response to redress the balance. One of the pioneers of its development was Ralph Nader, who criticised the safety of automobiles in the USA in his book *Unsafe at Any*

Speed (1965). Since then the movement has grown into a powerful force. As a result customers are increasingly able to communicate with organisations with powerful collective voices when products or promotions are considered unacceptable.

The advertising used by organisations to promote product benefits to target consumers is intended to influence choice, and can do so especially if the product relates to the consumer's wants and needs. Consumers, however, expect to receive more than this, and this desire is sometimes encompassed in what is described as the 'societal marketing concept'. This is where suppliers, in addition to trying to satisfy the needs and wants of consumers, are expected to at least maintain, if not improve, the well-being of society as a whole.

Furthermore, consumers are increasingly being given 'rights' and this trend needs to be appreciated by all marketers. Examples of this have been the development by the UK government of a Citizen's Charter, which was then used as the basis for the 'Patient's Charter' for the National Health Service, the 'Passenger's Charter' for rail travellers, and various other customer-focused initiatives.

The real start of consumerism was in the USA. Even before Nader's book President Kennedy highlighted the obligation that organisations owe their customers in his 'Consumer Bill of Rights'. This identified four basic consumer rights:

- The right to safety.
- The right to be informed.
- The right to choose.
- The right to be heard.

The idea of rights can be traced back to the 'inalienable rights' included in the US Declaration of Independence by Thomas Jefferson. The marketing profession of today must be aware of these rights and combine them where possible in any marketing plans for products and services. They form a good framework for considering all other associated issues.

Consumer rights

The right to safety

When a purchase is made the consumer has the right to expect that it is safe to use. The product should be able to perform as promised and should not have false or misleading guarantees. This 'right' is in fact a minefield for the marketing profession. Products that were at one time regarded as safe have subsequently been found by research not to be so. There was a time when cigarettes were not regarded as being particularly harmful to health, sugar in foods was not highlighted in television advertising as being bad for teeth, and everyone was encouraged to 'go to work on an egg'.

Legislation highlighting 'product liability' has been introduced in several countries. This has forced suppliers to reassess their responsibility for the safety of their products. As a result many organisations have developed a positive approach to product safety. Since failure to do so often results in complicated legislation it is obvious that marketers who fail to protect consumers do so at their peril.

The right to be informed

The right to be informed has far-reaching consequences: it encompasses false or misleading advertising, insufficient information about ingredients in products, insufficient information on product use and operating instructions, and information that is deceptive about pricing or credit terms. This negative approach to avoiding trouble is not sufficient. Marketers should take every opportunity to communicate with consumers and to inform them about the benefits and features of the product offered. It should be no protection to claim that consumers fail to read instructions. Marketers must develop effective communications between consumer and supplier. This 'right' is also crucial to customers having access to the information needed to effectively exercise the next right – the right to choose.

The right to choose

While the consumer's right to choose is central to the practice of marketing, this does involve trying to influence that choice. This is necessary, as in most western markets competition is encouraged, so this choice often involves comparing both different products and suppliers. This comparison can be effectively impossible if, for instance, similar products are not sold in standardised quantities. As a result some regulations have been introduced with this objective. However, it can be argued that such legislation restricts choice and is not considered important by customers. However, the major supermarkets in Britain have taken this on board – they now tend to display information on shelf tickets that enables comparison to take place.

The right to be heard

The right to free speech is present in all western countries. However, do organisations listen to consumers? In a well-focused marketing organisation such feedback should be encouraged, and it should be treated as a key input for the future. This right allows consumers to express their views after a purchase, especially if it is not satisfactory. When anything goes wrong with a purchase the customer should furthermore be able to expect complaints to be fairly and speedily dealt with. Many companies now have customer service departments that deal with complaints. However recent surveys have found that one in five people are dissatisfied with the service they receive and are starting to complain more.

Of course there will always be some unjustified complaints and others which, although justified, are not dealt with to the customer's satisfaction. This can often be minimised by using marketing principles to focus on the actual needs of customers.

Consumer groups

Consumerism is increasingly seen as the effect of formally organised consumer groups created to represent the rights of buyers to specific sellers. Since the early groups often formed as a result of customers becoming dissatisfied with an individual or group of suppliers many were initially considered unwelcome by suppliers. It was, however, found that such groups can provide organisations with opportunities both to respond to customers' changing needs and develop improved relationships with their customers. Because of this, developing a positive relationship with consumer groups is generally accepted as an important function of marketing. Six distinct types of consumer group can be identified:

1 Government-encouraged groups to monitor the behaviour of legalised monopolies, e.g. OFWAT, OFTEL (the offices set up by the UK government to regulate the water and telephone industries).

2 Independent groups campaigning for a change of product, such as the Campaign for

Real Ale (CAMRA) in the UK, which successfully persuaded UK brewers to continue brewing traditional types of beer.

3 Groups including some charities that campaign for legal restrictions to protect society. ASH (Action on Smoking and Health) and ROSPA (Royal Society for the Prevention of Accidents) are two examples. While some of these may be classified as pressure groups rather than consumer groups they need to be considered in the same category by a marketing function.

4 Groups formed after a major tragedy to influence future operating practices of organisations. Examples of such tragedies would be the Lockerbie Pan-Am air crash in Scotland, the *Herald of Free Enterprise* ferry accident at Zeebrugge, the Hillsborough football stadium disaster, the Dunblain tragedy where innocent children were shot – resulting in a move to outlaw handguns.

5 Commercial pressure groups, the Consumer's Association and *What Car?* magazine are such enterprises.

6 Media campaigners such as Ann Robinson with the *Watchdog* programme on UK television, and also Jeremy Clarkson, who had success via his TV programme and magazine *Top Gear* in the fight against very high car prices in the UK. The programme and the magazine were instrumental in bringing in the J. D. Power customer satisfaction survey to cover the British car market.

While some of these groups focus on trying to influence the government or organisations directly, others try to influence many groups and public opinion. An effective way of doing this is to have a 'national day' such as the national No-smoking Day promoted by ASH.

Consumerism and marketing

Consumer groups affect the marketing environment in which organisations operate. By working with such groups, organisations gain competitive advantage through the resulting PR. This can be particularly important for products subject to a wide range of customer taste, and contributed to the success achieved by CAMRA.

Organisations and indeed governments need to understand the influence that consumer groups can have in reflecting consumer attitudes and in shaping demand. Failure to do so can provide significant advantages for competitors. Consumers are no longer content to join a picket line but are willing to take action in many ways. These would include using the web, their mobile phones and organisational skills to achieve their desired response.

A good example of consumers supporting action was portrayed in Britain when groups of truck drivers, taxi drivers and farmers decided to take direct action with regard to the Labour government's tax on petrol. Key oil plants were blockaded and petrol stations were inundated with customers trying to buy fuel before supplies ran out. When supplies did run out, or were in scarce supply, many customers did not complain when the petrol was sold to emergency priority staff such as nurses, such was the feeling of public support for the protest.

Newspaper reports estimated that the blockades of the oil plants could cost British industry £250 million a day. To further add to the government's problem Esso made the announcement that it would increase petrol prices by 2p a litre and diesel by 4p, although this statement was subsequently retracted. On this occasion the action was against Labour government policy, but it should in no way lull big business into a false sense of security, as the consumers' wrath can be directed against them just as easily and cause bad publicity on a global scale.

Nike found itself being criticised for mistreating its workers in Indonesia, and the publicity spread easily because of technological advancements. The Internet is a high-speed information network that is being increasingly used, and is a very useful tool to spread consumer dissatisfaction.

The super-empowered consumer

The above examples show how technological advances have had an increasing impact on consumer power. Many of the activities carried out with regard to protests in today's environment are co-ordinated by mobile phone and e-mail, and appointed press officers give briefings to the television and newspaper reporters. The consumer of today is more voluble and determined than ever, the technological revolution is adding the previous missing ingredient – fast and reliable communication. It is likely that the consumer will be more ready to take action than ever before – consumers are it appears, becoming super-empowered.

Media communications that are incorrect may provide the impetus for consumers to fight together. A few examples of such possible situations are outlined below.

In September 1999 Argos offered television sets for £3 each on its website and refused to honour any orders placed. Likewise IBM refused to honour orders taken for laptops offered at $1 each via its US on-line store. In May 2000 about 100 people ordered more than 400 Ipaq Lite personal computers that had been mistakenly advertised for £1 each on the Compaq website. While refusing to honour the orders placed Compaq offered to supply a free printer worth £61 to any customer who wished to fulfil the order placed at the proper Ipaq Lite price of £530. One potential customer whose order had not been honoured by Compaq used the Internet to contact others in the same position with the objective of taking legal action against the company. Previous attempts to do this have failed owing to the legal costs that it would involve. Meanwhile in May 2000 the European Parliament approved the Electronic Commerce Directive, which seeks in part to clarify the contractual obligations resulting from errors such as these.

It will be interesting to note the level of activity in the coming years with regard to the Internet. This will undoubtedly affect organisations and the way in which they treat dissatisfied customers.

ETHICS

Ethics involves the application of moral principles to decisions made by individuals within an organisation. It is the study of what is 'right' in any activity, and is of course influenced by the collective values present in an organisation.

Ethical issues are inherently complicated. Inevitably they involve a number of individuals or groups and the situations to be resolved have no obviously right answer. Often ethical issues associated with marketing are further complicated by their relevance varying significantly between the groups involved.

Many of the issues becoming more important in Britain today include genetically modified foods, exploitation of Third World labour and globalisation of marketing messages. However, ethics has as much relevance to small business as to the large companies, and the following example shows how ethical behaviour can affect even the smallest firm.

All of the retailers in a small West Midlands village agreed that they would not sell fireworks provided one of the village organisations organised a 'Guy Fawkes' bonfire and fireworks display. For more than ten years there had not been a single accident involving fireworks in the village. One of the shops was sold and the new owner, having sold fireworks at his previous shop, saw no reason to respect the agreement. In order not to lose customers the other shops followed suit. As a result, at least in the short term, the new shopkeeper lost goodwill. What are the ethical issues? What are the marketing and business issues here? Who are the parties involved?

Ethics involves issues of human behaviour and human judgement applied in everyday situations.

Why is business ethics a problem that snares not just a few mature criminals, or crooks in the making, but a host of apparently good people who lead exemplary private lives while concealing information about dangerous products or systematically falsifying costs? Observation suggests that the problem of corporate ethics has three aspects:

■ the development of the executive as a moral person;
■ the influence of the corporation as a moral environment;
■ the actions needed to map a high road to economic and ethical performance – and to mount guard-rails to keep corporate wayfarers on track.

One problem in business, especially consumer markets, is that customers are often not technical professionals. They do not have the skills to fully assess the products they are offered except in a general way of judging the fitness of that product for the purpose for which it was purchased. But does the average consumer know how much water can be 'added' to a frozen chicken? The Trading Standards officers do, but is it appropriate for employees or their companies to ensure the maximum level is not exceeded or is this just good business practice?

Studies have shown that domestic laundry detergents are a significant source of environmental pollution. Because of this members of the Soap and Detergent Industry Association have adopted a voluntary Code of Practice called Washright. This is part of a Europe-wide scheme to inform consumers how they can minimise the effect on the environment when doing the laundry. Those manufacturers adopting the code are committed to improving the biodegradability of their products and including on their packs instructions for use. These instructions suggest such things as sorting laundry by colour, fabric and soiling, following dosing instructions carefully, using the minimum temperature for each wash, and using washing machines at full capacity, as many use the same amount of electricity, water and detergent whatever the load. This is clearly good advice for protecting the environment, but it is also likely to reduce rather than increase sales of detergent.

In another industry, how expert is an individual in assessing different life assurance policies? There is a regulator, the Securities and Investment Board (SIB) in the UK, but even with safeguards and periods after purchase when decisions can be changed, there are still opportunities for policies that pay the highest commission to be recommended more strongly than others.

When selling a house there is a legal restraint of caveat emptor – let the buyer beware. The ethical question for the seller is whether just to answer questions as asked or to volunteer information that might make a sale less likely.

With regard to choices made by individual executives to justify questionable conduct, Saul Gellerman (1986) suggests four 'rationalisations':

1 The activity is not 'really' illegal or immoral.
2 The activity is in the individual's, or the corporation's, best interest.
3 It will never be found out.
4 Because it helps the company, the company will condone it.

Individuals take the decisions reflected here but, as suggested by Andrews (1989), the influence of the corporation as a moral environment can put pressure on managers to act in a particular way. Andrews suggests that while an individual's initial values will come from family and school, most of the influence on ethical behaviour related to business 'will occur in the organisations in which people spend their lives'. Since many decisions are not clear-cut, it is the corporate influences that can determine the behaviour. In many cases behaviour is changed only as a result of a negative experience by a large enough group for it to be clear that something must be done. In this case we get:

Negative event
↓
Ethical view (what ought to be done)
↓
Code of behaviour

Such codes may be supported by law or enshrined in a voluntary agreement on appropriate industry practices. Because of this everyone involved with making marketing decisions needs to consider fully their ethical implications. In his book *Beyond the Bottom Line* Ted Tuleja asked the question, 'Can the good guys finish first?' His conclusion is one of hope that:

> the corporate villains will fall by the wayside, leaving the finish line to those businesses that play the game hard, but fairly. As democracy and competition both increase, earning the public's goodwill will become less and less an ancillary preoccupation, and move ever more forcefully to the forefront of managers' attention.
>
> (Tuleja 1987)

Although some of the comments made above are more than a decade old they still hold true. Time will tell whether the new super-empowered consumer of today will be able to make a difference to the way in which ethical behaviour develops.

Ethical marketing concept

In order to be successful companies must not only be able to sell a product or service, they need to be seen to adhere to high standards, both in the service offered and ethically. It appears that it may be the right time to move a stage higher than the societal marketing concept, and introduce an ethical marketing concept.

Individuals have their own standards of ethical behaviour and their own moral standards. Over the past decade some of these moral standards seem to have changed as circumstances alter, but the underlying beliefs tend to be more durable. A sense of what is fair permeates organisations as a result of their employees. There are exceptions to this fair play, and these should be the focus of the ethical concept. All employees are involved and need to accept responsibility for being ethical both with respect to the company itself and its customers. This involves being accurate when filling in expense claims, refusing to accept personal gifts at Christmas and many other similar day-to-day activities. These may involve the pricing of contracts where there are opportunities to make substantial profits from any subsequent amendments to the contract or through the supply of spare parts. Organisations have many opportunities to either promote or discourage ethical behaviour by their employees.

Other issues regarding the actual marketing of products also raise questions as to ethical standards. As an example: should a marketing manager suggest a bold flash on the front of his or her company's food product reading 'No added colours', and rely on consumers not reading the ingredients' panel to see that while this claim is true, there are many added flavourings?

There are other practices which, although not illegal, are aimed at gaining business regardless of what may be fair to customers. A code of conduct would be one way to encourage ethical marketing practices. This would effectively promote the ethical marketing concept but it will be difficult to achieve within the context of the European Union. What is considered acceptable in one country may well be considered unacceptable in another.

Social responsibility

Corporate social responsibility is generally considered to be the 'duty' of an organisation to conduct its activities with due regard to the interests of society as a whole. While no definition is given for the term 'social responsibility' in Michael Baker's dictionary of marketing terms, he does give the following definition for a social responsibility audit:

> An evaluation or assessment of the policies and practices of an organisation to establish how and to what extent it is behaving in a socially responsible manner, e.g. in terms of employment practices, relationships with its local community, environmental protection, etc.
>
> (Baker 1998)

From this it can be seen that corporate social responsibility covers issues of interest to marketing as well as to other business functions. However, anything that affects the way an organisation interacts with its stakeholders could be seen as a marketing issue.

Marketing has been defined in this book in terms of a satisfying exchange process between supplier and customer. The first part of this chapter shows that consumer groups can often demand more from organisations through organised pressure. It is perhaps appropriate that organisations attempt to achieve what Gordon Wills (1976) referred to when he said that efficiency and worth of marketing must be judged by what they do for society as a whole. An American chief executive officer described this by saying: 'A new dimension must be observed – a new 'bottom line' for business really is 'social approval'. Without this, economic victory would be pyrrhic indeed.'

However, perhaps the boundaries of social marketing have yet to be agreed. Social marketing can be seen as a direct reaction to consumerism. The question is whether it is enough just to react to consumerism or whether an organisation should go further in its relationship with its environment. An interesting viewpoint with regard to this question can be found in *Business as Unusual* by Anita Roddick (2000). The book looks at the development of The Body Shop and at the growth of vigilante consumerism. The range of topics covered is wide, and the book examines not only how businesses can evolve in the new millennium but also athuman rights abuses associated with globalisation. Roddick offers a vision for dealing with the demands of ethical business.

Consumers are now able to buy a wide range of publications that 'inform the public about the social, environmental and ethical policies of companies'. How much these are doing to change public opinion is open to question, but it is evident that more and more firms are introducing policies that will show them to be socially responsible.

Britain was in the throes of an environmental awakening during the late 1990s . Environmentalism and subsequent consumer actions have developed as society has changed; the degree of social responsibility expected from firms has also dramatically increased. The marketing response to two of these issues will be covered in the next section.

Social responsibility and marketing

Earlier in this chapter we explained how some consumers, having become aware of the marketing concept, now expect more than products and services that satisfy their needs and wants. They look for the added bonus of the societal marketing concept, where the well-being of society is also catered for. The situation has now arisen where it has become impossible in some industries to produce what customers want without an accompanying high cost in environmental terms.

The ozone layer

For more than two decades scientists have realised that the layer of ozone situated in the high atmosphere was becoming thinner. As a result the protection provided by this ozone layer against the sun's harmful ultraviolet radiation was being reduced. This is important, as this radiation is known to cause skin cancer. After much research a theory that the ozone layer was being damaged by chemicals known as chlorofluoro-carbons (CFCs) gained wide acceptance. As a direct result the US government banned these chemicals for use as aerosol propellant. This was an important development because at that time a significant proportion of the CFCs released into the atmosphere was from that source. Few other countries saw any need to follow the US example, partly because their market for aerosols had not been anything like as significant and the industry as a whole seemed to be following the lead of the US manufacturers that dominated the market.

Meanwhile CFCs continued to be used in the production of insulation materials and as the circulating liquid (refrigerant) used in refrigerators and air conditioners. One reason for this being permitted was that there was no acceptable 'ozone friendly' alternative, and it took many years before one was developed. Thus CFCs continued to be manufactured and released into the atmosphere as very few countries introduced the legislation that would have been needed to regulate the disposal of old refrigera-tors, freezers and cars fitted with air conditioners.

As governments did not implement such essential legislation, there has been increas-ing public concern, this has benefited the manufacturers of sunscreen products as people become aware that they must protect their skin from harmful ultraviolet radiation.

Even without legislation many organisations accepted the need to be seen as socially responsible by voluntarily eliminating their use of CFCs and by assisting other companies to do the same. As a result manufacturers of aerosols and most plastic pack-aging and insulation materials abandoned the use of CFCs and were able to actively promote this in their advertising campaigns. Unfortunately one of the most popular alternative aerosol propellants was subsequently condemned owing to it being classed as a 'greenhouse gas' (see global warming).

The problems associated with the use of CFCs have already provided both significant problems and opportunities with respect to marketing many different types of product. It will undoubtedly continue to be a significant marketing issue. To date it could be claimed that many of the opportunities were missed, so hopefully the marketing world will address similar problems more effectively in the future. It is becoming increasingly clear that both consumers and socially responsible companies will need to exercise what power they have, effectively, to bring about changes that are of long-term benefit to the environment.

Global warming

Packaging of goods uses up the raw material, wood, that is used for paper production. As there is a tremendous demand for paper the forests of the world are being depleted. Forests absorb carbon dioxide and emit oxygen, so reducing the harmful build-up of carbon dioxide in the upper atmosphere that leads to an increase in the earth's temperature. Although the majority of the general public do not want to return to the days when many products were not packaged, they do expect companies to act in a socially responsible manner with regard to the type and amount of packaging used.

Significant improvements have been made in the last few years, some firms even using their packaging policies as a selling point. Procter & Gamble have taken this one step further. Published on their Pampers nappies is the following information:

> Pulp: made with care for the environment. The traditional chlorine bleaching process is not used. Pampers pulp is purified with an oxidation process. With smaller bags Pampers saves raw materials and energy: less packaging, less waste and fewer lorries for transport.

CONCLUSION

This chapter has considered the wider implications for marketing within the field of consumerism, ethics and social responsibility. Certainly since the 1960s the consumerism movement has gathered pace, making an impact on corporate behaviour in general, and marketing in particular. Most categories of products on sale in western markets have been affected by consumer groups, making customers increasingly interested in quality, performance, value and related issues.

Ethics considers the morality of behaviour of individuals and groups that are party to decisions made within an organisation. Social responsibility encompasses arguably all activities, practices and policies through which a commercial organisation affects society at large and its interests.

While it is difficult to pass judgement on the multitude of 'grey' areas within corporate decision-making and behaviour, it can be clearly demonstrated that there is now a society-wide concern for responsible corporate behaviour and moral standards in business decisions. Marketers, no less than other business specialists, need to embrace these challenges as a facet of their own professionalism.

QUESTIONS

1 *Consider the view that consumerism would not have developed in the first place if marketers had been doing their job properly.*

2 *Obtain a copy of the mission statement of any organisation of your choice, and consider the extent to which it addresses the issues raised in this chapter.*

3 *What conflicts of morality and acceptable corporate behaviour might face a company operating across a spread of international markets?*

FURTHER READING

Adams, R., Carrathers, J. and Fisher, C. (1991) *Shopping for a Better World*. Kogan Page.

Andrews, K. (1989) 'Ethics in practice', *Harvard Business Review*, September–October.

Baker, M. (1998) *Dictionary of Marketing and Advertising*. Palgrave.

Brabbs, C. (2000) 'Web fuels consumer activism', *Marketing*, 21 Sept. 2000.

Fearnley, M. (1991) 'Companies find it pays to have a conscience', *The Independent on Sunday*, 14 July.

Gellerman, S. (1986) 'Why "good" managers make bad ethical choices', *Harvard Business Review*, July–August.

Grant, J. (1999) *The New Marketing Manifesto*. Texere Publishing.

Hill, G. (1991) 'Those we have loved to hate', *The Times*, 19 July.

Packard, V. (1960) *The Waste Makers*. Penguin.

Nader, R. (1965) *Unsafe at any Speed*. Grossman.

Quinn, J. B. (1991) 'Pilkington Brothers Plc case study', in H. Mintzberg and J. B. Quinn, *The Strategy Process*. Prentice-Hall.

Roddick, Anita (2000) *Business as Unusual*.

Sutherland, J. and Gross, N. (1991) *Marketing in Action*. Pitman.

Thornhill, J. (2000) 'The New Consumer is always right: Companies that fail to anticipate the desires of today's discriminating customer are doomed', *Financial Times*, 21 August.

Tuleja, T. (1987) *Beyond the Bottom Line*. Penguin.

Wills, G. (1976) 'Marketing's social dilemmas', *European Journal of Marketing*, vol. 8, no.1.

CASE STUDY

The New Consumer is always right:

Companies that fail to anticipate the desires of today's discriminating customer are doomed

In 1952 an American psychologist called Solomon Asch devised an experiment to test the impressionability of university students. He placed one student among a group of six others, who had all been instructed to give the same, wrong answer. He then asked the student to judge whether one line was longer, shorter, or the same length as another line.

Some 95 per cent of the individuals agreed with the group's false judgment even though it directly contradicted their own observation. But when the experiment was repeated decades later, the majority of the individual students refused to be swayed by their peers and stuck to their own interpretation of the truth.

In the same way, contends David Lewis, a respected marketing consultant, consumers have evolved from being conformist and deferential children, reared on wartime propaganda and prepared to trust mass advertising, into free-thinking, individualistic adults, who are sceptical of figures of authority and believe in what Sigmund Freud called 'the narcissism of small differences'.

Reflecting the change from an era of austerity to one of affluence, these consumers have largely exhausted the things they need to purchase and are now concentrating on what they want to buy. In this sense, shopping is not merely the acquisition of things but the buying of identity. For some people, consumption – in its widest sense – has even replaced religion as their main

►

source of solace and comfort. 'In their quest for authenticity, New Consumers are really seeking to discover themselves,' the author says.

While Old Consumers were constrained by cash, choice and the availability of goods, New Consumers are short of time, attention and trust. Mass society has shattered and been reduced to a mosaic of minorities. According to the author: 'In a hypercompetitive world of fragmented markets and independently minded, well-informed individuals, companies that fail to understand and attend to the needs of New Consumers are doomed to extinction. Currently, the average life of a major company only rarely exceeds 40 years. In the coming decade, any business that is less than highly successful will find that lifespan reduced by a factor of at least 10.'

This is frightening stuff, if true. How is a savvy consumer products manufacturer to confront such a daunting challenge? The first thing to do, says Lewis, is to reconnect with your customers. Even giant consumer products companies with excellent brands and long trading histories – such as Levi-Strauss, Kellogg, Marks & Spencer, and Coca-Cola – can lose touch with the New Consumers, whose behaviour often transcends categories such as age, ethnic identity and even income.

It is easy to make false assumptions about who customers are and what they want. One US record company was amazed to discover that the biggest purchasers of its rap and techno music were grandparents buying presents for their grandchildren.

The second main theme is that consumer products companies must become much better at directing their messages to increasingly critical audiences. In this game, technology can be an enemy as well as a friend. The proliferation of internet sites has enabled groups of consumers to publicise instantaneous, and often highly critical, reviews of new consumer products, services or films. These can carry more weight than the formal advertising campaign. For example, one such site, smartgirl.com, contains extensive reviews of personal care products, such as shampoos. 'Don't try! I tried it & it's all sticky & stiff. It may look cool, but it feels gross,' wrote Hippy Chick, 11, about one particular shampoo.

But improving technology and growing consumer sophistication also enable advertisers to become smarter. New advertising channels such as internet sites, video screens at supermarket check-outs and interactive television – which enables viewers to click on products shown in their favourite soap operas and find out how and where they can be bought – will enable suppliers to find more willing buyers. Companies are also becoming better at stimulating a street 'buzz' about their products by influencing select opinion formers, rather than by dousing their wares in mass advertising hype.

Some companies, such as Disney, Apple, Virgin, Starbucks and Body Shop, have already caught the zeitgeist, the author says, and have created innovative means of delivering their message to New Consumers.

Lewis concludes that New Consumers are above all else seeking 'authenticity' and prefer substance to hype. A less polite way of expressing the same thought is to say that consumers are fed up with being conned. In today's world, trying to flog customers over-priced CDs or over-hyped products is surely a finite game. But the future is still bright for those companies that can anticipate the demands of an unpredictable new breed of customers.

John Thornhill

Source: Financial Times; 21 Aug. 2000.

Question

What are your views? Can you identify ways in which consumers are becoming increasingly unpredictable?

International marketing

Why the world's mine oyster,
which I with sword will open.

William Shakespeare, *Merry Wives of Windsor*, **Act I, Scene II.2.**

INTRODUCTION

Most business enterprises start by meeting the needs of markets that are basically local
or, at most, national in character. That this should be so is not difficult to understand.
In all countries, whatever the state of economic development, there will be a ready
market for the community's basic and everyday requirements. With economic and technological advances, opportunities inevitably appear to supply markets further afield,
often in other countries. Indeed, strategically, it can be difficult to avoid acknowledging
that 'the world has become a smaller place'. Changes in technology, communications,
economic alignments and political geography encourage internationalisation and the
convergence of markets. Such a 'globalisation' process is likely to affect marketing no
less than other functions such as manufacturing, logistics, finance, or business in general. Nevertheless, it does not follow that the current level of globalisation allows
companies to adopt standardised marketing approaches across international boundaries. In spite of the march of globalisation, there remain innumerable and significant
environmental differences between markets across the globe. It is partly the enduring
complexity of these environmental contrasts (see Terpstra 2000) that underpins the case
for international marketing as a legitimate specialism within its parent field.

THE INTERNATIONAL MARKET ENVIRONMENT

While it is quite positive to consider the similarities in environment between an organisation's home market and prospective overseas markets, it is also good business sense
to be wary of those environmental differences that can cause major problems if they
are not heeded.

With increasing international experience, managers develop the necessary sensitivity and responsiveness to such issues. However, in the early stages of internationalisation, and certainly for those overseas markets that an organisation first enters, it
would be well advised to adopt a systematic approach for investigating specific market
environments.

Table 25.1 presents a framework for comparing differences in the market environment between countries. It should be stressed that this framework is not intended to
be a checklist for 'auditing' purposes, while it certainly cannot be seen as exhaustive.
Equally, it should be noted that :

Table 25.1   How to assess environmental differences between markets

Sector	Key elements

Economic	■ National income and wealth
	■ Economic development, e.g. industrialisation
	■ International trade:
	   – volumes, trade patterns and partners
	   – trade policies, e.g. tariffs, quotas
	■ Economic and trade affiliations, e.g. EU, NAFTA (North American Free Trade Association)
	■ Economic and investment policies, e.g. taxes, incentives
	■ Financial and monetary issues, e.g. monetary policy, financial infrastructure, currency

Political-legal	■ Type and stability of government ■ Government policy and attitude to overseas companies and investors ■ Framework and application of laws affecting marketing, e.g. competition, contract, agency law
Geographical	■ Physical features – dimensions of country/ territory, topography and climatic conditions, resources ■ Geocommercial – transport, infrastructure, population dispersion/ urbanisation, land use
Technological	■ Technological level – existing facilities and infrastructure, skills and training ■ Development potential, e.g. joint venture potential, investment incentives
Social-cultural	■ Demographic aspects, e.g. data on population age, ethnicity, health, education, religious, lifestyle profiles ■ Social – institutions, class influences ■ Cultural – language, regional and customary factors; attitude to work, materialism, business protocol

■ The less tangible factors such as culture will often prove the most durable, troublesome and unpredictable in international business.

■ Within-market environmental differences can be equally challenging, especially in large, diverse markets such as the USA and India.

■ There is an increasing dynamism and global interplay at work across the international market place that defies oversimplistic summaries or comparisons. Again, as LeClair (2000), Rowell (1994) and Hilton (1992) demonstrate in terms of the European Single Market, the same environmental spillover effects exist at the regional level.

COMPANY INTERNATIONALISATION

Companies involved in international business will tend to have different objectives, different orientations and different approaches to their markets. While a gradation or scale of activity may not be clearly apparent, the different approaches can be seen in the way organisations deal with overseas markets. At one end of the spectrum will be the organisation that seeks overseas sales only as a temporary measure: to keep its machinery running or to export surplus or redundant stock. This is typical of the periodic exporter.

In a totally different category is the organisation that plans to cultivate and exploit international opportunities to the mutual benefit of itself and its stakeholders. With a clearer view of some long-term future and a proven record of flexible marketing, such a 'global' organisation will identify as readily with the international market as with its country of origin.

Most companies actively engaged in international marketing will fit somewhere between these two extremes, and research indicates that company internationalisation involves a dynamic process of experimentation, experience and development.

A particular research focus has centred on the process by which interest in overseas markets develops, or evolves, what initiates this and what factors promote the 'internationalisation process' (Anderson 1993). A long-standing research question, of interest to academics and government policy-makers alike, concerns the process by which smaller firms enter export markets (see Coviello and McAuley 1999). One widely supported school of thought holds that smaller firms go through 'stages' or phases of export learning and business development, such that eventually there is a firm commitment to overseas marketing – as opposed to exporting or overseas selling. While many branches of enquiry have developed within the internationalisation literature – for example on the relation between firm size and international readiness or maturity (see Bonaccorsi 1992), it is worth mentioning that some commentators (e.g. Bell 1995) view the internationalisation of firms in terms of anything but a stage-wise development process.

Table 25.2 presents a view of some different guises of international marketing, from export (sales) activity to the full-blown global marketing that is associated with the larger 'transnational' corporations.

It should be noted that the variants of international marketing depicted in Table 25.2 are somewhat generalised stereotypes, and that they do not claim to represent the international development path taken by all companies. In recent years, too, competing theories have emerged in terms of the commercial wisdom or appropriateness of different strategies and the possible trade-offs involved, e.g. in terms of home market versus overseas market service levels.

There have always been companies that have accepted business from overseas on the same basis as from their home market. In doing this they have insisted on being paid in their local currency and that the buyer pays all packing, transportation and impor-

Table 25.2   Variants on international marketing

Activity	Characteristics
Exporting/export sales	Sales-led push into export markets, often dominated by short-term objectives
Export marketing	Export sales and distribution, supported by HO-directed marketing support
International marketing operations	A marketing-led approach to international business, co-ordinated from company HQ. Some overseas supply, i.e. no longer wholly exports
Multinational marketing	Wherever viable, market-based marketing and operations, i.e. multimarket approaches tailored to local conditions
Global marketing	Marketing on a worldwide scale, strategically co-ordinated to exploit global markets or customer groups.

tation charges. A few organisations operating in specialist markets have developed significant overseas business using this approach. Generally these companies have served specialist markets and thus benefited from their business being developed through the personal recommendation of their customers. By insisting on payment in local currency, often with the order, they have minimised the costs associated with overseas business to their benefit and that of their customers. More recently, the Internet has made it possible for any organisation serving a specialist market to expand its business using this approach. One of the first to benefit from this approach was a small company supplying spare parts for vintage motor cycles. By opening an internet website that listed the spares they currently had in stock, together with information regarding the cost of packing, shipping and payment, they were able to offer essentially the same service globally as they had previously offered locally.

DECISIONS WITHIN INTERNATIONAL MARKETING

On deciding to enter the international market place for the first time, or possibly considering adding new overseas markets, a company would do well to adopt a purposeful strategic approach, based on informed decisions. The major decision areas involved are outlined below:

- whether to market internationally
- which markets to enter
- how to enter selected markets
- marketing activities and strategy
- Organisation and management control.

Whether to market internationally?

This represents a critical decision, since it has major strategic implications. Many strategy-based arguments could be ranged in favour of international marketing. The list below presents a summary of the reasons that companies commonly cite for developing international markets:

- to gain more sales
- as (strategic) market diversification
- more profit potential overseas
- to counter depressed or declining home market
- to justify capacity increase, spread overheads
- to follow key customers abroad
- exploiting (new) products with world potential
- exploiting improved company competitiveness
- by invitation, through unsolicited business
- market internationalisation 'pull'
- as spin-off from sourcing/supply links overseas.

Aside from the profit opportunities that exist in selected markets, companies might be influenced by the need to strategically diversify their market base, to exploit a growing internationalisation in their prime market, or to capitalise on the overseas potential of new products or technologies. A classical marketing strategy might involve following key customers abroad – the stay-with-the-market strategy typified by leading international consultants, advertising agencies, insurance companies and other service-based organisations. More defensive strategies might involve efforts to counter seasonality or instability in the home market, or to justify capacity increases or seek scale economies.

Whatever strategic rationale a company may have for looking abroad, it would need to weigh up the 'downside' of the argument, especially the risks involved. It should be apparent from the earlier discussion that, in spite of accelerating globalisation, the business environment in many overseas markets will still be risky and unfamiliar in terms of economic and competitive conditions, legal factors, government policy and controls, and the social and cultural influences of the market place. The list below illustrates some of the more common difficulties and risks that await the unwary entrant to the international arena:

- credit risk
- cash flow problems
- exchange rate fluctuations, currency upheavals
- controls on profit repatriation
- taxation problems
- non-tariff barriers
- political problems
- legal traumas
- bureaucracy
- language and communications problems
- cultural resistance
- alien business culture.

While many of these difficulties can be minimised by careful research and good management, they nevertheless represent real potential pitfalls, even for the company seasoned in international business.

Which markets to enter

No less than mainstream marketing itself, international marketing will likely be more successful through careful targeting within selected markets. Especially in the early days of internationalisation, a company would be better to restrict its attentions, and resources, to at most a few promising markets, and to treat these as a learning and trialling ground for hopefully more ambitious steps later.

Mindful of the risks inherent in overseas ventures, many companies will seek initial customers, through export sales, in those markets that may have produced interest, enquiries or unsolicited orders in the recent past, or where they have contacts for other purposes, such as sourcing. Often there will be a tendency to approach markets that are 'psychologically' nearer, perhaps through language, cultural or even geographical proximity, e.g. German companies may relate more readily to Austria or Switzerland, Swedish companies to other Scandinavian markets (see Evans et al. 2000).

Such intuitive reasoning may well prove useful guidance to a company, but there may be a case for adopting a more rigorous and deliberate set of market selection criteria in order to objectively assess overseas opportunities in relation to company resources and capabilities. At its most basic there is a role for detailed SWOT (Strengths, Weaknesses, Opportunities, Threats) analysis approaches, while developments from this would lead to detailed research into market and competitor environments, albeit within a research budget constraint limited to a few selected 'shortlist' markets. Certainly within chosen target markets key entry and operating decisions will be better informed through market research efforts, perhaps involving a mix of secondary information sources and market-based primary research activities.

Marketing research for international marketing should be employed at least as regularly as within the domestic market, though a number of studies (e.g. Brown and Cook 1990) have shown that this is anything but the case, while even among companies using research many do not engage in regular or consistent market research efforts, use detailed fieldwork methodologies or enlist the services of professional market research agencies. Of course, it is possible to be too purist in research terms, especially in those overseas markets where all sorts of practical difficulties and constraints enforce the need for pragmatism and compromise in conducting research.

In terms of desk research, even first-time exporters should find for most markets a variety of sources for general economic/commercial data, ranging from UN and World Bank statistics to data provided by banks, chambers of commerce, professional and academic bodies, directory publishers, the world wide web and the media. However, especially for less-developed overseas markets, the exporter is likely to be faced with a number of problems and pitfalls in terms of data accuracy and consistency, coverage and currency, and sometimes difficulties in comparability. Equally, language and translation errors can cause difficulties (e.g. with definitions and classification terms), while care and time may need to be taken in converting measures and monetary values and dealing with difficulties such as broken (interrupted) data sets or conflicting data from equally plausible sources.

Primary research in international markets can also involve major problems. In terms of methodology, and research design, shortfalls in secondary data may affect the availability and reliability of sampling frames and so rule out probability sampling; while issues of language, literacy and wider cultural constraints may strongly influence the type of questions asked, their scope and accuracy (e.g. scales) and the whole issue of questionnaire design and use. Culture may limit the availability of certain respondents (e.g. female consumers in Muslim countries), while even in general terms it will influence behaviourial aspects of training and supervising research fieldworkers, the requirement for interviewer–respondent ethnic matching, and so forth. Of course, given that most primary research is customarily (and necessarily) completed by research agencies, most of these problems are of less direct concern to the international marketer. On using specialist agencies, though, a company would need to take care in appointing, briefing and dealing with a selected agency in order to ensure cost-effective, timely and reliable research outcomes.

How to enter selected markets

Exactly how a company enters and supplies a foreign market has major influences on the extent to which it capitalises on market potential, and on the strategic control it allows itself over market development.

Usually the early phases of internationalisation will lead the company into limited resource commitments, often facilitated by using indirect channels of market entry, which offer advantages of both risk- and knowledge-sharing. Such indirect channels will involve the use of third parties, or intermediaries, that may be based either in the exporter's market or the overseas territory. A variety of such intermediary entry routes, and more direct servicing channels, are presented in Table 25.3.

Table 25.3   Market entry and servicing channels

Indirect	Direct

■ Home-based export agents, traders, and buying offices
■ Overseas-based:
  – agents
  – distributors
	■ Export sales, HQ-based selling
	■ Overseas-based sales staff
	
	■ Full-scale manufacturing and marketing overseas
	■ Joint ventures:
	  – assembly, manufacture, full-scale joint ventures
	  – licensing/franchising

In principle, a company might 'travel far' in export markets through trading on its own doorstep with export merchants in its home market, specialist 'export houses' perhaps specialising in certain trades or geographical markets, or with buying offices of overseas interests (e.g. department stores) based in the home market. More commonly, companies will select and appoint foreign-based intermediaries such as agents or distributors, thereby at least achieving a closer representation at the market level. For practical purposes, it is worth pointing out that agents act 'on behalf' of the exporter (or legal 'principal'), while distributors buy and sell on their own behalf within the overseas market.

A common mistake made by exporters is to hurriedly appoint agents or distributors within overseas markets and subsequently adopt a low profile, optimistically awaiting a flourish of orders from the newly appointed intermediaries. In practice, to get the best out of any such third party approach, companies need to remain proactive and supportive from the very outset, taking care to treat the agent or distributor as a business partner and to develop an effective relationship based on responsive service and mutual respect (see Shipley et al. 1989).

In the case of both an agency or distributor arrangement, the exporting company should select and recruit carefully, ensuring that the chosen intermediary has local market knowledge, credibility (including financial probity), customer contacts, sales coverage and market experience, and has those marketing facilities (e.g. storage, transport, administrative system, service and support back-up) necessary to both adequately address agreed sales volume targets and contribute to subsequent market development. Obviously, in both cases, the export company would be advised to 'appoint' from a shortlist, and after a market visit involving observations, meetings and negotiation discussions at first hand. The legalities of a formal agreement should be treated as anything but a formality, since details on commission payments (for agents) or margins and allowances (for distributors) will necessarily relate to the duties and responsibilities expected of both parties, while these and other stipulations such as agreed products, territory coverage, competitive conflicts, contract duration and renewal arrangements will make for an effective working relationship, or alternatively occasion dissatisfaction and disputes, and even ultimately disengagement or litigation.

More direct representation in the overseas market will usually only be achieved by accepting the risk associated with the investment necessary. Obviously, the establishment of an overseas-based sales force, sales subsidiary or full-scale, full-service overseas subsidiary would involve heavy investments that would only be justified by major market opportunities, likely verified by a successful record through lower-risk trading channels such as agency or distributor operations. Within the overseas market, risk-sharing and investment-pairing may be served by collaborative approaches such as licensing, franchising or contractual joint venture arrangements, while among international companies (see Bronder and Pritzl, 1992; Taylor et al. 2000) the development of more informal strategic alliances has become popular.

Marketing activities and strategy

The marketing mix to be devised for an overseas market, and the strategy underlying it, will depend on a number of factors ranging from company resources and general marketing policies to local market conditions and chosen entry/servicing channel arrangements. Given the diversity to be met in overseas markets, in terms of cultural and social influences on purchasing, legal and trade constraints on marketing practices, and differing competitive scenarios, the design and implementation of an appropriate marketing mix is by no means a straightforward matter. Even in simple '4P' terms the marketing mix appropriate to one market may be totally unsuccessful in another. Some companies will seek to fine-tune their marketing programmes to local conditions, perhaps guided by research findings that indicate the scope for segmentation or differentiation strategies; while other companies will express a policy commitment to more standardised marketing across perhaps a wide spread of overseas markets. Certainly there is evidence (White and Griffith 1997) that those companies which carefully develop international marketing strategies consistent with their overall corporate strategy stand to gain in terms of global competitiveness. On a more everyday level, other companies will have little choice, in the early days at least, but to follow the advice of their local agents or to make nominal provision for marketing through offering discounts or other support incentives to their local distributors.

The exact make-up of the marketing mix may have to change, in whole or in part, according to market circumstances and company policy preferences. Interestingly, as distribution arrangements will be 'given' for any one time within any market, so too may be the basic logistics/supply arrangements, and the implications these hold for costings and price strategy. Not surprisingly, therefore, companies will often adapt their marketing mix along the apparently more discretionary dimensions of product and promotion/communications. These two dimensions will of course constitute a major element of the 'offer mix' in the market since they concern at once the product and how it is presented and communicated to the market.

Changes to the physical product may be required in many markets, for predictable reasons such as use circumstances, physical conditions (even climate, transit distances, etc.), and differences in industry standards, product and safety regulations, etc. Other product changes, more arguably, may be made for reasons of perceptual differences among target buyers, taste preferences, aesthetic and styling preferences and so on.

Within the communications mix, perceptual, cultural and linguistic differences may make for sometimes radical departures from the company's domestic advertising and promotion strategies and tactics. Indeed, it could be claimed that it is in the area of intangibles such as culture and social influences that companies will most often risk costly mistakes in overseas markets.

Organisation and management control

At least in principle, the distances, time differences and communications problems in international marketing perhaps call for better organisation and management control mechanisms than elsewhere within a company's business. However, experience suggests that many companies give less care and attention to managing overseas business than they do to their domestic markets. Not surprisingly, many failures in overseas marketing could be ascribed to a lack of management control, poor organisation or faulty strategy.

CONCLUSION

To be successful in international marketing a company should, from the outset, invest time, effort and resources into a strategic, planned approach, supported by dedicated staffing and organisational arrangements and effective information and communications systems. Without such commitment even speculative 'export' sales will be consigned to at best marginal activity, at worst costly misadventures.

QUESTIONS

1 *Consider the case for and against a company making an early start in exporting.*

2 *How might the international marketing environment vary in terms of the following products: motor cars; books; table wines; mobile phones.*

3 *Demonstrate with examples the influence of globalisation on any product field of your choice.*

4 *How might a company active in a number of markets approach its international marketing planning?*

5 *What kinds of international factors are likely to affect the new product development programme of a large company with trading and manufacturing interests overseas?*

FURTHER READING

Anderson, Otto (1993) 'On the internationalisation process of firms: a critical analysis', *Journal of International Business Studies*, vol. 24, no. 2, pp. 209–31.

Bell, J. (1995) 'The internationalisation of small computer software firms – a further challenge to "stage" theories', *European Journal of Marketing*, vol. 29, no. 8, pp. 60—75.

Bonaccorsi, A. (1992) 'On the relationship between firm size and export intensity', *Journal of International Business Studies*, vol. 23, no. 4, pp. 605—35.

Bronder, C. and Pritzl, R. (1992) 'Developing strategic alliances: a conceptual framework for successful co-operation', *European Management Journal*, vol. 10, no. 4, December.

Brown, Rick and Cook, David (1990) 'Strategy and performance in British exporters', *Quarterly Review of Marketing*, Spring, pp. 1–6.

Bush, Victoria Davies and Ingram, Thomas (1996) 'Adapting to diverse customers: a training matrix for international marketers', *Industrial Marketing Management*, vol. 25, no. 5, September.

Cavusgil, S., Tamer and Zou, Shaoming (1996) 'Global strategy: review and an integrated conceptual framework', *European Journal of Marketing*, vol. 30, no. 1, pp. 52–70.

Coviello, N. E. and McAuley, A. (1999) 'Internationalisation and the smaller firm: a review of contemporary empirical research', *Management International Review*, vol. 39, July.

Evans, J., Treadgold, A. and Mavondo, F. (2000) 'Explaining export development through psychic distance', *International Marketing Review*, vol. 17, issue 2.

Hilton, Andrew (1992) 'Mythology, markets and the emerging Europe', *Harvard Business Review*, Nov.–Dec., pp. 50–54.

LeClair, D. T. (2000) 'Marketing planning and the policy environment in the European Union', *International Marketing Review*, vol. 17, issue 2.

Rowell, R. (1994) 'Marketing laws: a European flavour', *Marketing Business*, February, pp. 34–35.

Shipley, D., Cook, D. and Barnett, E. (1989) 'Recruitment, motivation, training and evaluation of overseas distributors', *European Journal of Marketing*, vol. 23, no. 2, pp. 79–93.

Taylor, C. R., Zou, S. and Osland, G. E. (2000) 'Foreign market entry strategies of Japanese MNCs', *International Marketing Review*, vol. 17, issue 1.

Terpstra, V. (2000) 'The millennium and international marketing', *International Marketing Review*, vol. 17, issue 1.

White, D. S. and Griffith, D. A. (1997) 'Combining corporate and marketing strategy for global competitiveness', *Marketing Intelligence and Planning*, April–May, vol. 15.

CASE STUDY

Kingston Environmental Laboratories

Based at Kingston-upon-Hull, Humberside, Kingston Environmental Laboratories (KEL) is a private company, founded in 1974 by Dr Edmond Walker, a chemist formerly employed by Halifax Water Authority, now part of newly incorporated Yorkshire Water Plc.

From its inception, the company grew steadily for some 15 years, undertaking water sampling and purification analysis work for a range of clients, from process industry manufacturers such as brewing and soft drinks manufacturers, food companies, pharmaceutical, textile and chemical manufacturers, to utilities corporations, local authorities and specialist government agencies. Since the late 1980s, spurred by a growing national awareness of environmental standards, and increasingly stringent codes of conduct and legislation, company growth has accelerated rapidly.

Company turnover in 1999 topped £105m and pre-tax profits recorded a healthy £14.2m. Reflecting the changed nature of the company's business, in 1999 the traditional staple of water purity analysis laboratory work comprised some 55 per cent of this revenue figure, while the balance divided between a growing portfolio of research-funded projects (12 per cent), environmental consultancy contracts (15 per cent), and specialist laboratory equipment (18 per cent). The latter represents a recent (1994+) diversification into manufacturing/assembly, based on patented company know-how, through subcontract supply links with high tech instrumentation manufacturers in both the UK, Scandinavia and mainland Europe. While most company business (82 per cent) is still conducted within the UK, the company's burgeoning management team found early on in the manufacturing initiative that there existed hungry European export markets for their innovative equipment, from a mix of science-based organisations and process industries similar to their UK customer profile.

The ad hoc direct sales arrangements that supported the early development of this export trade have since been replaced by the appointment of commission agents, based in Germany, France, Italy, Sweden and Holland, which collectively account for some 75 per cent of export business. Export orders from elsewhere in Europe, including occasional orders from Eastern Europe, and a growing number from other countries (including the USA, South Africa and Australia), have so far been handled by direct market visits, where justified, or through catalogue-order transactions against cash payment.

At the company's December 1999 Annual Review Meeting Jack Mason, the appointee to the newly created post of Business Development Manager, suggested to the company board that radical and new representation arrangements be devised to cover all the company's overseas interests. He argued that the agency network so far developed was only a partial and patchy coverage of the potentially vast export market, and that anyway, agency arrangements were not necessarily the best approach to marketing high-value products such as their specialist equipment line. Citing the home market, where a dedicated sales representative had recently been taken on, he argued that the company should consider 'upgrading' to locally based sales representatives in leading markets. This, he argued, could also enable selective development of environmental consultancy work within overseas markets, in order to properly exploit a potential growth area that the company had for too long ignored.

Question

Consider the arguments put forward by Jack Mason, and review the alternative sales and marketing channels available to KEL, taking into account a possibly wider future overseas market for their products and services.

26 Marketing in action

The way to get things done is not to mind who gets the credit for doing them.
Benjamin Jowitt

INTRODUCTION

This chapter is designed to look at marketing in particular situations. A large number of ideas and techniques have been discussed in the main body of the book, and obviously not all are equally relevant in every application. To give some indication of the emphasis in several different contexts, the authors have drawn on their varying experience to look briefly at five areas:

- consumer product marketing
- organisational (B2B) marketing
- .com m@rketing
- services marketing
- non-business/ societal marketing.

Six case studies covering these areas are presented at the end of the chapter.

CONSUMER MARKETING

Fast-moving consumer goods

The first serious development of marketing techniques was in the so-called fast-moving consumer goods (fmcg) markets of the USA. Companies such as Procter & Gamble became the 'universities' of marketing where people learnt the elements of the marketing mix and devised plans to win market share. As these marketers moved to other companies and other industries they took with them the skills of product development, and the ability to create unique selling propositions and effective promotions. These skills have been modified in other industries, but the emphasis on the marketing mix still remains in fmcg markets. The major objective in such markets is to build brand loyalty, as the products are typically low-value regular purchases such as food, drink, confectionery, household and healthcare items, magazines, stationery and so on.

It was in one of these markets that Coca-Cola devised the tests of Acceptability, Affordability and Availability. This test is used in a wider context in this book, but for fmcg products the aim is to maximise all of the 'As' with the widest group of potential consumers. Information is continuously sought on product performance. This infor-

Table 25.1 Industry estimates of own-label share of grocery markets in 1998

	1998
Frozen poultry	80
Wrapped bread	57
Baked beans	38
Breakfast cereals	24
Granulated white sugar	4

mation comes in two basic forms, comparative data on market share and related issues from retailer and consumer panels, and acceptance/awareness data from tracking studies. It is such feedback that reveals small variations in performance and highlights trends that could require attention. These markets value the long-term investment to build brand names such as Mars, Kit Kat, Persil, Coke, Marlboro. Typically, mainstream media are used, requiring quite large advertising budgets (advertising/sales ratios can reach 10 per cent).

There have been a number of studies of the link between the share of grocery markets taken by retailer own brands and the advertising spend (adspend) by manufacturers on their proprietary brands (*The Grocer*, 28 March 1992, IGD Research Report 1995). In general there is a strong relationship, with low spending categories such as frozen poultry and bakery products having high penetration by own-label brands. Higher advertising expenditures, as in the case of breakfast cereals and pet food, have served to limit own-label penetration. However, in conversation with a retail buyer, one of the authors was recently told it was too obvious to equate advertising spend and market share, and certainly product innovation and customer perception of product quality are also important.

Exercise

1 These figures are now a few years old. Find the most up to date figures and suggest why own-label has not grown to dominate markets such as Sugar.

2 How has a company such as Heinz protected its market share in the face of competition from supermarkets selling their own-brand baked beans for as little as 9 pence?

One interesting development in the grocery market is the announcement by Migros, the large Swiss retailer, that it intends to launch Migros-branded products into UK retailers. In this case you could ask what is an 'own-label' brand. Migros contends that it does not want to compete with UK supermarkets, but by selling Migros brands in Tesco or Sainsbury it will be bringing a new brand to the market place. It might be an 'own-brand' in Switzerland but in the UK it would be a brand in its own right.

Advertising is no guarantee of success and many years of investment are usually necessary to develop strong brands. However, fmcg marketing does involve large promotional budgets and a great deal of care and effort in communicating with the millions of customers for any product. Contact with these customers is, of necessity, non-personal, and so sophisticated marketing research is needed to obtain feedback.

Typically, consumer goods companies will have large marketing departments covering all functional aspects of marketing such as advertising, marketing research and brand or product management. They will supplement this by use of agencies to provide specialist services, including promotional planning and new product development. The objective of fmcg marketing is to keep interest in the brands so that they remain relevant to customers, achieve high levels of awareness and become regular purchase items.

The low involvement associated with purchase of products in the fmcg category may offer opportunities for purchases to be undertaken remotely, for instance via an internet service. At present this tends to be somewhat time consuming, and thus potentially expensive if done directly on-line. To avoid this problem, Tesco Direct offer a CD-ROM that allows selection off-line prior to going on-line to place the order. This type of approach would seem to offer advantages to the customer, while allowing suppliers to use their web sites more effectively.

The situation becomes more complex, and interesting, when fast-moving consumer goods become organisational (or industrial) goods. Most fmcg products are sold through major supermarket groups such as Tesco or Sainsbury's. These retail groups purchase in large quantities, so that the marketing of chocolate bars or frozen chickens to a supermarket has more to do with (organisational) industrial marketing, intercompany relationships, and meeting the profit objectives of the powerful retailer than it has to do with the taste of the food or positive consumer feedback.

Consumer durables

Unlike fmcg, consumer durables are less frequently purchased. Consumers have to be able to identify available products when they are considering the purchase of a durable product. In order to reach such customers, communication is again vital.

Durables are typified by products such as washing machines, cars, video recorders or classic clothing. As discussed in Chapter 10, most consumer durables would fall into one of two categories: shopping goods or speciality goods. If the former, then the marketing task is determined by the consumer and the need for useful comparative 'shopping' information. The usefulness will come from providing facts about product benefits that are valued by customers and are the ('salient') ones used to make decisions. Considering how car companies communicate with their customers can provide an example of consumer durable marketing. At one level are to be seen evocative advertisements for Ford or Volvo creating a glamorous general position for their brands, using television and other mass media. This is complemented by press advertisements giving other details, say on performance or financial deals. Direct mail communication or sales promotion competitions are used to encourage customers to visit showrooms for the particular marque. Within the showroom the actual cars are supported by technical information in brochures and by the presentational skills of the direct sales staff.

Daewoo cars used a different, more direct approach when they entered the UK market. Their objective was to appeal to potential customers who felt they had been let down by the motor trade in general. This approach not only yielded a great deal of information but also a very large database of customer names and contact addresses. In a crowded competitive market it is vital to offer customers a reason for buying – or more precisely a reason for buying again if dealing with an existing customer, and a reason to switch for those customers previously buying from competitors.

By studying car distributors it is possible to see the range of techniques used to bring a potential customer to the point of purchase. The integrated programmes of communication will be designed to both inform and persuade. Sometimes information is given in a direct way, to compare one model with another and influence the comparisons of product suitability prior to actually seeing the product. The emphasis on information can be seen with many 'shopping' products.

Car dealers also reinforce decisions by direct communications with customers in the months and years after a sale. This is linked to the period of time between the purchase and the need to replace the durable. Not only is there an emphasis on after-sales service, but it is likely that other information on new models and other developments will be communicated to past customers. When the time comes for replacement the experience with the product will be very important in a customer's decision process. It was once said: 'The quality of a product is remembered long after the price is forgotten.' With durables it is certainly true that their performance rather than the purchase details is remembered. Therefore a consumer who has enjoyed excellent service from a product will remember that when the time comes for a replacement. The issue is a very personal one, as exemplified by the differing experiences of two of the authors regarding cars.

Example

One of the authors has a Vauxhall car, which was a former company car. It has already covered over 230 000 miles with few problems. However, it is nearing time for replacement and this person is convinced that a Vauxhall should be the next purchase. Another author also has a Vauxhall that has proved unreliable at times and recently required a new engine. He has had a poorer experience so is not so keen on this make next time round.

In the case above, the importance of the channel of distribution is highlighted, as it is the local distributor who gives the majority of after-sales service and this can build a strong position for the future. Of course there has been much media debate focusing on the high price of cars in the UK. This does not help the building of strong relationships, as the customer may lack trust in the dealer to make a fair offer. In addition 'switching costs' are low, i.e. it is quite easy for customers to go to buy elsewhere as they are not constrained in any way. This is especially marked in this market, where currently some 20 per cent of all new car sales are estimated to be taking place in continental Europe, for import back into the UK.

It must be remembered that durables are not only infrequent purchases, but they are also likely to involve substantial outlays of money. Issues of affordability are relevant, but perhaps value is a more important measure. Consumers do not necessarily buy the cheapest car or washing machine, but they buy the one that offers the features they require. The features offered with a durable product will vary enormously. There is likely to be much more variety than for a non-durable product. These features form what we have called the 'total product', or some authors call the 'augmented product'. Some of these features are important only at the point of purchase, such as free road fund licence or a full tank of petrol for a car, or free fitting for a carpet or washing machine. These are really promotional additions. Other features are more substantive and long-lasting, such as air conditioning in a car or a special economy programme with a washing machine, or a freeze-frame facility on a video recorder.

While purchasers may place differing values on various features, it has to be noted that all features cost money to provide within the manufacturing/distribution chain. Marketers responsible for consumer durables have to decide about such features and their role in a diverse market place. The ability of Toyota Motors to produce customised cars, with personally chosen features, while producing volume cars, is one way marketing and production can combine to make a very attractive offering to customers.

The facilities provided by e-commerce will increasingly allow potential customers not only to compare the offerings available from any relevant supplier, but also to match their specific requirements with what is actually available. This will increasingly allow customers to choose between waiting for a product with their exact specification, available to order at some time in the future, or choosing other, immediately available products that may cost more or less according to their standard specifications. These facilities will inevitably change the role of the retailer and the supplier/retailer/customer relationships.

Speciality goods are those where the exclusivity of the product is part of its appeal. A Jaguar or a Rolls-Royce car will be sold in small quantities at premium prices. While both these cars have many excellent features it is the intensity with which potential owners aspire to have one that is equally important to the marketing task. A famous study of Morgan cars by Sir John Harvey-Jones in his *Troubleshooter* TV series recommended increasing production to capitalise on the long waiting list (over two years) for a new car. Morgan rejected this advice, as they believed the actual scarcity of the product was part of its appeal to customers.

ORGANISATIONAL MARKETING

In earlier chapters distinctions have been made between products that are purchased for use by individuals, such as a can of Coca-Cola, and products that are purchased by organisations. The point was further made that many of the products purchased by organisations, such as toilet soap or stationery are the same as those purchased by consumers. Furthermore, most products purchased by consumers have in their turn been purchased by wholesale and retail organisations before reaching the final consumer.

Organisational marketing involves those products that are used by an organisation in the course of their business. It is sometimes termed B2B (business-to-business) marketing. Accordingly it involves three different types of products. First, there is the capital equipment required in all types of organisations, whether they are engaged in manufacturing or providing a service. Second, there are products which, either as raw materials or finished components, are used as part of the manufacturing process. Third, there are those products that are used in the manufacturing process but do not become part of the final product (e.g. consultancy services). These are discussed in Chapter 11.

Thus for the production of Coca-Cola drinks the following are all examples of industrial components or raw materials: the supply of the empty cans and bottles used by Coca-Cola to package their product; the sugar and other ingredients used to manufacture the syrup; the compressed carbon dioxide gas used to carbonate the drink; and the material in which the cans and bottles are subsequently packed – there are obviously many others. In contrast, the filter equipment used to process the water used in the drink, the machinery used to fill and print the cans and bottles, the conveyors used to transport the packed cans to the dispatch area and the lorries used to deliver the product are capital equipment and plant. The detergent used each day to clean the machinery is an example of industrial supplies.

Like consumer marketing, discussed earlier, organisational marketing involves optimising what is being offered to a potential buyer in terms of the product itself, the price of the product, the availability of the product and the method by which the potential customer is made aware of the product. Organisations differ from consumers in a number of important ways. In particular, there are fewer transactions and the value of each is generally much higher. There are also similarities, especially, as with consumer marketing, the importance of understanding the need that the potential customer wants the product to meet.

These needs depend upon a number of factors, in particular the reason that an organisational product is being purchased. Many issues affect this. For instance, the expertise within an organisation develops as a result of experience. This means that the routine purchases, particularly those which affect the final product, will be monitored very carefully. Thus it is likely that there will be a very good understanding of the relative values of the products offered by different suppliers. As a result of this knowledge it is quite likely that the preferred choice will not be the cheapest, but rather the most suitable offering, including such issues as the reliability and quality of the supplier. For less frequent purchases, or those not directly connected with the product being manufactured, it is likely that there will be less concern with value and as a result a tendency to consider price and specification as the main buying criteria.

It is the recognition that the buying criteria are likely to vary from organisation to organisation that is the key to successful organisational marketing. This is, of course, a form of market segmentation. Very often this segmentation involves not simply changing the product but changing the level of service provided by the organisation. Even suppliers of raw materials have found that by applying this approach they can not only increase their share of the market but can at the same time improve their profitability. What is required is the recognition that different types of customers are willing to accept different levels of service, and then finding a method by which this knowledge can be applied. This may involve setting up a separate division that specialises in supplying a specific segment of the market. Organisations adopting this approach usually have to overcome two problems. The first is that providing a different level of service is often against the culture of the organisation and strongly resisted by the staff. This is best overcome by ensuring that the staff can see the advantages that the organisation will offer its customers. The second problem can be associated with this, in that the old organisation is likely to compete with the new organisation, thereby putting at risk many of the potential advantages of the approach.

Where organisational products are ancillary to the production, such as might be the case with computers or delivery vehicles, it is possible that an organisation will buy on the reputation of the supplier rather than the suitability of the product. Hence the well-known adage, 'No one ever got fired for buying IBM!' (although this is now untrue as IBM has lost the dominant position it once held in the business computing market). It is for this reason that the creation of a brand within an industrial market can be so important. This involves, as it does in the consumer market, a single-minded approach to promotion. Also, as with some sectors of the consumer market, it is necessary to create this brand awareness within a small, specific market sector. Generally it is possible by using the technical press, not only to advertise but also to promote the brand through consistent editorial coverage. For most companies operating in B2B markets this can only be achieved by having a positive commitment to the use of public relations.

Many organisations are using e-commerce as a way of increasing the number of potential suppliers while limiting the number of actual suppliers who are thus having to face ever increasing competition. It allows purchasers to develop beneficial relationships with suppliers while potentially reducing the commitment that might be associated with such relationships. Suppliers are thus having to respond to the requirements of their customers and apply their organisational marketing skills in new ways. This is likely to be the key to success in the new world of B2B e-tr@ding.

In Chapter 6 the issues of organisational buying behaviour were discussed. In many circumstances there will be an emphasis on personal selling and building long-term relationships with customers. Routine reordering is often carried out without a sales call, in fact some organisations use on-line computer reordering to replenish stock levels.

Where strong relationships exist it becomes very difficult for a new supplier to get any business. A well-known UK purchasing director once said: 'I have all the suppliers I need, and, unless one of them starts to let me down, I see no prospect of changing these arrangements.'

This may be going too far, as changes do take place, but rarely is price the overriding stimuli; rather it is service levels that are critical. This is especially true with customers operating a JIT (just-in-time) policy for supplies. The best relationships are developed by not letting customers down. It is this area that is critical to success in organisational marketing.

.COM M@RKETING

There has been an explosion in internet @ctivity over the last decade. It is fast becoming the new way of doing business, and companies that ignore this area could be seriously challenged by new competitors. However it is very easy to get the whole market out of proportion, and students of marketing should remember that the most import aspect of business is to create a profitable exchange between a buyer and a seller. All offers must be Acceptable, Affordable and Available. It is no good ordering a book from Amazon.com and being told it will not arrive for 6–12 weeks. In fact orders are usually shipped within 24 hours but they can take a long time to arrive from the US if they are sent sea freight.

At the heart of e.business is the need to offer a customer more benefits than those offered by a competitor. This usually means utilising the Internet to:

- reduce costs and make an offering more *affordable*;
- offer a product to customers without their needing to leave their home or other location, thus making it more *available*;
- present the product or service in a way that is more *acceptable*.

This will be a challenge for marketers but one they should not shun.

There is no doubt that many new possibilities for trading in a very different way have been opened up by the explosion (e.xplosion) taking place as we enter the 21st century. However e.commerce should not be seen as a new marketing paradigm, it is simply another e.xciting and e.xtremely effective way of satisfying customers' needs.

The basic principles of marketing remain the same. It is still necessary to make offers to customers that are @cceptable, @ffordable and @vailable. In addition they must be superior in all these aspects when compared to the competition. If the Internet can help achieve these m@rketing objectives then it would be e.xtremely foolish to ignore the possibilities. However it should be approached with an open mind, as the role of m@rketing is to satisfy customers (created and retained), beat competitors and meet the objectives of the organisation. These usually involve making a profit sufficient to remain in business.

In Chapter 2 it was mentioned that Levi-Strauss jeans shut down its website in January 2000 as it was not cost effective. Web failure is also the subject of the case in Chapter 11 regarding fashion retailer 'boo.com' (now gone bust!). Other problems created by the power of the Net are affecting marketers' ability to control their market spaces – see the case of rock band piracy in Chapter 10. There are of course many e.xamples of good practice and e.xploitation given in this book, no doubt that the web offers really e.xciting opportunities for all marketers. These are well described by Michael Dell (founder of Dell Computers) writing in the Ford cars net magazine:

> Ford is one of Dell's premier customers and Dell is proud to be one of their business partners. The companies share many attributes, and one of the most important is a commitment to the Internet. We [both] are also dedicated to providing a superior customer experience, and share a strong desire to enhance our competitiveness in the connected global market place.
>
> I believe the Internet is the most powerful tool of our time. The potential of the Internet lies in its ability to transform relationships. It can bring communities together to create a network with shared interests. It is fuelling changes in how all businesses operate and how all people learn, buy goods, communicate, and are entertained.
>
> We are fast approaching the point where there will be no distinction between 'dotcom' businesses and traditional businesses. Ford has been quick to embrace this reality. Ford's website, complete with a custom configurator, is already receiving 25 million hits every month. In addition, Ford has made investments and created partnerships with strategic firms to secure its net-enabled future.
>
> Dell made a similar commitment to the Internet in 1994 (so long ago) when we launched *www.dell.com*. Sales now average $40 million per day, up from $14 million per day just one year ago.
>
> We have found that one of the keys to being successful on the Internet is a superior on-line customer e.xperience. To create sustainable relationships and loyalty over the web, your customer's web experience must be better than any experience in the physical world. Our goal at Dell is to deepen relationships with our customers by providing added convenience, efficiency, a wider array of services and tangible cost savings.
>
> From our supply chain to the end user, Dell's entire business is conducted on-line. We believe that 'three C's' are often the core steps to any sustainable internet endeavour, and to an improved on-line customer experience: *content, commerce, and community.*
>
> *Content* means putting compelling information on-line and making it available to customers 24 hours a day, seven days a week.
>
> *Commerce* refers to all aspects of an on-line transaction, including customised pages for placing and tracking orders, and on-line status checks.
>
> *Community* means building and supporting interactive, two-way relationships over the web with both customers and suppliers.
>
> the Internet is provoking a business revolution far greater than any change ever seen before, and that revolution reaches into every industry, from cars to computers.

These thoughts from a man at the centre of this revolution provide much for students of marketing to contemplate and absorb. By the time this book is published many more developments and initiatives will have occurred, so it is as well to try to relate to the basic principles of marketing and to reassess these in the light of the customer experience received via the Net or through some other link with a supplier.

SERVICES MARKETING

This book has emphasised the importance of marketing irrespective of whether it is applied to tangible products or intangible services. The difference between products and services is irrelevant from a general viewpoint, but there are some aspects of services that must be understood when one is involved in service marketing (see Chapter 11). At one level a service is a total product without a core.

Services can be offered to consumer markets, organisational markets, international markets, or be given in non-business situations. Therefore services can be seen as a subset of the marketing described in any of the other sections in this chapter. First and foremost it is important to decide if the service could be described as a service product or a product service.

The term service product refers to a service that is a self-standing offering and therefore fits the view taken in this book of a service that can be considered under the general heading of product. Examples of service products could be:

- a plumber mending a broken pipe
- an accountant auditing company accounts
- a doctor visiting a sick patient
- a taxi journey.

Product services are also subject to the distinctive factors introduced in Chapter 11 of intangibility, variability and perishability. However, product services are attached directly to a product and can be one of the added-value elements of the marketing offering. As a result it can be argued that with product services some form of ownership could be present. Kotler describes product services as: 'tangible goods with accompanying services'. He goes on to describe 'the offer which consists of a tangible good accompanied by one or more services to enhance its consumer appeal'.

The example given earlier related to two of the authors who both have a Vauxhall car. They have varying experiences, hence the variability of services received. The issue with product services is that the product is the fundamental core, car in the example or maybe a computer, and the service is an added element to increase the attractiveness of the offer. This is certainly the case when considering the service offered by the car salesman prior to and during the purchase period. The marketing emphasis at this time is then more on the product than on the accompanying service. In the post-purchase situation service becomes more important. The offer of an enhanced five-year 'parts and labour' warranty at a small extra charge is an example of a 'product service'. It is associated with the product although distinct from it. Had the author who owns the less reliable car had such a 'product service' he could have benefited more from his total purchase.

While with a 'service product' it is the service that dominates, a tangible product may be included to enhance the service. This might be the meal supplied on an air flight, the advice given by a doctor, or a guarantee provided by a builder.

NON-BUSINESS MARKETING

Just as marketing offers business organisations opportunities to be more successful so it has been realised that these same techniques could be applied with as great a benefit to non-business activities. This includes government organisations, providers of services such as the National Health Service, charities, and special interest groups such as political parties. The British Heart Foundation poster in the colour section shows the benefits of investing in heart research. This illustrates a benefit that a donor could acquire, but while the donor actually receives nothing tangible the charity is able to use the donation to invest to achieve its objectives. It is not unusual for many of these organisations to be referred to as non-profit making organisations; this has the disadvantage of denying them the expectation that through prudent management their income might exceed their costs, thereby yielding a surplus which can be invested in improved facilities or services.

The term non-business would seem to be preferable to non-profit, as the pursuit of a surplus is still important for any viable business. However profit is not the principal characteristic that separates businesses from other types of organisation. The real difference is that the fundamental objective of a business should be to achieve a return on the assets employed and thereby to increase the asset value of the owners at a rate that is commensurate with the risk involved. While to achieve this objective businesses must inevitably accommodate the interests of a wide range of stakeholders, this fundamental objective helps to focus the overall activity, since failure to meet this objective will ultimately lead to the organisation being disbanded or taken over. The term societal marketing is often used when the objectives of the organisation are based more on general principles of good citizenship. They sometimes also involve changing behaviour such as the campaigns to stop people smoking cigarettes.

One of the major benefits of applying marketing principles in the non-business context is that they provide effective alternatives to the financial surplus for measuring organisational performance. Examples of these can be seen in the various charters that have been implemented by the government in order to improve the accountability of organisations such as the National Health Service.

Another benefit of applying marketing principles in the non-business context is that it allows the often complicated transactions involved to be properly analysed. An example of where the failure to do this prevented an organisation from responding quickly enough to changing circumstances is the Blood Transfusion Service. For many years this organisation depended to a significant extent upon the co-operation of the many manufacturing companies that regularly provided facilities for blood donor sessions. This work-based collection of blood donations provided the basis for ensuring both constancy of supply and the efficiency of the collection service. During the 1980s many of the companies that provided these facilities reduced the size of their workforce to such an extent that they no longer justified having their own blood donor sessions. The Blood Transfusion Service responded by expanding the number of local sessions they ran in public buildings such as church halls and hospitals. However they were to find it was increasingly difficult to attract sufficient numbers of donors. What had not been appreciated was the actual cost incurred by the donor when giving blood. Time was a cost which had previously been 'paid' by the companies, which had not only provided the Blood Transfusion Service with the facilities it needed for the donor session but had also allowed their employees to attend during working hours. It was not until the real cost to the individual donor, giving in their own time at a less convenient location, was appreciated, and steps taken to minimise this by providing appointments and better information, that it was possible for the service to bring demand and supply back into balance.

Another common problem faced by non-business organisations is that of multiple publics. Just as business organisations have a number of stakeholders such as customers, employees and owners, so non-business organisations often have, in addition to staff and clients, donors and volunteers. The exchanges involved between each of these groups and the organisation is likely to differ both with the frequency and degree of the commitment. As a result, the organisation has to be especially careful to ensure that any changes made to improve the effectiveness of the exchanges between any two of these groups is acceptable to the others and to the public in general. This is one area where a lack of basic understanding of marketing has resulted in some very worthwhile charities losing support. By using dramatically strong adverts to improve awareness of it, and hopefully increase donations, a well-known charity actually upset both its staff and some existing supporters. By not taking proper account of the impact on the other groups upon which the organisation has to depend the result was negative, not positive.

There are, then, a number of benefits to be derived by non-business organisations 'taking a leaf' from the marketing approach. In addition to the examples already cited, the following areas offer prime potential for improved effectiveness:

- **Market research.** This is of no less relevance in non-profit organisations than in commercial companies. If non-profit bodies need to relate to and maintain a network of customers, users, sponsors and supporters, then market research techniques have a positive role to play in recognising trends and opportunities. These should help to identify better ways to reach and serve the organisation's various publics. On a general level, market research and analysis approaches will ensure that organisations do not lose sight of their wider environment.
- **Communications.** Historically this has been a major problem in non-business organisations, for a variety of reasons. Large public sector bodies have often been perceived as aloof and impersonal, occasionally intimidating and uncaring, even among the very groups they were mandated to 'serve'. Better external communications, adopting more marketing-led approaches, hold the promise of communicating and achieving a closer match between provider and user, a more responsive service and a more positive perception of it. Internal communications, too, have often been hampered by zealously administrative approaches to management, particularly within public sector organisations. Recent changes in structure and formal reporting relationships within the public sector may yet serve to improve internal communications and open new possibilities in terms of internal marketing.
- **Price and value.** Both of these are a continuing dilemma for some non-business organisations, where funding and resourcing provisions may be formally separate from the 'market' and the user. The classic example would be central and local government activities, organised as statutory or local monopoly supply arrangements. In such circumstances a customer or user focus may be all but totally absent, while notions of value and effectiveness may fall prey to the internal considerations of administrative convenience, producing sometimes a take-it-or-leave-it attitude among staff. The early attempts to establish customer charters, and a new-found interest in customer care and resource effectiveness, promise a radical if overdue rethink on issues such as market needs and the 'customer's' perceptions of value and preference.

Not surprisingly, many of the larger non-business organisations, particularly in the public sector, have proved to be slow and resistant to change. For some, the introduction of competitive practices has had to be painfully imposed, through internal markets, market testing and compulsory competitive tendering. Such resistance has also been apparent among non-government organisations such as charities and educational establishments, where perhaps a major obstacle has been the ideological opposition to what for long was dismissed as the 'vulgarity' of commercialism and marketing.

While marketing techniques are increasingly being adopted by non-business organisations they cannot offer any panacea or instant solutions. As is true of all functions, it is only as good as the management that drives it.

CONCLUSION

This final chapter has tried to give a flavour of the richness of marketing in many different types of organisations. It will be realised that the basic concept of an offer that is acceptable, affordable and available applies in all cases. It then needs to be promoted in the most appropriate way. It is not a question of placing advertisements all over the place, but deciding on a target market, deciding how to meet the needs, then finding an effective way of reaching the chosen customers.

The elements of the so-called marketing mix are important but the emphasis changes for different products/services and different situations. Understanding the exchange relationship is the key to marketing in all situations, and then resources and programmes can be devised to maximise the return.

QUESTIONS

1 *In many consumer goods markets it is more important to encourage repeat purchases by loyal customers than to achieve a one-off sale. What techniques might be used to build loyalty and what other factors related to the total marketing offering could affect repeat purchase?*

2 *'Companies do not make purchases; they establish relationships' (Charles S. Goodman). Discuss the validity of this observation on industrial marketing.*

3 *The last few years have seen an explosion in the Internet and in e-commerce. What are the key features that a marketer must appreciate when assessing an e-business opportunity?*

4 *'In service organisations, people come first.' Discuss this assertion in terms of the marketing concept.*

5 *Consider the potential value in adopting marketing techniques within a public sector organisation such as a public library.*

CASE STUDY 1

Satin Gold

Michelle Graham sat in her office deep in thought. She had just received the latest Neilsen research figures on Satin Gold, the long-established brand of bath oil that was the biggest contributor to her company's revenue. The trend was clear: in spite of strong promotional support the brand was continuing in long-term decline. Over the past few years new competitive brands with more trendy images had nibbled into the market. There were also the new aromatic products that offered health-enriching properties and now accounted for significant sales volumes, and of course there were the value-for-money, own-label products in Boots as well as some major grocery stores.

It was obvious that fewer customers were buying Satin Gold regularly, and the brand was not attracting new, younger consumers.

Just over a year ago the company had launched a new product – Bath Spice – that had a powerful aroma and was packaged in a bright, bulb-shaped orange bottle. The product had been well received in home placement research tests, and seemed to be favoured by the younger age groups who were not attracted by the more mature image of Satin Gold. However launching Bath Spice had involved some complex alterations to the production line and significant down time was experienced, giving rise to stock shortages with both the new and the established products. For Bath Spice this was particularly damaging as it led to the product not being available in key retail outlets at the time of the intensive launch advertising campaign. This was cited as one of the reasons why sales never achieved targets, and the product was withdrawn last month.

The problem with Satin Gold remained. It was obvious that the slow loss of sales required some action if the company was to maintain its sales and profit levels. At last week's management meeting Ken Jones, the production director, had proposed installing a high-speed automated packing line for Satin Gold. By including a small redesign of the bottle this new line would reduce the cost of manufacture by 10 per cent, which could be passed on to customers and help rekindle sales. He suggested the scheme would give a two-year pay back on the capital expenditure that met the company's financial requirements. However the new line would need to be located in the main building so the existing line would have to be taken out. The drawback of such a dedicated line was that all products packed by the company would have to use identical sized bottles, but such was the price of efficiency.

Ken did have an alternative, but it was twice as expensive; a more flexible line that could handle a range of different bottle shapes without any loss of speed or increased labour. However this expenditure could not be justified on grounds of productivity gains from more efficient production.

The finance director leant his weight to the new dedicated filling line by saying, 'we don't need a sophisticated line; we have just tried a new product in a fancy bottle and it failed. Customers can't be fooled by flashy shapes; it is only value for money that they understand, so that's why we need to reduce our costs.'

Following the withdrawal of Bath Spice a creative agency had been briefed to suggest the way forward. Their initial ideas had involved testing three different products, each in a different area of the country. Michelle reached across her desk to look at the proposals. The basic bath oil was not a problem; the technology of mixing a natural base with different essential oils, aromas and colours would also be no problem. The need to test the mixtures without using animals was in line with the comments made by young people during a number of qualitative focus groups, and that could be achieved. However the important part of the agency recommendations related to packaging. To achieve the excitement at the point of sale the product had to be dramatic, and all three proposals were based around packs that could not be accommodated on the proposed new production line.

Michelle looked at the idea rating screen that she had drawn up, and even scoring manufacturing at zero, the proposals totalled highly enough on all other criteria to make it look positive to proceed. The idea of comparing three different options instead of gambling on one single idea seemed realistic, but before taking the ideas into more detailed analysis and research it was necessary to consider the issue of variations in packaging against the benefits of low price. Michelle knew she was in a difficult position as the marketing department was being asked to resolve the future direction of the company, yet if she could not accommodate the views of finance and production while achieving a new product offering acceptable to a carefully chosen target market, there would continue to be a steady decline in the sales of Satin Gold.

Questions

1   *What lessons can be learnt from the failure of Bath Spice?*

2   *How can Michelle try to make a success of any future new product launches?*

CASE STUDY 2

Business-to-business

Linley Engineering Services is a small Coventry company providing a range of subcontract metalwork and engineering services including welding, profile cutting, flamecutting, grinding and fabricating. It also undertakes intermittent contract manufacture of a range of trolleys, an outwork arrangement made five years ago with the trolley manufacturer, a Birmingham-based company specialising in palletisation and materials-handling systems. This work, never particularly profitable or reliable, has for the last two years amounted to no more than an occasional batch order from the Birmingham company, which is itself now troubled by recessionary difficulties.

In 1999 Linley had a monthly turnover of approximately £60 000 and had 22 employees. However, since that date it has suffered severely from the effects of the local recession in manufacturing, and has not markedly recovered in spite of a recent industrial upturn. It now has only ten employees and turnover has fallen to £28 000 per month. It has recorded a small loss in each of the last three years.

There are some 1100 accounts in the sales ledger but only 120 have been active during the last 12 months. Of these, ten accounts produce 70 per cent of the company's sales. Order sizes vary from 'one-off' jobs costing £100 to a long-standing contract worth £10 000 per month. Profits per job are known to vary somewhat, though the company has not succeeded in its periodic attempts to plan profits or purposefully provide for future growth.

Sales contacts are currently handled by the managing director, John Linley. Apart from a listing in a local trades directory the company spends no money on advertising or publicity. The company has a secretary/works accountant who costs all jobs and prepares estimates and quotations. Design, production and purchasing are handled by a production foreman, under the direction of John Linley.

In recent months John Linley has been giving serious thought to the strategic avenues open to the company, and especially to the possibilities that might exist in new product fields and markets. He believes that, if only for survival purposes, the company needs to move away from dependence on the depressed subcontract sector, and the 'metal-bashing' image that sticks to it. In particular, he feels that opportunities lie in the development and commercialisation of a credible range of company-manufactured products, supplied to the open market. In this way, he reasons, the company would be in more direct control of its own destiny.

▶

To this end he has resolved to make a careful assessment of the company's situation, its strengths and limitations. From this he means to develop a shortlist of possible new product ideas for the intended line of manufactured products.

Question

Advise John Linley on the issues and guiding principles he might consider in developing a plan for the design and commercialisation of any new product line.

CASE STUDY 3

3 e.com

IT in M@arketing: effective strategies in an e-world

A report in the *Financial Times* on 9 October 2000 suggested that banks are reassessing the move from physical branches to internet banking. The report below by James Mackintosh explains why the physical branch is moving back into fashion.

On-line banks increasingly move from clicks back to bricks

The bank branch is back in fashion. Around the world on-line banks are going physical in an attempt to convince customers they can be trusted – and even the biggest brands have decided they must follow suit.

Merrill Lynch and HSBC, two of the world's most prominent banks, are to build a branch network for their new internet bank aimed at well-off investors.

The move highlights a shift in thinking among banks and stockbrokers away from the 'clicks-only' model and back to the physical, following the success of Charles Schwab, the giant US broker, in recruiting customers through branches. Schwab – which adopted on-line share-dealing early on – now does 80 per cent of its retail business on the web, but seven out of ten customers join after walking through the doors of its branch network.

Huw van Steenis, e-finance analyst at JP Morgan, believes the new focus on the branch is an attempt to persuade customers the on-line banks are trustworthy. 'Internet companies are here today, gone tomorrow, but seeing is believing,' he said. 'Just as banks in the 19th century had large marble halls to demonstrate their solidity the new asset management services are adopting a skinny branch network.'

TD Waterhouse, a Canadian-owned broker that uses branches to back its on-line services, adds that small offices with heavy branding on high streets also act as a cheap form of advertising.

The new mindset is clear from the approach taken by new up-market banking aimed at the well off. Credit Suisse, which has launched an internet-only bank for the 'mass affluent' in the UK, runs investor centres – branches by any other name – for the same customers in Italy, where it tested the concept. Deutsche Bank is also planning a Europe-wide branch network to go with its DB 24 operation.

Meanwhile, many of the big on-line brokers are building a physical presence, with E*Trade, the US number two, setting up 'investment centres' as well as buying a network of 8500 ATMs this year to back Telebank, its web-only banking arm. Some of the established internet banks have also started to switch back to bricks and mortar.

'You could say we are the ultimate in clicks and bricks,' said Tim Sawyer, marketing director of Cahoot, the Internet-only arm of Abbey National in the UK. It has done a deal with the Post Office to allow customers to pay in at branches. Egg, the largest UK internet bank, has moved slightly away from its clicks-only model by dropping charges on customers telephoning the call centre, and Dublin-based on-line bank First-e is considering opening physical outlets.

The attraction of the mixed model – known as clicks and bricks – showed up in hard data for the first time last month. A report by MMXI Europe, an on-line data company, showed Barclays, traditionally a branch-based bank, overtaking Egg for customer use in the UK, with Lloyds TSB close behind. Barclays and Lloyds are now the second- and third-most used sites in Europe, with German on-line stockbroker Comdirect the busiest. 'You need some degree of physical presence in the Internet world,' said Peter McNamara, managing director of mortgage bank Alliance & Leicester.

But customers bemoaning the loss of their village bank should not expect dotcoms to rush in. 'New entrants will be trying to move to a skinny branch model,' said Mr van Steenis. The branches will dispense advice, sell complex – and profitable – investment products and help customers with the web, not deal with mundane transactions like withdrawing cash. And there won't be very many of them.

TD Waterhouse covers the whole of the US with 170 branches. Stephen McDonald, CEO of TD Waterhouse, said: 'It is about perception. As long as the branch is within a short drive people are just happy to know it is there – they don't have to visit it.'

There are many internet banks trying to establish their place in the market. You might like to visit some of their sites because it is critical to have a user-friendly location.

Tasks

1 *Assess the advantages and disadvantages of the Internet as opposed to fixed sites for banks.*

2 *Why do you believe the mixed model of 'click @nd brick' is now being adopted?*

3 *What do you believe is the way forward for internet banking?*

website www.ukinternetbanking.co.uk lists the following providers of web banking in the UK in October 2000.

Pure internet banks – no high street retail branches

■ **Cahoot** (Current account and credit cards)
    URL: *http://www.cahoot.co.uk*
■ **Egg** (Savings, mortgages, credit cards, personal loans, ISAs)
    URL: *http://www.egg.co.uk*
■ **First-e** (Savings and current account)
    URL: *http://www.first-e.co.uk*
■ **First Direct** (Current account, savings, mortgages, credit card, insurance)
    URL: *http://www.firstdirect.co.uk*
■ **Intelligent Finance** (Current accounts, personal loans, credit card, mortgages and savings)
    URL: *http://www.if.com*
■ **Smile** (Full services)
    URL: *http://www.smile.co.uk*
■ **Virgin Direct**
    URL: http://www.virgindirect.co.uk

▶

High street retail banks and building societies

- **Abbey National** (Current accounts, savings, loans, mortgages and ISAs)
  URL: *http://www.abbeynational.co.uk*
- **Alliance & Leicester** (Current account and savings)
  URL: *http://www.alliance-leicester.co.uk*
- **Bank of Scotland**
  URL: *http://www.bankofscotland.co.uk*
- **Barclays Bank** (Full services – full integration with retail banking)
  URL: *http://www.barclays.co.uk*
- **CitiBank** (Current account and savings)
  URL: *http://www.citibank.co.uk*
- **Co-operative Bank** (Current, business – savings account, credit cards)
  URL: *http://www.cooperativebank.co.uk*
- **Halifax – On Line** (Credit card, mortgages and loans + free anti-virus software)
  URL: *http://www.halifax.co.uk*
- **HSBC** (Full services)
  URL: *http://www.hsbc.co.uk*
- **LloydsTSB** (Full services)
  URL: *http://www.lloydstsb.co.uk*
- **Nationwide**
  URL: *http://www.nationwide.co.uk*
- **Natwest** (Full services)
  URL: *http://www.natwest.co.uk*
- **Norwich Union** (Personal and business current accounts)
  URL: *http://www.norwichunion.co.uk*
- **Royal Bank of Scotland** (current account and savings)
  URL: *http://www.royalbankofscotland.co.uk*
- **The Woolwich** (Full services)
  URL: *http://www.thewoolwich.co.uk*

CASE STUDY 4

Services marketing

Following a takeover, an accountant friend of yours has been made redundant. He has decided to realise his ambition of running a sportswear retail shop. His redundancy payment (£25k) plus a loan guaranteed against his house will raise the £50 000 needed to purchase the business of Crown Sports. This business, started over 30 years ago by Charlie King after an undistinguished career as a professional footballer, trades from a 1000 sq ft shop about half a mile from the new Queen's Shopping Centre. Charlie is now 68 years old and is concerned that he is losing customers to the new Olympus shop in the shopping centre. In fact the Olympus shop seems to be doing about twice as much business compared with Crown Sports, and your friend has noticed that the typical Olympus customer is under 35, probably from social class A B, or C1. These customers like a particular style in the layout of a shop and it is obvious Crown Sports is rather too old fashioned, although perhaps this more traditional layout is preferred by Crown's loyal customers, which include parents buying for their children, officials from several local sports clubs and kit sales to a number of local schools.

Crown Sports did, however, achieve a turnover of £300 000 in 2000 which, after Charlie had drawn his salary of £16k, left a net margin of 2 per cent. Half the current turnover is in footwear with the rest split between equipment and clothes. Charlie has not specialised in any particular sport but rather covers the more popular ones, changing the emphasis depending on the relevant season, i.e. soccer/rugby in winter; cricket/tennis/golf in summer. He does, however, have a wide selection of footwear from such major manufacturers as Nike, Reebok, Fila, Puma and Hi Tec. There have been some past problems with Adidas, which insisted on minimum order quantities that Mr King felt excessive, so currently no Adidas equipment is stocked.

Your friend believes he can improve the financial control of the business. The major trends all seem to indicate that sports activities are thriving and in spite of the demographic decline in the teenage market and recent curbs on consumer spending there is every chance of this market continuing to grow ahead of the rate of inflation. There is, however, continuing development of 'high technology' specialist equipment that could involve stocking more expensive items. Also major competition for retail sports equipment is coming from the growth of sports chain stores (e.g. Olympus, JJB) and of buying groups (e.g. Intersport), which use their buying power to achieve significant deals that they advertise to attract customers.

Question

Before your friend acquires the business he needs to consider how he can develop it. He does not think he can compete on price with the likes of Olympus or specialists such as Footlocker but might be able to attract customers by specialising in particular parts of the market. Can you advise him on the marketing issues he should consider in this case, in particular suggesting how elements of superior service could assist an independent retailer to compete successfully against high profile multiple stores?

CASE STUDY 5

Societal marketing

Marketing and education – societal marketing or merely promotion?

Recognising the value that voters, and parents in particular, place on education, successive governments have, in recent years, given ever greater emphasis to education as a policy issue. Increasingly in the last few years, as if to mirror the public recognition of the need for educational improvements, a number of leading companies have begun to tie in their promotions to educational themes. A few examples may serve to show the growth in such activity within the UK – although parallel growth has been noted in other countries during the same period:

- In 1999 *The Times* and the *Sunday Times* launched a Books for Schools campaign that resulted in 2 million books being distributed to 28 000 schools. This initiative helped boost the circulation of both newspapers over a 16-week period.
- Another initiative was the Software for Schools campaign, which encouraged school children to collect tokens from *The Times*, the *Sunday Times* and the *Times Education Supplement*. The tokens could be exchanged for free software from leading software suppliers, including Microsoft and Lotus. W.H. Smith also supported the campaign with point-of-sale promotions.
- Early in the year 2000 Walkers crisps had a tie-up with News International in a Books for Schools scheme that had children and parents saving tokens printed on crisp packets.
- For several years Tesco has run a successful Computers for Schools promotion and rivals J Sainsbury have also run similar schemes.

In March 2000 the UK government launched a promotion – Maths Year 2000. The aim was to

▶

help improve the overall maths standards of children. This initiative was followed quickly by an education-based campaign spearheaded by United Biscuits, owner of the McVitie's and KP Foods brands, and linking with the Mirror Group investing £15m in providing maths equipment to schools. The United Biscuits promotion was called Maths Stuff for Schools and was supported by a large advertising campaign, with coupons appearing on many of United Biscuits' snacks, cakes and biscuit labels, as well as in Mirror Group newspapers. Schools could exchange the coupons for mathematical equipment such as protractors, compasses and calculators. Alison Head, chief communications officer at McVitie's, stated that, 'People believe in cause-related charity. We know that education in schools is a really strong motivator.' Arguably another factor may be that United Biscuits expected the promotion to generate £42m in extra sales across its McVitie's and KP Foods brands. However, in a recent survey by Mintel Research it was found that 60 per cent of consumers are cynical about companies' motives for cause-related marketing.

Notwithstanding this research, corporate interest in promoting products via education continues. Coca-Cola Schweppes Beverages (CCSB) is taking it a step further and providing teachers with an educational resource website. The aim of the website, which will be free to teachers at schools that have Coca-Cola brands in drinks machines and canteens, is to build awareness for the company's brands. Teachers will be able to download lesson plans and class handouts on a variety of curriculum subjects – but each handout will be linked to a different CCSB brand. A spokesperson from CCSB has stated: 'Each lesson plan has a brand affiliation, but only where it is appropriate, there is no requirement for the teacher to mention the brand.'

Questions

1 *Are the above promotional campaigns ethical?*

2 *Are the companies taking action that will benefit society?*

3 *What type of marketing management philosophy do you feel the above companies are following? Give reasons for your answers.*

4 *Do you think that this type of promotion could be effective within Further and Higher Education establishments? If so why?*

CASE STUDY 6

Non-profit marketing

Plea for blood donors as stocks slump to 'crisis level'

For the third time in five years a dramatic appeal has been launched for more people to come forward to give blood as stocks again slump to less than one day's supply for the country's hospitals.

The National Blood Service has warned that supplies are at a 'critically low level', and have asked regular donors who may not have given recently: 'Please come back this week as next week may be too late.'

There is also a need for those who have never donated blood to become new donors. The UK Blood Transfusion Service has, in the past, been successful at developing its operations to meet the ever increasing demand from hospitals for its products. However there are times when extra effort is required.

Although high profile appeals produce a good response in the short term, there are clearly issues that need to be dealt with on a longer time-scale to ensure 'such a worrying situation' does not occur again.

The BTS (Blood Transfusion Service) has begun to respond to this challenge and they now regularly advertise for donors. The use of advertising suggests that marketing concepts might provide a useful approach to analysing the problem.

Perhaps they need to start by asking: who is their customer? At first sight the obvious answer would seem to be the users of their product: hospitals and patients requiring blood transfusions. However, another way of looking at the operation is to consider the donor as a customer. This then leads to the next question: what is the product or benefit exchanged between the BTS and the donor? It is tempting to suggest that it is a pint of blood exchanged for a cup of tea and, if needed, a packet of iron tablets, which are given to donors at the end of their donation session. This, however, is supported by the provision of certificates to each donor and badges to recognise that a certain number of donations have been made. Perhaps the exchange involves blood for a 'done the right thing' feeling rather than for a cup of tea. Furthermore, as all donors know, the pint of blood is not actually missed. So if that 'done the right thing' feeling was not exchanged for the blood donated what was it exchanged for? The answer is not a simple one, but it might involve the sacrifice of time by the donor.

One reason for the Blood Transfusion Service being less able to keep up with demand now is the declining number of organisations large enough to co-operate with the BTS by providing facilities on site, thus allowing their employees to give blood during working hours. For these donors, the exchange had been a 'done the right thing' feeling in company time. This is often valued differently from personal time; if any waiting around was involved this was at least tolerated by the donors and often welcomed. Because of the reduction in company on-site giving, many of these donors were lost when the exchange started to require the time spent giving blood, and also the additional time spent travelling to and from a blood donation centre. To reduce the time involved meant introducing appointment systems and other approaches to ensure that the donor could see that what he or she was actually exchanging was treated as having value. It was not until this price element of the exchange had been addressed that steps could be taken that would ensure adequate supplies could be collected routinely.

Question

Consider the operations of the Blood Transfusion Service and suggest what is the product offering involved and how might the BTS develop this offering to appeal to the potential donors they require.

Glossary of marketing terms

Above the line A term applying to main media advertising expenditure and its traditional accounting treatment. Now used for all costs of advertising using traditional media.

Acceptability A test of a product offering from a customer's viewpoint.

ACORN (A Classification of Residential Neighbourhood) – a so-called, geodemographic database of residential locality types. Commercially available from CACI.

Ad hoc research Research which is conducted first hand on a one-off basis, for a particular research project.

Adoption Rate at which people accept and become users of a product. Often associated with the diffusion of innovation curve.

Advertisement A message from a person or an organisation to potential customers containing a specific message using paid-for media space. Sometimes shortened by practitioners to 'ad' and by the general public to 'advert'.

Advertiser A client placing 'paid-for' advertising.

Advertising An element of the marketing mix involving the use of paid media.

Advertising Agency An organisation which specialises in all forms of communication on behalf of clients.

Advertising Campaign A planned approach to communication over a defined period of time.

Advertising Media Communication channels such as radio, television, newspapers, magazines and posters.

Advertorial An advertisement written in an editorial style to attempt to give more credibility to the message.

Affordability A test of the value or pricing of a marketing offering from a customer viewpoint.

Agent An individual or company acting in a sales capacity on behalf of a principal. An agent does not at any stage of the transaction own the goods.

AIDA (Attention, Interest, Desire, Action) – a mnemonic used in advertising. First used by Strong in 1924. One of the hierarchy models.

Augmented Product *See* Marketing Offering.

Availability A test of the convenience of an offering from a customer viewpoint.

Awareness A measure of the proportion of a target audience who have heard of a particular product or service. Can be measured on a 'prompted' or 'unprompted' basis.

Below the line Expenditure on promotional activities which do not involve the use of traditional chargeable media or involves non-commission media.

BRAD (British Rate and Data) – the accepted tariff book of advertising in the EU.

Brand An article identified by a name, symbol, trade mark or other characteristic which differentiates it from competitive offerings.

Break-even point   Point at which the costs of production equal the revenue received from sales.

Budget   The amount of money allocated to performing a particular task.

Buyer behaviour   The way in which customers act, and the steps taken in the purchase decision process.

Communication Mix   *See* Promotional Mix.

Competitive Advantage   An element within a product offering that is particularly attractive to customers and not offered by competitors.

Consumer   The final user of a product or a service.

Consumer Goods   Products which are targeted at individuals in the general population, rather than at organisations.

Consumerism   A movement which aims to change the actions of organisations in favour of particular groups.

Consumer Panel   A research method using a group of consumers which continuously report on their purchases over an extended period of time. (*See* Panels.)

Continuous Research   Research that is conducted regularly over an extended period of time, used to monitor trends in the market place.

Controllable Factors   *See* Marketing Mix.

Convenience Sample   A market research sampling technique using any convenient method of selecting respondents. Results have no statistical validity although may be useful if sample can be shown as being 'typical' of the population from which it was drawn.

Copy   The written or broadcast words used in an advertisement.

Cost per Thousand (CPT)   Used in advertising as a measure of cost per 1000 people viewing or reading the advertisement.

Cost Plus Pricing   A pricing approach where an agreed percentage is added to the production cost of a product.

Coverage   The percentage of a selected target audience that have an opportunity to see a particular advertisement.

Customer   In marketing, it is generally anyone buying a product or service.

DAGMAR   (Defining Advertising Goals for Measured Advertising Results) – an acronym for one of the hierarchy of effects models of advertising.

Decider   A term used in industrial buying theory to classify the person who makes a specific purchase decision, usually in a formal capacity.

Delphi method   A forecasting technique using the opinions of a panel of experts to develop qualitative forecasts iteratively.

Demographic   Information relating to broad population statistics, such as age, gender, income, education level or marital status.

Depth Interviews   A research technique involving detailed discussions with individual respondents to explore issues such as motivation, beliefs, etc.

Derived Demand   The demand for a component or intermediate product dependent on sales of the final product or service.

Desk Research   Research which uses existing source of information, usually called 'secondary data'.

Differentiated   The separation of a marketing offering from those of competitors by using a specific marketing mix.

Differentiated Marketing   A marketing strategy which involves developing specific marketing offerings for each segment of a market.

Diffusion   The rate at which new products move through various adoption categories.

Direct Mail   A form of below-the-line advertising where personalised letters are sent directly from the advertiser to potential customers.

Direct Marketing   An approach offering products without intermediaries where the supplier sells directly to customers using direct mail or advertising.

Distribution Channel   The method used to make products available to consumers especially when using intermediaries.

Distributor   A person or organisation who distributes goods. Distributors take ownership from suppliers and are responsible for collecting payments from customers.

Diversification   A process of introducing new products into new markets unrelated to an organisation's current customers.

Elasticity   Sensitivity of customer demand to changes in price.

Exclusive Distribution   A policy adopted by organisations which limits product availability to a limited number of selected outlets.

Experiment   A research approach which evaluates alternatives to identify customer preferences. (*See* Hall Test.)

Exploratory Research   A limited marketing research review of a problem prior to committing significant resources to the study.

Fast-Moving Consumer Goods   (fmcg) – regularly purchased products, usually of low value.

Field Research   Primary research involving the use of a questionnaire based survey, observation or occasionally experimentation and conducted within the customer's usual environment.

Fieldwork   The activity of undertaking Field Research.

Focus Group   A quantitative market research technique whereby selected individuals discuss specific topics under the guidance of a moderator. Often involves the use of projective techniques to explore attitudes and beliefs.

Franchising   A contractual relationship between a seller and an outlet which uses the seller's format, product and name.

Global Brand   A brand which has universal appeal and is marketed in many countries with little modification to product or image.

Gross Profit Margin   The difference between the direct cost of production and the selling price.

Group Discussion   *See* Focus Group.

Hall Test   A market research experiment often carried out in a public hall close to a busy shopping area. Used to investigate customer preferences with respect to specific product attributers such as the shape or colour of a bottle or the packaging for a new product.

Hierarchy of need   A model of consumer behaviour, suggested by A. Maslow.

Image   The perceptions of a product, brand, or company by customers and consumers.

Industrial Goods   Products which are required by industrial organisations.

Intensive Distribution   A policy adopted by organisations to maximise the availability of their products.

Intermediary   A general name for a person who acts as a link in the flow of goods from a supplier to a final consumer.

Life Cycle   *See* Product Life Cycle.

Likert Scale   A scale which uses statements to indicate respondent agreement or disagreement in market research survey questionnaire.

Loyalty (also brand loyalty)   The extent to which customers repurchase a particular product or brand.

Macroenvironment   The general external business environment in which a firm functions.

Market Development   A strategy adopted by an organisation to increase sales by offering their existing product in new markets. Used by I. Ansoff in his matrix.

Market Leader   The organisation which has the greatest share of sales in a given market.

Market Penetration   A strategy an organisation may use to increase sales by offering more of their existing products in their existing markets. Used by I. Ansoff in his matrix.

Market Research   The specialist marketing research activity of using observational, survey and experimental social research techniques for marketing applications.

Market Segmentation   The identification of specific market segments within a market, and developing different marketing offerings for each of these segments.

Market Share   The relative sales of a product in relation to the overall market sales. Can be measured in either sales value or sales volume.

Marketing Audit   A systematic appraisal of the strengths and weaknesses of a company in relation to its market place, and the evaluation of the opportunities and threats in that market.

Marketing Concept   The theories developed to analyse the process of meeting customer needs and determine how this can be improved.

Marketing Environment   The social, economical, legal, political, cultural, competitive and technological factors which affect an organisation and its marketing decision. See PEST.

Marketing Information System   Information which is relevant to the company's marketing operations, including marketing research, intelligence and market analysis data. Often held and maintained as a computer database.

Marketing Mix   The controllable elements of the marketing offering which can often be considered under the headings known as the '4Ps' Product, Price, Place and Promotion.

Marketing Offering   What actually is selected by a customer. Includes the core product or service plus the additional values provided by promotion, availability, brand, image, etc.

Marketing Orientation   The focus of an organisation on both customers and competitors to develop a relevant marketing offering.

Marketing Planning   The systematic process of analysing the environment and a company's resources. Then developing objectives and suitable strategies and action plans to meet those objective. Also the feedback and control of such actions.

Marketing Philosophy   The recognition that organisations exist to meet the needs of their customers and that this should be the objective of every member of an organisation's staff.

Marketing Research   The collation of marketing information to improve marketing decisions. It is an aid to decision-making but not a substitute for it.

Market Strategy   The long-term direction of an organisation relating to marketing actions and the interaction of controllable variables.

Mark-up   A cost-plus price technique.

MEAL (Media Expenditure Analysis Limited)   A firm that collects and publishes information on major UK media use and cost by companies.

Media   Channels of communication such as television, radio, newspapers, etc.

Media Owners   The controllers of media who try to encourage the use of their channel and often provide comprehensive data about readers and viewers.

Multi-stage Sampling   A market research technique often used in political sampling where several random samples are used to give an easily accessed sample: for instance one street in one political ward in one constituency.

New Product Development   The process of identifying, developing and evaluating new marketing offerings.

Niche   A small discrete segment of a market which can be targeted with a distinct marketing strategy.

Non-price Competition   Other benefits such as warranties or additional features or merchandising which can give an offering a competitive advantage.

Objective   In planning, a target to be achieved.

Objective and Task Method   A method of establishing a promotional budget. It is based on the task to be achieved rather than money available. Good in theory but difficult in practice.

Observation (research)   A research approach which involves critically reviewing competitors' products and activities or the reactions and behaviour of customers.

Offer Mix   The mix of product, price and availability offered to a customer. Not including communication of that offer.

Omnibus Survey   A regular questionnaire-based field research survey with a large sample. Organisations can commission one or more questions to be asked; the survey includes questions from a number of different companies.

OTS (opportunity to see)   The average number of viewing occasions for a particular advertisement.

Panels (consumer panels)   Groups of consumers who regularly monitor buying or usage information, often through keeping diary records.

Pareto Effect   The 80/20 rule. The largest proportion of sales value or profit will often come from a small proportion of customers or range of products.

Perception (from psychology)   The way a product or event or stimulus is received and evaluated by a customer. The importance lies in the attempt to understand how people interpret messages.

Personal Interview   A research method where the researcher meets the respondent when carrying out a survey.

Personal Selling   An element of the promotional mix, where a supplier uses a trained representative to influence customers and increase sales.

PEST analysis (sometimes STEP)   Elements of the macro, external environment, political/legal, economic, social/cultural and technological.

Place   An element of the 4 Ps of the marketing mix. (*See* Distribution Channel.)

Point-of-sale   Usually in retail, the physical area where a customer selects a product.

Point-of-sale Material   Publicity material provided by a supplier for the use of a retailer at the point-of-sale.

Positioning, also Product Positioning   The determination of the main factors valued by consumers making purchase decisions and matching product features to those factors.

Postal Survey   Using the mail to distribute a specially prepared survey questionnaire.

Primary Data   Data obtained from primary research rather than secondary sources.

Product Development   A strategy adopted by organisations to increase sales by creating new products for existing markets used by I. Ansoff in his matrix. (*See also* New Product Development.)

Product Life Cycle   The different stages which are a characteristic of product sales rate as this develops over time. These are identified by the terms: development, birth (or introduction), growth, maturity and decline. Marketing mix decisions are influenced by the stage a product has reached in its life cycle.

Product Line   A number of related products offered by a supplier, which often cover the needs of several different segments.

Product Management   The function responsible for the tactical and strategic planning of a company's existing and new products.

Product Mix   The total range of products or services that an organisation offers.

Product Offering   *See* Marketing Offering.

Product Orientation   The focus of an organisation on product quality and production capability. This differs from marketing orientation.

Promotion   An element of the 4 Ps of the marketing mix, it covers the ways in which an organisation communicates with its market.

Promotional Mix   The elements of promotion enabling an organisation to communicate with its market. These include advertising, personal selling, sales promotion and publicity.

Prospecting   The identification of potential new customers by sales personnel.

Psychographics   A base for segmentation derived from attitudes and behavioural variables.

Publicity   An element of the promotional mix. (*See* Public Relations.)

Public Relations   A deliberate, planned and sustained effort to establish and maintain positive understanding between an organisation and its publics.

Pull Strategy   A marketing strategy by which the manufacture promotes directly to the final customers, and hopes that they will demand the product from intermediaries. The product is then 'pulled' through the distribution channels by customer demand.

Push Strategy   A marketing strategy in which the manufacturer promotes to the intermediaries, who in turn promote to their customers. The product is therefore 'pushed' through the distribution channels by manufacturer and distributor effort.

Qualitative Research   Marketing research which produces non numerical information such as may involve determining attitudes and beliefs.

Quantitative Research   Research which produces information-based numerical data. This may be obtained from secondary sources or surveys. This is sometimes referred to as 'hard data'.

Questionnaire   A prepared set of questions used to obtain information from a respondent.

Quota Sample   A sampling method where respondents are selected to match predetermined attributes such as gender, age, occupation.

Random sample   A sampling method where everyone within a defined population has an equal non-zero chance of being selected.

Rate Card   The published cost of advertising media.

Recall   *See* Awareness.

Research Brief   A structured document given to a research agency including background to the organisation and the objectives of the research.

Respondent   A person interviewed or contacted in a market research survey.

Retail Audit   The research undertaken in retail outlets involving checking invoices, delivery notes and sales records to determine the precise volume of goods sold. Results are often syndicated to several suppliers.

Sales Call   A visit made by a sales representative to a potential customer.

Sales Coverage   The percentage of customers and prospects allocated to a sales person visited within a set period, usually a year.

Sales Orientation   The focus of an organisation on to customers with the aim of achieving short-term sales.

Sales Promotion   An element of the promotional mix. Techniques and incentives used to increase short-term sales.

Sampling Frame   A defined population from which a sample is selected.

Secondary Data   Data used for marketing research although collated for other reasons. Includes external, published data such as population statistics and internal data such as sales by region collated to calculate sales commissions.

Segment   A grouping of customers who have common characteristics or features.

Shopping Good   Products which are considered purchases such as a consumer durable.

Skimming   A pricing strategy where an organisation introduces a product at a high price to maximise short-term profits.

Societal Marketing   Marketing which attempts to contribute to the improvement of society.

Socio-economic Group Classification   A grouping of the population according to the occupation of the head of the household: A, B, C1, C2, D, E.

Speciality Good   Shopping goods which are available from only a limited number of suppliers such as collectable compact discs.

Sponsorship   The funding of an event, programme, publication or participant as a promotional activity.

Strategy   An overall, long-term direction or approach which a company aims to follow, derived from the Greek words meaning to lead an army.

Stimulus   A 'trigger' that starts a purchasing process.

SWOT Analysis   SWOT is an acronym for Strengths and Weaknesses, Opportunities and Threats. The SW refer to internal resources of an organisation, the OT to the macroenvironment.

Syndicated Research   Research conducted on behalf of more than one organisation. Includes: consumer panels, retails audits and omnibus surveys.

Tactics   The specific operational activities undertaken in support of an organisation's strategy.

Target Market   The segment of a market at which a specific marketing offering is directed.

Test Marketing   The initial launching of a product into a limited area for a trial period to test its marketing mix prior to national sales.

Total Product   *See* Marketing Offering.

Trade Press   Published journals aimed at industrial and commercial readers.

TVR (Television Ratings)   A measure of coverage representing 1 per cent of a potential television audience. Calculated by using panel research information.

Undifferentiated Marketing   A common marketing strategy aimed at the total market without modifications for specific segments.

Unique Selling Proposition (USP)   A selling claim based on a distinctive product feature or unique element in the marketing mix.

Vertical Marketing Systems (VMS)   The integration of operators at different levels of a distribution chain to offer a co-ordinated package.

Wholesaler   An organisation which buys products in bulk, and resells them in smaller quantities to retailers.

Width (of a product line)   The variety and diversity of products offered in a product line.

The use of short case studies for studying marketing principles and practice

Most cases describe actual business situations although fictitious names are sometimes used. They are usually based on real management problems, although the facts may be modified to highlight particular situations. The problems described are therefore very similar to those that are encountered daily by managers. There are many benefits from using cases:

1 Cases can cover a range of organisations and industries and thus provide more varied range of problems than are likely to be experienced in day-to-day management.

2 They help to build knowledge of a number of specific situations by dealing intensively with problems of each case.

3 Case discussions provide opportunities for exchanging of experience. Using case situations effective approaches to addressing problems can often be developed by using the accumulated experience gained from the observation of actual events by those taking part. This is to be encouraged since the discussion of cases provides a way of reassessing the lessons of experience, and gaining additional learning from them.

4 Cases also help to develop analytical skills. You need to work with both facts and figures to produce quantitative and qualitative evidence to support recommendations and decisions. These could be challenged both by your instructors and your colleagues. It is important that you learn to defend your arguments and to develop an ability to think and reason in a rigorous way.

5 Cases are useful for developing principles and concept that can be applied in practice. Individual cases will identify specific concepts and approaches. Taken together, a series of cases should develop basic ideas that can then be applied in different managerial situations.

6 Perhaps the most important skill to be gained from studying cases and case situations is learning to ask the right questions. This is a really critical business skill. 'Discussion questions' could be suggested by your instructor, but that does not pre-empt the task of identifying the key problems. You must always still ask yourself: 'What really are the problems here?' It is too easy to just rearrange the facts and figures without defining the real problems in the case.

7 Often the greatest pedagogical benefit derived from the case studies is that they generate a high degree of involvement in the learning process. You will tend to learn the most from those things in which you are most deeply involved. It follows, too, there is little that can be learned from even the best cases without solid preparation.

There are, of course, major differences between cases and actual management. It is important to appreciate that:

- The 'facts' come in neatly written form. Managers in business rarely receive information in this way. Their knowledge usually comes through being in situ and via interactions with fellow managers, as well as memos, statistical reports; and even the external media.
- A case usually describes the situation at a single point in time. Real business problems usually develop over a period of time and their solution also takes time to implement. As a result, managers are seldom able to concentrate on one problem at a time.
- There is no responsibility for implementing the decisions or recommendations resulting from studying a case. This can result in ideal rather than pragmatic recommendations which means the need to implement decisions always needs to be discussed.
- A case is designed to fit a particular unit of study time. It will focus on certain categories of problems/marketing situations in order to explore them in more detail.

The marketing cases in this book are very short. They do not need great analysis. In fact they are really case-based examples. However, all will benefit from discussing the situations with other students. When studying them it might be helpful to follow the sequence below.

- First, read through the case quickly to put it into perspective. Initially the best preparation will come from working by yourself. Then, based on this, the next step is to decide whether the information is reliable. This will require a more thorough second reading, leading to an assessment of what is good or bad practice from the facts given. The aim is to try to isolate the real key problems which are there to be solved, or the lessons to be learnt.

- It is best that you note down the problems to be tackled and the relevant areas for analysis. For example, if the problems are 'Should we introduce Product X? To whom should it be sold? What should be our advertising strategy?', the areas for analysis might include:
  - trends in the market place
  - break-even analysis
  - buyer behaviour
  - segmentation
  - competition
  - communication needs.

- The information in the case should be considered to see what links together. In particular, it is necessary to see what helps the understanding of each area, and to draw some meaningful observations and conclusions. These may, in turn, provide the basis for answering the questions that have been suggested.
- The purpose of individual preparation is to enhance the learning opportunities when discussing the case in class. The more familiar you are with the case facts and the more ideas you have about the case problems, the better prepared you will be to take in, react to, and learn from the ideas of others in a group discussion. Through interchanging ideas and constructive debate you will build analytical skills, develop judgement and gain conceptual understanding.
- The next step is to present your arguments to other students and to listen to their views. This can be done in pairs, or in larger numbers, or in a seminar group. The purpose of the discussion of cases is to help refine, adjust and fill out your own

thinking. It is not to develop a consensus or a 'group' position. In fact it is not necessary, or even desirable that you agree at this stage.

■ In a seminar you will usually be allowed to take the case where you wish. This is where you fully explore the issues and problems which you have identified. The seminar group is for you to express, support and defend your conclusions and recommendations. Much learning comes from controversy and discussion. The effective use of cases as a learning vehicle depends on participation. This will benefit both your learning and that of other students. The more you contribute, the more you will get from it. It is therefore a responsibility of every student to get involved.

■ Discussion in class is also not only an effective way for you to think rigorously, but it allows you to develop skill in communicating, in 'thinking on your feet' and in responding to questions under pressure. Expressing your own views, and defending them, are all part of a distinctive experience.

■ However important it is to express your views, listening is even more important. It's easy to become so preoccupied with what we think that our minds become closed to the thoughts of other participants in the discussion. In class, as well as in business, it is just as important to be open-minded and to be willing to shift position when good arguments are presented.

■ The role of a seminar leader is to lead the discussion into considering other aspects that you may have missed, or even to require you to make a decision. At the end it is likely the discussions will be summarised to draw out the useful lessons and observations that come from class discussion comments, but please remember that there is no right answer in cases. The measure of your individual progress in any one case discussion does not depend on whether your ideas were 'right'. Instead it is more useful to ask: 'How much did I take away from the discussion that I didn't know when it started?'

Index